Communications in Computer and Information Science 1491

More information about this series at https://link.springer.com/bookseries/7899

Yuqing Sun · Tun Lu · Buqing Cao ·
Hongfei Fan · Dongning Liu · Bowen Du ·
Liping Gao (Eds.)

Computer Supported Cooperative Work and Social Computing

16th CCF Conference, ChineseCSCW 2021
Xiangtan, China, November 26–28, 2021
Revised Selected Papers, Part I

Springer

Editors
Yuqing Sun
Shandong University
Jinan, China

Tun Lu
Fudan University
Shanghai, China

Buqing Cao
Hunan University of Science and Technology
Xiangtan, China

Hongfei Fan
Tongji University
Shanghai, China

Dongning Liu
Guangdong University of Technology
Guangzhou, China

Bowen Du
University of Warwick
Coventry, UK

Liping Gao
University of Shanghai for Science
and Technology
Shanghai, China

ISSN 1865-0929 ISSN 1865-0937 (electronic)
Communications in Computer and Information Science
ISBN 978-981-19-4545-8 ISBN 978-981-19-4546-5 (eBook)
https://doi.org/10.1007/978-981-19-4546-5

This Springer imprint is published by the registered company Springer Nature Singapore Pte Ltd.
The registered company address is: 152 Beach Road, #21-01/04 Gateway East, Singapore 189721, Singapore

Preface

Welcome to ChineseCSCW 2021, the 16th CCF Conference on Computer Supported Cooperative Work and Social Computing.

ChineseCSCW 2021 was organized by the China Computer Federation (CCF) and co-hosted by the CCF Technical Committee on Cooperative Computing (CCF TCCC) and the Hunan University of Science and Technology, in Xiangtan, Hunan, China, during November 26–28, 2021. The theme of the conference was "Human-Centered Collaborative Intelligence", which reflects the emerging trend of the combination of artificial intelligence, human-system collaboration, and AI-empowered applications.

ChineseCSCW (initially named CCSCW) is a highly reputable conference series on computer supported cooperative work (CSCW) and social computing in China with a long history. It aims at connecting Chinese and overseas CSCW researchers, practitioners, and educators, with a particular focus on innovative models, theories, techniques, algorithms, and methods, as well as domain-specific applications and systems, covering both technical and social aspects in CSCW and social computing. The conference was initially held biennially since 1998, and has been held annually since 2014.

This year, the conference received 242 submissions, and after a rigorous double-blind peer review process, only 65 were eventually accepted as full papers to be orally presented, resulting in an acceptance rate of 27%. The program also included 22 short papers, which were presented as posters. In addition, the conference featured six keynote speeches, six high-level technical seminars, the 2nd Hengdian Cup ChineseCSCW Big Data Challenge, an award ceremony for senior TCCC members, and a forum titled "Mobile Computing and Social Computing" jointly hosted by CCF Changsha and CCF YOCSEF Changsha. We are grateful to the distinguished keynote speakers, Tianruo Yang from Hainan University, Bin Hu from the Beijing Institute of Technology, Jiade Luo from Tsinghua University, Jing Liu from the Guangzhou Institute of Technology, Xidian University, Peng Lv from Central South University, and Tao Jia from Southwest University.

We hope that you enjoyed ChineseCSCW 2021.

November 2021

Yong Tang
Jianxun Liu
Yuqing Sun
Dongning Liu
Buqing Cao

Organization

The 16th CCF Conference on Computer Supported Cooperative Work and Social Computing (ChineseCSCW 2021) was organized by the China Computer Federation (CCF) and co-hosted by the CCF Technical Committee on Cooperative Computing (CCF TCCC) and the Hunan University of Science and Technology.

Steering Committee

Yong Tang	South China Normal University, China
Weiqing Tang	China Computer Federation, China
Ning Gu	Fudan University, China
Shaozi Li	Xiamen University, China
Bin Hu	Lanzhou University, China
Yuqing Sun	Shandong University, China
Xiaoping Liu	Hefei University of Technology, China
Zhiwen Yu	Northwestern University of Technology, China
Xiangwei Zheng	Shandong Normal University, China
Tun Lu	Fudan University, China

General Chairs

Yong Tang	South China Normal University, China
Jianxun Liu	Hunan University of Science and Technology, China

Program Committee Chairs

Yuqing Sun	Shandong University, China
Dongning Liu	Guangdong University of Technology, China
Buqing Cao	Hunan University of Science and Technology, China

Organization Committee Chairs

Xiaoping Liu	Hefei University of Technology, China
Zhiwen Yu	Northwestern University of Technology, China
Tun Lu	Fudan University, China
Jianyong Yu	Hunan University of Science and Technology, China
Yiping Wen	Hunan University of Science and Technology, China

Publicity Chairs

Xiangwei Zheng	Shandong Normal University, China
Jianguo Li	South China Normal University, China

Publication Chairs

Bin Hu	Lanzhou University, China
Hailong Sun	Beihang University, China

Finance Chairs

Pei Li	Hunan University of Science and Technology, China
Yijiang Zhao	Hunan University of Science and Technology, China

Paper Award Chairs

Shaozi Li	Xiamen University, China
Yichuan Jiang	Southeast University, China

Program Committee

Zhan Bu	Nanjing University of Finance and Economics, China
Tie Bao	Jilin University, China
Hongming Cai	Shanghai Jiao Tong University, China
Xinye Cai	Nanjing University of Aeronautics and Astronautics, China
Yuanzheng Cai	Minjiang University, China
Zhicheng Cai	Nanjing University of Science and Technology, China
Buqing Cao	Hunan University of Science and Technology, China
Donglin Cao	Xiamen University, China
Jian Cao	Shanghai Jiao Tong University, China
Chao Chen	Chongqing University, China
Jianhui Chen	Beijing University of Technology, China
Long Chen	Southeast University, China
Longbiao Chen	Xiamen University, China
Liangyin Chen	Sichuan University, China
Qingkui Chen	University of Shanghai for Science and Technology, China

Ningjiang Chen	Guangxi University, China
Weineng Chen	South China University of Technology, China
Yang Chen	Fudan University, China
Shiwei Cheng	Zhejiang University of Technology, China
Xiaohui Cheng	Guilin University of Technology, China
Yuan Cheng	Wuhan University, China
Lizhen Cui	Shandong University, China
Weihui Dai	Fudan University, China
Xianghua Ding	Fudan University, China
Wanchun Dou	Nanjing University, China
Bowen Du	University of Warwick, UK
Hongfei Fan	Tongji University, China
Yili Fang	Zhejiang Gongshang University, China
Shanshan Feng	Shandong Normal University, China
Jing Gao	Guangdong Hengdian Information Technology Co., Ltd., China
Yunjun Gao	Zhejiang University, China
Liping Gao	University of Shanghai for Science and Technology, China
Ning Gu	Fudan University, China
Bin Guo	Northwestern Polytechnical University, China
Kun Guo	Fuzhou University, China
Wei Guo	Shandong University, China
Yinzhang Guo	Taiyuan University of Science and Technology, China
Tao Han	Zhejiang Gongshang University, China
Fei Hao	Shanxi Normal University, China
Chaobo He	Zhongkai University of Agriculture and Engineering, China
Fazhi He	Wuhan University, China
Haiwu He	Chinese Academy of Sciences, China
Bin Hu	Lanzhou University, China
Daning Hu	Southern University of Science and Technology, China
Wenting Hu	Jiangsu Open University, China
Yanmei Hu	Chengdu University of Technology, China
Changqin Huang	South China Normal University, China
Bo Jiang	Zhejiang Gongshang University, China
Bin Jiang	Hunan University, China
Jiuchuan Jiang	Nanjing University of Finance and Economics, China
Weijin Jiang	Xiangtan University, China

Yichuan Jiang	Southeast University, China
Lu Jia	China Agricultural University, China
Miaotianzi Jin	Shenzhen Artificial Intelligence and Data Science Institute (Longhua), China
Yi Lai	Xi'an University of Posts and Telecommunications, China
Dongsheng Li	Microsoft Research, China
Guoliang Li	Tsinghua University, China
Hengjie Li	Lanzhou University of Arts and Science, China
Jianguo Li	South China Normal University, China
Junli Li	Jinzhong University, China
Li Li	Southwest University, China
Renfa Li	Hunan University, China
Shaozi Li	Xiamen University, China
Taoshen Li	Guangxi University, China
Weimin Li	Shanghai University, China
Xiaoping Li	Southeast University, China
Yong Li	Tsinghua University, China
Lu Liang	Guangdong University of Technology, China
Hao Liao	Shenzhen University, China
Bing Lin	Fujian Normal University, China
Dazhen Lin	Xiamen University, China
Dongning Liu	Guangdong University of Technology, China
Hong Liu	Shandong Normal University, China
Jing Liu	Guangzhou Institute of Technology, Xidian University, China
Li Liu	Chongqing University, China
Shijun Liu	Shandong University, China
Shufen Liu	Jilin University, China
Xiaoping Liu	Hefei University of Technology, China
Yuechang Liu	Jiaying University, China
Tun Lu	Fudan University, China
Hong Lu	Shanghai Polytechnic University, China
Huijuan Lu	China Jiliang University, China
Dianjie Lu	Shandong Normal University, China
Qiang Lu	Hefei University of Technology, China
Haoyu Luo	South China Normal University, China
Zhiming Luo	Xiamen University, China
Pin Lv	Guangxi University, China
Hui Ma	University of Electronic Science and Technology of China and Zhongshan Institute, China
Keji Mao	Zhejiang University of Technology, China

Chao Min	Nanjing University, China
Haiwei Pan	Harbin Engineering University, China
Li Pan	Shandong University, China
Yinghui Pan	Shenzhen University, China
Lianyong Qi	Qufu Normal University, China
Jiaxing Shang	Chongqing University, China
Limin Shen	Yanshan University, China
Yuliang Shi	Dareway Software Co., Ltd, China
Yanjun Shi	Dalian University of Science and Technology, China
Xiaoxia Song	Datong University, China
Kehua Su	Wuhan University, China
Songzhi Su	Xiamen University, China
Hailong Sun	Beihang University, China
Ruizhi Sun	China Agricultural University, China
Yuqing Sun	Shandong University, China
Yuling Sun	East China Normal University, China
Wen'an Tan	Nanjing University of Aeronautics and Astronautics, China
Lina Tan	Hunan University of Technology and Business, China
Yong Tang	South China Normal University, China
Shan Tang	Shanghai Polytechnic University, China
Weiqing Tang	China Computer Federation, China
Yan Tang	Hohai University, China
Yiming Tang	Hefei University of Technology, China
Yizheng Tao	China Academy of Engineering Physics, China
Shaohua Teng	Guangdong University of Technology, China
Zhuo Tian	Institute of Software, Chinese Academy of Sciences, China
Dakuo Wang	IBM Research, USA
Hongbin Wang	Kunming University of Science and Technology, China
Hongjun Wang	Southwest Jiaotong University, China
Hongbo Wang	University of Science and Technology Beijing, China
Lei Wang	Alibaba Group, China
Lei Wang	Dalian University of Technology, China
Tao Wang	Minjiang University, China
Tianbo Wang	Beihang University, China
Tong Wang	Harbin Engineering University, China
Wanyuan Wang	Southeast University, China

Xiaogang Wang	Shanghai Dianji University, China
Yijie Wang	National University of Defense Technology, China
Zhenxing Wang	Shanghai Polytechnic University, China
Zhiwen Wang	Guangxi University of Science and Technology, China
Yiping Wen	Hunan University of Science and Technology, China
Ling Wu	Fuzhou University, China
Quanwang Wu	Chongqing University, China
Zhengyang Wu	South China Normal University, China
Chunhe Xia	Beihang University, China
Fangxion Xiao	Jinling Institute of Technology, China
Zheng Xiao	Hunan University, China
Xiaolan Xie	Guilin University of Technology, China
Zhiqiang Xie	Harbin University of Science and Technology, China
Yu Xin	Harbin University of Science and Technology, China
Jianbo Xu	Hunan University of Science and Technology, China
Jiuyun Xu	China University of Petroleum, China
Meng Xu	Shandong Technology and Business University, China
Heyang Xu	Henan University of Technology, China
Yaling Xun	Taiyuan University of Science and Technology, China
Jiaqi Yan	Nanjing University, China
Xiaohu Yan	Shenzhen Polytechnic, China
Yan Yao	Qilu University of Technology, China
Bo Yang	University of Electronic Science and Technology of China, China
Chao Yang	Hunan University, China
Dingyu Yang	Shanghai Dianji University, China
Gang Yang	Northwestern Polytechnical University, China
Jing Yang	Harbin Engineering University, China
Lin Yang	Shanghai Computer Software Technology Development Center, China
Xiaochun Yang	Northeastern University, China
Xu Yu	Qingdao University of Science and Technology, China
Zhiwen Yu	Northwestern Polytechnical University, China
Zhiyong Yu	Fuzhou University, China

Jianyong Yu	Hunan University of Science and Technology, China
Yang Yu	Zhongshan University, China
Zhengtao Yu	Kunming University of Science and Technology, China
Chengzhe Yuan	Guangdong Engineering and Technology Research Center for Service Computing, China
An Zeng	Guangdong Polytechnical University, China
Dajun Zeng	Institute of Automation, Chinese Academy of Sciences, China
Zhihui Zhan	South China University of Technology, China
Changyou Zhang	Chinese Academy of Sciences, China
Jifu Zhang	Taiyuan University of Science and Technology, China
Jing Zhang	Nanjing University of Science and Technology, China
Liang Zhang	Fudan University, China
Libo Zhang	Southwest University, China
Miaohui Zhang	Energy Research Institute of Jiangxi Academy of Sciences, China
Peng Zhang	Fudan University, China
Senyue Zhang	Shenyang Aerospace University, China
Shaohua Zhang	Shanghai Software Technology Development Center, China
Wei Zhang	Guangdong University of Technology, China
Zhiqiang Zhang	Harbin Engineering University, China
Zili Zhang	Southwest University, China
Xiangwei Zheng	Shandong Normal University, China
Jinghui Zhong	South China University of Technology, China
Ning Zhong	Beijing University of Technology, China
Yifeng Zhou	Southeast University, China
Huiling Zhu	Jinan University, China
Tingshao Zhu	Chinese Academy of Sciences, China
Xia Zhu	Southeast University, China
Xianjun Zhu	Jinling University of Science and Technology, China
Yanhua Zhu	The First Affiliated Hospital of Guangdong Pharmaceutical University, China
Jia Zhu	South China Normal University, China
Jianhua Zhu	City University of Hong Kong, China
Jie Zhu	Nanjing University of Posts and Telecommunications, China
Qiaohong Zu	Wuhan University of Technology, China

Contents – Part I

Domain-Specific Collaborative Applications

Contents – Part II

Social Media and Online Communities

Collaborative Mechanisms, Models, Approaches, Algorithms and Systems

Decentralized Predictive Enterprise Resource Planning Framework on Private Blockchain Networks Using Neural Networks

Zhijie Wu[1], Yangjie Qin[1], Yu Li[1], Bo Cheng[1], Zhihao Lin[1], and Jia Zhu[2(✉)]

[1] South China Normal University, Guangzhou, China
[2] Zhejiang Normal University, Jinhua, Zhejiang, China
jiazhu@zjnu.edu.cn

Abstract. Theoretically, cross-department predictive modeling can improve the operational efficiency of an enterprise, particularly on enterprise resource planning. For example, a model that predicts the volume of purchase goods will be more generalizable if the predication is based on the data from multiple departments. Most existing cross-department predictive models rely on a centralized technology, in which security and robustness are ignored, including unreliable single-point or malicious modification of records. Therefore, our works propose a decentralized framework to combine Blockchain technology with exited model so as to apply in predictive enterprise resource planning. In detail, model parameter estimation will be trained by without revealing any other information, which means only model-related data are exchanged across departments. In order to apply transaction metadata to disseminate models, we introduce neural networks combine with a private Blockchain network. In addition, we design an algorithm to train the neural networks that combine the loss function from each local model to achieve the smallest global level validation loss. Finally, we implement the experiments to prove the effectiveness of our framework by applying it to multi typical tasks in enterprise resource planning. Experimental results reveal the advantages of this framework on both tasks.

Keywords: Cross-department predictive · Blockchain · Neural networks

1 Introduction

Cross-department interoperable predictive modeling can improve the operational efficiency of an enterprise, particularly on enterprise resource planning. For example, as an important task of enterprise resource planning, a model that predicts the volume of purchase goods will be more generalizable if the predication is based on the data from multiple departments.

As we all know, parameters of the predictive model can be estimated with data that is not their own but from the other departments. However, it is

Y. Sun et al. (Eds.): ChineseCSCW 2021, CCIS 1491, pp. 3–13, 2022.
https://doi.org/10.1007/978-981-19-4546-5_1

non-trivial to use all data to train a predictive model because the data are from various departments with uncontrollable noise, which can lead to improper prediction outcomes. Furthermore, some departments may have the requirement of privacy-reserving which means they do not want to share data with others. Therefore, it is common to use some centralized algorithms to only transfer prediction models instead of disseminating data from individual department [1,2]. However, there are quite a few potential risks for a client-server architecture in an enterprise, e.g., single-point-of-failure [3]. In addition, In addition, participating departments have no permission to join/leave the network at all hours for the reason that server needs to repair problem if analysis process is interrupted. Furthermore, a new department will not be able to participate in the network if it have not authentication and reconfiguration of the central server [4]. Last but not least, it is valuable to know that synchronization issues are need to be solved on distributed networks, in which the participating departments need to agree on the aggregated model in the circumstance that each department maybe stop working due to accidents, which is the typical Byzantine Generals Problem [5].

To make up the above-mentioned defeats, we introduce the Blockchain technology [4,6,7] because a Blockchain-based distributed network is designed as a decentralized architecture as shown in Fig. 1. We utilize a certain mechanism to test every transaction, e.g., majority proof-of-work voting, therefore, each department is able to get control of their computational resources [3,4]. Obviously, the risk of single-point-of-failure will be decreased for this architecture, and each department is able to join/leave the network freely, during which the central server will not increase overhead, and there is no need to interrupt the machine learning process.

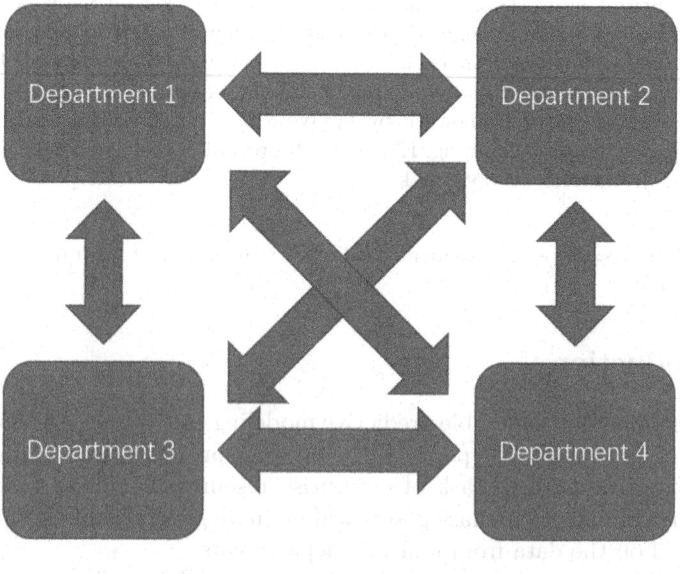

Fig. 1. Decentralized architecture

In our work, a decentralized framework is proposed to apply Blockchain technology in predictive enterprise resource planning. Model parameter estimation will be trained by participating department without revealing any other information, which means only model-related data are exchanged across departments. We combine online learning using neural networks with a private Blockchain network so as to utilize transaction metadata to disseminate models. In addition, we design an algorithm so as to train the neural networks. The relevant parameters will be updated back to the local learning model of each department when the training is finished. Through our intuitive analysis, it is valuable to know that the incremental feature of machine learning is helpful to adapt it to peer-to-peer networks such as Blockchain.

We show the effectiveness of our framework by applying it to a few traditional tasks on enterprise resource planning. Experimental results reveal the strength and robustness of this framework compared to exited typical approaches on all tasks. The three main contributions of our proposed works are below:

1. We innovatively propose a decentralized framework to adapt Blockchain technology for predictive enterprise resource planning. In this framework, each participating department is helpful to train model ability of parameter estimation without revealing any other information so that the cross-department predictive enterprise resource planning can be properly completed.
2. We integrate online learning combine neural networks with a private Blockchain network so as to utilize transaction metadata to disseminate models.
3. We design an algorithm so as to train the appropriate neural networks and update the information back to each department so that the concept of consensus can be realized.

The main content of this paper will be organized as follows. Section 2 describes related work on cross-department predictive modeling and Blockchain technology for various applications. Section 3 introduces the technical details of the model on our proposed framework. Section 4 reports the experiments of our model and discusses the results. Section 5 makes a conclusion for our work and has a talk about our future work.

2 Related Work

Cross-department predictive modeling and machine learning can improve the operational efficiency of an enterprise, particularly on enterprise resource planning. However, sensitive information may be exposed at risk if data have a unreasonable information exchange. Early, a lot of algorithms have been proposed in order to have a protection to the privacy of individuals, in which includes partially-trained machine learning models with transfer ability, but not disseminating data from personal departments [1,2,8,9]. Even though these machine learning models have been proposed, however, which exit some defects such as update the parameters of model in a batch and online fashion. These models are strongly dependent on a centralized network architecture, and inferiority of these algorithms are pointed out before such as single-point-of-failure.

Blockchain is widely sought after because of its new situation of distributed database, for the reason that it is able to store arbitrary data with transaction metadata form, so it is more suitable for financial transactions [10,11]. In detail, partially trained online machine learning models are disseminated by transaction metadata among participating departments. As a decentralized platform with smart contracts, Ethereum [12] becomes famous and popular Blockchain 2.0 system. The distributed database has a complex context, in which smart properties play the role of data entries and smart contract store procedures. In this paper, the proof-of-information algorithm model can be also achieved by Blockchain 2.0 architectures, which combine with smart contracts so as to update parameters and properly transfer the partial models.

Recently, in order to introduce applications for currency, economy, and markets, Blockchain 3.0 came into being [13,14]. Blockchain technology has broad application prospects, and medical healthcare system is a typical case. Early, Irving et al. proposed a distributed tamper-proof public ledger through Blockchain technology, which is helpful to save proof of endpoints of clinical trial [15]. Otherwise, McKernan make full of the feature of decentralized Blockchain, which proposed to utilize it to store genomic data [16]. Inspired by the application of genomic data, Jenkins proposed a novel framework with the bio-mining ability for biomarkers, which enhances data security through multi-factor authentication [17]. In the medical field, some researchers try to utilize Blockchain to store electronic health records [18] and to record the flow of drug transactions [19]. What's more, there are another kinds of application cases such as [20–24]. However, to the best of our knowledge, we are the first to utilize Blockchain to improve the performance of enterprise resource planning predictive modeling.

3 Proposed Framework

In this article, we propose a decentralized framework to adapt Blockchain technology for predictive enterprise resource planning. We first design a Block structure as shown in Fig. 2. As we can see from this Figure, each block has its own hash that is computed by the hash algorithm, and the status of the block is able to indicate the action a department has taken to a model. In addition, the hash of the model to save storage spaces, each block adjusts the model itself with relevant parameters setting and the validation loss of the model. Note that there are three types of actions we defined in the whole process, namely, "INIT", "TRAINED", and "UPDATE". We will explain them in the following sections.

Next, we give an overview of our proposed framework as shown in Fig. 3. In this framework, because each department is presented as a node in a Blockchain network, therefore, if we treat the Blockchain network as neural networks, then each department/node can be treated as an input at a certain time. Particularly, each time a node got updated in the Blockchain network, a transaction is created with the latest information from this node to other nodes until all nodes of

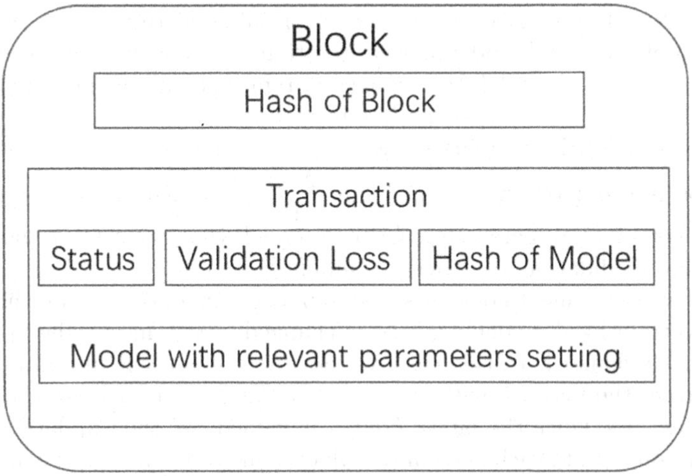

Fig. 2. Block structure

Blockchain network are synchronous using a certain consensus protocol. Since the information is propagated in a cycle manner, recurrent neural networks (RNN) [25] is suitable in this situation. In each time step t, we will use the information of current node X_t plus the output of last time step Y_{t-1} as input to get a output Y_t. Obviously, since the information is different in each department, the input vector X_t will also be different, which certainly can improve the comprehensiveness of the model.

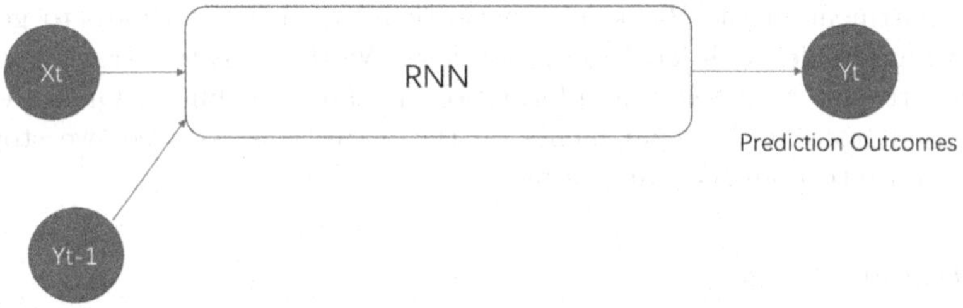

Fig. 3. Proposed framework

Though the framework is simple because we only use the traditional RNN in this framework according to the Fig. 3, but the training and testing steps are not common considering the Blockchain network concept is getting involved. We have explained the major points of this framework as below:

1. Assume there are N nodes in the Blockchain, and every node associated with a local model trained used local data, then each training iteration will have N time steps.

2. The RNN will be trained in the manner of online learning based on the loss function of each local model in each iteration. Since we have N local models, then for each local model M_i, we have θ_i represents all of the parameters to be trained to get the highest probability to get the correct answer, or say to have the smallest local validation loss $L(\theta_i)$. Therefore, we can define the loss function of the network $Loss_{all} = \min \sum_{i=1}^{N} L(\theta_i)$, which means our goal is to get the combination parameters from all models that can achieve the smallest global level validation loss during training.
3. Note that each time a node gets updated, e.g., the data used by the department to train local model, e.g. M_1, is changed, which means the θ_1 also will need to be changed. In this case, we borrow the concept of online learning and retrain the network with the new value in order to achieve the smallest validation loss. Once the latest $Loss_{all}$ is gained, we then update the latest information back to each node in the Blockchain network, e.g., the model with relevant parameters setting, according to Fig. 2. This process clearly shows the fact that we use the RNN as a consensus model to synchronize all nodes. Then, next time a new request comes to this node, e.g., predict the sales for next month, the node will use the new parameters setting to predict and get new validation loss.

Next, we will introduce relevant algorithms for different scenarios/actions.

3.1 Initialization Stage

Algorithm 1 shows the main algorithm for the initialization stage of the proposed framework. To initialize the framework, we first need to train each node/department in the Blockchain network using their own data to get the first learning model with local validation loss. We then create a transaction for each department with relevant information as shown in line 3. Once the loss information from all N departments on the network is received, we stop the process and return all the learning models M.

3.2 Training Stage

In this stage, we train the RNN using the data from each department in order to produce the model M_{all} that combines information from cross-department as shown in Algorithm 2. In each time step, we use the data X_i from a department plus the output Y_{i-1} from the previous department and perform a concatenation operation to put X_i and Y_{i-1} together to gain the embedding information as input of the RNN. After a certain time of iterations, until the RNN is converged, we can get the optimal model M_{all}. Similar to the initialization stage, we again create a transaction for each department with relevant information as shown in line 7. But this time, the θ_i is generated by the RNN, not from M_i.

Algorithm 1: Algorithm for Initialization Stage

Input: A set of participating departments D, Total number of participating departments N

Output: the latest models $M = \{M_1...M_n\}$, M_i is the learning model for each department

1 **for** *each department* $d_i \in D$ **do**
2   Learn the local data and compute the local validation loss $L(\theta_i)$;
3   Create a transaction from d_i to d_i itself with status= INIT, hash = $HASH(M_i)$, loss= $L(\theta_i)$, parameters= θ_i;
4 Wait until loss (status = INIT) from all N departments on the network are received;
5 **return** M

Algorithm 2: Algorithm for Training Stage

Input: Data X_i and loss function $L(\theta_i)$ from participating departments D, Total number of participating departments N

Output: the model M_{all} for RNN

1 **for** *each department* $d_i \in D$ **do**
2   **if** $i == 1$ **then**
3   Input the X_i to RNN and get the output Y_i;
4   **else**
5   Input the $X_i + Y_{i-1}$ to RNN and get the output Y_i;
6 Adjust θ_i and repeat the line 1-5 certain times until $Loss_{all} = \min \sum_{i=1}^{N} L(\theta_i)$;
7 **for** *each department* $d_i \in D$ **do**
8   Create a transaction from d_i to d_i itself with status= TRAINED, hash = $HASH(M_i)$, loss= $L(\theta_i)$, parameters= θ_i;
9 Wait until loss (status = TRAINED) from all N departments on the network are received;
10 **return** M_{all}

3.3 Update Stage/Testing Stage

As shown in Algorithm 3, once a node gets updated, we can either retrain the network with the new value in order to achieve the smallest validation loss or produce the prediction outcomes directly based on the new X_i. If we choose to retrain the network, once the latest $Loss_{all}$ is gained, we need to update the latest information back to each node in the Blockchain network as shown in line 4–7. This process clearly shows the fact that we use the RNN as a consensus model to synchronize all nodes. Note that the Algorithm 3 can also handle the situation for a new department to an existing network because it is the same situation as an existing department with new data.

Algorithm 3: Algorithm for Update Stage/Testing Stage

Input: New Data X_i from a departments d_i
Output: the model M_{all} for RNN

Learn the new local data X_i and compute the local validation loss $L(\theta_i)$;
if *We want to get prediction outcomes directly* **then**
  Input the X_i to M_{all} and generate the output Y_i;
else
  Adjust θ_i and retrain the M_{all} using X_i until $Loss_{all} = \min \sum_{i=1}^{N} L(\theta_i)$;
  for *each department* $d_i \in D$ **do**
    Build a transaction from d_i to d_i with status= UPDATE, hash = $HASH(M_i)$, loss= $L(\theta_i)$, parameters= θ_i;
  Wait until loss (status = UPDATE) from all N departments of network are received;
return M_{all}

4 Experiments

In this section, we discuss and analyze the empirical performance of proposed framework on two traditional enterprise resource planning prediction tasks: sales prediction and raw material purchase prediction.

4.1 Datasets and Preparation

We use the data from a clothing manufacturer to perform sales prediction and raw material purchase prediction The data contains the amount of daily sales and raw material purchase with associated information from five departments in the past ten years.

To simplify our evaluation, we use RBF neural networks [26] and RNN [25] as a learning model, and RMSE [27] as evaluation indicator for all departments. Since we use 80% data for training and 20% data for testing, therefore, we compare the average RMSE value from the 20% data.

4.2 Evaluation Results

According to Table 1, we can see whatever RBF neural networks or RNN, compared to running only based on the data from individual departments, our proposed framework can always perform well on both tasks. Our framework can achieve an average of 18.5 RMSE values for sales prediction, and 43.5 RMSE values for raw material purchase prediction, respectively, if using RNN. This result is at least 20% improvement to the department at the second place.

Table 1. Evaluation results

Models	Sales prediction		Raw material purchase prediction	
	RBF neural networks	RNN	RBF neural networks	RNN
Department 1	65	32.5	150	77
Department 2	70	50.5	148	91
Department 3	44	25.2	106	61
Department 4	65	48.5	78	51.6
Department 5	58	43.4	80	76
Proposed framework	**33.6**	**18.5**	57.6	**43.5**

5 Conclusion and Future Work

In our work, we describe our proposed decentralized framework to adapt Blockchain technology for predictive enterprise resource planning. Each participating department is helpful to train parameter estimation ability of model without revealing any other information. We integrate online learning combine neural networks with a private Blockchain network so as to utilize transaction metadata to disseminate models. In addition, we design an algorithm to train the neural networks combines the loss function with associated parameters from each local model to achieve the smallest global level validation loss. An online learning algorithm is also proposed to handle the case of new data or a new department joins the network. We show the effectiveness of our framework by applying it to two traditional prediction tasks on enterprise resource planning. With the help of Blockchain, we improve the quality of distributed enterprise resource planning predictive modeling.

In the future, we intend to test our framework in other areas, such as health care and government affairs, and hope to realize cross-institutional predictive modeling rather than only cross-department predictive modeling.

References

1. Wang, S., Jiang, X., Wu, Y., Cui, L., Cheng, S., Ohno-Machado, L.: Expectation propagation logistic regression (explorer): distributed privacy-preserving online model learning. J. Biomed. Inform. **46**, 480–496 (2013)
2. Wu, Y., Jiang, X., Kim, J., Ohno-Machado, L.: Grid binary logistic regression (GLORE): building shared models without sharing data. J. Am. Med. Inform. Assoc. **19**, 758–764 (2012)
3. Fromknecht, C., Velicanu, D., Yakoubov, D.: A decentralized public key infrastructure with identity retention. IACR Cryptology ePrint Archive, p. 803 (2014)
4. Luu, L., Narayanan, V., Zheng, K.B.C., Gilbert, S., Saxena, P.: SCP: a computationally-scalable byzantine consensus protocol for blockchains. Cryptology ePrint Archive Report, p. 1168 (2015)

5. Lamport, L., Shostak, R., Pease, M.: The byzantine generals problem. ACM Trans. Program. Lang. Syst **4**, 382–401 (1982)
6. Bissias, G., Ozisik, A.P., Levine, B.N., Liberatore, M.: Sybil-resistant mixing for bitcoin. Proceedings of the 13th Workshop on Privacy in the Electronic Society, pp. 149–158 (2014)
7. Garay, J., Kiayias, A., Leonardos, N.: The bitcoin backbone protocol: analysis and applications. In: Oswald, E., Fischlin, M. (eds.) EUROCRYPT 2015, Part II. LNCS, vol. 9057, pp. 281–310. Springer, Heidelberg (2015). https://doi.org/10.1007/978-3-662-46803-6_10
8. Jiang, W., et al.: WebGLORE: a web service for grid logistic regressions. Bioinformatics **29**, 3238–3240 (2013)
9. Yan, F., Sundaram, S., Vishwanathan, S., Qi, Y.: Distributed autonomous online learning: regrets and intrinsic privacy preserving properties. IEEE Trans. Knowl. Data. Eng. **25**, 2483–2493 (2013)
10. Vukolić, M.: The quest for scalable blockchain fabric: proof-of-work vs. BFT replication. In: Camenisch, J., Kesdoğan, D. (eds.) iNetSec 2015. LNCS, vol. 9591, pp. 112–125. Springer, Cham (2016). https://doi.org/10.1007/978-3-319-39028-4_9
11. Mainelli, M., Smith, M.: Sharing ledgers for sharing economies: an exploration of mutual distributed ledgers (aka blockchain technology). J. Finance Perspect. **3**, 38–69 (2015)
12. Buterin, V.: A next-generation smart contract and decentralized application platform. White Paper (2014)
13. Swan, M.: Blockchain: Blueprint for a New Economy. O'Reilly Media Inc., Sebastopol (2015)
14. Maesa, D.D.F., Mori, P.: Blockchain 3.0 applications survey. J. Parallel Distrib. Comput. **138**, 99–114 (2020)
15. Irving, G., Holden, J.: How blockchain-timestamped protocols could improve the trustworthiness of medical science. F1000Research **5**, 222 (2016)
16. McKernan, K.J.: The chloroplast genome hidden in plain sight, open access publishing and anti-fragile distributed data sources. Mitochondrial DNA **27**, 1–2 (2015)
17. Jenkins, J., Kopf, J., Tran, B.Q., Frenchi, C., Szu, H.: Bio-mining for biomarkers with a multi-resolution block chain. In: Spie Sensing Technology + Applications, pp. 1–10 (2015)
18. Baxendale, G.: Can blockchain revolutionise EPRs? ITNOW **58**, 38–39 (2016)
19. Witchey, N.J.: Healthcare transaction validation via blockchain proof-of-work, systems and methods. Patent 20150332283, A1 (2015)
20. Dubovitskaya, A., Xu, Z., Ryu, S., Schumacher, M., Wang, F.: Secure and trustable electronic medical records sharing using blockchain. In: AMIA Annual Symposium Proceedings, vol. 2017, p. 650. American Medical Informatics Association (2017)
21. Ekblaw, A., Azaria, A., Halamka, J.D., Lippman, A.: A case study for blockchain in healthcare: "medrec" prototype for electronic health records and medical research data. In: Proceedings of IEEE Open and Big Data Conference, vol. 13, p. 13 (2016)
22. Coelho, F.C.: Optimizing disease surveillance by reporting on the blockchain. bioRxiv, p. 278473 (2018)
23. Gem (2019). https://gem.co/health/. Accessed 30 Nov 2019
24. Healthcare working group (2019). https://www.hyperledger.org/industries/healthcare. Accessed 30 Nov 2019

25. Lai, S.W., Xu, L.H., Liu, K., Zhao, J.: Recurrent convolutional neural networks for text classification. In: Proceedings of the 29th International Conference on Artificial Intelligence, pp. 2267–2273 (2015)
26. Buhmann, M.D.: Radial basis functions: theory and implementations. Cambridge University, Cambridge (2003)
27. Hyndman, J.B., Koehler, A.B.: Another look at measures of forecast accuracy. Int. J. Forecast. **22**, 679–688 (2006)

Fine-Grained Diagnosis Method for Microservice Faults Based on Hierarchical Correlation Analysis

Yusi Tang[1], Ningjiang Chen[1,2](✉), Yu Zhang[1], Xuyi Yao[1], and Siyu Yu[1]

[1] School of Computer and Electronic Information, Guangxi University, Nanning 530004, China
chnj@gxu.edu.cn

[2] Guangxi Key Laboratory of Multimedia Communications and Network Technology, Nanning 530004, China

Abstract. With the expansion of application scale, the dependence of microservices becomes more and more complex, which makes it difficult to accurately locate the root cause of failure. At present, many microservices fault diagnosis methods have the problems of high cost of fine-grained location and difficult to predict the fault propagation path, which leads to more false positives and low diagnosis efficiency. Therefore, this paper proposes a microservice fault diagnosis method based on correlation analysis. Firstly, the historical exception and fault data of microservices is collected and processed, and the exception event is defined. Secondly, the machine learning algorithm is used to mine the correlation between microservices and abnormal events, and the hierarchical correlation graph is constructed. Finally, a microservice fault diagnosis mechanism based on a hierarchical correlation graph is designed to infer the root cause of the fault and provide effective diagnosis information for administrators. Experimental results show that the mechanism can quickly locate the fault location and infer the root cause of microservice failure in a more fine-grained way.

Keywords: Microservice · Correlation analysis · Fault diagnosis · Cloud computing

1 Introduction

With the rapid development of applications and the improvement of delivery requirements, microservice architecture to support fine-grained division and independent deployment has become one of the mainstream architectures in current project development. The application of lightweight container technology based on docker provides rapid packaging, flexible deployment and efficient management for microservices [1]. In the complex cloud environment, any software defects, configuration discomfort, network instability and other issues may lead to microservice failure. Secondly, failures may spread with the expansion of dependency relationships, which makes the application of microservices very fragile. According to the research data [2], the average downtime caused by faults may cause a loss of about 10 million RMB per 10 min.

Y. Sun et al. (Eds.): ChineseCSCW 2021, CCIS 1491, pp. 14–28, 2022.
https://doi.org/10.1007/978-981-19-4546-5_2

Container management tools (such as Kubernetes, Swarm, Mesos, etc.) provide container choreography and fault recovery management for microservices, but lack of enough dependency management on microservices. Therefore, it is necessary to combine link tracking tools to monitor and manage the call tracks and dependencies of microservices, such as Google dapper [3]. Administrators usually set alarm policies to check application exceptions and analyze the root cause of failure. But the diagnosis process is not simple. The faults may involve multiple related microservices, or show a variety of abnormal states, resulting in a large number of potential fault cause sets, and manual diagnosis will become very heavy, time-consuming and error prone. The more the number of microservices, the more complex the microservice dependency and the lower the diagnostic efficiency. Therefore, it is necessary to find a diagnosis method which can quickly locate the fault range and analyze the fault cause automatically.

This paper proposes a microservice fault diagnosis mechanism based on correlation analysis:

Firstly, a method of dynamic construction of a hierarchical correlation graph is designed. The dependence strength is evaluated according to the correlation between microservice failure events, and FP growth [4] algorithm is used to mine correlation rules between abnormal events. Then, the correct correlation rules are screened out by using a random forest algorithm, and the hierarchical correlation graph is constructed.

Secondly, a framework of Correlation-analysis based Diagnosis for Microservice Faults (CDMF) is designed. Based on the hierarchical correlation graph model to infer the suspicious source of the fault, and according to the inference results, further optimize the correlation graph to improve the accuracy of reasoning.

2 Related Work

In order to improve the efficiency of finding fault source, researchers have proposed a variety of diagnostic methods. In reference [5], the fault location was determined by tracking program frequently executing trajectory calculation program's suspiciousness. [6] identifies errors related to the document execution chain. These methods need to test the application, and focus on the detection of single process or internal call defects, which are difficult to deal with the distributed interaction problem of a large number of microservice applications.

Model based fault diagnosis method is a hot spot in recent years. Reference [7–9] studied the microservice dependency graphs for detecting microservice abnormal operations by tracking microservice call trajectories. However, they only focus on a single node and do not support fault correlation analysis between multiple nodes. Reference [5, 10] established the dependence probability graph model to analyze the correlation of not adjacent nodes. However, due to only considering the characteristics of path execution frequency, there is a lack of in-depth mining. In addition, some researches adopt the method of combining machine learning with graph model. In order to conduct more fine-grained fault diagnosis, literature [11] constructs a hybrid graph model of microservice dependency graph and program execution graph by mining the normal execution flow between and within microservices. The integrity of the graph mainly depends on the detail level of the log, and the resource overhead is high. At the same time, it is difficult to provide more failure cause analysis.

Compared with the existing fault diagnosis methods, the CDMF framework measures the microservice dependence from the correlation of fault events, which can predict the fault propagation path. Based on the application characteristics of microservices, it extracts the possible fault events from multiple dimensions as the cause analysis, and constructs the hierarchical correlation graph model to infer the root cause of the fault. The strategy can quickly locate the fault location and infer the root cause of microservice failure in a more fine-grained way.

3 Problem Analysis

The main work of this paper is to provide more detailed and instructive diagnostic information for administrators. The CDMF framework adopts the method from rough to detailed to establish the hierarchical correlation graph model, which can reduce the scope of fault location and quickly locate the fault source. The architecture of CDMF is shown in Fig. 1, which mainly includes monitor, the hierarchical correlation graph generator and fault diagnosis modules. Microservice dependency evaluation and event correlation rule mining is realized by using the hierarchical correlation graph generator.

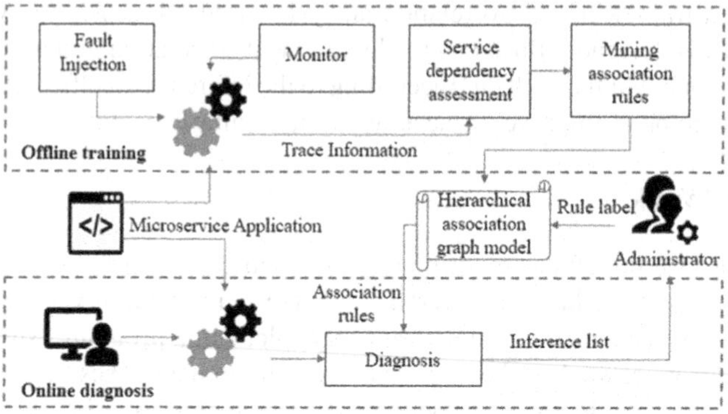

Fig. 1. CDMF architecture

The diagnosis process of CDMF framework is mainly divided into two parts, offline training and online diagnosis. In the training of offline model, the dependence strength between microservices is measured by calculating the correlation coefficient between historical fault events, and the microservice dependence graph is constructed to locate the fault range, so as to avoid the interference of a large number of unrelated abnormal events on fault diagnosis. FP growth algorithm is used to mine the correlation rules between the abnormal events in the historical fault scene, and the random Sen is used. In order to ensure the accuracy of correlation graph, a random forest algorithm is used to filter the rules. In the process of on-line diagnosis, according to the abnormal events collected from the fault scene and the hierarchical correlation graph model, the suspicious root cause of the fault is inferred, and the result tag feedback is used to further optimize the correlation graph, so as to achieve accurate and rapid fault location.

4 The CDMF Mechanism

4.1 Data Collection and Processing

Fault events are the main concern of diagnosis, and abnormal events are powerful clues for diagnosis. The collected fault events are described by multiple groups, and the basic characteristics of the events are recorded.

Definition 1: Fault event. *FaultEvent* = *(FName, FStarttime, FEndtime, FLocation, FType)* is used to describe the fault situation in the system, where *FName* represents the name of the fault event, *FStarttime* and *FEndtime* indicate the start time and end time of the fault respectively, *FLocation* represents the location of the fault, and *FType* represents the fault type.

In order to effectively analyze the root cause of the failure, we analyze the abnormal changes of each indicator from the three dimensions of node, container and microservice. The basic data information collected is shown in Table 1.

Table 1. Basic data information

Data dimension	Event description	Data type
Nodes	CPU consumption relative to its CPU limit; CPU utilization; Memory consumption relative to its memory limit; Memory utilization; Disk utilization; Bandwidth utilization; The number of microservice; CPU utilization;	Time series; event sequences
Container	Memory utilization; Bandwidth utilization; Port state; Running state, etc.	Time series; event sequences
Microservice	The CPU limit is relative to that of nodes; The memory limit is relative to that of nodes; The CPU consumption is relative to its CPU limit; The memory consumption is relative to its memory limit; The call frequency of microservice instance; Execution time of microservice call; HTTP response status of the call; Track operation condition; Microservice status; Microservice request failure rate; Configuration update; Microservice upgrade, etc.	Event sequences

In order to construct the fault cause set more comprehensively, we transform the collected time series and event sequence metrics into an event description of an abnormal state. Each abnormal state is a possible cause of failure.

Definition 2: Abnormal event. *AbnormalEvent* = *(AName, AStarttime, ALocation, AType)* is used to describe the abnormal state of system runtime data, where *AName* represents the name of the exception event, *AStarttime* indicates the timestamp when the event occurs, *ALocation* records the location of the event, and *AType* represents the event type.

4.2 Hierarchical Correlation Graph Modeling

In order to reduce the fault influence range according to the strength of the dependency relationship in the fault inference process. The dependency strength is measured by analyzing the correlation of fault events. The higher the dependency strength is, the more likely the fault will pass along with the dependency relationship. It supports correlation analysis and diagnosis of multiple nodes. Secondly, considering the direct or indirect correlation between the abnormal events, we construct the event correlation graph to describe the relationship between the fault cause sets. Next, this section describes the construction process of the hierarchical correlation graph.

Microservice Dependency Graph

If two microservices fail at the same time or successively, and they belong to a node or have a dependency relationship, then the two microservices are more likely to be affected. Therefore, the intensity of microservice dependence is measured by calculating the temporal and spatial correlation of fault events. Suppose that the time interval is equal $\{t_1, t_2, \ldots, t_{n-1}, t_n\}$, when microservice S_i and S_j at time t_n has a fault, and the exact fault time may be between t_{n-1} and t_n. If the fault time of microservice S_i and S_j is recorded as t_{ni} and t_{nj}, the average time between failures of all time periods of the system is as follows:

$$\Delta t = \frac{1}{n-1} \sum\nolimits_{m=1}^{n} \left| t_{mi} - t_{mj} \right| \tag{1}$$

Based on the consideration of time distance, this paper uses spherical covariance to calculate event correlation. Assuming that the time of each node is consistent and the time distance between f_{in} and f_{jm} is $df_{in,jm}$, the correlation $C_f(df)$ between fault events is calculated:

$$C_f\left(df_{in,jm}\right) = \begin{cases} 1 - \frac{3}{2}\left(\frac{df_{in,jm}}{\Delta t}\right) + \frac{1}{2}\left(\frac{df_{in,jm}}{\Delta t}\right), 0 \le df_{in,jm} \le \Delta t,\ \Delta t > 0 \\ 0,\ df_{in,jm} > \Delta t \end{cases} \tag{2}$$

$C_f(df_{in,jm})$ represents the correlation between the n th fault event on microservice S_i and the m th fault event on microservice S_j. When the distance df tends to 0, the event correlation degree reaches the maximum value, and the maximum value is 1. When the distance df is greater than the mean time between failures, the event correlation degree is 0. The greater the correlation coefficient of fault events between microservices is, the higher the dependence intensity is. In addition, there are spatial constraints between microservices, and the probability of fault propagation will increase when two microservices communicate frequently. In order to consider the influence of time and space, the dependence strength SR_{ij} between any two microservices S_i and S_j is expressed as:

$$SR_{ij} = \sum_{fin,jm} C_f\left(dfin,jm\right) \times P_{ij} \tag{3}$$

P_{ij} is the proportion of the total number of calls between microservices S_i and S_j. the larger the proportion value, the stronger the dependence between microservices. The graph theory is used to describe the microservice dependence structure and correlation strength of the whole microservice system:

Definition 3: Microservice dependency graph—*DGraph. DGraph* = (*Microservice, Edge*), *Microservice* is the collection of microservices in the system, *Edge* represents the set of dependencies between microservices, and each directed edge has a weight, that is, the dependency strength of microservices.

When $SR_{ij} \geq \alpha$ (the threshold set to measure the strength of dependency), it indicates strong dependency.

The current microservice failure is most likely to spread to other microservices which are closely related to it. Through the microservice dependency graph, the scope of fault influence can be preliminarily determined, and the microservice abnormal events within the scope can be associated together to analyze the cause of failure, and eliminate the interference of unrelated microservice abnormal events. Next, the fault cause is further analyzed by building event correlation graph. The example of Microservice dependency graph is shown in Fig. 2.

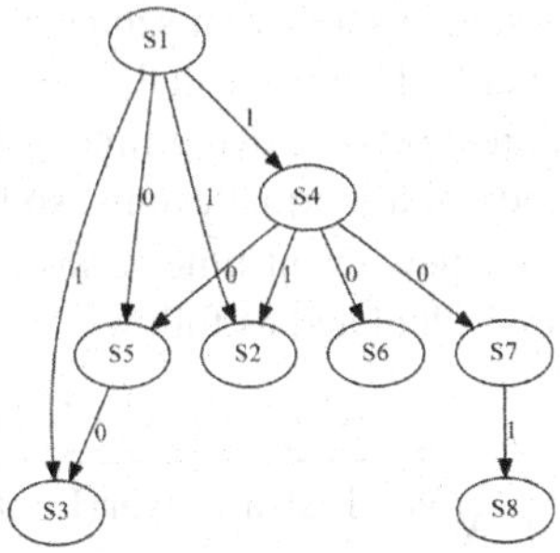

Fig. 2. Microservice dependency graph

Event Correlation Graph

There will be more abnormal events in the fault site. It will be a hard work to check all the abnormal events. This paper uses FP growth algorithm to mine correlation rules between historical abnormal events.

Definition 4: Abnormal symptom event rules—*AseRules*. If abnormal event a_i and a_j constitutes an correlation rule, that is, $a_i \rightarrow a_j$, which means that a_i occurs earlier than a_j, and a_i leads to the occurrence of a_j, then the $Rule(a_i \rightarrow a_j)$ is expressed as a *Rule*.

The abnormal events are sorted according to the time series and recorded as abnormal list. The time window is set to divide the abnormal list into transactions, and each of which is marked as $l_m = \{a_1, a_2, \ldots, a_i\}$, and $l_m \in AbnormalList$. The frequent itemsets of abnormal events that occur in the same transaction are counted, and the correlation characteristics of the events are mined, as shown in Table 2.

Table 2. Feature of rules

Rule$(a_i \rightarrow a_j)$	Feature description
Support	Event a_i and a_j the frequency of simultaneous occurrence of the same transaction
Confidence$_1$	Conditional probability $P(a_i \mid a_j)$
Confidence$_2$	Conditional probability $P(a_j \mid a_i)$
Lift	$P(a_i \mid a_j)/P(a_i)$
KULC	$P(a_i \mid a_j) * 0.5 + P(a_j \mid a_i) * 0.5$
IR	$P(a_i \mid a_j)/P(a_j \mid a_i)$
Pearson	*Pearson* correlation coefficient
Location relation	Event a_i and a_j Whether J occurs in the same host, node or microservice, or the dependency strength between microservices
$P_{correct}$	Probability of correct rules

Because the collection and statistics of event sequence data in database is not real-time, there is a problem of data delay. Therefore, in the calculation of Pearson correlation coefficient, this paper uses the method of moving time window to shift the time series $List(a_i)$ and $List(a_j)$ of two kinds of abnormal events, so that the start time of the two events is relatively equal to get a new event time series $List(a_i)^{\sim}$ and $List(a_j)^{\sim}$, The Pearson correlation coefficient is calculated as follows.

$$\text{Pearson} = \frac{\text{Cov}(\text{List}(\text{a}_\text{i})^{\sim}, \text{List}(\text{a}_\text{j})^{\sim})}{\sqrt{\text{Var}(\text{List}(\text{a}_\text{i})^{\sim})\text{var}(\text{List}(\text{a}_\text{j})^{\sim})}} \tag{4}$$

where $\text{Pearson} \in [-1, 1]$.

The closer the correlation coefficient of two events is to the value of both ends, the stronger the correlation is, and the closer to zero, the weaker the correlation is. In each time window WL, if a_i always occurs before a_j, we can infer that a_i causes the occurrence of a_j, and the correlation rule is expressed as $Rule(a_i \rightarrow a_j)$. If both always occur at the same time, a_i and a_j may interact with each other and save the rules $Rule(a_i \rightarrow a_j)$ and $Rule(a_j \rightarrow a_i)$.

In the mining correlation rules, there are a large number of weak correlation and redundant rules, which are easy to interfere with the accuracy of learning. Therefore, in this paper, a rule filter is established by using a random forest [12] algorithm to eliminate the error rules. Compared with Decision Trees [13] and Naive Bayes [14] and other representative machine learning classification algorithms, Random Forest method performs better in the face of multidimensional data features.

In the rule features, $P_{correct}$ is defined to record the correct probability of the rule, and its initial value is set to 0.5, indicating the uncertain state. The value of $P_{correct}$ is updated after getting the optimal classification result of correlation rules every time. When $P_{correct}$ is greater than 0.5, it means that the rule is more likely to be correct, while $P_{correct}$ less than 0.5 means that the rule is more likely to be wrong. After the correlation rules are trained, the correct rules are obtained. The support degree of each rule is taken as the weight of the edge to construct the abnormal event correlation graph dynamically, and then the subsequent fault cause inference is carried out. The mining and filtering process of correlation rules is shown in Fig. 3.

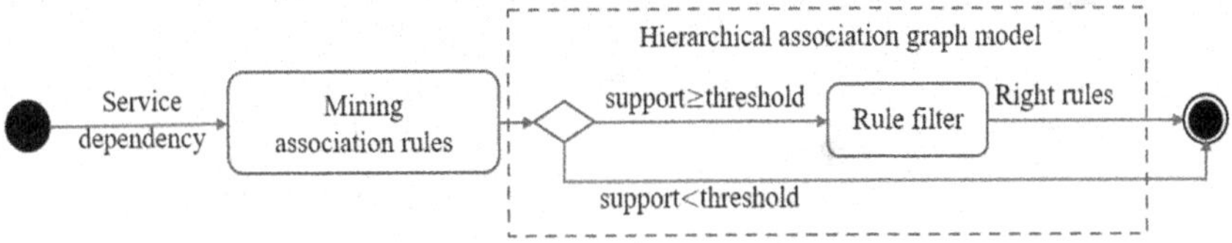

Fig. 3. The process of mining and classifying correlation rules

Definition 5: Event correlation graph—*EGraph*. $EGraph = (Event, Rule)$, *Event* is the set of exception events, and *Rule* is the set of correlation rules between events, and the support degree of each rule is taken as the value of the directed edge of the correlation graph, and then each exception event is linked to form a directed graph.

The hierarchical correlation graph, which is composed of microservice dependency graph and event correlation graph, can reduce the suspicious range of fault and provide effective information for analyzing the root cause of failure. Next, the process of fault inference will be described. The example of event correlation graph is shown in Fig. 4.

4.3 Fault Diagnosis

When a microservice failure occurs, the diagnostor first locks all related microservices which have strong dependence according to the microservice dependency graph. Then, based on the trained correlation rules, it collects the abnormal events of all related microservices on the fault site, and dynamically builds the correlation graph, and then infer the root cause of the fault according to the correlation path. The most observable case is that the real cause of the fault can be ranked first in the list.

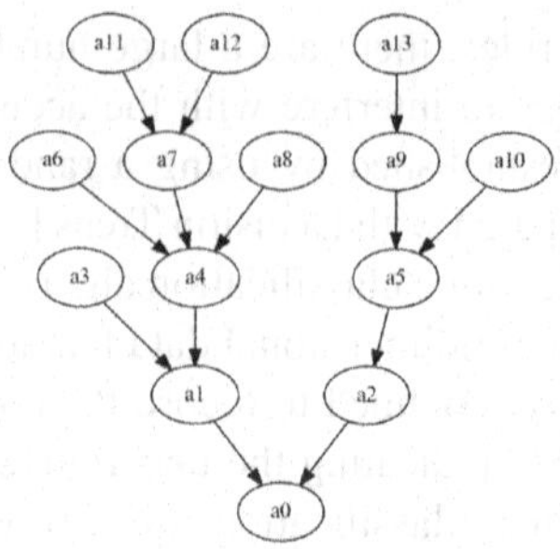

Fig. 4. Event correlation graph

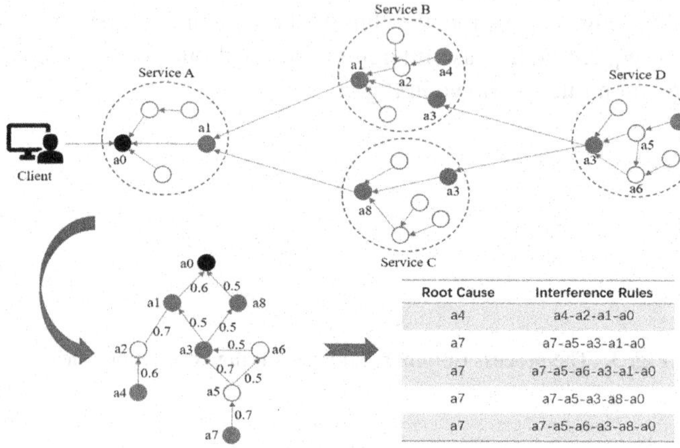

Fig. 5. Inference process of root cause of fault

In Fig. 5, the working process of microservice fault cause inference based on the hierarchical correlation graph is shown. The process of exception events mainly includes:

Step 1: Locate the fault range preliminarily. Suppose a_4,a_7 is the cause of failure a_0, When $SR > \alpha$, the microservice is saved to the related microservice collection (*RService*). In Fig. 3, all the microservices B, C, D related to fault microservice a_0 are locked. The search is continued until all related microservices are locked.

Step 2: Constructing the event correlation graph. The arrow symbol represents the direction of Event Correlation, and the event correlation graph with the support degree of each rule as the edge weight is built.

Step 3: Reason inference. To start with the fault event, the fault event a_0 as the starting node of the search, depth first search method is used to search the leaf node one by one from the directional edge with high weight. Then, the node is used as the starting point to find the nodes with higher weight and not visited, until all the root nodes and their access paths are saved, and the inference list of fault root causes is obtained.

In the process of diagnosis, the administrator checks the inference path and marks the correlation rules with classification errors, so as to update the event correlation graph in the next correlation rule learning. Next, the effectiveness of the proposed method is verified by experiments.

5 Experimental Evaluation

We verify the effectiveness of CDMF on a controlled Kubernetes cluster. Five physical servers with E5-2620 CPU and 32 GB memory are used as testing. Multiple virtual nodes are established in the cluster. Each node is configured with 4 CPU cores, 4 GB memory and 100 GB disk space, and Centos7.6 system and docker container are deployed. In the experiments, the sock Shop application [15] is deployed, which is an open source small and medium-sized microservice benchmark application, including 8 microservices and 10 tracking types. Secondly, it integrates Prometheus component for cluster state monitoring, and Jaeger component for microservice running track monitoring and dependency discovery. Finally, the CDMF diagnosis prototype system designed in this paper is deployed to the nodes for experimental verification.

In order to collect the fault event data, the faults are injected dynamically to simulate the CPU, memory, network and abnormal transmission conditions, resulting in application interruption. Each failure lasts for 30 s, and then returns to normal. The experiment simulates about 2260 microservice failures, and selects the most frequent fault event a_0 to simulate the collection of abnormal event data. The time window of the fault site is set as 15 min, and then the related abnormal events occur simultaneously or successively in this time period. The time interval between the two events is not more than 10 s, and some disturbing abnormal events are set randomly. Through this simulation method, the fault events are collected, and there are 42 kinds of abnormal events.

5.1 Data Collection and Processing

Evaluation of Microservice Dependence Intensity

The failure events are divided into three stages: 500, 1000 and 2000, and the microservice dependence intensity is calculated. The evaluation results are described in the form of thermal diagram, as shown in Fig. 6. The darker the color, the higher the dependence, otherwise the lower. Secondly, in order to eliminate the influence of Autocorrelation value on α, the value is set to 0.

According to the experiment, when the fault event is 500, the value of threshold α is 8.94. If the fault event is 1000, the value of threshold α is 17.35. And when the fault event is 2000, the value of threshold α is 33.39. In Fig. 6, when $SR \geq \alpha$, it indicates that there is a strong dependency between the two microservices and is marked with a red border. With the increase of fault events, the value of microservice dependence strength is continuously accumulated, and the relationship between microservice dependence strength and weakness is gradually stable.

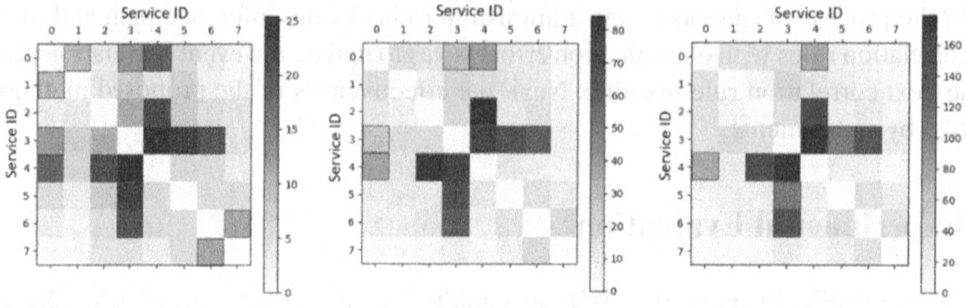

a. FaultEvent is 500 b. FaultEvent is 1000 c. FaultEvent is 2000

Fig. 6. Microservice dependency matrix heat map (Color figure online)

Through the evaluation of microservice dependence strength, the microservices which have strong dependence on each other are gathered, the scope of fault transmission is foreseen, and the correct direction for preliminary fault location is determined.

Trusted Rule Mining

42 kinds of abnormal events were collected in the experiments by simulating the fault event scene, and 1722 correlation rules were formed between the abnormal events. After mining the correlation features between them, the rules with support degree greater than 20 as the learning samples are selected, and 128 credible rules are screened. However, according to the professional domain knowledge, only 13 correct rules were involved, and these 13 positive rules were positive the correlation diagram composed of definite rules is shown in Fig. 7.

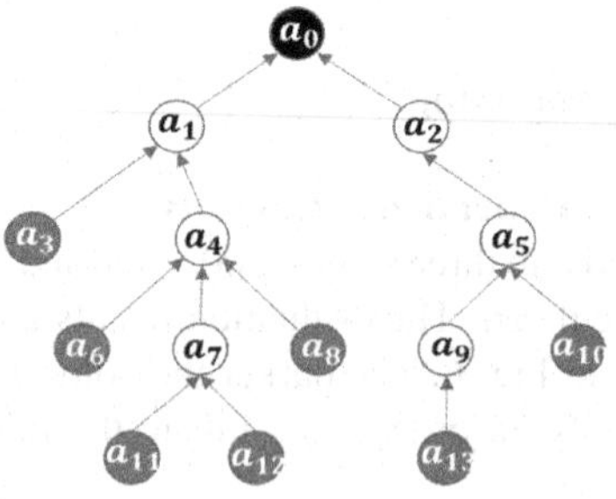

Fig. 7. Event causal legend

In Fig. 7, root node a_0 means fault event, $a_1 \sim a_{13}$ is the cause of the fault event, while the leaf node $a_3, a_6, a_{11}, a_{12}, a_8, a_{13}, a_{10}$ is the source of random triggering failure events. The possible triggering event a is listed in Table 3.

If a_1 (CPU utilization > 80%) and a_2 (memory utilization > 80%) is trigger a_0, and a_1 is defined by a_3 (HTTP response exception) or a_4 (response time delay), according to the relationship between the abnormal events, we can find out the root cause of the failure. Therefore, the more accurate the constructed correlation graph is, the higher

Table 3. Cause of triggering failure event a_0

Abnormal events	Description	Abnormal events	Description
a_0	The microservice is not available	a_7	The request failed
a_1	CPU utilization > 80%	a_8	The call frequency is too high
a_2	Memory usage > 80%	a_9	Microservice memory limit is higher than node memory limit
a_3	HTTP abnormal response	a_{10}	Microservice memory consumption is higher than node memory limit
a_4	Response time delay	a_{11}	The microservice network is abnormal
a_5	Execution time delay	a_{12}	Perform track offset
a_6	Microservice CPU consumption is higher than node CPU limit	a_{13}	Configuration update

the accuracy of the inference result is. Next, we need to use the rule learning model to identify the 13 correct rules, and to infer the fault cause accuracy.

5.2 Evaluation of Diagnosis Effect

In the inferential list, the higher the ranking of the root cause of the fault is, the more beneficial it is for administrator to check the real cause of the fault. The root cause of the fault is arranged in the top three of the inference list as the goal to verify the accuracy of the inference method. Every time the fault root cause is inferred, the correct rate of the inference results in the inference list and the ratio of top-3 as the fault root cause are recorded, and then the tag feedback is used to infer again. The correct fault source is obtained after multiple inference. The experimental results are shown in Fig. 8.

In the classification of correlation rules, correlation rules can be classified correctly after 6 times of learning and 24 times of inference. As shown in Fig. 8, the root cause of all suspected faults can be inferred after the 16th inference. At the same time, after 21 inferences, the top three of the list can completely list the suspected fault sources, which has both efficient and accurate inference results.

In order to verify that the CDMF framework has certain advantages in dealing with and inferring the relationship between more complex abnormal events, more abnormal events are added in the time window of 0, which increases the fault complexity of the whole system and the scale of event correlation graph. According to the three different scale rules listed in Table 4, the learning effect and inference accuracy are analyzed.

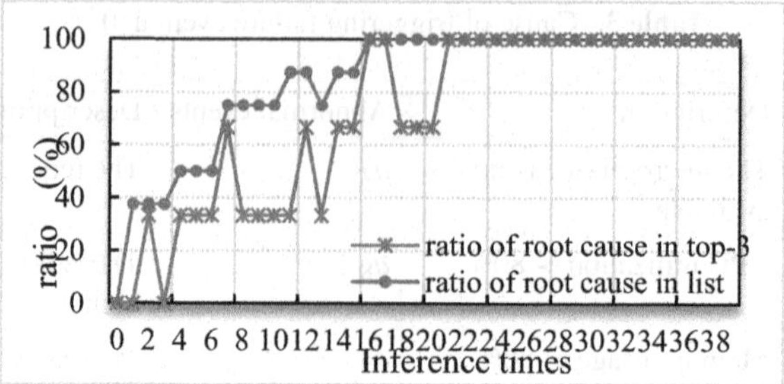

Fig. 8. Infer the accuracy of top-3 list

Table 4. Correct rules of different scales

Event nodes	Trusted rules	Correct rules	Root cause of failure
50	496	49	31
100	825	99	54
150	1247	149	81

By learning rules of different scales, the classification accuracy (the ratio of correct rules to all rules in correct class) and the coverage rate of correct rules (the probability that correct rules are divided into correct classes) are recorded, as shown in Fig. 9.

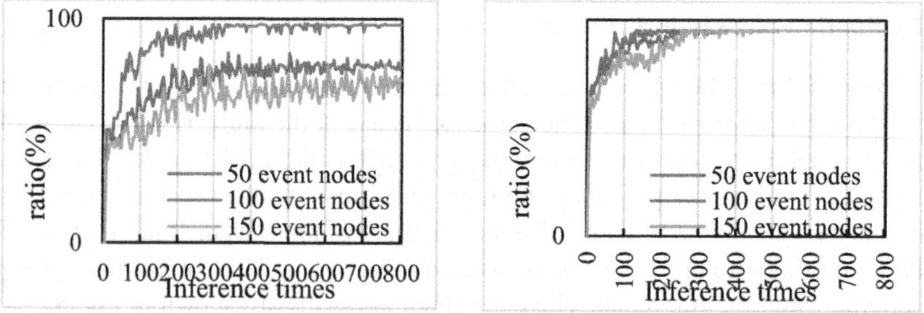

a. Accuracy of classification b. Coverage of correct rules

Fig. 9. Learning accuracy and inferential accuracy under different scale rules

As shown in the experimental Fig. 9(a), the more event nodes, the more complex the rule relationship formed, and the accuracy rate of rule classification is also relatively reduced. However, as shown in Fig. 9(b), the coverage rate of real rules of classification results can be maintained at a high rate. After 300 inferences, the correct coverage rate of rules of three scales is close to 100%. The probability comparison of fault source in top-3 inference list under different scale rules is shown in Fig. 10.

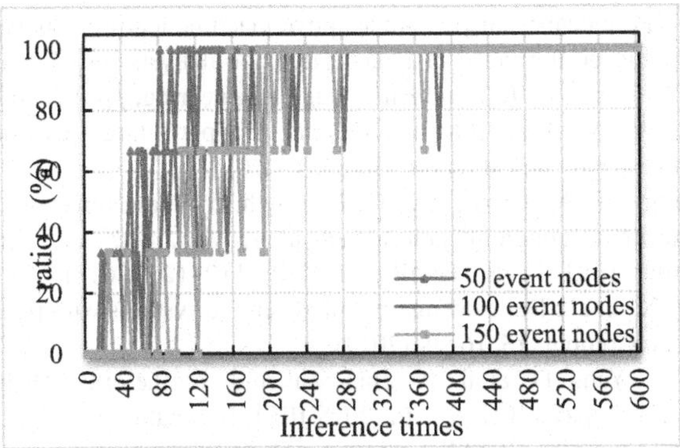

Fig. 10. Inferential accuracy under different scale rules

Experimental results show that with the increase of the number of event nodes, the inference effect of CDMF framework decreases. However, after 280 fault inferences, the correct fault source can be arranged in the top-3 of the inference list in most cases, which can still ensure the correctness of fault source inference.

6 Conclusion

Aiming at the problems that the existing fault diagnosis methods are not fine enough and the ability of correlation diagnosis is weak, a microservice fault diagnosis method based on correlation analysis is proposed. The CDMF framework fully considers the influence of the correlation of fault events in time and space on the strength of microservice dependence, and effectively predict the fault propagation path and narrow the scope of fault location. In addition, the rule features between abnormal symptom events are deeply mined, and the causal graph for fault suspicious root inference is dynamically constructed through rule learning, which provides accurate inference information for fault location. Through the experiment, results show that the mechanism can infer the root cause of the fault and effectively improve the diagnosis efficiency. In the future work, more effective features will be excavated from many aspects to describe the more accurate hierarchical correlation graph model and provide more accurate information for microservice fault diagnosis.

Acknowledgements. This work is supported by the Natural Science Foundation of China (No. 61762008), the National Key Research and Development Project of China (No. 2018YFB1404404), the Major special project of science and technology of Guangxi (No. AA18118047-7), and the Guangxi Natural Science Foundation Project (No. 2017GXNS-FAA198141).

References

1. Merkel, D.: Docker: lightweight linux containers for consistent development and deployment. Linux J. **2014**(239), 76–90 (2014)

2. Romsaiyud, W., Premchaiswadi, W.: An adaptive machine learning on Map-Reduce framework for improving performance of large-scale data analysis on EC2. In: 2013 Eleventh International Conference on ICT and Knowledge Engineering, pp. 1–7. IEEE (2013)
3. Sigelman, B.H., Barroso, L.A., Burrows, M., et al.: Dapper, a large-scale distributed systems tracing infrastructure. Technical report, Google (2010)
4. Mallik, S., Bhadra, T., Mukherji, A.: DTFP-growth: dynamic threshold based FP-growth rule mining algorithm through integrating gene expression, methylation and protein-protein interaction profiles. IEEE Trans. NanoBiosci. **17**(2), 117–125 (2018)
5. Zhou, X., Peng, X., et al.: Delta debugging microservice systems with parallel optimization. IEEE Trans. Serv. Comput. **15**, 16–29 (2019)
6. Guo, A., Mao, X., Yang, D., et al.: An empirical study on the effect of dynamic slicing on automated program repair efficiency. In: 2018 IEEE International Conference on Software Maintenance and Evolution (ICSME), pp. 554–558. IEEE (2018)
7. Ma, S.P., Fan, C.Y., Chuang, Y., et al.: Using service dependency graph to analyze and test microservices. In: 2018 IEEE 42nd Annual Computer Software and Applications Conference (COMPSAC), pp. 81–86. IEEE (2018)
8. Zhou, X., Peng, X., Xie, T., et al.: Latent error prediction and fault localization for microservice applications by learning from system trace logs. In: Proceedings of the 2019 27th ACM Joint Meeting on European Software Engineering Conference and Symposium on the Foundations of Software Engineering, pp. 683–694. ACM (2019)
9. Li, X., Li, W., Zhang, Y., et al.: DeepFL: integrating multiple fault diagnosis dimensions for deep fault localization. In: Proceedings of the 28th ACM SIGSOFT International Symposium on Software Testing and Analysis, pp. 169–180. ACM (2019)
10. Yu, X., Liu, J., Yang, Z., et al.: The Bayesian Network based program dependence graph and its application to fault localization. J. Syst. Softw. **134**(1), 44–53 (2017)
11. Jia, T., Chen, P., Yang, L., et al.: An approach for anomaly diagnosis based on hybrid graph model with logs for distributed services. In: 2017 IEEE International Conference on Web Services (ICWS), pp. 25–32. IEEE (2017)
12. Biau, G.: Analysis of a random forests model. J. Mach. Learn. Res. **13**(2), 1063–1095 (2010)
13. Xiao, J., Stolkin, R., Leonardis, A.: Single target tracking using adaptive clustered decision trees and dynamic multi-level appearance models. In: IEEE Conference on Computer Vision and Pattern Recognition, pp. 4978–4987. IEEE (2015)
14. Feng, X., Li, S., Yuan, C., et al.: Prediction of slope stability using Naive Bayes Classifier. KSCE J. Civ. Eng. **22**(3), 941–950 (2018)
15. Sockshop. https://github.com/microservices-demo/microservices-demo

Two-Stage Clustering for Federated Learning with Pseudo Mini-batch SGD Training on Non-IID Data

Jianqing Weng, Songzhi Su(✉), and Xiaoliang Fan

Xiamen University, Xiamen 361005, China
ssz@xmu.edu.cn

Abstract. Statistical heterogeneity problem in federated learning is mainly caused by the skewness of the data distribution among clients. In this paper, we first discover a connection between the discrepancy of data distributions and their model divergence. Based on this insight, we introduce a K-center clustering method to build client groups by the similarity of their local updating parameters, which can effectively reduce the data distribution skewness. Secondly, this paper provides a theoretical proof that a more uniform data distribution of clients in training can reduce the growth of model divergence thereby improving the training performance on Non-IID environment. Therefore, we randomly divide the clients of each cluster in the first stage into multiple fine-grained clusters to flatten the original data distribution. Finally, to fully leverage the data in each fine-grained cluster for training, we proposed an intra-cluster training method named pseudo mini-batch SGD training. This method can conduct general mini-batch SGD training on each fine-grained cluster with data kept locally. With the two-stage clustering mechanism, the negative effect of Non-IID data can be steadily eliminated. Experiments on two federated learning benchmarks i.e. FEMNIST and CelebA, as well as a manually setting Non-IID dataset using CIFAR10 show that our proposed method significantly improves training efficiency on Non-IID data and outperforms several widely-used federated baselines.

Keywords: Federated learning · Clustering · Non-IID data

1 Introduction

Federated Learning [1] is a novel distributed collaborative machine learning that can cooperatively train high-performance models. Unlike centralized machine learning, federated learning applies *model-to-data* strategy, in which the computation of the network training is largely conducted locally, hence data privacy protection can be encapsulated on the device. The conventional federated learning paradigm includes the following cyclical processes: (1) The server first distributes the initialize model to devices. (2) Each device receives a model from the server and continues the training process using its local dataset. (3) Each device uploads its trained model to the server. (4) The server aggregates models from all online devices to a single model using a weighted averaging. Representative algorithms for this paradigm are FedAvg [2] and FedProx [3].

Y. Sun et al. (Eds.): ChineseCSCW 2021, CCIS 1491, pp. 29–43, 2022.
https://doi.org/10.1007/978-981-19-4546-5_3

However, this paradigm poses a major challenge to federated learning: performance degradation occurred in *Non-Independent and Identically Distributed* (Non-IID) environment [4]. The IID sampling of the training data is important to ensure the stochastic gradient is an unbiased estimate of the full gradient [5,6]. But such IID assumption is hard to guarantee in reality. Moreover, federated learning tries to learn a globally shared model to fit all clients' data distribution, but when data across clients is heterogeneous, the model will deviate from its optimal direction, resulting in performance degradation.

In this paper, we no longer follow the conventional learning paradigm of federated learning. Scientifically, we mitigate the problem of data distribution skewness fundamentally by incorporating two-stage clustering into federated learning. We first employ K-Center clustering to group all the clients into multiple clusters, each of which corresponds to a different central server. Our first stage clustering strategy can train multiple disjointed models that are targeted to clusters of similar clients, which reduces the data distribution skewness. Then we randomly group clients in each cluster into multiple fine-grained clusters and each cluster conducts a pseudo mini-batch SGD to train a local model. Our second stage clustering strategy can flatten the data distribution among clients and reduce the growth of model divergence caused by Non-IID environment.

Major contributions are:

- We discover a connection between the discrepancy of data distributions and their model divergence. Therefore, a K-Center clustering method is adopted to build client groups, aiming to reduce the discrepancy of clients data distributions and speed up the convergence.
- We provide a theoretical proof that an uniform data distribution of clients in training is more likely to reduce the growth of model divergence, thereby improving the training performance on Non-IID environment. Hence, a fine-grained clustering method is further adopted to flatten the original data distribution.
- We propose an intra-cluster training method, named pseudo mini-batch SGD training, that can conduct general mini-batch SGD training on each fine-grained cluster with the data stored locally.
- We evaluate our method on two federated benchmarks and CIFAR10 given a manually Non-IID setting. The results show that superior performance is obtained by our two-stage clustering method compared to other baselines. Both theoretical and practical analysis is provided to prove the effectiveness and robustness of our method.

2 Related Work

Federated learning has become one of the most popular learning paradigms for its capability of learning a powerful shared model from massively distributed clients without having to access their local data. Albeit its popularity, many challenges of federated learning remain to be solved [7]. Among these challenges, four core challenges are (1) Communication Efficiency [2], (2) Systems Heterogeneity [3], (3) Statistical Heterogeneity [8] and (4) Privacy Concerns [9,10]. Other challenges [11], such as scalability [12] and personalized models [13] in federated learning have also attracted lots of interest from many researchers.

In recent years, there is rapidly growing attention on the non-IID problems in conventional federated settings. For example, Li et al. [14] analyzed the convergence of FedAvg algorithm on non-IID data and establish a convergence rate for strongly convex and smooth problems. Karimireddy et al. [15] proposed tighter convergence rates for FedAvg algorithm for convex and non-convex functions with client sampling and heterogeneous data. Some novel framework extended the existing FL framework to tackle the data heterogeneity problems. For example, Sattler et al. [16] proposed clustered federated learning (CFL) by integrating federated learning and bi-partitioning-based clustering into an overall framework. Thapa et al. [17] proposed a hybrid distributed learning approach, named SplitFed, that bring federated learning and split learning together to combine the advantages of both.

3 Background and Motivation

In this section, we introduce the model divergence problem in federated learning and demonstrate two enlightening thought that can help us to tackle Non-IID challenges.

3.1 Model Divergence in Federated Learning

Zhao et al. [18] analyzed the negative effect of Non-IID data on the performance from a unique perspective. He inferred from experiments that the *model divergence*, which quantifies the difference of weights from federated training setting and the centralized training setting with the same weight initialization is associated with the skewness of the data distribution. He further drew the conclusion that the root cause of the model divergence is the distance between the data distribution on each client and the population distribution, which can be formulated as **Proposition 3.1** in [18]:

$$\begin{aligned} \left\|\boldsymbol{w}_{mT}^{(f)} - \boldsymbol{w}_{mT}^{(c)}\right\| &\leq \sum_{k=1}^{K} \frac{n^{(k)}}{n} (a^{(k)})^T \left\|\boldsymbol{w}_{(m-1)T}^{(f)} - \boldsymbol{w}_{(m-1)T}^{(c)}\right\| \\ &+ \eta \cdot [\sum_{k=1}^{K} \frac{n^{(k)}}{n} \cdot \sum_{i=1}^{C} \left\|p^{(k)}(y=i) - p(y=i)\right\| \cdot \sum_{t=1}^{T-1} (a^{(k)})^t \\ &\times g_{max}(\boldsymbol{w}_{mT-1-k}^{(c)})] = \mathcal{P}_1 \cdot \left\|\boldsymbol{w}_{(m-1)T}^{(f)} - \boldsymbol{w}_{(m-1)T}^{(c)}\right\| + \mathcal{P}_2 \end{aligned} \tag{1}$$

$\boldsymbol{w}_{mT}^{(f)}$ denotes the weighted average global model after the m-th aggregation while $\boldsymbol{w}_{mT}^{(c)}$ denotes the weight after mT-th update in the centralized setting, $g_{max}(\boldsymbol{w}) = max_{i=1}^{C} \left\|\nabla_{\boldsymbol{w}} E_{\boldsymbol{x}|y=i} log f_i(\boldsymbol{x}, \boldsymbol{w})\right\|$ and $a^{(k)} = 1 + \eta \sum_{i=1}^{C} p^{(k)}(y = i)\lambda_{\boldsymbol{x}|y=i}$ with Lipschitz constanst $\lambda_{\boldsymbol{x}|y=i}$ for each class $i \in [C]$.

The term $\sum_{i=1}^{C} \left\|p^{(k)}(y = i) - p(y = i)\right\|$ is **earth mover's distance (EMD)** between the data distribution on client k and the population distribution. If the training data is IID, then the EMD is 0, which means no more model divergence between federated settings and centralized setting. In such case, federated learning is equivalent to centralized learning. If the training data is Non-IID, then the EMD will exist, causing the model divergence increase after each aggregation.

3.2 Federated Learning with Multiple Clusters

In traditional federated learning, data distributions among clients naturally diverge and only one identical global model will be learned, hence it is extremely challenging to provide every client with a model that optimally fits the local data distribution. To overcome this problem, we adopt a clustering algorithm to generate multiple clusters and each cluster contains clients with approximate IID data.

We provide a rationale for this observation. Defining our training loss with the widely-used cross-entropy loss, given the initial global model w_{init} at round t, the local model on client k after one iteration of SGD training can be represented by:

$$\boldsymbol{w}_1^{(k)} = \boldsymbol{w}_{init} - \eta \sum_{i=1}^{C} p^{(k)}(y=i) \nabla_{\boldsymbol{w}} E_{x|y=i}[log f_i(\boldsymbol{x}, \boldsymbol{w}_{init})].$$

Thus, the model divergence between client k and client k' can be measured as $\left\| w_1^{(k)} - w_1^{(k')} \right\|$. Following the same derivation process in [18], we can derive the upper bound of the model divergence after the first iteration at round t.

$$||\boldsymbol{w}_1^{(k)} - \boldsymbol{w}_1^{(k')}|| \leq \eta g_{max}(\boldsymbol{w}_{init}) \sum_{i=1}^{C} \left\| p^{(k)}(y=i) - p^{(k')}(y=i) \right\|$$

where $g_{max}(\boldsymbol{w}_{init})$ is only related to weights of centralized training. This implies that if different clients are initialized by an identical global model $\boldsymbol{w}_{init}$ at each round of training, then their discrepancy of data distributions can implicitly reflect the magnitude of their model divergence.

Based on the sights above, we design an experiment to show that this clustering strategy can reduce the discrepancy of clients data distributions and speed up the convergence.

We use the concept "Degree of Non-IID" from [19] as the metric, which is defined as:

$$\frac{1}{n} \sum_{k=1}^{n} \|\nabla f_k(\boldsymbol{x}) - \nabla f(\boldsymbol{x})\|^2, \forall x \in R^d \tag{2}$$

where $f_k(\boldsymbol{x}) := E_{\xi \sim \mathcal{D}_k}[F_k(\boldsymbol{x};\xi)]$ is the local objective function and $f(\boldsymbol{x}) := \frac{1}{n}\sum_{k=1}^{n} f_k(\boldsymbol{x})$ is the global objective function.

In this experiment, to create the Non-IID environment, we follow the data preprocessing steps in [3] that distribute the data among 1,000 devices such that each device has samples of only two digits and the number of samples per device follows a power law and train a two-layer CNN model.

We first perform 10 rounds of federated training for all clients and obtain the initial model $\boldsymbol{w}_{init}$. At the 11-th round, each client trains only one iteration of SGD using the local data to get $\boldsymbol{w}_1^{(k)}, k = 1, 2, .., 1000$. We then apply the K-Center clustering algorithm onto $w_1^{(1)}, ..., w_1^{(1000)}$ to group the 1000 devices into 3, 4 or 5 clusters. After clustering, each client cluster performs conventional federated learning independently.

As shown in Fig. 1, after 10 rounds of training, the clustering algorithm converges faster than FEDAVG algorithm with the degree of Non-IID dropped faster. This example implies that it is possible to reduce the discrepancy of clients data distributions and improve the performance of federated learning by grouping the clients into multiple clusters based on their weights.

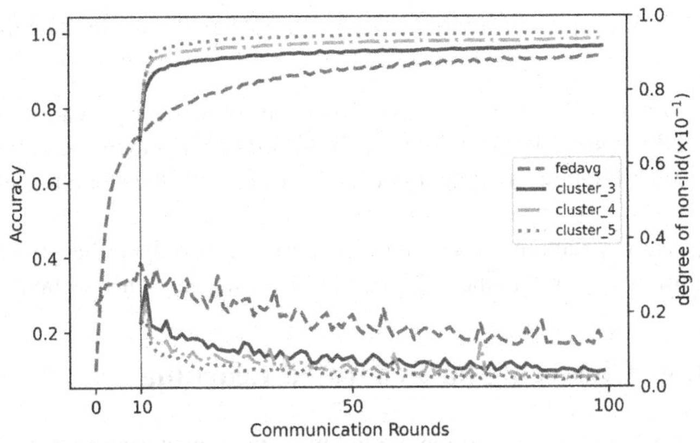

Fig. 1. Training a CNN model on non-IID MNIST data.

3.3 Reduction of the Growth of Model Divergence

Intuitively, if we flatten the data distribution among clients, we can improve the performance on Non-IID data. We think the explanation behind this intuition is that we can reduce the growth of model divergence by flattening the data distribution. We provide some mathematical reasoning for this explanation. Firstly, to obtain clients with more uniform data distribution, we simply divide all the clients into multiple groups of equal size and pool the data of clients in each group together to a new node.

Assume there are K clients participating training in federated learning, we divide every S clients into a group (we generate $\frac{K}{S}$ new nodes in total). Let $k_{s,j}$ represent the index of s-th client in the j-th group, where $s \in [S], j \in [\frac{K}{S}]$. Then, $\mathcal{N}_j = \{k_{1,j}, k_{2,j}, ..., k_{S,j}\}$ denotes the j-th node which contains the pooled data of clients in group j. Next the new upper bound of the model divergence in scenario where we let $\frac{K}{S}$ nodes participate in federated learning is derived.

Let $\boldsymbol{w}_t^{\prime(j)}$ denote the weights of node j at iteration t. Refer to formula (1), we can easily derive the new model divergence:

$$\begin{aligned}\left\|\boldsymbol{w}_{mT}^{\prime(f)} - \boldsymbol{w}_{mT}^{(c)}\right\| &\leq \sum_{j=1}^{K/S} \frac{n^{\prime(j)}}{n} (a^{\prime(j)})^T \left\|\boldsymbol{w}_{(m-1)T}^{\prime(f)} - \boldsymbol{w}_{(m-1)T}^{(c)}\right\| \\ &+ \eta \cdot [\sum_{j=1}^{K/S} \frac{n^{\prime(j)}}{n} \cdot \sum_{i=1}^{C} \left\|p^{\prime(j)}(y=i) - p(y=i)\right\| \cdot \sum_{t=1}^{T-1} (a^{\prime(j)})^t \\ &\times g_{max}(\boldsymbol{w}_{mT-1-j}^{(c)})] = \mathcal{P}'_1 \cdot \left\|\boldsymbol{w}_{(m-1)T}^{\prime(f)} - \boldsymbol{w}_{(m-1)T}^{(c)}\right\| + \mathcal{P}'_2\end{aligned} \tag{3}$$

Using mathematical tools, we can prove $\mathcal{P}_1' \leq \mathcal{P}_1$ and

$$\sum_{i=1}^{C} \|p^{\prime(j)}(y=i) - p(y=i)\| \leq \sum_{k \in \mathcal{N}_j} \sum_{i=1}^{C} \left\|p^{(k)}(y=i) - p(y=i)\right\| \tag{4}$$

We provide the detailed proof of $\mathcal{P}_1' \leq \mathcal{P}_1$ and inequality (4) in Appendix[1].

Inequality (4) indicates that the EMD between the data distribution on node j and the population distribution is less than before grouping clients into j-th group, which illustrates that such simple clustering strategy can help us flatten the data distributions.

Since $\mathcal{P}_2$, $\mathcal{P}_2'$ are constant, $sup\{\left\|w_{mT}^{(f)} - w_{mT}^{(c)}\right\|\}$ and $sup\{\left\|w_{mT}^{\prime(f)} - w_{mT}^{(c)}\right\|\}$ increase by factors of $\mathcal{O}(\mathcal{P}_1)$ and $\mathcal{O}(\mathcal{P'}_1)$ after each round of aggregation, which illustrate the model divergence when training with original clients increase more faster than when training with the new generated nodes (we train with the same initial weights in all settings).

To summarise up, flattening the data distribution can reduce the growth of model divergence to improve performance of federated learning in Non-IID environment.

4 Two-Stage Clustering for Federated Learning

Based on Sects. 3.2 and 3.3, we implemented two-stage clustering method both can be included in federated learning to solve the Non-IID problems.

4.1 The First Stage Clustering

First, given all the clients on the global joint model trained up to round $t-1$, at the clustering step(at round t), we perform a communication round involving all the trained clients. The updated local model from all clients is then used to judge the discrepancy of clients data distributions and we employed K-Center clustering algorithm to generate clusters of clients. The determined clusters of clients are trained independently but simultaneously, initialized with the joint model at its current state.

Assuming clusters are indexed by c, under the first stage clustering setting, a specialised global model $\boldsymbol{w}^{(f_c)}$ will be trained for every cluster c of similar clients, and each model has different objectives such that:

$$\forall c \in [C], E_{p^{(k)}}[\ell(\boldsymbol{w}^{(k)})] = \ell(\boldsymbol{w}^{(f_c)}), k \in c$$

4.2 The Second Stage Clustering

As illustrated in Sect. 3.3, to even out the data distribution, we simply divide all the clients into multiple groups of equal size. Unlike the first stage clustering, which we group all clients based on their model weights. In the second stage, the way to cluster the devices depends on the specific application scenario. We provide two representative clustering approaches as follows.

Random Clustering. The typical way is to group devices into multiple clusters of equal size uniformly at random, which is simple and does not require additional information.

[1] The appendix document can be viewed on https://gitee.com/JianqingWeng/appendix-ccscw2021.

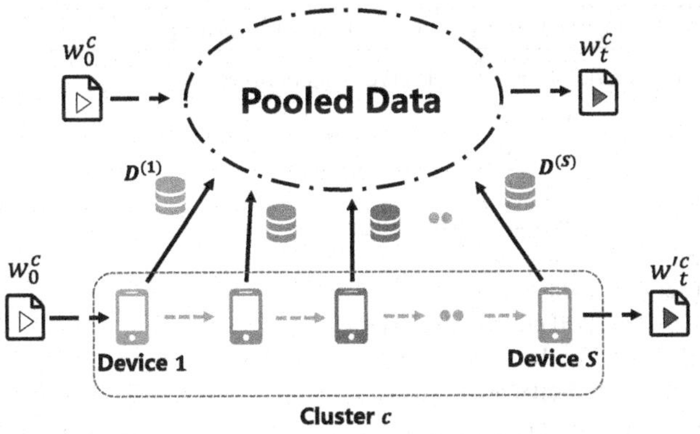

Fig. 2. Accessing the pooled data by using pseudo mini-batch SGD training.

Region-Based Clustering. Devices(or clients) are often distributed over the world, one can group the devices based on their geo-distribution. Such clustering strategy can usually reduce communication costs

4.3 Pseudo Mini-batch SGD Training

Having the second stage clustering completed, we need to pool the data of each cluster of clients to the new nodes as we demonstrated in Sect. 2.3. But in federated learning, to protect the data privacy, it requires data on devices can not be transferred to outside.

Since we cannot implement the operations of pooling data into one node, we find a way to achieve the purpose of accessing the pool data by transforming our original training method from *"data-to-model"* mode to *"model-to-data"* mode. Based on the new model, we proposed a novel training method called **pseudo mini-batch SGD training**, which allow us to fully leverage the pooled data in clusters of clients to train a model like the general mini-batch SGD training. The word *"pseudo"* indicates that it's not a real mini-batch SGD because the data of clients in each cluster still remain locally rather than pool together.

Assume we group S devices into cluster c. Each device $k, \forall k \in [S]$ possesses a local data set $\mathcal{D}^{(k)}$. Denote $\boldsymbol{w}_0^c$ as the initial model and t as the training iterations. As shown in Fig. 2, instead of using the pooled data $\mathcal{D} = \bigcup_{k=1}^{S} \mathcal{D}^{(k)}$ that we can't get to train a model $\boldsymbol{w}_t^c$, we can access the pooled data to train a model $\boldsymbol{w}_t'^c$.

We describe how pseudo mini-batch SGD training works. First, we pass $\boldsymbol{w}_0^c$ to the first device of cluster c as its initial model. Let device $k, \forall k \in [S]$ train with $t^{(k)}$ iterations where $\sum_{k=1}^{S} t^{(k)} = t$. Then, we pass the semi-trained model $\boldsymbol{w}_{t^{(k)}}^k$ to the next device $k+1$ as it's initial model $\boldsymbol{w}_0^{k+1}$ and keep training with $t^{(k+1)}$ iterations. When $k+1 > S$, we stop the training process and get the trained model $\boldsymbol{w}_{t^{(S)}}^S = \boldsymbol{w}_t'^c$.

To better understand pseudo mini-batch SGD training, we can think of each client as a *data storage station* that retains part of the data in the data pool. In distributed machine learning area, this form of data division is usually called *local shuffling*, which is: (1) shuffle the training data, (2) partition the data into non-overlapping subsets and

Algorithm 1. Two Stage Clustering For Federated Learning

1: Initialize clients' model $\left\{w^{(k)}\right\}$ and server's model $w_0^{(f)}$
2: **for** round $t \in [1, T_1]$ **do**
3: $w_t^{(f)} \leftarrow$ FederatedAveraging$(w_{t-1}^{(f)}, K)$
4: **end for**
5: Generate C clusters by K-Center Clustering ▷1st-stage
6: Initialize $\{w_0^{(f_c)}, c \in C\} \leftarrow w_{T_1}^{(f)}$
7: **for** each cluster $c \in C$ **do** ▷ In parallel
8: Generate fine-grained clusters in cluster c ▷2nd-stage
9: **for** round $t \in [1, T_2]$ **do**
10: $\{w^{(j,c)}\} \leftarrow$ PSEUDO-MB-SGD $(w_{t-1}^{(f_c)}, c)$
11: $w_t^{(f_c)} \leftarrow \sum_{j \in c} \frac{n^{(j,c)}}{\sum_{j \in c} n^{(j,c)}} w^{(j,c)}$
12: **end for**
13: **end for**
14:
15: **function** PSEUDO-MB-SGD$(w_{t-1}^{(f_c)}, c)$
16: **for** each fine-grained cluster $j \in c$ **do** ▷ In parallel
17: $w^{(tmp)} \leftarrow w_{t-1}^{(f_c)}$
18: **while** have not accessed all the data in j **do**
19: **for** each client $k_{s,j} \in j$ **do**
20: $w^{(k)} \leftarrow w^{(tmp)}$
21: $\{B_i\} \leftarrow$ Split $\mathcal{D}^{(k_{s,j})}$ into batches
22: **for** iteration $i \in [1, t_1^{(k_{s,j})}]$ **do**
23: $w^{(k)} \leftarrow w^{(k)} - \eta \nabla \ell(w^{(k)}, B_i)$
24: **end for**
25: $\mathcal{D}^{(k_{s,j})} = \mathcal{D}^{(k_{s,j})} - \{B_i\}$
26: $w^{(tmp)} \leftarrow w^{(k)}$
27: **end for**
28: **end while**
29: $w^{(j,c)} \leftarrow w^{(tmp)}$
30: **end for**
31: **return** $\{w^{(j,c)}\}$
32: **end function**

allocate each subset to a local worker. Batch size data can only be obtained from a specific data storage station (a random client) for training at each iteration.

4.4 The Entire Training Process

The entire training process is described in Algorithm 1. The function "FederatedAveraging" inputs a initialized model $w_{t-1}^{(f)}$ for round $t-1$ and K selected clients to perform the FedAvg algorithm, and outputs the weighted average model $w_t^{(f)}$ for round t.

To be noticed, in the second stage, we will not pass the model $w^k_{t^{(k)}}$ after training the whole $t^{(k)}$ iterations to the next client because continuous training of the same batch size of data will open up the possibility of over-fitting. We adopt a strategy called *multiple partial iterations* that we only train $t_1^{(k)}, t_1^{(k)} < t^{(k)}$ iterations on client k, but each client k need to train $t_2^{(k)}$ times so that $t_1^{(k)} \cdot t_2^{(k)} = t^{(k)}$.

5 Experiments

In this section, we evaluate our proposed Two-Stage clustering method on federated learning benchmarks in comparison with baseline and state-of-the-art methods. A detailed analysis is also provided.

5.1 Experiments Setup

Dataset and Local Model. In this experiment, we used two federated benchmarks datasets—FEMINST [20] and CelebA [21] in LEAF [22]. These two datasets have been pre-processed in advance so that they satisfy the federated setting environment well in realitys. In FEMNIST, we partitioned the handwritten images based on the writer of the digit/character. For CelebA, we partitioned the images by the celebrity on the picture and developed a classifier to recognize whether the person smiles or not. We provide statistics on these datasets in Table 1 and detailed network architecture in Table 2.

Table 1. Statistics on FEMNIST and CelebA datasets

Dataset	Number of devices	Samples	Samples per device	
			Mean	Stdev
FEMNIST	3200	678644	212.08	79.86
CelebA	9343	200288	21.44	7.63

Table 2. Network architecture of local model

FMNIST	CelebA
Input	Input
Conv1$(5 \times 5 \times 32)$[a]	Conv$(3 \times 3 \times 32)$
Pool1$(2 \times 2, strides = 2)$	BN
Conv2$(5 \times 5 \times 64)$	Pool$(2 \times 2, strides = 2)$
Pool2$(2 \times 2, strides = 2)$	Conv$(3 \times 3 \times 32)$
	BN
Fc1	Pool$(2 \times 2, strides = 2)$
Fc2	Fc
Softmax	Softmax

[a]Conv(H × W × N). H, W, N represent the height, width and number of filters.

Table 3. The comparison of our proposed method with other baselines on FEMNIST and CelebA. $\overline{Acc}$@Rounds denotes the average accuracy within a specific number of rounds.

Dataset	FMNIST				CelebA			
Metrics (%)	$\overline{Acc}$@Rounds			Top-Acc	$\overline{Acc}$@Rounds			Top-Acc
	30–50	50–100	100–150		30–50	50–100	100–150	
FedDist	16.9	35.8	59.7	66.0	61.8	64.4	72.7	78.5
FedProx	21.9	47.7	66.1	69.9	68.0	83.2	86.8	87.4
FedCluster	11.6	49.2	70.7	76.0	70.3	72.6	74.8	77.8
FL+HC	39.7	67.4	77.7	79.8	74.7	83.5	86.8	87.8
FedAvg(1)	35.9	62.1	73.7	75.8	68.0	82.9	86.7	87.6
FedAvg(3)	71.3	76.6	79.5	80.3	75.5	84.2	86.6	87.3
FedAvg(5)	74.4	77.9	80.1	80.8	**82.1**	86.1	87.3	87.8
FedSEM(2)	36.7	66.1	77.5	80.3	70.7	81.4	87.4	87.6
FedSEM(3)	32.7	62.1	75.1	77.7	67.1	71.7	79.1	84.1
FedSEM(4)	32.2	60.2	73.3	75.9	68.9	76.2	80.7	81.1
TSC+FL(3)	68.1	81.6	85.3	86.0	70.4	85.4	87.3	88.0
TSC+FL(5)	75.6	84.5	86.7	87.1	76.5	**87.1**	**88.2**	**89.0**
TSC+FL(10)	**82.8**	**87.2**	**88.1**	**88.3**	70.0	85.2	87.0	87.8

Baselines. We chose several classic and highly-relevant methods as baselines. (1) FedAvg(E): The traditional federated averaging algorithm from [2]. E denotes the local epoch. (2) FedDist: a distance based-objective function in Reptile meta-learning [23] to federated learning setting. (3) FedProx: Similar to FedAvg, but adding a proximal mapping term to constrain the local model from deviating too much from the global parameter [3]. (4) FedCluster: Enclose FedAvg into a hierarchical clustering framework [16]. (5) FL+HC: a modification to FL by introducing a hierarchical clustering step to separate clusters of clients [24]. (6) FedSEM(M): A multi-center federated learning method solved via federated SEM (FedSEM) with M centers [25].

Training Details. We randomly selected 355 clients on FEMINIST and 422 clients on CelebA at baseline experiment. For each client's data, we used 80% for training and 20% for testing. We used a batch size of 10 and a learning rate of 1e−3 for local optimizers. For our proposed two-stage clustering method, we set local epoch to 1 for all clients. In the second clustering stage, an increasing number of clients per fine-grained cluster will introduce additional communication overhead, hence we set the number of clients per cluster to 3,5 and 10. We trained 150 rounds on both datasets and report the average accuracy of 30 to 50 rounds, 50 to 100 rounds, 100 to 150 rounds as well as the top accuracy.

5.2 Empirical Results

Baseline Comparison Experiments. In this experiment, we use TSC+FL to represent our proposed method, two-stage clustering for federated learning. The number in brackets represents the number of clients in each fine-grained cluster. As shown in Table 3, our method outperforms other widely-used baselines, especially by a large margin in FEMNIST. In the FEMNIST experiment, when we set the number of clients in each fine-grained cluster to 3, the convergence rate of TSC+FL in 30–50 rounds is slower than FedAvg(3) and FedAvg(5). This is reasonable because the number of training iterations is less than FedAvg(3) and FedAvg(5) when we set the hyper-parameter to 3. After 50 rounds, the accuracy began to rise rapidly, exceeding FedAvg(3) and FedAvg(5). It shows our proposed method can effectively reduce the growth of model divergence than other baselines.

In the CelebA experiment, though the network performs a simple binary classification task, our proposed method still outperforms other baselines in the later stage of training. The experiment shows that our two-stage clustering strategy can significantly improve the training efficiency on Non-IID data.

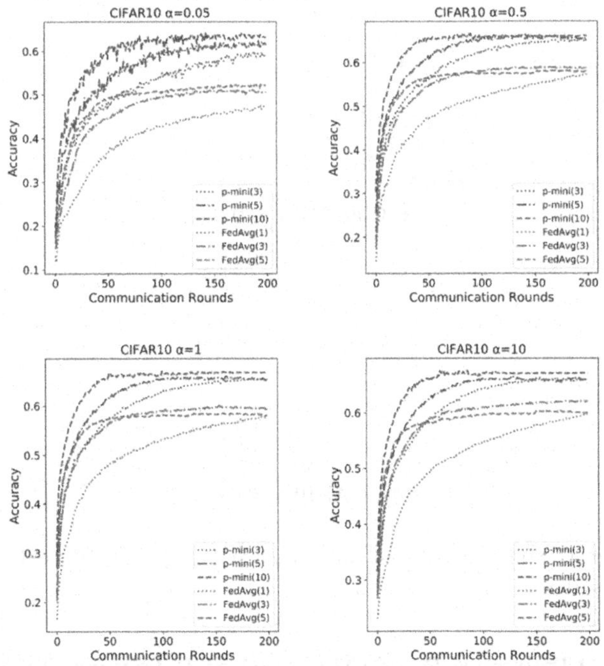

Fig. 3. Test set accuracy vs. communication rounds for the CIFAR10 dataset in manually setting non-iid environment. α control the skewness of the data distribution among client's data

Experiments on Manually Setting Non-IID CIFAR10 Dataset. We follow [26] to obtain a synthetic non-identical CIFAR10 dataset for 100 clients. We use a concentration parameter $\alpha, (\alpha > 0)$ to control the dependency of clients' data. The smaller α, the more skewness of the data distribution. *p-mini(N)* represents our pseudo mini-batch SGD training method with N clients per cluster. We skip the first stage clustering and directly adopt pusedo mini-batch SGD training on each cluster of clients. As shown in Fig. 3, FedAvg methods started to converge before reaching an accuracy of 0.6 and 0.5 (when $\alpha = 0.05$). While our proposed methods start to converge after reaching the accuracy of 0.64 and 0.6 (when $\alpha = 0.05$). Particularly, when the data is divided evenly, we can observe the similar growth curve in the early stage of training between FedAvg(3) and p-mini(3) as well as FedAvg(5) and p-mini(5). This is due to roughly the same amount of training iterations. But in the late stage of training, because of the slow rate of model divergence, our method can continuously improve the accuracy. The result intuitively shows our second clustering strategy with pseudo mini-batch SGD training effectively slow down the growth model divergence and thus improving training in Non-IID environment.

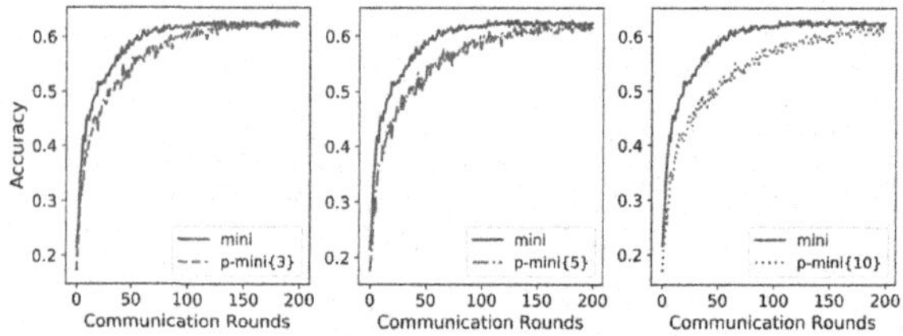

(a) CIFAR10 $\alpha = 0.05$

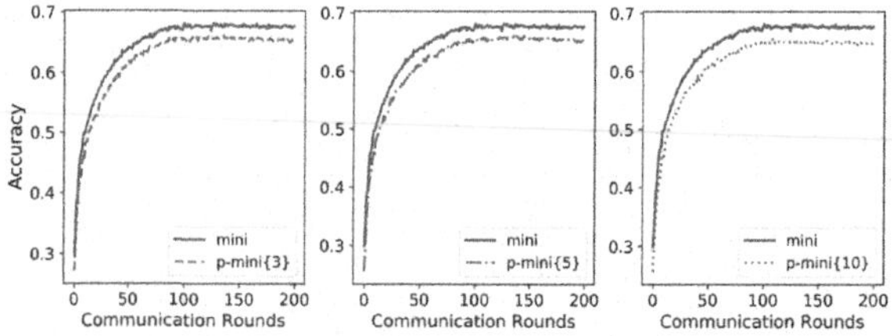

(b) CIFAR10 $\alpha = 0.5$

Fig. 4. Mini-batch SGD training vs Pseudo mini-batch SGD training for the CIFAR10 dataset in $\alpha = 0.05$ and $\alpha = 0.5$

Mini-batch SGD Training vs Pseudo Mini-batch SGD Training. To further demonstrate our pseudo mini-batch SGD training can train a model like the usual mini-batch SGD training, we compare their training performance in Non-IID environment. We use the same synthetic non-identical CIFAR10 dataset, seting α to 0.5 and 0.05. We divide every 5 clients into one cluster so that there are total 20 clusters. In the mini-batch SGD training, we pool the data of clients in each cluster to new devices and let these devices participate in training. In pseudo mini-batch SGD training, we can view each cluster of clients as a "new node" that we can access the data of all clients without transferring them, which achieve the goal of training a model using pooled data in another way. We let *mini* denote the mini-batch SGD training and let *p-mini*$\{M\}$ denote the pseudo mini-batch SGD training that each time we only train M iterations on each client.

As shown in Fig. 4, when $\alpha = 0.5$, the convergence rate of the two methods is roughly the same. The highest accuracy of mini-batch SGD training is only 0.05 higher than pseudo mini-batch SGD training. When $\alpha = 0.05$, although mini-batch SGD training converges faster, by the end of training, the accuracy of pseudo mini-batch SGD training gradually caught up. This experiments illustrate that our pseudo mini-batch training can replace mini-batch SGD in Non-IID environment and achieve the similar training effect.

Table 4. Ablation experiment on FEMNIST with different data size

Size	Stages	$\overline{Acc}$@Rounds(%)			Top-Acc
		30–50	50–100	100–150	
100	1st-stage	35.5	64.4	75.9	78.4
	2nd-stage	77.3	82.5	83.4	84.0
	Two-stage	**78.0**	**83.5**	**84.5**	**85.1**
200	1st-stage	42.0	67.3	77.3	79.2
	2nd-stage	79.2	83.8	85.3	85.7
	Two-stage	**81.5**	**85.7**	**87.2**	**87.7**
300	1st-stage	40.3	67.2	77.6	79.9
	2nd-stage	77.7	82.5	84.0	84.4
	Two-stage	**82.5**	**86.7**	**87.4**	**88.0**

5.3 Ablation Experiment

As we mentioned above, the two stages of clusterings are mutually beneficial and complementary with each other. With the execution of each stage, the negative effect of non-IID on training can be incrementally eliminated. To demonstrate the coupling and effectiveness between these two clustering stages, we separate each stage and compare each of them with the entire two-stage clustering method on FEMINIST with different data sizes.

As shown in Table 4, two-stage clustering for federated learning outperforms the methods with a single stage of clustering. To further compare the effectiveness of the two stages of clustering, the second stage shows better performance than using first stage clustering only, which indicates that reduction of the growth of model divergence has better effect than clusters clients according to the similarity of their model weight when training on non-IID data.

6 Conclusion

In this paper, we proposed a two-stage clustering method for federated learning to resolve the non-IID challenge in the traditional federated setting. Our approach first reduces the data distribution skewness by grouping the clients into clusters according to their weights. To eliminate the growth of model divergence, a fine-grained clustering is further conducted on clients of clusters and a pseudo mini-batch SGD is performed within each fine-grained cluster to simulate the mini-batch SGD training while ensure the data are kept locally in each device. This two-stage process is able to stabilise the gradient descent in Non-IID environments and improve the convergence of learning. The experimental results on FEMINST and CelebA datasets show our method outperform many federated baselines, especially by a large margin in FEMNIST. Other related analysis are also provided to support the effectiveness and robustness of our method.

References

1. McMahan, B., Ramage, D.: Federated learning: collaborative machine learning without centralized training data. Google Research Blog 3 (2017)
2. McMahan, B., Moore, E., Ramage, D., Hampson, S., Aguera y Arcas, B.: Communication-efficient learning of deep networks from decentralized data. In: Artificial Intelligence and Statistics, pp. 1273–1282. PMLR (2017)
3. Li, T., Sahu, A.K., Zaheer, M., Sanjabi, M., Talwalkar, A., Smith, V.: Federated optimization in heterogeneous networks. arXiv preprint arXiv:1812.06127 (2018)
4. Hsieh, K., Phanishayee, A., Mutlu, O., Gibbons, P.B.: The non-IID data quagmire of decentralized machine learning. arXiv preprint arXiv:1910.00189 (2019)
5. Bottou, L.: Large-scale machine learning with stochastic gradient descent. In: Lechevallier, Y., Saporta, G. (eds.) Proceedings of COMPSTAT'2010, pp. 177–186. Springer, Heidelberg (2010). https://doi.org/10.1007/978-3-7908-2604-3_16
6. Rakhlin, A., Shamir, O., Sridharan, K.: Making gradient descent optimal for strongly convex stochastic optimization. arXiv e-prints p. arXiv:1109.5647 (2011)
7. Li, T., Sahu, A.K., Talwalkar, A., Smith, V.: Federated learning: challenges, methods, and future directions. arXiv e-prints arXiv:1908.07873 (2019)
8. Smith, V., Chiang, C.K., Sanjabi, M., Talwalkar, A.S.: Federated multi-task learning. In: Advances in Neural Information Processing Systems, pp. 4424–4434 (2017)
9. Bhowmick, A., Duchi, J., Freudiger, J., Kapoor, G., Rogers, R.: Protection against reconstruction and its applications in private federated learning. arXiv preprint arXiv:1812.00984 (2018)
10. Geyer, R.C., Klein, T., Nabi, M.: Differentially private federated learning: a client level perspective. arXiv preprint arXiv:1712.07557 (2017)
11. Kairouz, P., et al.: Advances and open problems in federated learning. arXiv preprint arXiv:1912.04977 (2019)
12. Bonawitz, K., et al.: Towards federated learning at scale: system design. arXiv preprint arXiv:1902.01046 (2019)
13. Kulkarni, V., Kulkarni, M., Pant, A.: Survey of personalization techniques for federated learning. arXiv preprint arXiv:2003.08673 (2020)
14. Li, X., Huang, K., Yang, W., Wang, S., Zhang, Z.: On the convergence of FedAvg on non-IID data. arXiv preprint arXiv:1907.02189 (2019)

15. Karimireddy, S.P., Kale, S., Mohri, M., Reddi, S.J., Stich, S.U., Suresh, A.T.: SCAFFOLD: stochastic controlled averaging for federated learning. arXiv preprint arXiv:1910.06378 (2019)
16. Sattler, F., Müller, K.R., Samek, W.: Clustered federated learning: model-agnostic distributed multitask optimization under privacy constraints. IEEE Trans. Neural Netw. Learn. Syst. **32**(8), 3710–3722 (2020)
17. Thapa, C., Chamikara, M.A.P., Camtepe, S.: SplitFed: when federated learning meets split learning. arXiv preprint arXiv:2004.12088 (2020)
18. Zhao, Y., Li, M., Lai, L., Suda, N., Civin, D., Chandra, V.: Federated learning with non-IID data. arXiv preprint arXiv:1806.00582 (2018)
19. Li, X., Yang, W., Wang, S., Zhang, Z.: Communication-efficient local decentralized SGD methods. arXiv preprint arXiv:1910.09126 (2019)
20. Cohen, G., Afshar, S., Tapson, J., van Schaik, A.: EMNIST: an extension of MNIST to handwritten letters. arXiv preprint arXiv:1702.05373 (2017)
21. Liu, Z., Luo, P., Wang, X., Tang, X.: Deep learning face attributes in the wild. In: Proceedings of the IEEE International Conference on Computer Vision, pp. 3730–3738 (2015)
22. Caldas, S., et al.: LEAF: a benchmark for federated settings. arXiv preprint arXiv:1812.01097 (2018)
23. Nichol, A., Achiam, J., Schulman, J.: On first-order meta-learning algorithms. arXiv preprint arXiv:1803.02999 (2018)
24. Briggs, C., Fan, Z., Andras, P.: Federated learning with hierarchical clustering of local updates to improve training on non-IID data. arXiv preprint arXiv:2004.11791 (2020)
25. Xie, M., Long, G., Shen, T., Zhou, T., Wang, X., Jiang, J.: Multi-center federated learning. arXiv preprint arXiv:2005.01026 (2020)
26. Hsu, T.M.H., Qi, H., Brown, M.: Measuring the effects of non-identical data distribution for federated visual classification (2019). http://arxiv.org/pdf/1909.06335v1

Elastic Container Scheduling for Stochastically Arrived Workflows in Cloud and Edge Computing

Dong Wen[1], Lixin Zhu[2], Jian Xu[1(✉)], and Zhicheng Cai[1]

[1] School of Computer Science and Engineering, Nanjing University of Science and Technology, Nanjing 210094, China
dolphin.xu@njust.edu.cn

[2] 28th Research Institute of China Electronic Science and Technology Group Corporation, Nanjing 210007, China

Abstract. Many intelligent applications of Cloud and Edge can be modeled to be stochastically arrived workflows. Elastically provisioning resources such as containers to these applications is crucial to minimize resource costs while fulfilling deadlines. Most of existing workflow scheduling algorithms are either not for randomly arrived workflows from users of Edge Computing or only consider workflows in pure Cloud Computing. In this article, an elastic resource scheduling method, which integrates loosely coupled workflow scheduling with resource auto-scaling, is developed for stochastically arrived workflows in Cloud and Edge to minimize long-term operating costs while meeting deadline constraints. Experimental results illustrate that our approach achieves a lower overall cost and a higher success ratio compared with the state-of-art algorithm.

Keywords: Edge computing · Cloud computing · Microservice · Containers · Workflow scheduling

1 Introduction

The geography distribution of edge devices and real-time data processing requirements of intelligent applications in the field of Internet of Vehicles, smart cities, and augmented reality make traditional Cloud Computing face huge challenges in realtime response [1,2]. As a result, Edge Computing emerged, which is a new computing model that performs computing tasks at the edge of the network. Different from Cloud Computing, Edge Computing is geographically closer to users and is able to meet the low-delay requirements more easily [3]. However, resources of Edge Computing nodes are limited. Combining Edge Computing with Cloud Computing is a reasonable solution, because the flexibility and scalability of Cloud Computing is able to amend the shortcomings of Edge Computing. Each request of intelligent applications mentioned above usually consist of multiple tasks with dependencies which can be modeled to be workflows [4,5]. In the

Y. Sun et al. (Eds.): ChineseCSCW 2021, CCIS 1491, pp. 44–58, 2022.
https://doi.org/10.1007/978-981-19-4546-5_4

Cloud-Edge environment, a large number of requests from end users generally arrive randomly leading to stochastically arrived workflows. As a lightweight virtualization technology, containers are widely used to provide processing capacity to workflows [6] in the Cloud and Edge uniformly. Thereare many public Clouds provisioning container renting service directly rather than virtual machines [7]. From the perspective of application providers, it is crucial to develop container provisioning algorithms to minimize container renting costs while meeting deadline constraints.

The main challenge of workflow scheduling in Cloud-Edge is how to balance between fast response and making provisioning plans considering more workflow instances appropriately encountered with stochastically arrived workflows. Most of existing workflow scheduling algorithms are tailored for large-scale workflows which is not able to deal with such stochastically arrived instance-intensive small workflows [8,9]. Only a few of them are designed for stochastically arrived workflows. For example, resource renting and scheduling plans are made by accumulating multiple workflows of every fixed time interval in ESMS [6] and SCS algorithm [10] which is beneficial to saving cost by considering multiple workflows together. However, workflows are delayed and scheduled together increasing response times greatly. Meanwhile, these methods are designed for pure Cloud Computing environment without considering the selecting between Cloud and Edge resources of this paper. Further more, most of existing algorithms for the workflow scheduling in Cloud-Edge environments considered in this paper [11] are meta-heuristic algorithms which are very time consuming to find approximate optimal solutions. Their computation times will increase rapidly as the increase of the number of requests [12]. Therefore, they are not suitable for low-latency scheduling in Cloud and Edge Computing.

In this paper, an elastic workflow scheduling algorithm for Cloud-Edge environment is proposed, which consists of loosely coupled workflow scheduling and auto-scaling. The scheduling part schedules workflows based on priority and deadline distribution whenever they are received, and a scaling strategy is designed and invoked every fixed time interval to minimize the long-term cost which consists of rescheduling based scaling up and arrival-rate-proportion based scaling down. The main contributions of this paper are as follows:

1) A scheduling architecture for workflow applications in Cloud-Edge environment is proposed, which supports the scheduling of containers.
2) An online workflow scheduling algorithm is proposed to quickly assign tasks while reducing the waiting time of the stochastically arrived workflows.
3) A scaling strategy taking advantages of historical execution information and rescheduling of historical workflows is designed to avoid blind leasing and releasing of containers, which is loosely coupled with the scheduling algorithm.

The structure of the rest of this article is as follows. Section 2 introduces related work and Sect. 3 describes the workflow scheduling architecture in Cloud-Edge environment, and a detailed description of the two proposed algorithms. The experimental configuration and experiment results is introduced in Sect. 5. Section 6 includes the conclusion and future work.

2 Related Work

There are many workflow scheduling algorithms for traditional distributed systems such as grid computing. At the same time, many existing works are designed for workflow scheduling in Cloud and Edge Computing.

2.1 Workflow Scheduling in Cloud and Edge

Compared with traditional distributed systems, Cloud service providers charge users based on the performance and usage time of resources. As the budgets of users and application deadlines change, users need different algorithms to achieve specific requirements. Most of the list scheduling algorithms are based on the expansion or improvement of the HEFT algorithm [13–16]. The core idea of this type of algorithm is to generate a scheduling list by assigning priorities to tasks, and then map the tasks to appropriate resources according to the order in the scheduling list. These algorithms are mainly used in heterogeneous computing systems, and the optimization goal is the total execution time of the tasks. In addition, some list scheduling algorithms solve the problem of workflow scheduling in cloud computing through methods such as distributing sub-deadlines and searching for scheduling gaps [17–20].

Workflow scheduling algorithms in Edge Computing are mostly meta-heuristic algorithms, such as UARP algorithm [21], IGS algorithm [22] and SA-QL algorithm [23]. These algorithms are all improved on the basis of meta-heuristic algorithms, and the objective function is optimized through iteration. There are also some algorithms for workflow scheduling in a Cloud-Edge environment, such as the COM algorithm [5] and the DNCPSO algorithm [11]. However, the above meta-heuristic algorithms usually are very time consuming. Therefore, in this paper, fast heuristic algorithm are designed.

2.2 Scheduling of Stochastically Arrived Workflows

The aforementioned algorithms only consider scenarios where workflows are submitted once. However, in the real environment of edge computing considered in this paper, workflows arrive stochastically and the workload changes at any time, and resource scheduling should be a continuous process. The scheduling algorithm needs to deal with the lease and release of resources. The service processing stochastically arrived workflows is usually called WaaS (workflow-as-a-service) [12]. The above algorithms are difficult to solve this kind of problem. Mao et al. [10] proposed the SCS algorithm, which combines task scheduling and resource scaling to ensure that streaming workflows are completed within their deadlines with the least total cost. Wang et al. [6] proposed the ESMS algorithm, which determines the priority of tasks based on the urgency of tasks, and proposed an automatic scaling algorithm for a two-layer architecture of containers and VMs.

Compared to existing algorithms, the instance-intensive small-scale workflow considered in this article is characterized by large numbers and short execution time. In addition, The existing methods usually embed the scaling method into the scheduling algorithm, while they are loosely coupled and more flexible in our method.

3 Stochastically Arrived Workflow Applications

The number of user requests from the edge of the network changes over time, and each request sent to the Edge generates a corresponding workflow instance. This type of application is called stochastically arrived workflow application. Each workflow is represented by a directed acyclic graph (DAG). Let $G = (V, E)$ denote a DAG, where $V = \{v_i \mid 1 \leq i \leq m\}$ represents the set of m tasks in the workflow, $E = \{(v_i, v_j) \mid v_i, v_j \in V \wedge i \neq j\}$represents the dependency between tasks in the workflow. ω_i represents the computation load of task v_i, and $d_{i,j}$ represents the amount of data transmission between v_i and v_j. Let $pre(v_i)$ and $suc(v_i)$ be the direct predecessor task set and the direct successor task set of task v_i respectively. v_i can be executed only when all tasks in $pre(v_i)$ are executed. The tasks without a predecessor or successor task are called entry task v_{entry} or exit task v_{exit} respectively. Common notations are shown in Table 1. $R = \{r_1, r_2, ..., r_s\}$ represents s containers in the current resource pool provided by the Cloud and Edge, c_n represents the processing rate of r_n, and $b_{n,k}$ represents the bandwidth between r_n and r_k. The execution of each task needs to load a fixed image, and each container executes only one task at the same time [24,25].

In the workflow of a cross-media retrieval application [26], features of text and pictures in the request are firstly extracted respectively after data preprocessing, then the maximally correlated subspaces of these features are learned and the semantic spaces are produced by logistic regressors, and finally the retrieval results are obtained by text-image distance. In the process of workflow execution, both task execution time and data transmission time need to be considered. When a task v_i is assigned to the container r_n and its predecessor task v_j is assigned to the container r_k, the execution time of task v_i and the data transmission time from task v_i to task v_j are defined as:

$$ET(v_i, r_n) = \frac{\omega_i}{r_n} \tag{1}$$

$$TT(v_i, v_j) = \frac{d_{i,j}}{b_{n,k}} + l_{n,k} \tag{2}$$

where $l_{n,k}$ represents the delay that occurs when transmitting data.

The cost of the container r_n is $cost_n$, and changes according to the deployed location and configuration. Containers deployed in the Edge charge more than containers deployed in the Cloud:

$$cost_n = \begin{cases} P_e \times v_n, & r_n \text{ is deployed in the Edge} \\ P_c \times v_n, & r_n \text{ is deployed in the Cloud} \end{cases} \tag{3}$$

where v_n is the duration time of container r_n, including the initialization time of the container. P_e and P_c represent the price of containers in the Edge and Cloud respectively. According to the state of the container, the initialization $IT(r_n)$ time of container r_n has three values:

$$IT(r_n) = \begin{cases} 0, & r_n \text{ is running} \\ InitT, & r_n \text{ is initialized in the Edge} \\ InitT + PullT, & r_n \text{ is initialized in the Cloud} \end{cases} \quad (4)$$

When the container r_n is running, it can be used immediately. The edge environment has container images by default, and only the startup time is needed. When the container is initialized in the Cloud, additional pull time of image is required.

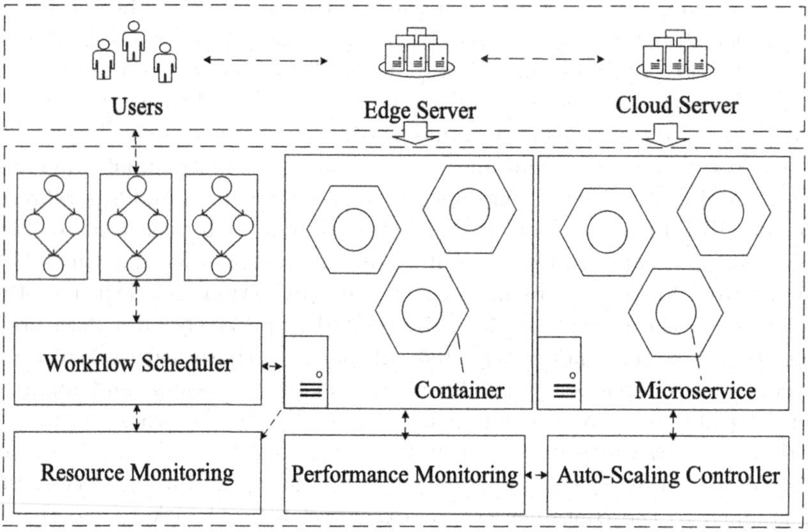

Fig. 1. Workflow scheduling architecture in Cloud-Edge environment

The workflow scheduling architecture in Cloud-Edge environment is shown in Fig. 1. The workflow scheduler accepts workflows from users and allocates workflows to resources based on scheduling algorithm. The auto-scaling controller starts periodically and scales the number of containers according to historical performance.

The earliest start time (EST) of task v_i is determined by two factors, one is the completion time and data transmission time of all its precursor tasks, and the other is the earliest available time $avail(r_n)$ of the container r_n, which is related to the state of the container:

$$EST(v_i, r_n) = max\{avail(r_n), max_{v_j \in suc(v_i)}\{AFT(v_j) + TT(v_i, v_j)\}\} \quad (5)$$

$$avail(r_n) = max\{IT(r_n), max_{v_j \in sche(r_n)}\{AFT(v_j)\}\} \quad (6)$$

where $AFT(v_j)$ is the actual completion time of task v_j. $sche(r_n)$ represents all tasks assigned to the container r_n. The estimated completion time $EFT(v_i, r_n)$ of the task can be calculated as follows:

$$EFT(v_i, r_n) = EST(v_i, r_n) + ET(v_i, r_n) \tag{7}$$

The overall completion time of the workflow WF_l is called makespan k_l, which is determined by the actual completion time of its exit task v_{exit}:

$$k_l = AFT(v_{exit}), v_{exit} \in WF_l \tag{8}$$

Let D_l represents the deadline of the workflow WF_l, so the optimization goal of this article can be defined as meeting the deadline constraints of each workflow while minimizing the overall cost:

$$\begin{aligned} &min. \sum_{r_n \in R} cost_n \\ &s.t.\ k_l < D_l, \forall WF_l, \end{aligned} \tag{9}$$

Table 1. Common notations

Parameter	Definition
v_i	The l-th task in a certain workflow
r_n	The n-th container
ω_i	The computation workload of v_i
c_n	The computation speed of r_n
$pre(v_i)$	The direct predecessor task set of v_i
$suc(v_i)$	The direct successor task set of v_i
v_{entry}	The entry task of a certain workflow
v_{exit}	The exit task of a certain workflow

4 Elastic Resource Scheduling Algorithm

In this article, a Loosely Coupled Stochastically arrived workflow Scheduling algorithm (LCSS) is proposed which is the hybrid of a rule based dynamic scheduling method and a prediction based resource auto-scaling method.

4.1 Rule Based Dynamic Scheduling

In LCSS, the workflow is scheduled to containers immediately after it is received, i.e., the First Come First Serviced rule (FCFS) is applied. In this article, a

Rule based Dynamic Scheduling method (RDS) is applied to schedule every stochastically arrived workflow which divide the workflow deadline into task deadlines first and schedule tasks to containers with the cheapest execution cost under deadline constraints.

In this paper, ready tasks are ordered based on the lengths of critical paths from each ready task to the exit task [13], which ensure that each task will not be assigned before its predecessor tasks are assigned. For each ready task v_i, $rank(v_i)$ is the length of the critical path from task v_i to v_{exit}, including the execution time of v_i as follows

$$rank(v_i) = ET(v_i, r^*) + max_{v_j \in suc(v_i)}\{TT(v_i, v_j) + rank(v_j)\} \tag{10}$$

where $ET(v_i, r^*)$ represents the average calculation time of task v_i on all containers. A higher rank value means a higher priority, and tasks are scheduled based on their priorities one by one.

Distributing the whole workflow deadline into tasks is the basic of workflow scheduling. It is a common method to assign sub-deadline sd_i to each task v_i according to the length of critical path [4,6] as follows

$$sd_i = S_l + (D_l - S_l) \times \frac{rank(v_{entry}) - rank(v_i) + ET(v_i, r^*)}{rank(v_{entry})} \tag{11}$$

where S_l is the submission time of workflow WF_l.

When a task is selected by the priority and to be scheduled to containers. There might be multiple containers fulfilling deadline constraints. In this paper, the container with the cheapest execution cost is selected.

$$C^i(v_i, r_n) = \frac{\omega_i}{c_n} \times P_{r_n} \tag{12}$$

If all current instances cannot complete the task within its deadline, the container with the smallest EFT is selected.

The formal description of the scheduling algorithm is shown in Algorithm 1. When a workflow WF_l arrives, the rank and sub-deadline of each task in WF_l are calculated. These tasks are sorted in descending order according to their ranks to satisfy the dependencies between tasks. For a task v_i, the EFT of v_i in each container that can execute it is calculated. For all containers that make EFT less than the deadline, find the container with lowest cost (Lines 4–11 in Algorithm 1). If two containers need the same execution cost, the one with lower EFT is chosen. Finally, if there is no container can fulfill the deadline constraint, the container with lowest EFT is chosen (Lines 12–14 in Algorithm 1). If each workflow has n tasks, the complexity of calculating EST and sd_i is $O(n^2)$. When there are s containers, the complexity of the task mapping step is $O(n^2 \times s)$. Therefore, the total complexity is $O(n^2 \times s)$.

4.2 Historical Success Ratio Based Resource Auto-scaling

Because the workload of stochastically arrived workflows changes with time, the type and number of rented containers should be adjusted dynamically to

Algorithm 1. RDS

Input: the l-th workflow, resources in the Edge and Cloud
Output: the scheduling solution M

1: Calculate rank and sub-deadline for each task in WF_l
2: Sort tasks in descending order according to their ranks
3: **for** each task v_i in the task ordering **do**
4: **for** each container r_n that can execute v_i **do**
5: calculate $EFT(v_i, r_n)$ via (7)
6: **if** $EFT(v_i, r_n) \leq D_l$ and $minCost \geq C^i(v_i, r_n)$ **then**
7: $minCost \leftarrow C^i(v_i, r_n)$
8: $minEFT \leftarrow EFT(v_i, r_n))$
9: $chosenC \leftarrow r_n$
10: **end if**
11: **end for**
12: **if** $chosenC =$ null **then**
13: $chosenC \leftarrow$ the container with the least EFT
14: **end if**
15: $M \leftarrow M + \langle v_i, chosenC \rangle$
16: **end for**
17: **return** M

minimize resource cost while fulfilling system performance requirement. In this paper, a Historical Success Ratio based Resource Auto-Scaling algorithm (HSR) is proposed to adjust the number of rented containers every time interval Δt.

Past information reflects the matching degree of tasks and resources, and can be used to determine whether resources need to be increased or decreased. At time t_0, the success ratio of the workflows in the last scheduling interval (SRL) is calculated to determine whether to lease or release the container:

$$SRL = \frac{\lambda}{\mu} \tag{13}$$

where λ is the number of workflows which meet the deadline within the scheduling interval $[t_0 - \Delta t, t_0]$, and μ is the total number of received workflows in the scheduling interval $[t_0 - \Delta t, t_0]$.

All workflows in the last scheduling interval are collected, assuming that these workflows are deployed in the current resource pool. For each workflow, the scheduling algorithm mentioned before is used for scheduling. The difference is that for a task v_i, if all current instances cannot complete the task, a new container needs to be created. The minimum calculation speed $minMips$ of the new container used to ensure that the task is completed within the deadline is calculated.

$$minMips = \frac{\omega_i}{sd_i - IT(r_n)} \tag{14}$$

The number of containers is adjusted according to the change trend of the workflow arrival rate. If the workflow arrival rate increases, the container will not be released. Otherwise, according to the proportion of the decrease in the arrival rate of the workflows, the corresponding proportion of the number of containers is released. When the leased resources of the scheduling algorithm are reasonable, this proportional resource adjustment is also reasonable. For all containers in the current resource pool, *Scale* is the scale of the containers to be released and Rel_k is the number of containers of each type that needs to be released.

$$Scale = 1 - \frac{\mu}{\nu} \tag{15}$$

$$Rel_k = Scale \times Type_k \tag{16}$$

where ν is the total number of workflows submitted in the scheduling interval $[t_0 - 2\Delta t, t_0 - \Delta t]$. $Type_k$ is the number of running containers of type k.

The formal description of the scaling algorithm is shown in Algorithm 2. In order to avoid blindly releasing the container, the number of containers of each type is counted. If SRL is less than 1, new containers need to be leased. For each workflow WF_l in the last scheduling interval, assuming that WF_l is deployed in the current resource pool by the RDS algorithm. If there is no container can meet the deadline, create a new container and calculate its $minMips$. When choosing where to deploy the new containers, the Edge has higher priority. For each host in the Edge, the host is selected according to the best fit (BF) strategy (Lines 6–13 in Algorithm 2). If the containers created in all hosts cannot meet the deadline constraints of the task, a container is applied for in the Cloud. If SRL is 1, some containers need to be released. *Scale* and Rel_k are calculated first. If *Scale* is greater than 0, for each type of container, release the corresponding number of idle containers according to Rel_k, and ensure that at least one container of each type is reserved (Lines 16–21 in Algorithm 2). When leasing a container, suppose the number of hosts of the Edge server is h, the number of containers is s, and the complexity of the leasing container step is $O(m^2 * n^2 * (s + h))$.

5 Performance Evaluation

In this section, the performance of the proposed algorithm is evaluated using a real cross-media information retrival application on a simulation platform established based on WorkflowSim [27], which supports workflow and deployment of multiple data centers [11]. By combining timestamps of user requests and events, the platform is modified to support stochastically arrived workflows. The platform runs on a Windows 10 computer with an i5 2.80 GHz CPU and 8 GB RAM.

5.1 Experiment Setting

The characteristics of the workflows generated by the cross-media retrieval application are shown in Table 2, where group A and group B respectively contain some workflows with short and long critical paths. The workloads used in this paper are generated according to the Wikipedia access rate [28], and these requests are converted into workflow submissions in proportion. In order to

Algorithm 2. HSR

Input: $Type_k$, SLR, workflow list WF in the last scheduling interval
Output: New container list NL, List of containers to be released RL

1: $Type_k \leftarrow \emptyset$
2: **for** each container r_n in the container list **do**
3: $Type_k \leftarrow Type_k + 1$, the type of r_n is k
4: **end for**
5: **if** $SLR < 1$ **then**
6: **for** each workflow WF_l in WF **do**
7: calculate $chosenC$ by Line 3 - 11 in Algorithm 1
8: **if** $chosenC =$ null **then**
9: calculate $minMips$ via (14)
10: selecte the host by the BF strategy;
11: $NL \leftarrow NL + r_n$
12: **end if**
13: **end for**
14: **else**
15: Calculate $Scale$ and Rel_k via (15) and (16)
16: **for** each container r_n in the container list **do**
17: **if** r_n is idle and $Rel_k \geq 1$ **then**
18: $RL \leftarrow RL + r_n$
19: $Rel_k \leftarrow Rel_k - 1$
20: **end if**
21: **end for**
22: **end if**
23: **return** NL, RL

obtain a reasonable deadline for each workflow, α is used to control the urgency of the deadline, which is a number greater than 1.

$$D_l = S_l + \alpha \times rank(v_{entry}) \tag{17}$$

The resource parameters in the Edge and the Cloud, such as the number of resources, bandwidth, and price, are shown in Table 3. Container initialization times in Edge and Cloud are set to be 6 s and 10 s based on experiments, respectively. LCSS is compared with ESMS which considers the scheduling of stochastically arrived workflows in pure Cloud Computing, because other scheduling algorithms are not aimed at the rapid deployment of stochastically arrived workflows in containers. Therefore ESMS is modified to support the running in Cloud-Edge environment by changing the cost calculation method and deployment strategy when the new container cannot complete the task.

Because the information of the last scheduling interval is used to run the auto-scaling algorithm, the scheduling interval has a great impact on the performance of the algorithm. In order to get the appropriate value of Δt, some experiments are carried out with different values of Δt while keeping the duration and load fixed. The Δt with the highest success ratio is chosen. If the highest success ratio

Table 2. Characteristics of the small-scale workflows

Type	Number of tasks	Average CP (s)	Average input data (KB)
CrossMedia	4	6.13875	468.69375
Group A	4	3.86	97.44
Group B	4	7.72	877.13

Table 3. Parameters of Cloud and Edge resources

Server	Number of hosts	Price per vCPU (USD/s)	Price per GB (USD/s)	Bandwidth (Mb/s)
Edge	4	0.0000144	0.0000015	100
Cloud	2000	0.000011244	0.000001235	50

corresponds to two different Δt, choose the one with lower cost. The success ratio and cost are important metrics to evaluate the performance of algorithms.

1) The success ratio is the ratio of the number of workflows completed within their deadlines to the number of all submitted workflows. The higher the success ratio, the better the performance of the algorithm.
2) The cost is the running cost of all containers leased and calculated by (3). The lower the cost, the better the performance of the algorithm.

5.2 Experimental Results

The Impact of Workloads. In order to evaluate the performance of each algorithm under workloads with different arrival rate. 20 workloads followed the same pattern are configured, and their arrival rate gradually increased. α is set to 1.4. The cost and success ratio of each algorithm varying with workload are shown in Fig. 2. Figure 2(a) shows that as the arrival rate of workload increases, the costs of the two algorithms also increase. The cost of LCSS is lower than that of ESMS, and the cost growth rate of LCSS is relatively slow. Figure 2(b) shows that LCSS has a stable and high success ratio. The success ratio of ESMS is relatively low and does not change much as the workload changes. Since ESMS transforms multiple workflows into a single workflow for scheduling, many tasks wait until the algorithm starts, which increases the urgency of these tasks [6]. In addition, the frequent expansion of renting and releasing containers in ESMS greatly increases the response time of the workflow. Using historical information and resource estimation based on rescheduling, LCSS guarantees a high success ratio.

The Impact of Deadlines. In order to evaluate the impact of deadlines on the performance of each algorithm, different values are used for α. From workload 1 to workload 4, the arrival rate gradually increases. The cost and SR of each

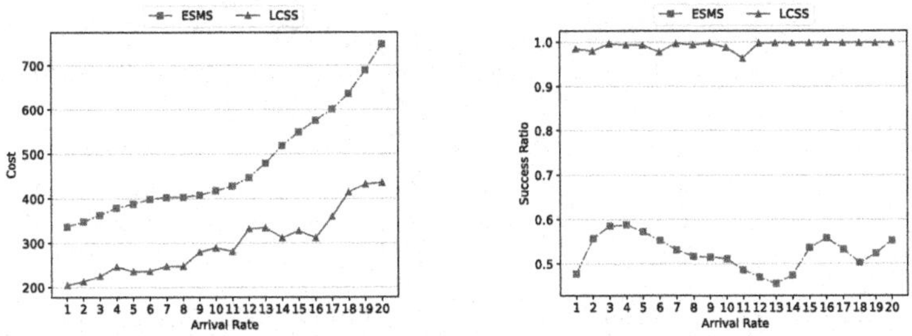

(a) The cost (b) The success ratio

Fig. 2. The cost and the success ratio with different workloads

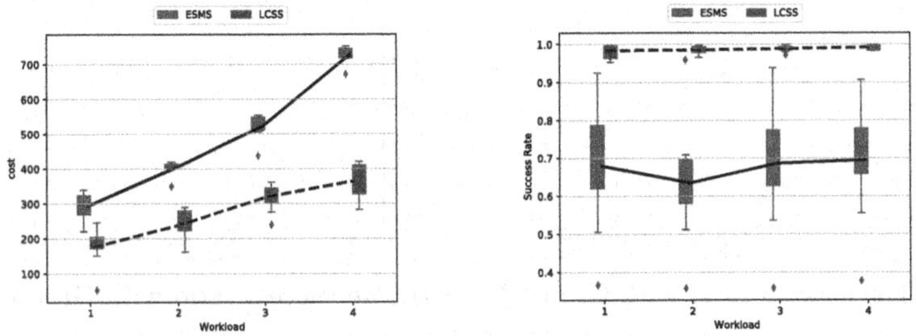

(a) The cost (b) The success ratio

Fig. 3. The cost and the success ratio with different deadlines

algorithm varying with the deadline are shown in Fig. 3. Figure 3(a) illustrates that LCSS is generally better than ESMS in terms of cost, and sometimes reach particularly low costs. Figure 3(b) shows that the success ratio of ESMS fluctuates greatly with the change of α. This is because the workflow in the workflow queue has a certain waiting time, which makes it difficult for the ESMS to perform well in the case of an urgent deadline. Only a more relaxed deadline can make the ESMS perform better. The success rate of LCSS is relatively stable and the performance of LCSS has a huge improvement over ESMS.

The Impact of Workflow Types. Workflows in group A and B are used to evaluate the impact of workflow types on the performance of each algorithm. In addition, the HSR is combined with ESMS as a new comparison algorithm, which is called ESMS-HSR. α is set to 1.4 and use the same workloads in Fig. 2. The results in Fig. 4(a) and 4(b) show that the cost-effectiveness of ESMS is inferior to the other two algorithms, and the average cost of each algorithm to process the workflows in group A is lower than that in group B. As shown in Fig. 4(c), the success ratio of LCSS is more stable than the other two algorithms. However, the success ratio of LCSS in Fig. 4(d) is not as stable as ESMS-HSR. When using small workflows, it is easier for LCSS to find the appropriate scheduling interval and thus LCSS has better performance. The conclusion is that in the

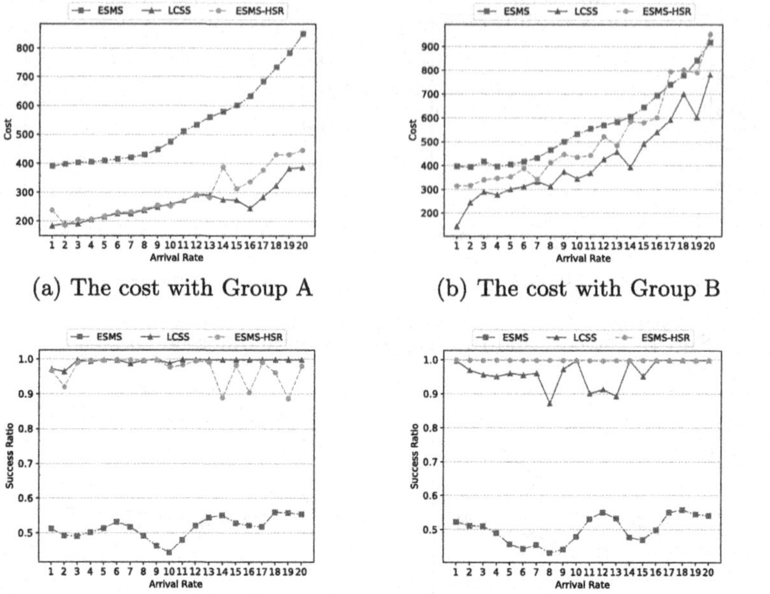

(a) The cost with Group A (b) The cost with Group B

(c) The success ratio with Group A (d) The success ratio with Group B

Fig. 4. The cost and the success ratio with different workflows

environment of directly renting containers, the expansion strategy for the two-tier architecture of containers and VMs in ESMS has poor performance.

6 Conclusion and Future Work

In the paper, an elastic resource scheduling method has been proposed to schedule stochastically arrived workflows in Cloud-Edge environment. Experimental results show that the LCSS reduces the overall cost of long-term operation and maintains a high success ratio. The online workflow scheduling algorithm is able to response to arrived workflows quickly and reduce the average waiting time of them, and the scaling algorithm is helpful to reducing the long-term running cost while ensuring the success ratio. Finding more accurate resource requirement estimating method is a promising future work.

Acknowledgments. This work is supported by the National Key Research and Development Program of China under Grant 2018AAA0102002, the National Natural Science Foundation of China (Grant No. 61872186, 61972202) and the Fundamental Research Funds for the Central Universities (No. 30919011235).

References

1. Blanchard, A., Kosmatov, N., Loulergue, F.: Integration of cloud computing and internet of things: a survey. In: 2018 International Conference on High Performance Computing and Simulation (2018)
2. Shi, W., Cao, J., Zhang, Q., Li, Y., Lanyu, X.: Edge computing: vision and challenges. IEEE Internet Things J. **3**(5), 637–646 (2016)
3. Tran, T.X., Hajisami, A., Pandey, P., Pompili, D.: Collaborative mobile edge computing in 5G networks: new paradigms, scenarios, and challenges. IEEE Commun. Mag. **55**(4), 54–61 (2017)
4. Quanwang, W., Ishikawa, F., Zhu, Q., Xia, Y., Wen, J.: Deadline-constrained cost optimization approaches for workflow scheduling in clouds. IEEE Trans. Parallel Distrib. Syst. **28**(12), 3401–3412 (2017)
5. Xiaolong, X., et al.: A computation offloading method over big data for IoT-enabled cloud-edge computing. Futur. Gener. Comput. Syst. **95**, 522–533 (2019)
6. Wang, S., Ding, Z., Jiang, C.: Elastic scheduling for microservice applications in clouds. IEEE Trans. Parallel Distrib. Syst. **32**(1), 98–115 (2021)
7. AWS fargate. http://aws.amazon.com/fargate/pricing/
8. Juve, G., Chervenak, A., Deelman, E., Bharathi, S., Mehta, G., Vahi, K.: Characterizing and profiling scientific workflows. Futur. Gener. Comput. Syst. **29**, 682–692 (2013)
9. Bharathi, S., Chervenak, A., Deelman, E., Mehta, G., Su, M.-H., Vahi, K.: Characterization of scientific workflows. In: 2008 Third Workshop on Workflows in Support of Large-Scale Science, pp. 1–10 (2008)
10. Mao, M., Humphrey, M.: Auto-scaling to minimize cost and meet application deadlines in cloud workflows. In: SC 2011: Proceedings of 2011 International Conference for High Performance Computing, Networking, Storage and Analysis, pp. 1–12 (2011)
11. Xie, Y., et al.: A novel directional and non-local-convergent particle swarm optimization based workflow scheduling in cloud-edge environment. Future Gener. Comput. Syst. **97**, 361–378 (2019)
12. Wu, F., Wu, Q., Tan, Y.: Workflow scheduling in cloud: a survey. J. Supercomput. **71**(9), 3373–3418 (2015). https://doi.org/10.1007/s11227-015-1438-4
13. Topcuoglu, H., Hariri, S., Wu, M.-Y.: Performance-effective and low-complexity task scheduling for heterogeneous computing. IEEE Trans. Parallel Distrib. Syst. **13**(3), 260–274 (2002)
14. Arabnejad, H., Barbosa, J.G.: List scheduling algorithm for heterogeneous systems by an optimistic cost table. IEEE Trans. Parallel Distrib. Syst. **25**(3), 682–694 (2014)
15. Zhou, N., Qi, D., Wang, X., Zheng, Z., Lin, W.: A list scheduling algorithm for heterogeneous systems based on a critical node cost table and pessimistic cost table. Concurr. Comput. Pract. Exp. **29**(5), e3944 (2016)
16. Djigal, H., Feng, J., Jiamin, L., Ge, J.: IPPTS: an efficient algorithm for scientific workflow scheduling in heterogeneous computing systems. IEEE Trans. Parallel Distrib. Syst. **32**(5), 1057–1071 (2021)
17. Abrishami, S., Naghibzadeh, M., Epema, D.H.J.: Cost-driven scheduling of grid workflows using partial critical paths. IEEE Trans. Parallel Distrib. Syst. **23**(8), 1400–1414 (2012)
18. Abrishami, S., Naghibzadeh, M., Epema, D.H.J.: Deadline-constrained workflow scheduling algorithms for infrastructure as a service clouds. Future Gener. Comput. Syst. **29**(1), 158–169 (2013)

19. Hao, W., Hua, X., Li, Z., Ren, S.: Resource and instance hour minimization for deadline constrained DAG applications using computer clouds. IEEE Trans. Parallel Distrib. Syst. **27**(3), 885–899 (2016)
20. Rimal, B.P., Maier, M.: Workflow scheduling in multi-tenant cloud computing environments. IEEE Trans. Parallel Distrib. Syst. **28**(1), 290–304 (2017)
21. Xu, X., Cao, H., Geng, Q., Liu, X., Wang, C.: Dynamic resource provisioning for workflow scheduling under uncertainty in edge computing environment. Concurr. Comput. Pract. Exp. **34**(14), e5674 (2020)
22. Jin Sun, L., Yin, M.Z., Zhang, Y., Zhang, T., Zhou, J.: Makespan-minimization workflow scheduling for complex networks with social groups in edge computing. J. Syst. Architect. **108**, 101799 (2020)
23. Lin, K., Lin, B., Chen, X., Lu, Y., Huang, Z., Mo, Y.: A time-driven workflow scheduling strategy for reasoning tasks of autonomous driving in edge environment. In: 2019 IEEE International Conference on Parallel Distributed Processing with Applications, Big Data Cloud Computing, Sustainable Computing Communications, Social Computing Networking (ISPA/BDCloud/SocialCom/SustainCom), pp. 124–131 (2019)
24. Bao, L., Chase, W., Xiaoxuan, B., Ren, N., Shen, M.: Performance modeling and workflow scheduling of microservice-based applications in clouds. IEEE Trans. Parallel Distrib. Syst. **30**(9), 2114–2129 (2019)
25. Mazlami, G., Cito, J., Leitner, P.: Extraction of microservices from monolithic software architectures. In: IEEE International Conference on Web Services (2017)
26. Rasiwasia, N., et al.: A new approach to cross-modal multimedia retrieval. In: Proceedings of the 18th ACM International Conference on Multimedia. Association for Computing Machinery (2010)
27. Chen, W., Deelman, E.: Workflowsim: a toolkit for simulating scientific workflows in distributed environments. In: 2012 IEEE 8th International Conference on E-Science, pp. 1–8 (2012)
28. Wikipedia access traces. http://www.wikibench.eu

Modeling Method for Function Trees Guided by the Symmetric Quintuple Implicational Controller

Yiming Tang[1,2](✉), Xiaopeng Han[1], Xi Wu[1], and Li Zhang[1]

[1] Anhui Province Key Laboratory of Affective Computing and Advanced Intelligent Machine, School of Computer and Information, Hefei University of Technology, Hefei 230601, China
tym608@163.com

[2] Engineering Research Center of Safety Critical Industry Measure and Control Technology, Ministry of Education, Hefei University of Technology, Hefei 230601, China

Abstract. In product conceptual design, and/or/not function tree is a very common functional model, but the modeling of functional tree is often a tough problem in this field. Previous modeling was done manually by domain experts, which can be difficult for larger function trees. For this reason, the symmetric quintuple implicational method is introduced, and then the symmetric quintuple implicational controller is proposed, and the function tree modeling method guided by the symmetric quintuple implicational controller is put forward. Firstly, the theoretical structure of fuzzy and/or/not function tree is described, and the symmetric quintuple implicational method is reviewed. Secondly, a symmetric quintuple implicational controller is proposed from the point of view of rule base, fuzzier, inference machine, fuzzier and numerical determination. Thirdly, based on the requirement of functional tree modeling, a new fuzzy and/or/not function tree establishing method has been put forward by using the symmetric quintuple implicational controller as the core. Finally, the whole process of functional tree modeling is demonstrated through an application example, and the validity of the scheme is verified. It provides a new breakthrough direction for solving the problem of fuzzy and/or/not function tree modeling, and promotes the progress of product collaborative conceptual design, fuzzy control and related fields.

Keywords: Conceptual design · Collaborative design · Fuzzy reasoning · Function tree

1 Introduction

Conceptual design is a design method that uses design concept and takes it as the main line throughout the whole design process, which has a very important impact on the whole life cycle of the product [1]. This impact is not only reflected in the performance, reliability and safety of products, but also in the cost of product development and many other aspects [2, 3]. According to some data, although the actual input cost in this stage only accounts for 5% of the total product development cost, it has the decision power of

Y. Sun et al. (Eds.): ChineseCSCW 2021, CCIS 1491, pp. 59–71, 2022.
https://doi.org/10.1007/978-981-19-4546-5_5

70–80% of the total product cost [4]. Therefore, how to get the scheme more efficiently and quickly to form a stronger competitiveness is hurdle to be overcome in the current conceptual design domain [5].

The core problem of conceptual design [6] lies in the process of functional modeling and functional solution of conceptual design, that is, forming a function-structure model (referred to as functional model) and transforming it into a design scheme that can be realized. A large number of scholars have proposed many functional models, among which the and/or/not function tree model is the most typical and widely used [7].

At present, a large number of experts have conducted large-scale studies on different models of and/or/not function trees. Among them, Chakrabarti and Bligh [8] discussed the inference method of functional method tree. Ren et al. [9] proposed the optimal solution of multicast tasks supported by network function virtualization based on service function tree embedding problem, which greatly reduced the cost of multicast traffic transmission. Luo et al. [10] proposed to combine multiple service function chains into a function tree of security services, so as to reduce the demand for resources when allocating virtual security functions.

For function tree, the conventional language was used to describe. But in fact, this often leads to less detailed analysis of the problem. Moreover, it is difficult to consider the problem thoroughly only by relying on human thinking, so the artificial function tree model often exposes the problem of incomplete information. To make clear the function tree in more detail, we introduce the idea of fuzzy inference. The specific fuzzy values are added to the nodes of the and/or/not function tree, and it is known as the fuzzy and/or/not function tree.

There exist lots of schemes of fuzzy inference, in which some typical ones are the CRI algorithm, the BKS algorithm [11], the triple I algorithm [12], the universal triple I algorithm [13, 14], the symmetric implicational algorithm [15, 16] and so on. Among them, the newly proposed symmetric quintuple implicational algorithm [17] is recognized as a relatively advanced method in this field.

In the aspect of function tree modeling, the previous modeling is mainly manually established by domain experts, which is quite difficult for large scale function tree. To this end, a novel scheme of function tree modeling is studied here. In this study, the symmetric quintuple implicational algorithm is token as the intrinsic inference mechanism, and is developed to the category of fuzzy controller, thus we propose the modeling method of function tree guided by symmetric quintuple implicational algorithm.

2 Modeling Method of Function Tree via the Symmetric Quintuple Implicational Algorithm

2.1 Fuzzy and/or/not Function Trees

Definition 1. A and/or/not function tree is the superposition of and, or, note operations on a functional trees. "And" gate decomposition is denoted by $\wedge$, "or" gate decomposition is equivalent to $\vee$ and "not" gate is expressed by negation operation $'$.

Definition 2. The function tree uses the same variable to express the same leaf nodes, referred to as a basic variable. It is expressed by an atomic proposition x_i. If $x_i = 1$, then it means that the node satisfies the demand. If $x_i = 0$, then it implies that the node does not satisfy the demand. We use extension variable M_j to express the gate node of the function tree. The variables and extension variables are collectively referred to as a tree proposition. $H(M_i)$ denotes the function for a function tree with the top node M_i.

Definition 3. The logical function $\phi_{M_1}(X) = \phi(x_1, \ldots, x_m, M_1, \ldots, M_n)$ is a tree function for a function tree $H(M_1)$. If $\phi_{M_1}(X) = 1$, then it means the total demand is satisfied. Otherwise, $\phi_{M_1}(X) = 0$ implies that the total demand is not satisfied. The function tree containing only basic variables is called the target tree function.

Definition 4. A fuzzy membership value is added to the nodes in the and/or/not function tree, then the new tree is known as fuzzy and/or/not function tree.

Functional solution is an important part of conceptual design. To be precise, it is to obtain the corresponding concrete implementation scheme from the functional requirements, in which its core is to obtain the structural scheme. Therefore, functional structure deduction is the most important in this process. The previous function structure deduction is mainly carried out by the user. Here we deal with it through the computer aided way.

In particular, assume that there is a fuzzy function tree, which has nothing but function nodes. The fuzzy function tree is quantized by numerical filling, so the structure of the function tree can be realized by the symmetric quintuple implicational algorithm in the fuzzy controller.

2.2 The Symmetric Quintuple Implicational Algorithm.

The basic fuzzy inference model is FMP (Fuzzy Modus Ponens) problem. As shown below:

$$\text{FMP}: \text{ For } A \to B \text{ and input } A^*, \text{ calculate the output } B^*. \quad (1)$$

For the FMP problem, its outcome is the minimum fuzzy set such that the following formula gets its maximum value:

$$(A(x) \to B(y)) \to ((A^*(x) \to A(x)) \to (A^*(x) \to B^*(y))). \quad (2)$$

Definition 5. Let $B \in F(Y)$, $A, A^* \in F(X)$. If B^* makes

$$(A(x) \to_1 B(y)) \to_2 ((A'(x) \to_1 A(x)) \to_2 (A'(x) \to_1 B'(y))) \quad (3)$$

get the maximum for all $x \in X, y \in Y$. Then B^* is referred to as a FMP-symmetric quintuple implicational solution. The minimum solution is called a MinP-symmetric quintuple implicational solution.

Theorem 1 [17]. If $\to_1, \to_2$ are two R-implications, and $\otimes_1$ is the operation associated with $\to_1$, and $\otimes_2$ is the operation associated with $\to_2$, then the MinP-symmetric quintuple implicational solution of the symmetric quintuple implicational algorithm is

$$B^*(y) = \sup_{x \in X}\{A^*(x) \otimes_1 ((A^*(x) \to_1 A(x)) \otimes_2 (A(x) \to_1 B(y)))\}, y \in Y \quad (4)$$

2.3 Symmetric Quintuple Implicational Controller

Based on the symmetric quintuple implicational algorithm, a symmetric quintuple implicational controller is proposed here. Specifically, the fuzzy controller is dealt with from five aspects: knowledge base of fuzzy controller, fuzzier, inference machine (i.e., the symmetric quintuple implicational algorithm), defuzzier and numerical determination.

Firstly, in the aspect of knowledge base design, triangular fuzzy set clan (i.e., the structure composed of several triangular fuzzy sets) is mainly used to process. It is used to express the required inputs and outputs. Let the peak distances of the fuzzy sets in the fuzzy set clan be equal. As shown in Fig. 1, the leftmost and rightmost are right triangle fuzzy sets, and the middle ones are isosceles triangle fuzzy sets.

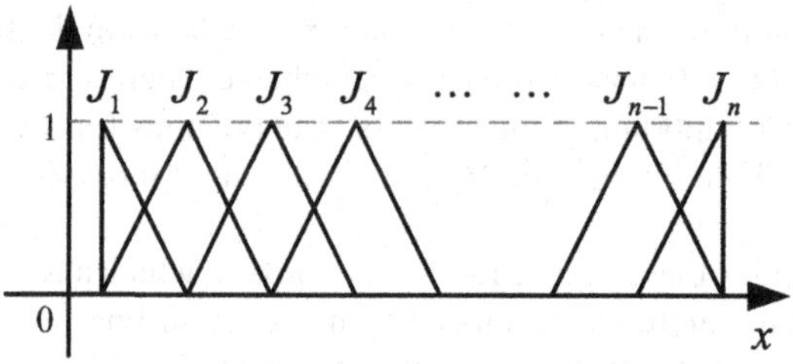

Fig. 1. Fuzzy set clan

Secondly, the singleton fuzzier is used. Specifically, a singleton is adopted for the input as follows:

$$A^*_{x'} = A^*(x) = \begin{cases} 1, & x = x' \\ 0, & x \neq x' \end{cases}. \tag{5}$$

Thirdly, according to the requirements of product conceptual design field, the symmetric quintuple implicational algorithm is used for fuzzy inference.

In actual processing, we employ $\rightarrow_1 = I_{LK}$ and $\rightarrow_2 = I_{FD}$. In the symmetric quintuple implicational algorithm, such combination of implication possesses great reducibility together with response property.

For the case of $\rightarrow_1 = I_{LK}, \rightarrow_2 = I_{FD}$, according to Theorem 1, the MinP-symmetric quintuple implicational formula is:

$$B^*(y) = \sup_{x \in E}\{A^*(x) \otimes_2 ((A^*(x) \rightarrow_2 A(x)) \otimes_2 R_1(x', y))\} \tag{6}$$

in which $E_y = \{x \in X | (A^*(x) \rightarrow_{FD} A(x)) + R_1(x', y) > 1, ((A^*(x) \rightarrow_{FD} A(x)) \wedge R_1(x', y) + A^*(x) > 1, A\left(x'\right) > R_1(x', y)\}$.

For the input x', considering that $A^*_{x'} = A^*(x) = \begin{cases} 1, & x = x' \\ 0, & x \neq x' \end{cases}$. We easily find

$$B^*(y) = \begin{cases} R_1(x', y), & x' \in E_y \\ 0, & x' \notin E_y \end{cases}.$$

For any x', we let $x' \in E_y$. It is easy to find two fuzzy sets $A_m A_{m+1}$ satisfying $A_m\left(x'\right), A_{m+1}\left(x'\right)$ correspondingly. Then one has:

$$\begin{aligned} B^*(y) = R_1(x', y) &= (A_m(x') \rightarrow_1 B_m(y)) \vee (A_{m+1}(x') \rightarrow_1 B_{m+1}(y)) \\ &= (A_m(x') \times B_m(y)) \vee (A_{m+1}(x') \times B_{m+1}(y)) \\ &= (a_m \times B_m(y)) \vee (a_{m+1} \times B_{m+1}(y)) \\ &= \begin{cases} a_m \times B_m(y), & a_m \times B_m(y) \geq a_{m+1} \times B_{m+1}(y) \\ a_{m+1} \times B_{m+1}(y), & \text{else} \end{cases} \end{aligned} \tag{7}$$

where $m, m+1 \in \{1, 2, \ldots, n\}$, and $A_m\left(x'\right), A_{m+1}\left(x'\right) > 0, A_1\left(x'\right) = \ldots A_{m-2}\left(x'\right) = A_{m-1}\left(x'\right) = A_{m+2}\left(x'\right) = A_{m+3}\left(x'\right) = \cdots = A_n\left(x'\right) = 0$, meanwhile we let $a_m \cong A_m\left(x'\right)$, $a_{m+1} \cong A_{m+1}\left(x'\right)$.

Here A_m, A_{m+1} are two consecutive fuzzy sets. According to the rules $A_m \rightarrow B_m$,$A_{m+1} \rightarrow B_{m+1}$ in the knowledge base, we can get B_m, B_{m+1}. So B_m, B_{m+1} are not necessarily two consecutive fuzzy sets (it may also occur $B_m = J_3, B_{m+1} = J_1$). The following is similar.

In addition, there are other possible results, that is, if there is only one fuzzy set A_m such that $A_m\left(x'\right) > 0$ (let $A_m\left(x'\right) = 1$). Then $B^*(y) = a_m \times B_m(y) = B_m(y)$ can be obtained.

The above two cases correspond to simple single-input single-output (SISO) scenarios, while the symmetric quintuple implicational algorithm is used for fuzzy inference. In order to solve the relatively complex single input and multiple outputs problem, the above two cases cannot be satisfied, and the following calculation ideas can be adopted:

For $A \rightarrow (B_1, B_2, \ldots, B_m)$ and A^*, find $(B_1{}^*, B_2{}^*, \ldots, B_m{}^*)$.

This can be treated separately according to the subterms. In detail, we get $B_1{}^*$ with $A \rightarrow B_1$ andA^*, and get $B_2{}^*$ with $A \rightarrow B_2$ andA^*. Thus we obtain$B_1{}^*, B_2{}^*, \ldots, B_m{}^*$, and finally synthesize the full solution $(B_1{}^*, B_2{}^*, \ldots, B_m{}^*)$.

Following that, the center average defuzzier is used in the defuzzier.

Specifically, the corresponding values $B^*(y)$ can be obtained by using a central average defuzzier, in which M represent the union or intersection of multiple fuzzy sets. Its formula is as below:

$$y^* = \sum\nolimits_{p=1}^{M} \bar{y}^p \omega_p / \sum_{p=1}^{M} p, \tag{8}$$

where $\bar{y}^p$ stands for the center of the p-th fuzzy set, meanwhile the weight ω_p is its height $(p = 1, 2, \ldots, M)$. From (7), one has

$$B^*(y) = (a_m \times B_m(y)) \vee (a_{m+1} \times B_{m+1}(y)), \tag{9}$$

$$y^* = \frac{\sum_{i=1}^{n} y_i B^*(y_i)}{\sum_{i=1}^{n} B^*(y_i)} = \frac{\bar{y}^p B^*(\bar{y}^p) + \bar{y}^{p+1} B^*(\bar{y}^{p+1})}{B^*(\bar{y}^p) + B^*(\bar{y}^{p+1})} = \frac{\bar{y}^p a_m + \bar{y}^{p+1} a_{m+1}}{a_m + a_{m+1}}, \tag{10}$$

where $\overline{y}^p$, $\overline{y}^{p+1}$ respectively are the center of the fuzzy set B_m, B_{m+1}.

Finally, we carry on numerical determinations. After we gety^*, the general function and structure can be considered to boil down to concrete classes. It is convenient to calculate the distance from y^* each $B_i(y)$ to the center y_i $(i = 1, \ldots, n)$. Let $d = \min\{|y_i - y^*|, i = 1, \ldots, n\}$, and then we take

$$y^{**} = \max\{y_i \big| d = |y_i - y^*|, i = 1, \ldots, n\}. \tag{11}$$

For multiple outputs $y^*{}_1, \ldots, y^*{}_r$, the corresponding output $y^{**}{}_j$ can be obtained by processing according to (11). At the end, we achieve $y^{**} = (y^{**}{}_1, \ldots, y^{**}{}_r)$.

2.4 Modeling Process of Function Tree Guided by the Symmetric Quintuple Implicational Controller

The main steps of function tree modeling are as follows. To begin with, we design and input a fuzzy and/or/not function tree containing only functional nodes. Then we carry out the function-structure deduction by symmetric quintuple implicational controller. Finally we can build a complete fuzzy function tree with complete functional nodes. Based on this process, we come up with a modeling scheme guided by the symmetric quintuple implicational controller.

Algorithm 1: A function tree modeling method guided by the symmetric quintuple implicational controller.

Input: Initializes the fuzzy and/or/not function tree.

Output: Expanded tree.

Step 1: We use breadth traversal to transform the fuzzy and/or/not function tree. The initial node is the first leaf node in the fuzzy and/or/not function tree.

Step 2: We deal with the leaf node demanded to be processed. Otherwise, jump to Step 7.

Step 3: We transform leaf nodes into $A^*(x)$.

Step 4: We deduce $A^*(x)$ to $B^*(y)$, and find the corresponding fuzzy rules of the sub-knowledge base in the rule base. Then carry out the fuzzy inference of the symmetric five-element implication algorithm.

Step 5: We calculate $B^*(y)$ according to the center average defuzzier.

Step 6: We carry on numerical determination, and save the structure nodes corresponding to the current leaf nodes. So a function-structure deduction is completed.

Step 7: For the original tree, we make the current node employ the next leaf node, and jump to Step 2. If not, go on.

Step 8: We put the resulting structural nodes to the final tree.

3 An Application Example

The conceptual design of maglev train is a case study of showing the steps of modeling. Among them, the maglev function and drive function are mainly described in two aspects. Maglev function is divided into magnetic repulsion and magnetic suction. We just discuss the case for the magnetic repulsion. In the meantime, for functional integrity, the implementation strategy of the driver is also given. The realization of magnetic repulsion function mainly includes magnetic-magnetic mode and magnetic-inductor mode.

Around the functions discussed above, assume that the initial tree have already obtained, which is shown in Fig. 2.

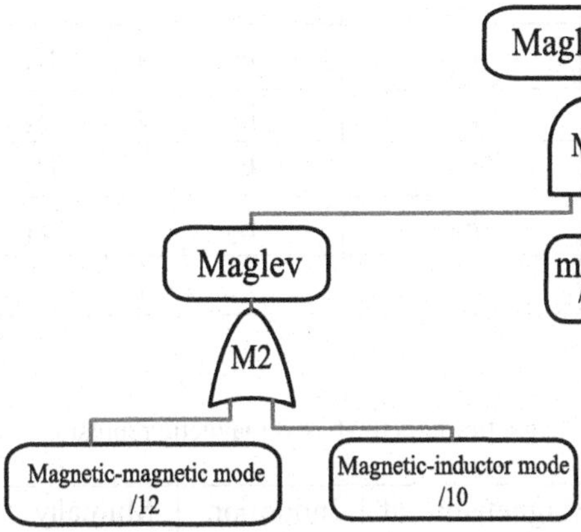

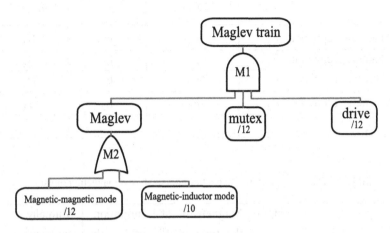

Fig. 2. Initial tree for maglev train

Firstly, function requirement and fuzzy inference rule library are constructed as follows.

1) Magnetic repulsion function by virtue of magnetic-magnetic mode.
   Such mode can be used to make the train bottom and track have magnetic properties. The input of this function is the magnetism at the train bottom (based on magnetic-magnetic mode), mutually exclusive magnetism and rail magnetism. The relevant results are Y^*_1, Y^*_2, Y^*_3. Among them, the magnetism at the train bottom takes five-fuzzy set clan (that is, the combination composed of 5-triangular fuzzy sets). The mutually repulsive magnetism employs 2-fuzzy set clan, the rail magnetism takes 3-fuzzy set clan. Table 1 shows the fuzzy inference rule library of homologous parts.
2) Magnetic repulsion function by virtue of magnetic-inductor mode
   To realize the track sensing the magnetism at the train bottom while keeping the cost low, the magnetic repulsion function by virtue of the magnetic-inductive method can be adopted. Three conditions including the magnetism at the train bottom (via magnetic-inductor mode), the induction of the track, and the mutually repulsive magnetism, are used for input. The output results W^*_1, W^*_2, W^*_3 are taken as 5-fuzzy set clan, 3-fuzzy set clan and 2-fuzzy set clan respectively. Table 2 shows the fuzzy inference rule base of relevant parts.

Table 1. The rule library for magnetic-magnetic-based magnetic repulsion

Input / Output	Magnetism at the train bottom	Track magnetism	Mutually exclusive magnetism
Magnetic repulsion F_1	F_1	E_1	D_1
Magnetic repulsion F_1	F_1	E_2	D_2
Magnetic repulsion F_2	F_2	E_0	D_1
Magnetic repulsion F_2	F_2	E_2	D_1
...	...	...	...

Table 2. The rule library for magnetic-inductor-based magnetic repulsion

Input / Output	Magnetism at the bottom of the train	Induction of the track	Mutually exclusive magnetism
Magnetic repulsion E_1	F_1	E_1	D_1
Magnetic repulsion E_1	F_2	E_1	D_1
Magnetic repulsion E_2	F_3	E_1	D_1
Magnetic repulsion E_2	F_3	E_2	D_1
...	...	...	...

The inference steps of functional structure on the strength of fuzzy inference is as follows:

1) Deduction of magnetic repulsion function-structure by virtue of magnetic-magnetic mode
According to Fig. 2, for the input "magnetic repulsion by virtue of magnetic-magnetic/12", i.e., $x^{'} = 12$. The fuzzy inference step is as follows.
For $x^{'}$, we employ $A^{*}_{x^{'}} = A^{*}(x) = \{ \begin{matrix} 1, x = 12 \\ 0, x \neq 12 \end{matrix}$. Then we have $a_{m+1} = A_{m+1}\left(x^{'}\right) = F\left(x^{'}\right) = 0.65$ and $a_m = A_m\left(x^{'}\right) = F_2\left(x^{'}\right) = 0.35$. From Table 1, one has $A_m = F_2$ and $A_m = F_3$ each has two output schemes denoted as B_1^1, B_1^2 and B_2^1, B_2^2. Therefore, 4 schemes can be obtained.

(i) Firstly, we take $A_m \rightarrow B_1^1, A_{m+1} \rightarrow B_2^1$ as an example, where $B_1^1 = (B_{11}, B_{12}, B_{13}) = (F_1, E_1, D_1), B_2^1 = (B_{21}, B_{22}, B_{23}) = (F_2, E_0, D_1)$ (referring to Table 1). We're going to do a calculation here to gain (B^*_1, B^*_2, B^*_3). That is, we use $A_m \rightarrow B_{11}, A_{m+1} \rightarrow B_{21}$ to calculate B^*_1. Others are calculated in a similar way. We get:
$B^*_1(y) = (a_m \times B_{11}(y)) \vee (a_{m+1} \times B_{21}(y)) = (a_m \times F_1(y)) \vee (a_{m+1} \times F_2(y))$,
$B^*_2(y) = (a_m \times B_{12}(y)) \vee (a_{m+1} \times B_{22}(y)) = (a_m \times E_1(y)) \vee (a_{m+1} \times E_0(y))$,
$B^*_3(y) = (a_m \times B_{13}(y)) \vee (a_{m+1} \times B_{23}(y)) = (a_m \times D_1(y)) \vee (a_{m+1} \times D_1(y))$.
Then, according to the center average defuzzier, the following results can be obtained:
For B^*_1, we have

$$y^*_1 = \frac{y^{-p}a_m + y^{-(p+1)}a_{m+1}}{a_m + a_{m+1}} = \frac{8 \times 0.65 + 10 \times 0.35}{0.65 + 0.35} = 8.7;$$

For B^*_2, we have

$$y^*_2 = \frac{y^{-p}a_m + y^{-(p+1)}a_{m+1}}{a_m + a_{m+1}} = \frac{12 \times 0.65 + 6 \times 0.35}{0.65 + 0.35} = 9.9;$$

For B^*_3, we have

$$y^*_3 = \frac{y^{-p}a_m + y^{-(p+1)}a_{m+1}}{a_m + a_{m+1}} = \frac{12 \times 0.65 + 12 \times 0.35}{0.65 + 0.35} = 12;$$

So, we can gain $y^* = (y^*_1, y^*_2, y^*_3) = (8.7, 9.9, 12)$.
Then, with regard to the classification question of y^*, i.e., y^* is transformed into $y^{**} = (y^{**}_1, y^{**}_2, y^{**}_3)$. One has $y^{**}_1 = \max_{i \in \{1,\ldots,n\}} \{y_i | \min_{j \in \{1,\ldots,n\}} |y_i - y^*_1| = |y_i - y^*_1| = 8\}$, $y^{**}_2 = 10$, $y^{**}_3 = 12$.
Lastly one has $y^{**} = (y^{**}_1, y^{**}_2, y^{**}_3) = (8, 10, 12)$.

(ii) For $A_m \rightarrow B_1^1, A_{m+1} \rightarrow B_2^2$, and $B_1^1 = (F_1, E_1, D_1), B_2^2 = (F_2, E_2, D_1)$, we similarly get $y^{**} = (y^{**}_1, y^{**}_2, y^{**}_3) = (8, 12, 12)$.

(iii) For $A_m \rightarrow B_1^2, A_{m+1} \rightarrow B_2^2$, we get $y^{**} = (y^{**}_1, y^{**}_2, y^{**}_3) = (8, 7, 10)$.

(iv) For $A_m \rightarrow B_1^2, A_{m+1} \rightarrow B_2^2$, we get $y^{**} = (y^{**}_1, y^{**}_2, y^{**}_3) = (8, 8, 10)$.
So here are the four schemes.

2) Deduction of magnetic repulsion function-structure by virtue of magnetic-magnetic mode.
According to Fig. 2, for the input "magnetic repulsion by virtue of magnetic-inductor/10", that is, $x' = 10$. We can use a singleton fuzzy set, that is $A^*_{x'} = A^*(x) = \{\begin{matrix} 1, & x = 10 \\ 0, & x \neq 10 \end{matrix}$. Similar to the above process, corresponding conclusions can be drawn. Finally, two schemes can be obtained, which are (7, 6, 8) and (7, 7, 8).

3) The complete fuzzy function tree is obtained.
According to the implementing schemes of the drive, we complete the drive through the linear motor, ac linear induction motor driver board, dynamo armature. Finally,

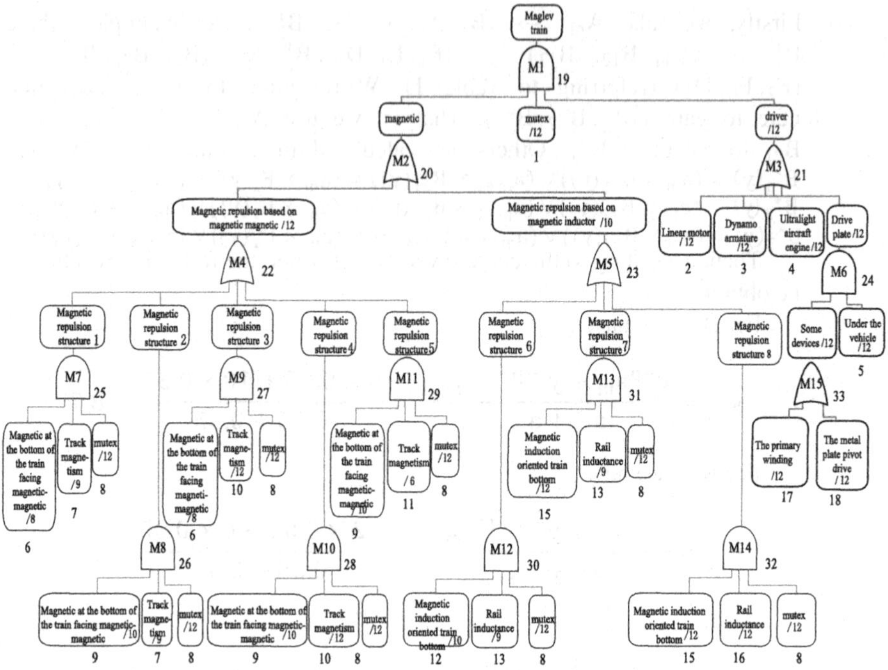

Fig. 3. Entire fuzzy function tree of train

a complete fuzzy function tree can be obtained by combining the function-structure deduction with the fuzzy function tree, we can see this in Fig. 3.

The method of function solving is not expanded here due to space limitations, but can be carried out by lossless solving algorithm [18], as shown in Fig. 4. As you can see from Fig. 4, 30 concepts of function solving can be obtained here. For example, $x_1 \wedge x_3 \wedge x_8 \wedge x_{15} \wedge x_{16}$ is an example. The specific meaning of the structure is that x_{15} is used to represent the equipped with superconducting electromagnet. x_{16} represents the aluminum closed loop on the track. When the train is moving, x_8 denotes the exclusion of the induced current in the closed loop. Finally x_3 represents the dynamo armature. The cost of the improved design scheme is high, and it is not an ideal scheme for the optimization study of maglev train.

In fact, another function-structure design can be adopted. For example, $x_1 \wedge x_5 \wedge x_8 \wedge x_9 \wedge x_{11} \wedge x_{18}$ is a better idea. Its structure includes the bottom of the car body, magnetic field mutual repulsion, drive board and other magnetic excitation track and dynamic tracking operation. The results show that the cost of such scheme is low, which is a relatively ideal design scheme.

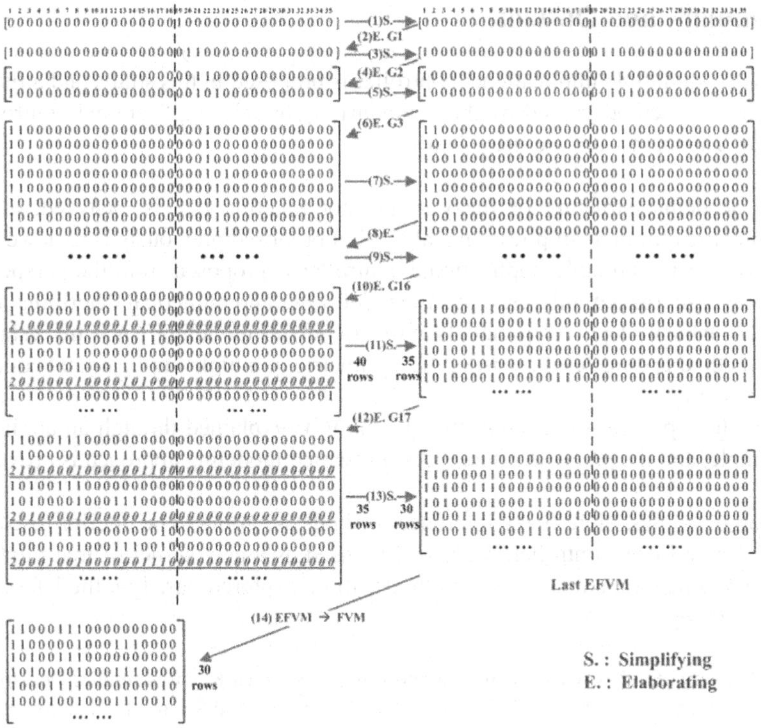

Fig. 4. Matrix display of EFVM reduction algorithm

The advantages of this study are mainly reflected in the following aspects:

1) A symmetric quintuple implicational controller is proposed from the perspectives of rule base, fuzzier, inference machine, defuzzier and numerical determination. The symmetric quintuple implicational algorithm (which is advanced in the field of fuzzy inference) is adopted.
2) A new modeling method of fuzzy and/or/not function tree is proposed, which employs the symmetric quintuple implicational controller as the core and takes it as the driving strategy of function tree expansion.
3) The knowledge of experts is described in the way of fuzzy set clan to form a fuzzy rule base, which is applied to the modeling of function tree as a pointcut.
4) The idea of fuzzy control is taken as the driving mode of function tree modeling. On the one hand, it makes full use of the knowledge of experts, and on the other hand, it can intelligently and automatically build fuzzy and/or/not function trees. This is particularly significant for large function trees.

4 Summary and Outlook

Asymmetric quintuple implicational controller is proposed in this study, and a function tree modeling method guided by the symmetric quintuple implicational controller is proposed. The main work are listed below:

1) The academic structure of fuzzy and/or/not function tree is analyzed, and the symmetric quintuple implicational algorithm proposed previously is reviewed.
2) A symmetric quintuple implicational controller is proposed from the perspectives of rule base, fuzzier, inference machine, defuzzier and numerical determination.
3) Based on the in-depth requirements of functional tree modeling, a new tree establishing method is developed by using the symmetric quintuple implicational controller as the core.
4) The whole process of function tree modeling is explained through an application example, and the practical effect of the presented modeling approach is proved.

In future studies, more fuzzy inference methods are going to be ulterior researched to build a new fuzzy controller. They will be used as a new kernel of tree modeling. In addition, a new function solving method will be explored based on the latest fuzzy inference strategy.

Acknowledgement. This work received support by the National Key Research & Development Program of China (No. 2020YFC1523100) and the National Natural Science Foundation of China (Nos. 62176083, 61673156, 61877016, 61976078), the Fundamental Research Funds for the Central Universities of China (No. PA2021GDSK0092), the Natural Science Foundation of Anhui Province (Nos.1408085MKL15, 1508085QF129).

References

1. Shai, O., Reich, Y., Rubin, D.: Creative conceptual design: extending the scope by infused design. Comput. Aided Des. **41**(3), 117–135 (2009)
2. Tang, Y.M., Li, L., Liu, X.P.: State-of-the-art development of complex systems and their simulation methods. Complex Syst. Model. Simul. **1**(4), 271–290 (2021)
3. Self, J.A.: Communication through design sketches: implications for stakeholder interpretation during concept design. Des. Stud. **63**(1), 1–36 (2019)
4. Wu, Y.L., Zhou, F., Kong, J.Z.: Innovative design approach for product design based on TRIZ, AD, fuzzy and Grey relational analysis. Comput. Indust. Eng. **140**, Article 106276 (2020)
5. Song, Y.T., Wu, S.T., Wan, Y.X., et al.: Concept design on R H maintenance of CFET R Tokamak reactor. Fus. Eng. Des. **89**(9), 2331–2335 (2014)
6. Pahl, G., Beitz, W.: Engineering Design. The Design Council, London (1984)
7. Tang, Y.M., Liu, X.P.: Task partition for function tree according to innovative functional reasoning. In: Proceedings of the 12th International Conference on Computer Supported Cooperative Work in Design, pp. 189–195, Xian (2008)
8. Chakrabarti, A., Bligh, T.P.: A scheme for functional reasoning in conceptual design. Des. Stud. **22**(6), 493–517 (2001)
9. Ren, B., Guo, D., Shen, Y., et al.: Embedding service function tree with minimum cost for NFV-enabled multicast. IEEE J. Sel. Areas Commun. **37**(5), 1085–1097 (2019)

10. Luo, J., Yu, S.Z., Peng, S.: SDN/NFV-based security service function tree for cloud. IEEE Access **8**, 38538–38545 (2020)
11. Tang, Y.M., Pedrycz, W.: Oscillation bound estimation of perturbations under Bandler-Kohout subproduct. IEEE Trans. Cybern. (2021). https://doi.org/10.1109/TCYB.2020.3025793
12. Wang, G.J.: Full implication of fuzzy reasoning triple I algorithm. Sci. China (Ser. E) **29**(1), 43–53 (1999)
13. Tang, Y.M., Ren, F.J.: Universal triple I method for fuzzy reasoning and fuzzy controller. Iranian J. Fuzzy Syst. **10**(5), 1–24 (2013)
14. Tang, Y.M., Pedrycz, W.: On continuity of the entropy-based differently implicational algorithm. Kybernetika **55**(2), 307–336 (2019)
15. Tang, Y.M., Pedrycz, W.: On the α(u, v)-symmetric implicational method for R- and (S, N)-implications. Int. J. Approx. Reason. **92**, 212–231 (2018)
16. Tang, Y.M., Pedrycz, W., Ren, F.J.: Granular symmetric implicational method. IEEE Trans. Emerg. Top. Comput. Intell. **6**(3), 710–723 (2021) https://doi.org/10.1109/TETCI.2021.3100597
17. Tang, Y.M., Bao, G.Q., Chen, J.J., et al.: On the symmetric quintuple implicational method of fuzzy reasoning. Iranian J. Fuzzy Syst. **18**(4), 113–129 (2021)
18. Tang, Y.M., Liu, X.P.: Lossless solving of two-valued propositional logic. Chin. J. Comput. **36**(5), 1097–1114 (2013)

An Adaptive and Collaborative Method Based on GMRA for Intrusion Detection

Shaohua Teng(✉), Yongzhi Zhang, Wei Zhang, and Lu Liang

School of Computer Science and Technology, Guangdong University of Technology, Guangzhou 510006, China
shteng@gdut.edu.cn

Abstract. Generally, the detection configuration in the normal state cannot cope with the detection during sudden network peaks. Moreover, a kind of attack detection algorithm is suitable to detect some attack types. Based on the two cases, we formally present the above-mentioned problems by applying Group Multi-Role Assignment (GMRA) model and propose an adaptive detection model that is composed of many parallel detection algorithms.

The formalization of the above questions makes it easier to solve by applying the IBM ILOG CPLEX optimization package (CPLEX). In order to find the optimal parallel algorithms, we assign legitimately detection resources in real time according to the detection time of different attack. The proposed approaches are verified on two different data sets of UNSW-NB15 and NSL-KDD. Comparative experiments verify the effectiveness and advantages of the proposed model.

Keywords: Role-Based Collaboration (RBC) · Group Multi-Role Assignment (GMRA) · Intrusion detection · UNSW-NB15 · IBM ILOG CPLEX optimization (CPLEX) package

1 Introduction

Intrusion detection is an important means to ensure network security. Many researchers develop various intrusion detection algorithms and achieve some excellent results. However, with the explosive growth of data transmission and the wide application of high-speed networks, especially under the modern multimedia network that integrates voice and video services in the big data and cloud computing environment, the real-time data traffic of the network during peak periods has skyrocketed. The detectors cannot efficiently cope with these emergencies. In order to effectively save cost, adaptive adjustment of detection resources is very important.

Generally, in order to deal with such emergencies, traditional method can only use historical data to make statistics analysis, and many resources are used to detect the real-time transmission traffic. This also causes invalid consumption of the detection

This work is supported in part by the Key-Area Research and Development Program of Guangdong Province under Grant 2020B010166006, and by the National Natural Science Foundation of China under Grant 61972102.

Y. Sun et al. (Eds.): ChineseCSCW 2021, CCIS 1491, pp. 72–84, 2022.
https://doi.org/10.1007/978-981-19-4546-5_6

resources. Being idle for time causes a waste of resources. Moreover, for some common types of attacks, some more adaptive detection algorithms have not been chosen.

In fact, in real-time intrusion detection, we can deploy multiple detection systems with different numbers on different servers, and then one detection system can detect multiple attack types, and one attack type can also be detected by multiple detection systems. Then each test system can be responsible for testing one or more attack performance that is more suitable for itself (Considering from the two aspects of detection time and detection rate), in addition detection resources can be adjusted according to the size of real-time traffic (The number of test servers open). On this basis, through group multi-role assignment (GMRA), we form the real-time adaptive parallel intrusion detection problem.

In fact, GMRA [1] is a sub-model of Environments – Classes, Agents, Roles, Groups, and Objects (E-CARGO) [2–4], which is a general model of Role-Based Collaboration (RBC) [3, 4]. RBC is a collaboration methodology that uses roles to facilitate an organizational structure to collaborate, and coordinate group activities with or within systems. Through RBC and its E-CARGO model, complex problems can be formalized and solved efficiently. It has been revealed as complex processes through the life cycle of RBC, that is, role negotiation, agent evaluation, role assignment, role playing, and role transfer, where role negotiation is a complex and highly domain-oriented task.

According to RBC, in order to solve the above-mentioned intrusion detection problem, we use the attack types in the two UNSW-NB15 [19] and NSL-KDD [20] data sets and different detection systems to form roles and agent sets respectively, and then reasonably evaluate the roles of different agents. Finally, more efficient and flexible allocation algorithms are used to improve the overall detection rate and make it adaptive in a reasonable time.

More exactly, different detection systems can be used as agents, and the types of attacks contained in the data set are roles. Based on these abstractions, this paper formalizes the intrusion detection problem through Group Role Assignment (GMRA), and proposes a role negotiation method based on the AHP algorithm. The formalization of the intrusion detection problem makes it easy to find a solution using the IBM ILOG CPLEX [5] optimization package (CPLEX).

The main contributions of this paper include the following aspects:

1) A concise formalization of Intrusion detection problem based on GMRA;
2) A pertinent role negotiation way to make the Intrusion detection problem be solved reasonably and efficiently;
3) A practical Intrusion detection problem solution based on the IBM ILOG CPLEX optimization package (CPLEX) [5], and a thorough simulation experiment.

The structure of this paper is as follows. It describes the real-world scenarios related to the proposed problem in Sect. 2; the GMRA and E-CARGO models are presented in Sect. 3. The Sect. 4 introduces the CPLEX solution and simulation experiments, the results of which prove that the proposed solution is feasible. The Sect. 5 reviews the related work and summarizes and points out the future work.

2 Related Work

In the computer network intrusion detection, many efficient and feasible detection methods have been proposed.

A. Ahmim *et al.* [7] proposed a classifier method based on decision trees and rules, which was composed of REP tree, JRip algorithm and ForestPA. The REP tree algorithm and JRip algorithm were used to classify network traffic data into anomaly or normal data. In addition to taking the output of the REP tree algorithm and JRip algorithm as its own input, ForestPA also uses the characteristics of the initial data set as labels. Compared with the current state-of-the-art solutions, they have certain advantages in terms of accuracy, detection rate, false alarm rate and time overhead.

In order to make full use of the advantages of misuse detection and anomaly detection, Chun Guo *et al.* [8] combined the two and focused on intrusion detection. This method is a two-stage hybrid solution consisting of two anomaly detection components and one misuse detection component. In phase one, an anomaly detection method with low computational complexity is developed, and the detection component is constructed using this method. The k-nearest neighbor algorithm becomes crucial when the two detection components are established in the second stage. The detection component of stage one participates in the process of establishing the two detection components of stage two. These two detection components reduce the false positives and false negatives generated by the detection components of stage 1. The experimental results on the KDD 1999 data set [19] and the Kyoto University benchmark data set [20] show that the hybrid method can effectively detect network anomalies, and it has a low false positive rate.

Teng *et al.* [9] introduced Collaborative computing and Particle computing to intrusion detection, and proposed a cooperative multi-agent intrusion detection model, in which each agent plays a role of a detector, and these agents form a distributed intrusion detection model.

Table 1. The detection rate of different detection systems for different types of attacks (unit: Percent)

	BayesNet	JRip	DTNB	DescisionTable	J48Consolidated	MLP	LogitBoost	PART
Normal	81.08	99.99	99.99	100.0	100.0	100.0	100.0	100.0
Backdoor	19.20	11.67	18.17	7.38	26.29	0	12.55	21.86
Analysis	11.40	11.94	21.20	16.81	43.78	0	15.18	23.21
Fuzzers	63.52	86.46	83.13	78.54	86.77	0	84.20	87.96
Shellcod	65.89	57.32	57.74	53.14	88.70	0	5.23	60.25
Reconnaissance	69.34	57.32	71.99	74.99	81.21	99.31	68.24	75.44
Expoits	42.30	69.20	56.95	85.89	49.00	40.10	89.64	80.00
Dos	72.67	0	70.50	6.49	38.62	0	5.200	23.25
Worms	87.09	35.48	8.06	1.61	78.50	0	0	45.16
Generic	97.80	98.06	97.79	97.80	97.96	97.81	97.84	98.47

Table 2. The detection time of different detection systems for different types of attacks (unit: s)

	BayesNet	JRip	DTNB	DescisionTable	J48Consolidated	MLP	LogitBoost	PART
Normal	0.551	0.152	0.490	0.194	0.105	3.007	0.598	1.217
Backdoor	0.016	0.004	0.014	0.005	0.003	0.090	0.018	0.036
Analysis	0.019	0.054	0.174	0.068	0.003	0.106	0.021	0.043
Fuzzers	0.179	0.049	0.159	0.063	0.034	0.979	0.195	0.396
Shellcod	0.011	0.003	0.010	0.004	0.002	0.064	0.012	0.026
Reconnaissance	0.103	0.028	0.092	0.036	0.019	0.566	0.112	0.229
Expoits	0.327	0.090	0.291	0.115	0.062	1.788	0.356	0.723
Dos	0.12	0.033	0.10	0.04	0.02	0.66	0.13	0.27
Worms	0.001	0.0004	0.001	0.0005	0.002	0.008	0.001	0.003
Generic	0.395	0.109	0.352	0.139	0.075	2.157	0.429	0.873

Collaboration research is a challenging topic in a variety of domains [10–13]. In collaboration research, roles and agents are used to describe collaboration activities [15–17]. Zhu et al. define the relationship between roles and agents. They develop an engineering methodology for RBC [3, 4] and their E-CARGO [2–4] model. Current RBC research focuses on accurate task assignment and task transfer to save the workload of later collaboration [18–21]. One of the kernels of RBC is Group Multi-Role Assignment (GMRA). In GMRA, the process of task assignment aims to propose an assignment with optimal team performance based on agent evaluations. Many studies focus on assignment problems with various constraints tailored to different applications. Roles and agents have many constraints, including mutual exclusion, number, time and etc. which make assignment problems complex.

3 Problem Formalizations with E-CARGO Model

In order to clarify the problem that each detection system in intrusion detection has multiple attack type more suitable for its own detection, we model it through GMRA, which is a sub-model of E-CARGO. The E-CARGO model abstractly describes the components of the collaboration system with a 9-tuple $\sum$ ::= < $\mathcal{C}, \mathcal{O}, \mathcal{A}$, M, $\mathcal{R}, \mathcal{E}, \mathcal{G}, \int\prime, \mathcal{H}$>. Among them, $\mathcal{C}$ indicates a class; $\mathcal{O}$ indicates an object; $\mathcal{A}$ (Agent) indicates a collection of individual units; $\mathcal{M}$ indicates a message set; $\mathcal{R}$(Role) indicates a set of roles (that is, abstraction of tasks and requirements) $\mathcal{E}$ is used for an abstract collaboration environment; $\mathcal{G}$ (Group) Indicates the group set; $\int 0$ is the initial state of the system; $\mathcal{H}$ is a group of users.

When discussing group multi-role assignment [1, 2], the environment (e) and group (g) are formalized with vectors and matrices. Among them, this paper uses a non-negative integer m (=$|\mathcal{A}|$) to indicate the size of set $\mathcal{A}$; $n(= |\mathcal{R}, |)$ indicates the size of set $\mathcal{R}$; $i_0,\ i_1,\ i_2,\ i_3 \ldots$ to indicate the subscript of an agent, specifically referring to each agent; $j_0,\ j_1,\ j_2,\ j_3 \ldots$ to indicate the subscript of a role, specifically referring to each role.

In particular, regarding the allocation of different detection systems, the attack types can be regarded as roles, and different detection systems can be regarded as agents.

Definition 1 [4]: A role is defined as *r*:: = <*id*, ®> where *id* is the identification of *r* and ®*r* is the attribute set of the role.

In the intrusion detection problem, different types of attacks in a data set is used as the role, then a data set usually contains different types of attacks.

Note that Table 1 and Table 2 are based on UNSW-NB15 data set as an example, the NSL-KDD data set is similar.

Definition 2 [4]: An agent is defined as *a*:: = <*id*, Q>, *id* is the identification of *a*, and ® is the set of values corresponding to the required attributes for matching a role. $Q =$ {"detection time", "detection rate"} is shown in Table 1 and Table 2. For example, the "detection time", "detection rate" of role *r* are named *r.k* and *r.d* respectively.

Note that in the intrusion detection problem, an agent refers to different types of intrusion detection system.

Definition 3 [4]: An *ability limit vector* $\boldsymbol{L^a}$ is an *m*-vector, where $L^a[i]$ $(0 \le i < m)$ indicates how many roles can be assigned to agent *i* at most.

In the intrusion detection problem, in order to better adapt to changes in network traffic, we divide the network traffic state into normal state, busy state and peak state. Based on the mining and analysis of data sets and historical traffic data, we can get the total traffic size and the proportion of various attack types in the total traffic in a certain period of time under normal conditions. Therefore, taking UNSW-NB15 as an example, we can get an initial range vector $\boldsymbol{L^a} = [3, 1, 1, 1, 1, 1, 1, 1, 1, 2]$, NSL-KDD is similar.

Note that when the amount of network traffic changes from the normal state to the busy state, the range vector $\boldsymbol{L^a}$ will correspondingly change to $\boldsymbol{L^a} = [6, 2, 2, 2, 2, 2, 2, 2, 2, 4]$; when the network traffic changes from the busy state to the peak state, the range vector $\boldsymbol{L^a}$ will change to $\boldsymbol{L^a} = [12, 4, 4, 4, 4, 4, 4, 4, 4, 8]$.

Definition 4 [4]: A *role range vector* **L** is a vector of the lower bound of the ranges of roles in environment *e* of group *g*.

Based on Definition 3, we set $\boldsymbol{L} = [2, 2, 2, 2, 2, 2, 2, 2]$ in the normal state, $\boldsymbol{L} = [2, 2, 2, 2, 2, 2, 2, 2]$ in the busy state and $\boldsymbol{L} = [4, 4, 4, 4, 4, 4, 4, 4]$ in the peak state to deal with the detection demand of different network conditions. The above values have all been UNSW-NB15 as an example, NSL-KDD is similar.

Definition 5 [4]: The *role weight vector W* indicates the weight of each role and is indicated by a vector *W*, where $W[j] (0 \le j < n)$ indicates the weight of r_j.

In different application scenarios, different types of attacks will have different impacts on it. Public websites should pay more attention to some types of denial of service attacks such as DDOS, while individual users should pay more attention to attacks such as worms. Therefore, different attack types have different weights in different scenarios. In this article, we use the AHP algorithm [21] to evaluate the general weights of different attack types in the UNSW-NB15 data set, which is $W[j] = [0.099, 0.095, 0.083, 0.097, 0.142, 0.107, 0.079, 0.102, 0.095, 0.101]$.

Note that in different data sets, the types of attacks included are different, so the corresponding weights are also different. This article takes the UNSW-NB15 data set as an example, and the NSL-KDD data set is similar.

Definition 6 [4]: A *qualification matrix* $\boldsymbol{Q}$ is an $m \times n$ matrix. $Q[i,j] \in [0, 1]$ indicates that $a_i (0 \le i < m)$ is responsible for the performance score of r_j $(0 \le j < n)$. $Q[i,j] = 0$ indicates the lowest value, $Q[i,j] = 1$ represents the highest.

In the intrusion detection problem, we need to obtain the Deterate (detection rate) and Detetime (detection time) of different detection systems for different types of attacks in the data set, which can be known from Table 1 and Table 2. Secondly, we combine the W vector in Definition 5 to obtain the Q matrix.

Normalizing the values of the Deterate and Detetime;

$$\text{Detetime}[i,j] = \frac{\text{Detetime}_{initial}[i,j] - min\{\text{Detetime}_{initial}\}}{max\{\text{Detetime}_{initial}\} - min\{\text{Detetime}_{initial}\}} [0, 1]$$

$$\text{Detetime}[i,j] = \frac{\text{Detetime}_{initial}[i,j] - min\{\text{Detetime}_{initial}\}}{max\{\text{Detetime}_{initial}\} - min\{\text{Detetime}_{initial}\}} [0, 1]$$

Based on Table 1 and Table 2, as well as the weight of a role, $\boldsymbol{Q_{initial}}$ is the sum of different detection systems' scores for different types of attacks.

Table 3. Represents the scoring matrix Q obtained after the normalization process

	REPTree	JRip	J48Consolidated	DecisionTable	J48	SPAARC	LogitBoost	Bagging
Normal	0.160000	0.098629	0.124684	0.142663	0.154221	0.127895	0.133674	0.136884
Backdoor	0.384332	0.000000	0.084975	0.022915	0.404859	0.095000	0.067789	0.380513
Analysis	0.059000	0.000000	0.112500	0.029500	0.029500	0.029250	0.029500	0.031908
Fuzzers	0.150963	0.077744	0.109733	0.124747	0.148949	0.106598	0.137800	0.126642
Shellcod	0.205207	0.100534	0.142000	0.143791	0.196992	0.200708	0.111714	0.217138
Reconnaissance	0.168354	0.099393	0.135444	0.128995	0.156943	0.127837	0.140406	0.147244
Expoits	0.187997	0.079000	0.056314	0.090943	0.160198	0.084287	0.081311	0.115544
Dos	0.136545	0.000000	0.108480	0.074831	0.145026	0.080130	0.036545	0.144636
Worms	0.156623	0.104123	0.095000	0.112248	0.137623	0.047123	0.035500	0.153874
Generic	0.06500	0.060308	0.124853	0.132146	0.160166	0.131524	0.098224	0.140999

$\boldsymbol{Q_{initial}}$ is as follows:

$$Q_{initial}[i,j] = (\text{Deterate}[i,j] + \text{Detetime}[i,j]) \times W[j]$$

It is then normalized in [0, 1]

$$Q[i,j] = \frac{Q_{initial}[i,j] - \min\{Q_{initial}\}}{\max\{Q_{initial}\} - \min\{Q_{initial}\}} \in [0, 1]$$

Definition 7: A *role assignment matrix* $\boldsymbol{T}$ is an $m \times n$ matrix. That $T[i,j] \in \{0, 1\} (0 \le i < m, 0 \le j < n)$ indicates whether or not a_i is assigned to role r_j. The value of $T[i,j] = 1$ means yes and 0 no.

Based on Table 3 $\boldsymbol{Q}$ matrix, Fig. 1 represents the role assignment matrix $\boldsymbol{T}$ obtained after the normalization process;

0	0	0	0	0	0	0.187997	0	0	0
0	0	0	0	0	0	0	0	0	0
0	0	0.112500	0	0	0	0	0	0	0
0.142663	0	0	0	0	0	0	0	0	0
0	0.404859	0	0	0	0	0	0	0	0
0	0	0	0	0.200708	0	0	0	0	0
0	0	0	0.137800	0	0	0	0	0	0
0	0	0	0	0	0	0	0.144636	0	0
0	0	0	0	0	0.168354	0	0	0	0
0	0	0	0	0	0	0	0	0	0
0	0	0	0	0	0	0	0	0	0
0.142663	0	0	0	0	0	0	0	0	0
0	0	0	0	0	0	0	0	0	0.160166
0	0	0	0	0	0	0	0	0	0.131520
0.133674	0	0	0	0	0	0	0	0	0
0	0	0	0	0	0	0	0	0.153874	0

Fig. 1. *T* matrix

We can get the role assignment matrix T of the UNSW-NB15 data set through the IBM ILOG CPLEX optimization package (CPLEX), σ = 2.221414.

Definition 8: The *group performance σ* of group **g** is defined as the sum of the assigned agent' qualifications.

$$\sigma = \sum_{i=0}^{m-1}\sum_{j=0}^{n-1} Q[i,j] \times T[i,j]$$

Definition 9: Role *j* is *workable* in group *g* if it has been assigned i.e.

$$\sum_{i=0}^{m-1} T[i,j] = L[j]$$

Definition 10: $\boldsymbol{T}$ is *workable* if each role *j* is workable, i.e. $\sum_{i=0}^{m-1} T[i,j] = L[j](0 \leq j < n)$, Group **g** is workable if $\boldsymbol{T}$ is workable. From the above definitions, group **g** can be expressed by $\boldsymbol{Q}$, $\boldsymbol{L}$ and $\boldsymbol{T}$.

Definition 11: The problem of assigning the number of different types of charging piles is finding a feasible $\boldsymbol{T}$ that:

$$\max\sigma = \sum_{i=0}^{m-1}\sum_{j=0}^{n-1} Q[i,j] \times T[i,j]$$

Subject to

$$T[i,j] \in N(0 \leq \mathrm{i} < m, 0 \leq j < n) \tag{1}$$

$$\sum_{j=0}^{n-1} T[i,j] \leq L^a[i](0 \leq i < m) \quad (2)$$

$$\sum_{j=0}^{n-1} T[i,j] \leq L[j](0 \leq j < n) \quad (3)$$

Where expression (1) is a natural number constraint; (2) denotes that the sum of the rows of the role assignment matrix cannot greater than the respective values of the vector $\boldsymbol{L^a}$; (3) indicates that the sum of the number of each column of the role assignment matrix, is equal to each value of the vector $\boldsymbol{L}$ respectively.

From this formalization, the intrusion detection problem is formalized with GMRA, which can be processed by the IBM ILOG CPLEX optimization package.

4 Solution and Experiments

4.1 The Solution and Flow Chart

The whole project model can be divided into the construction of intrusion detection part and the adaptive part. Among them, the construction of intrusion detection includes two parts: Event generator and Event detector. The adaptive part is composed of Response unit of ECARGO adaptive mechanism. As shown in Fig. 2, the Event generator in the intrusion detection part is composed of Agent Evaluation, Role Assignment and the preselected Li in Historical date; Event detector is composed of Parallel detection; Response unit is composed of response unit. The intrusion detection part uses parallel detection model based on ECARGO to detect real-time traffic data. When the Q Matrix has been calculated and the Role Assignment Matrix has been calculated, when the traffic data enters the detection model through the TAP device [24], it will be copied into the same number of copies to enter the detection modules located on different hosts. After that, through the linkage of the firewall and rules of the host, the data corresponding to its Role is taken in each black box, and other data will be filtered out.

In addition, the response unit will activate ECARGO adaptive mechanism according to the size of the real-time traffic, and readjust the value of the L vector according to whether the pre-selected Li satisfies the ratio of various attack types in the real-time traffic to change the number and types of agents participating in the detection. The model diagram under the UNSW-NB15 data set is similar to it.

4.2 The Results and Analysis

A detection model with better performance should have a higher detection rate and a lower false alarm rate. Therefore, in order to evaluate the effectiveness of the proposed model and make meaningful comparisons with other detection models, we choose false positive rate (FPR) and detection rate (DR) as evaluation metrics. These measurement methods are described below.

$$FPR = \frac{FP}{FP + TN}$$

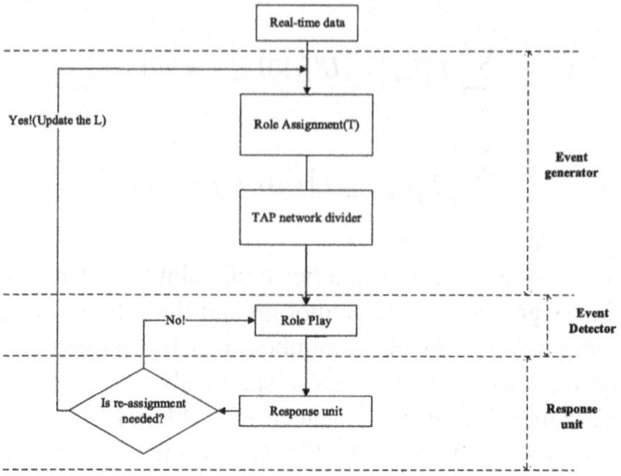

Fig. 2. The overall detection flow chart based on the NSL-KDD data set

$$DR = \frac{TP}{TP + FN}$$

In this comparative study, in addition to FPR and DR, we also compared the detection time.

The composition of the training and testing subsets using the UNSW-NB15 dataset in this paper is shown in Table 1. In fact, 20.4M have been used in the experimental data of the Role Assignment The UNSW-NB15 test set respectively simulates the initial flow, so as to obtain $L = [3,1,1,1,1,1,1,1,1,2]$ for the extreme point with a total preselected flow of 20M, without loss of generality, it is assumed that the preselected L vector is exactly the ratio of the various attack types in the current actual traffic Roughly the same. Table 2 summarize the overall performance of our model and other classifiers under two data sets. our model gives the highest overall detection rate (DR overall) of 82.02% and 93.69%, false alarm rate (FAR) of 18.60% and 2.45%, and test time of 0.20 s shown in Table 4.

Table 4. Our comparison of the overall performance of our detection model and other detection models on the NSL-KDD dataset

Date set	UNSW-NB15								
Model	Our model	REPTree	JRip	J48Consolidated	DescisionTable	J48	SPAARC	LogitBoost	Bagging
FPR	2.45%	4.7%	7.9%	0.5%	3.5%	1.0%	1.0%	1.4%	1.1%
DR	93.69%	65.30%	79.00%	84.70%	87.3%	86.40%	85.80%	75.50%	87.40%
Test time	0.60s	0.48s	0.69s	0.60s	0.59s	0.5s	0.59s	0.58s	0.56s

4.3 Detection Under Real-Time Network

The experiment verifies the following two scenarios, taking the NSL-KDD data set as an example. From the above paper 16.2M NSL-KDD data set test set are used to simulate the real-time traffic of two different scenarios.

***Scene One*:**
When the real-time traffic enters the model, the initial $L = \{3, 1, 1, 1, 1\}$, and the number of Agents participating in the Role Assignment is 8. After finishing the assignment after 0.003s. Details are shown in Table 5.

For example, Table 4 is the detection time and detection rate after the Parallel detection module. It can be seen that when $L = \{3, 1, 1, 1, 1\}$, the number of Agents is 8. The overall detection accuracy of the model is 82.83%, and the detection time is 0.31 s. From this, the actual detection data volume of the entire model is 26.13 M/s ($8.1 \times 0.3226 = 26.13$ M/s). After the Response Unit, it can be concluded that the actual attack type ratio in the real-time traffic within 1s is $L = [2, 2, 1, 1, 1]$. The adaptive mechanism will re-adjust the value of the L vector, and Re-assign the Agent within 0.004 s, such as Table 6.

Table 5. Parameters of adaptive multi-agent parallel cooperative intrusion detection model at L = {3, 1, 1, 1, 1}.

	NSL-KDD				
L	3	1	1	1	1
Role	Normal	DOS	PROBE	R2L	U2R
The distribution of the agent	DescisionTable + ForestPA + JRip	LogitBoost	SPAARC	PART	J48Consolidated
Average accuracy	97.28%	82.31%	84.20%	7.5%	24.46%
Average detection time	0.23s	0.31s	0.13s	0.15s	0.14s

For example, Table 5 is the detection time and detection rate after the Parallel detection module. It can be seen that when $L = \{3, 1, 1, 1, 1\}$, the number of Agents is 8. The overall detection accuracy of the model is 82.83%, and the detection time is 0.31 s. From this, the actual detection data volume of the entire model is 26.13 M/s ($8.1 \times 0.3226 = 26.13$ M/s). After the Response Unit, it can be concluded that the actual attack type ratio in the real-time traffic within 1 s is $L = [4, 4, 2, 2, 2]$. The adaptive mechanism will re-adjust the value of the L vector, and Re-assign the Agent within 0.004 s, such as Table 6.

It can be drawn from the table that after adaptive adjustment between $L = \{5, 3, 4, 2, 1\}$ the longest detection time is 0.25 s as the final time, the model detection time is 0.25s, and the detection rate is 81.9%. It can also be obtained that under the configuration of $L = [4, 4, 2, 2, 2]$. Compared with before the adjustment, while maintaining the detection

Table 6. The model after adjusting the L vector.

	NSL-KDD				
L	2	2	1	1	1
Role	Normal	DOS	PROBE	R2L	U2R
The distribution of the agent	DescisionTable + ForestPA	LogitBoost + JRip	SPAARC	PART	J48Consolidated
Average accuracy	97.67%	82.01%	84.20%	7.5%	24.46%
Average detection time	0.21 s	0.25 s	0.13 s	0.15 s	0.14 s

rate basically unchanged, the detection time is reduced by optimizing the configuration, so that the detection capability of the entire model is increased.

***Scene Two*:**
When the real-time traffic enters the model, the model will mine according to the historical data and determine $L = \{5, 3, 4, 2, 1\}$, and the number of Agents participating in the Role Assignment is 16. After finishing the assignment after 0.014 s. Details are shown in Table 7.

Table 7. Parameters of adaptive multi-agent parallel cooperative intrusion detection model under the state of 200% traffic.

	NSL-KDD				
L	5	3	4	2	1
Role	Normal	DOS	PROBE	R2L	U2R
The distribution of the Agent	2 × DescisionTable + 2 × JRip + ForestPA	2 × LogitBoost + PART	2 × SPAARC + 2 × ForestPA	J48Consolidated + PART	J48Consolidated
Average accuracy	97.38%	82.43%	82.80%	9%	24.46%
Average detection time	0.20s	0.25s	0.25s	0.145s	0.14s

For example, Table 7 is the detection time and detection rate after the Parallel detection module. It can be seen that when $L = \{5, 3, 4, 2, 1\}$, the number of Agents is 16. The overall detection accuracy of the model is 81.99%, and the detection time is 0.25 s. After passing the Response Unit, it can be concluded that the actual attack type ratio in the real-time traffic within this 1s is $L = [4, 4, 2, 2, 2]$. The adaptive mechanism will re-adjust the value of the L vector, and Re-assign the Agent within 0.014s, such as Table 8.

It can be concluded from Table 7 that after adjusting the matching between $L = [4, 4, 2, 2, 2]$ and Agent, the overall detection time is maintained at 0.25 s, and the

Table 8. Parameters of adaptive multi-agent parallel cooperative intrusion detection model under the state of 200% traffic.

	NSL-KDD				
L	4	4	2	2	2
Role	Normal	DOS	PROBE	R2L	U2R
The distribution of the Agent	2 × DescisionTable + 2 × ForestPA	2 × LogitBoost + 2 × JRip	2 × SPAARC	PART × 2	J48Consolidated × 2
Average accuracy	97.67%	81.80%	84.20%	7.5%	24.46%
Average detection time	0.21s	0.25s	0.13s	0.15s	0.14s

overall detection accuracy of the model is 82.02%. It can also be obtained that under the configuration of $L = [4, 4, 2, 2, 2]$, the actual detection data volume of the model is 64.8 M/s (16.2 × 4 = 32.4 M/s). Compared with before the adjustment, while maintaining the detection rate and detection time basically unchanged, optimizing the configuration to reduce the number of Agents participating in the Role Assignment can reduce idle detection resources.

5 Conclusion

This paper uses GMRA [1, 2] to formalize the intrusion detection problem, and based on this, proposes a parallel detection model. This formalization can be mapped to a linear programming problem, and then a solution can be obtained through a commercial platform such as CPLEX [5].

In the future, we may conduct research as follows:

1) The first is to study the application of role transfer in the detection model of this article.
2) Last but not least, there are more general relationships and additional constraints between roles, which can be studied in the future.

References

1. Zhu, H., Liu, D., Zhang, S., Yu, Z., Teng, L., Teng, S.: Solving the Many to Many assignment problem by improving the Kuhn–Munkres algorithm with backtracking. Theoret. Comput. Sci. **618**, 30–41 (2016)
2. Zhu, H., Alkins, R.: Group role assignment. In: International Symposium on Collaborative Technologies and Systems, pp. 431–439 (2009)
3. Zhu, H., Alkins, R., Alkins, R.: Group role assignment via a Kuhn–Munkres algorithm-based solution. In: IEEE Transactions on Systems Man and Cybernetics - Part A Systems and Humans, pp .739–750 (2012)

4. Zhu, H., Zhou, M.C.: Role-based collaboration and its kernel mechanisms. In: IEEE Transactions on Systems Man & Cybernetics Part, pp. 578–589 (2006)
5. IBM: ILOG CPLEX Optimization Studio (2019). http://www01.ibm.com/software/integration/optimization/cplex-optimization-studio/. 2019
6. Ahmim, A., Maglaras, L.: A novel hierarchical intrusion detection system based on decision tree and rules-based models. In: 2019 15th International Conference on Distributed Computing in Sensor Systems, pp. 228–233 (2019). https://doi.org/10.1109/DCOSS.2019.00059
7. Guo, C., Ping, Y.: A two-level hybrid approach for intrusion detection. Neurocomputing **214**, 391–400 (2016)
8. Teng, S., Wu, N., Zhu, H.: SVM-DT-based adaptive and collaborative intrusion detection. IEEE/CAA J. Autom. Sin. **5**(1), 108–118 (2018), https://doi.org/10.1109/JAS.2017.7510730
9. Zhu, H., Hou, M., Wang, C., Zhou, M.C.: An efficient outpatient scheduling approach. IEEE Trans. Autom. Sci. Eng. **9**, 701–709 (2012)
10. Luo, L., Zhang, Y., Fang, Q., Ding, H., Shi, Y., Guo, H.: A discrete event simulation approach for reserving capacity for emergency patients in the radiology department. BMC Health Serv. Res. **18**, 452 (2018)
11. Sheng, Y., Zhu, H., Zhou, X., Hu, W.: Effective approaches to adaptive collaboration via dynamic role assignment. IEEE Trans. Syst. Man Cybernet. Syst. **45**, 76–92 (2016)
12. Zhu, H.: Avoiding conflicts by group role assignment. IEEE Trans. Syst. Man Cybernet. Syst. **46**, 535–547 (2016)
13. Ten.g, S.H., Du, H.L., Wu, N.Q., Zhang, W., Su, J.Y.: A cooperative network intrusion detection based on fuzzy SVMs. J. Netw. **5**(4), 475−483 (2010)
14. Çaliş, B., Bulkan, S.: A research survey: review of AI solution strategies of job shop scheduling problem. J. Intell. Manuf. **26**(5), 961–973 (2013). https://doi.org/10.1007/s10845-013-0837-8
15. Zhu, H., Zhou, M.C.: Role-based collaboration and its kernel mechanisms. IEEE Trans. Syst. Man Cybernet. Part C. **36**, 578–-589 (2006)
16. Zhu, H.: Role-based collaboration and E-CARGO: revisiting the developments of the last decade. IEEE Syst. Man Cybernet. Mag. **1**, 27–36 (2015)
17. Zhu, H., Zhou, M.C.: Efficient role transfer based on Kuhn–Munkres algorithm. IEEE Trans. Syst. Man Cybernet. Part A Syst. Hum. **42**(2), 491–496 (2002)
18. Tian, Z.P., Zhu, H.P., Shao, X.Y.: A fast discrete small-world optimization algorithm. In: Proceedings of the 2015 5th International Conference on Computer Sciences and Automation Engineering, pp. 560–564 (2016)
19. Sheng, Y., Zhu, H., Zhou, X., Hu, W.: Effective approaches to adaptive collaboration via dynamic role assignment. IEEE Trans. Syst. Man Cybernet. Syst. **46**, 76–92 (2016)
20. Moustafa, N., Slay, J.: UNSW-NB15: a comprehensive data set for network intrusion detection systems (UNSW-NB15 network data set). In: 2015 Military Communications and Information Systems Conference, pp. 1–6 (2015)
21. KDD Cup 1999 Dataset. http://kdd.ics.uci.edu/databases/kddcup99/kddcup99.html
22. Kyoto University Benchmark Data. http://www.takakura.com/Kyoto_data
23. Lai, V.S., Wong, B.K., Cheung, W.: Group decision making in a multiple criteria environment: a case using the AHP in software selection. Eur. J. Oper. Res. **137**(1), 134–144 (2002)

The Scheduling Model of Forest Fire-Extinguishing Resources and Its Simulation

Guoxiong Zhou, Chao Lu(✉), and Mingxuan Li

Central South University of Forestry and Technology, Changsha, China
1244414754@qq.com

Abstract. A scheduling model of forest fire extinguishing suitable for Southern forests is proposed in this paper. First of all, according to forest fire fighting strategy, we can determine the extinguishing points that can divide the fire field and break them one by one. Then, quantum particle swarm optimization is used to calculate the optimal path. If there are "flying fire" and other emergencies in the fire extinguishing process, the improved Ant Colony algorithm based on periodically pheromone updating is used to schedule resources including personnel and fire extinguishing materials, so as to improve the efficiency of forest fire-extinguishing resources scheduling in southern China. The simulation results show that compared with the conventional scheduling model of forest fire extinguishing, the proposed model has more iterations per unit time, and the operation time is greatly reduced, which indicates that the efficiency of fire extinguishing resource dispatching has been significantly improved.

Keywords: Quantum particle swarm algorithm · Improved Ant Colony algorithm · Forest fire-extinguishing resources scheduling · Path planning

1 Introduction

Forest fire is the main factor that is destructive to forest resource. It appears to be suddenly and randomly. Thus, it can make tremendous damage to both human and environment in a short time, causing huge loss of economy and social resource. The safety of fire fighter will be threatened and much fire-extinguishing resource will be wasted if there is no scientific dispatching [1, 14, 15]. Therefore, it is necessary to take emergency measures scientifically according to the situation, use scientific and reasonable methods to systematically dispatch various fire extinguishing resources, and put out the fire with the best scheduling plan. Kemballeook and Stephenson suggested that the demand of resources should be estimated when dispatching rescue resources, so as to improve the scheduling efficiency. Then Ray Wael, Rathi and Eqi studied the resource dispatching problem to minimize the resource consumption based on different constraints of the fire. But the model did not consider the resource cost due to time delay [6]. In China, Jiang Lizhen et al. proposed an improved model of forest fire extinguishing resource dispatching with the objective function as the minimum area [7]. Dai Gengxin et al. established a mathematical model that can efficiently solve the multi resource dispatching

Y. Sun et al. (Eds.): ChineseCSCW 2021, CCIS 1491, pp. 85–101, 2022.
https://doi.org/10.1007/978-981-19-4546-5_7

problem by deeply studying the multi resource-multi rescue point scheduling problems [2]. He et al. proposed a multi-objective scheduling model with the shortest scheduling time and the least number of rescue points based on the multi resource-multi rescue point scheduling problem. They used fuzzy planning as the main method to deal with the problem and gave the corresponding algorithm out [4]. Renqiang et al. used multiple resource types, multiple demands, multiple resource points and supply points provides collaborative resources for demand points as constraints, designed an improved multi-objective scheduling model. Based on Wang Zhengfei's forest fire spread model [11]. Feng Xue et al. made out the algorithm of resource dispatching which is one-time consuming and multiple emergency rescue points [3].

It can be seen from the above that the basic theoretical research on forest fire extinguishing resource dispatching problem in China is less than overseas, and it started later as well. These researches were mainly aimed at specific problems and algorithms. Moreover, it has strong limitations and can not adapt to the dispatching conditions of Southern Forest in China. In this paper, the southern forest is taken as the object. Due to the situation of southern forest fire is complex and there may be a sudden fire at any time, it will not be able to solve the fire point which is the greatest threat to firefighters and national property in a short time if using only one of the heuristic algorithms mentioned above. So, it is necessary to use multi scheduling algorithms and specify the switching conditions in order to switch methods under different conditions. This paper proposed to use quantum particle swarm optimization (QPSO) [13] in the scene of conventional enclosure and segmentation fire extinguishing. When there are some emergencies that need to dispatch a large number of resources in a short time, the improved ant colony algorithm [8] can solve the optimal path selection problem.

2 General Idea of the Algorithm

The scheduling model of forest fire-extinguishing resources can dispatch the fire-fighting personnel and materials scientifically when the forest fire occurs. Taking Huang Fengqiao forest farm in You County of Hunan province as an example, considering that it has obvious southern forest characteristics: stacked mountains, vertical and horizontal streams, densely distributed forest roads, and there are man-made barriers including houses, roads, drinking water projects, which can be connected into fire extinguishing network when dispatching resources, and the scheduling model of forest fire-extinguishing resource proposed in this paper is established. When a fire occurs, firstly locate each fire extinguishing point and the demand for fire extinguishing personnel and material resources, and then dispatch them. Due to the obvious regional characteristics of the southern forest, the optimization efficiency of the existing scheduling model of forest fire-extinguishing resources is low when dispatching resources. When it is used in the complex forest fire-extinguishing scheduling system, the scheduling results can not be obtained in the best time. In view of the fire extinguishing points used in forest fire extinguishing scheduling are separated and of large quantities, and the road conditions from the fire extinguishing resource points to each fire extinguishing point are different, the main way to improve the efficiency of emergency scheduling is to plan the path reasonably. PSO [10] algorithm has low iterative efficiency when it is applied in practice, which leads to low optimization efficiency. Based on the PSO, this paper proposes a QPSO which combines the

PSO with the relevant theories of quantum mechanics. However, in the case of "flying fire" and other emergencies requiring large-scale scheduling in a short period of time, the conventional heuristic algorithm and the QPSO mentioned above will lead to congestion and slow down the scheduling rate due to the non-uniform traffic capacity of forest roads. At this time, the improved ant colony algorithm is used. In this paper, the pheromone updates periodically to optimize the traditional ant colony algorithm, so that the large-scale scheduling in a short time will not lead to low scheduling efficiency due to road congestion. The simulation results of Huang Fengqiao forest farm in You county of Hunan province show that the algorithm above can greatly improve the convergence speed and the quality of optimization solution, and improve the efficiency of resource scheduling in forest fire extinguishing.

3 Scheduling Model of Fire-Extinguishing Resources

The scheduling model of fire-extinguishing resources is mainly to simulate the vehicle routing problem in scheduling. It means that a resource point provides services for multiple fire extinguishing points. Each fire extinguishing point has a certain demand, and can only get the service from one vehicle. All vehicles start from the resource distribution center and finally return. The vehicles participated in have limited constraints such as transporting speed, capacity and distance. The purpose of scheduling vehicles is to minimize the total transporting time. In this paper, the capacity of vehicles participated in the forest fire extinguishing resource scheduling, the demand of each fire extinguishing points, and the distance between the fire extinguishing points and the resource gathering points are quantified and then substituted into the mathematical model. The model is as follows.

Suppose Z is the resource point of fire extinguishing resources, P is the collection of N fire-extinguishing points, the distance between the fire extinguishing resources gathering point and the fire- extinguishing point is $D_1, D_2 \cdots D_{\mathrm{n}}$, and the number of fire extinguishing resources needed is respectively $\mathrm{p}_1, p_2 \cdots p_n$. Generally, the definition of vehicle routing problem is given a network $G = (V, E)$ with a total of nodes $N + 1$, where V is the set of nodes, $\mathrm{V} = \{0, \cdots, N\}$, Node 0 represents the resource point, and the rest are fire extinguishing points. Under the condition of limited capacity, the vehicles shall find the circuit passing through all fire extinguishing points with the minimum total time. This process shall meet the following limited conditions:

(1) It can meet the needs of each fire extinguishing point;
(2) Each fire extinguishing point can get served and only once;

(3) The total demand of fire extinguishing points should not be greater than the maximum loading capacity of the vehicles. The mathematical model is as follow

$$\begin{cases} \underset{X_{ijk},y_{ik}}{Min} \sum_{i,j\in V} \sum_{k\in K} c_{ij}x_{ijk} \\ s.t. \sum_{i\in K} q_i y_{ik} \le W, \forall k \in K \\ \sum_{k\in K} y_{ik} = \begin{cases} |K|, i = 0 \\ 1, i \ne 0, i \in V \end{cases} \\ \sum_{k\in K} x_{ijk} = y_{ik} \\ x_{ijk} \in \{0, 1\}, y_{ik} \in \{0, 1\}, \forall i, j \in V, k \in K \end{cases} \tag{1}$$

where: V is the collection of fire extinguishing points; K is the collection of vehicles; 0 is the storage center of fire extinguishing resources; W is the capacity of vehicles; q_i is the demand of fire extinguishing point i; c_{ij} is the distance from distribution point i to fire extinguishing point j; if vehicle K reaches fire-extinguishing point j and passes through fire-extinguishing point i, $x_{ijk} = 1$ otherwise $x_{ijk} = 0$; if fire point i is served by vehicle K, $y_{ik} = 1$; in other cases, $y_{ik} = 0$.

4 Scheduling Path Planning Based on Quantum Particle Swarm Optimization

In the actual fire extinguishing action of southern forest with complex road conditions, it is difficult to solve the fire extinguish path planning problem in a short time by using the conventional optimization algorithm. Scholars related found that this kind of combinatorial optimization problems can be solved by heuristic algorithm, but most of them have more parameters and complex modulation, while PSO has fewer parameters and simple modulation, which belongs to the optimization algorithm of iterative evolution of heuristic algorithm. Therefore, this paper chooses PSO as the southern forest fire path planning optimization.

4.1 Conventional Particle Swarm Optimization (PSO)

Particle swarm optimization (PSO) is a kind of Swarm Intelligence Optimization algorithm to simulate the movement of biological groups. In this paper, the Scheduling Model of Southern Forest Fire-Extinguishing Resources, each scheduling particle updates and adjusts its position while searching space based on the experience of itself and other particles in the population, all particles gradually move to the best target of the solution and converge without a fixed leader by sharing experience and group constraints. In the simulation model of forest fire-extinguishing scheduling, the PSO used distribute uniformly in the whole solution space at the beginning. In the process of particle flight, the following formulas are used to calculate the vector value of the next particle flight.

$$\vec{p}(k+1) = \vec{p}(k) + \vec{v}(k) \tag{2}$$

$$\vec{v}(k+1) = c_1 \times \vec{v}(k) + c_2 \times r(0,1) \times (\vec{p}_{selfbest}(k) - \vec{p}(k)) + c_3 \times r(0,1) \times (\vec{p}_{groupbest}(k) - \vec{p}(k)) \tag{3}$$

where: the vector $\vec{p}$ represents a particle; the vector $\vec{v}$ represents the velocity of the particle; $p_{selfbest}$ is the optimal solution experienced by a single particle in the flight process; $p_{groupbest}$ is the optimal solution experienced in the whole particle population; r(0, 1) is a random number in the range [0, 1]. c_1, c_2, c_3 are the weighting coefficients. The inert coefficient c_1 represents the level at which the particle believes itself. The social learning coefficient c_2 represents the level at which the particle believes in experience. The social cognition coefficient c_3 represents the level at which the particle believes the surrounding individuals.

4.2 Path Planning Based on Quantum Particle Swarm Optimization

Due to the uncertainty, suddenness and unconventionality of forest fire, the Path Scheduling Model of forest fire dispatching path involves many problems, such as how to timely mobilize the fire dispatching resources from fire dispatching stations to meet the demand. It is necessary to consider that how to transport resources to the certain point as soon as possible while scheduling resources. PSO algorithm has the disadvantages of low efficiency and slow operation speed in single iteration when solving these problems with equality constraints. In this paper, a scheduling model of forest fire fighting based on QPSO with the advantages of fast iterative speed, high precision and strong robustness is proposed. QPSO is a new optimization algorithm which combines quantum mechanics theory with PSO. The basic idea is to introduce the concept of potential well to the particles in the search space and take the optimal solution as the center of the potential well, that is, the lowest point of energy in the potential well, and search through the mechanism of particles moving towards the center of potential well in quantum mechanics. The particle moves in the potential well and its position can be determined by the following stochastic equation.

$$P_{ij} = p_{i,j} \pm \frac{L_{i,j}}{2} \ln(\frac{1}{u_{i,j}}) \tag{4}$$

In the formula, P_{ij} represents the dimensionality of the position of particle i, $p_{i,j}$ represents the attractor, $L_{i,j}$ represents the characteristic length of the potential well, and $u_{i,j}$ represents the random numbers uniformly distributed in the interval (0, 1). When $u_{i,j} > 0.5$ the formula above is positive, otherwise it is negative. Among them, attractors

$$p_{i,j} = \phi_j P_{best,i,j} + (1 - \phi_j) G_{best,j} \tag{5}$$

$$L_{i,j} = 2\alpha \bullet \left| m_{best,j} - X_{i,j} \right| \tag{6}$$

where: ϕ_j is for random numbers uniformly distributed over (0, 1); $P_{best,i,j}$ represents the individual historical optimal position of the "i"th particle; $G_{best,j}$ is for the global optimal position of the particle population; $m_{best,j}$ represents the average optimal position of all the particles in the population. Then

$$m_{best,j} = \frac{1}{M}\sum_{i=1}^{M} P_{best,i,j} \tag{7}$$

α is called contraction expansion factor. It is an important parameter for convergence of the algorithm, and usually made to decrease linearly with iteration.

$$\alpha = 1 - 0.5\frac{\mathrm{k}}{\mathrm{K}} \tag{8}$$

where: k – current iteration number; K – maximum iteration number.

The optimization efficiency of forest fire extinguishing path planning can be improved effectively by the QPSO algorithm which combines quantum mechanics with particle swarm optimization.

5 Scheduling Path Planning Based on Improved Ant Colony Algorithm

In southern forest fires, there are strong advection gas, high convective column, high levels of thermal radiation, and whirlwind caused by bridges, culverts and steep slopes under roads and railways, because of which "flying fire" may occurs. This special forest fire behavior will lead to heavy casualties and economic losses without being handled properly. The principle of correct disposal of "flying fire" is to send enough fire-fighting forces at one time, or even use more than 90% of the current fire-fighting forces to eliminate "flying fire" quickly and thoroughly without leaving any hidden danger. Therefore, many scholars focus on choosing the scheduling path of shortest time to the "flying fire" point. When using the QPSO algorithm for large-scale scheduling path planning, however, it can not compare the traffic capacity of roads in the southern forest, resulting in road congestion, which in turn slowing down the speed of vehicles on these roads, leading to low scheduling efficiency. Therefore, a new algorithm that can periodically compare and update road conditions for selecting a path to avoid blocking is needed. Ant Colony algorithm is a kind of heuristic algorithm that can effectively solve combinatorial optimization problems. It has the characteristics of positive feedback, parallelism and so on. It is a population-based algorithm with strong robustness, which can solve complex optimization problems. In addition, it can also update pheromones periodically to solve the problem of low efficiency in large-scale scheduling. Therefore, this paper proposes an emergency scheduling model based on improved Ant Colony algorithm to deal with the phenomenon of "flying fire".

5.1 Improved Ant Colony Algorithm

Conventional Ant Colony algorithm derives from the behavior of ants seeking food. It is designed to allow ants finding many paths and leave pheromone evaporating over time. According to the principle that the path with thicker pheromone is closer, the best path can be selected out after a period of time. But in practice, the phenomenon of slow convergence even stagnation is prone to occur. That is, when the ants search to a certain extent, all the individuals involved in the search get the same solution, so they will not search the solution space further, resulting in no more new solutions, which is called premature phenomenon. Moreover, when many ants choose the same path, the pheromone concentration in the path will explode in a sudden, which makes a large number of ants concentrate on one path, resulting in blocking of the scheduling path that reduces the scheduling efficiency. What's more, it is found that the speed of convergence and when the stagnation will occur will affect each other. Increasing the convergence speed will make the stagnation phenomenon appear in advance. In order to obtain an optimal solution between improving the convergence speed and avoiding the stagnation phenomenon, this paper adopts the method of dynamically updating pheromone in the searching progress of Ant Colony algorithm to solve the problem of slow convergence speed and stagnation phenomenon. The method is as follows.

Firstly, let ant k$(k = 1, 2 \cdots m)$ determine the direction of its next transfer according to the pheromone concentration in each path during the search. Taboo table tabu$_{\mathrm{k}}(k = 1, 2 \cdots m)$ is used here to record the set of locations that Ant k currently travels through, and the set is dynamically adjusted with the evolution process of tabu$_{\mathrm{k}}$. In the searching process, the ant calculates the probability of state transition according to the pheromone concentration and heuristic information of each path. $P_{ij}^{\mathrm{k}}(t)$ represents the transfer probability of ant k from site i to site j at time t.

$$P_{\mathrm{ij}}^{K}(t) = \begin{cases} \frac{\tau_{ij}^{\partial}(t)\eta_{ik}^{\beta}(t)}{\sum\limits_{s\in allowed} \tau_{is}^{\partial}(t)\eta_{is}^{\beta}(t)}, j \in allowed_k \\ 0, j \notin allowed_k \end{cases} \tag{9}$$

where, $\tau_{\mathrm{ij}}(t)$ is the pheromone concentration on the path (i, j) at time t; $allowed_k$ represents the location allowed to be selected by ant k in the next step; α and β are the tradeoff between pheromone concentration and control visibility; $\eta_{\mathrm{ij}}(t)$ is the value of heuristic information associated with path (i, j), and its expression is $\eta_{\mathrm{ij}}(t) = 1/d_{ij}$. d_{ij} is for the distance between adjacent points i and j. For ant k, the smaller d_{ij} is, the bigger $\eta_{\mathrm{ij}}(t)$ will be, $\mathrm{p}_{ij}^{k}(t)$ as well. The heuristic function represents the expected degree of ant's transfer from site i to site j. In order to avoid the heuristic information from covering by too many residual pheromones, the residual information should be updated every time an ant completes a cycle. Therefore, the pheromone concentration on the path (i, j) at time $t + n$ can be adjusted according to the following formula:

$$\tau_{\mathrm{ij}}(\mathrm{t} + n) = (1 - \rho) \cdot \tau_{ij}(t) + \Delta\tau_{ij}(t) \tag{10}$$

$$\Delta\tau_{\mathrm{ij}}(t) = \sum_{k=1}^{m} \Delta\tau_{ij}^{k}(t) \tag{11}$$

where, ρ represents the volatilization coefficient of pheromone and 1-ρ represents the residual factor of pheromone. In order to prevent information coverage, the range of ρ is:

$\rho \subset [0, 1]$; $\Delta\tau_{\mathrm{ij}}(t)$ represents the pheromone increment on the path (i, j) in this cycle. The initial $\Delta\tau_{\mathrm{ij}}(0) = 0$; $\Delta\tau_{\mathrm{ij}}^{k}(t)$ represents the amount of pheromone left in the path (i, j) of the "k"th ant in this cycle.

The value of $\Delta\tau_{\mathrm{ij}}^{k}(t)$ adopts the Ant-Cycle model:

$$\Delta\tau_{\mathrm{ij}}^{k}\pi \begin{cases} \frac{Q}{L_K}, \text{pheromones left by the k - th ant between T and T + 1} \\ 0, \mathit{else} \end{cases} \quad (12)$$

where, Q is a constant and it represents pheromone strength, which can affect the convergence speed of the algorithm; $\mathrm{L_k}$ represents the total distance of the "k"th ant's path in this loop. The improved method of ant colony algorithm is to update pheromone dynamically according to the quality of different solutions, which means that only enhance the information on the better path, and reduce the amount of information on the other paths. The time $t_{AVG} = \sum_{k=1}^{m} t_k/m$, which is taken to find the path will be averaged each time the ants complete a cycle. For the ants whose time cost is less than t_{AVG}, a relatively large coefficient is given when updating pheromones left on the path; for those whose time cost is greater than t_{AVG} or equal to it, we give a stable coefficient. Pheromone $\Delta\tau_{\mathrm{ij}}^{k}(t)$ the "k"th ant left on the path (i, j) of this cycle changed to:

$$\Delta\tau_{ij}^{\mathrm{k}} \begin{cases} \frac{\lambda Q}{L_k}, \text{pheromones left by the k - th ant between T and T + 1} \\ 0, \text{else} \end{cases} \quad (13)$$

where λ is solved as follow:

$$\lambda = \begin{cases} \frac{t_{AVG} - t_k}{t_{AVG}}, t_k < t_{AVG} \\ 0, t_k \geq t_{\mathrm{AVG}} \end{cases} \quad (14)$$

5.2 Dynamic Calculation of Value of Heuristic Information

Fire-fighting personnel need to carry a large number of fire extinguishing tools, so they tend to choose roads with short traffic time and good traffic capacity. However, forest roads are complex and changeable. Sometimes a forest road is open for cars, the next second it becomes a footpath narrow for only one man to go through. In view of the diversity of forest road capacity, a dynamic method is used to calculate the value $\eta_{\mathrm{ij}}(t)$ of heuristic information associated with the road. The variable $\eta_{\mathrm{ij}}(t)$ is used to realize the transfer probability $\mathrm{p}_{ij}^{k}(t)$ to the road node. The specific description is that the road with higher traffic capacity is easier to be selected in the selection of the optimal path. So that, the reciprocal of the time t_{ij} passing through a road can be used to represent the heuristic information value $\eta_{\mathrm{ij}}(t)$ of the road, among them, $\mathrm{t}_{ij} = L_{ij}/v_{ij}$. The four speed levels of passing through the road are respectively v1 to v4. The speed on road from node i to j is v_{ij}, and the calculation formula is as follows:

$$\eta_{\mathrm{ij(t)}} = \begin{cases} \frac{v_{ij}}{L_{ij}}, v_{(i-1)(j-1)} \in \{v_1, v_2\} \\ \eta_{ij}^{r}(t), v_{(i-1)(j-1)} \in \{ v_3, v_4\} \end{cases} \quad (15)$$

$$\eta_{ij}^{\mathrm{r}}(t) = \begin{cases} \frac{\nu_3}{L_{ij}}, \nu_{ij} \in \{\nu_1, \nu_2, \nu_3\} \\ \frac{\nu_4}{L_{ij}}, \nu_{ij} \in \{\nu_4\} \end{cases} \tag{16}$$

5.3 Concrete Steps of Improving the Algorithm

In order to meet the requirements of southern forest fire-extinguishing dispatching, the conventional ant colony algorithm is improved according to the following steps.

(1) Parameter initialization. Let the number of iterations is nc, and initial $nc = 0$, maximum $nc = NC$; set the number of scheduling vehicles participating in forest fire fighting as m, and put m scheduling vehicles on the initial vertex; make the initial information amount $\tau_{\mathrm{ij}}(t) = C$ for each edge (i, j) on the road topology map and at the initial time $\Delta\eta_{\mathrm{ij}}(0) = 0$.
(2) The starting point of each vehicle participating in fire-extinguishing scheduling is put into the current solution.
(3) According to the improved state transition rule $\mathrm{p}_{ij}^{k}(t)$, each vehicle $k(k = 1, 2, \cdots)$ participating in fire-extinguishing scheduling is moved to the next location j, and the vertex j is placed in the current solution.
(4) If the current solution set of all vehicles participating in fire-extinguishing scheduling contains the end point, go to step 5, otherwise turn to step 3.
(5) The travel time of each vehicle participating in fire-extinguishing dispatching is calculated, and the shortest time cost path is recorded.
(6) The pheromone update method is used to update pheromone of each side of the shortest time cost path.
(7) For each side arc (i, j), set $\Delta\tau_{\mathrm{ij}} = 0$, $nc = nc + 1$.
(8) If $nc < NC$, turn to step 2, otherwise terminate the iteration and get the optimal path.

6 Simulation Experiment

In order to compare the advantages and disadvantages of the improved algorithm in task completion speed and performance, in the experimental environment of windows 10 operating system, Intel Core i7 processor, 8G memory and MATLAB, the running results of southern scheduling model of forest fire extinguishing using different algorithms and different constraints were compared.

6.1 Total Distance Test of Objective Function

To compare the performance of the improved Particle swarm optimization (QPSO) with conventional one, the following simulation experiments were carried out. Supposed $c_1 = c_2 = c_3$ in the standard Particle swarm optimization (PSO), assuming that there are 50 fire points and 4 fire engines, the QPSO algorithm was compared with the Basic GA (Harish et al. 2015) algorithm and the conventional Particle swarm optimization

(QPSO). In the Basic GA algorithm, the probability of crossover and mutation was taken as $p_c = 0.7$, and $c_1, c_2 = 0.2, c_3 = 0.6$ in both PSO and QPSO. Each algorithm runs 10 times and gets the average value of its optimal solution. The objective function values of each algorithm in the evolution of 10, 30, 50 and 70 generations are shown in Fig. 1.

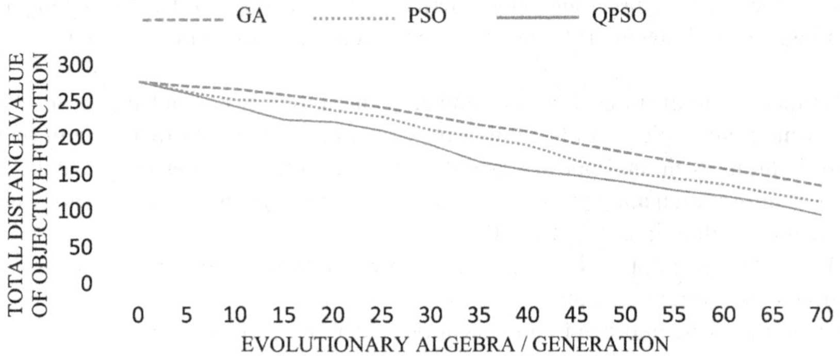

Fig. 1. Simulation of total distance test of objective function

As shown in Fig. 1, the results of QPSO in the 10th, 30th, 50th and 70th generations are better than those of the other two. It illustrates that the proposed optimization algorithm, QPSO, can bring better results than other algorithms, and it has faster convergence speed and higher quality solutions.

6.2 Verify the Efficiency of the Improved Ant Colony Algorithm

The traditional ant colony algorithm and the improved ant colony algorithm were used to carry out the simulation experiment [9]. The parameters were set as follows: number of vehicles participating in fire-extinguishing scheduling was 20; initial pheromone $\tau_{ij}(0) = 20$; the volatilization factor of pheromone $\rho = 0.5$; the influence parameter of pheromone on the selection probability $\partial = 0.5$; the influence parameter of length of path on the selection probability $\beta = 5$; number of pheromones updated each time by vehicles participating in the scheduling was 1; and the maximum number of iterations was 100. This experiment was repeated 50 times, the maximum number of iterations reached by each algorithm during the simulation was taken as the termination condition. The results of comparing the conventional Ant Colony algorithm with the improved Ant Colony algorithm were shown in Fig. 2.

It can be seen from the results of the simulation experiment in Fig. 2 that compared with the conventional Ant Colony algorithm, the improved Ant Colony algorithm can get a solution with less scheduling time when the same number of iterations is carried out, which can make the convergence to the global optimal solution faster. It illustrates that the improved Ant Colony algorithm has faster global convergence speed than the conventional one.

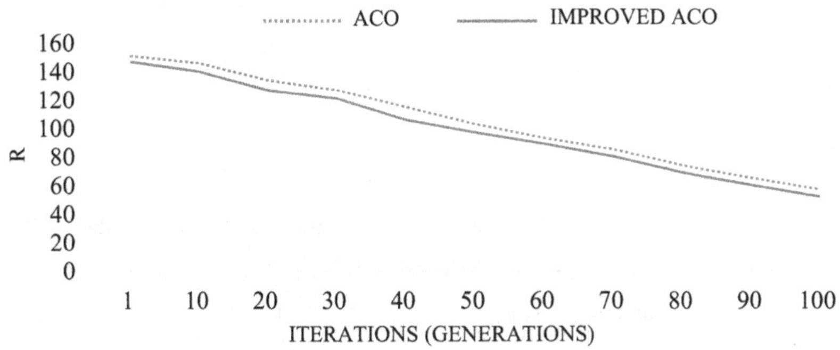

Fig. 2. Time cost of conventional Ant Colony algorithm and improved Ant Colony algorithm in same iteration times

6.3 Comparison of Iteration Rates

(1) In order to compare the number of iterations per unit time (MS) between QPSO and PSO in the same time, the following experiment was designed, with $c_1 = c_2 = c_3 = 1$.

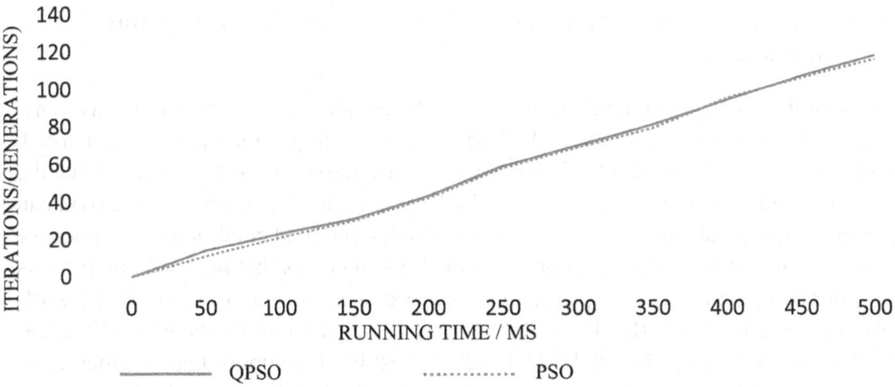

Fig. 3. Comparison of iteration times of QPSO and PSO in the same running time

The simulation results are shown in Fig. 3. It can be seen that there is no obvious difference in the number of iterations between QPSO and PSO in unit time. The main reason for this result is that QPSO improves the efficiency of a single iteration by changing the iteration method rather than taking increasing the number of iterations as the main improvement goal.

(2) The same simulation experiment was done to compare the conventional Ant Colony algorithm and the improved Ant Colony algorithm. Make the number of vehicles participating in the fire control operation 20. $\tau_{ij}(0) = 20$, $\rho = 0.5$, $\partial = 0.5$, $\beta = 5$.

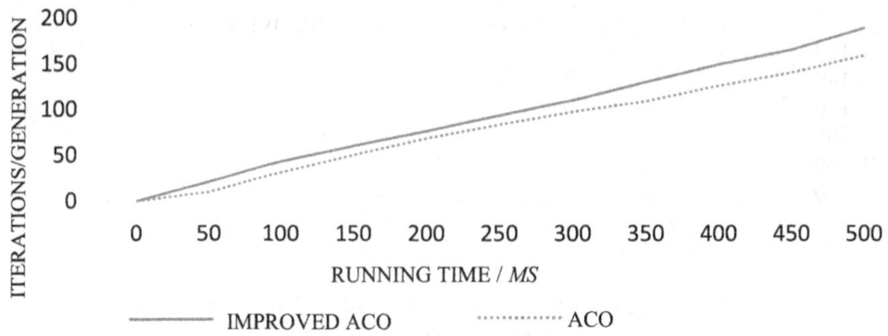

Fig. 4. Comparison of the iterations between improved ACO and ACO in same running time

As shown in Fig. 4, the improved Ant Colony algorithm always has more iterations than the conventional Ant Colony algorithm in the same running time. The main reason is that its volatility coefficient ρ has a direct relationship with the number of iterations, and the lower ρ is, the higher the number of iterations. In the improved Ant Colony algorithm, the pheromone is kept at a low level by periodically updating pheromone, so that the number of iterations per unit time is more than that of conventional Ant Colony algorithm.

6.4 Verify the Advanced Nature of the Improved Ant Colony Algorithm in Topological

In a forest fire-extinguishing scheduling example, the local road distribution was transformed into a topology diagram, and 32 adjacent fire-extinguishing points are marked. As shown in Fig. 5 below, the road capacity is divided into four levels: v1 means that the road is in good condition and can be used by large vehicles; v2 means that the road can generally allow small vehicles to pass; v3 means that the road condition is too poor for vehicles to go but normally for people to travel; v4 indicates that the road condition is very poor that people can only pass at a slow speed. The capacity of roads 11-12 is v4; capacity of roads 19-32, 18-31, 16-30, 13-27 is v3, capacity of roads 30-31-32, 2-29-27-12, 3-24-25-26-27, 5-6-7, 9-10-11 is v2; the rest is v1. Suppose that an emergency such as "flying fire" suddenly occurs at point 11, and point 1 is the gathering point of fire-fighting resources. Conventional Ant Colony algorithm and improved Ant Colony algorithm are respectively used to optimize the path.

The simulation experiment shows that the path selected by the conventional Ant Colony algorithm is 1-2-29-27-12-11, the path length is 15 km, and the travel time is 0.665 h. The path selected by the improved Ant Colony algorithm is 1-2-3-4-5-6-7-8-9-10-11, the path length is 23 km, and the travel time is 0.467 h. It can be seen from the result, the conventional Ant Colony algorithm selected the path with the shortest length but relatively poor traffic capacity so that it takes a long time. The path selected by the improved Ant Colony algorithm was longer, but due to the good traffic capacity, vehicles can travel at a much higher speed, so that the time required is shorter, that is to say, the path found is better.

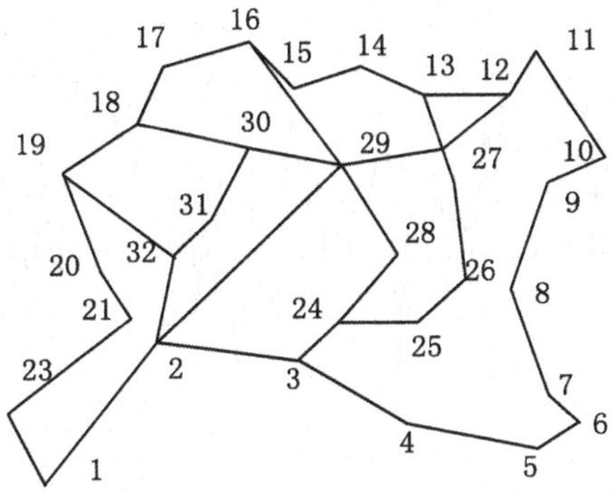

Fig. 5. Roads topology

6.5 Time Comparison Test of Optimal Solution

This experiment is to compare which of the two algorithms presents the optimal solution earlier and the quality of the optimal solution under the same iteration times. For each test function, let the space dimension of the model is 20, there are 30 vehicles participating in fire-extinguishing dispatching, the maximum number of iterations is 100, $c_1 = c_2 = c_3 = 0.1$. The convergence curves of PSO and QPSO are respectively shown in Fig. 6 and Fig. 7.

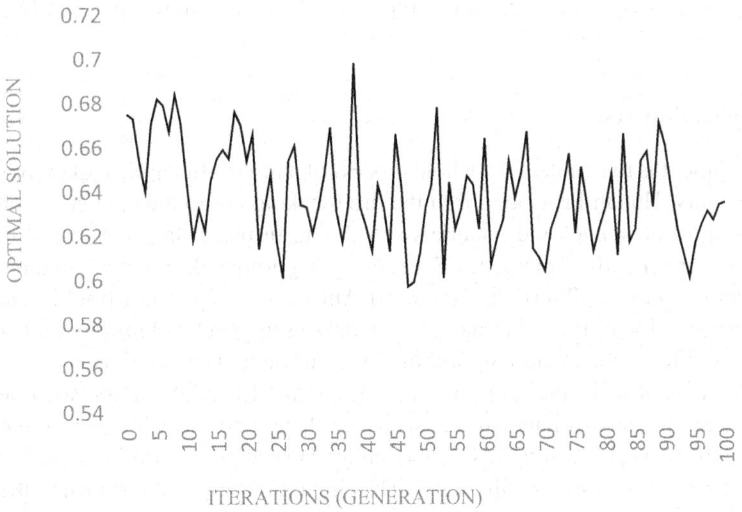

Fig. 6. The average path length and the shortest path length obtained by PSO

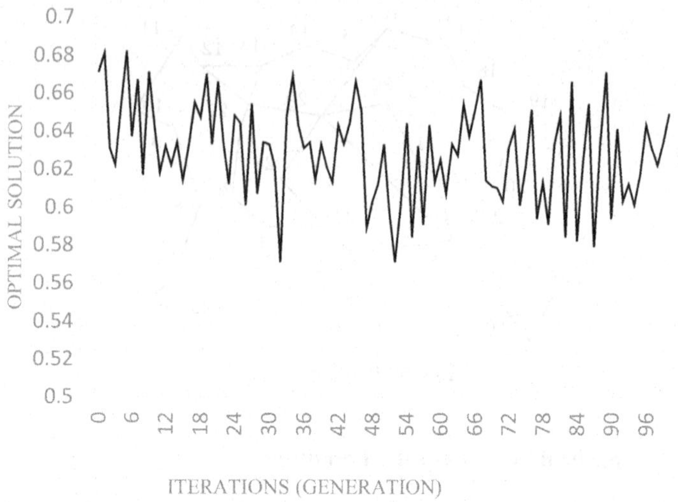

Fig. 7. The average path length and the shortest path length obtained by QPSO

From the example simulation, we can see that the improved quantum particle swarm optimization has fewer iterations than the basic particle swarm optimization. It can converge to the global optimal solution at a faster speed. In terms of solution, the shortest path found by quantum particle swarm optimization is 0.599. The optimal solution found by the basic particle swarm optimization is 0.581, which shows that QPSO is more effective.

6.6 Application Test

This experiment is to simulate the whole process of a fire in Huang Fengqiao forest farm of You County, Hunan Province, from the fire breaking out to the emergency situation and then to all personnel and materials scheduling in place. In order to test the path scheduling capacity, the Emergency Scheduling Algorithm Based on quantum particle swarm optimization (QPSO) and improved Ant Colony algorithm (multi algorithms 1) was compared with the combination of widely used genetic algorithm and artificial potential field algorithm (multi algorithms 2) in this paper [12] (Fig. 8).

It can be seen from the map that there are natural barriers of forests, rivers and hills in the South and artificial barriers such as villages and roads. Moreover, the traffic capacity of roads is also diversified, so it is suitable to use the scheduling model of forest fire extinguishing proposed in this paper. The simulation results are shown in the figure below.

Fig. 8. Map of Huang Fengqiao forest farm and its surroundings in You County, Hunan Province

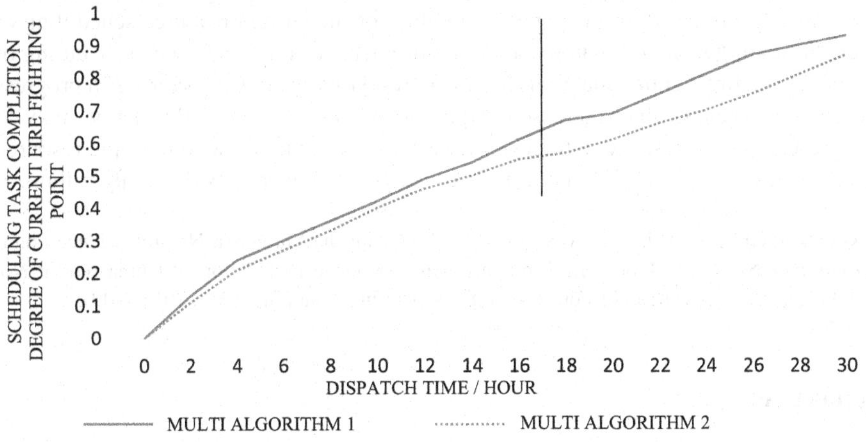

Fig. 9. Comparison of the completion degree of multi algorithm 1 and multi algorithm 2 at the same time

15 h after a forest fire, a fire-extinguishing point burst into a "flying fire" emergency. It was necessary to dispatch all personnel and materials to the this point. Two algorithms were used in the model. As can be seen from Fig. 9, when scheduling the resources of all the fire-extinguishing points, the scheduling speed of QPSO is higher than that of the combination of genetic algorithm and artificial potential field algorithm. Because QPSO encodes all the variables, which can improve the computational efficiency. What's more, in the case of large-scale single demand point scheduling after 15 h, the improved ant

colony algorithm which periodically updating pheromone can avoid low scheduling efficiency in a short period of time. Therefore, using the combination of the two algorithms, multi algorithms scheduling strategy, can greatly improve the scheduling efficiency.

7 Conclusion

Aiming at the shortcomings of the forest fire-extinguishing resources scheduling model, such as long operation time, unable to select a better path in time and low scheduling efficiency in emergency due to the complexity of forest terrain in southern China. In this paper, the resource scheduling model of forest fire-extinguishing based on quantum particle swarm optimization (QPSO) is proposed, and the model is improved from the following three aspects: combining the theory of quantum mechanics with the conventional particle swarm optimization (PSO) to improve the operation efficiency; in the searching process, the pheromone of the ant colony algorithm is updated periodically to delay the search stagnation time; and the conditions of algorithm switching are defined, so that the algorithm can be flexibly applied to various situations. The model was applied to a forest fire simulation experiment in Huang Fengqiao forest farm of You County, Hunan Province. The simulation result shows that the resource scheduling model of forest fire-extinguishing proposed in this paper is suitable for the current resource scheduling of forest fire-extinguishing. It can meet the requirements of high-efficiency scheduling of personnel and fire-fighting materials in forest fire-extinguishing and short-term progress in case of emergency, which increased the practicability of the model. Besides, we may do more research on forest fire-extinguishing resources scheduling with multiple resource points and experiment in different forests to verify the universality of the algorithm.

Acknowledgements. This work was supported by Changsha Municipal Natural Science Foundation(Grant No. kq2014160), the National Natural Science Foundation of China (Grant No. 61703441), the State Bureau of Forestry "948" project in China (Grant No. 2014-4-09).

References

1. Cui, Y.P., Yang, H.X.: Promote the development of forest fire prevention system to improve the comprehensive capacity of forest fire prevention. Forest Fire Prev. **20**(3), 6 (2014)
2. Dai, G.X., Da, Q.L.: The study of combinatorial scheduling problem in emergency systems. Syst. Eng.-Theory Pract. **8**(9), 52–55 (2000)
3. Feng, X., Wu, D.S., Luo, W.J.: A multi-depot emergency scheduling algorithm for forest fire prevention. J. Zhejiang A & F Univ. **30**(2), 257–262 (2013)
4. He, J.M., Liu, C.L.: Fuzzy programming problem for vehicle dispatch under time restriction. Decis. Control **16**(3), 318–321 (2001)
5. Harish Garg.: A hybrid PSO-GA algorithm for constrained optimization problems. Appl. Math. Comput. **2**(274), 292–305 (2015). (0096-3003)
6. Inbar, A., Lado, M., Sternberg, M., Tenau, H., Ben-Hur, M.: Forest fire effects on soil chemical and physicochemical properties, infiltration, runoff, and erosion in a semiarid Mediterranean region. Geoderma **221**, 131–138 (2014)
7. Jiang, L.Z., Liu, M.: Research of optimal allocation model of forest fire materials. China Public Secur. **24**(3), 97–100 (2008)

8. Liu, D.W., Guan, X.B.: Application of Ant Colony algorithm in forest fires fighting path selection. Comput. Eng. **37**(14), 214–217 (2011)
9. Li, B., Chen, A.B., Zhou, G.X., Zhou, T.: Wolves optimization algorithm based on Cell-DEVS for forest fire-fighting resource scheduling. J. Comput. Appl. **38**(5), 1494–1499 (2018)
10. Pan, F., Zhong, W.J.: Modeling and simulation of complex emergency scheduling based on particle swarm optimization. Stat. Decis. **21**, 18–21 (2014)
11. Renqiang, W., Shaobo, Z., Hongyong, Y., Quanyi, H.: Emergency resource multi-objective optimization scheduling model and multi-colony ant optimization algorithm. J. Comput. Res. Dev. **50**(7), 1464 (2013)
12. Sharafi, M., ELMekkawy, T.Y.: Multi-objective optimal design of hybrid renewable energy systems using PSO-simulation based approach. Renew. Energy **68**, 67–79 (2014)
13. Wang, H., Ai, Q.: Voltage quality control for DC-AC hybrid system with DGs based on improved quantum particle swarm optimization. Electr. Energy Manag. Technol. **30**(15), 79–88 (2018)
14. Zhou, G.X., Wu, Q., Chen, A.B.: Research of cellular automata model for forest fire spreading simulation. Chin. J. Sci. Instrum. **38**(2), 288–294 (2017)
15. Zhou, G.X., Wu, Q., Chen, A.B.: Forestry fire spatial diffusion model based on multi-agent algorithm with cellular automata. J. Syst. Simul. **30**(3), 824–830, 839 (2018)

Research on Data Dynamic Adjustment Method Considering Security Requirements in Cloud Computing Environment

Yinzhang Guo[1(✉)], Xiaoyan Li[2], and Xinyu Zhao[1]

[1] School of Computer Science and Technology, Taiyuan University of Science and Technology, Taiyuan 030024, China
guoyinzhang@263.net

[2] Staff Department of Beijing Armed Police Corps, Beijing 100027, China

Abstract. Data storage is widely used as a basic service of cloud computing. How to improve the efficiency of data use under the premise of ensuring data security is one of the current research hotspots in the cloud computing environment of multi-copy storage. In view of the problem of storage location adjustment caused by the dynamic change of data resources during the operation of cloud computing, this paper first presents a data request habit detection strategy RT to detect the rationality of the data storage scheme in the current environment in real time. By using the optimization ability of genetic algorithm, users and related applications can obtain data safely and efficiently. Experiments show that this method can improve the security of data storage and the efficiency of data acquisition under the changeable data request mode.

Keywords: Cloud computing · Data storage · TC-GA strategy · Dynamic adjustment

1 Introduction

As a new computing paradigm, cloud computing has been widely used in medical care, finance, education and other fields. Its core lies in IT resource as a service. While the key problem of cloud computing, security, had never been solved completely. According to a survey by IDC in the first half of 2020, security issues in cloud computing are still serious. Nearly 80% of companies have experienced at least one cloud data breach in the past 18 months, while 43% have reported 10 or more breaches. The provision of cloud services depends on basic functions including data interaction and storage, Ali M [1] et al. state that the challenges of cloud security focus on network communication, cloud architecture, and related laws. The security of architecture mainly contains virtual machines, data storage, cloud applications, and identity management and control.

The current literature on data backup and dynamic adjustment in the cloud mostly adopts evolutionary algorithms and hierarchical iterative methods, mainly focusing on saving energy consumption, reducing the cost of data storage and transmission, and

Y. Sun et al. (Eds.): ChineseCSCW 2021, CCIS 1491, pp. 102–112, 2022.
https://doi.org/10.1007/978-981-19-4546-5_8

adjusting the location of data backup to adapt to different data acquisition modes in the cloud environment, without full consideration on of data security. However, literatures focus on the security of actual location of data are inadequate in realizing load balancing, backup storage and adapting to the dynamic change of data request mode. Thus, in order to provide secure and efficient cloud services, dynamic adjustment of data storage location in cloud computing environment to adapt to changing data request patterns is an urgent need for in-depth research.

2 Related Work

Some of the current mainstream cloud storage [2–4] mainly adopt the static method with a copy of the data storage and management: when the number of copies is 3, they will be stored on three nodes respectively, including two nodes on the local rack and one node randomly selected on different racks [5], and the data will be called nearby when need-ed. G E et al. [6] put forward the cost-based allocation (CBA) resource allocation algorithm under the premise of guaranteeing the lowest availability for various relationships between servers and service instances. Reddy K H K [7] proposed the DPPACS strategy to divide data fragments based on task requirements, put relevant fragments into a single cluster as far as possible, and assign related tasks to clusters with the most required data fragments, so as to reduce the cost of data migration. According to the characteristics of workflow in cloud computing, Yuan D [8] divided data on the basis of whether it was fixed storage and allocated. These proposed static storage schemes studies mainly pursue benefits, while behaved poor in load balancing, security, backup storage and other aspects, and fail to adapt to changing cloud service requirements.

In order to cope with the characteristics of multiple backup storage and variable data request modes in the cloud environment, file [9] conducted a large number of comparative experiments starting from various boxing methods and scenarios, aiming to demonstrate that the combination of on-demand initial allocation and dynamic redistribution in the cloud can effectively save energy consumption. Xu J P et al. [10] designed resource scheduling algorithm in cloud environment by combining triangular fuzzy number analysis and genetic algorithm, which reduced the time consuming of cloud storage process. These methods adapt to dynamically changing access patterns, but lack a copy management strategy. These methods are appropriate for dynamically changing access patterns, but lack a copy management strategy. Shao B L et al. [11] solved the problems of availability, load balancing and energy consumption caused by multi-copy storage by using MODE/A algorithm. The Dynamic Replica Management Scheme (DRM) is proposed to reduce storage resource consumption, ensure storage availability, and improve system load balancing through copy Management [12]. Such type of replica management strategy can greatly improve the availability of the system and the application of the particular scenario performance, but it does not take into account the risk of data leakage at physical nodes caused by multi-replica storage.

From what has been discussed above, this paper proposes the data request habit detection strategy RT and the data adjustment scheme generation algorithm TC-GA. RT is used to detect the request mode of data stored on each node. When a large change in the data request pattern is detected, the TC-GA algorithm will be triggered. On the purpose of improving access efficiency, the GA algorithm can effectively avoid the potential security risks caused by improper data storage location and improve the efficiency of data acquisition service in the system.

3 Problem Description and Modeling

3.1 Definition of Cloud Data Storage Nodes and Bandwidth

Cloud computing is distributed storage environment, where data is stored in different geographical position on each node (server, data center). This article mainly focuses on the performance change of cloud service according to storage node and the network status.

Definition 1: Definition of data storage node:

$$\begin{aligned} Node &= \bigcup_{i=0}^{N-1} node[i], node[i] \\ &= \text{<size}, \mathit{remain}, \mathit{site}, \text{state>} \end{aligned} \tag{1}$$

$$size, remain, site \in R+, state \in \{0, 1\}$$

N represents the number of nodes in the current research network, I represents the label of node. Size Represents the storage capacity of the node, and remain indicates the available capacity of that node. Site indicates the position of location, state is used to distinguish the security status of nodes in the current round process of data distribution, "1" indicates safe, "0" indicates unsafe.

Definition 2: The communication bandwidth between nodes in a network is defined as $\boldsymbol{B}[\boldsymbol{N}][\boldsymbol{N}]$.

$$\boldsymbol{B} = \begin{bmatrix} B[1][1] & B[1][2] & \ldots & B[1][N] \\ B[2][1] & B[2][2] & \ldots & B[2][N] \\ \ldots & \ldots & \ldots & \ldots \\ B[N][1] & B[N][2] & \ldots & B[N][N] \end{bmatrix} \tag{2}$$

In the above formula, $B[i][j] \in \{0, R+\}$, $B[i][j]$ represents the communication bandwidth between nodes labeled i and j, and the value range is non-negative real numbers. $B[i][j] = 0$ means that node i cannot reach j directly. Similarly, the communication distance matrix $dis[N][N]$ can be defined to represent the communication distance between nodes.

3.2 Definition of Cloud Data Storage Scheduling Object

The study of dynamic adjustment scheme for single data should be considered referred to the relationship among data request, storage location of fragment and backup, and storage status of each node.

Definition 3: The data dynamic adjustment problem can be described as a triple: $DAP = $ <***Data***, ***Node***, ***Request***>, in which ***Data*** represents data sets, ***Node*** represents node sets, ***Request*** represents the data request set.

Definition 4: Data size: ***Data***

$$\begin{aligned} \boldsymbol{Data} &= \bigcup_{i=0}^{M-1} \bigcup_{j=0}^{r-1} data[i][j], date[i][j] \\ &= \text{<size}, f\_n, \boldsymbol{f\_size}[], \boldsymbol{site}[], ave\_rc\text{>} \end{aligned} \tag{3}$$

$$date[i][j] = \text{<}size, f\_n, f\_size[], site[], ave\_rc\text{>}$$

M is the number of data involved in problem analysis, R represents the backup number of each data, and i, j and k are labels. $data[i][j]$ is the jth backup of the ith data, $size$ is the size of data, f_n is the number of data slice. $f\_size[k]$ and $size[k]$ represent the kth position of fragment and size. ave_rc is used in the request pattern detection policy and represents the average cost of a single acquisition of the data over a period of time.

Definition 5: Definition of data request set:

$$\boldsymbol{Rq} = \bigcup_{i=0}^{l-1} rq[l], rq[i] = \text{<}site, d, ti\text{>} \tag{4}$$

l is the number of data requests participating in the statistics, $site$ is the location of the node sends the request. d is the label of the requested data, ti shows the time of requesting.

4 Cloud Data Dynamically Adjusts Policies

4.1 Data Request Pattern Detection Policy

The data request mode detection policy RT periodically checks the data request mode in the cloud computing environment to determine whether the data request cost time of the system changes significantly due to the change of the request mode. If the request mode reaches the threshold, the dynamic adjustment policy TC-GA is triggered. Therefore, it is necessary to define the evaluation basis for the change of data request mode. This part mainly considers the short-term change and the long-term cumulative change, and the more detailed contents of the values of the two parts are explained in Definition 1.

Definition 1: When the change rate of data request mode exceeds the threshold, the TC-GA algorithm is called:

$$\begin{aligned} &\left\{ \begin{array}{l} rate\_a = \dfrac{ave\_RC\_now}{ave\_RC\_last} > \alpha \\ rate\_b = \dfrac{ave\_RC\_now}{ave\_RC\_past} > \beta \end{array} \right., \alpha > \beta > 1; \\ &\text{if } rate\_a || rate\_a == 1,\ call \text{ TC - GA} \end{aligned} \tag{5}$$

The time interval is represented by *TI* (Time interval), in the above formula, *ave_RC_now*, *ave_RC_last*, *ave_RC_past* represent the average cost of data acquisition in recent *TI*, last TI and so far respectively. *rate_a* is the change rate of *ave_RC* between two adjacent *TI*, which is used to judge whether the data request mode changes greatly in a short time interval. *rate_b* is the current rate of change compared to historical *ave_RC*, which is used for supplement evaluation of changes in long-term data request patterns. Since the long-term rate of change causes greater overhead change to the overall communication and requires more sensitive processing, $\alpha > \beta$. If any of the comparison results in the above formula is true, it means that the data request mode has changed greatly, and the TC-GA algorithm is invoked for processing. The values of *TI*, α and β need to be set according to the specific application environment, and the algorithm flows shown below.

Algorithm 1: RT strategy

1. Input: $Node, Data, Rq, B[N][N], dis[N][N]$;
2. Output: invoke TC-GA or not;
3. For each TI;
4. Invoke function $Freude(dis[N][N])$;
5. Calculate the shortest access path between data $\min p[N][N]$;
6. For each data in Data requested in Rq
7. For each rq in Rq
8. Call $Dijkstra(rq[l], \min p[N][N], B[N][N])$;
9. Obtain every RC;
10. End for;
11. For each rq in every TI
12. Calculate ave_RC_now;
13. Sum(ave_RC_now);
14. End for;
15. Figure out $rate\_a$、$rate\_b$ according to definition 1.
16. If($rate\_a \,||\, rate\_b == 1$)
17. Invoke TC-GA
18. End if;
19. End for;
20. End for;

4.2 Algorithm TC-GA

(1) Model evaluation
The two objectives pursued in this paper are the security of data storage location and the efficiency of data access. The security is incorporated into the location

selection criteria based on T-color idea as one of the constraints for genetic TC-GA algorithm. The optimization objective problem is defined as follows:

Object: maximize (fitness).

Subject to:

$$\begin{cases} hop >= h > 0; \ \ldots\ldots\ldots\ldots\ldots\ldots\ldots\ldots\ldots\ldots 1 \\ data[i][j].f\_size[k] < node[m].remain; \ \ldots\ldots\ldots\ldots 2 \\ \sum data[i][j].f\_size[k] == data[i][j].size; \ \ldots\ldots 3 \end{cases} \quad (6)$$

$$fitness = 1/ave\_RC;$$

Fitness is the reciprocal of ave_RC, the average access time of the data to be adjusted, as the optimization objective to reduce the data access time. Constraint 1 indicates security requirements: hop must be greater than h, and all data fragments from the same data cannot be stored on the same node, which means $h > 0$. Constraint 2 indicates that the nodes to be stored have enough storage space. Constraint 3 means that the sum of data fragment sizes is equal to the data size.

(2) Coding rules and the selection of related operations

TC-GA algorithm mainly studies the storage location of data fragments. In order to conveniently describe the location of each data fragment in a network containing several nodes, the encoding length is set as the number of data fragments f, and array $data[i][j].site[fn]$ represents the location of each data fragment with data of label i and backup of label j, according to Definition 4. Suppose that node size N is 100 and data fragment $fn = 7$, a possible coding example for the storage locations of the data is {21,34,76,37,23,18,3}.

Selection is mainly depending on the size of the fitness and using elite strategy, retains the highest fitness plan directly in the forefront of population, the left individual is selected by "roulette wheel" method.

This coding method is suitable for single point crossover and single point mutation operation. Crossover operation considers exchanging the first half of adjacent coding segmentation points, and randomly selects a fragment of the code for redistribution when mutation occurs.

(3) Strategies for conflict resolution

Due to the existence of constraint conditions, the above coding methods and related operations, especially in the process of crossover and mutation, are easy to produce unreasonable schemes. Unreasonable schemes mainly include two types:

I. In violation of the constraint condition 1, the condition of breach depends on the values of h. Such as plan {21,34,76,37,23,21,3} will lead to different data fragment stored in the same node 21, which makes hop = 0. Adjustment strategy: only one of the conflicting nodes will be reserved, the others will be store in the node randomly selected from the node set that meets hop > h and other constraints. Repeat the above tests and selection until the solution is reasonable.

II. When constraint condition 2 is violated, node re-selection should be carried out for the fragments that fail to be stored, and random selection should be adopted, considering constraint condition 1. The detailed strategy is similar to that mentioned inI.

(4) Formal description of algorithm TC-GA

Algorithm 2: TC-GA

1. Input: $data[i][j], \min p[N][N], TI, Node, Rq, ave\_RC\_now, iteration = 0$, ite;
2. Output: $data[i][j]$ fragment' position adjustment scheme $pop[p][f\_n]$;
3. Generate the initial population $pop[p][f\_n]$; according to the number of population p;
4. While iteration<ite;
5. For each $pop[x][:]$ in $pop[p][f\_n]$;
6. If(conflict test($pop[x][f\_n]$))
7. Conflict solve($pop[x][f\_n]$);
8. End if;
9. End for;
10. Sort ($pop[p][f\_n]$);
11. Selction ($pop[p][f\_n]$);
12. For each $pop[x][:]$ in $pop[p][f\_n]$;
13. Intersection(); repeat 4-9;
14. Variation(); repeat 4-9;
15. End for;
16. End while;
17. If $ave\_RC < ave\_RC\_now$
18. Return $pop[0][fn]$;
19. Else return $data[i][j].site[f\_n]$;
20. End if;

When the data access time of the optimal scheme is shorter than that of the scheme to be adjusted significantly, implement the scheme; otherwise, no adjustment will be executed.

5 Simulation Experiment

The experiment in this paper mainly uses numerical simulation method to simulate the cloud environment to generate scheduling scheme, and evaluates the cost of the scheme in the cloud environment in terms of security and data access efficiency. The main experiments involved in the comparison include ① general genetic algorithm (GA), ② DROPS (Division and Replication of Data in Cloud for Optimal Performance and Security), ③ greedy-random strategy (GR) and ④ Fathest-First strategy (FF).

5.1 Experimental Environment

Hardware: one 8-generation Core I5 dual-core CPU notebook computer; Software: Eclipse-2018;

In order to simulate the actual interconnection between nodes in the cloud environment (Fig. 1), considering the existence of bus topology, the interconnection ratio of nodes in the hybrid network of various topologies is calculated to be about $1/(N-1)$ magnitude. In the connected graph randomly generated in this experiment, the interconnection probability between nodes is $4/N$. Due to the uneven quality of the equipment used to build the cloud computing platform, parameters such as node capacity and remaining capacity are randomly assigned in a given interval. In order to ensure the reliability of the results, the experimental comparison data are the median of multiple experimental results, and the random distribution strategy is adopted for the initial distribution of data.

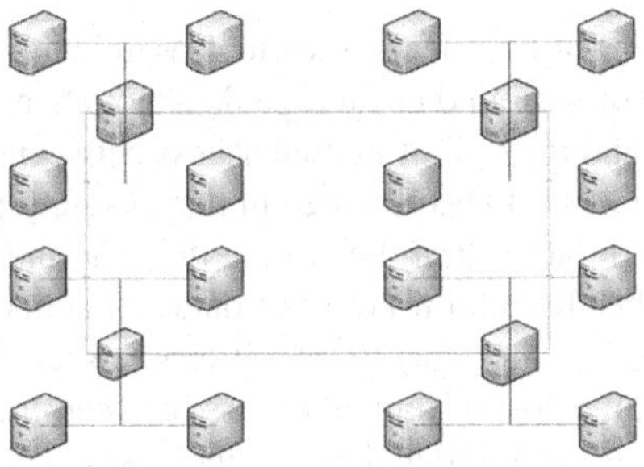

Fig. 1. Star + ring topology

5.2 Security

System security: Since some strategies in the comparison scheme adopt different security indexes from this scheme or do not consider security, this paper establishes unified security indexes to conduct security comparison.

Definition 9:

$$sc = \frac{\sum_{i=0}^{M-1} \sum_{j=0}^{n-1} \sum_{k=0}^{n-2} min(d(ij, k))}{M \cdot n \cdot (n-1)} \tag{7}$$

$d(x, y)$ is the shortest distance between node x and y, M and n represent the number of data and fragment respectively. The shortest distance between the *jth* data fragment of the *ith* data and other fragments is divided by the product of the number of data, the number of fragments and the number of handshakes in a single round, which represents the average minimum cost of mutual visits between fragments of each data and is defined as the security indicator *sc* to represent the system.

TC-GA algorithm and DROPS algorithm set the hop limit to 2, and observe the changes of the system security performance by changing the node scale and the number of fragments. After normalization, the experimental results are shown in Fig. 2.

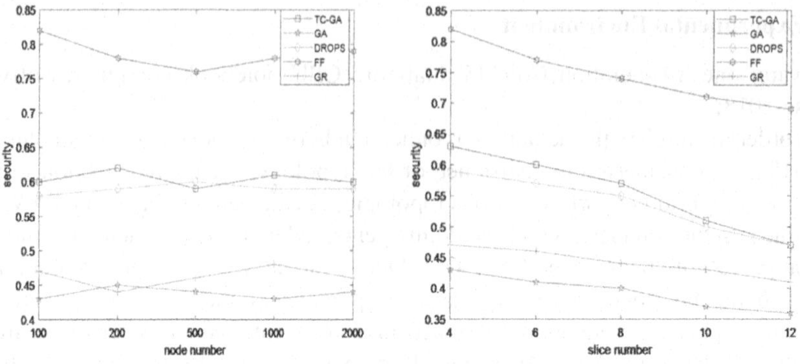

(a) (b)

Fig. 2. (a) Safety comparison (b) Safety comparison

In Fig. 2(a), the number of fragments is set to 4. Within a fixed geographical range, the security performance of system data storage does not change significantly with the expansion of node scale, and the cost of mutual access between data fragments remains basically unchanged.TC-GA and DROPS are similar in safety performance, which are better than ordinary genetic algorithm, but worse than FF and GR. However, TC-GA guarantees the hop number limitation between data, its actual security perference is better. In Fig. 2(b), the node scale is set to 200. It can be seen that with the increase of the number of fragments, the cost of mutual access between fragments of a single data decreases, the probability of overall data leakage increases, and the guarantee ability of system security becomes weaker. It is worth noting that TC-GA still outperforms other schemes in terms of safety in this situation. Through further experiments, it is found that TC-GA and DROPS generation schemes are far safer than other algorithms when the hop = 3. However, with its increasing, the possibility of rejection storage will increase. Therefore, hop is suggested to be selected appropriately according to the node size.

5.3 Data Access Efficiency

The evaluation of data adjustment strategy on service quality improvement ability mainly depends on formula (6) and (7). The change rate of formula (6) can well reflect the improvement degree of data access efficiency after the implementation of adjustment plan, and formula (7) can reflect whether data adjustment effectively improve service quality for all users. In this experiment, the number of data fragments is set as 8, node size as 200, hop limited as 2, $\alpha = 1.3$, $\beta = 1.2$, and the effect of the adjustment strategy is observed by adjusting the *Rq* set. The experimental results are normalized and shown in Fig. 3.

As the proportion of data to be adjusted increases, it can be seen from Fig. 3(a) that the scheduling scheme generated by TC-GA algorithm improves the data access efficiency to the same extent as the ordinary GA algorithm, significantly better than DROPS and FF, and slightly worse than GR. However, the GR policy may increase data leakage risks and uneven load. Therefore, it is not recommended for scenarios with high

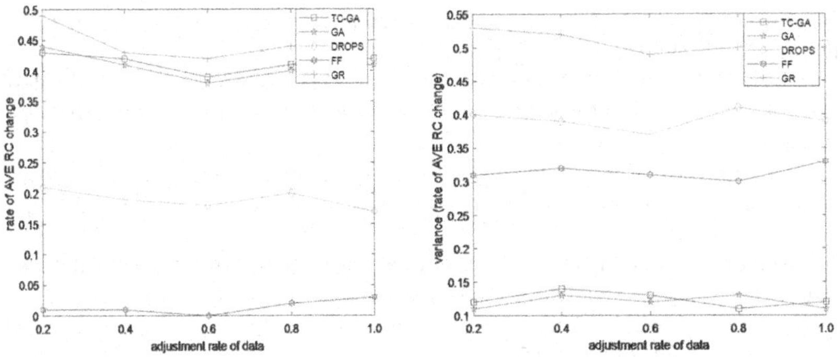

(a) (b)

Fig. 3. (a) Data request efficiency comparison (b) Data request efficiency comparison

security requirements. It can be seen from Fig. 3(b) that the algorithm proposed in this paper can protect the rights and interests of each user after data dynamic adjustment to a greater extent, while the other methods perform poorly in this respect.

The above experiments show that the data distribution adjustment scheme generated by TC-GA algorithm effectively avoids the security risk of data storage location, and greatly improves the quality of data access service in the system.

6 Conclusion

This paper studies the dynamic adjustment strategy for the storage nodes during the operation of data services in cloud computing environment. RT request detection strategy and TC-GA dynamic scheduling algorithm are designed to detect the rationality of the data storage scheme and adjust the unreasonable storage scheme in time respectively. Experiments show that the TC-GA algorithm can effectively realize the purpose of dynamic adjustment of cloud storage nodes under the premise of ensuring data security when the data request mode changes periodically. However, this method is not suit for the case where the data request pattern changes frequently. Also, the strategy can be adjusted for a single data fragment to further reduce the scheduling cost, improve the efficiency of the algorithm and broaden the application scenarios of the algorithm in future.

References

1. Ali, M., Khan, S.U., Vasilakos, A.V.: Security in cloud computing: opportunities and challenges. Inf. Sci. **305**, 357–383 (2015)
2. Piper, B., Clinton, D.: Amazon Simple Storage Service and Amazon Glacier Storage. AWS Certified Solutions Architect Study Guide (2019)
3. Mckusick, K., Quinlan, S.: GFS: evolution on fast-forward. Commun. ACM **53**(3), 42–49 (2010)
4. Karun, A.K., Chitharanjan, K.: A review on Hadoop — HDFS infrastructure extensions. In: Information & Communication Technologies, pp. 132–137 (2013)

5. Melorose, J., Perroy, R., Careas, S.: Hadoop definitive guide. O'rlly Media Inc Gravenstn Highway North **215**(11), 1–4 (2015)
6. Gonçalves, G.E., Endo, P.T., Rodrigues, M., Sadok, D.H., Kelner, J., Curescu, C.: Resource allocation based on redundancy models for high availability cloud. Computing **102**(1), 43–63 (2019)
7. Reddy, K.H.K., Roy, D.S.: DPPACS: a novel data partitioning and placement aware computation scheduling scheme for data-intensive cloud applications. Comput. J. **59**(1), 64–82 (2016)
8. Yuan, D., Yang, R., Liu, R., et al.: A data placement strategy in scientific cloud workflows. Futur. Gener. Comput. Syst. **26**(8), 1200–1214 (2010)
9. Wolke, A., et al.: More than bin packing: dynamic resource allocation strategies in cloud data centers. Inf. Syst. **52**, 83-95 (2015)
10. Xu, J.P., Li, X., Zhao, X.F.: Improved resource scheduling algorithm in cloud storage. Appl. Res. Comput. **36**(7), 2015–2019 (2019)
11. Shao, B.L., He, J.N., Bian, G.Q.: Research on replica layout algorithm based on multi-objective decomposition strategy. J. Front. Comput. Sci. Technol. **14**(9), 1490–1500 (2020)
12. Tao, Y.C., Ba, Y., Shi, L., et al.: Management mechanism of dynamic cloud data replica based on availability. J. Chin. Comp. Syst. **39**(03), 92–97 (2018)

Optimal Storage Cloud Data Recoverability Audit Method Based on Regenerative Code

Xiaoyan Li[1], Yinzhang Guo[2(✉)], and Ting Han[2]

[1] Staff Department of Beijing Armed Police Corps, Beijing 100027, China
[2] School of Computer Science and Technology, Taiyuan University of Science and Technology, Taiyuan 030024, China
guoyinzhang@263.net

Abstract. In cloud data security storage, when data holders store locally controllable data resources in the cloud, they lose control of data integrity and availability. For data holders, the cloud service provider CSP is untrustworthy, and it may damage the data stored in the cloud or forge and deceive the integrity of the damaged data. Aiming at the data recoverability problem after detecting data integrity damage in cloud data storage, an audit method of optimal storage cloud data recoverability based on regeneration code is proposed. This solution not only supports the third-party audit agency to verify whether the data block is damaged and locate the exact location of the damaged data block, but also realizes the data integrity recovery function. In the process of data processing and auditing, the privacy and safety of data are guaranteed. Experiments have proved that the program has a certain degree of safety and effectiveness.

Keywords: Cloud data storage · Integrity audit · Recoverability proof POR · Tamper detection and localization

1 The Introduction

Cloud computing has efficient and convenient computing and storage resources, saving users a lot of data storage burden [1]. The most concerned issue for data owners is whether the data stored in the cloud server will be accidentally damaged or deliberately attacked, and whether the original data can be restored once it is damaged [2, 3]. If the MDS-based solution is used to complete the recovery of damaged data, the entire file needs to be detected first, which will greatly increase the cost of recovering data, and the data storage method based on multiple copies will increase the storage cost [4]. Therefore, for the data owner, only by correctly holding the data stored in the cloud server and being able to repair the original data when the integrity of the data is damaged, can the user trustably store the data in the cloud server. This chapter proposes an audit method of optimal storage cloud data recoverability based on regeneration codes. This method can solve the problem of restoring the user's damaged data and support the trusted TPA to verify the integrity of the data. Once the data is found to be tampered with, the cloud server is immediately required to locate the specific location of the damaged data block and complete the data recovery. Theoretical analysis and experimental results show that the program has a safe and efficient data recovery function.

Y. Sun et al. (Eds.): ChineseCSCW 2021, CCIS 1491, pp. 113–123, 2022.
https://doi.org/10.1007/978-981-19-4546-5_9

2 Cloud Data Integrity Audit System Model to Support Data Recovery

The system model in this scheme is usually composed of three entities, which are user, CSP, and TPA. The specific model is shown in Fig. 1. The user is the actual owner of cloud data and has a large number of original data files; CSP is the actual storage service provider of user data, provides storage services according to user needs, has strong computing power and sufficient storage space; TPA is trusted and independent A third-party organization that can verify the integrity of data on behalf of users and feed back the true results to users. TPA can be any secure and trusted entity in the cloud. The cloud servers in this model can be provided by CSPs with different identifiers, and data holders store their own data files in different cloud servers. In the model, by effectively identifying the unique identifier of the cloud server, TPA and users can easily identify each cloud server. If it is found that the data on some cloud servers has been tampered with or lost, the identifiers found the data is distinguished, and the original file will be recovered from the copy of the data stored on other cloud servers.

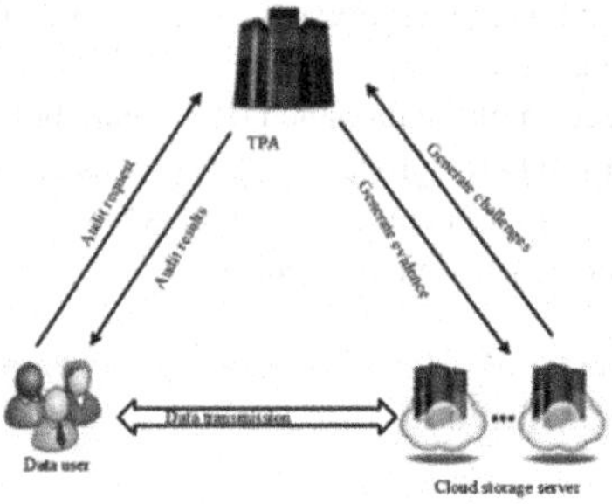

Fig. 1. A model for a third-party audit approach that supports data recovery.

3 Cloud Data Integrity Audit Technologies to Support Data Recovery

3.1 Optimal Storage Regeneration Code (MSR)

Regeneration code is one of erasure codes that can support data recovery technology. Aiming at the problem of excessive storage capacity and repairing traffic overhead, Dimakis et al. [5] first proposed the concept of regeneration codes. The regeneration code is divided into minimum storage regeneration code (MSR) and minimum bandwidth regeneration code (MBR). Assuming that the data block is only occasionally abnormal, then the chance of using the regeneration code to repair will be reduced, resulting in higher repair costs, but increasing the storage overhead and auditing overhead in the system [6]. Compared with MBR, the total bandwidth recovery of MSR is relatively high, and the storage capacity of each node is relatively weak, so the final storage cost will be reduced.

The scheme proposed in this paper combines the optimal storage regeneration code proposed by Rashmi [7] and others. The use of the precise repair regeneration code can significantly reduce the storage redundancy of the system, so that the repaired data block can achieve the same effect as the damaged data block. The basic principle of the optimal storage regeneration code (MSR) [8]: Suppose a cloud server is set up in cloud storage, and when the user uploads a file, the divided data blocks are sequentially encoded. In the data recovery phase, as long as any one of the storage nodes is selected and connected in this storage node, the recovery task can be completed. If the optimal storage regeneration code can be successfully constructed, then it can be constructed successfully for any value. Assuming that a file of size F is to be stored in a cloud server, the file is divided into data blocks, and then these data blocks are allocated to different cloud server storage nodes, so that each storage node can be allocated to Data blocks. It can be seen from the properties of the regeneration code that if the data in a storage node is randomly selected from all storage nodes, the recovery of the entire data file can be completed, which also satisfies the maximum length that can be allocated between n and k.

3.2 Bilinear Mapping Encryption

Bilinear mapping belongs to a concept in cryptography and is the basic function for performing data block authentication [9]. A bilinear mapping function refers to elements on two different vector spaces, and the mapping generates an element on the third vector space.

Let G and G_T be the multiplicative cyclic groups of order prime q, If have a mapping $e : G_1 \times G_2 \rightarrow G_T$ satisfies the following attributes, the mapping is called bilinear mapping.

(1) Bilinear. There are all $u \in G$, $v \in G$, $a \in Z_P{}^*$, $b \in Z_P{}^*$, meet the $e\left(u^a, v^b\right) = e(u, v)^{ab}$. This property also satisfies multiplication, For all the $u_1, u_2 \in G$, Meet the $e(u_1 \cdot u_2, v) = e(u_1, v) \cdot (u_2, v)$.
(2) The degenerative. If g is a generator on G_1, g_2 is a generator on G_2, there must be $g_1, g_2 \in G_T$, meet $e(g_1, g_2) \neq 1$.
(3) Computability. For any $u, v \in G$, there is an efficient algorithmic calculation $e(u, v)$.

A similar definition can be made for a bilinear pair map of an additive group.

Let G and G_T be additive cyclic groups of order prime q, The attribute of bilinear pair mapping can be obtained as: there are all $u \in G$, $v \in G$, $a \in Z_P{}^*$, $b \in Z_P{}^*$, meet the $e(au, bv) \cdot e(u, v)^{ab}$.

3.3 Regeneration Code Allocated to Cloud Storage Nodes

Different storage nodes or implemented in clusters [10]. The cloud storage system contains a large number of storage nodes, the purpose is to be able to effectively select the required number of nodes to store data and code blocks. During the selection process, if the overall bandwidth and disk space availability of the storage system are low, the storage node repair will fail. Another factor that affects overall performance is the choice of extreme remote storage node computing load. Therefore, balancing the system load is very critical, which can only be solved by selecting a suitable storage node set and efficient node allocation.

If the regenerative code storage system is regarded as a complete storage system, the availability of storage nodes with bandwidth and other parameters, the distance between nodes, the available space of the hard disk, and the computing load on the storage nodes can be better selected. Data and code nodes. When a data block (or data set) is stored in a regeneration code storage system, the system must select the storage node with the best available state. The maximum bandwidth guarantees the speed of data transmission, the largest disk storage space, and the smallest calculation load, so as to deal with the problem of no delay and the smallest distance between storage nodes. The distance between storage nodes uses the number of hops. In addition to the distance between nodes, other parameters can be changed frequently. Therefore, the node allocation should be carefully changed in each storage situation. Similarly, when a node in the regenerative code cloud storage system fails, the best new node is to select a node called a new node from the available storage nodes. Therefore, there is a need for efficient processing of allocated protocols.

4 Cloud Data Integrity Audit Policy Solution for Data Recovery

4.1 Initialization Phase

1. To Choose Parameters;
2. Generate the key KeyGen(1^k) $\rightarrow$ (pk, sk): executed by the user, enter a security parameter k, generate the public and private keys and system parameters for the user. Set G_1 and G_T is a multiplicative cyclic group of order prime q, if we have bilinear mapping properties, there are e : $G_1 \times G_1 \rightarrow G_T$. Pick an arbitrary element g in G_1, The user's private key is randomly selected from x $\leftarrow Z_q{}^*$, The public key is calculated using $X = g^x$. The public and private key pair of the third-party auditor is (y, Y), the public and private key pair of the cloud server is (z, Z). The user selects an arbitrary element s in G_1, and calculate the $\mu = g^s$.

4.2 File Upload Phase

1. Coding Encode(F, X) $\rightarrow$ C:
   Performed by the user, using the regeneration code technology to encode the file F.

   a. Partition file F, divided into N data blocks, represented as a F = $\{m_1, m_2, \ldots m_N\}$, and distribute N blocks of data into the matrix M:

$$M = \begin{bmatrix} S_1 \\ S_2 \end{bmatrix}$$

   In this matrix M, both S_1 and S_2 are symmetric matrices, and the number of rows and columns is α. In the two matrices of S_1 and S_2, different data blocks form the upper triangular part and include all the divided data M blocks; the data block of the lower triangular part can be randomly selected from all the data blocks.

b. Choose a matrix $n \times d$ of coding coefficient: $\varphi = [\varnothing \wedge \varnothing]$. Where $\varnothing$ is a matrix with n rows and α columns, and $\wedge$ is a diagonal matrix with n rows and columns.
c. The encoded file is $C = \varphi M = [\varnothing S_1 + \wedge \varnothing S_2]$.

2. Encryption Encrypt$(C, k_e) \rightarrow C'$.
When the user encrypts the data block, he chooses $K_e \in Z_p$ as his private key and outputs the encrypted data block.
3. Label generation TagGen$(e_{ij}, x) \rightarrow \sigma_{ij}$:
Before generating the homomorphic label, the user first signs C_i with the private key, and performs the homomorphic label calculation on each data block of e_{ij} to form a set σ_i. When the user establishes n MHTs, he selects a set of homomorphic tags as its leaf nodes. In the process of constructing a single MHT, the calculation is performed from the bottom to the top from the bottom of the leaf node, the left and right child nodes are concatenated and the hash operation is performed to obtain the value of the non-leaf node, and finally the uniqueness of each MHT is obtained. Root node value M_{root}. The signature is calculated based on the private key for the root node value and timestamp.
4. User upload data:
Users upload their data encoding collection, homomorphic tag collection, and signature collection to different cloud servers as needed. Each cloud server calculates the data information as its leaf node, establishes a separate MHT, and obtains the unique root node value M_{root} respectively. When verifying the user tag information, if the verification results are equal, the user will be returned with a success message; otherwise, a failure message will be returned and the user will be required to upload the data again.

4.3 Integrity Verification Phase

This stage is divided into three parts: TPA confirms the user's identity; TPA sends a challenge to the CSP; TPA verifies the CSP return value. When the user needs to verify the data, it sends a verification request to the TPA, and the TPA first verifies whether the user has access rights and identity authentication. After the verification is passed, the user sends the data file to be verified to the TPA. After receiving the data information that the user needs to audit, the TPA marks it as a flag, constructs the MHT and calculates its root node value M_{root}', and challenges the CSP. After the CSP receives the challenge information sent by the TPA, it finds the data copy stored in the cloud server, calculates the root node value of the same MHT, and then sends the data block that is also marked as flag in the copy with the calculated root node value M_{root}' To TPA. After the TPA receives the relevant information sent by the CSP, it first verifies the integrity of the root node value M_{root}'. If the root node value M_{root}' is the same, it means that the data is not damaged; if the root node value is not the same, it means that the data in the cloud server is incomplete. Data is tampered or lost, and then perform a partial check on the data block.

4.4 Data Recovery Phase

This stage is executed by the user. When TPA detects that a certain data block of the user is damaged, it immediately requires an inspection of all data in the cloud server and finds the number of the cloud server where the damaged data block is located. After receiving the cloud server number returned by TPA, the user randomly downloads the data in any m complete cloud servers to restore the cloud server with data corruption.

1. First, the user randomly selects m cloud servers among the remaining complete cloud servers and expresses them as a set: $Q_2 = \{1, 2, \ldots, m\}$.
2. Generate corresponding proof values for the data blocks divided by the user file and the generated homomorphic tags:

$$\sigma_i = \prod_{j=1}^{m} \sigma_{ij}$$

$$\theta_j = \sum_{j=1}^{m} e_{ij}$$

3. Server S_i sends $\{\sigma_i, \theta_i\}$ to the user
4. Users use the following formula to calculate:

$$e\left(\prod_{i=1}^{Q_2} \sigma_i, g\right) = e\left(\prod_{i=1}^{Q_2} \mu^{\theta_i} \prod_{i=1}^{Q_2} \prod_{j=1}^{m} h(e_{ij}), X\right)$$

   If the formula holds, go to the next step; otherwise, go back to the first step and re-select the cloud server set.
5. If the encoding vector of the storage node f of the damaged data block is set to φ_f, the data previously stored in this node is $\left[\varnothing_f{}^t \wedge_f \varnothing_f{}^t\right] M = \varnothing_f{}^t S_1 + \wedge_f \varnothing_f{}^t S_2$. All the data received by the user from these m server nodes is $\psi_{repair} M \varnothing_f$, where ψ_{repair} is a matrix composed of m rows of matrix ψ and set Q_2, and is the inverse matrix of ψ_{repair}. Therefore, Mr can be calculated by multiplying (ψ_repair)$^{-1}$ to the left, and $\varnothing_f{}^t S_1$ and $\varnothing_f{}^t S_2$ can be obtained after transposition, and finally the damaged data storage node can be restored by calculating $\varnothing_f{}^t S_1 + \wedge_f \varnothing_f{}^t S_2$.

5 Security Analysis of Cloud Data Integrity Audit Scheme Supporting Data Recovery

5.1 Correctness Analysis

Based on the basic properties and algorithm principles of bilinear mapping, the program is analyzed to prove that the third party can accurately verify the integrity of cloud storage data [11]. For the correctness of uploaded files, it is necessary to ensure that users will not encounter data corruption or loss when uploading data on the cloud server. If the data is tampered with by the cloud server privately, the user can request the cloud server to return a response and verify it, and at the same time initiate a password to the user to re-upload the data. In the process of data integrity auditing, the data holder is the first to upload important files to the cloud. If they are intercepted and destroyed by internal or external attackers during the upload process, when the cloud receives the file, the relevant algorithm is called and the data block is used as the value of the leaf node is calculated layer by layer from bottom to top. After concatenating the left and right child nodes, the Hash operation is performed to obtain the value of the non-leaf node, and finally an MHT is obtained to generate the unique root node value. Determine whether the relevant verification equation is established. If it is established, the data is not damaged. If it is not established, the user is notified to upload the data again.

5.2 Unforgeability Analysis

In this solution, suppose that when a user requests TPA audit data, TPA sends a challenge request for related data to the CSP. At this time, the challenge data block stored in the CSP is tampered with or lost, and the CSP tries to conceal the true state of the data block. Choose to use other complete data instead, so that it will not pass the TPA audit. If the CSP's privately forged proof value passes the TPA audit and conceals the user, it is equivalent to a solution to the CDH assumption problem, which is obviously inconsistent with this assumption. Under normal circumstances, if the TPA issues a challenge, what you get should be the correct proof value returned by the CSP. Set the proof value forged in the cloud, assuming that the proof value can safely pass the integrity audit of TPA, because P is correct $e(\sigma, g) = e\left(\sigma', g\right)$. According to the nature of the bilinear mapping, there is $e\left(\sigma'/\sigma, g\right) = e\left((\mu)^{\Delta C}, X^{\gamma}\right)$. If a solution to the CDH problem can be found, it will contradict the assumption that the problem is computationally infeasible in G. In summary, in the process of TPA auditing data, the cloud server cannot forge the proof value.

5.3 Data Privacy Protection Analysis

In the process of verifying data, the third-party audit institution cannot obtain the user's data block information based on the audit evidence $P = (\theta, \sigma)$ sent by the cloud. θ_i cannot be derived fromμ. According to the DL hypothesis, since $pr[A(g, g^x) = x : x \leftarrow Z_q{}^*]$ can be omitted and cannot be calculated from $\theta_i = u^{\sum_j^J = a_{ij}e_{ij}}$, it can be guaranteed that the information will not be leaked $\sum_j^J = a_{ij}e_{ij}$, and data related information cannot be obtained from $\sigma = \prod_{i=1}^{I}\sigma_i = \prod_{i=1}^{I}\prod_{j=1}^{d}\sigma_{ij} = \left(h\left(e_{ij}\right)\cdot u^{e_{ij}}\right)^x$. Because the files have been processed during the upload stage, it is impossible for a third-party auditor to successfully restore the user's original data without the user's key, thus realizing data privacy protection.

5.4 Identity Authentication Analysis

This scheme supports identity authentication. Identify the data holders, third-party auditors, and CSP to avoid DDoS attacks as much as possible. DDoS attack is embodied in the fact that the attacker illegally uses a botnet to transmit a large amount of verification information to the cloud, thereby occupying a lot of storage space of the cloud server, causing the Internet to malfunction and making the cloud server unable to operate normally. Reflect identity authentication by proving the establishment of the following equation:

$$Auth = h\left(e(Y, Z)^x, W||VID\right)$$

$$= h\left(e\left(g^y, g^z\right)^x, W||VID\right)$$

$$= h\left(e(X, Z)^z, W||VID\right)$$

In order to avoid DDoS attacks as much as possible, CSP can identify among the three to resist most illegal verification requests.

6 Experimental Verification and Performance Analysis

This chapter analyzes the performance of the algorithm by analyzing the communication cost and calculation cost. The experimental environment is implemented on a 64-bit Ubuntu 18.14 operating system with two 4-core CPUs, model Intel(R) Xeon(R) CPU E5630, 2.53 GHz, and 8 GB of RAM in VMware 15, using Python programming. In the experiment, the elliptic curve is type A, and the security level is selected as 80bit.

6.1 Algorithm Timeliness Analysis

The data sample size in this solution is 1 GB. Assuming that the data damage rate is 1%, only 460 data blocks are selected arbitrarily to complete the audit to ensure that the detection rate of damaged data blocks reaches 99%. In this experiment, the files were divided into fixed-size blocks of 1 KB, 2 KB, 4 KB, 8 KB, and 16 KB, respectively, and the influence of different numbers of data blocks in the data partition on the length of the response message was analyzed, as shown in Fig. 2. It can be seen from the figure that the impact of data blocks of different lengths on the length of the response message is relatively small. As the number of data blocks increases, the impact of the data block size on the length of the response message is also more obvious.

6.2 Communication Cost Analysis

The communication consumption required by the third-party auditor and CSP to complete the audit task is analyzed. Assume that when verifying the data, each cloud server is arbitrarily selected 460 data blocks and divided into 50 blocks. In the actual verification process, when the size of the verification data block changes, the size of the communication cost will also change. To evaluate the pros and cons of an audit method, the cost of communication is a crucial performance indicator.

The scheme proposed in this paper is compared with the scheme proposed in scheme [12], scheme [13] and scheme [14] in simulation experiments. These methods all use regenerated codes as coding techniques, but they are quite different in design. For more convenient comparison, the number of audit blocks for all audit methods is unified to 460. Under normal circumstances, in order to ensure the integrity of user data, it is necessary

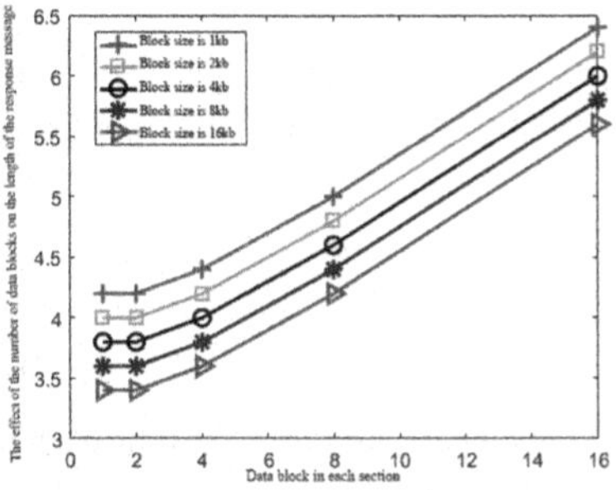

Fig. 2. The effect of the number of different data blocks in the partition on the length of the generated response message.

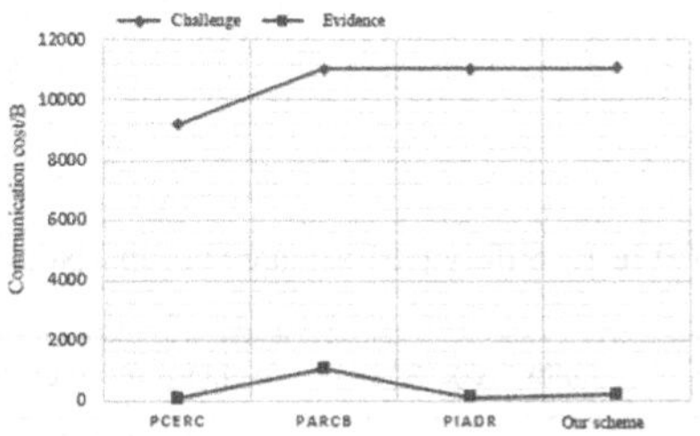

Fig. 3. Communication cost comparison of each method

to periodically review the data in the cloud server, so the size of the communication cost will directly affect the audit process. As shown in Fig. 3, the communication cost of each method can be intuitively compared.

It can be seen from the figure that, except for the relatively small communication cost of the PCERC scheme that generates the challenge, the communication costs of other methods are similar. The only difference in the communication cost of the evidence generated by the cloud server is obvious. The communication cost of the evidence generated by the PARCB scheme is relatively large compared to other schemes. When the number of reviews is larger, this method is not applicable, but the method in this chapter is within an acceptable range.

6.3 Calculation Cost Analysis

In the audit stage, generating and verifying evidence requires a relatively large amount of calculation, and the calculation cost is the most concerned issue in the audit method. Verify that the probability of data file corruption has nothing to do with the file size. Set the number of data blocks to be randomly checked as divided into the number of blocks for each data block (Fig. 4).

It can be seen from the figure that under the premise of using the same settings as in the previous section, the calculation cost difference between each method is not very large. Only the PARCB and PCERC schemes have relatively high calculation costs. On the

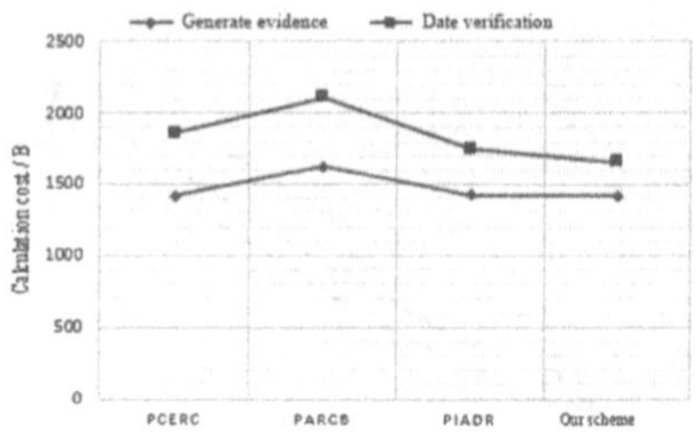

Fig. 4. Cost comparison is calculated by each method

whole, compared with other solutions, this solution has a slightly higher communication overhead, but the amount of calculation is smaller (Table 1).

6.4 Function analysis

Table 1. Safety performance comparison

Heading level	Data recoery[15]	Data recovery[16]	Our scheme
Public audit	√	√	√
Data privacy Protection	×	×	√
The identity authentication	√	×	√
Dynamic update	√	√	√
Homomorphic validation	×	√	√
Data recovery	√	√	√

7 Concluding Remarks

This paper proposes an optimal storage cloud data recovery audit method based on regenerative code. The system model and related technologies are introduced, and the audit strategy scheme including initialization, file uploading, integrity verification and data recovery is elaborated in detail. In the verification process, the scheme can locate the exact location of the damaged data block, recover the data by using the knowledge of matrix inverse operation, and verify the security of the scheme from four aspects. Experimental results show that the security performance of this scheme is better than other schemes, although the communication cost is a little worse, but the calculation cost has a big advantage.

References

1. Mell, P.M., Grance, T.: SP 800-145. The NIST Definition of Cloud Computing. National Institute of Standards and Technology vol. 53, issue 6, pp. 50–50 (2011)
2. Xuelong, L., Haigang, G.: Overview of big data system. Sci. China Inf. Sci. **45**(1), 1–44 (2015)
3. Chaosheng, F., Zhiguang, Q., Ding, Y.: Cloud data security storage technology. Chin. J. Comput. **38**(001), 150–163 (2015)
4. Dengguo, F., Min, Z., Hao, L.: Big data security and privacy protection. Chin. J. Comput. **01**, 246–258 (2014)
5. Dimakis, A.G., Godfrey, P.B., Wu, Y., et al.: Network coding for distributed storage systems. IEEE Trans. Inf. Theory **56**(9), 4539–4551 (2010)
6. Chen, L.: Using algebraic signatures to check data possession in cloud storage. Future Gener. Comput. Syst. FGCS **29**(7) (2013)
7. Rashmi, K.V., Shah, N.B., Kumar, P.V.: Optimal exact-regenerating codes for distributed storage at the MSR and MBR points via a product-matrix construction. IEEE Trans. Inf. Theory **57**(8), 5227–5239 (2011)
8. Miao, B., Song, M., et al.: A transformation principle of regenerated code for heterogeneous distributed storage. Mod. Electron. Techn. **42**(24), 104–107(2019)
9. Diffie, W., Hellman, M.: New directions in cryptography. IEEE Trans. Inf. Theory **22**(6) (1976)
10. Shah, N.B., Rashmi, K.V., Kumar, P.V.: A flexible class of generating codes for distributed storage. In: Proceeding of IEEE International Symposium on Information Theory (1SIT), pp. 1943–1947. Austin, Juru (2010)
11. Qing, Z., Wang, S., et al.: An auditing protocol for data storage in cloud computing with data dynamics. J. Comput. Res. Develop. **52**(10), 2192–2199 (2015)
12. Jing, C., Peng, Y., Du, R., et al.: Regenerating-codes-based efficient remote data checking and repairing in cloud storage. In: 2015 IEEE Trustcom/BigDataSE/ISPA, pp. 20–22. IEEE (2015)
13. Liu, J., Huang, K., Rong, H., et al.: Privacy-preserving public auditing for regenerating-code-based cloud storage. IEEE Trans. Inf. Forensics Secur. **10**(7), 1 (2015)
14. Kai, H., Huang, C., Shi, J., et al.: Public integrity auditing for dynamic regenerating code based cloud storage. Computers & Communication. IEEE (2016)
15. Liu, C., Chen, J., Yang, L.T., et al.: Authorized public auditing of dynamic big data storage on cloud with efficient verifiable fine-grained updates. IEEE Trans. Parallel Distrib. Syst. **25**(9), 2234–2244 (2014)
16. Liu, C., Ranjan, R., Yang, C., et al.: MuR-DPA: top-down levelled multi-replica merkle hash tree based secure public auditing for dynamic big data storage on cloud. IEEE Trans. Comput. **64**(9), 2609–2622 (2015)

A Three-Way Group Decision-Making Approach Based on Mixture Risk

Zhihang Yu[1], Libo Zhang[1(✉)], Wentao Li[1], and Jiubing Liu[2]

[1] School of Artificial Intelligence, Southwest University, Chongqing 400715, People's Republic of China
lbzhang@swu.edu.cn

[2] School of Business, Shantou University, Shantou 515063, People's Republic of China

Abstract. The three-way decision (3WD) using probabilistic rough set (PRS) and 3WD using decision-theoretic rough set (DTRS) are both effective decision-making methods. However, in the group decision-making problem, it will bring challenges to the consistency of decision-making, if different experts utilize diverse models based on their own considerations. Therefore, we propose a three-way group decision-making model which combines these two kinds of models and eliminate the inconsistency in measurement. Firstly, the probabilistic risk cost function is formulated based on the decision rules in the 3WD using PRS model. Then, the total risk cost is defined as the mixture of the probabilistic risk costs in PRS model and the Bayesian risk costs in DTRS model. The best option is selected according to the Bayesian minimum risk rule. Finally, the proposed model is verified by an illustration example.

Keywords: Group decision-making · Three-way decision · Bayesian risk

1 Introduction

Three-way decision (3WD) theory is effective to deal with imprecise and incomplete information in decision-making problem [15]. It originates from the probabilistic rough set (PRS) and the decision-theoretic rough set (DTRS) [12]. The boundary decision (temporary non-commitment) is the most distinctive feature of 3WD [8]. When there is not enough information to make a definite decision, non-commitment is a suitable choice, because decision mistake leads to higher costs.) Therefore, 3WD has received increasing attentions in decision making [2,10,20], conflict analysis [4,5], and fuzzy system [3,19]. 3WD-PRS and 3WD-DTRS are both effective and popular [11], but they are constructed from different perspectives. The former considers probability as the most important factor, while the latter is constructed based on the Bayesian risk [14,21].

Group decision-making (GD) method can integrate the wisdom of the different experts, which is effective to deal with the risk decision problem [1,6,22]. During recent years, GD method has induced heightened attentions in linguistic

Y. Sun et al. (Eds.): ChineseCSCW 2021, CCIS 1491, pp. 124–132, 2022.
https://doi.org/10.1007/978-981-19-4546-5_10

assessment [9,13], fuzzy system [7,17], etc. Based on different considerations and preferences, different experts tend to use diverse models and give different suggestions in the same problem. In decision-making problems, different people may tend to use different tools to evaluate decision risks. Some experts may prefer 3WD-PRS while some others adopt 3WD-DTRS. It will bring challenges to the consistency of decision-making, if different experts utilize diverse models based on their own considerations. However, there is few methods to combine these two kinds of models in the field of GD.

To eliminate the inconsistency in measurement, we propose a novel three-way group decision-making model. Considering experts may have different preferences, the proposed method aggregates probabilistic information and decision-theoretic loss information together. To achieve that, the 3WD with PRS model is analyzed from the perspective of decision risk and the probabilistic risk cost of different decisions are calculated. Then, the total risks of three decisions are computed, which is the mixture of probabilistic risk cost and Bayesian risk cost. The best option for the instance is the one with the least total risk. At last, an illustration example is utilized to demonstrate the efficiency of the proposed approach. The proposed method combines the 3WD-PRS and 3WD-DTRS from the perspective of decision risk.

2 Preliminary

Suppose the set of states is denoted as $\Omega = \{X, \neg X\}$. In the traditional models, a set of actions is given by $AC = \{a_P, a_N\}$. The positive decision a_P means classifying the sample into the positive region of X, i.e., POS(X). The negative decision a_N means the sample is believed to be in the negative region of X, i.e., NEG(X). 3WD offers another option: the boundary decision a_B, which indicates the sample is in the boundary region of X, i.e., BND(X) [16,18].

In 3WD-PRS, the decision thresholds ν and μ ($0 \leq \nu < \mu \leq 1$) are usually directly given by experts. Suppose that the conditional possibilities $Pr(X|[x])$ and $Pr(\neg X|[x])$, ($Pr(X|[x]) + Pr(\neg X|[x]) = 1$) have been computed. The thresholds μ and ν divide the whole probabilistic space into three regions, which are presented as:

$$\begin{aligned}
&(\text{P1})\ \text{POS}(X) = \{x \in U | P(X|[x]) \geq \mu\},\\
&(\text{B1})\ \text{BND}(X) = \{x \in U | \nu < P(X|[x]) < \mu\},\\
&(\text{N1})\ \text{NEG}(X) = \{x \in U | P(X|[x]) \leq \nu\}.
\end{aligned} \tag{1}$$

Based on cost-sensitive learning, different decisions lead to different costs. For instances, in category $\neg X$, the cost of decision a_P is denoted as λ_{PN}. Similarly, λ_{NN}, λ_{BN}, λ_{PP}, λ_{NP} and λ_{BP} are defined. By resorting the Bayesian risk theory, the expected losses of three decisions are presented as follows:

$$\begin{aligned}
R(a_P|[x]) &= \lambda_{PP} Pr(X|[x]) + \lambda_{PN} Pr(\neg X|[x]),\\
R(a_B|[x]) &= \lambda_{BP} Pr(X|[x]) + \lambda_{BN} Pr(\neg X|[x]),\\
R(a_N|[x]) &= \lambda_{NP} Pr(X|[x]) + \lambda_{NN} Pr(\neg X|[x]),
\end{aligned} \tag{2}$$

Table 1. The probabilistic thresholds of m experts

$E^{(1)}$	(μ, ν)	
	μ	ν
$e_1^{(1)}$	μ_1	ν_1
$e_2^{(1)}$	μ_2	ν_2
$\vdots$	$\vdots$	$\vdots$
$e_m^{(1)}$	μ_m	ν_m

Table 2. The cost information table for n experts

	$e_1^{(2)}$		$e_2^{(2)}$		$\ldots$	$e_n^{(2)}$	
	X	$\neg X$	X	$\neg X$	$\ldots$	X	$\neg X$
a_P	λ_{PP}^1	λ_{PN}^1	λ_{PP}^2	λ_{PN}^2	$\ldots$	λ_{PP}^n	λ_{PN}^n
a_B	λ_{BP}^1	λ_{BN}^1	λ_{BP}^2	λ_{BN}^2	$\ldots$	λ_{BP}^n	λ_{BN}^n
a_N	λ_{NP}^1	λ_{NN}^1	λ_{NP}^2	λ_{NN}^2	$\ldots$	λ_{NP}^n	λ_{NN}^n

where $R(a_k|[x]), k \in \{P, N, B\}$ is the Bayesian risk loss of an action a_k. The optimal result for the instance x can be put as below:

$$\phi^*(x) = \arg\min_{k\in\{P,N,B\}} R(a_k|[x]). \tag{3}$$

3 Problem Formulation

In group decision problems, different experts may have different considerations or preferences. Denote $E^{(1)} = \{e_1^{(1)}, e_2^{(1)}, \ldots, e_m^{(1)}\}$ as a set of m experts who prefer the 3WD-PRS. The probabilistic thresholds are supposed to be determined by the experts in $E^{(1)}$, which are tabulated in Table 1. The thresholds all satisfy that $0 \le \nu < \mu \le 1$. $E^{(2)} = \{e_1^{(2)}, e_2^{(2)}, \ldots, e_n^{(2)}\}$ is denoted as the set of n experts, who tend to utilize the 3WD-DTRS. Suppose the cost matrix has been given by the experts in $E^{(2)}$, which is tabulated in Table 2.

4 Model Construction

3WD-PRS evaluates the decision risk from the perspective of the probabilistic, while the 3WD-DTRS concentrates on the Bayesian decision risk. They are both effective decision-making methods. In group decision problems, some experts prefer 3WD-DTRS, while some others tend to adopt 3WD-PRS. The acquired decision rules may be different, which may cause a conflict. Therefore, a three-way group decision method is proposed to integrate the two kinds of models.

4.1 The Decision Risk Analysis of 3WD-PRS

If the conditional probability of sample x stratifies $Pr(X|[x]) < \mu$, the decision a_P will result in decision risk, because it is not correspondent with the decision rule in probabilistic rough set. Similarly, other decisions also might lead to risks, such as classifying x into $\text{BND}(X)$ when $Pr(X|[x]) \geq \mu$ or $Pr(X|[x]) \leq \nu$, or sorting an object into $\text{NEG}(X)$ when its conditional probability satisfies $Pr(X|[x]) > \nu$.

Denote $C(a_i|[x])$ as the decision risk of taking action $a_i, i \in \{P, N, B\}$. If the conditional probability of the object satisfies $Pr(X|[x]) \geq \mu$, the risk $C(a_P|[x]) = 0$. If the conditional probability satisfies $Pr(X|[x]) < \mu$, the risk $C(a_P|[x]) > 0$ because it violates the probabilistic decision rule. Moreover, if $Pr(X|[x])$ further decreases, the risk $C(a_P|[x])$ of taking action a_P will increase. The trends of $C(a_B|[x])$ and $C(a_N|[x])$ are similar to $C(a_P|[x])$. For simplicity, denote $p = Pr(X|[x])$. To sum up, the decision risk is related to the divergence between the conditional probability and the corresponding threshold.

The decision risk function expressed as follows:

$$\begin{aligned} C(a_P|[x]) &= \begin{cases} g(\mu - p), & p < \mu; \\ 0, & p \geq \mu; \end{cases} \\ C(a_B|[x]) &= \begin{cases} g(\nu - p), & p \leq \nu; \\ 0, & \nu < p < \mu; \\ g(p - \mu), & p \geq \mu; \end{cases} \\ C(a_N|[x]) &= \begin{cases} 0, & p \leq \nu; \\ g(p - \nu), & p > \nu. \end{cases} \end{aligned} \tag{4}$$

where $g(x)(x \in [0, 1])$ is a monotone non-decreasing function. For $i = 1, 2, \ldots, m$, by resorting thresholds (μ_i, ν_i) from expert $e_i^{(1)}$, the risk function of taking actions $a_k, (k \in \{P, N, B\})$ is denoted as $C^i(a_k|[x])$. Rely on Eq. (4), the total risk loss of all experts from $E^{(1)}$ can be defined as:

$$C^{St}(a_k|[x]) = C^1(a_k|[x]) + C^2(a_k|[x]) + \cdots + C^m(a_k|[x]), k \in \{P, N, B\}. \tag{5}$$

4.2 Total Risk in Group Decision Problems

In the last subsection, the 3WD-PRS is analyzed from the perspective of cost. By combining the risk loss function of PRS with DTRS, the decision information from all experts is utilized to make decision for instances.

For expert $e_j^{(2)}$, the expected loss of taking action $a_k, k \in \{P, N, B\}$ is denoted as $R^j(a_k|[x])(j = 1, 2, \ldots, n)$. According to the Bayesian risk decision theory, $R^j(a_P|[x])$, $R^j(a_B|[x])$ and $R^j(a_N|[x])$ are computed as:

$$R^j(a_k|[x]) = \lambda_{kP}^j p + \lambda_{kN}^j (1 - p), k \in \{P, N, B\}. \tag{6}$$

The total expected loss of all experts from $E^{(2)}$ can be expressed as follows:

$$R^{St}(a_k|[x]) = R^1(a_k|[x]) + R^2(a_k|[x]) + \cdots + R^n(a_k|[x]), k \in \{P, N, B\}. \tag{7}$$

Table 3. The probabilistic parameters given by experts

Parameter	Project					
	x_1	x_2	x_3	x_4	x_5	x_6
μ	0.81	0.78	0.61	0.74	0.50	0.80
ν	0.20	0.10	0.40	0.49	0.00	0.30

The total expected losses can be computed as follows:

$$R^T(a_k|[x]) = w * C^{St}(a_k|[x]) + (1-w) * R^{St}(a_k|[x]), k \in \{P, N, B\}. \quad (8)$$

where $w \in [0,1]$. When $w = 0$, it means all the experts choose the 3WD-DTRS. When $w = 1$, it means all the experts choose the 3WD-PRS.

$R^T(a_i|[x])$ balances the Bayesian loss and probabilistic loss. Therefore, we can utilize the decision information from all the experts to make decisions. According to the minimum risk rule, the decision rule for sample x is presented as below:

(P2) If $R^T(a_P|[x]) \leq R^T(a_B|[x])$ and $R^T(a_P|[x]) \leq R^T(a_N|[x])$, decide $x \in \text{POS}(X)$;
(B2) If $R^T(a_B|[x]) \leq R^T(a_P|[x])$ and $R^T(a_B|[x]) \leq R^T(a_N|[x])$, decide $x \in \text{BND}(X)$;
(N2) If $R^T(a_N|[x]) \leq R^T(a_P|[x])$ and $R^T(a_N|[x]) \leq R^T(a_B|[x])$, decide $x \in \text{NEG}(X)$.

5 Illustrative Example

The above discussions are verified by didactic examples about the investment project. An investment case may bring losses or gains. According to the market research and feasibility analysis, the decisions of investment manager will be investment, waiting or rejection. In these investment decisions, some experts consider that the probability of success is crucial, and tend to utilize 3WD-PRS. Some others take the possible profits or losses as the most important factor in investment. They prefer the 3WD-DTRS. Suppose we have a set of two states and a set of three actions for the investment.

The set of state is defined as $\Omega = \{X, \neg X\}$. X and $\neg X$ denote the project is profitable or not, correspondingly. The action set is $AC = \{a_P, a_B, a_N\}$. The three elements denote three actions: invest, wait and reject, respectively. 6 different projects (or investment plans) are denoted as $\{x_1, x_2, \ldots, x_6\}$. The probabilistic thresholds given by 2 experts are all shown in Table 3. For 3WD-DTRS, the decision costs for 6 different investment projects are given in Table 4.

Suppose there are two different project managers defined as i_1 and i_2. The probabilistic risk $g(x)(x \in [0,1])$ is assumed to be a linear function,

Table 4. The cost items given by expert using DTRS

	λ_{PP}	λ_{BP}	λ_{NP}	λ_{PN}	λ_{BN}	λ_{NN}
x_1	4	7	11	7	4.5	2
x_2	6	9	12	9	3	1.5
x_3	3	6	9	12	9	6
x_4	2	2	4	3	1	1
x_5	0	2	8	6	3	0
x_6	1	2	3.5	5	3	2

Table 5. The decision rules of the second investor i_1

p	Invest	Wait	Reject
0	$\emptyset$	$\emptyset$	$\{x_1, x_2, x_3, x_4, x_5, x_6\}$
0.1	$\emptyset$	$\emptyset$	$\{x_1, x_2, x_3, x_4, x_5, x_6\}$
0.2	$\emptyset$	$\{x_2\}$	$\{x_1, x_3, x_4, x_5, x_6\}$
0.3	$\emptyset$	$\{x_1, x_2, x_5\}$	$\{x_3, x_4, x_6\}$
0.4	$\emptyset$	$\{x_1, x_2, x_4, x_5, x_6\}$	$\{x_3\}$
0.5	$\emptyset$	$\{x_1, x_2, x_3, x_4, x_5, x_6\}$	$\emptyset$
0.6	$\{x_3, x_5\}$	$\{x_1, x_2, x_4, x_6\}$	$\emptyset$
0.7	$\{x_1, x_3, x_5\}$	$\{x_2, x_4, x_6\}$	$\emptyset$
0.8	$\{x_1, x_2, x_3, x_5, x_6\}$	$\{x_4\}$	$\emptyset$
0.9	$\{x_1, x_2, x_3, x_4, x_5, x_6\}$	$\emptyset$	$\emptyset$
1	$\{x_1, x_2, x_3, x_4, x_5, x_6\}$	$\emptyset$	$\emptyset$

i.e. $g(x) = kx$. For different projects, the linear coefficient is not supposed to be the same. For $e_1^{(1)}$, the coefficient set for 6 projects is $\{10, 15, 8, 4, 5, 4\}$. For $e_2^{(1)}$, the coefficient set is $\{40, 45, 15, 20, 40, 30\}$. Based on (P2) to (N2), one can make a reasonable decision for each investment project given the proper probability p in a real problem. When p ranging from 0 to 1 with step size 0.1, the decisions of the managers are tabulated in Table 5 and 6. The approach provides a reasonable way to solve the practical group decision problems.

Table 6. The decisions of the first investor i_2

p	Invest	Wait	Reject
0	$\emptyset$	$\emptyset$	$\{x_1, x_2, x_3, x_4, x_5, x_6\}$
0.1	$\emptyset$	$\{x_5\}$	$\{x_1, x_2, x_3, x_4, x_6\}$
0.2	$\emptyset$	$\{x_2, x_5\}$	$\{x_1, x_3, x_4, x_6\}$
0.3	$\emptyset$	$\{x_1, x_2, x_5\}$	$\{x_3, x_4, x_6\}$
0.4	$\emptyset$	$\{x_1, x_2, x_5, x_6\}$	$\{x_3, x_4\}$
0.5	$\emptyset$	$\{x_1, x_2, x_3, x_4, x_5, x_6\}$	$\emptyset$
0.6	$\{x_3, x_5\}$	$\{x_1, x_2, x_4, x_6\}$	$\emptyset$
0.7	$\{x_3, x_5\}$	$\{x_1, x_2, x_4, x_6\}$	$\emptyset$
0.8	$\{x_1, x_2, x_3, x_4, x_5, x_6\}$	$\emptyset$	$\emptyset$
0.9	$\{x_1, x_2, x_3, x_4, x_5, x_6\}$	$\emptyset$	$\emptyset$
1	$\{x_1, x_2, x_3, x_4, x_5, x_6\}$	$\emptyset$	$\emptyset$

6 Conclusion

3WD-PRS and 3WD-DTRS are both effective decision-making methods, but they are constructed from diverse perspectives. The assumed given information and decision rules are also different. In group decision-making problems, different experts prefer different models based on their own considerations and favored factors, which will lead to inconsistency. Therefore, it is necessary to formulate group decision model to integrate different types of information. By formulating the probabilistic risk cost function, a novel 3WD approach is developed to analyze the comprehensive decision risk in group decision-making problem. Then the best option for one sample is selected based on the minimum Bayesian risk decision rule. A case study demonstrates the feasibility of the proposed group decision-making approach. In the future, we will further explore the inconsistencies and conflicts in group decision-making problems.

Acknowledgement. This work is supported by the National Nature Science Foundation of China (Nos. 62106205, 62106135 and 61903346), the Guangdong Basic and Applied Basic Research Foundation (No. 2020A1515110434), the Young innovative talents project of colleges and universities in Guangdong Province (No. 2019WQNCX027), and the Fundamental Research Funds for the Central Universities (Nos. SWU119043 and SWU119063), the Youth project of science and technology research program of Chongqing Education Commission of China (No. KJQN202100207).

References

1. Brownlee, E., Zhu, H.B.: Group role assignment with busyness degree and cooperation and conflict factors. In: 2020 IEEE International Conference on Systems, Man, and Cybernetics (SMC). pp. 1479–1484 (2020)
2. Dai, D., Li, H., Jia, X., Zhou, X., Huang, B., Liang, S.: A co-training approach for sequential three-way decisions. Int. J. Mach. Learn. Cybernet. **11**(5), 1129–1139 (2020). https://doi.org/10.1007/s13042-020-01086-7
3. Huang, B., Li, H.X., Feng, G.F., Zhou, X.Z.: Dominance-based rough sets in multi-scale intuitionistic fuzzy decision tables. Appl. Math. Comput. **348**, 487–512 (2019)
4. Lang, G.M., Luo, J.F., Yao, Y.Y.: Three-way conflict analysis: A unification of models based on rough sets and formal concept analysis. Knowl.-Based Syst. **194**(2020)
5. Lang, G.M., Miao, D.Q., Fujita, H.: Three-way group conflict analysis based on Pythagorean fuzzy set theory. IEEE Trans. Fuzzy Syst. **28**(3), 447–461 (2020)
6. Liang, D.C., Pedrycz, W., Liu, D., Hu, P.: Three-way decisions based on decision-theoretic rough sets under linguistic assessment with the aid of group decision making. Appl. Soft Comput. **29**, 256–269 (2015)
7. Liu, P.D.: A weighted aggregation operators multi-attribute group decision-making method based on interval-valued trapezoidal fuzzy numbers. Exp. Syst. Appl. **38**(1), 1053–1060 (2011)
8. Luo, C., Li, T.R., Huang, Y.Y., Fujita, H.: Updating three-way decisions in incomplete multi-scale information systems. Inf. Sci. **476**, 274–289 (2019)
9. Pedrycz, W., Song, M.L.: A granulation of linguistic information in ATM decision-making problems. Inf. Fusion **17**, 93–101 (2014)
10. Qian, J., Liu, C.H., Miao, D.Q., Yue, X.D.: Sequential three-way decisions via multi-granularity. Inf. Sci. **507**, 606–629 (2020)
11. Qian, J., Liu, C.H., Yue, X.D.: Multigranulation sequential three-way decisions based on multiple thresholds. Int. J. Approx. Reason. **105**, 396–416 (2019)
12. Tan, A.H., Wu, W.Z., Qian, Y.H., Liang, J.Y., Chen, J.K., Li, J.J.: Intuitionistic fuzzy rough set-based granular structures and attribute subset selection. IEEE Trans. Fuzzy Syst. **27**(3), 527–539 (2019)
13. Xu, Z.S.: An automatic approach to reaching consensus in multiple attribute group decision making. Comput. Ind. Eng. **56**(4), 1369–1374 (2009)
14. Yao, J.T., Azam, N.: Web-based medical decision support systems for three-way medical decision making with game-theoretic rough sets. IEEE Trans. Fuzzy Syst. **23**(1), 3–15 (2015)
15. Yao, Y.Y.: Three-way decisions with probabilistic rough sets. Inf. Sci. **180**(3), 341–353 (2010)
16. Zhan, J.M., Jiang, H.B., Yao, Y.Y.: Three-way multi-attribute decision-making based on outranking relations. IEEE Trans. Fuzzy Syst. **29** (2020). https://doi.org/10.1109/TFUZZ.2020.3007423
17. Zhang, L., Zhan, J.M., Xu, Z.S., Alcantud, J.C.R.: Covering-based general multi-granulation intuitionistic fuzzy rough sets and corresponding applications to multi-attribute group decision-making. Inf. Sci. **494**, 114–140 (2019)
18. Zhang, L.B., Li, H.X., Zhou, X.Z., Huang, B.: Sequential three-way decision based on multi-granular autoencoder features. Inf. Sci. **507**, 630–643 (2020)
19. Zhang, Q.H., Yang, C.C., Wang, G.Y.: A sequential three-way decision model with intuitionistic fuzzy numbers. IEEE Trans. Syst. Man Cybernet. Syst. **51**(5), 2640–2652 (2021)

20. Zhang, X., Zhang, Q., Cheng, Y., Wang, G.: Optimal scale selection by integrating uncertainty and cost-sensitive learning in multi-scale decision tables. Int. J. Mach. Learn. Cybernet. **11**(5), 1095–1114 (2020). https://doi.org/10.1007/s13042-020-01101-x
21. Zhou, B., Yao, Y., Luo, J.: Cost-sensitive three-way email spam filtering. J. Intell. Inf. Syst. **42**(1), 19–45 (2013). https://doi.org/10.1007/s10844-013-0254-7
22. Zhu, H.B., Zhou, M.C.: Role-based collaboration and its kernel mechanisms. IEEE Trans. Syst. Man and Cybernet. Part C (Appl. Rev.) **36**(4), 578–589 (2006)

Fog Computing Federated Learning System Framework for Smart Healthcare

Yang Guo(✉), Xiaolan Xie, Chengyou Qin, and Yueyue Wang

College of Information Science and Engineering, Guilin University of Technology, Guilin 541006, Guangxi, China
237290696@qq.com

Abstract. With the continuous growth of medical big data, the use of remote cloud servers for big data analysis becomes more and more complicated and difficult, and it is susceptible to security and privacy issues. In response to the above problems, a fog computing federated learning system for smart healthcare is proposed. The system uses the iFogSim simulation platform to establish a smart fog computing layer between sensor nodes and remote cloud servers to improve data analysis and processing capabilities; at the same time, the federated learning idea is introduced to integrate the federation. Combine learning and fog computing to build a fog federation framework to ensure the privacy of data interaction. Aiming at the redundancy and high dimensionality of medical big data, principal component analysis and variance analysis are used for preprocessing; fully considering the disaster tolerance of the system, an improved election algorithm and detection mechanism are proposed to improve the security of data interaction. Ensure the normal operation of the system. In this way, the problem of "data islands" and resource imbalance in the medical field can be solved. Using real cardiovascular data sets and simulated data sets for testing, the experimental results show that the fog computing federated learning system has a significant improvement in network usage, system delay, system energy consumption, and system accuracy.

Keywords: Smart healthcare · Data islands · Federated learning · Fog computing · Privacy protection

1 Introduction

With the popularity of IoT devices in the medical field, various wearable body sensors and medical devices are used in medical services. These IoT devices can collect a large amount of medical data and use remote cloud servers to analyze the data to advance. The development of smart medical field. However, with the rapid increase in IoT devices, it also brings unprecedented amounts of data. According to the latest Cisco report, the Internet Data Center (IDC) estimates that by 2023, the number of connected devices worldwide will reach 48.9 billion. The average monthly data usage of a computer will be close to 60 GB. Therefore, only analyzing and processing a large amount of data through remote cloud servers will inevitably lead to serious network congestion and delay [1], which may cause serious medical accidents.

Y. Sun et al. (Eds.): ChineseCSCW 2021, CCIS 1491, pp. 133–147, 2022.
https://doi.org/10.1007/978-981-19-4546-5_11

Fog computing was proposed by Flavio Bonomi et al. [2] of CISCO in 2012. As an extension of cloud computing in edge networks, fog computing is not a substitute for cloud, but as an intermediate layer between cloud and the Internet of Things. Fog nodes can exist anywhere between the terminal device and the cloud, and provide users with more responsive services by using the computing and storage resources of routers, gateways, and small edge servers near the data source. Therefore, adding fog computing to the medical field can effectively reduce network delay and congestion, and scholars have also made great contributions to the development of fog computing and the Internet of Things in the medical field [3–6].

In order to improve the sustainable and high-quality intelligent medical services of the medical system and alleviate the increasing cost of manual services, the majority of researchers have introduced machine learning into the medical care system to provide patients with more intelligent and automated medical services [7–9].

In addition to considering the issues of network latency and service intelligence, security and privacy issues are also an aspect that must be paid attention to. With the proliferation of Internet of Things devices, the attack surface of data and information has been expanded. According to the results of Cisco's Global Network Trends Survey 2020, 43% of global network teams have prioritized improving network security capabilities. How to protect the large amount of sensitive data exposed during the transmission from source to fog to cloud is the primary issue we must consider. With the rapid rise of medical data and the continuous growth of medical databases, patient information, as privacy-sensitive data, must be guaranteed not to be leaked to reduce the risk of data being attacked and leaked. Therefore, it is urgent to build a credible and efficient smart medical system. The contributions of this article are as follows:

1. On the basis of the cloud-things of the previous smart medical architecture, the middle layer of smart fog computing is added, and a decentralized ring network topology is used in the fog computing layer. In order to improve the efficiency of resource allocation to fog nodes, the leader election method is used to select credible leaders for node resource management and allocation, so that fog nodes can dynamically allocate edge server resources to achieve load balancing effects, reduce latency, and improve efficiency.
2. In order to improve the disaster tolerance of the system, the heartbeat detection mechanism is introduced into the fog node ring network, and the neighbour node heartbeat detection mechanism is designed to ensure that the fog nodes participating in the calculation can operate normally when the system is running, and pass the leader immediately after failure Nodes adopt solutions to provide reliable computing services.
3. In order to solve the problem of "data islands" and realize the provision of intelligent medical services for hospitals with poor medical resources, federal machine learning [10] is introduced into the framework, and medical institutions with different geographical locations in a region are formed into a medical institution. federal. Participating institutions do not exchange data, only upload the gradients of local medical model training, and calculate the aggregation results by integrating the gradients provided by multiple parties and using the federal average algorithm, etc., and return them to the medical institutions. This not only ensures the privacy of data,

but also promotes the sharing of medical resources among various institutions, and provides effective help for exchanges and cooperation between different hospitals.

The rest of this article is organized as follows. The second section introduces the development status and related work of the smart medical field, the third section introduces the system architecture design, the fourth introduces the system mechanism, and the fifth section is the experimental design and result evaluation of the system, finally summarizes the article.

2 Related Work

At present, e-health is being popularized globally, and many smart medical systems (SHS) have been born. For example, Algarni A [11] proposed a three-tier smart medical system based on a human sensor layer, a cloud server layer, and a data analysis layer. Conduct a certain investigation and analysis of security attacks in the intelligent medical system. M. Fazio et al. [12] used the FIWARE cloud platform constructed by the European Commission to combine cloud computing and the Internet of Things to establish an electronic health remote patient monitoring system to help medical staff perform remote patient assistance work. However, with the continuous increase of patient data and the typical geographical differences between sensors and various mobile devices and back-end cloud servers, the drawbacks of mobile cloud computing (MCC) have gradually emerged, and a large amount of data has been continuously uploaded, resulting in cloud resources. Problems such as shortages, communication delays, network congestion, high energy consumption, etc. So in order to alleviate these problems, IBM and Nokia Siemens proposed the concept of mobile edge computing (MEC). MEC as a variant of MCC has also been applied to the field of smart medical care. Madukwe KJ et al. [13] proposed a patient-centric approach. The architecture for remote monitoring of patients includes a biosensor, a smart phone and an edge analysis platform for data analysis. By processing the data at its source, the data communication delay problem of cloud computing is eliminated. Awaisi K S et al. [14] proposed an efficient fog-based architecture for a healthcare system based on the Internet of Things, and proposed a user authentication method to prevent security vulnerabilities through identity management. Peng Shaoliang et al. [15] proposed an edge computing architecture for smart medical care, and the architecture built with edge computing provides a certain solution to the privacy protection problem of medical big data. With the development of artificial intelligence, machine learning and deep learning methods have also been applied to the medical field. Thaha M et al. [16] used edge computing, deep learning, Internet of Things and other methods to build the UbeHealth electronic health care system; Aujla GS, etc. [16, 17] designed a medical recommendation system (DLRS) based on deep learning. After dimensionality reduction of medical data, a classification scheme based on decision trees was used and convolutional neural networks were used to provide health advice to patients.

It can be seen from the above introduction that the field of smart medical care is constantly moving forward, but there are still certain problems worthy of our attention. First, the combination of smart medical care and fog computing lacks a certain disaster tolerance mechanism. The fog node exists at the edge of the network, and it is prone to network instability and loss of connection, which affects the normal operation of the system. Second, in order to ensure data security, a series of laws have been promulgated one after another, and the domestic legal system for data supervision is gradually becoming stricter and more comprehensive. The promulgation of various laws and regulations has strengthened the protection of data privacy, but it has also made the originally feasible data cooperation very difficult and the phenomenon of "data islands" has appeared. The protection of patients' privacy guarantees the safety of patients' personal sensitive information, but it also brings certain difficulties to medical research cooperation between medical institutions, especially for medical institutions with relatively biased geographical locations and lack of medical resources., The number of patients is significantly less than in other regions, and it is impossible to build smart healthcare through scarce medical data.

Therefore, in response to such problems, this paper designs a Smart fedrated fog-Health (SFFH) system that applies federated learning in fog computing. It is hoped that fog computing can reduce network latency and improve service efficiency, while combining machine learning and federated learning to improve The system's intelligence and privacy protection have further promoted medical cooperation between different regions and brought more convenience to people's daily lives.Mike's schoolbag.

3 System Overview

Today, the lack of medical resources has developed into a global problem. Moreover, a large number of medical staff and high-quality medical services are concentrated in central cities, which also brings about the problem of imbalance of medical resources. In order to promote the popularization of smart medical services, while ensuring that sensitive medical data is not leaked, the SFFH system is proposed. The system aims to establish a credible medical federation composed of multiple medical institutions with a regional unit. Through collaborative cooperation in the medical federation, a smart medical model can be jointly trained to solve the problem of geographic limitation of medical service quality. Medical institutions provide high-quality and efficient smart medical services. As shown in Fig. 1, the SFFH system includes a four-layer architecture: (1) Medical data collection layer (2) fog computing layer (3) federated server layer (4) cloud computing layer.

The medical data collection layer mainly completes the collection of patient medical data. Different medical institutions have different geographic locations. As shown in Fig. 1, medical institutions A, B, and C have different medical resources due to different geographic locations. A can represent a city-level hospital, B can represent a district-level hospital, and C can represent a county-level hospital. The medical conditions received by patients a, b, and c are also different. Medical institutions mainly collect patient data in two ways. The first is to configure body sensors, upload patient data through a sensor network, and perform real-time health monitoring. The second is to upload patient data through medical facilities. Medical facilities and body sensors can be used in a complementary manner. When medical facilities are in short supply, they can be replaced with lower-priced body sensors.

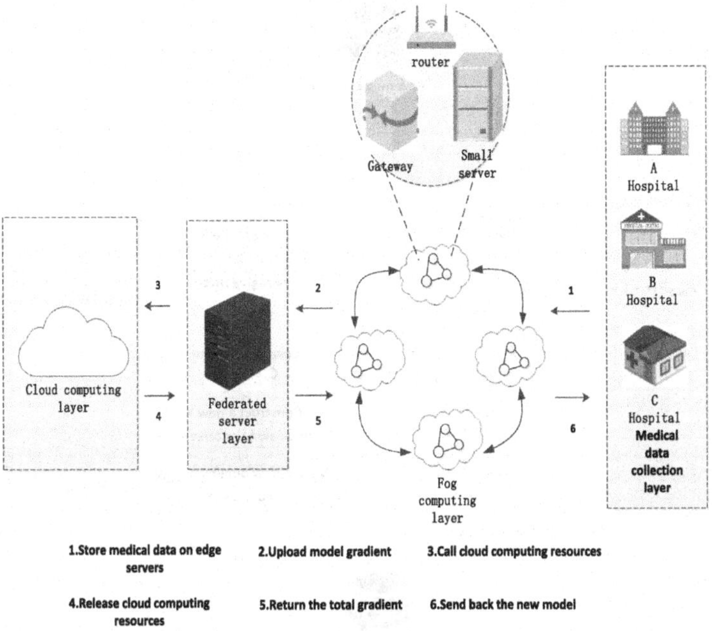

Fig. 1. SFFH architecture design

The fog computing layer deploys medical equipment, body sensors, routers, and small edge servers of medical institutions as local fog nodes to provide medical institutions with low-latency and fast-response services to ensure the emergency medical service needs of medical institutions. And we introduce cluster domain network technology in this layer to connect multiple fog nodes to form a cluster. The cluster domain structure facilitates offloading tasks to edge servers for different computing tasks to optimize the total task execution time. In this framework, the fog node resource is mainly responsible for two pieces of content: (1) As a participant in federated learning, use its own computing resources to help medical institutions complete local machine learning tasks. (2) Use the transmission function to communicate with the federated server Layer interaction model gradient.

The federated server layer receives the model gradients from the fog computing layer, aggregates the model gradients and averages the total gradients, and then returns the total gradients to each medical institution. The cloud computing layer has powerful computing power resources. When the federated server layer needs more powerful computing power, resources can be released to serve it.

4 System Mechanism

4.1 Data Preprocessing Mechanism

According to the case data collected by medical institutions, there are two problems: (1) High-dimensional case data can easily lead to heavy calculation load on the fog node

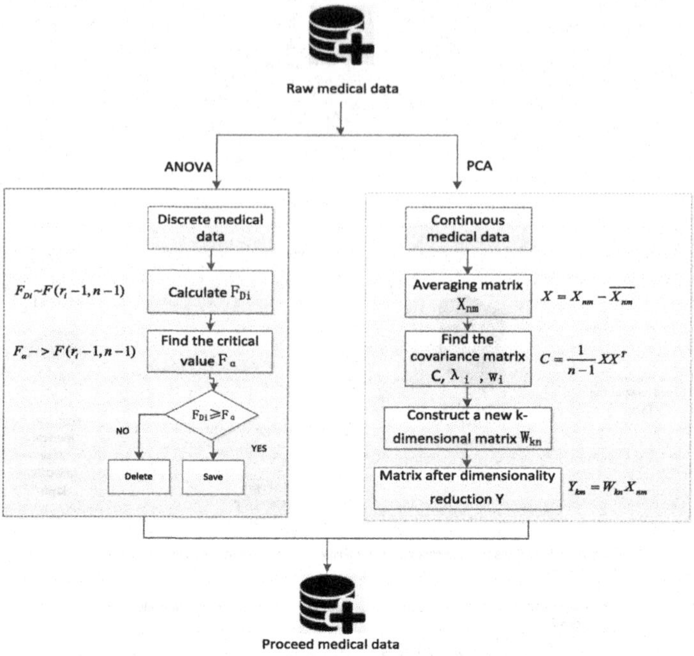

Fig. 2. Data preprocessing mechanism

(2) The heterogeneity of medical equipment leads to unstructured data, which makes data preprocessing become more difficult. Considering the redundancy of information, we implement dimensionality reduction to reduce the resource consumption of fog computing. This article uses principal component analysis (PCA) and analysis of variance (ANOVA) for the above two problems, as shown in Fig. 2. The specific description is as follows:

(1) We use PCA to analyze continuous health data. In many medical fields, case data is often continuous, but while multi-dimensional samples provide rich information, it also increases the workload of data processing. Therefore, we use principal component analysis to explain most of the variables in the original data with fewer variables. Assuming that the original medical data is n-dimensional features of m sample data, the target dimension is k ($k < n$), first do the mean value of the original data matrix, and then find the covariance matrix C, eigenvalueλ_i and eigenvector w_i, choose the largest Construct a new k-dimensional matrix W_{kn} from the k eigenvalues, and finally get the reduced-dimensional matrix.
(2) We use analysis of variance for discrete health data. Principal component analysis pays attention to the characteristics of obvious difference, and it is easy to ignore rare abnormal indicators. Suppose there are n discrete features, and the series of the first discrete feature is r_i. We first calculate the test statistics F_{Di}. Then, the significance level α is defined as the dimensionality reduction threshold, and Di will be retained only when $F_{Di} \geq F_\alpha(r_i - 1, n - 1)$.

4.2 Fog Federation Mechanism

In order to ensure the security of data, a series of laws have been promulgated one after another, and the domestic legal system for data supervision has gradually become more stringent and comprehensive. In this way, the privacy protection of data is strengthened, but it also makes it very difficult for the originally feasible data cooperation to become very difficult, and many enterprises have appeared in the phenomenon of "data islands". As sensitive information of patients, it is difficult to share medical data among medical institutions. However, in order to train an intelligent medical model, sufficient training data must be guaranteed. Therefore, Google proposed the concept of federated learning in 2016 [18, 19], has become the key technology to solve this problem.

Federated learning includes two models, one is a client-server model, and the other is a (peer-to-peer,P2P) network model. This article is chosen to ensure the stability of the system and reduce excessive computing operations. Use a client-server model. The client-server model is a distributed architecture. The architecture consists of two roles: the client and the central server. Each client trains the local data locally instead of uploading the server for centralized training, and the model is encrypted by means of encryption. Gradient exchange (does not violate data privacy laws and regulations), the central server updates and aggregates the gradient data uploaded by each client (for example, the federated average algorithm [10]), and returns the updated gradient to the client after the aggregation is completed. The end updates the local model according to the new gradient after aggregation. By repeating the above steps and continuously updating iteratively, the model can continuously move closer to the training model in the data set. In terms of performance, we allow the performance of the federated learning framework V_{FED} Slightly worse than the performance of the data set model V_{SUM}, that is to satisfy the formula (1), δ, Which is a non-negative number can be changed according to the situation.

$$V_{SUM} - V_{FED} < \delta \tag{1}$$

Figure 3 shows the fog federation description diagram of the framework. The terminal medical equipment is composed of smart sensors, medical equipment, and computer terminals of various medical institutions in different geographical locations to complete data collection. When the federated server initiates a notification of collaboration, each medical institution can choose whether to join the federated collaboration. When the agreement between each institution and the server is reached, the federation server can broadcast the initial model parameter 0 to the medical institutions participating in the collaboration (we assume here that the total number of medical institutions participating in the collaboration is K), and each medical institution starts to notify the fog server to mobilize the edge device Computing resources, the fog server mobilizes the resources of the fog node according to the request of the medical structure to start computing, storage, transmission and other services from the bottom up. After the local training task is completed, the fog server uploads the trained model parameters to the federated server. The federated server uses the weighted average algorithm shown in formula (2) to aggregate the model parameters and sends them back to the medical institution. The medical institution will use the updated model. The gradient calls the fog server resources to update the local model. By repeating this process, the local training model is continuously optimized.

$$\overline{\omega}_{t+1} \leftarrow \sum_{k=1}^{K} \frac{n_k}{n} \omega_{t=1}^{(k)} \tag{2}$$

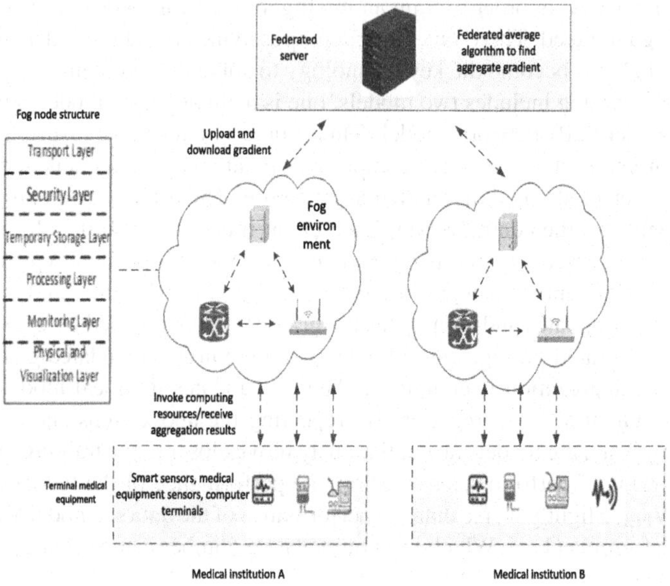

Fig. 3. Fog federation architecture

4.3 Fog Node Management Mechanism

As a part of cloud computing in the edge environment, fog computing has relatively weak communication capabilities, storage capabilities, and computing capabilities. Therefore, how to reasonably use fog resources in a fog environment, improve resource utilization, and enhance users' QOS constraints is The content that the smart framework must pay attention to. The fog computing model includes a centralized model and a decentralized model. This article uses a decentralized model. As shown in Fig. 4, the fog nodes in a cluster use a decentralized model. Compared with the centralized model, decentralized The transformation model enables the interconnection of fog nodes to facilitate gradient interaction as a participant in federated learning. However, in order to facilitate the allocation of fog resources, a management node still needs to be selected. Therefore, we use the leader election model to select the leader node (Leader) to effectively manage the fog node, realize the dynamic allocation of edge server resources by the fog node, realize the load balancing effect, and ensure that the task instances do not conflict.

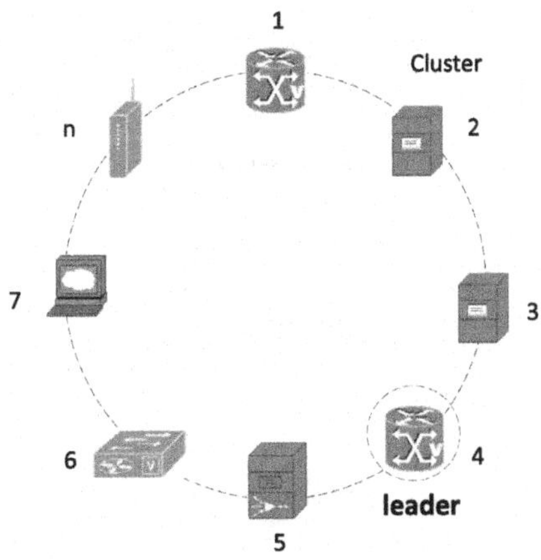

Fig. 4. Decentralized ring model

(1) Leader election mode-improved LCR ring election algorithm

This article uses a decentralized ring network structure, using an improved LCR ring election algorithm to select the leader node, that is, based on the original only one UID parameter for each node, a new parameter, namely trust score, is added. As shown in Fig. 5, in the ring network, each fog node has a unique identifier. We set it as UID and the node's Trust Points (TP). If a node has errors or unfriendly records in the system's operating records, its TP value will be reduced. At the beginning of the election, a node is randomly selected, and its UID is assigned to UID_send, its TP is assigned to TP_max, and then UID_send and TP_max are sent around the ring to the next node. The next node compares the received UID_send and TP_max with its own UID and TP, and first judges whether the UID value is the same, and judges whether it is the same node. Secondly, the TP is compared. The node with the higher TP value updates the TP_max value and sends the new UID_send and TP_max to the next node, and the node with the lower TP value continues to send the current UID_send and TP_max without change. When the UID_send received by a node is the same as its own UID, it indicates that the information of the node has circled the circle, and the node is appointed as the leader node.

(2) Heartbeat detection mechanism of neighboring nodes.

Regardless of whether it is a cloud computing model or a fog computing model, we must consider the disaster tolerance mechanism of the model and monitor the health of the fog nodes. When a node failure causes communication interruption, the leader node needs to re-allocate node resources to ensure communication Normal operation. Therefore, in order to ensure the normal operation of the framework service, we introduce a heartbeat mechanism into the cluster, because the ring network structure used is not suitable for the PUSH heartbeat detection model, that is, let each fog node actively send a heartbeat to the leader node at a set time interval Signal, so here is designed to use the neighborhood heartbeat detection mechanism. The fog node in operation sends heartbeat

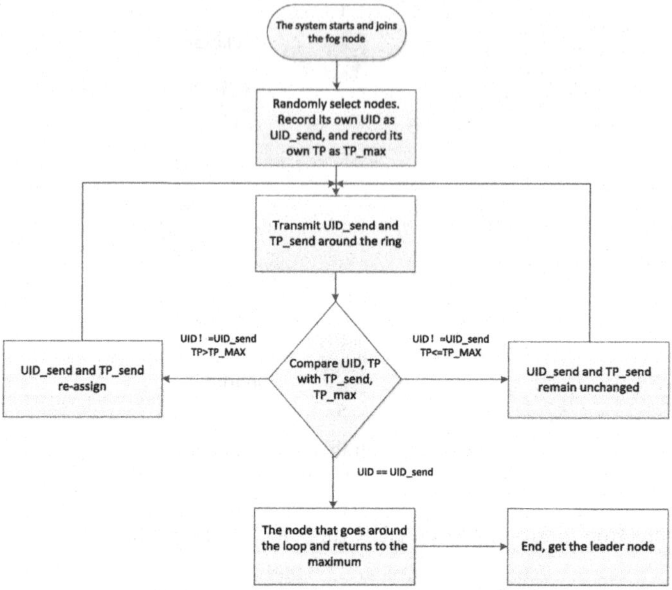

Fig. 5. Leader node election flowchart

signals to its left and right nodes at a certain time interval, and also receives heartbeat signals from the left and right nodes. Each fog node receives the two from the left and right. A heartbeat signal indicates that all fog nodes are operating normally. When the fog node is abnormal and does not send a signal to the left and right nodes, the left and right nodes will only receive one signal, so that the abnormal node can be accurately located, which is convenient for the leader. The node deletes the abnormal node and reallocates resources.

5 Experimental Design and Evaluation

The fog computing federal smart medical system proposed in this paper uses the iFogSim [20] platform for simulation experiments, using the Kaggle dataset Cardiovascular Disease dataset and the iFogsim simulator simulation dataset for testing. The real dataset contains Data records of 70,000 patients, with a total of 11 characteristics and one goal. In order to evaluate the effectiveness of the framework, we will simulate two experimental scenarios based on cloud and fog medical scenarios, and compare the two scenarios to prove the effectiveness of the fog framework.

In the framework, we will design four role entities: cloud server, federation server, fog server, and user sensor. The parameter configuration of the role entity is shown in Table 1. Three different medical institutions are simulated by setting three fog servers, and the topological results are shown in the system startup interface in Fig. 6.

Table 1. Entity parameter settings

	Cloud server	Federated server	Fog server	users
Mips	40000	2800	4000	1000
Ram	40000	4000	4000	1000
UpBw	40000	10000	10000	10000
DownBw	10000	10000	10000	270
Level	0	1	2	3
BusyPower	16 * 103	107.339	107.339	87.53
IdlePower	16 * 83.25	83.4333	83.4333	82.44

The experiment process is as follows:

(1) Topology mapping: Map the topological results to the code, and configure parameters for cloud servers, federated servers, and IoT devices, such as link speed, memory, Mips, power, etc.
(2) Define the sensor type: In this medical case, we integrated an electrocardiography (ECG) sensor [21] to generate ECG simulation data. ECG characteristics play an important role in the field of medical care and have been applied in many studies, which can help doctors monitor and treat many cardiovascular-related diseases more effectively.
(3) Configure the fog server strategy, build a ring network topology, and realize the leader election and neighbor node detection mechanism.
(4) Configure federated server parameters, including the number of nodes used in the process, the number of iterations, and the size of local batch processing.
(5) Add a controller and integrate all codes to run two types of environments.
(6) Calculate energy consumption, network usage and delay, etc.

Figures 7 and 8 are the running results of the fog scene and the cloud scene respectively. In the end, we will get the results of energy consumption, execution time, delay, and network usage. Based on the obtained experimental results, we will draw and evaluate them. We evaluate the effect of our experiment by using network usage, energy consumption,delay, and accuracy.

According to the topology shown in Fig. 6, each fog server is connected to three user devices, and the number of tasks 3 that each user device can perform is set to 10,000. We increased the number of user devices, increased experimental batches, from 3 user devices in turn, and compared multiple parameters of the experimental results to compare the results of the two systems.

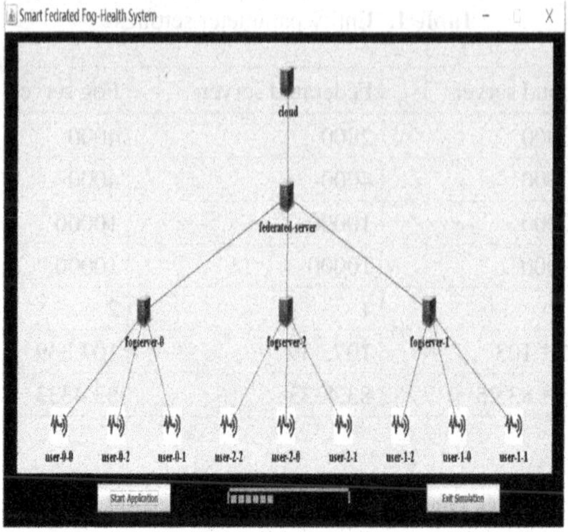

Fig. 6. System startup interface

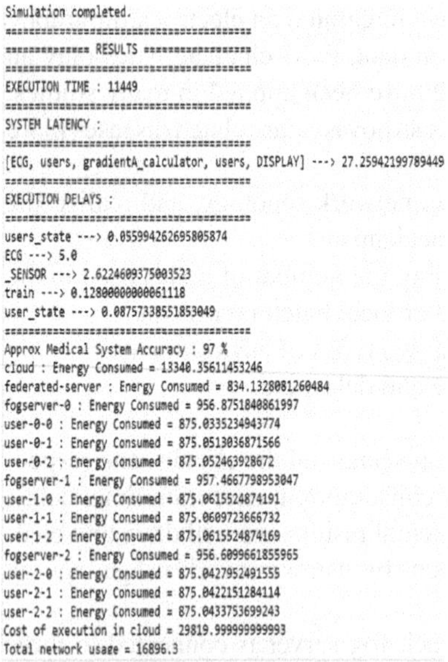

Fig. 7. Fog results

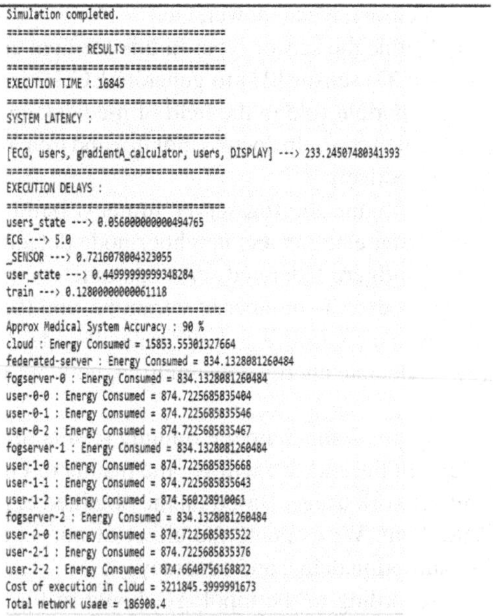

Fig. 8. Cloud results

Experimental evaluation:

(1) According to the comparison of network usage in Fig. 9, as the number of connected devices increases, the network load based on the cloud environment increases significantly, while the network load based on the fog environment increases slowly. But the changes in the two environments are linear, which shows the efficiency

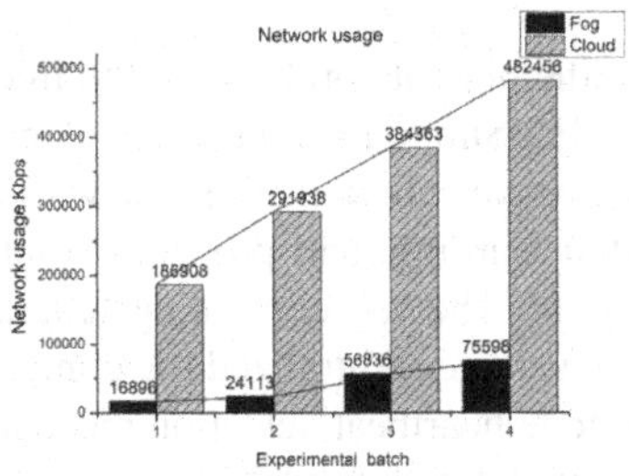

Fig. 9. Comparison of network usage

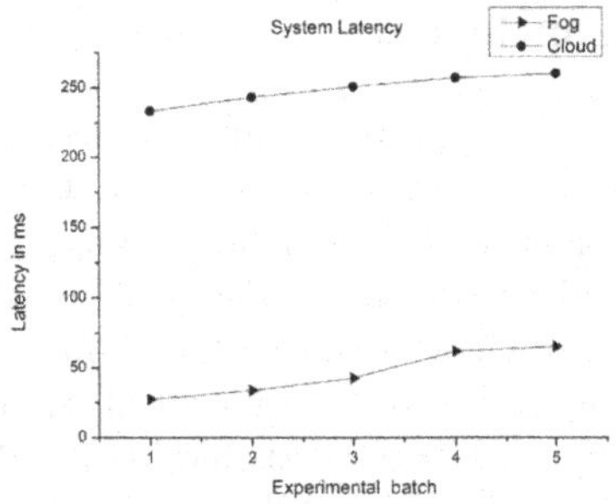

Fig. 10. System delay comparison

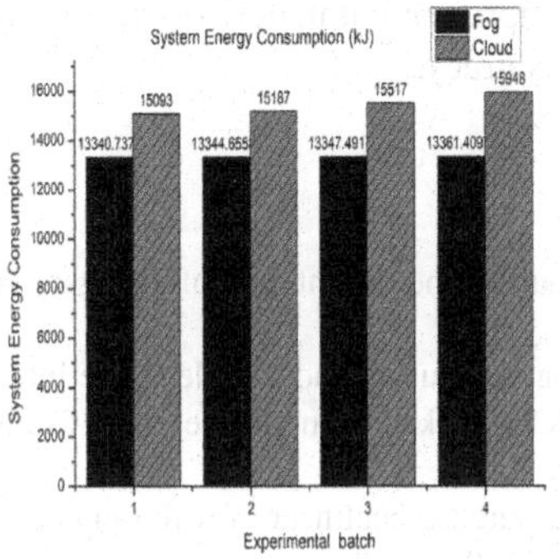

Fig. 11. System energy consumption

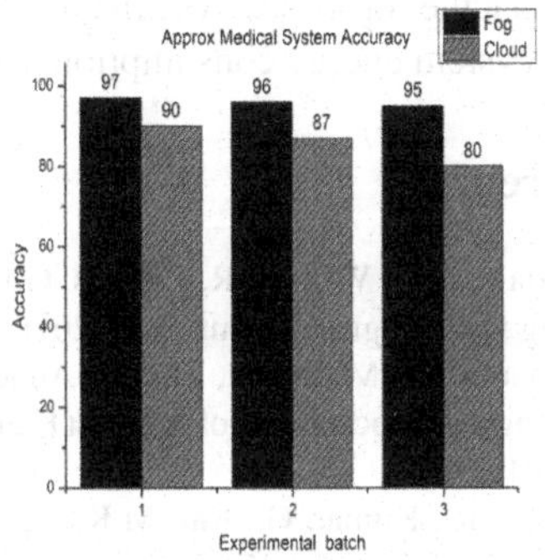

Fig. 12. Accuracy comparison

of data preprocessing. Even if we add a lot of gateways, the simulation can be performed in an acceptable time.

(2) According to the system delay line chart of Fig. 10, when the medical system is simulated in a fog environment, the system delay is significantly lower than that in the cloud environment. The delay of the fog-based system can reach 27 ms, and the delay of the cloud-based system is 233 ms. It can be seen that the response speed of the fog architecture in experimental calculations is much higher than that of the cloud architecture. The reduction of system latency not only reduces the response time of the system, but also protects the system's scalability issues in the face of big data. Therefore, when used for specific services, such as fog-based smart electronic health, smart home, and smart wireless systems, they all perform well.

(3) As shown in Fig. 11, in terms of system energy consumption, the fog-based system still consumes less energy than the cloud-based system. It is worth noting that after the increase in the number of devices, the upward trend is slower than that of the cloud-based system.

(4) Figure 12 shows the comparison of the accuracy of the medical system. The accuracy is calculated in real time through the processing response time of the system, and it is deducted from 100 based on the processing result.

6 Conclusion

Fog computing has become a powerful solution to the big data problem of the Internet of Things. This paper uses the simulation platform iFogSim to model the cloud and fog environment, focuses on how to implement smart medical care in institutions with poor medical resources, introduces the idea of federated learning, and proposes solutions to the problem of "data islands" in the medical field. The fog computing federation learning system for smart medical care is simulated, using decentralized fog computing topology, leader election algorithm, and neighbor node heartbeat detection mechanism to build an efficient, real-time, disaster-tolerant fog federation model. Provide reliable smart medical models for institutions with scarce medical resources, promote medical cooperation, and solve the problem of medical resource imbalance. Experimental results show that the fog-based system has a significant improvement in network usage, system delay, system energy consumption, and system accuracy.

References

1. Atlam, H.F., Walters, R.J., Wills, G.B.: Fog computing and the Internet of Things: a review. Big Data Cogn. Comput. **2**(2) (2018)
2. Bonomi, F., Milito, R., Zhu, J., Addepalli, S.: Fog computing and its role in the internet of things In: Proceedings of the First Edition of the MCC Workshop on Mobile Cloud Computing (2012)
3. Saha, R., Kumar, G., Rai, M.K., et al.: Privacy ensured e-healthcare for fog-enhanced IoT based applications. IEEE Access **7**, 44536–44543(2019)
4. Mutlag, A.A., Abd Ghani, M.K., Arunkumar, N., et al.: Enabling technologies for fog computing in healthcare IoT systems. Future Gener. Comput. Syst. **90**, 62–78(2018)
5. Akshat, et al.: A smart healthcare monitoring system using smartphone interface. In: 2018 4th International Conference on Devices, Circuits and Systems (ICDCS), pp. 228–231(2018)
6. Qiu, J., Liang, X., Shetty, S. Bowden, D.: Towards secure and smart healthcare in smart cities using blockchain. In: 2018 IEEE International Smart Cities Conference (ISC2), pp. 1–4 (2018)
7. Chkirbene, Z., Mohamed, A., Erbad, A., Guizani, M.: Smart edge healthcare data sharing system. In: 2020 International Wireless Communications and Mobile Computing (IWCMC), pp. 577–582 (2020)
8. Nalinipriya, G., Priyadarshini, P., Puja, S.S., Raja Rajeshwari, K.: BayMax: a smart healthcare system provide services to millennials using machine learning technique. In: 2019 International Conference on Smart Structures and Systems (ICSSS), pp. 1–5 (2019)
9. Newaz, A.I., Sikder, A.K., Rahman, M.A., Uluagac, A.S.: HealthGuard: a machine learning-based security framework for smart healthcare systems. In: 2019 Sixth International Conference on Social Networks Analysis, Management and Security (SNAMS), pp. 389–396 (2019)
10. McMahan, B., Moore, E., Ramage, D., et al.: Communication-efficient learning of deep networks from decentralized data. In: Artificial Intelligence and Statistics, pp. 1273–1282 (2017)
11. Algarni, A.: A survey and classification of security and privacy research in smart healthcare systems. IEEE Access **7**, 101879–101894 (2019)
12. Fazio, M., Celesti, A., Márquez, F.G., Glikson, A., Villari, M.: Exploiting the FIWARE cloud platform to develop a remote patient monitoring system. In: 2015 IEEE Symposium on Computers and Communication (ISCC), pp. 264–270 (2015)

13. Madukwe, K.J., Ezika, I.J.F., Iloanusi, O.N.: Leveraging edge analysis for Internet of Things based healthcare solutions. In: 2017 IEEE 3rd International Conference on Electro-Technology for National Development (NIGERCON), pp. 720–725 (2017)
14. Awaisi, K.S., Hussain, S., Ahmed, M., et al.: Leveraging IoT and fog computing in healthcare systems. IEEE Internet Things Magaz. **3**(2), 52–56 (2020)
15. Peng, S., Bai, L., Wang, L., et al.: Trusted edge computing for smart medical care. Telecommun. Sci. 56–63 (2020)
16. Muhammed, T., Mehmood, R., Albeshri, A., Katib, I.: UbeHealth: a personalized ubiquitous cloud and edge-enabled networked healthcare system for smart cities. IEEE Access **6**, 32258–32285 (2018)
17. Aujla, G.S., et al.: DLRS: deep learning-based recommender system for smart healthcare ecosystem. In: ICC 2019 - 2019 IEEE International Conference on Communications (ICC), pp. 1–6 (2019)
18. Konen, J., Mcmahan, H.B., Ramage, D., et al.: Federated Optimization: Distributed Machine Learning for On-Device Intelligence (2016)
19. Konen, J., Mcmahan, H.B., Yu, F.X., et al.: Federated Learning: Strategies for Improving Communication Efficiency (2016)
20. Gupta, H., Vahid Dastjerdi, A., Ghosh, S.K., et al.: iFogSim: a toolkit for modeling and simulation of resource management techniques in the Internet of Things, Edge and Fog computing environments. Software Pract. Exper. **47**(9), 1275–1296 (2017)
21. Akrivopoulos, O., Chatzigiannakis, I., Tselios, C., et al.: On the deployment of healthcare applications over fog computing infrastructure. In: 2017 IEEE 41st Annual Computer Software and Applications Conference (COMPSAC), pp. 288–293 (2017)

Research on Temporal Workflow Task Assignment Strategy

Tianhong Xiong, Yang Xu, Yang Yu(✉), and Dingjun Lou

School of Computer Science and Engineering, Sun Yat-sen University, Guangzhou, China
yuy@mail.sysu.edu.cn

Abstract. Work efficiency and stability of QoS (quality of service) are required in real-word business process. The purpose of this paper is to propose a feasible task assignment strategy based-on temporal workflow, aiming to improve the on-time completion rate in the multi-process and multi-case scenarios to enhance the flexibility of the workflow system. To achieve this purpose, we represent the needed temporal constraints used in the assignment, including both static and dynamic properties. Differing from the best-effort scheduling, our strategy recognize the priority of work items, assign the work item into the various level queue and select the optimal resource giving a global view of the temporal constraints of three dimensions (process, task and resource). During the assignment, we make some efforts like reserve the flexible and critical resource for the task that may be delayed in the future. We evaluate our strategy on YAWL by comparing with other three popular scheduling algorithms (Random Assignment, Fastest Complete Assignment and the Shortest Queue Assignment), which shows that our strategy performs more effective and stable.

Keywords: Temporal workflow · Workflow · Task assignment · Temporal constraint

1 Introduction

Time is a component that can't be ignored during the management and execution of business processes in real life. There are many excellent reviews in the literature dealing with the related problems. [1] introduces time into workflow as a dimension and presents a concept temporal workflow. [2] revisits a serious works of workflow time management and summarize main topics of this field. Moreover, time is also associated with work efficiency and service quality which has become the focus of public attention. The research on temporal conceptual modeling, planning, scheduling or assignment of workflow has made great progress especially in best-effort scheduling to improve average completion time of each case.

However, chasing the minimum average completion time can't meet the stability of QoS probably. Several researchers have proposed some creative and meaningful ideals as inspiration for the temporal task assignment problem, especially resource selection criteria, such as task priority [3, 4], resource competence [5, 6], preference [5], workload,

Y. Sun et al. (Eds.): ChineseCSCW 2021, CCIS 1491, pp. 148–163, 2022.
https://doi.org/10.1007/978-981-19-4546-5_12

resource time availability [5, 25], etc. What they mainly focus on during the scheduling is the process dimension aiming at finishing each task as soon as possible. In the current study, the deadline of a case is often defined by the task duration time and agents finish their work list according to "first come, first served" rule without distinguishing the time requirement of different cases. Furthermore, the scenario discussed or experimented in most research is usually one process with multiple instances while multi-process and multi-cases with resource competition is much closer to real-life business scenario.

Therefore, we will argue the following aspects in this work.

Firstly, it must also be mentioned that stability is an important indicator of QoS so we use on-time completion rate as our evaluation criterion in our experiments. [7] mentions on-time completion rate becomes one of the most important QoS dimensions that pervade the design, development, and running of business process management systems in data flow. Some works [8, 9] use the success rate of process instances or time-targeted that is similar to on-time completion rate in this work.

Secondly, every case has its life cycle and varies from different emergency level. That is, each case may be normal, slack or urgent. For instance, given a process, obtaining a passport, which contains several procedures (tasks), common approaches only concern about time constraint of each task and tend to make best-effort scheduling on each task to finish the case as soon as possible. It is likely to lead to congestion with finite resources. Besides, in our daily life we often determine a case deadline first and then arrange the tasks instead of in reverse order. Most research define case deadline by the deadline of its task and ignore the independent life cycle of the case. Much research describes temporal constraints on task or activities in detail while few research pays attention to giving a global view of the temporal constraints of three dimensions (process, task and resource) during the task assignment. In this work, we try to explain the task assignment strategy by considering temporal constraints for three dimensions of the workflow model.

Thirdly, there generally exist parallel working processes in enterprises, thus having resource conflicts among them [10]. So multi-process and multi-case are an indispensable consideration of the task assignment in the man-involved business process. In Sect. 4, we validate our strategy under a multi-process and multi-case circumstance.

Therefore, we aim to propose a flexible strategy based on temporal constraints for different dimensions of the man-involved business process in order to increase the on-time completion rate in this work. We achieve this by answering the following research questions:

1. How to represent the needed temporal constraints used in the assignment, including both static and dynamic properties?
2. How to choose a resource to assign that cases can be finished on time as many as possible in order to increase the on-time completion rate in the multi-process and multi-case scenarios?
3. How to make some efforts to avoid the time violation during the assignment?

The rest of this paper is organized as follows. Section 2 defines the needed temporal constraints used in the strategy. Section 3 explains the full strategy we proposed using the former temporal constraints. Section 4 shows experiments of different situations comparing with typical algorithms. In Sect. 5, we provide an overview of prior studies closely related to our work. Finally, Sect. 6 concludes the paper with a summary and outlook in Sect. 6.

2 Research Problem and Temporal Constraints

Workflow model has three dimensions: process dimension, case dimension and task dimension [11]. In this section, we make a description of our problem and give the definitions of temporal constraints for three dimensions of workflow model, which will be used in the following sections.

2.1 Problem Description

Given a group of process instances $\boldsymbol{I} = \{\boldsymbol{case_1}, \boldsymbol{case_2}, \boldsymbol{case_3}, \ldots, \boldsymbol{case_n}\}$, whose arrival obeys a certain probability distribution. $\boldsymbol{I}$ may come from different processes. For $\mathbf{case}_i$, it has a series of work items that are created one by one during the running cases and each work item will be assigned to one participant to execute using task assignment strategy π. When $\mathbf{case}_i$ is finished, it turns into a finished case σ_i. The temporal constraints become one of the dimensions in temporal workflow model, which leads to the requirement of presenting, calculating and refreshing temporal information.

$$\boldsymbol{case_i} \xrightarrow{\pi} \boldsymbol{\sigma_i}$$

Just as the questions we put forward in Sect. 1, the main problem of this paper is to consider the temporal constraints for different dimensions of workflow model, the priority of work items and the capabilities and history properties of resources synthetically and assign each work item to a certain participant, aiming to increase the on-time completion rate of the workflow system.

Note that we pay attention the individual and historical properties of resources (i.e., capability, preference, experience, etc.) and not take too much social properties like collaborations into considerations in this work.

2.2 Temporal Constraints

Process, case, task and resource all have temporal constraints in temporal workflow. A task is reflected as a work item or activity in the running case. We use work item to denote the specific task in the following sections.

Based on the actual observation in practice and a review of the workflow literature, temporal constraints for three dimensions of workflow model are proposed as follows. We use parts of definitions in related works [17, 18, 20] as basis of our concepts and pay more attention to the real scenario to enrich our definitions.

3 Assignment Strategy

To solve the problem mentioned above, a new work item scheduling strategy is needed. It should consider the dependency of tasks, the dependency of resources and the availability of resources and finally reach a best result.

In the workflow system, work items will be created after starting a case. In order to use the strategy in this article, the strategy can be split into two steps. Recognize the priority of the work items and decide which one to assign using the two-level feedback queue triggering algorithm. Then, select a local optimal resource from the candidates to finish the work item, considering the dependency of resources and work items as well as the availability of resources.

The outline of this strategy is shown in Fig. 1. We'll walk through these steps in detail in the upcoming section.

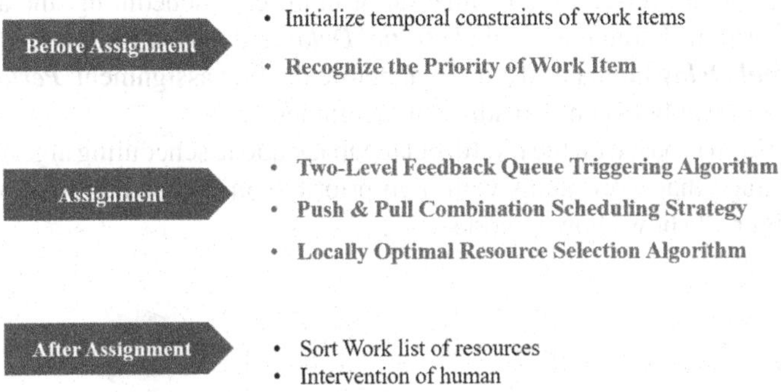

Fig. 1. Outline of the strategy

3.1 Recognize the Priority of Work Item

A work item is an instance of a task in a case. Here, the priority of work item depends on the criticality of task. Some works [3, 4] have mentioned the priority or the preference for the task during the scheduling. Tasks can be categorized into ***critical task*** and ***normal tasks*** in this work according to whether it's on the critical path and whether it's timeout in the past.

Definition 1. (*Critical Task*) Critical task includes critical path task and once-timeout task. Any task that is included in critical path is called ***critical path task*** [26, 27]. Task that has ever expired the latest start timer or the latest finish timer is called ***once-timeout task***.

Definition 2. (*Normal Task*) A task in this work is either a critical task or a normal task.

In addition to whether it's a critical task, the extent of delay will affect the priority of work items. Therefore, we add a delay rate property to work item. The definition is as follows.

Definition 3. (*Delay Rate*) For any work item w, its delay rate is:

$$dr(w) = \begin{cases} 100(t - w.rst)/(w.lst - w.rst),\ t < w.lst \\ 100,\ t \geq w.lst \end{cases} \quad (1)$$

where ***w.rst*** is regular start time, ***w.lst*** is latest start time, ***w.et*** is execute time and ***t*** is current time. As a result, ***dr(w)*** < 0 means that the work item ***w*** begins earlier than expected. On the contrary, 0 < ***dr(w)*** < 100 means that the work item ***w*** is late than expected. A work item has higher priority if it is critical and it has a higher delay rate.

3.2 Two-Level Feedback Queue Triggering Algorithm

We design the Two-level Feedback Queue Triggering Algorithm to handle the work items in the waiting queue. Based on the situation of multi-case scheduling, the assignment algorithm is periodic. Parameters include ***Initial Delay*** and ***Period Interval***, which can be changed. ***Initial Delay*** indicates the interval before the first assignment. ***Period Interval*** indicates the interval between two adjacent assignments.

This algorithm is based on the multilevel feedback queue scheduling algorithm which has the advantage that work items with high priority can be handled first even if they reach late. Figure 2 shows how it works.

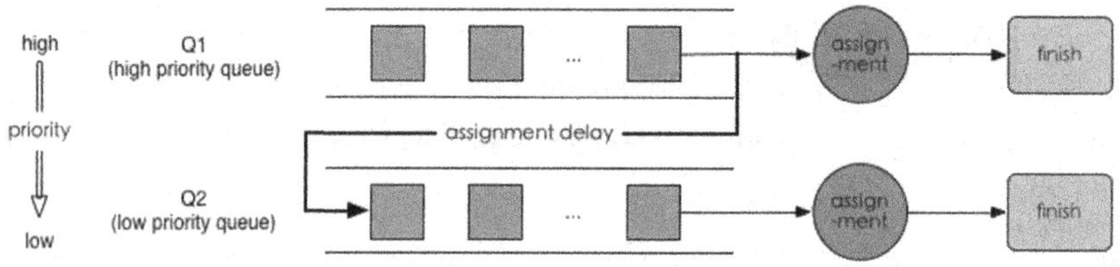

Fig. 2. System assignment queue

The algorithm firstly adds the newly created work items into ***Q1***, which is the high priority queue. Then it triggers the task dispatcher and starts a assignment periodically. During the assignment, the work items in ***Q1*** will be assigned front the head of ***Q1*** one by one while putting the unqualified work items into ***Q2***, the lower priority queue. For the waiting items in ***Q1***, an item is qualified means it satisfies at least one of the following conditions:

1) $\mathbf{0 < \mathit{dr}(w_i) < 100}$
2) the work item is critical and $\mathbf{\mathit{dr}(w_i) \leq 100}$ while there are non-critical or non-flexible resources in resource candidates set. (The definition of critical resource and flexible resource are shown later in Sect. 3.3)

Algorithm 3–1 is the pseudo code for the Two-level Feedback Queue Triggering Algorithm.

3.3 Locally Optimal Resource Selection Algorithm

Resources are divided into ***critical resource***, ***flexible resource*** and ***normal resource*** in our paper.

Definition 4. (***Critical Resource***) Any resource whose work list contains allocated task or start task with delay rate larger than 80% is a critical resource.

Definition 5. (***Flexible Resource***) Any resource with multiple roles is a flexible resource.

Definition 6. (***Normal Resource***) Any resource that is neither a critical resource nor a flexible resource is a normal resource.

In order to select a local optimal resource, we define a formula to calculate its average capability.

Definition 7. (***Average Capability of Resource***) For any resource *r*, its average capability for task *t* is:

$$a_r = f(r.workload, r.historicalExecuteTime(t)) \tag{2}$$

where ***r.workload*** is the current of ***r***, ***r.historicalExecuteTime*** is ***r***'s histroical average execute time of task ***t*** and function ***f*** is:

$$f = \begin{cases} -historicalExecutionTime(t), \ workload = 0 \\ 0.7 * workload + 0.3 * historicalExecutionTime(t), \ workload \neq 0 \end{cases} \tag{3}$$

During the running of workflow system, it maintains a ***Task-Role (TR) Denpendency Graph*** in which depics dependency between task and task, dependency between task and role and dependency between role and resource. Using the strategy in Sect. 3.4, we can get a resource candidate set $R(w_i)$ from TR graph.

An example of graph is shown in Fig. 3. Task 1 (***t1***) and task 2 (***t2***) are executed by the participants of role 1 (***r1***) while task 3 (***t3***) corresponds with role 2 (***r2***). Participant 1, 2, 6 (***p1, p2, p6***) belongs to ***r1*** and participant 3, 4, 5 (***p3, p4, p5***) belongs to r2. Note that ***p3*** is flexible resource. For instance, if $R(w_1)$ can not contain flexible resource then $R(w_1) = \{p1, p2, p6\}$.

Given a work item ***w*** and its resouce candidates set $R(w)$, we can calculate the capability of each resource using formula (2). For resource set $R_1(w) = \{r|r \in R(w), a_r < 0\}$, choose the participant with largest a_r if $R_1(w)$ is not empty. Else, for resource set $R_2(w) = \{r|r \in R(w), a_r = 0$, choose the participant randomly if $R_2(w)$ is not empty. If both $R_1(w)$ and $R_2(w)$ are empty, choose the pariticipant with smallest a_r as the optimal resource. Algorithm 3–1 is the pseudo code for the Local Optimal Resource Selection Algorithm.

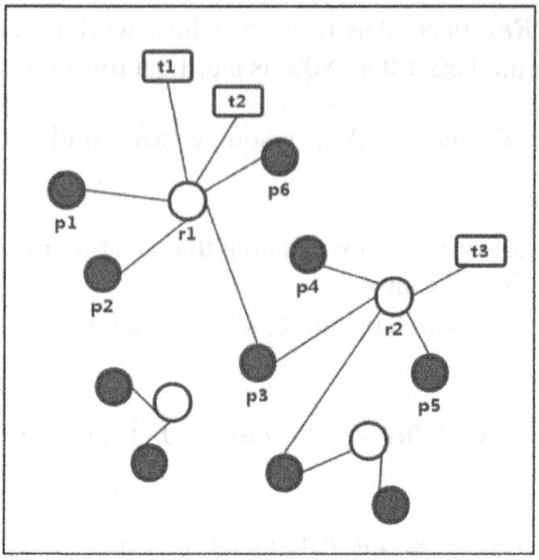

Fig. 3. A task-role graph example

Algorithm 3-1 (Local) Optimal Resource Selection Algorithm

Input :
workitem: work item to be assigned
PL: resource candidates list,
PL = R(workitem)

Output :
best_performer: best resource to execute the work item

Algorithm Description :

```
sublist1, sublist2 ← new Array()
best_performer ← None

for each p in PL:
   if a_p < 0:
      sublist1.add(p);
   else if a_p = 0:
      sublist2.add(p);

if sublist1 is not empty:
   best_performer = chooseMaxAbility(sublist1, workitem);
else if sublist2 is not empty:
   best_perfomer = chooseRandom(sublist2, workitem);
else
   best_perfomer = chooseMinAbility(PL, workitem);

return best_performer
```

3.4 Push & Pull Combination Scheduling Strategy

Task Dispatcher will start scheduling work items after the Two-level Feedback Queue Triggering Algorithm picks one to assign. While scheduling, the dispatcher chooses the participant to assign the work items from the resource candidates set $R(w_i)$. This section introduces how to get $R(w_i)$ and the corresponding scheduling strategy in different situations.

1) For a normal work item w_i:

   a) If, $dr(\mathbf{w}_i) \leq \mathbf{0}$, w_i are in a slack status. Then the work item will be offered to all participants who belong to the specified role and waiting for a participant to accept it, which is to pull work items.
   b) The critical resources and the flexible resources will be excluded from $\mathbf{R}(\mathbf{w}_i)$ first. They are reserved for the future critical work items. Then participants that are estimated not to be able to start or finish work item in time will be excluded from $\mathbf{R}(\mathbf{w}_i)$. And it finally returns a new candidate set $\mathbf{R}(\mathbf{w}_i)'$ from which the dispatcher chooses a participant if $\mathbf{0} < dr(\mathbf{w}_i) < \mathbf{100}$ The dispatcher chooses participant from the original $\mathbf{R}(\mathbf{w}_i)$ if $\mathbf{R}(\mathbf{w}_i)'$ is empty. After choosing the participant, dispatcher makes it accept the work item directly, which is to push work items.

2) For a critical work item w_i:

   a) The critical resources will be excluded from $\mathbf{R}(\mathbf{w}_i)$ first and then participants that are estimated not to be able to start or finish work item in time will be excluded. It returns a new set $\mathbf{R}(\mathbf{w}_i)'$ for dispatcher to choose a participant. The dispatcher chooses a participant from the original $\mathbf{R}(\mathbf{w}_i)$ if $\mathbf{R}(\mathbf{w}_i)'$ is empty. Dispatcher makes the participant accept the work item immediately if $dr(\mathbf{w}_i) \leq \mathbf{0}$. It's to push work items.
   b) Else it makes the participant start work item at once.

To evaluate whether a participant can start before latest start time of work item or finish before latest finish time, the algorithm calculates the start timepoint and finish timepoint according to the known availability of participants and execute time of the work item.

4 Experiments

4.1 Evaluation Criterion

We use the ***on-time completion rate*** (***OCR***) as a criterion to evaluate the performance of different algorithms. The set of completed cases in one test case is denoted by ***CCase.*** For any case $\sigma \in$ ***CCase,*** the ***OCR*** of σ is the ratio of the number of completed cases on time n_σ to the number of total cases N. $CCT(\sigma)$ is the processing time of case σ and $\sigma.cvt$ is the valid time of case σ.

$$OCR = \frac{n_\sigma}{N}, CCT(\sigma) \leq \sigma.cvt$$

4.2 Experiments Plan

OCR is used as the evaluation criterion explicitly in [5] but it is used in the field of data flow. [6] mentions the success rate of process instances but it doesn't take the dependency between resource role and task into consideration. Most of other similar strategies are experimented in different specific environment or without engineering experiments. As a result, it's hard to compare with the results of other methods and we plan to make comparisons with three typical scheduling algorithms.

We evaluate our strategy on YAWL system (a workflow system based on Java) by comparing with other three algorithms of YAWL: Random Assignment (RA), Fastest Complete Assignment (FCA) and the Shortest Queue Assignment (SQA).

Firstly, we design a resource organizational model shown as Fig. 4 taking real energy company as a reference for our experiments. It contains the department, position, role and capacity for each participant. There are 5 customers, 6 customer-service staff, 6 maintenance directors, 6 maintenance managers, 6 junior engineers, 5 scheduling clerks, 5 designers and 7 senior engineers; 2 purchasing directors, 2 purchasing managers, 2 inventory analysts, 2 purchasing analysts and 5 buyers. And we set 4 participants hold two positions to be flexible resources in some time. They are set between senior engineer and maintenance director, senior engineer and maintenance manager, purchasing manager and maintenance manager.

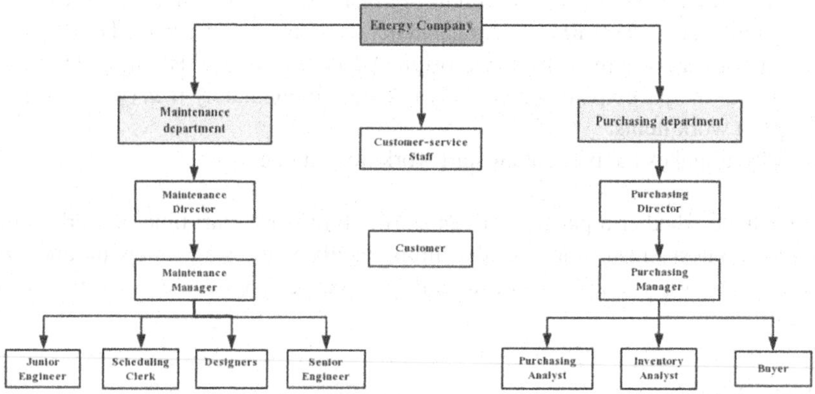

Fig. 4. Resource organizational model

Secondly, we use 2 processes for our experiments. Process 1, ***maintenance***, is showed as Fig. 5, which contains six workflow control mode (i.e. Sequence, Parallel Split, Synchronization, Multiple Choice and Synchronizing Merge). The effective time of the case is 3 days or 72 h and each task will be processed for 2 h. Process 2, ***purchasing***, is showed as Fig. 6. The main purpose of the process design is to compete with the tasks of the maintenance process, and to analyze the ability of the 4 strategies to handle the bottleneck resources.

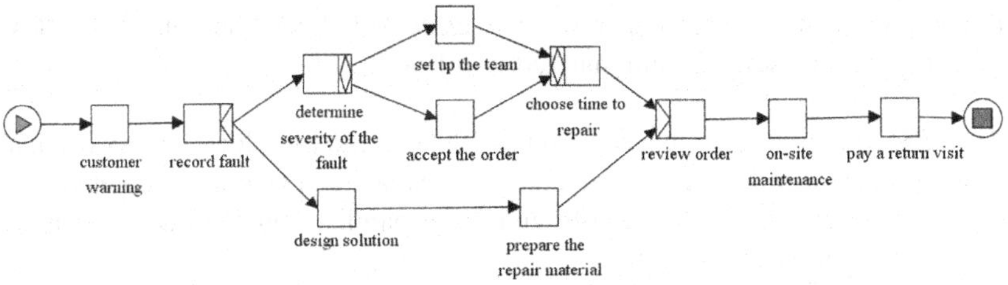

Fig. 5. Maintenance process

Fig. 6. Purchasing process

Time constraints of human resources are set as: work days are from Monday to Friday and work hours a day are from 9:00 to 12:00 and from 14:00 to 18:00. To get more convincing results, two flexible participants are set private holidays from 9:00 to 12:00 for one day and another two are set extra work from 18:00 to 21:00 for two days. Besides, our processes may arrive through the public holidays for 3 days. We use coefficients, from 0.5–1.0, multiplying by task expected execution time (the result will be within the task max and min execution time) to simulate different participants with different capacities. We launch 10, 26 and 50 cases (50% of Maintenance Process and 50% of Purchasing Process) respectively in two hours, which corresponds to light, medium and heavy load with the limited resources. In the case of each load, the historical records of each participant are generated with the progress of the experiment. Then, we simulate 10 times for each strategy and take the mean value as the result shown as Table 1.

Table 1. Experiments results

Case number	New strategy	RA	FCA	SQA
10	100% (10/10)	31% (3.1/10)	63% (6.3/10)	80% (8/10)
25	95.6% (22.8/25)	28.1% (7.3/26)	50% (13/26)	50.8% (13.2/26)
50	44.8% (22.4/50)	12.6% (3.4/50)	25.6% (12.8/50)	22.6% (11.3/50)

4.3 Results and Observation

The results of experiments are shown as follows. Table 2, 3 and Fig. 7, 8 show the experiment results of different load, with the X axis showing the order and the Y axis the number of completed cases. Table 1 shows the overall results, it can be inferred that the RA is unstable because it chooses the resources randomly. Both FCA and SQA perform better than RA and our strategy performs more effectively than other three regardless of light or high load. Reasons are summarized as follows:

1) The ***ORC*** of our strategy reaches around 100% in the light load with coordinating the temporal constraints, historical record and capacity of resources. Later cases can refer to the previous timeout record and the capability values of each resource to learn from failure experiences.
2) When system load is high, the ***OCR*** of our strategy is imperfect. Because of a huge gap between the number of work items and resources, the large workload of resources causes the waiting time of latter work items will be longer and resources cannot be released in time so that many cases can't be finished before their valid time. According to the results, the maximum capacity of this organization may be around 25 cases.
3) We can find a tendency that the results are often lower at first, then increased and finally steady in three situations because at first there is no historical records as a reference for the strategy. With the progress of the experiment, it can use these records to select a more appropriate resource.

In conclusion, we argue that our strategy can improve the OCR significantly in comparison with the other three typical strategies.

Table 2. Results of light load

	1	2	3	4	5	6	7	8	9	10	Average
RA	2	5	0	3	0	2	1	5	5	8	3.1
FCA	7	7	8	6	6	6	7	6	5	5	6.3
SQA	9	8	8	8	8	7	8	7	9	8	8
New strategy	8	8	9	10	10	10	10	10	10	10	10

Table 3. Results of heavy load

	1	2	3	4	5	6	7	8	9	10	Average
RA	0	2	4	3	0	4	1	11	9	0	3.4
FCA	15	13	10	11	13	13	13	13	14	13	12.8
SQA	12	15	10	14	12	10	12	9	11	8	11.3
New strategy	23	26	24	20	22	24	23	19	22	21	22.4

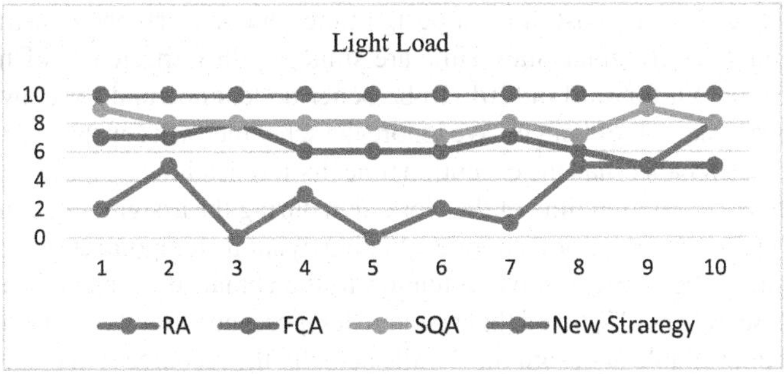

Fig. 7. Results of light load

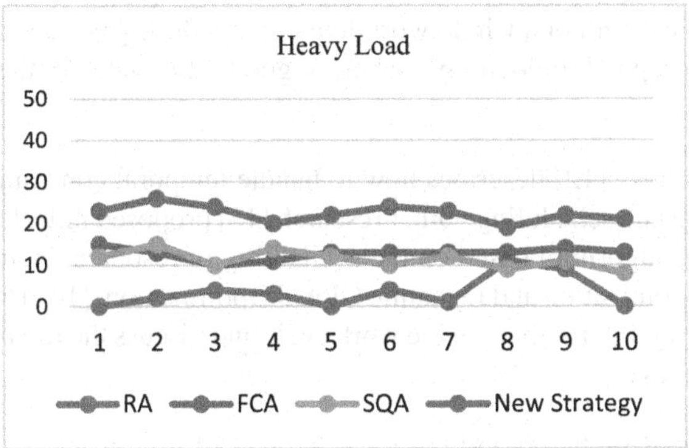

Fig. 8. Results of heavy load

5 Related Works

Managing temporal requirements is important for business processes management. This has led to a number of researches on temporal workflow in many aspects. Many proposals have been put forward to address various aspects of temporal workflow including temporal information representation and scheduling. In this section, we first introduce temporal constraints modeling, then discuss the task assignment strategies from three aspects: selection criteria, resource behavior and intervention strategies.

Temporal Constraints Modeling. The topic of the management of temporal aspects in the definition of workflows has been only considered by the literature recently. Eder et al. [17–19] has made a serious works of the temporal properties. [17] specify the temporal properties for a task (namely, "activity node"), considering the duration, and the earliest finish and latest finish times, and extend the model by adding the best and the worst case of execution to cope with possible conditional branches [18]. The earliest and latest finish times of activities adopted in this work is proposed in [18]. More deeply, a technique for modeling, checking and enforcing temporal constraints in workflow processes containing conditionally executed activities is proposed in [19]. Combi et al. [20] defined a taxonomy of temporal constraints including task constraints, schedule-task constraints and inter-task constraints at design time. In our work, the constraints, Task Max Execution Time, Regular Start Time are similar with ExpectedTaskDuration and MaxTaskDuration put forward in [20]. To be better understood and for convenience of our strategy, we make some changes. We ignore the schedule-task constraints in our work because it is much smaller than the execution time. Its soft deadline and firm deadline also inspire us to make escalation time of the work item during the assignment to monitor the execution. [21] presents an approach for evaluating dynamic temporal constraints during process execution. Few research pay attention to the actual life especially in resource dimension. Researchers [25] noted that resource temporal constraints can be divided into available and unavailable at design time while actually the resource will change his time temporarily during the execution of the case. In this work we discriminate the resource availability and the static or dynamic constraints. [22] discussed how to manage six time constraints in the critical path of a workflow *process* and proposed two algorithms to determine the critical path of a whole workflow process during build time and run time.

All these conceptual modelling makes a good reference to the planning and scheduling works.

Assignment Strategies. [12] describes how to handle temporal constraints in workflow model for planning and scheduling. Other research [13] proposed three kinds of business process scheduling algorithm based on the availability of resource, including Min Gap, Dynamic Local Optimization and Dynamic Global Optimization. [14–16] notice the task selecting algorithm for participant in the work cycle and discuss the temporal constraints during the scheduling.

Selection Criteria. Role-based and the measurement of the resource are the common *thoughts* when selecting a resource. [25] proposes a temporal workflow scheduler which considers most temporalities affecting task assignment policies. The time constraints of resources in [25] are divided into availability and unavailability and in their algorithm, they consider the selection criteria in the following order: role, effective availability, number of unavailabilities, presence at task start and task completion time. Using task preference, [3] designs a mechanism to provide dynamic resource support in multi-instance contexts, making the study more comprehensive and realistic. [23] proposed a multi-criteria assessment model (i.e., capabilities, social relationships and task relationships) capable of evaluating the suitability of individual workers. And in our work, we also consider the workers with different skills and expertise may share the same role in an organization while what we emphasize is their time contributions to the whole system.

Resource Behavior Measurement. [5, 6] tried to measure resource behavior based on process mining. Presents an approach of measuring resource behavior from four important perspectives, i.e., preference, availability, competence and cooperation. Aalst et al. [6] present a framework for analyzing and evaluating resource behavior through mining event logs with new categories: skills, utilization, preference, productivity and collaboration. Some other research also has measure the resource capacity by statistical method. In our work, we focus on the experience of the resource.

Intervention Strategies. Some approaches provide flexibility solutions in order to adapt a process that may potentially violate the case life cycle. We preserve the flexible resource for urgent cases and in this work we haven't discuss the intervention strategies in detail. In our experiment, if a work item is timeout, the managers will get the alarm and make decisions for compensation. [21] mentioned some design time and runtime intervention strategies. For the same purpose, [24] proposes a framework, 3D (detect, decide, do) approach for deadline escalation from four perspectives: process, task, data and resource, which extends the ECA (event-condition-action) rules approach.

6 Conclusion and Future Works

In this paper, we propose a task assignment strategy considering of temporal constraints for case, task and resource dimension of the workflow model at the same time and pay attention to the on-time completion rate of man-involved process, which may meet the needs of task assignment in actual life and increase the flexibility of the work flow system. Besides, our experimental results show that our strategy can be more effective in the situation of multi-process and multi-case.

What's more, the social and psychological attributes (such as work pressure, collaborations, etc.) of human resources can also directly affect the efficiency of business processes. The task assignment strategy of this paper focuses on the individual attributes (such as capability and historical experience) of resources. In future work, the flexibility of human resources can be taken into consideration in the improved algorithm. How to compare with similar methods persuasively is also a problem worth considering in the future.

Acknowledgements. This work was Supported by the NSFC-Guangdong Joint Fund Project under Grant No.U20A6003; the National Natural Science Foundation of China (NSFC) under Grant No.61972427; the National Key Research and Development Program of China under Grant No.2020YFB1707603; the Research Foundation of Science and Technology Plan Project in Guangdong Province under Grant No.2020A0505100030.

References

1. Yu, Y., Tang, Y., Liang, L., et al.: Temporal extension of workflow meta-model and its application. In: The 8th International Conference on Computer Supported Cooperative Work in Design, Proceedings, vol. 2, pp. 293–297. IEEE (2004)
2. Eder, J., Panagos, E., Rabinovich, M.: Workflow time management revisited. In: Bubenko, J., Krogstie, J., Pastor, O., Pernici, B., Rolland, C., Sølvberg, A. (eds.) Seminal Contributions to Information Systems Engineering, pp. 207–213. Springer, Heidelberg (2013). https://doi.org/10.1007/978-3-642-36926-1_16
3. Zhao, W., Liu, H., Dai, W., et al.: An entropy-based clustering ensemble method to support resource allocation in business process management. Knowl. Inf. Syst. **48**(2), 305–330 (2016)
4. Byun, E.K., Kee, Y.S., Kim, J.S., et al.: BTS: Resource capacity estimate for time-targeted science workflows. J. Parallel Distrib. Comput. **71**(6), 848–862 (2011)

5. Huang, Z., Lu, X., Duan, H.: Resource behavior measure and application in business process management. Expert Syst. Appl. **39**(7), 6458–6468 (2012)
6. Pika, A., Leyer, M., Wynn, M.T., et al.: Mining resource profiles from event logs. ACM Trans. Manage. Inf. Syst. **8**(1), 1 (2017)
7. Liu, X., Wang, D., Yuan, D., et al.: Workflow temporal verification for monitoring parallel business processes. J. Softw. Evol. Process **28**(4), 286–302 (2016)
8. Xu, J., Liu, C., Zhao, X., et al.: Resource management for business process scheduling in the presence of availability constraints. ACM Trans. Manag. Inf. Syst. **7**(3), 9 (2016)
9. Jung, I.Y., Chang, S.J.: Selective task scheduling for time-targeted workflow execution on cloud. High PERFORMANCE Computing and Communications, 2014 IEEE, International Symposium on Cyberspace Safety and Security, 2014 IEEE, International Conference on Embedded Software and System, pp. 1055-1059. IEEE (2015)
10. Yanhua, D.U.: Real-time model checking of dynamic temporal consistency for multi-process of workflow. J. Mech. Eng. **46**(2), 185–191 (2010)
11. van der Aalst, W.M.P., Desel, J., Oberweis, A.: Business Process Management Models. Techniques and Empirical Studies (2000)
12. Zhang, W., Wang, L., Wang, N., et al.: Handling temporal constraints in workflow model for planning and scheduling. In: 2010 2nd International Asia Conference on Informatics in Control, Automation and Robotics (CAR), vol. 2, pp. 467–471. IEEE (2010)
13. Xu, J., Liu, C., Zhao, X., Yongchareon, S.: Business process scheduling with resource availability constraints. In: Meersman, R., Dillon, T., Herrero, P. (eds.) OTM 2010. LNCS, vol. 6426, pp. 419–427. Springer, Heidelberg (2010). https://doi.org/10.1007/978-3-642-16934-2_30
14. Yang, H., et al.: A task selecting algorithm for personal schedules in workflow systems. In: Huang, Z., Liu, C., He, Jing, Huang, G. (eds.) WISE 2013. LNCS, vol. 8182, pp. 133–143. Springer, Heidelberg (2014). https://doi.org/10.1007/978-3-642-54370-8_12
15. Senkul, P., Toroslu, I.H.: An architecture for workflow scheduling under resource allocation constraints. Inf. Syst. **30**(5), 399–422 (2005)
16. Baggio, G., Wainer, J., Ellis, C.: Applying scheduling techniques to minimize the number of late jobs in workflow systems. In: Proceedings of the 2004 ACM Symposium on Applied Computing, pp. 1396–1403. ACM (2004)
17. Eder, J., Panagos, E., Rabinovich, M.: Time constraints in workflow systems. In: Bubenko, J., Krogstie, J., Pastor, O., Pernici, B., Rolland, C., Sølvberg, A. (eds.) International Conference on Advanced Information Systems Engineering, pp. 286–300. Springer, Heidelberg (1999). https://doi.org/10.1007/978-3-642-36926-1_15
18. Eder, J., Panagos, E., Pozewaunig, H., et al.: Time Management in Workflow Systems. BIS 1999, pp. 265–280. Springer, London (1999)
19. Eder, J., Gruber, W., Panagos, E.: Temporal modeling of workflows with conditional execution paths. In: Ibrahim, M., Küng, J., Revell, N. (eds.) International Conference on Database and Expert Systems Applications, pp. 243–253. SpringerHeidelberg (2000). https://doi.org/10.1007/3-540-44469-6_23
20. Combi, C., Pozzi, G.. Temporal conceptual modelling of workflows. In: Song, IY., Liddle, S.W., Ling, TW., Scheuermann, P. (eds.) International Conference on Conceptual Modeling. LNCS, vol. 2813, pp. 59–76. Springer, Heidelberg (2003). https://doi.org/10.1007/978-3-540-39648-2_8
21. Wondoh, J., Grossmann, G., Stumptner, M.: Dynamic temporal constraints in business processes. In: Proceedings of the Australasian Computer Science Week Multiconference, p. 34. ACM (2017)
22. Li, W., Fan, Y.: A time management method in workflow management system. In: Workshops at the Grid and Pervasive Computing Conference, pp. 3–10, GPC 2009. IEEE, (2009)

23. Shen, M., Tzeng, G.H., Liu, D.R.: Multi-criteria task assignment in workflow management systems. In: Proceedings of the 36th Annual Hawaii International Conference on System Sciences, 9 pp. IEEE (2003)
24. van der Aalst, W.M.P., Rosemann, M., Dumas, M.: Deadline-based escalation in process-aware information systems. Decis. Support Syst. **43**(2), 492–511 (2007)
25. Carlo, C., Pozzi, G.: Task scheduling for a temporal workflow management system. In: Thirteenth International Symposium on Temporal Representation and Reasoning, pp. 61–68. TIME 2006. IEEE (2006)
26. Kelley, J.E.: The critical-path method: resources planning and scheduling. J.f.muth G.l.thompson Indust. Schedul. **37**(11), 108–111 (1963)
27. Kelley, J.E.: Critical-path planning and scheduling: mathematical basis. Oper. Res. **9**(3), 296–320 (1961)

Intrusion Detection Algorithm of Industrial Control System Based on Improved Bloom Filter

Yanru Chen[1], Yuanyuan Zhang[1], Youlin Lin[1], Xinmao Huang[2], Bin Xing[3], Ping Long[3], Yang Li[4], and Liangyin Chen[1(✉)]

[1] Sichuan University, Chengdu, Sichuan, China
chenliangyin@scu.edu.cn
[2] Sichuan GreatWall Computer System Company Limited, Luzhou, Sichuan, China
[3] Chongqing Innovation Center of Industrial Big-Data Co., Ltd., Chongqing, China
[4] Institute of Southwestern Communication, Chengdu, Sichuan, China

Abstract. With the upgrading of industrial manufacturing, industrial control system (ICS) is gradually changing from closed island to open, and it adopts network automation. Meantime, this change brings many risks and constant threats to ICS security. ICS is widely used in many fields closely related to people's livelihood. Once the ICS in these fields is threatened, it may cause very serious consequences. As an active system security protection technology, intrusion detection technology can effectively make up for the shortcomings of firewall and other traditional security protection technologies. It is considered as the second security defense line of ICS. In view of limited resources of ICS equipment, there are no more resources to store the intrusion feature database and carry out complex calculation, this paper proposes an intrusion detection algorithm of ICS based on improved bloom filter (IDA-ICS-IBF). The experimental results show that the IDA-ICS-IBF algorithm has low memory occupation, fast detection speed, and can be applied to ICS environment.

Keywords: Intrusion detection · Industrial control system · Bloom filter · Misuse-based

1 Introduction

Nowadays, all the industrial powers worldwide are trying their best to build industrial Internet, and based on industrial Internet platform, they are exploring new models for the transformation of industrial manufacturing industry to intelligent and digital. At present, several major industrial countries focusing on this transformation have not released relevant security documents, but they all emphasize the importance of ICS and infrastructure security [1]. ICS is widely used in many fields closely related to people's livelihood, such as natural gas, electric power, petroleum and petrochemical, civil aviation, urban rail transit, urban water supply and heating, etc. [2, 3]. Once ICS is threatened, it may cause serious consequences, and even threaten national security.

In 2010, Iran's nuclear power plant was attacked by the "Stuxnet" virus, resulting in the leakage of radioactive materials [4]. In 2011, the urban water supply system of

Y. Sun et al. (Eds.): ChineseCSCW 2021, CCIS 1491, pp. 164–175, 2022.
https://doi.org/10.1007/978-981-19-4546-5_13

Illinois was invaded, resulting in water supply pump. "Duqu" virus collected intelligence data from ICS manufacturers. "Conficker" virus attacked control system of Daqing Petrochemical refinery. In 2017, "WannaCry" virus ravaged the world.

However, "Stuxnet" virus has really attracted attention from many countries for ICS safety, and some research results were obtained. For example, the US published relevant guidance literature and standards, and established several key ICS labs, such as Sandia National Lab. and Idaho National Lab. NIST has also issued safety standards in ICS field, which are constantly updated with change of safety situation.

Traditional intrusion detection has many problems, such as incompatibility of protocol type, complexity of computation, long detection time and large memory occupation. Therefore, traditional intrusion detection cannot be directly applied to ICS. To sum up, it is an urgent problem to design and develop an intrusion detection system which can effectively ensure ICS security. In order to overcome the above problems, this paper proposes an intrusion detection algorithm for ICS based on improved bloom filter (IDA-ICS-IBF). The main contributions are as follows:

1. This paper applied bloom filter to intrusion detection in ICS. Bloom filter is a kind of data structure with high space efficiency. Its bottom layer is composed of a bit array, so memory occupation of Bloom filter is very small, which can meet requirements of limited storage resources of ICS. Moreover, the query of Bloom filter is realized by a set of hash operations, and its detection speed is faster than string matching and other algorithms, and the hash operation is relatively simple, so bloom filter is also suitable for high real-time and computing resource limited environment.
2. In order to further improve the query speed of Bloom filter, this paper uses one hash operation and a set of bit operations instead of multiple hash operations in standard bloom filter to implement bloom filter.

The rest of the paper is arranged in the following manner: Sect. 2 presents the review of literature, Sect. 3 presents the methods and materials used by the current study, Sect. 4 contains the results and analysis, and Sect. 5 concludes the paper.

2 Related Work

Intrusion detection of ICS is mainly divided into four categories: misuse-based (also known as signature-based, feature-based) detection, anomaly-based detection, specification-based detection, and mixed detection [5]. The misused intrusion detection technology [6, 7] firstly analyze and summarize attack behaviors and features, and then establish attack feature database [8]. Finally, the matching technology is adopted to match and compare the data to be detected, so as to detect the intrusion behavior. Misuse-based intrusion detection has a high detection rate for known intrusion types [9], but it can't do anything for unknown intrusion behaviors [10]. Anomaly-based intrusion detection firstly establishes database of normal behavior, and then matches the behavior to be detected to find abnormal behavior data. It can detect unknown attacks [9, 11], but its detection rate is low. The hybrid intrusion detection method is the combination of the above methods, which can detect new attacks and ensure the detection rate at a high level, and further improve detection effect. Although there are many researches implementing intrusion detection based on misuse and anomaly, considering limited resources and high real-time features of ICS, it is difficult to apply any of them, and impossible to use them at the same time. Therefore, this paper deeply discusses intrusion detection technology based on misuse, and proposes an intrusion detection algorithm based on misuse.

In 2018, Farhad et al. [12] studied how hackers use sensor channels to send malicious commands to ICS, and proposed to use these sensing channel information to generate corresponding intrusion features. However, it is only carried out in experimental environment, and only realizes detection of some injection attacks, and does not explain detection effects. Menachem [13] proposed a distributed intrusion detection framework based on intrusion feature in IOT field in 2020. Considering poor computing power, limited memory size and storage space of IOT devices, they proposed a string matching technology framework that can adapt to IOT environment. However, the detection speed of the framework and the storage space of intrusion feature database still have room for improvement, and it is not suitable for ICS environment. Jayashree [14] et al. proposed an intrusion detection system based on KMP (Knuth Morris Pratt algorithm) for wireless sensor network (WSN) environment. In this system, the intrusion feature database is composed of a series of feature strings. Although the algorithm has a high detection rate, the memory occupation of intrusion feature database is large and detection speed is slow. According to the fact that most network packets will not match any signature in intrusion detection system, Weizhi [15] proposed an intrusion detection algorithm based on blockchain and single character frequency exclusive signature matching (ESM). The main idea of ESM is to identify the mismatches in the process of signature matching, not to find the exact matching. Although experimental results show that detection time can be reduced by 16% to 32.5%, however, it can be concluded that this intrusion detection method occupies a large amount of memory and detects intrusion slowly. Firoz et al. [16] proposed a hierarchical feature-based computer network intrusion detection system. According to the intrusion frequency as the priority, the system divides intrusion feature database into several different priority databases. In order to improve detection efficiency, priority is matched from high to low. Although the system improves detection efficiency to a great extent, memory space occupied is large, and computing resources required are also high.

To sum up, the existing intrusion detection technology based on misuse has problems of large memory occupation and complex calculation of intrusion detection, which can not meet the resource limitation and high real-time requirements of ICS.

3 The IDA-ICS-IBF Algorithm

3.1 Intrusion Signature of ICS

The data set used in this experiment is the public data set published by Mississippi State University in 2014 [17]. The data set includes the data collected by SCADA in the laboratory level ICS. The data comes from network application layer of natural gas pipeline control system. The data includes normal data and intrusion data. The normal data includes network traffic, process control and process measurement data during normal operation. The abnormal data contains four types of attacks, namely reconnaissance, response injection, command injection and denial of service (DoS). These attacks can be subdivided into seven sub categories, including 27 different attacks. In the above data sets, each data has a category label, and the rest includes 26 features. As shown in Eq. (1), f_i represents the feature and y represents the label .

$$\mathrm{D} = \{\mathrm{f}_1, \mathrm{f}_2, \ldots, \mathrm{f}_{26}, \mathrm{y}\} \tag{1}$$

Reconnaissance attack is usually used by attackers to obtain information on SCADA system, and can reflect network architecture of system and collect equipment information. The response injection attack injects or changes the response packet, and sends error message to response device to interfere with normal operation of system. Command injection attacks force the system to change execution state by sending error messages, which will affect normal operation of system. The purpose of DoS attack is to exhaust the resources on device, resulting the device cannot run normally.

Each type of attack has a specific mode. In terms of function code scanning attack, in Modbus protocol, function code is used to represent the function of information frame, that is, to tell the requested device what task to perform. Three types of function codes are defined in MODBUS specification, which are public function code, user-defined function code and reserved function code. Therefore, the blacklist of function codes can be established according to the function codes supported by the server, and the function codes not supported by the server are in the blacklist. Each unsupported function code of the server corresponds to a feature of the function code scanning attack. The features of the function code scanning attack are as follows:

$$FuntionCode : Invalid\ FunctionCode$$

$$(FunctionCode \in FunctionCode\ Black\ List)$$

Other types of attack features are similar. As shown in the following formula, each attack feature consists of two parts, namely, the field type and the corresponding value of the field.

$$Field\ type : Value$$

3.2 Improved Bloom Filter

Although bloom filter is a data structure with high space efficiency and high time efficiency, considering the high real-time requirements of ICS, this paper uses single hash combined with bit operation to improve bloom filter. It is the same as the idea of standard bloom filter, which improves the matching speed by sacrificing a certain accuracy. The matching speed of standard bloom filter depends on the number k of hash functions and the complexity of hash functions, and has nothing to do with the amount of data. The function of hash function is to map the data to different bits of bit group evenly. Therefore, in order to ensure that the error rate of Bloom filter is at a low level, in practical application, hash function usually takes multiple. Considering that the speed of in place operation is higher than that of hash operation, and bit operation can also make the data evenly mapped to different bits of bit group. Therefore, this paper uses bit operation instead of hash operation to improve the bloom filter, in order to improve the matching speed of Bloom filter.

The standard and improved bloom filters are shown in Fig. 1. The standard bloom filter uses a set of hash functions for element insertion and query. When inserting, the values of the bits corresponding to the calculation results are changed to *1*. When querying, it is judged whether the values of the bits corresponding to the calculation results are all *1*. The improved bloom filter not only uses hash operation, but also uses a group of bit operations in element insertion and query. The original hash function of a group is replaced by a hash function and a group of bit operations. The hash function is used to generate an intermediate value, and the bit operation is to map the intermediate value to different positions of the bit group. When the improved bloom filter inserts an element, it first performs hash operation on the element to get a hash value, then performs k-group bit operation on the hash value, and finally gets k values corresponding to *1*. When the improved bloom filter is used to query elements, the calculation method is the same as that of insert. Finally, it is judged whether the values on the corresponding bits of the calculation results are all *1*. It can be seen from Fig. 1 that the mapping method of the standard bloom filter is $X \rightarrow Y$, while the mapping method of the improved bloom filter is $X \rightarrow Y \rightarrow Z$. Many bit operations can be used in the mapping of $Y \rightarrow Z$. The methods used in this paper are as follows:

1. If the length of the bit array is 2^x, the hash result of the data d to be inserted is T;
2. Shift T to the right for i bits and add a prime number to get t;
3. XOR T and t, and take the last x bits as the result s;
4. Set the value at s address to *1*;
5. Judge whether i is greater than k. if i is less than k, repeat step 2. If i is greater than k, it ends.

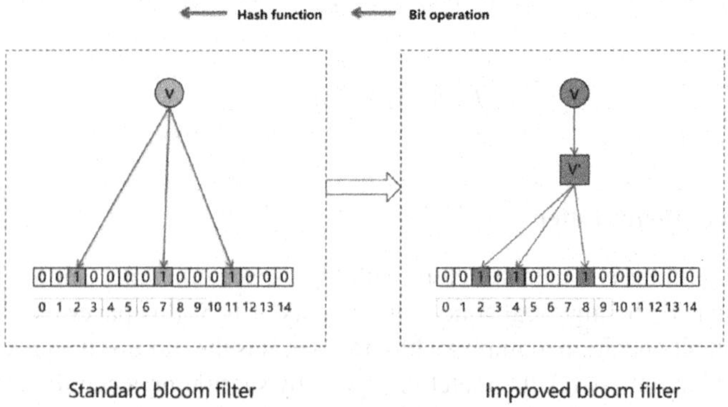

Fig. 1. Standard and improved bloom filters.

In the process of inserting as mentioned above, only one hash operation is performed on the inserted data to obtain the hash value of the data $h(x) = R$, and then the bit operation and XOR operation are performed to set the calculated values at k positions to 1. The method of searching is similar to that of inserting. If the calculated values of k positions are all 1, the data is considered to exist in the improved bloom filter; On the contrary, if at least one position is not 1, it is considered that the data does not exist in the bloom filter.

3.3 Intrusion Feature Database

Taking bloom filter as the intrusion detection database of ICS, we need to define a bit group A with the length of m (according to the actual situation), select a hash function $H = h_1$, and extract all the intrusion data $F = \{f_1, f_2, \ldots, f_n\}$ $(1 \le i \le n)$. Secondly, the extracted features in F are stored in the improved bloom filter, as shown in Fig. 2. The steps of storing the data in the improved bloom filter are as follows:

1. Initialize bit group A, and set all positions in it to 0;
2. The hash function will be operated in turn by $f_i$to get the intermediate value G_i;
3. The intermediate value G_i is carried out by bit operation in turn, and the obtained values are mapped between $[0, m\text{-}1]$, and finally k results $b_1(G_i), b_2(G_i), \ldots, b_k(G_i)$ are obtained;
4. Check the value of corresponding positions in digit group A, i.e. $A[b1(G_i)]$, $A[b_2(G_i)], \ldots, A[b_k(G_i)]$. If the value of corresponding position is 0, set it to 1; If the value in the corresponding position is 1, no modification is made;
5. Repeat steps 2 and 3 until all intrusion features are mapped to bit group A.

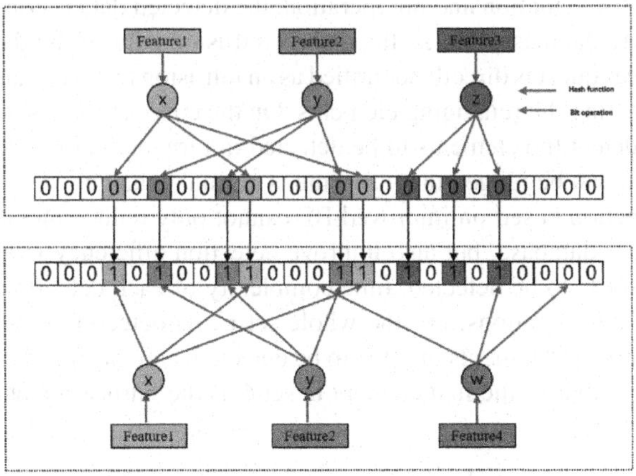

Fig. 2. Example of IBF storage and query.

The data stored in industrial control intrusion database based on the improved bloom filter is only the mapping of real data, not real data. No matter the intrusion features are "address: 0x0f", "function code: 0x03" or "exception code: 05", they are only represented by k bits with a value of *1* in bloom filter, and some bits are used by multiple elements, Therefore, it can greatly improve the utilization of space.

3.4 Intrusion Detection

The detection process of industrial control intrusion detection based on Bloom filter is similar to the above writing process, as shown in Fig. 3. Firstly, the industrial control data packet to be detected is processed, and the effective data fields are extracted, such as F*unction Code, Address, Setpoint, Pump, relief Value*, and these fields are regarded as a set to be detected $C = \{c_1, c_2, \ldots, c_j\}$ $(1 \leq i \leq j)$. The detection steps are as follows:

1. Initialize *count* to *0;*
2. The field to be detected $c_i$is operated on the above hash function to obtain the intermediate value G_i;
3. The calculated G_i is mapped between *[0, m-1]* by bit operation, and finally, k results are obtained $b_1(G_i), b_2(G_i), \ldots, b_k(G_i)$;
4. Check the values of corresponding positions in digit group A, i.e. $A[b1(G_i)]$, $A[b_2(G_i)], \ldots, A[b_k(G_i)]$. If the value of corresponding position is *1*, add *1* to the *count* value. If the value of corresponding position is *0*, no operation is performed;
5. Judge whether *count* is equal to number of hash functions k. if *count* and k are equal, it means the data to be detected exists in the database, that is, the behavior is an intrusion behavior, and detection ends; If *count* and k are not equal, go to step 5;
6. Repeat the above four steps until all data in the set to be detected are detected.

In a word, if the value of detected data in the corresponding position of array is *1* after hash function calculation and bit operation, the detected data is considered to exist in intrusion feature database, that is, the data is intrusion data. If the data is judged as intrusion data, the request is directly identified as an intrusion behavior, and the detection ends without detecting the remaining elements. On the contrary, if it is normal behavior data, it needs to detect the elements to be detected in turn, and all the detection results are normal, then it can be judged that this time is normal behavior.

Intrusion detection based on improved BF cannot only reduce memory occupation of intrusion feature database, but also improve detection efficiency in some level. For each element in set C to be detected, time complexity of each detection is $O(k)$, and k is the number of bit operations. For the whole set C, its detection time complexity is $O(n)$, n is the number of elements in set C to be detected, and the optimal detection time complexity is $O(1)$, that is, the first element in set C is the intrusion feature.

4 Experiment and Analysis

This section mainly evaluates the performance of IDA-ICS-IBF through experiments and comparison with other three intrusion detection algorithms (Menachem [13], jayashree [14], Weizhi [15]). The experimental environment is java8, and result graph is drawn by python. The data set used is the public data set released by Mississippi State University in 2014, and the data has been annotated. The experiment will evaluate IDA-ICS-IBF from the following aspects: detection time efficiency, memory occupation, accuracy, false alarm rate, and missing report rate. Memory occupation refers to the size of memory space required by intrusion feature database; Accuracy represents the proportion of data whose results are consistent with the actual results; False alarm rate indicates the result detected is abnormal behavior data, which is actually normal behavior data, accounting for the proportion of total normal behavior data; Missing report rate indicates detection result is normal behavior data, which is abnormal behavior data, accounting for proportion of total abnormal behavior data.

The parameters involved are shown in Table 1, where *b* represents average storage space occupied by each intrusion feature, in bytes. The default encoding mode of experimental environment is UTF-8, with English and Chinese characters accounting for *1* and *2–3* bytes respectively. The detection process is simulated by multiple devices, where *d* represents number of simulated devices and used in Menachem [13].

Table 1. Experimental parameters.

Parameter name	Meaning	Value
n	The number of intrusion features	50–2500
q	Detection times	10^2–10^5
k	Number of bit operations	12–14
b	Size of intrusion feature	11–49
d	Number of analog devices	4

4.1 Improving Query Speed of Bloom Filter

As can be seen from Fig. 3, for query operation, the query speed of the improved bloom filter (IBF) is much better than that of the standard bloom filter (BF). And as shown in Fig. 4, the error rate of the improved bloom filter is similar to that of the standard bloom filter, but the query efficiency has been improved to a certain extent.

4.2 Improving the Performance of Bloom Filter

In the web field, there is no high requirement for detection time efficiency. However, due to high real-time requirements of ICS, it is one of the important indicators to measure intrusion detection algorithm. The parameters that affect detection time include features number in database and detection times. This section evaluates the average detection time efficiency of IDA-ICS-IBF from above two dimensions.

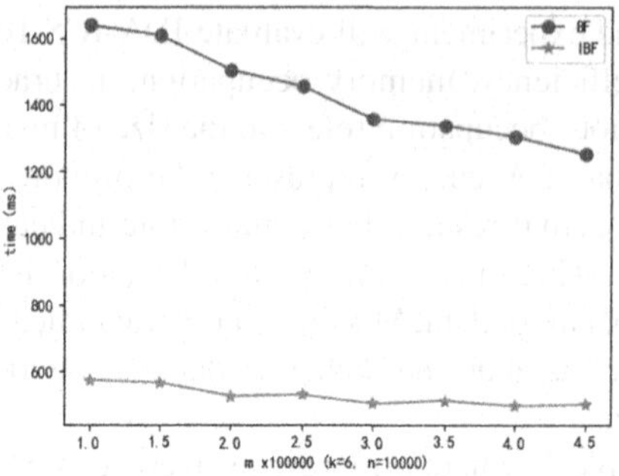

Fig. 3. Comparison of query speed between IBF and BF

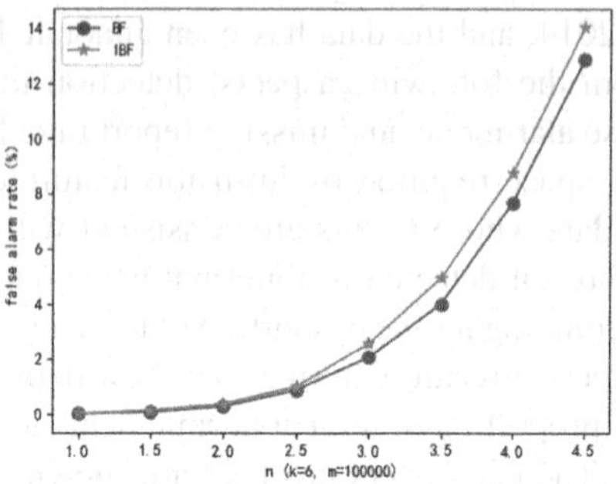

Fig. 4. Comparison of false alarm rates of IBF and BF.

The first group of experiments evaluated detection time efficiency from detection times. The overall detection times of four algorithms increases with the increase of detection times, but increase degree is different. *n* is set to 400, *k* is set to 14, and detection number is increased from 10^2 to 10^5. In Fig. 5, IDA-ICS-IBF has the fastest detection speed, and the more detection times, the greater the gap. When it is 10^2 queries, detection time is 14.29%, 9.09% and 16.67% of other three algorithms. When it is 10^5 queries, the average detection time of IDA-ICS-IBF is the shortest of 9.70%.

The second group of experiments evaluated detection time efficiency based on features number in database. The detection time of IDA-ICS-IBF is almost not affected by features number, while detection time of other three algorithms increases with the increase of features number. q is set to 10^4, and then the number of intrusion features is increased continuously, taking 500 as the initial value, increasing 250 each time, until 2500. In Fig. 6 IDA-ICS-IBF has much less detection time than other three algorithms when dealing with different number of intrusions, and is very stable.

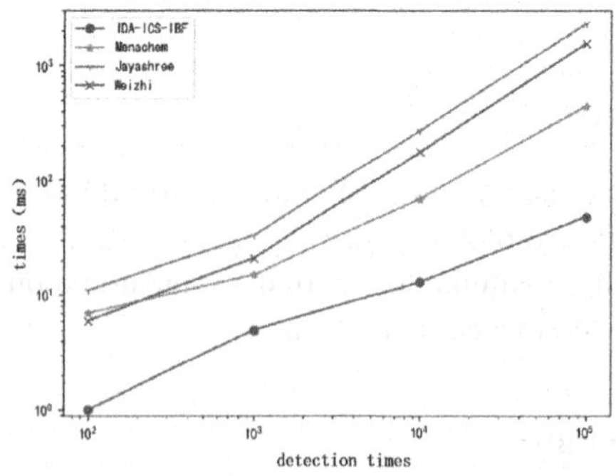

Fig. 5. Comparison of detection time (n = 400).

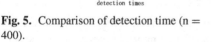

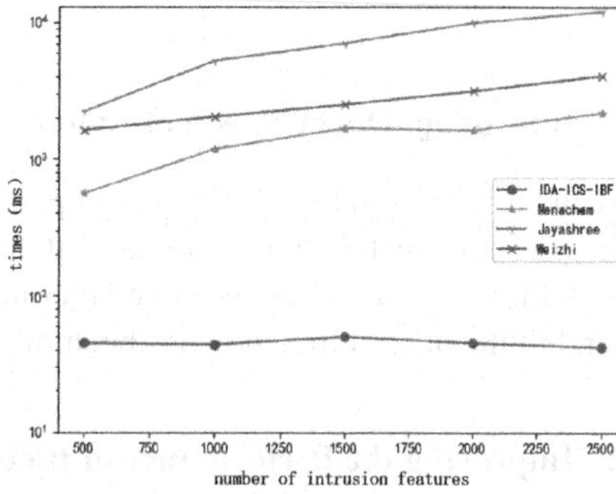

Fig. 6. Comparison of detection time (q = 10^4).

To sum up, IDA-ICS-IBF algorithm is much more efficient than the other three intrusion detection algorithms in terms of the number of features or detection times.

4.3 Memory Occupation of Intrusion Feature Database

Similar to detection time efficiency, memory occupation of feature database is one of the important indicators to measure feature-based intrusion detection algorithm. This section compares memory consumption of four algorithms by features number.

The independent variable is intrusion feature number, and the dependent variable is the space occupied by intrusion feature database. In the experiment, feature number is initially 50, and each experiment increases by 50 until 450. In Fig. 7, when feature number is small, the space occupied by database of IDA-ICS-IBF, Menachem [13] and Weizhi [15] is the same. When feature number increases gradually, memory consumption of Weizhi is about twice of IDA-ICS-IBF. Although memory consumption of Menachem is only slightly larger than that of IDA-ICS-IBF, the database of Menachem is composed of multiple devices. Therefore, space consumption of Menachem is much larger than IDA-ICS-IBF. When feature number is small, the space of jayashree is larger than the other three algorithms, and with the increase of features, the gap between jayashree and the other three algorithms is larger. However, in actual ICS environment, the variety of attacks is increasing with new attacks, so feature number is bound to increase. The memory occupation of Menachem and Weizhi feature database will not meet the needs of ICS environment.

To sum up, IDA-ICS-IBF has the smallest memory occupation of intrusion feature database, and has the best space efficiency compared with the other three algorithms.

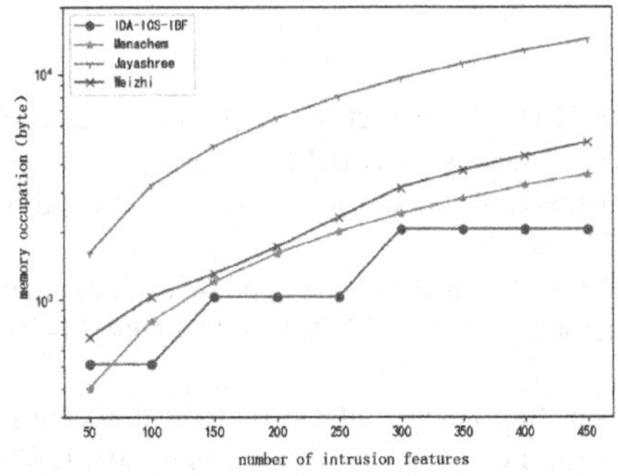

Fig. 7. Memory occupation of intrusion feature database.

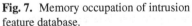

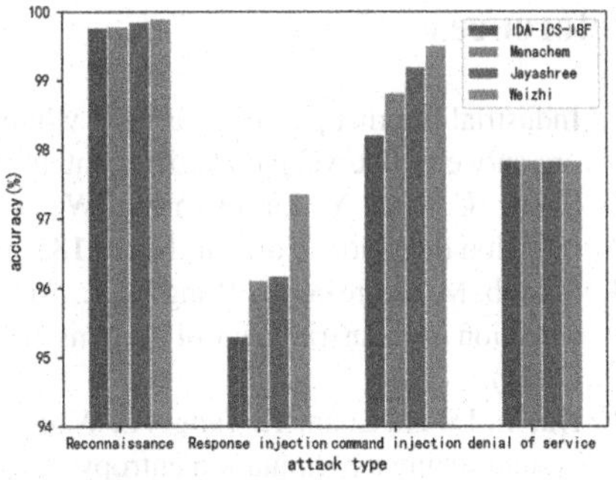

Fig. 8. Comparison of accuracy.

4.4 Detection Effect

Accuracy rate, false alarm rate and missing alarm rate are important indicators to measure the performance of intrusion detection algorithm, and they all play a decisive role in algorithm quality. The comparison results of detection accuracy, false alarm rate and missing report rate are shown in Fig. 8, 9 and 10. Although these results of IDA-ICS-IBF's are slightly inferior to the other three algorithms, they are still very excellent.

As real-time and availability being the primary goals of ICS, due to the comprehensive consideration of detection speed, memory occupation and detection effect, IDA-ICS-IBF is more suitable for intrusion detection in ICS environment.

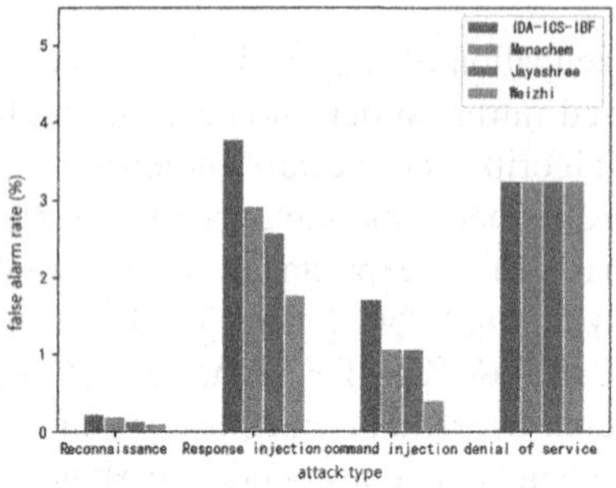

Fig. 9. Comparison of false alarm rate.

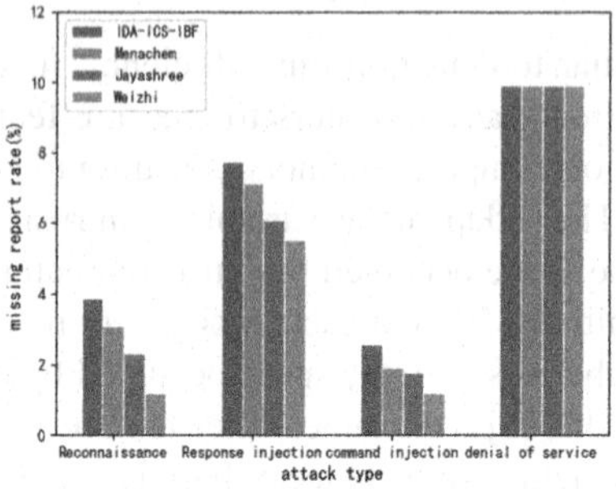

Fig. 10. Comparison of missing report rate.

5 Conclusion

Although the IDA-ICS-IBF algorithm proposed in this paper is slightly inferior to the other three methods in detection effect, it has advantages in detection speed and memory occupation. Thus, it is more suitable for ICS environment with real-time and availability as the primary goal. However, feature database cannot be automatically updated according to new attack type. Thus, future work will be devoted to this area.

References

1. Industrial Internet platform security white paper (2020)[R/OL] (2020). http://www.cics-cert.org.cn/web_root/webpage/articlecontent_102003_1338419755761012738.html
2. Sheng, C., Yao, Y., Fu, Q., Yang, W.: A cyber-physical model for SCADA system and its intrusion detection. Comput. Netw. **185**, 107677 (2021)
3. Sohrab, M., Alireza, A., Kang, K.Y., Arman, S.: A Machine learning approach for anomaly detection in industrial control systems based on measurement data. Electronics **10**(4), 4–407 (2021)
4. Hu, Y., Li, H., Luan, T., Yang, A., Wang, R.: Detecting stealthy attacks on industrial control systems using a permutation entropy-based method. Futur. Gener. Comput. Syst. **108**, 1230–1240 (2020)
5. Hajiheidari, S., Wakil, K.M., Navimipour, N.J.: Intrusion detection systems in the Internet of Things: a comprehensive investigation. Comput. Netw. **160**(4), 165–191 (2019)
6. Yan, Y., Zou, C.: Industrial control system IDS technology research review. Cyberspace Secur. **10**(2), 62–69 (2019)
7. Wang, Y., Meng, W., Li, W., et al.: A fog-based privacy-preserving approach for distributed signature-based intrusion detection. J. Parallel Distrib. Comput. **122**(DEC), 26–35 (2018)
8. Liu, J., Deng, Q., Dong, W.: Network intrusion detection of industrial control system based on flow characteristic fingerprint. J. Wuhan Univ. (Eng. Sci.) **52**(07), 642–650 (2019)
9. Maruthi, R.A., Nishtha, K., Munish, K., Krishan, K.: Intrusion detection techniques in network environment: a systematic review. Wireless Netw. **27**, 1269–1285 (2021)

10. Eirini, A., Lowri, W., Pete, B., Kevin, J.: A three-tiered intrusion detection system for industrial control systems. J. Cybersecur. **7**(1) (2021)
11. Wang, C., Wang, B., Liu, H., Qu, H.: Anomaly detection for industrial control system based on autoencoder neural network. Wireless Commun. Mobile Comput. (2020)
12. Farhad, R., Hoda, M.: Misusing sensory channel to attack industrial control systems. In: Proceedings of the Eighth ACM Conference on Data and Application Security and Privacy, pp. 158–160. ACM (2018)
13. Menachem, D.: A framework of signature-matching-algorithms for IoT intrusion detection. In: Proceedings of the Future Technologies Conference, pp. 889–898. Springer (2020). https://doi.org/10.1007/978-3-030-63092-8_60
14. Khammassi, C., Krichen, S.: A GA-LR wrapper approach for feature selection in network intrusion detection. Comput. Secur. **70**, 255–277 (2017)
15. Meng, W., Li, W., Tug, S., Tan, J.: Towards blockchain-enabled single character frequency-based exclusive signature matching in IoT-assisted smart cities. J. Parallel Distrib. Comput. **112**(3), 2023–2045 (2020)
16. Firoz, N.F., Arefin, M.T., Uddin, M.R.: performance optimization of layered signature based intrusion detection system using snort. In: Touhid Bhuiyan, Md., Mostafijur Rahman, Md., Ali, A. (eds.) Cyber Security and Computer Science: Second EAI International Conference, ICONCS 2020, Dhaka, Bangladesh, February 15-16, 2020, Proceedings, pp. 14–27. Springer International Publishing, Cham (2020). https://doi.org/10.1007/978-3-030-52856-0_2
17. Thomas, M., Wei, G.: Industrial control system traffic data sets for intrusion detection research. In: International Conference on Critical Infrastructure Protection, vol. 441, pp. 65–78. Springer, Heidelberg (2014)

A Novel Traversal Search-Based D2D Collaborative Offloading Approach for Workflow Application in Dynamic Edge Environment

Cheng Qian[1,2], Gansen Zhao[1,2], and Haoyu Luo[1,2](✉)

[1] School of Computer Science, South China Normal University, Guangzhou 510631, China
{qiancheng,gzhao,hluo}@m.scnu.edu.cn

[2] Key Lab On Cloud Security and Assessment Technology of Guangzhou, Guangzhou 510631, China

Abstract. D2D (Device-to-Device) collaborative offloading is a kind of offloading paradigms in the Mobile Edge Computing (MEC) environment, which allows edge devices to offload workflow tasks to the adjacent mobile devices with idle resources. As a supplement to the End-Edge-Cloud collaborative offloading paradigms, the D2D collaborative offloading can relieve the MEC's performance bottleneck caused by the limited capacity of edge servers and increased offloading requirements. However, the mobility and capacity fluctuation of mobile devices makes it difficult to guarantee the quality of service of the D2D collaborative offloading of workflow application. For this issue, we propose a dynamic environment oriented D2D collaborative offloading approach to ensure that the workflow offloading requirements in edge devices can be responded with a minimum cost before the deadline. Specifically, we first encode the feasible offloading strategy in a rough order of cost, and then perform Fibonacci traversal to fast approximate the optimal offloading strategy. In the remaining iterations, a uniform traversal is performed in the neighborhood of the optimal offloading strategy. Finally, the best offloading strategy ever traversed is applied to practice. We do not pursue optimality but real-time performance, so as to adjust the offloading strategy online with the same procedure. Experimental results show that our proposed approach is highly cost-effective with low decision overhead and high success rate.

Keywords: Workflow · D2D · Collaborative offloading · Mobile Edge Computing

1 Introduction

Recent years have witnessed the great potential of workflow applications in mobile devices. For example, in the UAV last-mile delivery application, the process of confirming recipient can consist of frame filtering, target detection, image segmentation, face recognition, and other computation intensive tasks [1]. Many researchers focus on

Y. Sun et al. (Eds.): ChineseCSCW 2021, CCIS 1491, pp. 176–190, 2022.
https://doi.org/10.1007/978-981-19-4546-5_14

the Mobile Edge Computing (MEC), where mobile users can offload their computational tasks either to the near-to-user edge facilities (e.g., base stations from network providers) or to the cloud servers for energy-saving and meeting the delay requirement [2]. However, with the explosive increase of mobile devices with offloading requests, edge facilities with limited processing capacity may reach performance bottlenecks.

The Device-to-Device (D2D) collaborative offloading [3, 4] is a supplement to the End-Edge-Cloud collaborative offloading paradigms, where mobile users can dynamically offload the workflow computation tasks to the adjacent mobile devices with idle resources. On the one hand, the computing capacity of mobile devices is continuously enhanced, many devices have the preliminary capacity to deal with deep learning tasks. On the other hand, a large number of mobile devices remain idle for most of the time. The D2D collaborative offloading not only reduces the workload of edge facilities, but also improves the utility of mobile devices, which is helpful to improve the collaborative ecology in the MEC environment.

Nevertheless, the dynamic environment makes the D2D collaborative offloading to face great challenges, such as **1) Mobility:** The position of mobile users as well as the availability of computing providers are stochastic and unpredictable; and **2) Capacity fluctuation:** The network speed and CPU frequency of mobile devices are not stable, which make the duration and cost of workflow offloading stochastic and unpredictable. Therefore, it is very significant to investigate how the D2D collaborative offloading can be made efficient and economic in the dynamic environment.

Most studies assume that mobile devices are constantly available with stable capacity, while they have some limitations in reality. Based on predicted mobility or reliability of mobile devices, evolutionary algorithms were used in some studies to search optimal offloading strategy. However, evolutionary algorithms usually have high computational overhead. Besides, the performance of an optimal offloading strategy depends on the accuracy of prediction, which has limitation in an unpredictable environment.

This paper presents a dynamic environment oriented D2D collaborative offloading approach for workflow applications, where workflow offloading requirements can be responded before the deadline with a minimum cost, even in an unpredictable environment. The core of the proposed approach is the online adjustment triggered by the real-time state monitor. The online adjustment is made to search the best offloading strategy for the current state and to replace the existing offloading strategy. The online adjustment is made in two main steps:

Step 1: Estimating the duration and cost under a specific offloading strategy, so as to compare which strategy is better. Since the estimate in a dynamic environment cannot be precise, the results are obtained according to a confidence level.

Step 2: Traversing the decision space to search the best offloading strategy. Since the optimal strategy in a dynamic environment cannot maintain the optimality up to the end, only limited strategies are traversed, and the best offloading strategy is chosen from them. Therefore, the offloading strategy in the decision space is specially encoded, so that the estimation (from **Step 1**) in the decision space is roughly in order. The Fibonacci traversal and uniform traversal are used to maximize the efficiency under the limited traversal.

We conduct comprehensive experiments in a simulated unpredictable environment. Experimental results show that in various scenarios, our approach is the best from a comprehensive point of view.

2 Related Work

2.1 Collaborative Offloading Paradigms in Mobile Edge Computing

MEC provides an IT service environment and cloud-computing capabilities at the edge of the mobile network [5], which enables collaborative offloading in the close proximity to mobile users.

The paradigms of MEC include the End-Edge collaboration, End-Edge-Cloud collaboration, and End-End collaboration. For the purpose of execution, the computational tasks of mobile devices are offloaded to the edge server by the End-Edge collaboration [6], to both edge servers and cloud servers by the End-Edge-Cloud collaboration [2], and to the adjacent mobile devices by the End-End collaboration [3]. The End-End collaboration is usually combined with the D2D (Device-to-Device) communication technology. So, it is also called as the D2D collaboration.

Various works focused on the D2D collaboration. For example, Pu *et al.* [3] proposed tit-for-tat constraints for incentive and preventing free-riding behaviors. Baek *et al.* [7] proposed the addition of redundant tasks in the D2D collaboration to verify the trustiness and also to preserve privacy in the meantime. Li *et al.* [8] proposed an End-to-End encrypted D2D offloading approach for data security in the D2D collaboration.

2.2 D2D Collaborative Offloading Approach in Dynamic Edge Environment

The D2D collaborative offloading approach in a dynamic environment usually adopts an offline decision or online adjustment. For example, Zhang [9] used real-world mobility datasets to predict the contact time between mobile devices, so as to improve the success rate of the offline decision. Wang *et al.* [10] adopted an offline expert policy and an online agent policy to minimize the average task completion time in a fully decentralized environment with the Manhattan mobility model. Li *et al.* [8] simulated the fluctuation of device performance. Pu *et al.* [3] simulated both mobility and performance fluctuation, where they adjusted the offloading decision online according to the real-time environment status to minimize the overall energy consumption. However, the above offloading approaches cannot be applied directly to the workflow application as they do not consider the dependencies between tasks.

Only a few of the D2D collaborative offloading approaches considered both workflow and dynamic environment. For example, Peng *et al.* [11] first modeled the reliability of mobile devices in the MEC environment, and then used Krill-Herd algorithm to maximize the reliability of the workflow offloading strategy. Peng *et al.* [4] first predicted the mobility of mobile devices to obtain continuously available candidate devices for a workflow instance, and then made the offloading decision by an evolutionary algorithm. However, the above approaches have limited adaptability to environmental changes as they assume that the reliability or mobility can be predicted accurately, whereas the adaptability is limited by predictability. Besides, the above approaches have a high computational overhead. Therefore, this paper not pursues accurate prediction and optimization, but real-time performance, and compensates the final performance by online adjustment.

3 Scenario Description and Problem Definition

3.1 Scenario Description

As shown in Fig. 1, the MEC scenario includes a sufficient number of mobile devices and a few base stations. The mobile devices can move freely within the service range of any base station. Any mobile device may run workflow applications. When a certain device (offloading requestor) cannot complete the workflow locally in time due to poor performance, high energy consumption, or any other factor, then it offloads all workflow tasks to the adjacent mobile devices with idle resources. The offloading requestor performs only two virtual tasks locally: sending the initial data and receiving the final results. Note that this paper only focus on the D2D collaboration. But in other scenarios, some workflow tasks with high resource requirements may need to be offloaded to edge servers or even cloud servers. In that case, the approach proposed in this paper can be combined with the existing End-Edge-Cloud multi-level collaborative offloading approach to meet the offloading requirements of workflow applications.

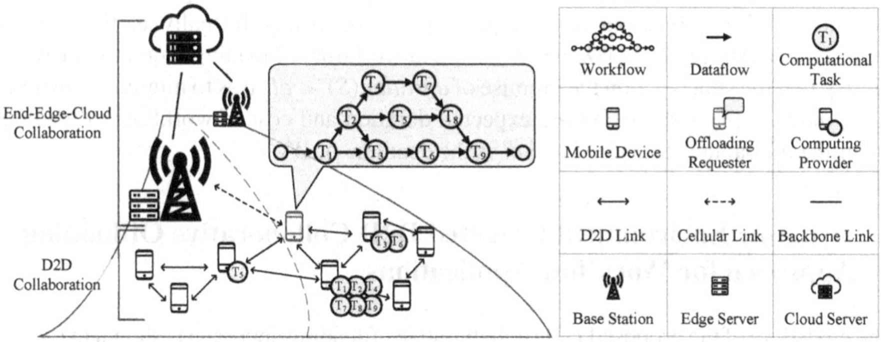

Fig. 1. D2D collaborative offloading in the MEC scenario

In this scenario, the base station acts as the offloading decision-maker and manager, and it does not execute workflow tasks. The offloading requester releases the workflow offloading requirements through the base station. The base station decides the mapping between workflow tasks and computing providers based on the real-time state of the mobile devices and workflow instance. The D2D link is used for dataflow transmission, and the cellular link is used for real-time state collection. Since the mobile devices are owned by individuals who will not provide computational service free of charge, the offloading requester needs to pay remuneration to computing providers according to the unit time price and calculation duration of the computing provider. Since device security and trust are not the focus of this paper, it is assumed that the mobile devices involved in the D2D collaborative offloading scenario are trusted.

Generally speaking, a higher capacity of computing providers leads to a shorter completion time. Accordingly, the offloading cost will also be higher. From the perspective of the offloading requester, the offloading approach should ensure that the workflow instance can be completed within the time constraint with the lowest offloading cost.

However, in real scenarios, the geographical location and the CPU frequency along with the network speed of the mobile devices will get changed all the time. These are difficult to predict, which makes the offloading decision face great challenges.

3.2 Problem Definition

The workflow offloading requirement is represented by the directed acyclic graph $W = \{\mathcal{T}, \mathrm{E}\}$, where $\mathcal{T} = \{T_i | 1 \le i \le L\}$ is the set of computational tasks, $\mathrm{E} = \{T_i \to T_j | 0 \le i < \mathrm{j} \le L+1\}$ is the set of dataflows, and $T_i \to T_j$ is the dataflow from task T_i to task T_j. In addition, T_0 and T_{L+1} are two virtual tasks executed locally by the offloading requester, and $T_i \in \mathcal{T}$ are the tasks that need to be offloaded. T_i can start execution only when all $T_x \to T_i \in E$ transfer is completed, all $T_i \to T_y \in E$ can start transfer only when T_i execution is completed.

The workflow offloading strategy is represented by the vector $\mathrm{S} = [s_1, s_2, \ldots, s_L]$, where s_i is the computing provider of task T_i. For example, if device D_2 is the computing provider of tasks $\{T_1, T_2, T_4\}$, and device D_6 is the computing provider of tasks T_3, then this strategy can be represented by $[D_2, D_2, D_6, D_2]$, abbreviated as [2, 2, 6, 2].

The workflow offloading decision problem can be defined formally as: For a given set of mobile devices $\mathcal{D} = \{D_i | 1 \le i \le N\}$ and workflow offloading requirement $W = \{\mathcal{T}, \mathrm{E}\}$, find the strategy S on the premise of $duration(S) < dl$ so as to minimize $cost(S)$. Here, $duration(S)$ and $cost(S)$ are expected duration and cost of workflow offloading under the offloading strategy S, and dl is the deadline of W.

4 Dynamic Environment Oriented D2D Collaborative Offloading Approach for Workflow Applications

The procedure of the proposed D2D collaborative offloading approach is shown in Fig. 2. It is used to yield an offloading strategy for the problem defined in the previous section. The approach is lightweight and optimal so that it can be applied to large numbers of users and complicated workflows.

In the proposed approach, the online adjustment would be triggered according to the real-time state of the workflow instance and adjacent mobile devices. Once the online adjustment is triggered, a limited number of offloading strategies would be traversed and estimated, and the best strategy ever traversed would replace the current offloading strategy. Three practical problems will be solved in this section: 1) When to trigger the online adjustment, 2) How to estimate a specific offloading strategy, and 3) How to traverse effectively under the number limit.

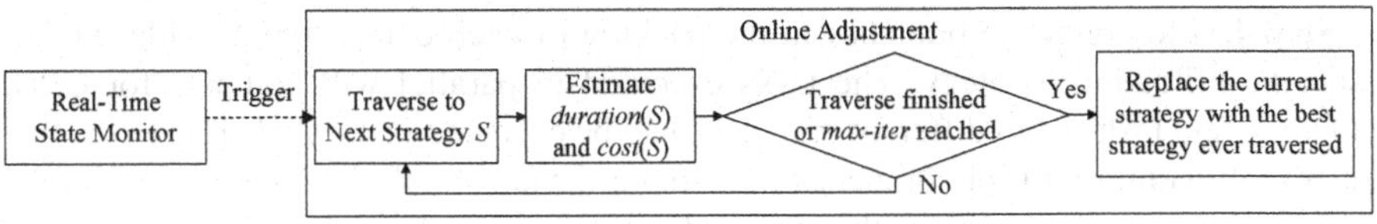

Fig. 2. The procedure of the D2D collaborative offloading approach

4.1 State Monitor of Workflow Instance and Adjacent Mobile Devices

The real-time state monitor is to collect information about the workflow instance and adjacent mobile devices as shown in Fig. 3.

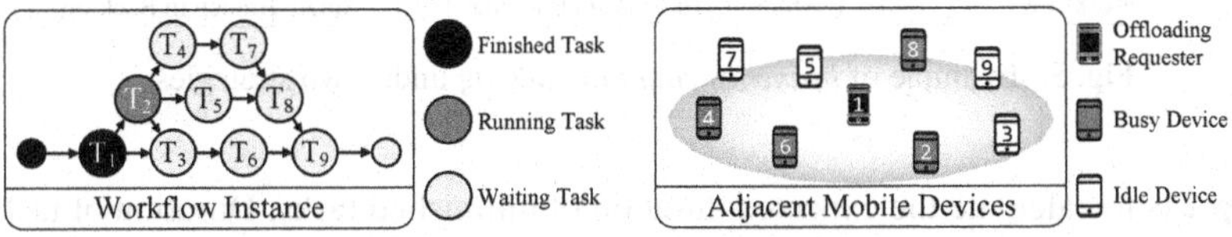

Fig. 3. Real-time state of workflow instance and adjacent mobile devices

For the workflow instance, the collected information includes the real-time progress of each task and dataflow, incurred offloading cost of each task, and timestamps of starting and finishing tasks.

For adjacent mobile devices, the collected information includes the unit time price, backlog, mean and standard deviation of the CPU instruction frequency, communication bandwidth and power, and geographic coordinates.

The online adjustment will be triggered in three cases: 1) There is an unfinished task without a computing provider, 2) There is a new task just completed, and 3) There is a computing provider failure.

4.2 Estimating Duration and Cost of Workflow Under Specific Strategy

Estimating the duration and cost of workflow under a specific offloading strategy is critical to offloading decision-making. The process is shown in Fig. 4. Note that the final duration and cost are impossible to be estimated accurately under the unpredictable environment, until the workflow is actually finished. Therefore, in order to pursue the real-time performance, some compromises on accuracy are made in the following steps, so that the accuracy can be compensated in the next online adjustment.

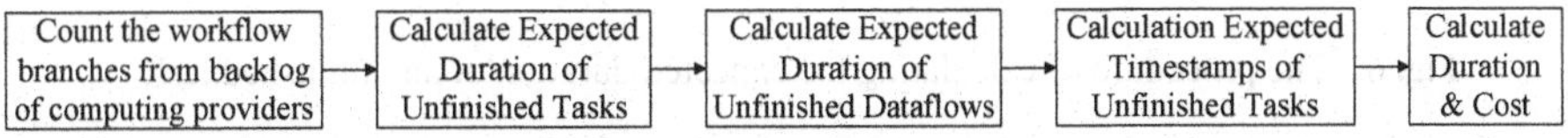

Fig. 4. The procedure of measuring the duration and cost

Step 1 is to count the branches in the backlog of each computing provider under a specific offloading strategy. The tasks executed in parallel will compete for CPU resources, and tasks from different branches may be executed in parallel. Therefore, the strategy offloading multiple branches to a single device should be avoided. A simple and effective way is to increase the expected duration according to the *branches count in backlog*. The example of *branches count in backlog* is shown in Fig. 5.

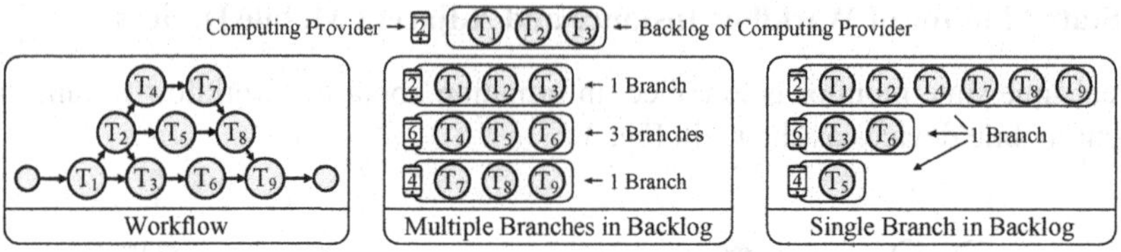

Fig. 5. Example of *branches count in backlog* under two strategies

Step 2 is to calculate the expected duration of unfinished tasks. Duration of tasks is hard to calculate due to the fluctuation of the CPU frequency. Therefore, we propose a confidence-based duration measuring method as shown in Fig. 6. It has four steps: 1) The probability distribution of the CPU frequency is modeled. Without losing generality, we assume that the CPU frequency of mobile devices follows normal distribution. 2) We calculate the probability distribution of the finish time based on the formula in the upper right corner of Fig. 6. 3) We calculate the cumulative distribution of the finish time to get the probability distribution of the maximum finish time (makespan). 4) The inverse function of the previous step is the function of expected duration,which input is the confidence level, and the output is the expected duration of the task. The confidence level is preset by the offloading demander.

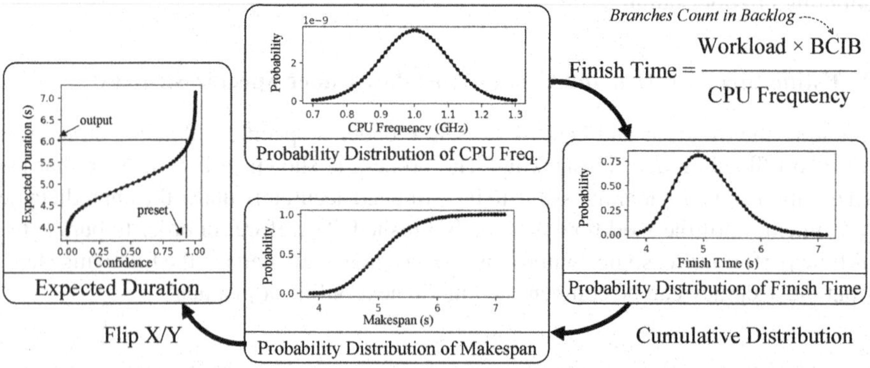

Fig. 6. The procedure of calculating the expected duration of an unfinished task

There are two practical difficulties in the above process: 1) How to calculate the probability distribution of the finish time as the CPU frequency is a variable. The derivation process is shown in Eq. (1). 2) How to calculate the inverse function of cumulative distribution of the finish time as it involves a nearly unsolvable integral equation. We discretize the integral equation for obtaining an approximate result by segmentation and summation.

$$g(t) = f(c)\left|\frac{dc}{dt}\right| = f\left(\frac{w}{t}\right)\left|\frac{d\frac{w}{t}}{dt}\right| = f\left(\frac{w}{t}\right)\frac{w}{t^2} = \frac{w}{t^2}\frac{1}{\sqrt{2\pi}\sigma}e^{-\frac{\left(\frac{w}{t}-\mu\right)^2}{2\sigma^2}} \quad (1)$$

where c is the real-time CPU frequency; $c \sim \mathrm{N}(\mu, \sigma)$; t is the finish time; f and g are the probability distribution functions of c and t, respectively; and w is the unfinished workload times the *branches count in backlog* of the computing provider of the task.

Step 3 is to calculate the expected duration of the unfinished dataflow. Duration of dataflow is hard to calculate due to the network fluctuation and user mobility, which is more variable than task duration. Therefore, we make some compromises on confidence, otherwise the expected duration of dataflow with a high confidence will be even longer than the workflow deadline. The calculation of dataflow duration is as follows:

$$t = \frac{d}{B_{eff} B_w log_2\left(1+\frac{P_m K_d r^{-\alpha_d}}{N_0 B_w \theta_{eff}}\right)} \quad (2)$$

where t is the expected duration of the dataflow, d is the unfinished data size, B_{eff} is the bandwidth efficiency,B_w is the bandwidth of device, P_m is the transmission power, K_d is the path-loss factor for a distance in meters, r is the distance between the two devices of dataflow, α_d is the path-loss exponent, N_0 is the noise power spectrum density, and θ_{eff} is the SNR efficiency.

Step 4 is to calculate the expected timestamp of each unfinished task as follows:

$$\begin{aligned} \mathrm{ts}_c(T_i) &= \max_{T_x \in Pred(T_i)} \left(\max\left(\mathrm{ts}_p(T_x), \mathrm{ts}_{\mathrm{now}}\right) + t_{trans}(T_x, T_i)\right) \\ \mathrm{ts}_p(T_i) &= \max(\mathrm{ts}_c(T_i), \mathrm{ts}_{\mathrm{now}}) + t_{comp}(T_i) \end{aligned} \quad (3)$$

where $\mathrm{ts}_c(T_i)$ is the timestamp of task T_i starting computing, $\mathrm{ts}_p(T_i)$ is the timestamp of task T_i finishing computing, $\mathrm{ts}_{\mathrm{now}}$ is the timestamp of the current time, $t_{trans}(T_x, T_i)$ is the expected duration of dataflow $T_x \rightarrow T_i$, and $t_{comp}(T_i)$ is the expected duration of task T_i.

Step 5 is to calculate the duration and cost of workflow as follows:

$$\begin{aligned} duration(S) &= \mathrm{ts}_c(T_{L+1}) \\ cost(S) &= \sum_{i=1}^{L}(cost_R(T_i) + tl(T_i) \times price(s_i)) \end{aligned} \quad (4)$$

where $cost_R(T_i)$ is the incurred offloading cost of task T_i, $price(s_i)$ is the unit time price of device s_i, s_i is the computing provider of task T_i under the strategy S, and $tl(T_i)$ is the remaining billing time of task T_i. The calculation of $tl(T_i)$ is as follows:

$$tl(T_i) = \max_{T_x \in Pred(T_i)} (t_{trans}(T_x, T_i)) + \max_{T_x \in Succ(T_i)} (t_{trans}(T_i, T_x)) + t_{comp}(T_i) \quad (5)$$

4.3 Traversal Search for the Best Offloading Strategy

Searching the optimal strategy is the core of the offloading decision-making, the procedure of which is shown in Fig. 6. Note that the optimal offloading strategy of the current moment may not be the optimal of the next moment. It is impossible to search an offloading strategy which keeps the optimal from the beginning to the end under the unpredictable environment, until the workflow is actually finished. Therefore, in order to pursue the real-time performance, some compromises on the optimality are made in the following steps, so that the cost-effectiveness and QoS can be improved with the best effort in each online adjustment.

Step 1 is to determine the decision space, specifically to find and sort adjustable branches and available devices.

An adjustable branch is a subset of a workflow branch. The adjustable branch consists of tasks which are waiting for starting. The adjustable branch does not consist of tasks which are already running, so as to reduce the loss of progress due to the adjusting strategy. The adjustable branches are sorted in descending order of their workloads.

An available device is an adjacent mobile device near the offloading requester. Available devices have no task in backlog, so as to avoid that previous tasks could not be finished in time due to competing CPU resources with new tasks. The available devices are sorted in ascending order of their unit time prices.

The decision space is the cartesian product of the combination and permutation, where the combination is the selection of new computing providers from available devices and the permutation is the arrangement of adjustable branches into new computing providers. Since the adjustable branches and available devices are sorted, the duration and cost of strategies in the decision space are roughly in order (Fig. 7).

If strategy $S_{i,k}$ is the product of the i-th combination and k-th permutation, n is the number of available devices and m is the number of adjustable branches at this moment, then we have $1 \leq i \leq C_n^m$ and $1 \leq k \leq m!$. When i or k increases, $cost(S_{i,k})$ tends to increase and $duration(S_{i,k})$ tends to decrease. When i or k decreases, $cost(S_{i,k})$ tends to decrease and $duration(S_{i,k})$ tends to increase.

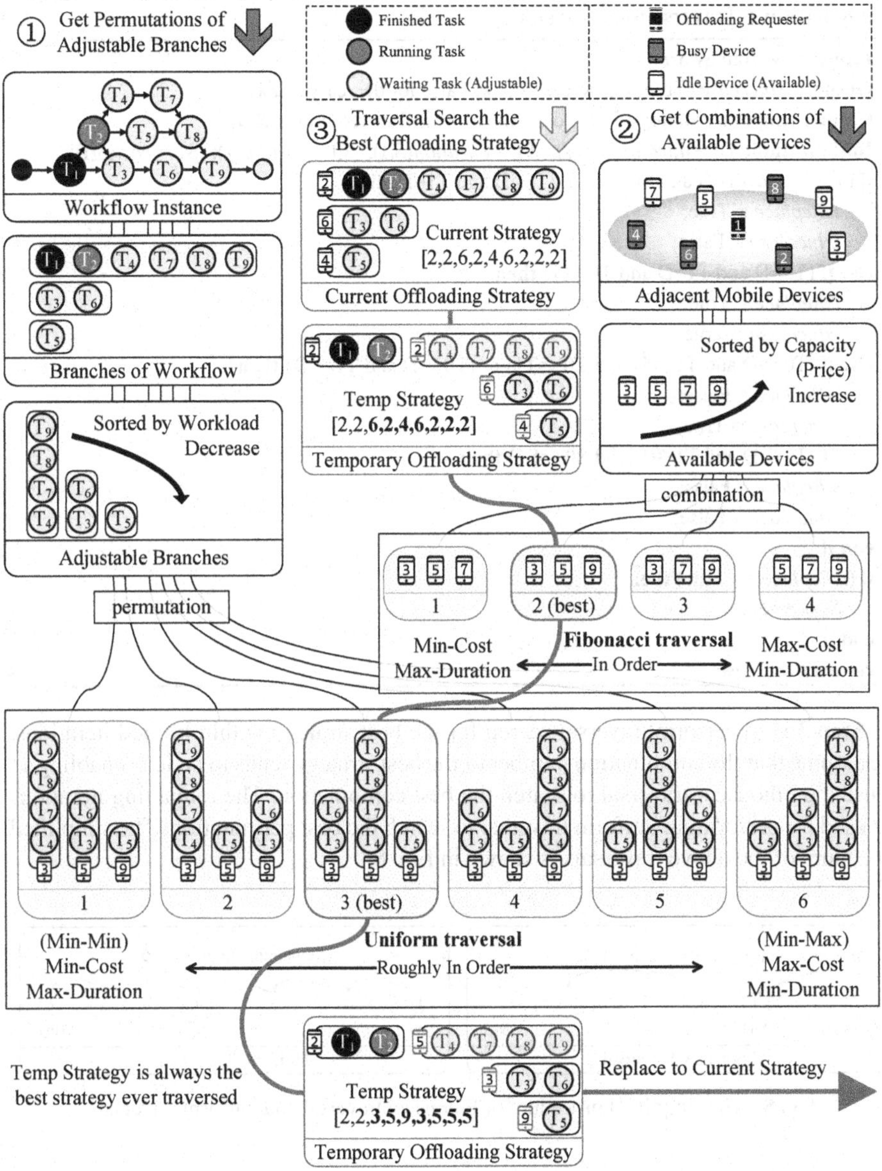

Fig. 7. The traversal procedure searching the best strategy

Step 2 is to determine the traversal rule, specifically to decide whether to increase or decrease i or k for the next traverse and whether this strategy is the best. Therefore, a temporary offloading strategy S_{temp} is initiated as current offloading strategy and used for temporary storage of the best strategy ever traversed. The implementation of the traversal rule is given in Algorithm 1.

Algorithm 1 Traverse to a new strategy

Input: new strategy $S_{i,k}$
Output: *isIncrease* (True for increase *i* or *k*; False for decrease *i* or *k*)
Global: temporary strategy S_{temp} , deadline of workflow requirement *D*;
Initialization: T0 = $duration(S_{temp})$; T1 = $duration(S_{i,k})$; S0 = $cost(S_{temp})$; S1 = $cost(S_{i,k})$;
if (T0<D and T1<D and S0>S1) or (T0>D and T1<D) **then**
  isReplace = True;
  isIncrease = False;
else if (T0>D and T1>D and T0>T1) **then**
  isReplace = True;
  isIncrease = True;
else if (T0>=D and T1>=D and T0<=T1) or (T0<=D and T1>=D) **then**
  isReplace = False;
  isIncrease = True;
else if (T0<=D and T1<=D and S0<=S1) **then**
  isReplace = False;
  isIncrease = False;
end if
if (*isReplace* == True) **then**
  $S_{temp} \leftarrow S_{i,k}$;
end if
return *isIncrease*;

Step 3 is to perform traversal search for the best strategy within limited iterations. We assume that the combination number of the best strategy tends to be low, enabling us to use the Fibonacci traversal to search the best combination. The remaining iterations are used for performing uniform traversal to search the best permutation. The simplified procedure of the above traversals is shown in Fig. 8.

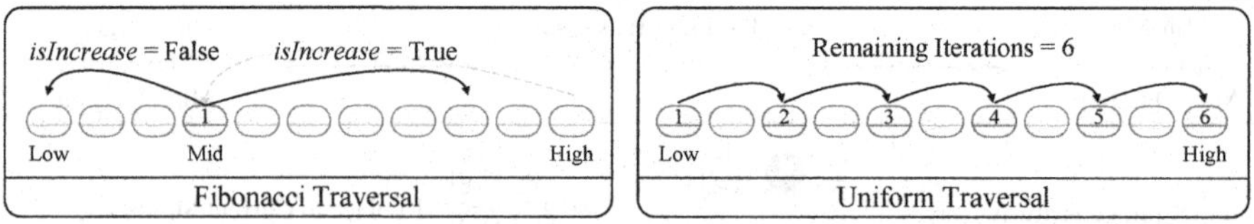

Fig. 8. The simplified procedure of Fibonacci traversal and uniform traversal

5 Evaluation

5.1 Experimental Setting

A SimPy-based script is used to simulate a workflow of the D2D offloading scenario.

Mobility: We adopt the Gauss-Markov Mobility Model [14] to simulate the movement of users. This model has no restriction on the movement path. The speed and direction of a device are affected by its past speed, past direction, and a random variable, so as to simulate an unpredictable environment.

Network: We adopt the modified Shannon capacity formula proposed in [12] and the network parameters reported in [13] to simulate the network speed. The max D2D communication distance is set to 200 m.

Computing: The mean and standard deviation of the real-time CPU frequency of device D_i are set randomly as $c_\mu(D_i) \sim N(1.5, 0.3)$ GHz and $c_\sigma(D_i) = 0.1 \times c_\mu(D_i)$, respectively. The parallel executed tasks will divide the real-time CPU frequency equally.

Pricing: The unit time price of device D_i is set to $price(D_i) = c_\mu(D_i)^2$ as it can make the duration of the workflow offloading inversely proportional to the offloading cost, which can better fit the actual demand.

Workflow: We adopt four scientific workflows from [15] for simulation, the structures of which are shown in Fig. 9. The workload of task T_i is set randomly as $w_i \in \{1, 2, 5\}$ G, and the data size of dataflow $T_i \rightarrow T_j$ is set randomly as $d_{i,j} \in \{1, 2, 5\}$ M. The deadline of workflow is set to be the ideal minimum duration of workflow multiplied by a ratio. The ideal refers to the situation of the CPU frequency to be stable at 1GHz without any communication delay. The default ratio is 1.5. For communication intensive workflows such as CyberShake and Sipht, enlarge the ratio by one half.

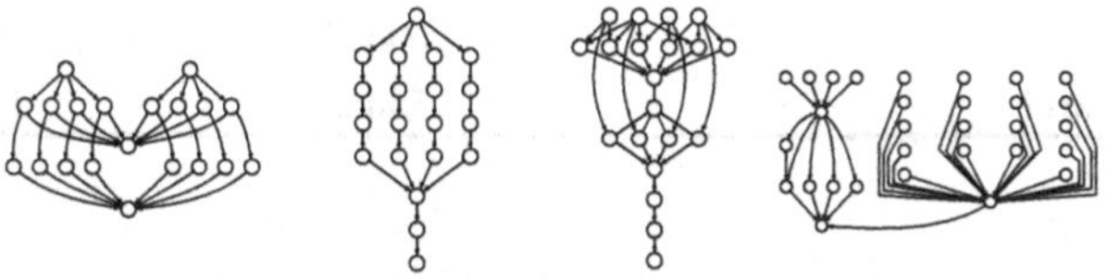
(a) CyberShake (b) Epigenomics (c) Montage (d) Sipht

Fig. 9. The structures of scientific workflows

Simulation: Mobile devices move freely on $1000 \times 1000\ m^2$ ground. Their real-time coordinates, speed, direction, communication speed, CPU frequency, dataflow transmission progress and task execution progress are refreshed at every second. From the 1st second to the 10th second of the simulation, there are 10 devices with the lowest c_μ release of the workflow offloading requirements, and the simulation ends at the 300th second. Each simulation offloads only one class of workflow. Each offloading approach runs four simulations with different scientific workflows, and averages the result. In order to reduce the interference of irrelevant factors, the parameters and the seed of random number are kept the same as those in the first simulation.

Comparisons: We consider HEFT [16], PSO, GA and GRASP [17] for comparisons of the proposed traversal search algorithm. HEFT is used for optimizing the duration of workflow, and the others are used to optimize the cost in the premise of the workflow that can be finished before the deadline. PSO and GA use the encoding scheme reported in [4] and the default parameters of scikit-opt [18].

Evaluating Indicator: We adopt decision overhead, offloading cost, and success rate as evaluating indicators. The decision overhead is the number of offloading strategies ever estimated in all the online adjustments. The offloading cost is the final cost when the workflow is actually finished. The success rate is the proportion of the workflows finished before the deadline of all the workflows.

5.2 Performance Evaluation

Table 1 shows the performance of the following case: number of mobile devices is 1000, the maximum iteration number is 20, and the confidence level of expected duration is 95%. From a comprehensive point of view, our approach is the best. Compared with the lowest-cost-approach (PSO), our approach reduces the decision overhead by 98.36%, increases the success rate by 2.5%, and increases the offloading cost by 0.014% only.

Table 1. Performance comparison of different offloading approaches

Offloading Approach	Decision Overhead	Offloading Cost	Success Rate
HEFT	**14.8**	961.24	**100%**
GA	16616.6	552.56	**100%**
PSO	13160.0	**536.17**	97.5%
GRASP	255.4	606.88	**100%**
Traversal Search	**216.4**	**536.25**	**100%**

HEFT has the minimum decision overhead and the maximum offloading cost as it straightly uses high-capacity devices without considering offloading cost.

GA and PSO have the maximum decision overhead. But compared with the Traversal Search which has a low decision overhead, their performances are not improved significantly. The reason is that the decision process does not take auxiliary information, such as workflow branches and device capacity, into consideration, and hence leads to inefficiency.

GRASP has a low decision overhead and good performance. The reason is that the decision process takes workflow branches into consideration, and searches strategies by branches. However, GRASP is a type of random search, and it does not consider device information. So, its performance is limited by the maximum iteration number.

The performance comparison in terms of different numbers of mobile devices is shown in Fig. 10. We can find that 1) The decision overhead is not affected by the number of mobile devices. 2) With increasing number of mobile devices, the offloading cost of HEFT is increased, others are decreased, which indicates that HEFT is not suitable for the scenario with many devices. 3) Traversal search can keep the lowest cost and the highest success rate from the beginning to the end with a low decision overhead.

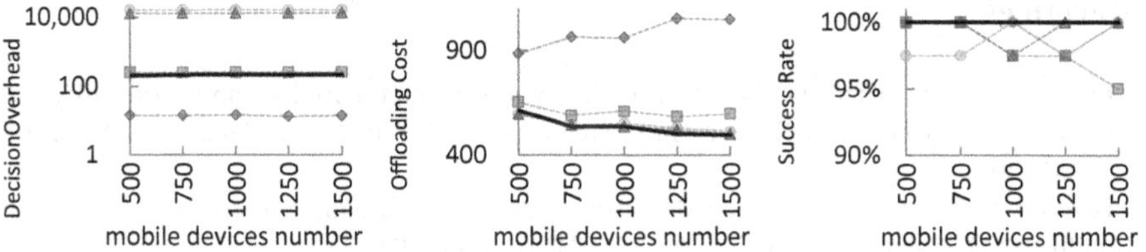

Fig. 10. Performance comparison in terms of different number of mobile devices

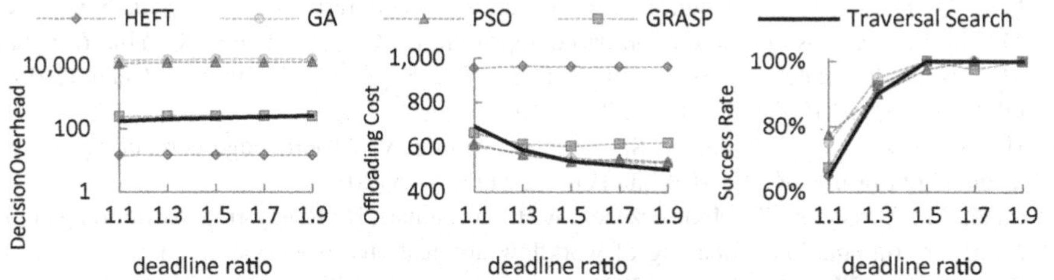

Fig. 11. Performance comparison in terms of different deadline ratios

The performance comparison in terms of different deadline ratios is shown in Fig. 11. The deadline ratio is the ratio of the deadline to the ideal minimum duration of workflow. We can find that 1) When the deadline ratio is greater than 1.5, the traversal search is the best choice. 2) When the deadline ratio less than 1.5, GA and PSO are the best from the perspective of offloading cost and success rate. However, the high decision overhead is a fatal disadvantage when the deadline is such urgent. As a result, when the deadline ratio is less than 1.5, the traversal search is still the acceptable best choice.

6 Conclusions

In this paper, we have studied the problem of D2D collaborative offloading for workflow in an unpredictable dynamic environment. In order to make the workflow to be finished before the deadline with the minimum cost, we propose a D2D collaborative offloading approach. In this approach, the real-time state monitor triggers the online adjustment based on the estimation of the traversal to search the best strategy. We conduct simulations to evaluate the performance of our proposed offloading approach. The simulation results show the significant improvement in performance achieved by the proposed offloading approach.

Acknowledgements. This work is supported by the National Natural Science Foundation of China (No. 62002123), Guangdong Basic and Applied Basic Research Foundation (No. 2019A1515110212), Key-Area Research and Development Program of Guangdong Province (No. 2020B0101650001), National Key-Area Research and Development Program of China (No. 2018YFB1404402). Haoyu Luo is the corresponding author.

References

1. Li, X., Chen, T., Yuan, D., Xu, J., Liu, X.: A novel graph-based computation offloading strategy for workflow applications in mobile edge computing. arXiv Preprint ArXiv:2102.12236 (2021)
2. Hossain, M.D., et al.: Fuzzy decision-based efficient task offloading management scheme in multi-tier MEC-enabled networks. Sensors **21**(4), 1484 (2021)
3. Pu, L., Chen, X., Xu, J., Fu, X.: D2D fogging: An energy-efficient and incentive-aware task offloading framework via network-assisted D2D collaboration. IEEE J. Select. Areas Commun. **34**(12), 3887–3901 (2016)
4. Peng, Q., He, Q., Xia, Y., Chunrong, W., Wang, S.: Collaborative workflow scheduling over MANET, a user position prediction-based approach. In: Gao, H., Wang, X., Yin, Y., Iqbal, M. (eds.) CollaborateCom 2018. LNICSSITE, vol. 268, pp. 33–52. Springer, Cham (2019). https://doi.org/10.1007/978-3-030-12981-1_3
5. Hu, Y.C., Patel, M., Sabella, D., Sprecher, N., Young, V.: Mobile edge computing—a key technology towards 5G. ETSI White Paper **11**(11), 1–16 (2015)
6. Shadi, M., Abrishami, S., Mohajerzadeh, A.H., Zolfaghari, B.: Ready-time partitioning algorithm for computation offloading of workflow applications in mobile cloud computing. J. Supercomput. **77**(6), 6408–6434 (2021). https://doi.org/10.1007/s11227-020-03528-z
7. Baek, H., Ko, H., Pack, S.: Privacy-preserving and trustworthy device-to-device (D2D) offloading scheme. IEEE Access **8**, 191551–191560 (2020)
8. Li, Z., Hu, H., Hu, H., Huang, B., Ge, J., Chang, V.: Security and energy-aware collaborative task offloading in D2D communication. Future Generation Comput. Syst. **118**, 358–373 (2021)
9. Zhang, X.: Enhancing mobile cloud with social-aware device-to-device offloading. Comput. Commun. **168**, 1–11 (2021)
10. Wang, X., Ning, Z., Guo, S.: Multi-agent imitation learning for pervasive edge computing: a decentralized computation offloading algorithm. IEEE Trans. Parallel Distrib. Syst. **32**(2), 411–425 (2020)
11. Peng, Q., Jiang, H., Chen, M., Liang, J., Xia, Y.: Reliability-aware and deadline-constrained workflow scheduling in mobile edge computing. In: 2019 IEEE 16th International Conference on Networking, Sensing and Control (ICNSC), pp. 236–241. IEEE, Banff (2019)
12. Mogensen, P., et al.: LTE capacity compared to the Shannon bound. In: 2007 IEEE 65th Vehicular Technology Conference-VTC2007-Spring, pp. 1234–1238. IEEE, Dublin (2007)
13. Anamuro, C.V., Varsier, N., Schwoerer, J., Lagrange, X.: Distance-aware relay selection in an energy-efficient discovery protocol for 5G D2D communication. In: IEEE Transactions on Wireless Communications (2021)
14. Camp, T., Boleng, J., Davies, V.: A survey of mobility models for ad hoc network research. Wireless Commun. Mobile Comput. **2**(5), 483–502 (2002)
15. Bharathi, S., Chervenak, A., Deelman, E., Mehta, G., Su, M.H., Vahi, K.: Characterization of scientific workflows. In: 2008 Third Workshop on Workflows in Support of Large-scale Science, pp. 1–10. IEEE, Austin (2008)
16. Topcuoglu, H., Hariri, S., & Wu, M. Y.: Performance-effective and low-complexity task scheduling for heterogeneous computing. IEEE Trans. Parallel Distrib. Syst. **13**(3), 260–274 (2002)
17. Blythe, J., et al.: Task scheduling strategies for workflow-based applications in grids. In: CCGrid 2005. In: IEEE International Symposium on Cluster Computing and The Grid, 2005, vol. 2, pp. 759–767. IEEE, Cardiff (2005)
18. Scikit-opt (2021). https://github.com/guofei9987/scikit-opt

A Road Congestion Detection Model Based on Sequence Change of Vehicle Feature Matrix

Zhi-bing Fu, Qing-kui Chen(✉), and Ming-ming Wang

University of Shanghai for Science and Technology, Shanghai, China
chenqingkui@usst.edu.cn

Abstract. In order to solve the problem of urban road congestion, this paper proposes a road congestion detection model based on the sequence change of vehicle feature matrix. The model uses the YOLO_V3 deep learning model to extract features from the images of the traffic area, calculates the eigenvalues of each vehicle, uses these eigenvalues to construct a road vehicle eigenvalue matrix, and finally uses the eigenvalue matrix sequence changes to analyze the displacement of vehicles in each lane. Then, the congestion situation of each lane is judged. The model can not only quickly obtain multiple information such as vehicle flow state and state duration in the lane area, such as straight, left-turn, and right-turn vehicles, but also can interpret the speed of traffic flow, especially at low speeds, so it is more suitable for road congestion detection. The experimental results finally show that the accuracy of the model for the vehicle flow state of a single lane is more than 84%.

Keywords: Road congestion · Congestion detection · Urban traffic · Eigenmatrix sequence · YOLO_V3

1 Introduction

With the improvement of people's living standards and the acceleration of the urbanization process, the number of motor vehicles in my country has increased sharply, and the traffic volume has also continued to increase, making the problem of urban road traffic congestion increasingly serious. More and more attention has been paid to urban intelligent traffic management and control, and road congestion detection is an important content of intelligent transportation [1].

At present, the common methods of road traffic congestion monitoring include sensing based on electronic induction coils [2, 3], based on vehicle GPS data analysis [4–6], and video traffic monitoring based on artificial intelligence [7–9], etc. There are problems such as high cost, easy damage or inability to accurately predict road vehicle congestion. Based on the above problems, this paper proposes a road congestion detection model based on the sequence change of vehicle feature matrix. Interpret the speed of traffic flow, especially at low speed, it is more obvious. Therefore, it is more suitable for road congestion detection. The experimental results finally show that the accuracy of the model for the vehicle flow state of a single lane is more than 84%.

Y. Sun et al. (Eds.): ChineseCSCW 2021, CCIS 1491, pp. 191–198, 2022.
https://doi.org/10.1007/978-981-19-4546-5_15

2 Related Work

2.1 Road Congestion Detection Method

Document [2] collects data information through the induction coil detector, and uses the fuzzy clustering judgment algorithm to judge the road traffic status of the collected data. Literature [3] proposed a method of integrating induction coils and video data for road traffic detection. This method can make full use of the information of different sensor data, so as to effectively predict the reliability of traffic events. Literature [4–6] collects the information of the vehicle GPS, and judges the congestion of the road through the feedback information of the third-party platform. Reference [7] uses the YOLO_V3 deep learning method for vehicle target detection, establishes a traffic flow counting model, and realizes vehicle tracking. Reference [8] uses the basic SSD deep learning method for vehicle target detection, and realizes road congestion monitoring by establishing a vehicle flow model. Reference [9] explores three machine learning techniques (logistic regression, random forest, neural network) for short-term traffic congestion prediction. Most of these AI-based video traffic monitoring cannot distinguish lane information, which in turn affects road traffic congestion monitoring.

In the YOLO series, YOLO_V3 solves the problem of low target recognition accuracy for small targets and occlusions [7,10]. Therefore, this paper selects YOLO_V3 to detect objects on the road. In order to solve the problem of high cost and inability to accurately predict road vehicle congestion. This paper proposes a road congestion detection model based on the sequence change of vehicle feature matrix.

3 Model Design

3.1 Model Architecture

In this paper, a road congestion detection model based on the sequence change of vehicle feature matrix is proposed. The model architecture is shown in Fig. 1. The model architecture includes five parts: clock drive system, video information acquisition system, initial marking system, image feature extraction system, congestion monitoring and analysis system, and alarm system. In Fig. 1, the dotted box is information, the solid box is the function, the dotted arrow line is the control flow, and the solid arrow line is the information.

In order to better describe the basic data structure of the corresponding model in Fig. 1, the basic data structure in Fig. 1 is described in detail in Table 1.

3.2 Vehicle Eigenvalue Matrix Sequence

In order to detect the vehicle congestion in the lane, the method uses deep learning model to extract features from the images of traffic areas, thereby calculating the eigenvalues of each vehicle, and finally using these eigenvalues to construct a road vehicle eigenvalue matrix, and then using the eigenvalue matrix sequence changes to analyze the displacement of vehicles in each lane condition.

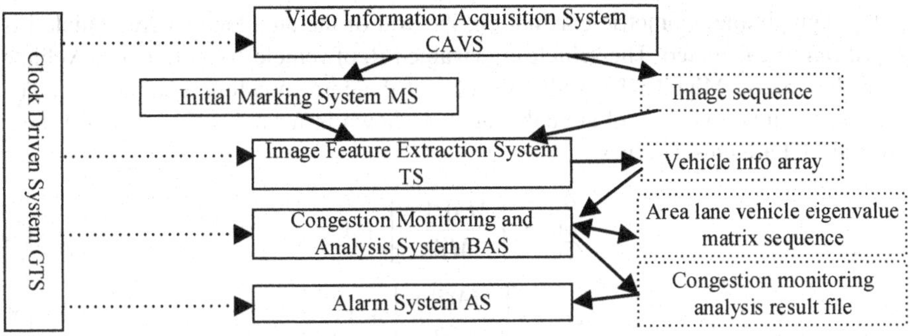

Fig. 1. Model architecture diagram

Table 1. Symbolic description of basic data structure

Symbol	Meaning
CA	The camera area
MR	Area lane, an area lane MR is a vehicle flow motion flow function Sub-area contained in the main body of a certain camera area CA
SL	Area lane dividing line, in the camera coordinate system of CA
$minfo_i$	The feature vector of vehicle i
FR_i	The eigenvalue of vehicle i is used to extract the vehicle in the Camera area CA by using the method of target detection
MA[i]	The information array of vehicle i
MRR_{t_i}	The eigenvalue matrix of the area lane vehicle at time t_i
arid	Represents different area lanes
f_{arid}	Create a congestion monitoring analysis results file per zone lane
sta_{arid}	The general flow state of vehicles in the area lane arid

Traditional machine learning [11–14] has computationally complex problems in extracting vehicle features from images, here we use a simple and fast vehicle feature extraction method. The calculation method of the eigenvalue FR_i of vehicle i is shown in formula (1), where in the eigenvector $minfo_i$ of vehicle i, pinfo is the weight vector occupied by each component of minfo, and the sum of each component of the vector is 1. MA[i].minfo is the row vector in formula (1), MA[i].pinfo is the column vector in formula (1), and N is the length of the feature vector.

$$FR_i = \begin{bmatrix} P_1 \; P_2 \cdots P_N \end{bmatrix} \times \begin{bmatrix} Q_1 \\ Q_2 \\ \vdots \\ Q_N \end{bmatrix} \tag{1}$$

Through simple geometric calculation, the arid of the area lane where vehicle i is located can be calculated. The vehicle eigenvalue FR_i of vehicle i is stored in the vehicle eigenvalue matrix MRRTMP1[arid] (row,col) of the corresponding area lane aid. The matrix subscripts row and col are calculated as shown in formulas (2) and (3), Where MW and MH are preset values.

$$row = \left\lfloor \frac{MA[i].x}{MW} \right\rfloor + 1 \tag{2}$$

$$col = \left\lfloor \frac{MA[i].y}{MH} \right\rfloor + 1 \tag{3}$$

Let a time series be t_1, t_2, t_3..., at time t_i (i >= 1), a vehicle eigenvalue matrix composed of the vehicle eigenvalues of all vehicles in the lane in the area at time t_i, then corresponding to the above time series, we can obtain a regional lane vehicle eigenvalue matrix sequence MRR_{t_1},MRR_{t_2},..., MRR_{t_i}. Here we calculate the variance value sv of the vehicle eigenvalue matrices MRRTMP1[arid] and MRRTMP2[arid] at two adjacent moments of each area lane arid. For the specific process, see Step 7 in Algorithm 2.

4 Model Implementation

4.1 Clock-Driven System GTS

The clock-driven system is a time series generator, which can generate a time series according to the application requirements. All subsystems of the system run synchronously according to this time series, and the time series interval is t.

4.2 Video Information Acquisition System CAVS

According to the time series provided by the GTS system, the image sequence P_1, P_2, P_3,... P_t of the camera area (CA) is formed by using a commercial camera, image capturing and preprocessing system.

4.3 Initial Marking System MS

The MS displays the camera area CA on the display according to the image sequence provided by CAVS, and the user uses the mouse to successively give the area lane dividing lines SL_1, SL_2,..., SLs, and divide the camera area CA into s + 1 disconnected areas. The system is represented by the equation of SL_1, SL_2,..., SLs at the points marked by the dividing line, denoted as $YF_i(x,y)(0 <= i <= s)$.

4.4 Image Feature Extraction System TS

Here, after passing the image obtained from the camera area CA through the target detection network YOLO_V3, the x and y coordinates of the corresponding vehicle i and the feature vector $minfo_i$ can be obtained. The method of the image feature extraction system TS is Algorithm 1.

Algorithm 1. Image Feature Extraction System TS Algorithm

Start

Step1 : Gets the current time t from system GTS.

Step2 : System CAVS obtains the image P_t of the camera area CA at time t.

Step3 : Feature extraction is carried out on image P_t to obtain the information of all vehicles and store it in the vehicle information MA[i][j].

```
For i=0; i++;i<Q
    For j=0;j++;j<5
        MA[i][j]= vehicle information for vehicle i
End for
```

Step4 : Vehicle information MA[i][j] is sent to the system BAS.

Step5 : Turn to Step1 for the next moment of image processing.

End

4.5 Congestion Monitoring and Analysis System BAS

The BAS method of the congestion monitoring and analysis system is as follows, and Algorithm 2 is its corresponding algorithm.

Algorithm 2. Congestion Monitoring and Analysis System BAS Algorithm

Start

Step1 : Obtain the regional lane divider SL_1, SL_2.. of the camera regional CA.

Step2 : Create a congestion monitoring analysis result file f_{arid} for each regional lane.

Step3 : Create two matrixes MRRTMP1[$arid_k$], MRRTMP1[$arid_k$] for each regional lane arid, and create a temporary exchange variable TTMP.

Step4 : According to the GTS clock sequence, the vehicle information MA[i] of the image P is obtained.

Step5: The vehicle eigenvalue matrix MRRTMP1[$arid_k$] of $arid_k$ is calculated.

Step6 : The vehicle eigenvalue matrix MRRTMP2[$arid_k$] of $arid_k$ is calculated at the next moment, like Step5.

Step7 : The variance values sv of the vehicle eigenvalue matrices MRRTMP1 [$arid_k$] and MRRTMP2 [$arid_k$] at two adjacent moments were calculated.

```
For a=0; a<n;a++
    For b=0; b<m;b++
        sv=sv+abs(MRRTMP2 [arid_k]- MRRTMP1 [arid_k])
sv=sv/(n+m)
```

Step8 : According to the sv value, the current traffic flow state(sta) of regional lane is judged, and put the individual attribute values into f_{arid}.

End

4.6 Alarm System AS

1) Obtain from the congestion monitoring and analysis system BAS the number of regional lanes s + 1 in the camera area CA and the congestion monitoring and analysis result file $f_{arid}(0 <= arid <= s)$ corresponding to each regional lane;
2) Read the current clock of GTS;
3) For 0 <= arid <= s + 1, do the following:
   Read the state sta and duration ptime of the area lane arid at the current moment from the f_{arid}, if the state sta duration ptime exceeds the normal value, the state sta alarm will be thrown to the area lane arid.
4) Turn to 2) to perform the next moment alarm analysis.

5 Experiment and Analysis

5.1 Evaluation Indicators

A_i represents the total time of the actual situation of a certain state in a certain lane unit time, F_i represents the time sum of the experimental analysis of a certain state in a certain lane unit time, n represents the number of different states (n = 1, 2, 3, 4). Here, the accuracy of the overall flow state of vehicles in different lanes (left-turn lane, middle straight lane, right-turn lane) is counted separately, and MAPE is used to evaluate the accuracy of the experimental results, as shown in formulas (4).

$$\mathrm{MAPE} = \left(\frac{1}{n}\sum_{i=1}^{n}\left|\frac{A_i - F_i}{A_i}\right|\right) \times 100\% \tag{4}$$

5.2 Experiment and Analysis

Divide the video into several 1-minute videos for analysis in the model in this paper. Figure shows the detection results of vehicle feature values within a certain minute. Figure 2 represent the characteristics of vehicles at the intersection of Jinqiao Road. The detection result of the value, which corresponds to the corresponding eigenvalue matrix.

Taking the vehicle flow state per unit time at the Jinqiao Road intersection as an example, Table 2 shows the experimental results of the vehicle flow state per unit time at the Jinqiao Road intersection. Specifically, it includes the left-turn lane, the middle straight lane, and the right-turn lane in the time t of a certain vehicle flow state sta and the corresponding duration (units). The blank part in Tables 2 and 3 indicates the end of the video analysis.

The experimental results of the vehicle flow state in the intersection unit time and the actual collection results of the vehicle flow state in the intersection unit time are analyzed. At the same time, according to the evaluation indicators of formula (4), we obtained the accuracy rates of vehicle flow states in the left turn lane, middle straight lane, and right turn lane at the Jinqiao intersection, respectively 98%, 84%, and 97%. The road congestion detection model based on the change of the vehicle feature matrix sequence has an accuracy rate of more than 84 for the vehicle flow state of a single lane.

Fig. 2. Vehicle characteristic value detection results

Table 2. Experimental results of vehicle flow state at Jinqiao Road intersection in unit time

Lane	Sta_{t1}	T1	Sta_{t2}	T2	Sta_{t3}	T3	Sta_{t4}	T4
Left turn lane	1	57.2	2	4.1				
Middle straight road	1	19.0	2	9.0	1	11.0	1	21.0
Right turn lane	1	58.1	2	2.4				

Table 3. Actual collection results of vehicle flow state in unit time at Jinqiao Road intersection

Lane	Sta_{t1}	T1	Sta_{t2}	T2	Sta_{t3}	T3	Sta_{t4}	T4
Left turn lane	1	60.0						
Middle straight road	1	22.0	2	8.0	1	19.0	1	11.0
Right turn lane	1	57.5	2	2.5				

6 Summary

Aiming at the problem of urban road congestion, this paper proposes a model with low implementation cost, strong global information, and fast and accurate prediction of lane vehicle congestion. The model can not only quickly obtain multiple information such as vehicle flow state and state duration in the lane area, such as straight, left-turn, and right-turn vehicles, but also can use the vehicle eigenvalue matrix sequence transformation difference. The speed of traffic flow is more obvious especially at low speed, so it is more suitable for road congestion detection.

The training and test data in this paper contain images of day and night, due to factors such as the complexity of urban road intersections and the influence of large trucks, some vehicles may appear blocked. The phenomenon of occlusion leads to deviations in vehicle target detection. These are the directions for further research in our next work.

References

1. Zheng, Y.: Road Traffic Flow Prediction Model and Road Network Flow Optimization Based on Deep Learning. Guizhou University, Guiyang (2020)
2. Chen, X., Chen, R.: A review on traffic prediction methods for intelligent transportation system in smart cities. In: 2019 12th International Congress on Image and Signal Processing, BioMedical Engineering and Informatics (CISP-BMEI), pp. 1–5. IEEE (2019)
3. Jiang, Z.: Traffic operation data analysis and information processing based on data mining. Autom. Control. Comput. Sci. **53**(3), 244–252 (2019)
4. Guo, J., Liu, Y., Yang, Q., et al.: GPS-based citywide traffic congestion forecasting using CNN-RNN and C3D hybrid model. Transportmetrica A Transport Sci. **17**(2), 190–211 (2021)
5. Wahid, A., Rao, A.C.S., Goel, D.: Server communication reduction for GPS-based floating car data traffic congestion detection method. In: Krishna, A.N., Srikantaiah, K.C., Naveena, C. (eds.) Integrated Intelligent Computing, Communication and Security. SCI, vol. 771, pp. 415–425. Springer, Singapore (2019). https://doi.org/10.1007/978-981-10-8797-4_43
6. Sui, X., Zhang, Y.: Entropy-based traffic congestion propagation pattern mining with GPS data. In: 2021 IEEE 6th International Conference on Big Data Analytics (ICBDA), pp. 128–132. IEEE (2021)
7. Lai, J., Wang, Y., Luo, T., Chen, Y., Liu, S.: A YOLO_V3-based road-side video traffic volume counting method and verification. J. Highw. Transp. Res. Dev. **38**(01), 135–142 (2021)
8. Al Okaishi, W., Zaarane, A., Slimani, I., et al.: A vehicular queue length measurement system in real-time based on SSD network. Transp. Telecommun. **22**(1), 29–38 (2021)
9. Elfar, A., Talebpour, A., Mahmassani, H.S.: Machine learning approach to short-term traffic congestion prediction in a connected environment. Transp. Res. Rec. **2672**(45), 185–195 (2018)
10. Redmon, J., Farhadi, A.: Yolov3: an incremental improvement. arXiv preprint arXiv:1804.02767 (2018)
11. Li, T., Lai, Y., Fang, T., Yuan, T., Yongtao, L.: Research of driving sight distance detection algorithm based on procurement of special points. J. Chongqing Univ. Technol. (Natural Science) **33**(07), 37–43 (2019)
12. Qitian, W.: Highway parking event detection based on improved Haar-like+Adaboost. Chongqing University (2019)
13. Liu, H., Liu, H., Yu, M., Zhao, Z.: Research and implementation of vehicle tracking algorithm based on multi-feature fusion. J. Chinese Comput. Syst. **41**(06), 1258–1262 (2020)
14. El-Khoreby, M.A., Abu-Bakar, S.A.R., Mokji, M.M., et al.: Performance comparison between SVM and K-means for vehicle counting. In: IOP Conference Series: Materials Science and Engineering, vol. 884, no. 1, p. 012077. IOP Publishing (2020)

Resource Scheduling Method Based on Microservices

Zhuo Tian[1], Changyou Zhang[1](✉), Shuai Tang[2], and Jiaojiao Xiao[1,2]

[1] Institute of Software, Chinese Academy of Sciences, Beijing 100190, China
changyou@iscas.ac.com
[2] Beijing Forestry University, Beijing 100083, China

Abstract. The rapid growth of access and data traffic on the Internet has led to the need for IT construction to cope with the high concurrent access of a large number of users to network applications. Servers need to have the ability to provide a large number of concurrent access services to achieve high availability and high fault tolerance. When a large number of users access concurrently, the access server faces problems such as access load pressure and resource scheduling among back-end services. This paper proposes a resource scheduling algorithm based on microservices, comprehensively considers the performance indicators of each server, and uses a quantitative scoring model to implement load balancing algorithms. Experimental results show that the load balancing algorithm implemented in this paper reduces resource scheduling time and improves The utilization of server resources increases the concurrent access capability of distributed systems.

Keywords: High concurrency · Resource scheduling · Microservices · Load balancing · Distributed

1 Introduction

Behind the high concurrent traffic access of the network is the scheduling of a large number of service resources [1]. The most widely used method is to build a server cluster to improve system performance to deal with huge access requests [2]. Resource scheduling is an effective adjustment of resources, so that resources can be used reasonably to the maximum extent [3]. The current method is generally to load balance the request to the back-end server through load balancing technology, and let the back-end server handle it [4, 5].

Microservice is a tiny service that can be deployed independently and it is more suitable for contemporary service architecture [6]. If you use Eureka for load balancing [7, 8], you will face a problem: if you want to adjust the load balancing scheme, such as complex weighting, then the entire system will face the embarrassment of stopping the service [9, 10]. So can we delegate load balancing to middleware outside the system? This article realizes that the initiative of the load is handed over to the reverse proxy server, and the load balance is realized through a third-party scheduling algorithm [11].

Y. Sun et al. (Eds.): ChineseCSCW 2021, CCIS 1491, pp. 199–204, 2022.
https://doi.org/10.1007/978-981-19-4546-5_16

2 Background

In the current era of rapid Internet development, more and more users have become netizens. The "epidemic health code" launched by the national integrated government service platform has been applied for by a total of 900 million people, and the number of uses has exceeded 40 billion times [12]. Currently, the most widely used method is to build a server cluster to improve system performance to deal with the huge traffic demand [13]. Nginx is a high-performance reverse proxy server produced under this background. Usually can carry tens of thousands of concurrent connections at the same time. It also supports a variety of load balancing strategies, and also supports third-party module extensions to achieve load balancing functions [14, 15].

3 Scheduling Algorithm

3.1 Scheduling Algorithm Module

This algorithm combines the three factors of single server connection (conn), weight (weight), and last successful completion request time (delta) for comprehensive evaluation, and the best score (score) is preferred. If the number of connections of a person's server is small, it means that the available processing power of the server is strong, so it is preferred. If the time difference of a server is small, it indicates that the server has a fast response time and strong processing capacity, and it should be preferred. Among these factors, due to the large changes in the time factor, in order to reduce the impact of the large changes in time, a parameter A is added to adjust the overall score, and in order to increase the influence of other factors, the conn and weight are squared, and the formula 1.

$$\text{score} = \text{A} \cdot \text{delta} \cdot \frac{\text{conn}^2}{\text{weight}^2} \tag{1}$$

3.2 Data Structure Design

This paper proposes an improved load balancing algorithm conntime, the structure ngx_http_upstream_sugar_peer_data_t, which contains members such as the polling structure, the number of attempts, the current time, and the adjustment factor. Among them, since the network data transmitted by the socket communication is forcibly converted into the data in the structure, the polling structure should be placed first, and space should be opened for all members.

```
typedef struct{
    ngx_http_upstream_rr_peer_data_t rrp;
    u_char tries;
    time_t now;
    ngx_uint_t coefficient;
    ngx_event_get_peer_pt get_rr_peer;
}ngx_http_upstream_sugar_peer_data_t;
```

3.3 Registration Structure Design

Since the load balancing algorithm name needs to be written in the nginx.conf configuration file, there should be registration information inside the load balancing algorithm. If a new load balancing algorithm named conntime wants to register to the upper layer, then the nginx instruction structure, the http subordinate module structure, and the nginx registration structure containing the first two must be declared. As shown in Table 1.

Table 1. Registration structure.

Type of data	Variable name	Comments
static ngx_command_t	ngx_http_upstream_conntime_commands[]	Instruction
static ngx_http_module_t	ngx_http_upstream_conntime_module_ctx	http module
ngx_module_t	ngx_http_upstream_conntime_module	ngx module

3.4 Function Design

In nginx, all scheduling algorithms except for the main scheduling module have a fixed process, which is the main algorithm function, the initialization algorithm, the initialization of the back-end server, the obtaining of the optimal back-end server id and the marking, and the end. After calling the initialization algorithm function in the main function, proceed in sequence.

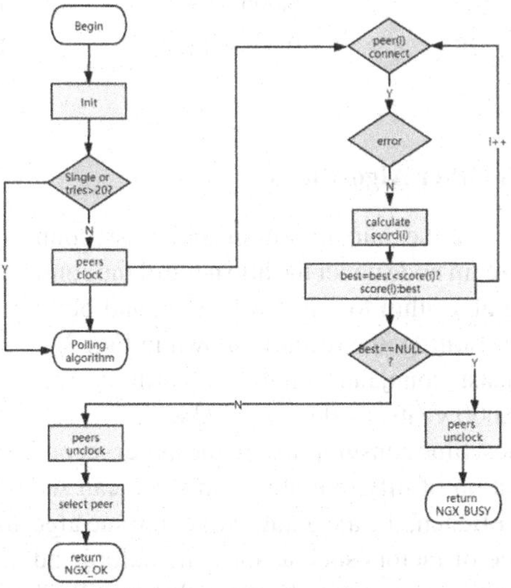

Fig. 1. The relationship between the structure of ngx-http-upstream scheduling algorithms.

Obtaining the optimal back-end server is the core of the entire scheduling algorithm, the simplified algorithm flow is shown in Fig. 1. After the necessary initialization, all servers must be locked to prevent errors. Then try to see if all available servers are available or if there are other errors. If there is no problem, the score is calculated. The server with the best score is marked. Regardless of whether the optimal server is found, unlock it and return the corresponding result.

4 Results and Discussion

4.1 Load Balancing Algorithm Test

If you want to use a certain load balancing algorithm in nginx, you must first add an upstream node under the http node of the nginx.conf configuration file. We add three back-end servers to the nginx server, namely 192.168.142.141, 192.168.142.142, and 192.168.142.143. And the load balancing algorithm used is the self-developed conntime algorithm. The ApacheBenc(ab) command has very low requirements on the computer issuing the load. The test uses 50 users to access the nignx server 2000 times. The total time is 0.259 s, 1336000 bytes are transmitted, the average time per request is 0.130ms, and the transmission rate is 5032.24 Kbytes/s (Table 2).

Table 2. Statistics details of each server.

Server IP	Numbers	ups_resp_time/ms	request_time/ms
124.16.131.141	695	0.006608633	0.006585612
124.16.131.142	579	0.006740933	0.006734024
124.16.131.143	728	0.006303571	0.006300824

4.2 Comparing with Other Algorithms

Use ApacheBench to test the fair algorithm and least_conn algorithm in the same way.That is, in the upstream node under the http node of the configuration file Nginx.conf, change the scheduling algorithm to fair, least_conn, and polling for testing. When the scheduling algorithm is polling, the result is shown in Fig. 2.

By comparing the least_conn, fair, conntime algorithms, we can get the instantaneous data of 50 users with 2000 visits, as shown in Table 3.

By comparing the test time consumption, requests per second, average time consumption and other information of different algorithms, we can see that under the negative pressure tool of ApacheBench, the advantages of conntime algorithm are more obvious. Excluding the influence of factors such as the time before and after the test, the small data size, and the overall low test time, the algorithm is still relatively advantageous.

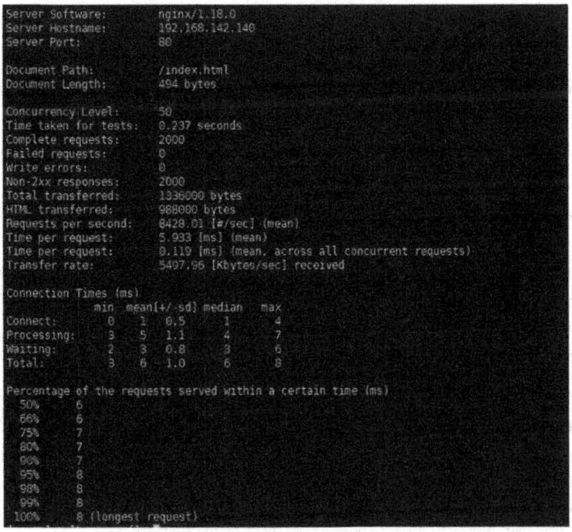

Fig. 2. Test comparison-least_conn.

Table 3. Comparison test details.

	Test time(s)	Number of requests (#/s)	Average time (ms)	Transfer rate (KB/s)
least_conn	0.312	6416.01	0.156	4185.45
fair	0.345	5789.32	0.173	3776.62
conntime	0.259	7714.09	0.130	5032.24
polling	0.237	8428.01	0.119	5497.96

5 Conclusions

This article implements an nginx-based technology resource scheduling system, which combines self-developed scheduling algorithms, jQuery framework, and Ajax technology. The article explains the self-developed replacement steps and related usage of the load balancing algorithm. Realize the combination of load balancer and microservice registry. Designed and implemented a self-developed load balancing scheduling algorithm. Under the ApacheBench negative pressure tool, the conntime algorithm improves the scheduling efficiency of the system.

Acknowledgments. This work was partially supported by National Key Research and Development Project—R&D and application demonstration of comprehensive technology service platform for Beibu Gulf city group (2018YFB1404400).

References

1. Wei, W., Qi, W., Heyang, X., Yang, L.: Highly complex resource scheduling for stochastic demands in heterogeneous clouds. J. Grid Comput. **19**(1), 12 (2021)
2. Ramana, K., Ponnavaikko, M.: A multi-class load balancing algorithm (MCLB) for heterogeneous web cluster. Stud. Inform. Control **27**(4) (2018)
3. Lin, W., Qi, D.: Survey of resource scheduling in cloud computing. Comput. Sci. **39**(010), 1–6 (2012)
4. Xiaoni, C, Bichuan, L., Qi, N., Qiuxuan, W.: Web load balance and cache optimization design based Nginx under high-concurrency environment, pp. 1029–1032 (2012)
5. Ramana, K., Ponnavaikko, M.: Web cluster load balancing techniques: a survey. Int. J. Appl. Eng. Research **10**(19), 39983–39998 (2016)
6. AI-Debagy, O., Martinek, P.: A microservice decomposition method through using distributed representation of source code. Scalable Comput. Pract. Exp. **22**(1), 39–52 (2021)
7. Jayswal, A.K.: Hybrid load-balanced scheduling in scalable cloud environment. Int. J. Inf. Syst. Model. Des. **11**(3), 62–78 (2020)
8. Hsieh, H.-C., Chiang, M.-L.: The incremental load balance cloud algorithm by using dynamic data deployment. J. Grid Comput. **17**(3), 553–575 (2019). https://doi.org/10.1007/s10723-019-09474-2
9. Junhua, F., Rong, Z., Aoying, Z.: Load balance for distributed real-time computing systems. East China Normal University Scientific Reports 13, WorldScientific, ISBN 9789811216145, pp. 1–260 (2020)
10. Phi-Le, N., Thanh-Hung, N., Kien, N.: A path-length efficient, low-overhead, load-balanced routing protocol for maximum network lifetime in wireless sensor networks with holes. Sensors **20**(9), 2506 (2020)
11. Ramnath, S., Gunturij, V.M.V.: Optimal load balanced demand distribution under overload penalties. CoRR abs/2009.01765 (2020)
12. China Internet Network Information Center. Statistical Report on Internet Development in China (No. 47) [EB/OL]. http://www.cnnic.net.cn/,2021.02
13. Chiang, M.-L., Cheng, H.-S., Liu, H.-Y., Chiang, C.-Y.: SDN-basedserverclusters with dynamic load balancing and performance improvement. Clust. Comput. **24**(1), 537–558 (2021)
14. Rajpoot, P., Dwivedi, P.: Optimized and load balanced clustering for wireless sensor networks to increase the lifetime of WSN using MADM approaches. Wireless Netw. **26**(1), 215–251 (2018). https://doi.org/10.1007/s11276-018-1812-2
15. Yin, M., Sun, D., Sun, H.: Dynamic load balance strategy for parallel rendering based on deferred shading. Int. J. Comput. Sci. Eng. **18**(3), 286–293 (2019)

A Novel Construction Approach for Dehazing Dataset Based on Realistic Rendering Engine

Shizhen Yang, Fazhi He(✉), Jiacheng Gao, and Jinkun Luo

School of Computer Science, Wuhan University, Wuhan, China
fzhe@whu.edu

Abstract. Image dehazing is an important pre-processing for computer vision systems. Modern dehazing techniques are based deep learning and training data. Typical datasets are constructed with depth camera for indoor scene. However, it is challenging to construct outdoor dataset because the limitation of depth information devices. This paper presents a novel construction approach for outdoor dehazing dataset. In our approach, we propose to adopt realistic rendering engine to generate pairs of both hazy and clear images for outdoor scene. Initial experiments on typical dehazing networks confirm the proposed idea and construction method.

Keywords: Image dehazing · Dataset design · Realistic rendering engine · Convolutional neural network · Atmospheric scattering model

1 Introduction

During the past few decades, with pollution in industrial production and the popularity of cars, hazy weather happens frequently especially in metropolitans like Beijing. In a haze scene, small particles condensed by water vapor in air will cause scattering of light, resulting in serious degradation of images obtained through the camera, which may reduce the accuracy of subsequent advanced vision tasks, such as image segmentation and pedestrian re-identification. Therefore, removing haze from hazy images has become a hot research topic of computer vision and artificial intelligence.

Modern dehazing techniques are based on neural network models, in which the dataset is the foundation of dehazing algorithms. In the field of dehazing based on deep learning, there are several common datasets, such as NYU Depth V2 dataset [1], RESIDE dataset [2], and so on. However, the method of constructing hazy images by depth maps is limited by the capability of the device and is very costly for outdoor scenes. Thus, existing outdoor hazy images was generated by depth estimation [3], which may lead to big errors.

Therefore, we propose a method based on realistic sense engine simulation to construct pairs of both hazy and clear images for one same outdoor scene at the same time, which is impossible to be collected in real-world.

Y. Sun et al. (Eds.): ChineseCSCW 2021, CCIS 1491, pp. 205–214, 2022.
https://doi.org/10.1007/978-981-19-4546-5_17

This manuscript has 5 sections: Sect. 2 discusses the related works of dehazing algorithms and datasets of deep learning dehazing. Section 3 describes our approach how to construct pairs of both hazy and clear images for outdoor scene based on the realistic engine. In Sect. 4, initial experiments are conducted to confirm the proposed idea and technique. Section 5 summarizes this work with future directions.

2 Related Works

2.1 Atmosphere Light Model

Theoretical studies have shown that the reasons for atmospheric light scattering are two respects [4]. Firstly, in hazy days, particles in the atmosphere, as dust and water droplets, will scatter the light in different directions. This scattering makes the light appear to be split and thinner in different directions. Secondly, the incident light is reflected to some extent by these particles, causing a direct change in the direction of the incident light. Further validation and refining by other scholars supplement the conversion mechanism between hazy and clear images.

The scattering mechanism of an image is shown in Fig. 1 [5].

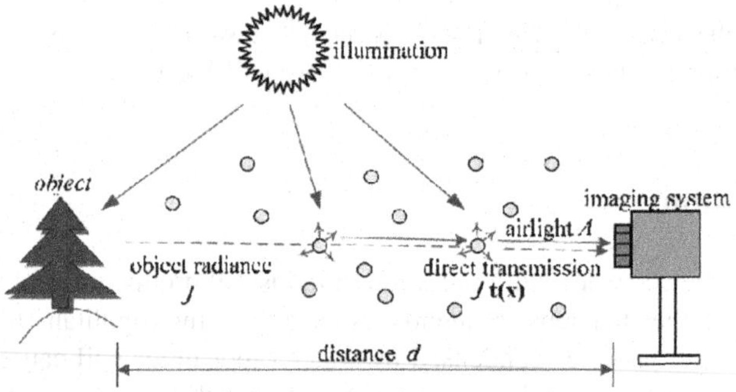

Fig. 1. Atmosphere scattering model

The mathematical equation of the model is expressed as Eq. (1) and Eq. (2).

$$I(x) = J(x)t(x) + A(1 - t(x)) \tag{1}$$

where,

$$t(x)= exp^{-\beta d(x)} \tag{2}$$

In Eq. (1), $J(x)$ is the dehazed image, $I(x)$ is the image with haze, $t(x)$ is the transmittance map, and A represents the atmospheric light.

Equation (2) illustrates that transmittance $t(x)$ can be estimated with depth information. $d(x)$ is the depth information value of the scene, and β is the atmospheric scattering coefficient, which is usually small. The formula shows that $t(x)$ and $d(x)$ show a negative correlation.

2.2 Dehazing Algorithms

There are two catalogues of image dehazing techniques: techniques based on handcrafted priors and techniques based on deep learning methods.

Based on Handcrafted Priors. These methods only based on physical models of atmospheric scattering is applied by measuring or estimating parameters such as atmospheric transmittance and scattering intensity.

Fattal et al. analyzed various components of the image separately thus achieving the effect of dehazing [3, 6]. Tan et al. chose to regionally adjust the image contrast of haze image [7]. S. G. Narasimhan et al. proposed a binary scattering model with image depth and the intensity of atmospheric scattering considered [8]. He et al. proposed the dark channel prior theory and estimate the transmission map according to the prior [9].

Based on Deep Learning Methods. Cai et al. introduced a CNN model called DehazeNet for dehazing. [10] Li et al. constructed an end to-end network and combined the atmosphere light and transmission into a K-estimation module to reduce the error in training. [11] Zhang et al. developed a densely connected network optimizes the Atmosphere, transmission map and the original image at the same time. [12]. FFA-Net is a state-of-art method using the attention-based feature fusion structure of different levels that is adaptive to learn feature weights and give more weight to important features [13].

2.3 Dehazing Datasets

The widely used dehazing datasets include NYU Depth V2 dataset, RESIDE dataset and Middlebury Stereo dataset.

NYU Depth V2 Dataset. The dataset contains more than one thousand RGBD images and the raw images of this data are acquired by Microsoft's Kinect depth camera as shown in Fig. 2.

It consists of the label information of the objects which is used for semantic segmentation, the RGB and depth data provided by the original camera, and functions set used for manipulating the data and annotation.

Fig. 2. NYU Depth V2 dataset images samples. The three images are the output from the RGB camera (left), preprocess depth (center) and a set of labels (right) for the image.

Some popular networks such as DCPDN and AOD-Net adopt NYU Depth V2 to generate hazy indoor images. In these works, the indoor hazy images are created by using the atmosphere light model and the depth information from RGBD images.

RESIDE Dataset. The RESIDE dataset (REalistic Single Image Dehazing) includes both indoor images and outdoor images as show in Fig. 3. The indoor images of RESIDE come from NYU Depth V2. The indoor hazy images are created by using atmosphere light model and depth information of RGBD images.

For outdoor scenes, it is difficult to find the accurate depth information for hazy image. Therefore, the depth estimation has to be used in atmosphere light model to create hazy images, which are inaccurate.

RESIDE dataset is used in networks such as FFA-Net and MSBDN-DFF for training and testing.

RESIDE dataset adopts two evaluation criteria, no-reference metric and human subjective rating, which are used to evaluate the dehazing results on real-world blurred images as a complement to the widely used PSNR and SSIM.

Fig. 3. RESIDE dataset image samples

Middlebury Stereo Dataset. In addition to the above datasets, there is a dataset called Middlebury Stereo dataset [14], which consists of high-quality images of real indoor scenes and depth maps as Fig. 4.

It's used for indoor images dataset construction in RESIDE, too. Due to the small number of images, it's not used alone.

3 Dataset Construction

Though hazy images can be captured directly in the real environment, it is impossible to get the corresponding ground-truth non-haze scene images at the same time, which brings difficulty in dehazing based on the supervised learning. Furthermore, most of the time we can't acquire hazy images under extreme conditions in the real world.

Therefore, we propose to use Flightgear, a flight simulation engine, to simulate pairs of scenes with haze and without haze. We also adopt the Simulink tool component in MATLAB to control with same flight parameters. Finally, we use Auto Screen Cap to collect images pairs of the same scene under different weather to construct the dataset.

Fig. 4. Middlebury Stereo dataset image samples

3.1 Simulate Engine and Capture Tools

The proposed approach adopt three related tools as follows.

Flightgear. Flightgear is a flight simulator well established for realistic scenes, which is released as free open-source GPL software [15]. Many aviation control data researchers choose it for flight parameter acquisition and calculation. Therefore, we adopt this flight simulation engine to generate both the haze weather scenes and clear scenes.

MATLAB and Simulink. MATLAB is a widely used mathematical software, which can realize the calculation and simulation of some complex mathematical formula. Simulink is a visual development component for MATLAB, which has specific functions to achieve dynamic system modeling and digital signal simulation.

In the proposed approach, we use the Simulink component in MATLAB to generate the states of the aircraft, such as velocity, gesture and position coordinates. These states can be used to drive the aircraft scenes in Flightgear.

Auto Screen Cap. It's a utility used to collect the pair images of hazy scenes and clear scenes with a fixed frequency [16]. It starts up with simulator simultaneously to keep the consistency of the flight trajectory in different weather.

3.2 Data Capture

The proposed capture process of dehazing data is shown as Fig. 5.

(1) First, Start the Flightgear with the Script. By setting specific aircraft startup parameters in the startup file, the initial position of the aircraft is fixed in the air, so it has a certain scenery in the initial state. The flight parameters of the aircraft are transmitted to port 5502 via UDP protocol and stored using Flightgear's official tool provided.

(2) Next, Start the Simulink to Control the Flight Trajectory of the Aircraft. The simulation is repeated with same aircraft's velocity and trajectory in scenes under different weather.

The model structure of Simulink is shown in the Fig. 6.

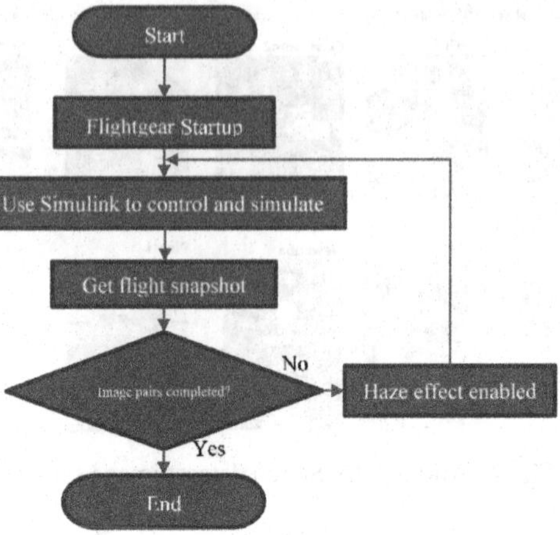

Fig. 5. The overall process of dehazing data capture

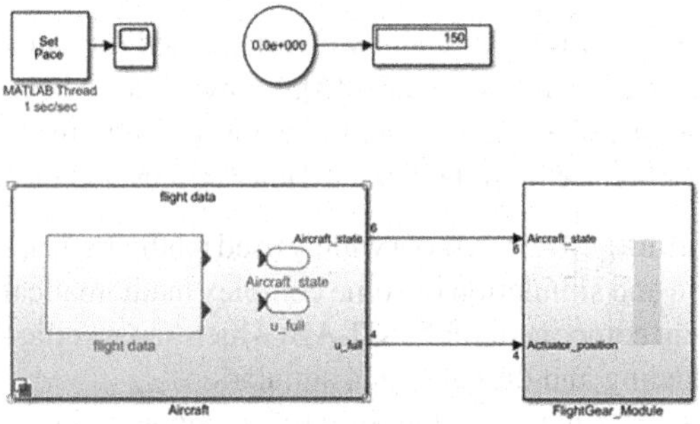

Fig. 6. Simulink model structure

(3) Get the Clear Images. During the first simulation, Flightgear runs without haze effect, and images such as in Fig. 7 are collected.

Fig. 7. Non-haze scene

(4) Get the Haze Images. Since the haze effect of Flightgear's default weather engine satisfies the Eqs. (1) and (2). Therefore, to obtain the corresponding haze images, we enable the haze options of Flightgear and rerun the simulator with other parameters unchanged, then collect the hazy-images as the same way above. We can get the corresponding image as Fig. 8.

Fig. 8. Hazy scene

3.3 Dataset Construction

After image pairs collected, we can use them to construct our dataset. Different works may need dataset in different format. The dataset can be easily constructed by separate images into different folder with same filename for corresponding image.

Because of the lack of landscape model, we only construct a test dataset for the following experiment at present. A larger dataset contains training set will be created after more model collected in future.

4 Initial Experiments

Our initial experiments are designed to test and confirm the proposed idea with limited scene data. Therefore, we use the captured data as testing samples in this paper. In the future, we will use our data for training samples.

The experiment is based on the Pytorch 0.4.0, Python 3.6.0, and all the training and testing runs on the Nvidia GTX 1070Ti GPU.

4.1 Testing Network

We use AOD-Net as the basic training and testing network and NYU-Depth V2 dataset as training set to examine the effect of our constructed test set. Except the test on AOD-Net, there are some additional examples tested on other net-works, which include GCA-Net [17], DCPDN, FFA-Net.

4.2 Dehazing Quality Metrics

After referring to recent studies on dehazing, we design experiment to examine the haze removal performance of the constructed dataset from the aspect of quality and confirm the effectiveness of the dataset.

To measure the quality of dehazing test, four kinds of hazy images are included in the test as follows:

- white objects or areas
- low brightness image dehazing
- building dense scene image dehazing
- dense haze scene dehazing

After comparing and observing the factors of the recovered images in these scenes, such as the color and the outline of objects and other vision effect of the dehazed images of this dataset, the testing effect of this self-built dataset is confirmed.

4.3 Qualitatively Analysis of Dehazing Visual Effects

The results of dehaze test on different networks are shown in Fig. 9, though the light haze is removed in all images, there exist some problems such as lightness decreasing in GCA-Net, and oversaturation in AOD-Net and DCPDN. The comparison shows that the dehaze net trained on real-world images dataset can be applied to test the simulator-generated haze images with dense buildings.

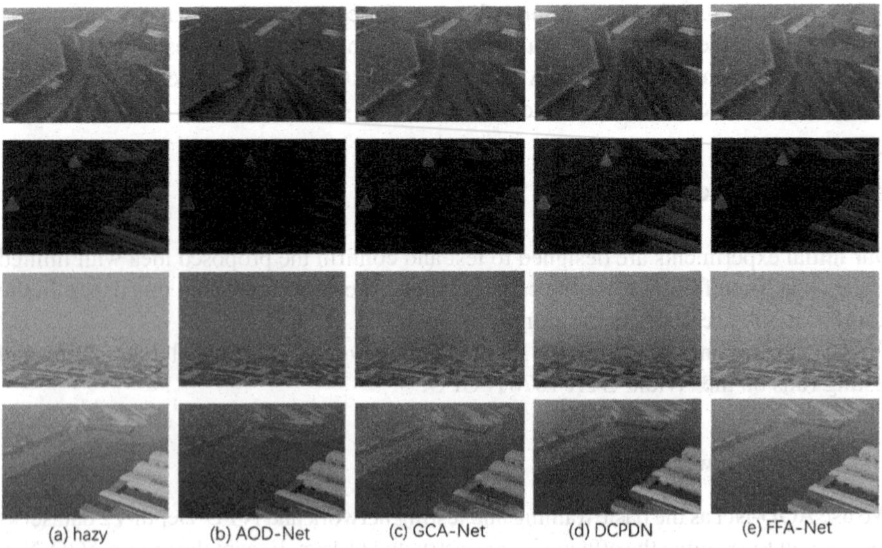

Fig. 9. The dehazing effect under different scenes

4.4 Quantitively Analysis of Dehazing Visual Effects

We added an experiment which using our generated dataset as the training set of the AOD-Net and compare its' effect with AOD-Net's default training dataset.

The compared results are shown in Table 1.

Table 1. The PSNR & SSIM of AOD-Net with same test set when trained on different dataset

	Default training dataset	Our generated training dataset
PSNR	19.6954	21.5742
SSIM	0.8478	0.7998

5 Conclusion and Future Work

This paper presents a new method for generating dehazing data. Haze scenes are generated with Flightgear, a flight simulation engine and MATLAB Simulink. The corresponding haze-free image of the same scenes are collected and tested with haze image on several different networks. The initial experiment results confirm the proposed idea and approach.

In the future, we will continue the work as follows. Firstly, the default landscape model of Flightgear is limited in size, which makes it difficult to simulate long-distance flight paths and limit the size and quality of the generated dataset. We aim to solve this problem by importing model with larger scale and higher quality in the future. Secondly, the frequent manual operations of flight path switching increase the burden of image collecting. So, auto flight with complex preset path is need. Thirdly, due to the feature of flight simulation, most of the landscape scenes are observed from a top view in the sky. We will decrease the flight altitude and deal with the problems of aircraft clipping through the mountain in low altitude flight.

References

1. Silberman, N., Hoiem, D., Kohli, P., Fergus, R.: Indoor segmentation and support inference from RGBD images. In: Fitzgibbon, A., Lazebnik, S., Perona, P., Sato, Y., Schmid, C. (eds.) ECCV 2012. LNCS, vol. 7576, pp. 746–760. Springer, Heidelberg (2012). https://doi.org/10.1007/978-3-642-33715-4_54
2. Li, B., et al.: Benchmarking single-image dehazing and beyond. IEEE Trans. Image Process. **28**(1), 492–505 (2019)
3. Liu, F., Shen, C., Lin, G., Reid, I.: Learning depth from single monocular images using deep convolutional neural fields. IEEE Trans. Pattern Anal. Mach. Intell. **38**(10), 2024–2039 (2015)
4. McCartney, E.J.: Optics of the Atmosphere: Scattering by Molecules and Particles. New York (1976)
5. Xing, L., Yang, L.: Image restoration using prior information physics model. In: 2011 4th International Congress on Image and Signal Processing, vol. 2, pp. 786–789. IEEE (2011)

6. Fattal, R.: Single image dehazing. ACM Trans. Graph. **27**(3), 1–9 (2008)
7. Tan, R.T.: Visibility in bad weather from a single image. In: 2008 IEEE Conference on Computer Vision and Pattern Recognition, pp. 1–8. IEEE (2008)
8. Narasimhan, S.G., Nayar, S.K.: Chromatic framework for vision in bad weather. In: Proceedings IEEE Conference on Computer Vision and Pattern Recognition. CVPR 2000 (Cat. No. PR00662), vol. 1, pp. 598–605. IEEE (2000)
9. He, K., Sun, J., Tang, X.: Single image haze removal using dark channel prior. IEEE Trans. Pattern Anal. Mach. Intell. **33**(12), 2341–2353 (2010)
10. Cai, B., Xiangmin, X., Jia, K., Qing, C., Tao, D.: Dehazenet: An end-to-end system for single image haze removal. IEEE Trans. Image Pro-cess. **25**(11), 5187–5198 (2016)
11. Li, B., Peng, X., Wang, Z., Xu, J., Feng, D.: Aod-net: all-in-one dehazing network. In: Proceedings of the IEEE international conference on comput-er vision, pp. 4770–4778 (2017)
12. Zhang, H., Patel, V.M.: Densely connected pyramid dehazing network. In: Proceedings of the IEEE conference on computer vision and pattern recognition, pp. 3194–3203 (2018)
13. Qin, X., Wang, Z., Bai, Y., Xie, X., Jia, H.: Ffa-net: Feature fusion attention network for single image dehazing. Proc. AAAI Conf. Artif. Intell. **34**, 11908–11915 (2020)
14. Scharstein, D., et al.: High-resolution stereo datasets with subpixel-accurate ground truth. In: Jiang, X., Hornegger, J., Koch, R. (eds.) GCPR 2014. LNCS, vol. 8753, pp. 31–42. Springer, Cham (2014). https://doi.org/10.1007/978-3-319-11752-2_3
15. FlightGear: Flightgear flight simulator – sophisticated, professional, open-source. https://www.flightgear.org/. Accessed 29 June 2021
16. Autoscreencap download—sourceforge.net. https://sourceforge.net/projects/autoscreencap/. Accessed 29 June 2021
17. Chen, D.: Gated context aggregation network for image dehazing and deraining. In: 2019 IEEE Winter Conference on Applications Of Computer Vision (WACV), pp. 1375–1383. IEEE (2019)

Cooperative Evolutionary Computation and Human-Like Intelligent Collaboration

Differential Evolution Algorithm Based on Adaptive Rank Exponent and Parameters

Weijie Mai(✉), Mingzhu Wei, Fengshan Shen, and Feng Yuan

Institute of Software Application Technology, Guangzhou and Chinese Academy of Sciences, Guangzhou, China
maiweijie@gz.iscas.ac.cn

Abstract. Differential evolution algorithm is a very useful and impactful method for handling global numerical optimization issue in the evolutionary algorithm family. However, there are still some shortcomings. Such as, the performance of DE is depend on its mutation strategy and parameters setting. In this article, we present a new fashione differential evolution algorithm which called AFP-DE with adaptive rank exponent and parameters. Compared with the update variant DE algorithms, the experiment shows that performance of AFP-DE is better than them with good performance.

Keywords: Differential evolution algorithm · Adaptive rank exponent and parameters · Mutation strategy

1 Introduction

Differential evolution algorithm (DE) is a simple yet powerful evolutionary algorithm firstly introduced by Storn and Price for dealing with global optimization over continues space [1, 2]. The merits of DE are its simple of use, compact, speed, and robustness. So far, DE has obtained many successful applications in different engineering fields. However, like other smart algorithm, Differential evolution algorithm also can't escape its own shortcomings. For example, it is easy to fall into local optimum, the presence of contradictory of convergence speed and accuracy as well as appear the trend of the stalemate with the algorithm advance. recently, lots of researcher both here and abroad have put forward many methods to improve DE, which can be major summarized for two aspects:

1. Mutation strategies. Scholars have put forward a lot of classical variation strategies by far, such as DE/rand/1, DE/best/1, DE/rand-to-best/1. However, different strategies have different characteristics, which means that there are different effects when solving different problems. It only lists some of the frequently used strategies, a large number of mutation strategies are put forward,such as [3–9].
2. Parameter setting. The classical differential evolution algorithm has three control parameters, namely the scaling factor F and the cross factor CR as well as the population size NP, which obviously affect the performance of DE. Therefore, scholars have

Y. Sun et al. (Eds.): ChineseCSCW 2021, CCIS 1491, pp. 217–229, 2022.
https://doi.org/10.1007/978-981-19-4546-5_18

projected a number of parameter improvement methods to improve the capability of DE. Such as [10–14].

In this paper, we are interested in the DE/rand/1, DE/rand/2, DE/best/1variation strategies to improve the performance of DE. We present adaptive Rank mutation strategy for the DE algorithm, which called AFP-DE.

The rest of the article is organized as follows. In Sect. 2, we briefly describes the original DE algorithm and some related work to the mutation operators in DE. The details of our proposed algorithm is described in Sect. 3. The experiment and evaluation of our proposed algorithm are presented in Sect. 4. Section 5 gives the summary of this article and the related research in the next step.

2 The Original Differential Evolution Algorithm

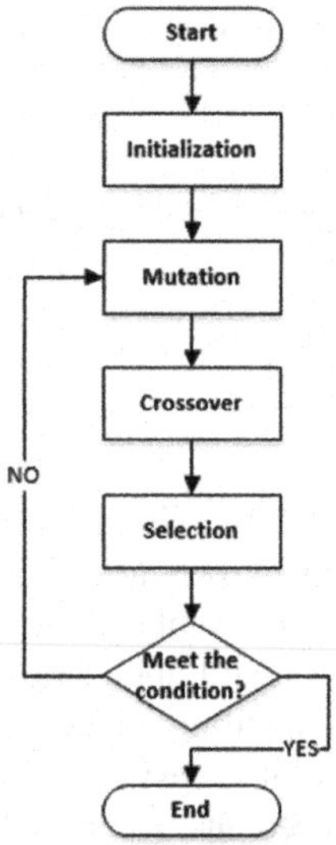

Fig. 1. The flow-process diagram of standard DE

Differential evolution was first proposed by Storn and Pricein in 1995 to deal with complex optimization problems, and it is a heuristic algorithm. On the one hand, DE as a kind of swarm intelligent algorithm, which is not affected by the nature and structure of the problem, with a simple principle, few parameters involved, easy to understand and in parallel in a given space search. On the other hand, Differential evolution algorithm with only three control parameters, as well as variation, crossover and selection operator, which greatly simplify the parameter setting process and running time of the algorithm. Figure 1 shows the flow chart of the original DE algorithm.

2.1 Initialization Population

At the beginning of DE, a set of D optimization parameters is called an individual, which is represented by a D-dimensional parameter vector. DE contains a total of three control parameters NP, F and CR. NP is also the size of the population. The parameters F is the scaling factor, which is generally restricted in the range of (0,1]. CR is the crossover rate, which restricted in range [0,1]. For each target vector $X_{i,G}$, generally, which is defined as follows:

$$X_{i,g} = (X_{i,1}^{g}, X_{i,2}^{g}, \cdots, X_{i,D}^{g}) \quad i = 1, 2, \cdots, NP \tag{1}$$

the initialization methods are used for each solution is:

$$X_{i,j}^{0} = X_{j}^{\min} + rand\,(0, 1) \cdot (X_{j}^{\max} - X_{j}^{\min}) \tag{2}$$

where *rand(0,1)* is a uniformly distributed random in [0,1], $X_j^{\min}$ and $X_j^{\max}$ are the minimum and the maximum of the *jth* dimension of the search space respectively.

2.2 Mutation

In the DE algorithm, the kernel operator is the differential mutation operator. Lost of mutation operators that have been proposed [15, 16]. Here we outline some of the major variation strategies.

1) DE/rand/1

$$V_i = X_{r1} + F \cdot (X_{r2} - X_{r3}) \tag{3}$$

2) DE/rand/2

$$V_i = X_{r1} + F \cdot (X_{r2} - X_{r3}) + F \cdot (X_{r4} - X_{r5}) \tag{4}$$

3) DE/best/1

$$V_i = X_{best} + F \cdot (X_{r1} - X_{r2}) \tag{5}$$

4) DE/current-to-rand/1

$$V_i = X_i + F \cdot (X_{r1} - X_i) + F \cdot (X_{r2} - X_{r3}) \tag{6}$$

5) DE/current-to-best/1

$$V_i = X_i + F \cdot (X_{best} - X_i) + F \cdot (X_{r2} - X_{r3}) \tag{7}$$

where X_{best} indicate optimal solution in the current generation; $r1$, $r2$, $r3$, $r4$, and $r5 \in \{1, 2, \cdots, NP\}$; and $r1 \neq r2 \neq r3 \neq r4 \neq r5 \neq i$. The parameter F is the scaling factor for controlling the mutation scale, which is generally restricted in (0,1].In the literature [17], the author used a large number of experiments to point out that the effects of mode 1) and mode 5) are equivalent.

2.3 Crossover

After mutation, a binomial crossover operation forms the trial vector $U_i^G = (U_{i,1}^G, U_{i,2}^G, \cdots, U_{i,D}^G)$ as follows:

$$U_{i,j}^G = \begin{cases} V_{i,j}, ifrand(j) \leq cr, or(j == j(rand) \\ X_{i,j} \end{cases} \tag{8}$$

Here, $j_{rand} = 1, 2, \cdots, D$.

2.4 Selection

For Selection step pick the better solution from the parent vector x_i^g and the trial u_i^g in the light of a greedy selection scheme. For example, we select the lower fitness for a minimization problem, which is given by

$$X_{i,j}^G = \begin{cases} U_{i,j}, if, fit(u) \leq fit(x) \\ X_{i,j} \end{cases} \tag{9}$$

2.5 Discussion on the Parameter of DE Algorithm

The scaling factor F and the cross factor CR are the major research directions, which control the mutation and cross operation of DE algorithm respectively.

The scaling parameter F is very sensitive to the characteristics of the algorithm, it controls the size ratio of the difference vector and adjusts the search range of the algorithm [18]. Generally, the value range of scaling parameter F is between 0 and 2. Fan and Lampinen [19] advised that the value of F in [0.5, 1.1]. Ronkkonen [20] believe that 0.9 is a fine option to regulate the relationship between precision and speed rate.

Like F, the cross factor CR is also sensitive to the performance of the DE algorithm and is an important parameter of DE. Bigger values of CR tend to promote the local search capacity of the algorithm and accelerate the speed rate of the algorithm, But it may be possible to measure the diversity of populations [21]. The smaller CR value increases the global search capacity of DE and improves the diversity of population, but weakens the space utilization capacity of the algorithm and slows down the convergence speed of the algorithm. Ronkkonen et al. [20] believe that the value of CR depends on the characteristics of the problem. The range of CR is 0.9 to 1 is applied to non-separable and multi-problems, while the range of 0 to 0.2 is just for separable problems.

3 Our Improved Approach

In this section, we put forward a new DE algorithm, which called AFP-DE algorithm with adaptive rank exponent and parameters to enhance the performance of DE.

3.1 Rank-DE

In nature, excellent individuals usually have good genes, and they have more opportunities to produce offspring. In other words, in evolutionary algorithm, the unpacking of good information that they should have more opportunities to generate new solutions. Based on this natural phenomenon, Gong et al. [6] proposed a differential evolution algorithm based on rank selection, which is called Rank-DE. Specifically, in differential mutation operator, vector of parent variation not random from the population choice, but according to a selected based on the probability level. The higher the individual level, the higher the probability that the individual will be selected to produce variation. Probability is calculated as follows [6]:

$$p_i = \frac{R_i}{NP} \tag{10}$$

where R_i is its ranking that the *ith* vector X_i is sorted according to its fitness. NP is the population size and p_i is the probability of the *ith* vector X_i. After computing the selection probability of each individual in (10), Gong gives algorithm for how to choose individual according to the section probability, as Algorithm I [6]. Note that the function rand is used to generate random numbers from 0 to 1.

Algorithm I: Ranking-based vector selection for 'DE/rand/1'

1: **Input**: The current solution index i

2: **Output**: The select vector indexes r_1, r_2, r_3

3: Randomly select $r_1 \in \{1, NP\}$ {base vector index}

4: **while** $rand > Pr_1$ or $r_1 == i$

5: Randomly select $r_1 \in \{1, NP\}$

6: **end while**

7: Randomly select $r_2 \in \{1, NP\}$ {terminal vector index}

8: **while** $rand > Pr_2$ or $r_2 == r_1$ or $r_2 == i$

9: Randomly select $r_2 \in \{1, NP\}$

10: **end while**

11: Randomly select $r_3 \in \{1, NP\}$

12: **while** $r_3 == r_2$ or $r_3 == r_1$ or $r_3 == i$

13: Randomly select $r_3 \in \{1, NP\}$

14: **end while**

3.2 AFP-DE

3.2.1 Adaptive Parameters for F and CR

In standard DE, there are two important parameters, *F* and *CR*, which control the scaling of the difference vector and the component of the trial vector from the basic individual or the mutated individual. Formula (3)–(7) shows that Scaling parameters very affect the performance of DE. Generally speaking, In the process of algorithm, the larger f value is conducive to global exploration, while the compared value is useful to local search. Formula (8) shows Capability of parameterCR dominates the "gene" of trial individual that it comes from the mutant individual or the parent individual. Yet, when CR valube get little one, the global search of DE will becomes powerful.

Based on the above analysis, the values of *F* and *CR* should be tune-up dynamically as the population evolves, then two relatively simple parameter adaptive strategies are raised:

$$\mathrm{F} = g_{\max} - (fg_{\max} - fg_{\min}) \cdot (\frac{g}{G_{\max}}) \tag{11}$$

$$\mathrm{CR} = cr_{\max} - (cr_{\max} - cr_{\min}) \cdot (\frac{g}{G_{\max}})^2 \cdot (\frac{g}{G_{\max}}) \tag{12}$$

where, the maximum value of and the minimum value of the scaling factor are setted $fg_{max} = 0.9, fg_{min} = 0.2$, respectively. This paper takes $\mathrm{cr}_{max} = 0.9$, $\mathrm{cr}_{min} = 0.3$, $G_{max} = 1500$ is the maximum number of iterations.

3.2.2 Adaptive Parameters for F and CR

Shortcomings in literature [6] is that it uses a fixed probability calculation model, which means that the superiority is the same of a better solution with respect to the worse one in each generation. But in nature, the superiority of good individuals to produce offspring with respect to a poor individual should be variable. Based on this natural phenomenon, this paper proposes an adaptive exponential model (AFP-DE) to highlight the differences between the two.

In this section, we put forward the selection probability p_i of the *ith* individual X_i is computed as:

$$p_i^g = \left(\frac{R_i}{NP}\right)^{\alpha(g)} \tag{13}$$

where $\alpha(g)$ is a an adaptive exponential of the *gth* generation in population, and initialize the value of $\alpha(1) = 1$, which is renewed according to the following formula:

$$\alpha(g+1) = \begin{cases} k_1 \cdot sample(upper, 1) \ if \ RT(g+1) \geq \eta \cdot RT(g) \\ k_2 \cdot sample(low, 1) \qquad\qquad else \end{cases} \tag{14}$$

$$RT(g+1) = \frac{n(g+1)}{NP} \tag{15}$$

where $n(g+1)$ represents the number of the $(g+1)th$ generation successfully produce a better solution, which is initialized to 0 in every generation; in the parameter setting, we suggest that $k1 = 4$, $k2 = 2$, $\eta = 0.85$ and $RT(0) = 0.5$. *upper* and *low* are the top *NP/2* and bottom NP/2 of the uniform distribution *rand(1,NP)* in descending order. *Sample* means to randomly select a value from *upper* or *low*.

The Fig. 2 shows curve with the change of the exponential α (here just list $\alpha = 1/3$, $\alpha = 1$, $\alpha = 3$), the difference of the individual level is also changed. As can be seen from the figure, when $\alpha = 3$, it means that condition $RT(g + 1) \geq \eta \cdot RT(g)$ in the formula is true. It is obvious that $\alpha = 1$ is a special case of the literature [6], at this time, the differences of all individuals level are the same.

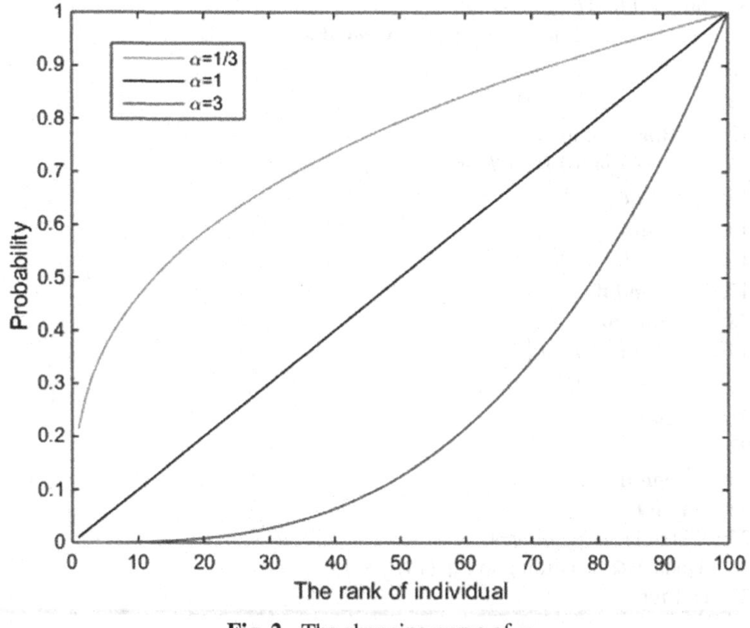

Fig. 2. The changing curve of α

3.2.3 The Procedure AFP-DE Algorithm

Our adaptive rank exponent and parameters govern method are merged into classical DE for compose the AFP-DE algorithm. The pseudo-code of the whole AFP-DE base on the mutation strategy of DE/rand/1/bin is demonstrated in Algorithm II.

Algorithm II: the procedure of the AFP-DE algorithm for 'DE/rand/1/bin'

Initialize $k_1 = 4$, $k_2 = 2$ $\eta = 0.85$, $RT(0) = 0.5$, fg_{max}=0.9 , fg_{min}=0.2, cr_{max}=0.9 ,
$\mathbf{cr}_{min}$=0.3 , NP=100, $\alpha(1) = 1$.
for g=*1 to* G_{max}
  Set n=0;
  Sort individuals according to the fitness of the function from worst to best.
  Compute the probability of each solution according to Eq. (13).
  Calculate *g-th* value of *CR* and *F* according to Eq. (11-12).
  for $i = 1$ to NP
    Select $r1$, $r2$ and $r3$ according **Algorithm I**
    $V_i^G = X_{r1}^G + F \cdot \left(X_{r2}^G - X_{r3}^G\right)$
    $j_{rand} = rand\,\mathrm{int}(1, D)$
    for $j = 1$ to D
      if $rand(0,1) \le CR$ or $j == j_{rand}$
        $U_{i,j}^G = V_{i,j}^G$
      else
        $U_{i,j}^G = X_{i,j}^G$
      end if
    end for
    if $f\left(U_i^G\right) \le f\left(X_i^G\right)$
      $X_i^{G+1} = U_i^G$, n=n+1;
    else
      $X_i^{G+1} = X_i^G$
    end if
  end for
  RT(g+1)=n/NP; g=g+1;
  Update α according to Eq. (14).
end for

4 Experimental Results

Ten out of twenty-two functions [15] with 30D were hired to test the ability of our algorithm. The benchmark functions are given in Table 1.

In order to ensure fairness, the functions selected above include both continuous and discontinuous functions, as well as unimodal and multi-peak functions, etc. In addition to Rank-DE, we also compare with the state-of-art DE, SADE [16], The parameter settings for DE, SADE, Rank-DE and AFP-DE base on mutation strategy DE/rand/1 respectively are shown in Table 2.

In our experiments, the average and the standard deviation of the function value are applied to evaluate the optimization performance. The maximal function evaluation (max_FES) is adopted as the termination criterion, which is set to $5000 \cdot D$(Dimension of solution). For all the compared algorithms, 25 independent runs are executed on each test function. The accuracy of our algorithm is measured here by Wilcoxon's statistics. For simple, the optimal solution for each test issue are signed in boldface as Table 3.

Table 1. Benchmark functions in experiments

Name	Function	Range	Min
Sphere	$f_1(x) = \sum_{i=1}^{D} x_i^2$	$[-100, 100]^D$	0
Elliptic	$f_2(x) = \sum_{i=1}^{D} (10^6)^{\frac{i-1}{D-1}} x_i^2$	$[-100, 100]^D$	0
SumSquare	$f_3(x) = \sum_{i=1}^{D} ix_i^2$	$[-10, 10]^D$	0
Step	$f_7(x) = \sum_{i=1}^{D} (\lfloor x_i + 0.5 \rfloor)^2$	$[-100, 100]^D$	0
Quartic	$f_9(x) = \sum_{i=1}^{D} ix_i^4 + random[0, 1]$	$[-1.28, 1.28]^D$	0
Rosenbrock	$f_{10}(x) = \sum_{i=1}^{D-1} \left[100\left(x_{i+1} - x_i^2\right)^2 + (x_i - 1)^2 \right]$	$[-5, 10]^D$	0
Rastrigin	$f_{11}(x) = \sum_{i=1}^{D} \left[x_i^2 - 10\cos(2\pi x_i) + 10 \right]$	$[-5.12, 5.12]^D$	0
NCRastrigin	$f_{12}(x) = \sum_{i=1}^{D} \left[y_i^2 - 10\cos(2\pi y_i) + 10 \right]$ $y_i = \begin{cases} x_i & \lvert x_i \rvert < \frac{1}{2} \\ \frac{round(2x_i)}{2} & \lvert x_i \rvert \geq \frac{1}{2} \end{cases}$	$[-5.12, 5.12]^D$	0
Griewank	$f_{13}(x) = 1/4000 \sum_{i=1}^{D} x_i^2 - \prod_{i=1}^{D} \cos\left(\frac{x_i}{\sqrt{i}}\right) + 1$	$[-600, 600]^D$	0
Schwefel 2.2	$f_{14}(x) = 418.98288727243380 * D - \sum_{i=1}^{D} x_i \sin\left(\sqrt{\lvert x_i \rvert}\right)$	$[-500, 500]^D$	0

Table 2. The parameter settings

Algorithms	Parameter settings
DE(DE/rand/1/bin)	$NP = 100, F = 0.5, CR = 0.9$
Rank-DE(DE/rand/1/bin)	NP = 100, F = 0.5, CR = 0.9
SADE(DE/rand/1/bin)	NP = 100, k = 4, $\varepsilon = 0.01$, L = 50
AFP-DE(DE/rand/1/bin)	NP = 100, $fg_{max} = 0.9$, $fg_{min} = 0.2$, $cr_{max} = 0.9$, $cr_{min} = 0.3$, $k_1 = 4$, $k_2 = 2$, $\alpha(1) = 1, RT(0) = 0.5, \eta = 0.85$

Table 3 clearly indicates experimental results. For the "DE/rand/1" mutation operator, it is clearly found out that AFP-DE is better than classic DE except *f13* on ten test functions. Compared with Rank-DE, AFP-DE wins in all test functions exclude *f13*. At the same time, we found that the optimization results of AFP-DE and Rank-DE are equal on the function f_7, and they have achieved the best value is 0. In addition, the performance advantages and disadvantages of SADE and AFP-DE in the test functions are each half.

The specific instructions are as follows: AFP-DE is superior to SADE on the continuous unimodal functions *f1*–*f3* and the Rosenbrock *f10* which is unimodal for $D = 2$

Table 3. Comparisons of the state-of-art DE algorithms with AFP-DE on 10 test functions with 30D

Fun	Metric	DE DE/rand/1/bin	Rank-DE DE/rand/1/bin	SADE DE/rand/1/bin	AFP-DE DE/rand/1/bin
f_1	Mean	5.61e−14	2.51e−29	1.56e−37	**2.41e−59**
	std dev	4.81e−14	2.47e−29	1.97e−37	**5.96e−59**
f_2	Mean	3.79e−11	3.19e−26	4.12e−34	**2.24e−56**
	std dev	3.10e−11	3.88e−26	1.15e−33	**4.06e−56**
f_3	Mean	4.55e−15	2.21e−30	5.37e−38	**1.17e−61**
	std dev	3.08e−15	2.53e−30	7.24e−38	**2.71e−61**
f_7	Mean	**0.00e+00**	**0.00e+00**	**0.00e+00**	**0.00e+00**
	std dev	**0.00e+00**	**0.00e+00**	**0.00e+00**	**0.00e+00**
f_9	Mean	9.37e−03	4.82e−03	**3.31e−03**	3.62e−03
	std dev	2.18e−03	1.64e−03	**1.41e−03**	1.57e−03
f_{10}	Mean	1.61e+01	4.16e+00	2.12e+01	**5.13e−01**
	std dev	9.72e−01	1.52e+00	1.90e+01	**1.67e+00**
f_{11}	Mean	1.67e+02	1.13e+02	**2.83e−14**	2.05e+01
	std dev	1.05e+01	3.06e+01	**6.96e−14**	5.71e+00
f_{12}	Mean	1.55e+02	1.09e+02	**1.11e−07**	1.95e+01
	std dev	1.33e+01	2.57e+01	**1.62e−07**	3.74e+00
f_{13}	Mean	**1.72e−13**	4.92e−04	6.86e−04	4.49e−03
	std dev	**2.51e−13**	2.15e−03	2.37e−03	2.78e−03
f_{14}	Mean	7.13e+03	5.45e+03	**0.00e+00**	1.31e+03
	std dev	2.77e+02	1.03e+03	**0.00e+00**	1.09e+02
-/+/ =	—	8/1/1	8/1/1	5/4/1	—

"−", "=" and "+" respectively indicate that the running algorithm is worse, similar or better than AFP-DE according to the Wilcoxon's rank test at a 0.05 significance level.

and $D = 3$, while it may have multimodal optimal solutions. On the other hand, AFP-DE is inferior to SADE on the noisy function *f9* and the multimodal functions *f11–f14*. Further, they have the same value of 0 at the function f_7. Overall, on ten test functions, AFP-DE is obviously better than DE and Rank-DE base on mutation strategy DE/rand/1, and has also better robustness. Meanwhile, it has advantages over SADE in some of the above functions. The evolution curves of the best mean function values comes from DE, rankDE, SADE, AFP-DE versus number of iterations are plotted in Fig. 3.

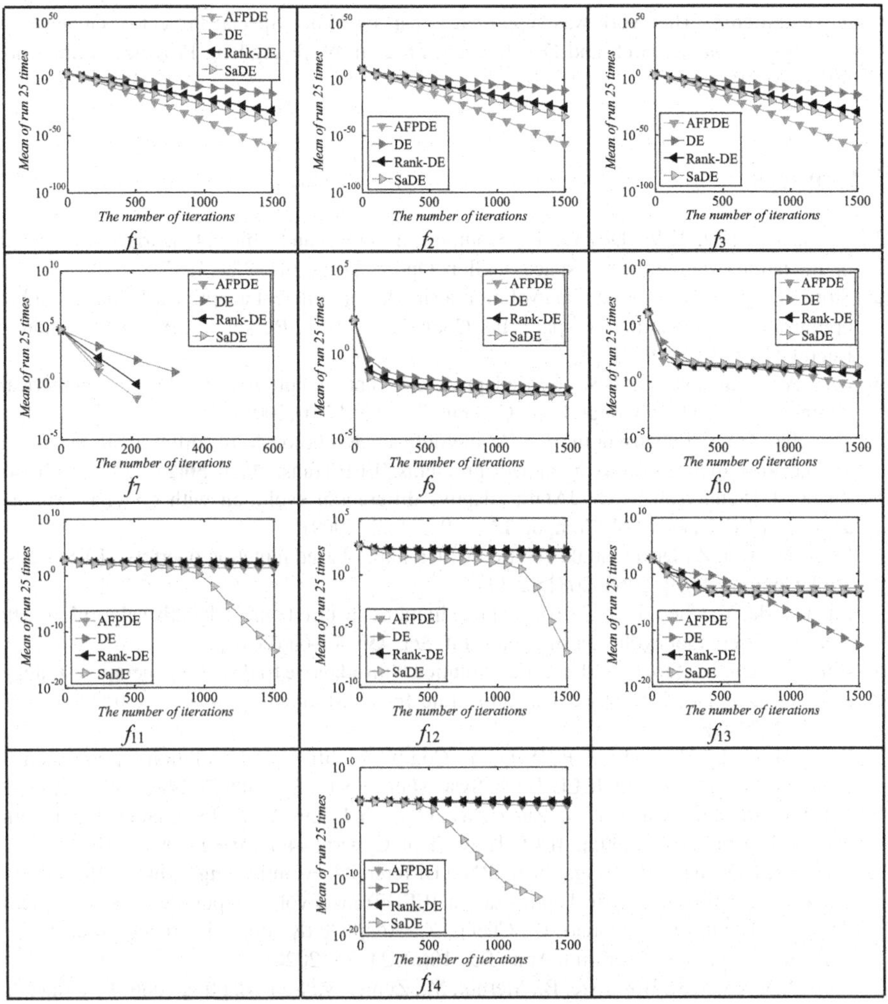

Fig. 3. Evolution curve of AFP-DE, DE, Rank-DE and SADE

5 Conclusion

In the article, a novel DE variant algorithm called AFP-DE, is raised to promote the ability of DE, which is compared with DE, rankDE, SADE algorithms base on mutation operator DE/rand/1. they have been tested on a series of typical benchmark functions than they are used on the literature. Experimental results shows AFP-DE is better or at least competitive performance just for the speed rate and the robustness, compared with the latest DE algorithm. Considering the future work, the AFP-DE will be compared with same kind of algorithm base on DE/rand/2/bin, DE/best/1/bin. At the same time, Both new mutation strategy and sensitivity analysis of parameter (Eq. 14) should be proposed to enhance the optimization performance of AFP-DE algorithm.

Acknowledgments. This work was supported in part by Major Special Project of Guangdong Province "Key-Area Research and Development Program of Guangdong Province" (Grant no. 2020B010166005).

References

1. Storn, R., Price, K.V.: Differential evolution: a simple and efficient heuristic for global optimization over continuous space. J. Glob. Optim. **11**(4), 341–359 (1997)
2. Storn, R., Price, K.: Differential evolution-a simple and efficient adaptive scheme for global optimization over continuous space. Int. Comput. Sci. Inst., Berkeley ,CA, USA, Technical Report TR-95-012 (1995)
3. Qin, A.K., Suganthan, P.N.: Self-adaptive different evolution algorithm for numerical optimization. Pro EEE Congr. Evol. Comput. **2**, 1785–1791 (2005)
4. Tenaglia, G.C., Lebensztajin, L.: A multiobjective approach of differential evolution optimization applied to electromagnetic problems. IEEE Trans. Magn. **50**(2), 625–628 (2014)
5. Zhang, J., Sanderson, A.C.: JADE: adaptive differential evolution with optional external archive. IEEE Trans. Evol. Comput. **13**(5), 945–958 (2009)
6. Gong, W., Cai, Z.: Differential evolution with ranking-based mutation opertors. IEEE Trans. Evol. Comput. **43**(6), 2066–2081 (2013)
7. Lin, Q., Ma, Y., Chen, J., et al.: An adaptive immune-inspired multi-objective algorithm with multiple differential evolution strategies. Inf. Sci. **430**, 46–64 (2018)
8. Bin, X., Chen, X., Tao, L.: Differential evolution with adaptive trial vector generation strategy and cluster-replacement-based feasibility rule for constrained optimization. Inf. Sci. **435**, 240–262 (2018)
9. Wang, B.-C., Li, H.-X., Li, J.-P., Wang, Y.: Composite differential evolution for constrained evolutionary optimization. IEEE Trans. Syst. Man Cybern. Syst. **49**(7), 1482–1495 (2018)
10. Yu, W.J., Shen, M., Chen, W.N., Zhan, Z.H., Gong, Y.J., Lin, Y.: Differential evolution with two-level- parameter adaption. IEEE Trans. Evol. Cybern. **44**(7), 1080–1099 (2014)
11. Qin, A.K., Huang, V.L., Suganthan, P.N.: Differential evolution algorithm with strategy adaptation for global numerical optimization. IEEE Trans. Evol. Comput. **12**(1), 64–79 (2008)
12. Wang, T., Kaijun, W., Tiaotiao, D., Cheng, X.: Adaptive dynamic disturbance strategy for differential evolution algorithm. Appl. Sci. **10**(6), 24–35 (2020)
13. Brest, J., Greiner, S., Boskovic, B., Mernik, M., Zumer, V.: Self-adapting control parameters in differential evolution : a comparative study on numerical benchmark problems. IEEE Trans. Evol. Comput. **10**(6), 646–657 (2006)
14. Huang, P.-Q., Wang, Y., Wang, K., Yang, K.: Differential evolution with a variable population size for deployment optimization in a UAV-assisted IoT data collection system. IEEE Trans. Emerg. Top. Comput. Intell. **4**(3), 324–335 (2020)
15. Gao, W.-F., Liu, S.-Y.: Artificial bee colony algorithm based on information learning. IEEE Trans. Cybern. **36**(5) (2015)
16. Qin, A.K., Suganthan, P.N.: Self-adaptive differential evolution algorithm for numerical optimization. Proc. IEEE Congr. Evol. Comput. **9**(2), 1785–1791 (2005)
17. Price, K.V.: An Introduction to Differential Evolution. New Ideas in Optimization, pp. 79–108 (1999)
18. Qin, A.K., Huang, V.L., Suganthan, P.N.: Differential evolution algorithm with strategy adaptation for global numerical optimization. IEEE Trans. Evol. Comput. **13**(2), 398417 (2009)
19. Fan, H.-Y., Lampinen, J.: A trigonometric mutation operation to differential evolution. J. Global Optim. **27**(1), 105–129 (2003)

20. Ronkkonen, J., Kukkonen, S., Price, K.V.: Real-parameter optimization with differential evolution. Proc. IEEE Congr. Evol. Comput. 506–513 (2005)
21. Storn, R.: On the usage of differential evolution for function optimization. Proc. North Amer. Fuzzy Inf. Process. 519–523 (1996)

Information Centrality Evaluation Method Based on Cascade Topological Relevance

Yuting Shen[1,2,3](✉), Kaixuan Wang[4,5], Yueqing Gao[6,3], Lulu Chen[7,3], and Chu Du[3]

[1] National Space Science Center, Chinese Academy of Sciences, Beijing 100190, China
rebeccashenstudy@yeah.net

[2] University of Chinese Academy of Sciences, Beijing 100039, People's Republic of China

[3] The 54th Research Institute of China Electronics Technology Group Corporation, Shijiazhuang 050000, People's Republic of China

[4] China Academy of Launch Vehicle Technology, Beijing 100076, People's Republic of China

[5] School of Automation Science and Electrical Engineering, Beihang University, Beijing 100191, People's Republic of China

[6] Beijing Jiaotong University, Beijing, China
18111069@bjtu.edu.cn

[7] Center for Future Multimedia and School of Computer Science and Engineering, University of Electronic Science and Technology of China, Chengdu 610051, China

Abstract. Unmanned systems can be abstracted as dynamic and complex systems of multi-agent competition and cooperation. Its quantitative and qualitative characteristics are naturally similar to those in network science. Therefore, we can explore how to form a dynamic and efficient adjustment of the link relationship between nodes, based on studying of structural complexity, node complexity, and interactions between structure and nodes in network science. The aforementioned outputs can accordingly support the efficiency of information interaction and dissemination between nodes. To solve the problem of information cooperation in weak communication connection of unmanned systems, this paper proposed an information centrality evaluation method based on the degree of cascaded topology correlation (CTRICE, Cascade Topological Relevance Information Centrality Evaluation). The evaluation method and strategy of cascading topology association degree based on local neighborhood were formed through the evaluation of cascading information aggregation ability within the neighborhood and the evaluation of intimacy based on topology and interaction behavior. Consequently, the results of the assessment would provide support for information fusion and decision-making. This paper first proves the feasibility of this method in terms of information synergy consistency. Meanwhile, it compares and analyzes the convergence efficiency through simulation experiments between the proposed method with assessment methods of mean value and degree centrality. Compared with the traditional method, the proposed method has better robustness and robustness under the condition of low quality communication connections. The method presented in this paper provides an idea for the realization of information self-organization and collaboration based on topological relations in unmanned systems.

Keywords: Complex network · Multi-agent system · Information collaboration · Cascade topology · Centrality evaluation

Y. Sun et al. (Eds.): ChineseCSCW 2021, CCIS 1491, pp. 230–242, 2022.
https://doi.org/10.1007/978-981-19-4546-5_19

1 Background

In the multi-agent system (MAS), there are continuous interaction processes between intelligent individuals and their environment [1]. Whether the linking and dissemination of information in these interactive processes has the consistency and completeness of information among multiple nodes is the basis for realizing collaboration and decision-making among multi-agents [18–21].

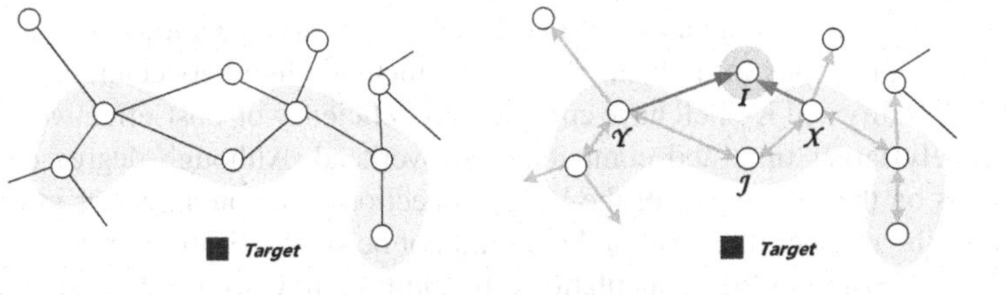

(a) Example of direct observation area (b) Example of information propagation and fusion

Fig. 1. Schematic diagram of cluster direct observation and information dissemination.

For example, in the process of information perception and transmission of unmanned clusters: Due to the fact that agents in close proximity to the information source would own relatively complete target information, when the agents initially perceive the existence of the information source, and then spread the observation to neighborhood (Fig. 1), the preference connection establishment tend to these key nodes, in regenerative processes of multi-agent network. This preferred link feature is in line with the characteristics of the BA scale-free network. Therefore, the unmanned system can be abstracted into a cluster network, which simultaneously according to topological centrality of scale-free networks and their nodes in the neighborhood (Fig. 2), the information dissemination between nodes can be measured. As a consequence, the endogenous confidence level and the attenuation level of the information propagation would be used as the basis for information acceptance, supporting the integration of multi-agent information interaction and group organization in a dynamic communication environment.

Since the 1940s, multi-disciplinary scholars have carried out continuous research on the centrality description methods of nodes in complex networks. For example, Matjaž Krnc et al. described and implemented group decentralization and centralized modeling in networks through a greedy approximation algorithm [2]. A. Samad et al. proposed the betweenness centrality measurement method (SAM) based on hop-count to analyze user rankings in social networks [3]. Gaoshi Li et al. worked on the identification of essential proteins via neighborhood closeness consistency model [4]. Zhenzhen Shao et al. improved the efficiency and effectiveness of centrality calculation for dynamic graph changes through incremental update of proximity centrality detection [5]. In terms of the k-shell method, Alighanbari et al. proposed the SLPA algorithm based on K-shell decomposition to detect and identify communities in the network [6]. Taras Agryzkov et al. built an analysis model of urban transportation network based on eigenvector centrality, by means of fusion of node data and topology information [7]. The main indicators [8–11] are shown in the table below.

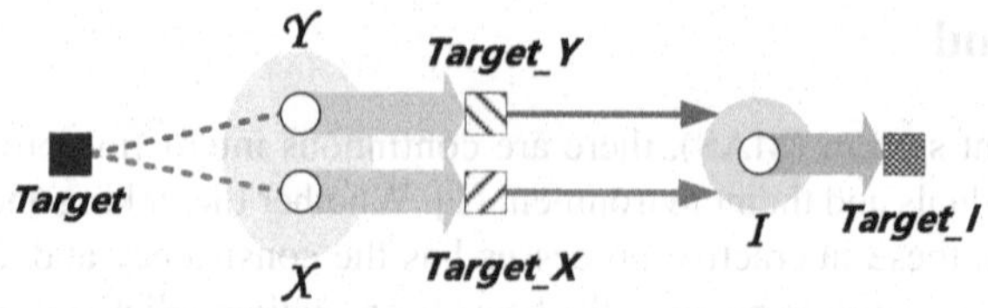

Fig. 2. Schematic diagram of target information fusion based on observation of neighbors.

On account of requirements of global calculations, when facing uncertain weak and unstable connections in unmanned systems, methods like betweenness centrality, proximity centrality and K-shell have conspicuous deficiency on cost-effectiveness, due to its relatively larger time and computational overhead. Although degree centrality only depends on the calculation of the local connection situation, however in practical applications, the number of global nodes would not be stable. Feature vector centrality is relatively expensive in local calculations. In addition, how to use the importance of neighbor nodes to characterize materiality of central nodes requires specific design in combination with practical applications (Table 1).

Table 1. Main importance indicators of undirected network nodes.

Appellation	Definition	Calculation formula	Calculation range	Complexity
Degree centrality	The degree of the node is used to characterize the importance of the node, and normalization is generally performed	$DC_i = \frac{k_i}{N-1}$	Local/Global	$O(n)$
Betweeness centrality	The importance of the node is characterized by the number of shortest paths passing through the node, describing the influence of the node on information flow in the network to a certain extent	$BC_i = \sum_{s \neq i \neq t} \frac{n_{st}^i}{g_{st}}$ [16]	Global	$O(n^3)$

(*continued*)

Table 1. *(continued)*

Appellation	Definition	Calculation formula	Calculation range	Complexity
Closeness centrality	The inverse of the average distance from a node to other nodes in the entire network	$CC_i = \frac{1}{d_i} = \frac{N}{\sum_{j=1}^{N} d_{ij}}$	Global	$O(nm + n^2 logn)$
K-shell decomposition	Through the k-shell decomposition method, the shell decomposition process is carried out layer by layer. The complex network is decomposed into cores, peer-to-peer connected pieces, isolated pieces, etc. for coarse-grained division	\	Global	$O(n + m)$
Eigenvector centrality	The importance of the neighbor node is used to characterize the importance of the node	$x_i = c\sum_{j=1}^{N} a_{ij}x_j$	Local/Neighborhood	$O(n^2)$

According to the above, information interaction requirements of unmanned multi-agent systems could be measured from two aspects: information content and network topology. Therefore, an information centrality evaluation algorithm based on cascade topological relevance in extend the neighborhood (CTRICE) is proposed in this paper. The cascading neighborhood information relevance of an agent jointly characterized by associated evaluating the intimacy between neighboring nodes and cascading information aggregation ability. The results of simulation experiment verify the effectiveness of the method, and its promotion of the robustness of synergy in multi-agent systems in the face of unstable topological connections.

2 Information Interaction Consensus Theory of Multi-agent Topology

Based on the basic Vicsek model [14], when N autonomous individuals constitute a discrete-time system. The initial positions and directions of movement of the individuals are randomly distributed. All individuals move freely in the plane area of $L \times L$ with periodic boundary conditions at a constant speed. The individual's cognitive estimation information will be updated according to the broadcast information of all neighbors in update processes with noise which mean value is zero. Each individual with its own current location $\overrightarrow{x_t}(t) \in R^2$ can only perceive the information of other neighbouring individuals. Neighbors of individual i are composed of agents whose Euclidean distance between themselves less than the sensing and communication range $R > 0$ (perception range and communication range capability and size are the same). Let $\Gamma_i(t)$ [15] represent the set of neighbors of individual i at time t, namely.

$$\Gamma_i(t) = \left\{ j \| \| \overrightarrow{x_j}(t) - \overrightarrow{x_i}(t) \| \le R, j = 1, 2, \ldots, N \right\} \tag{1}$$

The information interaction between individuals can be transmitted as follows

$$I_i(t+1) = \langle I_i(t) \rangle_\Gamma + \zeta_i(t) \tag{2}$$

wherein, $\zeta_i(t)$ is the uniformly distributed noise signal on $[-\eta, \eta]$, and $\langle I_i(t) \rangle_\Gamma$ represents the information fusion result based on individual local observations. Consequently, it is easily obtainable that there must be a certain moment $t_0 > 0$ for $t \ge t_0$, any $I_i(0)$ when $I_i(t) = I_j(t), \forall i, j = 1, 2, \ldots, N$. at $t \to \infty$ satisfying.

$$\lim_{t \to \infty} I_i(t) = \lim_{t \to \infty} I_j(t), \forall i, j \tag{3}$$

Accordingly, the cluster can gradually reach the consistency of information exchange. Hence, regardless of whether there are discrete subgraphs in the topological relationship of the group at current moment, the attenuation and distortion noise between information interactions can be uniformly distributed to achieve consistent cognition, after information accumulation during a certain amount of time. Then, when there is noise based on probability and observation error in the information interaction between agents, it is necessary to consider whether the cluster information interaction can achieve global consistency, so as to ensure the local dynamic information interaction process can be competent for comprehensive estimation of global information on the cumulative time scale.

3 Cascade Topological Relevance Information Centrality Evaluation (CTRICE)

3.1 Method for Defining Cascaded Neighborhoods Based on Cluster Topology

In the definition of cascaded neighborhood based on cluster topology, there are mainly two problems as follows:

(1) Influence Maximization.

In a given network diagram $G(V, E)$, maximization of influence is how to construct the Influence Spread Model and the strategy of selecting k spreading base nodes on current topology structure of G and find the seed node set $N_{set}(N_{set} \subseteq V)$. Through Expected Influence Spread Evaluation (EISE), the final node activation seed set is$\sigma(N_{set})$. According to analysis of actual networks [13], the influence of information transmission would been attenuated to a negligible level when the number of hops transmitted exceeds 3–4 hops. Therefore, when defining the cascaded neighborhood, the number of link hops ($Hop_{threshold}$) of the neighborhood computing node should not be greater than 3, in order to balance calculation efficiency and data validity.

(2) Information Backflow.

According to the proof in Sect. 2, in information transmission process of target perception, interference of information noise can be effectively integrated reduced by fusion, when multiple agents produce observations of the same target with different confidence levels. For example, processes of target reconnaissance with different payloads can provide different dimensions of information, thereby improving the full-dimensional grasp of target information. However, when it is impossible to determine whether it is direct observation or indirect observation, the multipath backflow of information is often disturbed by the diffusion of cluster information. As shown in the following figure, when agent X performs neighborhood node evaluation, neighbor agent I and J's information about target M comes from the same agent Y. Which is obvious that the correlation calculation would own highest utility with trimming backflow nodes when the non-X neighborhoods of I and J have no difference (Fig. 3).

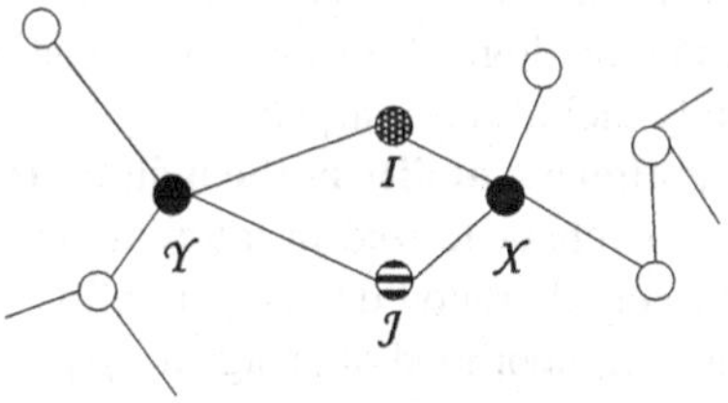

(a) Example of information backflow

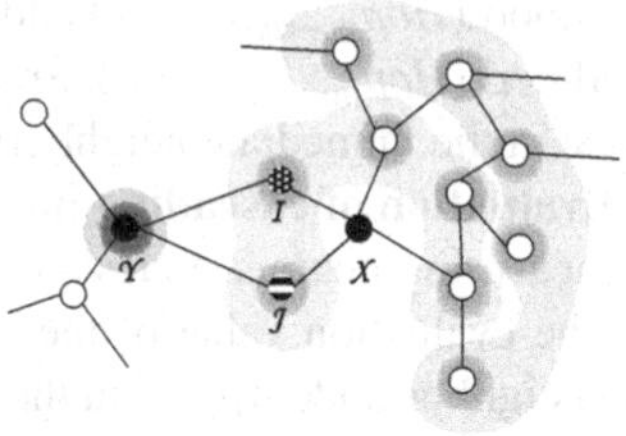

(b) Example of local neighborhood definition

Fig. 3. Schematic diagram of information backflow and local neighborhood definition.

Hence, for the multi-agent cluster network $\mathcal{N}_{ICE}(A_{ICE}, E_{ICE})$ (we assuming that the multi-agent cluster network $\mathcal{N}_{ICE}$ is an unpowered and undirected network)- where A_{ICE} represents the set of agents contained in the network and $E_{ICE\,ij}$ represents the communication connection state between agent node i and agent node j - the local neighborhood hop count ($Hop_{threshold}$) should defined as 1 to 2 hops based on the above analysis, namely $Hop_{threshold} \in [1, 2]$ and $Hop_{threshold} \in \mathbb{Z}$. That is, for any agent A_{ICE-X}, the neighborhood range $S_{neighbors_{A_{ICE-X}}}$ at time t is

$$S_{neighbors\_t}{}_{A_{ICE-X}} = \{A_{ICE-v} | A_{ICE-v} \in \{S(A_{ICE-X})_{Hop_1\_t} \cup S(A_{ICE-X})_{Hop_2\_t}\}, \forall A_{ICE-X}, A_{ICE-v} \subseteq A_{ICE}\} \tag{4}$$

where

$$S(A_{ICE-X})_{Hop_1\_t} = \{A_{ICE-v} : (A_{ICE-X}, A_{ICE-v}) \in E_{ICE}\} \tag{5}$$

$$S(A_{ICE-X})_{Hop_2\_t} = \left\{A_{ICE-w} | A_{ICE-w} \in \{S(A_{ICE-X})_{Hop_2\_Naive\_t} - S(A_{ICE-X})_{Hop_2\_BackFlow\_t}\}\right\} \tag{6}$$

$$S(A_{ICE-X})_{Hop_2\_Naive\_t} = \{A_{ICE-w} : (A_{ICE-w}, A_{ICE-v}) \in E_{ICE}, A_{ICE-w} \neq A_{ICE-X}\} \tag{7}$$

$$\begin{aligned} S(A_{ICE-X})_{Hop_2\_BackFlow\_t} &= \{A_{ICE-w} : (A_{ICE-w}, A_{ICE-v}) \in E_{ICE}, S(A_{ICE-v1})_{Hop_1} \\ &= S(A_{ICE-v1})_{Hop_1}, \forall A_{ICE-v1}, A_{ICE-v2} \subseteq S(A_{ICE-X})_{Hop_1}\} \end{aligned} \tag{8}$$

As shown in the figure above, based on the current real-time cluster topology link situation, the green part is $S(A_{ICE-X})_{Hop_1\_t}$, the blue part is $S(A_{ICE-X})_{Hop_2\_t}$, and the red part is the trimmed part $S(A_{ICE-X})_{Hop_2\_BackFlow\_t}$ at time t for agent A_{ICE-X}.

3.2 Evaluation Method of Cascaded Topological Relevance Based on Local Neighborhood

The method of local neighborhood-based topological relevance evaluation is mainly used in assessment and acceptance processes of neighborhood received information for each agent node. The process can be divided into the direct relevance evaluation of the neighborhood ($Hop_{threshold} = 1$) and the indirect relevance evaluation of the extended neighborhood ($Hop_{threshold} = 2$). Specifically, the topological correlation evaluation of each node in the immediate neighborhood mainly includes two aspects:

(1) Evaluation of cascading information gathering ability in the neighborhood

By measuring degree, nodes' influence can be characterized in information interaction. The evaluation value of the normalized neighborhood degree centrality of the one-hop neighbor node A_{ICE-i} in the immediate neighborhood of an agent A_{ICE-X} is

$$C_{D\_NDRX\_i} = \frac{k_i}{\sum_{u \in \Gamma_X(t)} k_u} \tag{9}$$

where $k_i = |N(i)| = |\{j : (i, j) \in E_{ICE}\}| = \sum_{i \in A_{ICE}} \mathbb{1}_{[(i,j) \in E_{ICE}]}$ and $\sum_{u=1}^{r} k_u$ are the sum of the degrees of other one-hop neighbor nodes in the immediate neighborhood. After cascading the extended neighborhood, the evaluation value of the extended neighborhood degree centrality of the one-hop neighbor node A_{ICE-i} is

$$C_{D\_ENIRX\_i} = \mu \sum k_j \tag{10}$$

Among them, $A_{ICE-j} : \left(A_{ICE-j}, A_{ICE-i}\right) \in E_{ICE}, A_{ICE-j} \neq A_{ICE-X}$ and μ are used to adjust the influence of the extended neighborhood degree centrality evaluation on the cascade evaluation. In summary, the comprehensive information aggregation ability evaluation value with considering a node A_{ICE-i} in the direct neighborhood of A_{ICE-X} and its associated expanded neighborhood is defined as

$$C_{DX\_i} = C_{D\_NDRX\_i} * C_{D\_ENIRX\_i} \tag{11}$$

Evaluation Strategy of Information Aggregation Ability in Cascade Neighborhood:

(a) If the one-hop neighbor nodes in the direct neighborhood is not trimmed, the cascade evaluation value of the information aggregation ability of each node based on direct and corresponding extended neighborhood. Which equals the information aggregation capability value of direct neighborhood multiply by its extended neighborhood evaluation value. If the extended neighborhood of a one-hop neighbor does not exist, only the degree centrality of the direct neighborhood would be calculated.
(b) If clipping operations occur (meaning that the node has a high risk of information backflow), the information aggregation capability evaluation value of the clipped node in extended neighborhood would be used as the information aggregation capability evaluation value of the node in its connected immediate neighborhood, with doing information fusion processing for its connected one-hop neighbor nodes.

(2) Intimacy evaluation based on topology and interactive behavior

The computing spectrum of intimacy evaluation is confined to immediate neighborhood based on topological relationship and interaction frequency per unit time [22, 23]. Concretely, the intimacy between any agent node A_{ICE-X} and its neighbor node A_{ICE-i} in the immediate neighborhood is defined as follows

$$C_{IX\_i} = \beta_1 C_{I\_TX\_i} + \beta_2 C_{I\_IX\_i} \tag{12}$$

where $C_{I\_TX\_i}$ represents the topological intimacy between A_{ICE-X} and A_{ICE-i}, $C_{I\_IX\_i}$ represents the interaction frequency intimacy between A_{ICE-X} and A_{ICE-i}. β_1 and β_2 are adjustment coefficients. The interaction frequency intimacy is characterized by average information interaction time interval. The specific definitions of the two aspects of intimacy are as follows

$$C_{I\_TX\_i} = \frac{\Gamma_X(t) \cap \Gamma_i(t)}{\{\Gamma_X(t) \cup \Gamma_i(t)\} - 1} + 1 \tag{13}$$

$$C_{I\_IX\_i} = \frac{1}{f_{X\_i} - 1} \sum_{n=1}^{f_{X\_i}} t_n - t_{n-1} \tag{14}$$

Among them, $\Gamma_i(t)$ represents the set of neighbor nodes of i at time t, f_{X_i} represents the total times of information exchanges between A_{ICE-X} and A_{ICE-i} before the current moment, and t_n represents the time of the n th information exchange.

(3) Information centrality evaluation method based on cascade topological relevance

Synthetically, taking any agent node A_{ICE-X} as an example, the cascade topological relevance evaluation $E_{Local\_TAX\_i}$ of neighbor node A_{ICE-i} in the immediate neighborhood of A_{ICE-X} is defined as follows

$$E_{Local\_TAX\_i} = \alpha_1 * C_{DX_i} + \alpha_2 C_{IX\_i} \tag{15}$$

where, α_1 and α_2 are adjustment coefficients.

Then the formula for neighborhood information fusion based on the evaluation of the local association degree of the central agent node A_{ICE-X} is defined as follows

$$I_X(t) = \sum_{i \in \Gamma_X(t)} \frac{E_{Local\_TAX\_i}}{\sum_{u \in \Gamma_X(t)} E_{Local\_TAX\_u}} I_i(t) \tag{16}$$

where, $\Gamma_X(t)$ represents neighbor nodes of agent node A_{ICE-X} at time t, $I_i(t)$ represents the information transmitted by neighbor A_{ICE-i}, and $E_{Local\_TAX\_i}$ represents the topological relevance evaluation of neighbor A_{ICE-i}. The evaluated relevance results would be used as the basis for information admissibility after unified processing.

4 Simulation Verification

Initial simulation environment based on the Barabási-Albert model with 200 agent nodes which initial positions of which generation obeyed Poisson distribution were $\left(pos_{A_{ICE-i}}\right)_t = \left[pos_{x_{t_i}}, pos_{y_{t_i}}, pos_{z_{t_i}}\right], \forall pos\_x_{t\_i}, pos\_y_{t\_i}, pos\_z_{t\_i} \in [-1000, 1000]$. The initial network topology was shown in Fig. 4 below. Simulation took one agent owned largest current connections as the direct observation node to spread real target position $(700, 400, -200)$. The initial target positions held by other nodes were randomly generated obeying Poisson distribution on $[-1000, 1000]$.

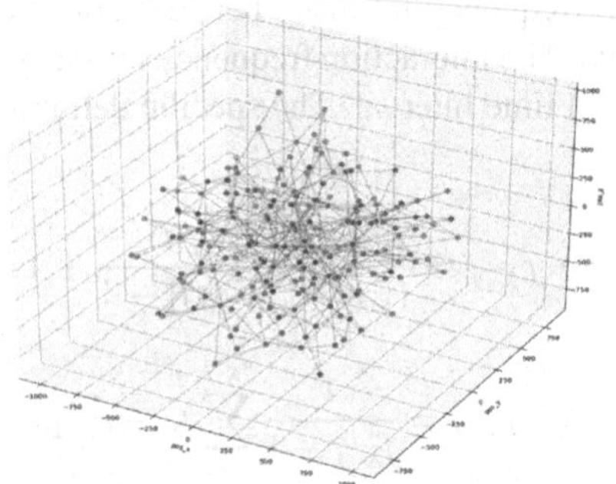

Fig. 4. Schematic diagram of the initial network connection topology of the experiment.

The simulation work of this article mainly focused on the following two aspects:

(1) Convergence efficiency of information collaboration consistency.

It could be seen in Fig. 5 that the cascaded topology relevance evaluation method can make the cluster shared information converge uniformly, possessing almost indistinguishable efficiency with mean evaluation and degree centrality evaluation.

(2) Robustness of information collaboration under weak connection conditions.

Simulation experiment added a Poisson-distributed connection interruption that obeyed [0, 5]. During connection interruption, the agent cannot interact with its neighbors. We made comparative observation on synergy status during information fusion with disparate evaluation method between degree centrality and the proposed method. As shown on the left side of Fig. 6, when there were a large number of intermittent interruptions, under the degree centrality assessment, initial information could converge to a certain extent, but could hardly achieve global uniform convergence.

Using the proposed evaluation method based on local neighborhoods, when the communication connection status was weak, the weight of acceptance during information fusion can be adjusted through historical interactive information and interactive topological relationships. So that the system could handle weak connection conditions with better robustness. At the same time, because of the expansion of the scope of information evaluation, the loss of information can be compensated when some connections are interrupted to enhance the robustness of the system. As shown on the right side of Fig. 6, information centrality evaluation method based on cascade topological relevance

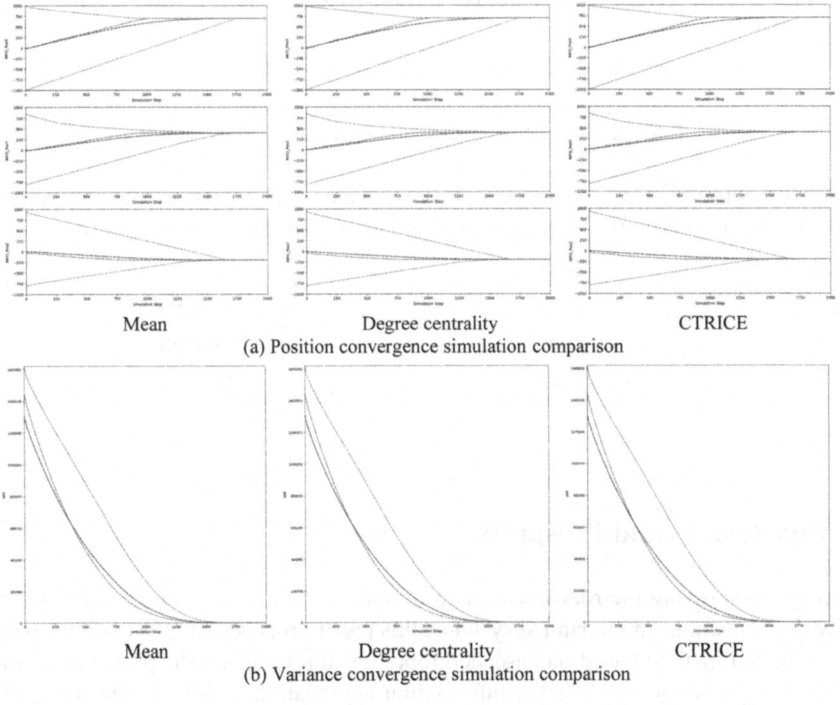

Fig. 5. Convergence efficiency comparison of information collaboration consistency.

can still ensure convergence of information at a better level. Finally, the experiment basically converged to the set threshold value range when the simulation step is about 2600. When one node entered target's direct observation range, its could become a direct observation node to accelerate convergence process.

All lines are metabolic curves along with time. In position convergence simulation comparison, the gray ones are extreme values, the blue ones are mean values, and the red ones are median values. In variance convergence simulation comparison, gray, blue and green lines each represent positions of x, y and z for its statistical variance.

Simulation experiments were carried out at four levels of connection interruption and conducted 30 trials for each level by adjusting the normalized parameters. The average convergence time and efficiency reduction are shown in Table 2.

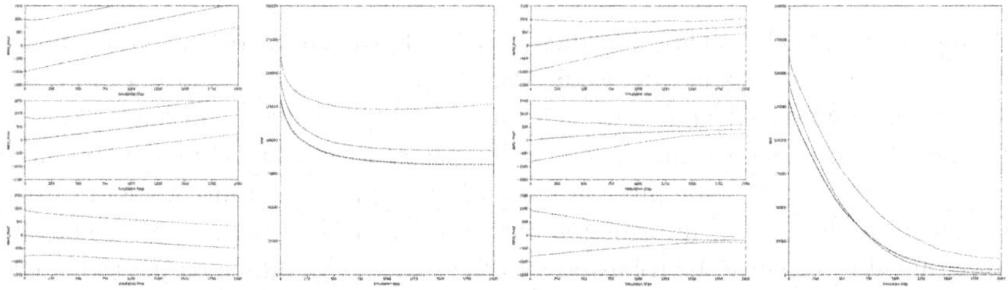

(a) Degree centrality assessment

(b) Information centrality evaluation method based on cascade topological relevance

Fig. 6. Comparison of information collaboration under weak connection conditions.

Table 2. Statistics of connection interruption simulation.

Connection interruption (obey poisson distribution)	Convergence time/simulation steps (average used of 30 trials for each)	Average efficiency decline
No interruption	1683	\
[0, 3]	1976	14.828%
[0, 5]	2186	23.010%
[0, 10]	2249	25.167%

5 Conclusions and Prospects

Aiming at improving the robustness of information collaboration under the condition of weak connections in unmanned systems, this paper proposes an information centrality evaluation method based on cascaded topological relevance. The proposed method adopts the evaluation of cascaded information aggregation capability and the assessment of intimacy in the neighborhood to estimate information centrality and contribute to form information fusion strategy. This paper verified the feasibility of this method in terms of information coordination consistency, efficiency and robustness of information collaboration under the condition of low-quality communication connections through simulation experiments. Further work will be carried out on more diverse dynamic changes of topological relations.

References

1. Jennings, N.R., Sycara, K., Wooldridge, M.: A roadmap of agent research and development. Auton. Agent. Multi-Agent Syst. **1**(1), 7–38 (1998)
2. Krnc, M., Škrekovski, R.: Group degree centrality and centralization in networks. Mathematics **8**(10), 1810 (2020). https://doi.org/10.3390/math8101810
3. Samad, A., Qadir, M., Nawaz, I., et al.: SAM centrality: a hop-based centrality measure for ranking users in social network. Indust. Netw. Intell. Syst. **7**, 163985 (2020)
4. Li, G., Li, M., Wang, J., et al.: United neighborhood closeness centrality and orthology for predicting essential proteins. IEEE/ACM Trans. Comput. Biol. Bioinform. 1–1 (2018)
5. Shao, Z., Guo, N., Gu, Y., Wang, Z., Li, F., Yu, G.: Efficient closeness centrality computation for dynamic graphs. In: Nah, Y., Cui, B., Lee, S.-W., Yu, J.X., Moon, Y.-S., Whang, S.E. (eds.) DASFAA 2020. LNCS, vol. 12113, pp. 534–550. Springer, Cham (2020). https://doi.org/10.1007/978-3-030-59416-9_32
6. Bagheri, A.E.: An Influence maximization algorithm in social network using K-shell decomposition and community detection (2020)
7. Agryzcov, T., Tortosa, L., Vicent, J.F., et al.: A centrality measure for urban networks based on the eigenvector centrality concept. Environ. Plan. B: Urban Anal. City Sci. **46**(4), 239980831772444 (2017)
8. Das, K., Samanta, S., Pal, M.: Study on centrality measures in social networks: a survey. Soc. Netw. Anal. Min. **8**(1), 1–11 (2018). https://doi.org/10.1007/s13278-018-0493-2
9. Klein, D.J.: Centrality measure in graphs. J. Math. Chem. **47**(4), 1209–1223 (2010)
10. Wan, Z., Mahajan, Y., Kang, B.W., et al.: A Survey on Centrality Metrics and Their Implications in Network Resilience. (2020)
11. Walsh, T.: Algorithms and Experiments for Betweeness Centrality in Tree-Like Networks Bachelorarbeit (2017)
12. Lu, Z., Fan, L., Wu, W., Thuraisingham, B., Yang, K.: Efficient influence spread estimation for influence maximization under the linear threshold model. Comput. Soc. Netw. **1**(1), 1–19 (2014). https://doi.org/10.1186/s40649-014-0002-3
13. Goyal, A., Lu, W., Lakshmanan, L.V.S.: SIMPATH: an efficient algorithm for influence maximization under the linear threshold model. In: The 2011 IEEE International Conference on Data Mining, pp. 211–220 Vancouver, Canada (2011)
14. Vicsek, T., Czirok, A., Ben-Jacob, E., et al.: Novel type of phase transition in a system of self-driven particles (2006)
15. Duan, H.B., Qiu, X.H.: Unmanned Aerial Vehicle Swarm Autonomous Control Based on Swarm Intelligence. China Science Publishing & Media Ltd, Beijing (2018)
16. Freeman, L.C.: A set of measures of centrality based on betweenness. Sociometry **40**(1):35–41 (1977)
17. Kitsak, M., Gallos, L.K., Havlin, S., et al.: Identifying influential spreaders in complex networks. Nat. Phys. **6**(11), 888–893 (2010)
18. Park, M.J., Lee, S.H., Kwon, O.M.: An eigenvector-centrality based consensus protocol design for discrete-time multi-agent systems with communication delays. In: Park, J.H. (ed.) Recent Advances in Control Problems of Dynamical Systems and Networks. SSDC, vol. 301, pp. 61–81. Springer, Cham (2021). https://doi.org/10.1007/978-3-030-49123-9_3

19. Myeong-Jin, P., et al.: Weighted consensus protocols design based on network centrality for multi-agent systems with sampled-data. IEEE Trans. Autom. Control **62**, 2916–2922 (2017)
20. Xie, B., Lu, X.: A distributed algorithm based on local centrality for dynamic social network reconstruction in multi-agent systems. In: 2020 4th CAA International Conference on Vehicular Control and Intelligence (CVCI), pp. 481–486 (2020)
21. Julian, Z., et al.: Social adaptation in multi-agent model of linguistic categorization is affected by network information flow. PLoS ONE **12** (2017)
22. Ma, Y.-Y., Han, H., Qu, Q.-Q.: Importance evaluation algorithm based on node intimate degree. Comput. Sci. **48**(5), 140–146 (2021)
23. Tian, Y.P., Li, Y., Wang, X.Q., et al.: Suppress the diffusion of rumors with nodes closeness mining. Chin. J. Netw. Inf. Secur. (2016)

Marine Predators Algorithm with Stage-Based Repairment for the Green Supply Network Design

Zhaobin Ma[1], Bowen Ding[1], Xin Zhang[1(✉)], Pengjiang Qian[1(✉)], and Zhihui Zhan[2]

[1] Jiangnan University, Wuxi 214000, China
zhangxin@jiangnan.edu.cn, qianpjiang@126.com
[2] South China University of Technology, Guangzhou 510006, China

Abstract. Green supply chain network design (GSCND) has become a hot topic in many manufacturing industries today, since it is an environmentally friendly manufacturing mode and is significantly related to the sustainable development of enterprises. The GSCND problem always has multiple complex constraints, which makes it difficult for traditional methods to search for feasible solutions within the limited time. Therefore, this paper designs a four-echelon green supply chain network model, and proposes a Marine Predators Algorithm with the Stage-based Repairment (MPA-SR) to solve the complex constrained problem. For infeasible solutions that violate the constraints, MPA-SR repairs its logistics routes firstly, and then allocates the freight volume to the routes. Besides, an adaptive repair probability variable is designed to control the probability of the repair operator. In order to prove the efficacy of MPA-SR, the experiment is carried out on nine instances with three different scales. The experimental results show that MPA-SR performs better than other compared algorithms in terms of both the solving speed and the solution quality.

Keywords: Green supply chain network · Marine predators algorithm · Constrained optimization

1 Introduction

Supply chain network management has become more and more important for many industries. Supply chain network generally consists of suppliers, manufacturers, warehouses, customers, and so on, which are connected to form a whole functional network chain structure [1–3]. The main purpose of supply chain network design (SCND) is to minimize the whole cost of the network and to satisfy the demand of customers. A well-designed SCND can save the operation time and cost, and improve customer satisfaction and the competitiveness of enterprises.

Y. Sun et al. (Eds.): ChineseCSCW 2021, CCIS 1491, pp. 243–258, 2022.
https://doi.org/10.1007/978-981-19-4546-5_20

As the green and low-carbon manufacturing has become more and more important for the sustainable development, the green supply chain network design (GSCND) has received widespread attention [4]. The concept of GSCND was first proposed by the Manufacturing Research Association of Michigan State University in 1996 in an "Environmentally Responsible Manufacturing" study [5]. GSCND considers both the environmental impact and the resource efficiency in the system, and has become a modern popular management model. It pursues economic benefits and green benefits at the same time to achieve sustainable economic development.

In order to extend the SCND problem to the GSCND problem, many models and algorithms were proposed, but they still have some shortcomings. Qian Tao proposed the Green Agri-food Supply Chain Network and used Chaotic PSO Algorithm to solve this problem [6]. However, the proposed model contains few constraints and is not realistic. Essam Kaoud proposed the Dual-Channel Closed Loop Supply Chain with E-Commerce, and used GAMS-CPLEX to prove the validity of the model [7]. But, due to the large scale of the problem and complex constraints, it is time-consuming to use software to solve the problem. Y.T. Chen designed an integrated closed-loop supply chain model, and applied a two-stage genetic algorithm (GA) algorithm to solve it [8]. Since the complex constraints of the problem, it is difficult for the two-stage GA to produce the feasible solutions without the repair operator.

To solve the above problems, this paper proposes a new green supply chain model and a Marine Predators Algorithm with the Stage-based Repairment. The model takes the green factor (i.e. the pollution) as a new constraint, so it can be easily applied to various fields in manufacturing. This algorithm combines marine predators algorithm (MPA) [9] and the repair operator to quickly find feasible solutions. And the repair operator can randomly generate feasible logistics routes, which can help the solution search in feasible space. Experimental results show that the proposed algorithm can obtain higher-quality solutions within the shorter time.

2 GSCND Problem Definition

With the continuous promotion of the concept of green environmental protection in recent years. In order to reduce the pollution from the source, this paper proposes a green supply chain model composed of a logistics system, a supply system, and a distribution system [10].

Green design of GSCND is an important part of the model in [11–13], and the pollution is taken as a constraint in the proposed model. In the condition of satisfying the pollution discharge requirements, this model is to minimize the whole cost of the system, and improve the economic efficiency as much as possible.

The workflow of the proposed model is shown as follows:

1) Suppliers provide materials for manufacturers.
2) Manufacturers produce products and transports them to warehouses.
3) Warehouses transport products to customers.

In order to make the model more closed to the reality, this paper considers the following assumptions and constraints:

1) The materials provided by suppliers are subject to proportional restrictions. The supply relationship constrained by proportion is more in line with the actual situation. For example, if the ratio of material a to material b required to produce a new product is 1:1. The ratio of material a to material b provided by suppliers to manufacturers must also be 1:1.
2) This model has the several capacity limitations. For example, the freight volume of materials provided by a supplier should not exceed its capacity; the quantity of products produced by a manufacturer and the freight volume of products provided to warehouses by the manufacturer cannot exceed its capacity; the inventory of a warehouse and the freight volume of products provided to customers by the warehouse cannot exceed its capacity.
3) Customers' demands are preset, and the demand of each customer must be satisfied.
4) A supplier can supply for different manufacturers, a manufacturer can supply for different warehouses, also a warehouse can supply for different customers, and vice versa.
5) According to the types of materials required by the product, suppliers are divided into multiple categories. Suppliers of the same category provide the same materials for manufacturers, but their materials prices are not the same. Generally speaking, the prices are related to the pollution. Similar to the situation for manufacturers. Different manufacturers use different production processes, so their production prices and pollution are also different.

The notations of indices, parameters and decision variables about this model are shown as follows:

Indices:

p	index of materials	w	index of warehouses
s	index of supplies	c	index of customers
m	index of manufacturers		

Parameters:

MT	number of material types
S_p	number of suppliers who supplies material p
M	number of manufacturers
W	number of warehouses
C	number of customers
$M\_fixedCost_m$	fixed cost of manufacturer m
$W\_fixedCost_w$	fixed cost of warehouse w
$T\_sup2manu_{p,s,m}$	unit freight cost of material p from supplier s to manufacturer m
$T\_manu2ware_{m,w}$	unit freight cost from manufacturer m to warehouse w
$T\_ware2cus_{w,c}$	unit freight cost from warehouse w to customer c
$S\_price_{p,s}$	unit price of material p supplied by supplier s
M_price_m	unit price of a product produced by manufacturer m
$S\_pollution_{p,s}$	unit pollution of material p supplied by supplier s
$M\_pollution_m$	unit pollution of a product produced by manufacturer m
P_norm	unit pollution of a product
$S\_capacity_{p,s}$	capacity of supplier s supplying material p
$M\_capacity_m$	capacity of manufacturer m
$Q\_component_p$	proportion of material p in a new product
C_demand_c	demand of customer c
TC	total cost of the supply chain
$materialCost$	material cost of the supply chain
$productionCost$	production cost of the supply chain
$fixedCost$	fixed cost of the supply chain
$frightCost$	freight cost of the supply chain

Decision variable:

$Q\_sup2manu_{p,s,m}$	quantity of material p shipped by supplier s to manufacturer m
$Q\_manu2ware_{m,w}$	quantity of products shipped by manufacturer m to warehouse w
$Q\_ware2cus_{w,c}$	quantity of products shipped by warehouse w to customer c
$Q\_manuprocess_m$	quantity of products produced by manufacturer m
M_open_m	whether manufacturer m is selected
W_open_w	whether warehouse w is selected

The total cost TC consists of the material cost, the production cost, the fixed cost, and the freight cost.

The material cost $materialCost$ can be calculated as

$$materialCost = \sum_{p=1}^{MT}\sum_{s=1}^{S_p}\sum_{m=1}^{M} S\_price_{p,s} \times Q\_sup2manu_{p,s,m} \tag{1}$$

The conversion cost $productionCost$ can be calculated as

$$productionCost = \sum_{m=1}^{M} Q\_manuprocess_m \times M\_price_m \tag{2}$$

The fixed cost *fixedCost* can be calculated as

$$fixedCost = \sum_{m=1}^{M} M\_open_m \times M\_fixedcost_m + \sum_{w=1}^{W} W\_open_w \times W\_fixedcost_w \quad (3)$$

Finally, the freight cost *freightCost* can be calculated as

$$\begin{aligned} freightCost = & \sum_{p=1}^{MT}\sum_{s=1}^{S_p}\sum_{m=1}^{M} T\_sup2manu_{p,s,m} \times Q\_sup2manu_{p,s,m} \\ & + \sum_{m=1}^{M}\sum_{w=1}^{W} T\_manu2ware_{m,w} \times Q\_manu2ware_{m,w} \\ & + \sum_{w=1}^{W}\sum_{c=1}^{C} T\_ware2cus_{w,c} \times Q\_ware2cus_{w,c} \end{aligned} \quad (4)$$

So, the final objective function of this problem is calculated as follows:

$$\text{Minmize } TC = materialCost + productionCost + fixedCost + freightCost \quad (5)$$

Subject to:

$$\sum_{s=1}^{S_p} Q\_sup2manu_{p,s,m} = Q\_component_p \times Q\_manuprocess_m \quad \forall p \in MT, \forall m \in M \quad (6)$$

$$Q\_manuprocess_m = \sum_{w=1}^{W} Q\_manu2war_{m,w} \quad \forall m \in M \quad (7)$$

$$\sum_{c=1}^{C} Q\_war2cus_{w,c} \le \sum_{w=1}^{W} Q\_manu2war_{m,w} \quad \forall w \in W \quad (8)$$

$$\sum_{w=1}^{W} Q\_war2cus_{w,c} = C\_demand_c \quad \forall c \in C \quad (9)$$

$$\sum_{m=1}^{M} Q\_sup2manu_{p,s,m} \le S\_capacity_{p,s} \times S\_open_s \quad \forall p \in MT, \forall s \in S_p \quad (10)$$

$$\sum_{w=1}^{W} Q\_manu2war_{m,w} \le M\_capacity \times M\_open_m \quad \forall m \in M \quad (11)$$

$$\sum_{c=1}^{C} Q\_war2cus_{w,c} \le W\_capacity_w \times W\_open_w \quad \forall w \in W \quad (12)$$

$$Q\_sup2manu_{p,s,m} \in N^* \quad \forall p \in MT, \forall s \in S, \forall m \in M \tag{13}$$

$$Q\_manu2ware_{m,w} \in N^* \quad \forall m \in M, \forall w \in W \tag{14}$$

$$Q\_ware2cus_{w,c} \in N^* \quad \forall w \in W, \forall c \in C \tag{15}$$

$$M\_open_m, W\_open_w \in \{0, 1\} \quad \forall m \in M, \forall w \in W \tag{16}$$

$$\sum_{p=1}^{MT}\sum_{s=1}^{S_p}\sum_{m=1}^{M} T\_sup2manu_{p,s,m} \times S\_pollution_{p,s} + \sum_{m=1}^{M} Q\_manuprocess_m \times M\_pollution_m \leq \sum_{m=1}^{M} Q\_manuprocess_m \times P\_norm \tag{17}$$

Constraint (6) indicates that for each material required by each manufacturer, the sum of materials provided by suppliers must satisfy the requirements for the production of new products. Constraint (7) indicates that for each manufacturer, the freight volume of the provided product must be equal to the quantity of the new produced product. Constraint (8) restricts that for each warehouse, the inflow is great than or equal to the outflow. Constraint (9) shows that for each customer, its demand must be satisfied. Constraints (10), (11) and (12) formulate the capacity constraints of suppliers, manufacturers and warehouses respectively. Constraints (13), (14), and (15) represent the integer limit. Constraint (16) represents the binary limit. Constraint (17) represents the pollution limit.

3 Marine Predators Algorithm (MPA)

MPA, developed by Faramarzi, is a nature-inspired metaheuristic. It mimics the optimal foraging mechanism of Marine predators searching for prey. When the concentration of prey in the environment is low, predators use Lévy strategy to search for prey; otherwise, predators will employ Brownian movement. Predators make tradeoffs between Lévy and Brownian strategies based on the velocity ratio between predators and prey:

1) At low-velocity ratio ($v = 0.1$), whether the prey is moving in Brownian or Lévy, the best strategy for the predators is Lévy.
2) At unit velocity ratio ($v = 1$), if the prey moves in Lévy, the predators will move in Brownian.
3) At high-velocity ratio ($v \geq 10$), regardless of whether the prey is moving in Brownian or Lévy, the best strategy for the predators is to keep still.

The mathematical model of MPA is described as follows:

At the first step, a group of prey will be generated by the following formula:

$$\vec{X}_0 = \vec{X}_{\min} + \overrightarrow{rand} * \left(\vec{X}_{\max} - \vec{X}_{\min}\right) \tag{18}$$

where $\overrightarrow{rand}$ is a uniform random vector generated between 0 and 1, and $\vec{X}_{\min}$ and $\vec{X}_{\max}$ are the lower and upper bound vectors of variables in the optimization problem.

After the initialization, each solution will be evaluated based on the objective function, where the solution with the highest fitness is defined as the top predator. Based on survival of fittest theorem, the top predator is used to build up a matrix which is called *Elite*. *Elite* is consisted of *n* $\overrightarrow{X^I}$, the dimensions of *Elite* is n × d, $\overrightarrow{X^I}$ represents the top predator, d is the dimensions of $\overrightarrow{X^I}$.

The predators will update their position through a matrix called *Prey*, which has the same dimensions as the matrix *Elite* and constructed of prey.

3.1 High-Velocity Ratio

This is the exploration phase, where the prey use Brownian strategy to explore the search space. This phase happens in the beginning of the iterative process and is calculated as follows:

$$\begin{aligned} \overrightarrow{SS}_i &= \vec{R}_B \otimes \left(\overrightarrow{Elite}_i - \vec{R}_B \otimes \overrightarrow{Prey}\right) \\ \overrightarrow{Prey}_i &= \overrightarrow{Prey}_i + P * \vec{R} \otimes \overrightarrow{SS}_i \end{aligned}, \text{ if } t < \frac{1}{3}Max\_t \tag{19}$$

where $\vec{R}_B$ is a normally distributed random vector which represents Brownian motion, $\otimes$ represents the entry-wise multiplication, P is a constant number, the original paper recommend $P = 0.5$, $\vec{R}$ is a uniformly distributed random number vector in [0–1], t is the current iteration, and Max_t is the maximum one.

3.2 Unit-Velocity Ratio

This is the transitional phase between exploration and exploitation, where half of the population (prey) use Lévy strategy to exploitation and the other half (predators) use Brownian strategy to exploration. This phase happens in the middle iterative process.

($\frac{1}{3}Max\_t < t < \frac{2}{3}Max\_t$) and is calculated as follows:

For the first half of the population

$$\begin{aligned} \overrightarrow{SS}_i &= \vec{R}_L \otimes \left(\overrightarrow{Elite}_i - \vec{R}_L \otimes \overrightarrow{Prey}_i\right) \\ \overrightarrow{Prey}_i &= \overrightarrow{Prey}_i + P * \vec{R} \otimes \overrightarrow{SS}_i \end{aligned} \tag{20}$$

For the second half of the population

$$\overrightarrow{SS}_i = \vec{R}_B \otimes \left(\vec{R}_B \otimes \overrightarrow{Elite}_i - \overrightarrow{Prey}_i\right)$$

$$\overrightarrow{Prey}_i = \overrightarrow{Elite}_i + P * CF \otimes \overrightarrow{SS}_i \tag{21}$$

where $\vec{R}_L$ is a random vector based on Lévy distribution representing Lévy movement, and CF is an adaptive parameter and is used to control the step size of the predator and is formulated as follows:

$$CF = \left(1 - \frac{t}{Max\_t}\right)^{\left(2\frac{t}{Max\_t}\right)} \tag{22}$$

3.3 Low-Velocity Ratio

This phase is for the exploitation, where the predators use Lévy strategy to catch prey. This phase happens in the end of the iterative process and is formulated as follows:

$$\begin{aligned}\overrightarrow{SS}_i &= \overrightarrow{R}_L \otimes \left(\overrightarrow{R}_L \otimes \overrightarrow{Elite}_i - \overrightarrow{Prey}_i\right) \\ \overrightarrow{Prey}_i &= \overrightarrow{Elite}_i + P * CF \otimes \overrightarrow{SS}_i\end{aligned}, \text{ if } t > \frac{2}{3}Max\_t \quad (23)$$

According to research, the environment can influence the behavior of marine predators, such as the eddy formation or Fish Aggregating Devices (FADs) effects. So MPA designed FADs to jump out of local optima solution, the FADs effect is formulated as follows:

$$\overrightarrow{Prey}_i = \begin{cases} \overrightarrow{Prey}_i + CF\left[\overrightarrow{X}_{\min} + \overrightarrow{R} \otimes \left(\overrightarrow{X}_{\max} - \overrightarrow{X}_{\min}\right)\right] \otimes \overrightarrow{U}, \text{if } r \le FADs \\ \overrightarrow{Prey}_i + \left[FADs(1-r) + r\right]\left(\overrightarrow{Prey}_{r1} - \overrightarrow{Prey}_{r2}\right), \text{if } r > FADs \end{cases} \quad (24)$$

where r is the uniform random number in [0,1], $FADs = 0.2$ represents the influence of FADs on the optimization process, and $\overrightarrow{U}$ is a binary vector containing arrays of 0 and 1. For each array in $\overrightarrow{U}$, it is constructed by generating a random vector in [0,1]. And if the array is less than $FADs$, then it is set to 0, otherwise, it is set to 1. $r1$ and $r2$ are random integers in the range of population size.

Besides, MPA has an operator called memory saving, this operator saves the previous solutions. After a solution is updated, the current solution is compared to the previous solution, if the previous solution is better, the current solution is replaced with the previous solution.

4 Proposed Algorithm MPA-SR

4.1 Solution Encoding

The dimension of a solution is equal to $\left(\sum_{p=1}^{MT} S_p \times M\right) + M \times W + W \times C$. An example of the encoding of solutions is shown in Fig. 1.

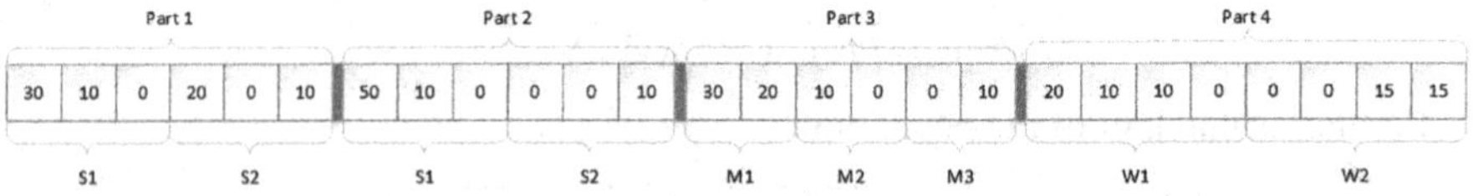

Fig. 1. Illustration of the encoding schemes of solution.

In this example, $MT = 2$, $S_1 = 2$, $S_2 = 2$, $M = 3$, $W = 2$, $C = 4$. The solution is divided into four parts. Part 1 represents the delivery of material 1. The first three variables represent that supplier 1 delivers 30 units of material 1 to manufacturer 1 and 10 units of material 1 to manufacturer 2 and does not deliver materials to manufacturer 3. Part 2 represents the transportation of material 2, Part 3 represents the delivery of products from manufacturers to warehouses, Part 4 represents the delivery of products from warehouses, and the principle is the same as Part 1.

4.2 Stage-Based Repairment

The penalty function method is widely used to solve constrained optimization problems because of its simplicity and easy implementation. However, with the expansion of the problem scale and the sharp increase in the number of constraints, it is difficult for the penalty function method to find feasible solutions. In order to solve this problem, this paper designed a stage-based repairmen (SR) to help find feasible solutions.

For each solution, the check algorithm is used to determine which part of the solution is illegal. If the solution is feasible, the algorithm returns 0, otherwise the check algorithm returns the indices of the illegal part of the solution, the procedure of the check is shown in Algorithm 1.

After the solution is checked, if the solution is infeasible, the solution will be repaired. Since the repair operator is time-consuming, an adaptive parameter p_{repair} is designed to control the repair probability. At the beginning, the value of p_{repair} is small, so as to not limit the search ability of the algorithm. After that, in order to increase the number of feasible solutions and accelerate the convergence, the value of p_{repair} keeps increasing. The formula of p_{repair} is as follows:

$$p_{repair} = 0.01 * e^{(p_l - 1)} \tag{25}$$

where e is an Euler's number, and approximately equals to 2.718, and p_l is the proportion of feasible solutions in the population.

Algorithm 1: Check

```
Input: x: solution; MT: the number of materials types
Output: the indices of the illegal part of the solution
if x violates constraint (9) and (12) then
    return MT+2;
else if x violates constraint (8) and (11) then
    return MT+1;
else
    t is a empty list;
    for p = 1 to MT do
        if x violates constraint (6) and (10) then
            add p to the list t;
    if len(t)>0 then
        return t;
    else
        return 0;
```

Firstly, the repair operator randomly generates a logistics route represented by binary string, and then it is determined whether the logistics route is legal. If the logistics route is illegal, a new logistics route will be regenerated until the logistics route is legal. Since logistics routes are generated randomly, this operator helps to protect the diversity of the solutions.

An example of the binary encoding of the logistics route is shown in Fig. 2. The first three variables represent that supplier 1 provides material 1 to manufacturer 1 and does not provide materials to manufacturer 2 and manufacturer 3.

The judgment rules of the logistics route are as follows:

1. For each receiver, the sum of the quantities of products that all its providers can provide must be larger than or equal to the receiver's demand.
2. The sum of the quantity of products from all providers must be larger or equal to the sum of demands of the receivers.

Then, after the logistics route is legal, the repair operator will allocate freight volume to the logistics route. The allocation steps are shown in Algorithm 2.

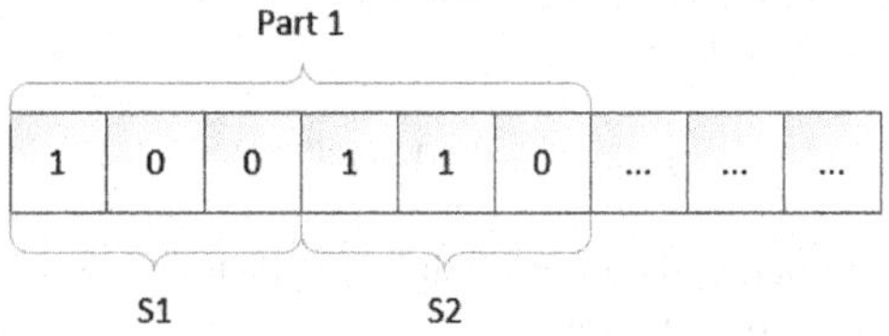

Fig. 2. Illustration of the binary encoding schemes of route.

The complete steps of the repair operator are shown in Algorithm 3.

Algorithm 2: Allocation

---

while *receivers' demand is not met* **do**
  Allocate freight volume to receivers with only one provider according to demand;
  Update demand and supply capacity;
  For receivers with multiple providers, sort their providers according to unit transportation cost. The lower the transportation cost, the higher the ranking;
  High-ranking providers are assigned first;
  if *there are multiple providers in the same ranking* **then**
    if *supply capacity is greater than demand* **then**
      Randomly divide demand into multiple parts and distribute them to the providers;
    else
      The freight volume is equal to supply capacity;
  Update demand and supply capacity;

Algorithm 3: Repair

```
Input: x: solution; t: the index of stage that needs to be repaired;
       demand: demand of receivers
Output: the legal solution
Flag=False;
while Flag==False do
    Randomly generate a binary route information in the part t of x;
    Determine whether the route is legal according to the judgment
     rule;
    while route is illegal do
        Randomly generate binary route information in the part t of x;
        Determine whether the route is legal according to the judgment
         rule;
    Allocate freight volume to the route using Algorithm 2;
    if allocation is successful then
        Flag=True;
    else
        Flag=False;
if t==MT+2 then
    Calculate warehouses' demand for products w_demand;
    Repair(x, t − 1, w_demand);
else if t==MT+1 then
    for i = 1 to MT do
        Calculate manufacturers' demand for material i m_demand;
        Repair(x, i, m_demand);
else
    Return x.
```

4.3 Complete MPA-SR

The complete MPA-SR is shown in Algorithm 4. Since the problem has many constraints and a large solution space, it is difficult for the original MPA algorithm to obtain the feasible solutions. The advantage of MPA-SR is that it can quickly find a feasible solution through the repair operator, which greatly reduces the time required for the algorithm. Then MPA-SR can find higher-quality solutions through powerful search capabilities.

Algorithm 4: MPA-SR

```
Initialize Prey populations i=1,2,...,n;
Set parameters' value;
while t < Max_t do
    Calculate P_repair according to Eq.(25);
    for each Prey_i do
        index=Check(Prey_i);
        if not(index==0) then
            r=random(0,1);
            if r<=P_repair then
                if index is a list then
                    for each id in index do
                        Calculate the corresponding demand;
                        Prey_i=Repair(Prey_i,id,demand);
                else
                    Calculate the corresponding demand;
                    Prey_i=Repair(Prey_i,index,demand);
            Calculate the fitness of Prey_i by using penalty function
             method;
    Construct the Elite matrix and accomplish memory saving;
    for each Prey_i do
        if t < 1/3 * Max_t then
            Update Prey_i according Eq.(19);
        else if 1/3 * Max_t < t < 2/3 * Max_t then
            if i <= 1/2 n then
                Update Prey_i according to Eq.(20);
            else
                Update Prey_i according to Eq.(21);
        else
            Update Prey_i according to Eq.(23);
    Accomplish memory saving and update the Elite matrix;
    Apply FADs effect and update based on Eq.(24);
```

5 Experimental Results

To validate the performance of the MPA-SR algorithms for solving the GSCND problem, three different scales are considered. Each scale includes three instances. There are 3 (scales) × 3 (instances) = 9 instances in total. The details of each scales are reported in Table 1.

Four compared algorithms were implemented, including MPA, the social learning particle swarm optimization (SLPSO) [14], the competitive swarm optimizer (CSO) [15] and the Red deer algorithm (RDA) [16]. The optimal parameter settings of all algorithms are shown in Table 2.

Each instance was tested with 30 replications, and both the best and worst and average values were recorded. All the algorithms were implemented in python 3.8 and run on a PC with the Intel Core i7-11700 and 16.0 GB memory.

Table 1. Scale configuration and execution time.

No.	S1	S2	M	W	C	Dimension	Execution time (Seconds)
1	3	2	4	2	5	38	40
2	5	4	5	5	6	100	120
3	6	6	8	6	10	204	300

Table 2. Optimal parameter settings of all algorithms.

Algorithm	Tuned parameters
MPA-SR	$N\_pop = 140, Max\_t = 300, P = 0.5, FADs = 0.2$
MPA	$N\_pop = 140, Max\_t = 300, P = 0.5, FADs = 0.2$
SLPSO	$N\_pop = 200, \alpha = 0.5, \beta = 0.01$
CSO	$N\_pop = 300$
RDA	$N\_pop = 200, N_{male} = 30, \alpha = 0.9, \beta = 0.4, \gamma = 0.8$

The results of the instances are shown in Tables 3, 4 and 5. Results in italics type indicate that the global optimal solution is illegal. The best solutions among all the algorithms are in bold.

In Table 3, MPA-SR can find the minimum total cost in each instance, followed by MPA and SLPSO. CSO sometimes cannot find feasible solutions, because its exploration capabilities are not enough to deal with complex constraints. RDA cannot search for feasible solutions at all.

As shown in Table 4, in the medium scale, only MPA-SR, MPA and SLPSO can obtain better solutions, and other algorithms cannot find feasible solutions. Among the three algorithms with the better performance, MPA-SR is better than other two algorithms.

Table 5 shows that as the scale expands to a large scale, only MPA-SR can search for feasible solutions and converge to better values. Other algorithms cannot find feasible solutions in the face of a large number of constraints.

In order to analyze the convergence of all algorithms, the convergence curves of three scales are drawn, as shown in Figs. 3, 4 and 5. It can be seen that after some iterations, the evolution of CSO, RDA, SLPSO quickly stagnates, falling into a local optimum. Due

Table 3. The results on small-scale instances.

Instance		MPA	SLPSO	CSO	RDA	MPA-SR
1	Best	146146.5	147341.5	146612.0	1.54E + 12	**139754.0**
	Avg	147572.1	147826.6	*3346729.0*	2.28E + 12	**139833.0**
	Worst	149401.0	148707.0	*9146192.0*	3.10E + 12	**139890.0**
2	Best	153338.0	154280.0	154417.0	1.46E + 12	**147785.0**
	Avg	153881.8	154389.5	*1954532.7*	2.42E + 12	**148561.3**
	Worst	154819.5	154475.0	*6154840.0*	3.55E + 12	**149108.5**
3	Best	153241.0	154624.0	154903.5	1.37E + 12	**147158.0**
	Avg	154242.9	155724.3	*355337.7*	1.70E + 12	**147535.8**
	Worst	154700.5	156366.5	*1152664.0*	2.30E + 12	**147890.0**

Table 4. The results on medium-scale instances.

Instance		MPA	SLPSO	CSO	RDA	MPA-SR
1	Best	216110.6	226819.9	*5.33E + 12*	*3.20E + 12*	**204356.1**
	Avg	221470.4	233918.4	*6.59E + 12*	*4.13E + 12*	**205541.9**
	Worst	226840.6	238286.7	*9.20E + 12*	*6.69E + 12*	**206475.8**
2	Best	219051.8	227241.4	*5.67E + 12*	*7.40E + 12*	**205323.0**
	Avg	225112.1	235312.2	*6.85E + 12*	*3.13E + 13*	**206385.9**
	Worst	230742.5	238973.5	*7.62E + 12*	*6.53E + 13*	**208554.5**
3	Best	219120.3	225126.5	*4.53E + 12*	*4.23E + 12*	**205532.5**
	Avg	224862.4	234531.8	*6.42E + 12*	*6.52E + 12*	**205933.2**
	Worst	233688.4	237942.1	*8.74E + 12*	*2.75E + 13*	**207850.5**

Table 5. The results on large-scale instances.

Instance		MPA	SLPSO	CSO	RDA	MPA-SR
1	Best	1406839.1	*4.76E + 9*	*7.51E + 12*	*8.31E + 12*	**393962.8**
	Avg	*15005174.6*	*8.63E + 9*	*9.79E + 12*	*1.32E + 13*	**394956.5**
	Worst	*51402879.9*	*1.94E + 10*	*1.26E + 13*	*1.53E + 13*	**395940.7**
2	Best	*445827.2*	*5.09E + 10*	*7.24E + 12*	*2.36E + 13*	**423359.4**
	Avg	*10452323.1*	*7.72E + 10*	*8.45E + 12*	*5.35E + 13*	**424451.6**
	Worst	*31443358.4*	*1.02E + 11*	*1.43E + 13*	*8.35E + 13*	**425734.6**
3	Best	*5425123.0*	*5.88E + 9*	*3.15E + 13*	*1.68E + 13*	**434526.9**
	Avg	*55775270.0*	*7.44E + 9*	*4.45E + 13*	*3.85E + 13*	**435843.2**
	Worst	*87403555.0*	*9.52E + 9*	*6.39E + 13*	*5.72E + 13*	**437020.7**

to the characteristics of MPA, in the first third generation, the entire population is in the exploratory stage. Its convergence speed is slow in the early stage. In the last two-thirds of the generation, the algorithm uses Lévy strategy to accelerate convergence. MPA-SR can quickly converge to a feasible value in the early stage through the repair operator, because the repair operator can help to find more feasible solutions and speed up the convergence speed of the algorithm.

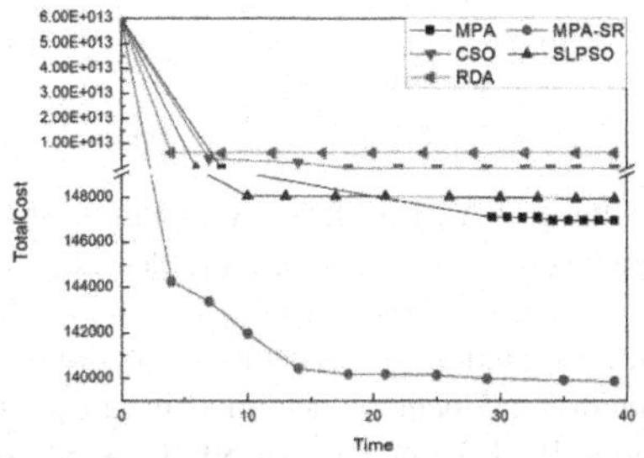

Fig. 3. Convergence curves of all algorithms (small-scale)

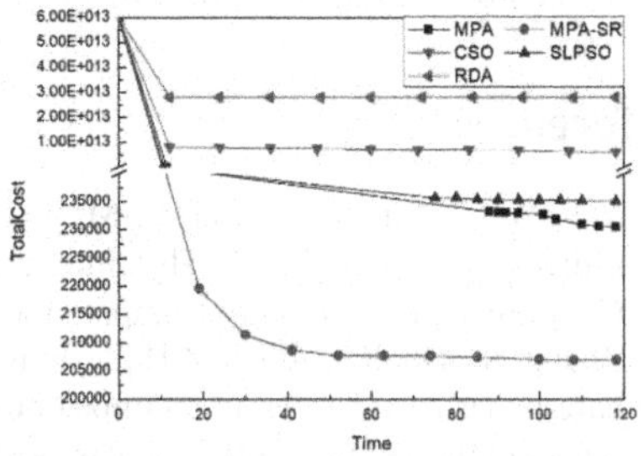

Fig. 4. Convergence curves of all algorithms (medium-scale)

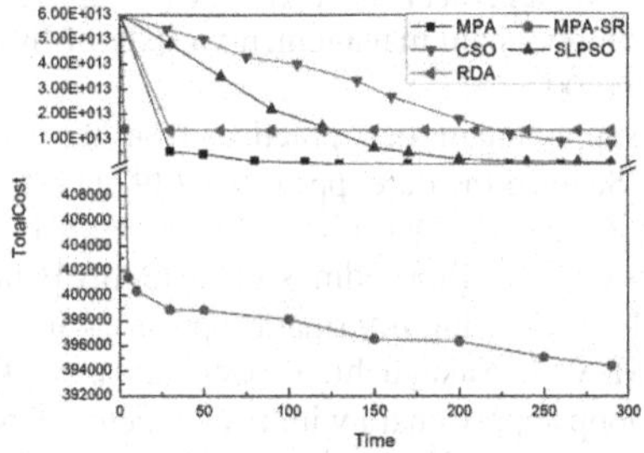

Fig. 5. Convergence curves of all algorithms (large-scale)

6 Conclusions

Based on the concept of green and environmental protection, this paper proposes a new GSCND model. The model is more closed to the real needs and can be applied to different manufacturing industries. However, due to the complex constraints of the model, it is hard for the existing algorithms to solve the problem. This paper proposes an efficient algorithm MPA-SR to deal with the complex constrained optimization problem. In order to find feasible solutions, this paper proposes a stage-based repair operator. According to the corresponding judgment rules of the logistic routes and distribution rules of the freight volume of routes, the infeasible solutions can be transformed into the feasible solutions. Since the repair operator is time-consuming, in order to balance the running time and the performance of the operator, an adaptive parameter P_{repair} is proposed to control the probability of the repair operator.

Nine instances with three different scales are randomly generated to verify the performance of the MPA-SR algorithm. The results show that MPA-SR is significantly better than other algorithms in different scales of the problem. Besides, the increase in the data size and the number of constraints will not influence the performance of the proposed algorithm.

Acknowledgements. This research work is supported by the National Natural Science Foundation of China (NSFC) under Grant 62106088.

References

1. Yeh, W.-C., Lin, W.-T., Lai, C.-M., Lee, Y.C., Chung, Y.Y., Lin, J.-S.: Application of simplified swarm optimization algorithm in deteriorate supply chain network problem. In: IEEE Congress on Evolutionary Computation (CEC), pp. 2695–2700 (2016)
2. Zhang, X., Du, K.J., Zhan, Z.H., Kwong, S., Gu, T.L., Zhang, J.: Cooperative coevolutionary bare-bones particle swarm optimization with function independent decomposition for large-scale supply chain network design with uncertainties. IEEE Trans. Cybern. **50**(10), 4454–4468 (2020)
3. S. Bandyopadhyay, R.B.: NSGA-II based multi-objective evolutionary algorithm for a multi-objective supply chain problem. In: IEEE-International Conference on Advances in Engineering, Science and Management (ICAESM-2012), pp. 126–130 (2012)
4. Srivastava, S.K.: Green supply-chain management: a state-of-the-art literature review. Int. J. Manag. Rev. **9**(1), 53–80 (2007)
5. Handfield, B.R.: Green supply chain: best practices from the furniture industry. In: Annual Meeting of the Decision Science Institute, pp. 1295–1297 (1996)
6. Qian Tao, Z.H., Gu, C., Zhang, C.: Optimization of green agri-food supply chain network using chaotic PSO algorithm. In: Proceedings of 2013 IEEE International Conference on Service Operations and Logistics, and Informatics, pp. 462–467 (2013)
7. Kaoud, E., Abdel-Aal, M.A.M., Sakaguchi, T., Uchiyama, N.: Design and optimization of the dual-channel closed loop supply chain with E-commerce. Sustainability **12**(23) (2020)
8. Chen, Y.T., Chan, F.T.S., Chung, S.H.: An integrated closed-loop supply chain model with location allocation problem and product recycling decisions. Int. J. Prod. Res. **53**(10), 3120–3140 (2015)
9. Faramarzi, A., Heidarinejad, M., Mirjalili, S., Gandomi, A.H.: Marine predators algorithm: a nature-inspired metaheuristic. Expert Syst. Appl. **152** (2020)
10. Silva, C.A., Sousa, J.M.C., Runkler, T.A., da Costa, J.M.G.S.: Distributed supply chain management using ant colony optimization. Eur. J. Oper. Res. **199**(2), 349–358 (2009)
11. Glantschnig, W.J.: Green design: an introduction to issues and challenges. In: IEEE Transactions on Components, Packaging, and Manufacturing Technology, pp. 508–513 (1994)
12. Jayaraman, V., Guide, V.D.R., Srivastava: a closed-loop logistics model for remanufacturing. J. Oper. Res. Soc. **50**, 497–508 (1999)
13. Arena, U., Mastellone, M.L., Perugini: The environmental performance of alternative solid waste management options: A life cycle assessment study. Chem. Eng. J. **96**, 207–222 (2003)
14. Cheng, R., Jin, Y.: A social learning particle swarm optimization algorithm for scalable optimization. Inf. Sci. **291**, 43–60 (2015)
15. Cheng, R., Jin, Y.: A competitive swarm optimizer for large scale optimization. IEEE Trans. Cybern. **45**(2), 191–204 (2016)
16. Fathollahi-Fard, A.M., Hajiaghaei-Keshteli, M., Tavakkoli-Moghaddam, R.: Red deer algorithm (RDA): a new nature-inspired meta-heuristic. Soft. Comput. **24**(19), 14637–14665 (2020). https://doi.org/10.1007/s00500-020-04812-z

Compressed-Coding Particle Swarm Optimization for Large-Scale Feature Selection

Jia-Quan Yang[1], Zhi-Hui Zhan[1](✉), and Tao Li[2]

[1] School of Computer Science and Engineering, South China University of Technology, Guangzhou 510006, China
zhanapollo@163.com

[2] School of Computer and Information Engineering, Henan Normal University, Xinxiang 453007, China

Abstract. Particle swarm optimization (PSO) is a popular method for feature selection. However, when dealing with large-scale features, PSO faces the challenges of poor search performance and long running time. In addition, a suitable representation for particles to deal with the discrete binary optimization problem like the feature selection is still in great need. This paper proposes a PSO algorithm for large-scale feature selection problems named compressed-coding PSO (CCPSO). It uses the *N*-base encoding method for the representation of particles and designs a particle update mechanism based on the Hamming distance, which can be performed in the discrete space. It also proposes a local search strategy to dynamically shorten the length of particles, thus reducing the search space. The experimental results show that CCPSO performs well for large-scale feature selection problems. The solutions obtained by CCPSO contain small feature subsets and have an excellent performance in classification problems.

Keywords: Particle swarm optimization · Large-scale feature selection · Compressed coding · Hamming distance

1 Introduction

Feature selection is to select an optimal feature subset related to the problem from the whole feature set [1]. It can not only reduce the number of large-scale features and shorten the processing time of data but also reduce the interference of redundant features on the results [2]. With the rapid development of big data and deep learning technology, the number of features contained in the data has also increased dramatically. Since the number of feature combinations increases exponentially as the number of features increases, feature selection faces the difficulties brought by the massive combination search space and is still a very challenging problem.

There are three main methods of feature selection: the filter method, the wrapper method, and the embedded method [3]. The filter method has a wide range of applications and a high calculation efficiency but generally performs worse than the wrapper method in feature selection problems [4]. The embedded method embeds the feature selection

Y. Sun et al. (Eds.): ChineseCSCW 2021, CCIS 1491, pp. 259–270, 2022.
https://doi.org/10.1007/978-981-19-4546-5_21

into a specific machine learning training process, so it is more restricted than the wrapper method when used. Particle swarm optimization (PSO) has the advantage of simple implementation and fast convergence. As one of the wrapper methods, PSO is often applied to solve feature selection problems [5, 6]. However, there still exist the following problems when using PSO for feature selection. First, in the existing PSO algorithms, a suitable representation and an effective evolution mechanism are still in great need to handle discrete binary optimization problems [5]. Second, when dealing with large-scale features, due to the huge search space, it is easy for particles to fall into local optima and lead to a bad search performance, i.e., PSO faces the challenge of "the curse of dimensionality" [6].

Focusing on the challenges faced by PSO in large-scale feature selection problems, the main contributions of this paper can be summarized as follows:

(1) Proposing a compressed-coding representation for particles. The compressed-coding method adopts the N-base encoding instead of the traditional binary encoding for representation. It divides all features into small neighborhoods. The feature selection process then can be performed comprehensively on each neighborhood instead of on every single feature, which provides more information for the search process.
(2) Developing an update mechanism of velocity and position for particles in discrete space based on the proposed compressed-coding representation and the Hamming distance. The update mechanism overcomes the difficulty that most PSOs search in real-value space so it is hard to explain their search process in discrete space.
(3) Proposing a local search mechanism based on the compressed-coding representation for large-scale features. The local search mechanism can shorten the length of particles dynamically, which not only decreases the search space but also improves the search performance when dealing with large-scale feature selection problems.

The rest of this paper is organized as follows. In Sect. 2, the related work of applying PSO to feature selection is introduced. The proposed PSO for large-scale feature selection problems is introduced in detail in Sect. 3. In Sect. 4, the experimental results and analysis compared with other state-of-the-art algorithms are given. Finally, the work of this paper is summarized in Sect. 5.

2 Related Work

2.1 Discrete Binary PSO

The feature selection optimization problem is a discrete binary optimization problem. Therefore, the original PSO algorithm [7] proposed for continuous space cannot be used directly to solve feature selection problems. The discrete binary PSO (DBPSO) that can be used for feature selection was first proposed by Kennedy and Eberhart [8]. In DBPSO, each particle has a position vector and a velocity vector. Each dimension of the position vector can only be 0 or 1, i.e., the value of the position is discrete. However, the value of the velocity is still continuous. For the optimization process in the discrete space, DBPSO defines velocity as the probability that its corresponding position value is 1, and uses the Sigmoid function to map any velocity value to the range of [0, 1]. DBPSO updates the velocity $\boldsymbol{v_i}$ with Eq. (1) as

$$\boldsymbol{v_i} = \boldsymbol{v_i} + c_1 r_1 (\boldsymbol{pbest_i} - \boldsymbol{x_i}) + c_2 r_2 (\boldsymbol{gbest} - \boldsymbol{x_i}) \tag{1}$$

where $\boldsymbol{x_i}$ is the current position of the i-th particle, $\boldsymbol{pbest_i}$ is the best position found by the particle so far and represents the personal historical experience, $\boldsymbol{gbest}$ is the best position found by all particles and represents the historical experience from other particles, c_1 and c_2 are acceleration constants and always set to 2, r_1 and r_2 are random values uniformly sampled from [0, 1].

Then, DBPSO updates the position with Eq. (2), where *rand* is a random value uniformly sampled from [0, 1] and d is the dimension index of the position vector. If the value of v_i^d is large, then its corresponding position x_i^d is likely to be 1.

$$x_i^d = \begin{cases} 0, rand > v_i^d \\ 1, rand \le v_i^d \end{cases} \tag{2}$$

2.2 Two Main Design Patterns for Applying PSO to Feature Selection

At present, most discrete PSOs for feature selection are mainly designed in two patterns. The PSOs using the first pattern is to follow the idea of DBPSO and define the velocity v as the probability that position x takes a certain discrete value, such as DBPSO and Bi-Velocity Discrete PSO (BVDPSO) [9]. Although the value of the position vector is discrete, the value of the velocity vector is continuous and is limited to the interval [0, 1].

The second design pattern is to discretize the existing PSOs which are proposed to solve continuous optimization problems. Since feature selection is described as a 0/1 optimization problem, binarizing the continuous value of x can represent the solution of the feature selection problem. Decoding x from continuous space to discrete space usually uses Eq. (3):

$$x_i^d = \begin{cases} 1, x_i^d > \lambda \\ 0, x_i^d \le \lambda \end{cases} \tag{3}$$

where λ is a user-defined threshold. In the search process of the particle swarm, each particle still searches in continuous space, and its values of position and velocity are continuous. Only when evaluating the particle, its position x will be decoded into a discrete value according to the given threshold. Most existing PSOs used for feature selection adopt the second design pattern [10–13].

It is not complicated to convert the continuous PSO into the discrete PSO and it only needs to perform the decoding step on x before evaluating the particles. However, the meanings of the position and velocity in continuous PSOs are different from those in discrete PSOs, which makes the update process of position and velocity hard to be explained. The PSOs implemented by the first design pattern are more reasonable and suitable to solve feature selection problems. However, the performance of the DBPSO is usually worse than the PSOs designed by the second pattern [5]. Therefore, how to find a more reasonable design pattern for PSO to handle feature selection problems still remains to be solved [5, 6].

2.3 PSO for Large-Scale Feature Selection

With the rapid increment of the feature number contained in the data, PSO faces the challenge of the "dimensional curse" when it is used for feature selection. Proposing a new PSO for large-scale feature selection problems has become a new research focus. Gu et al. [11] discretized the competitive swarm optimizer (CSO) which performs well on large-scale continuous optimization problems for the large-scale feature selection problems. Tran et al. [12] proposed the variable-length PSO to assign different lengths to particles in different subswarms, and dynamically change the lengths of particles according to fitness values, which prevents particles from being trapped in local optima for a long time. Song et al. [13] adopted the co-evolution mechanism in PSO and proposed the variable-size cooperative coevolutionary PSO, which divides the feature search space based on the importance of features and adaptively adjusts the sizes of subswarms to search important feature subspaces adequately. However, due to the huge search space, many challenges like premature convergence and huge time consumption still remain to be solved when using PSO for feature selection on high-dimension data.

3 The Proposed Compressed-Coding PSO for Large-Scale Feature Selection

In this section, a compressed-coding representation for particles is first proposed. Then, based on the proposed representation, a discrete update mechanism for the velocity and position of particles is designed. Especially for the large-scale feature selection problems, a local search strategy is also proposed. Finally, the overall framework of the proposed PSO, named compressed-coding PSO (CCPSO), is given.

3.1 Compressed-Coding Representation of Particle Position

The traditional representation of the particle position for feature selection problems is to use a binary bit to represent the selection of a feature. Therefore, in an optimization problem with D features, the encoding length of a particle is D. If there are thousands of or even more features contained, the encoding length also needs to be thousands or longer, which increases the difficulty of encoding and searching for the optimal solution. In order to shorten the encoding length of particles, the compressed-coding representation uses N-base ($N > 2$) encoding method and each bit can represent a segment of 0/1 string. The value N should satisfy $N = 2^n$, where $n =$ 2, 3, 4, and so on.

The process of compressing a 0/1 string with the N-base representation is shown in Fig. 1. When $N = 8$, every three bits under the binary representation are compressed into one 8-base bit. If the original binary bits are not sufficient, the remaining bits will be randomly filled in. During the search process of the swarm, all particles adopt the compressed-coding representation method. Only when evaluating particles, the N-base representations will be decoded into binary representations to represent solutions of feature selection problems for evaluation. With the compressed-coding representation, multiple features in the same neighborhood can be selected as a whole. That is to say, not only the selection state of the feature itself but also the selection state of the features in its neighborhood can be learned from the representation. Therefore, the information used in the search process for the optimal solution has increased.

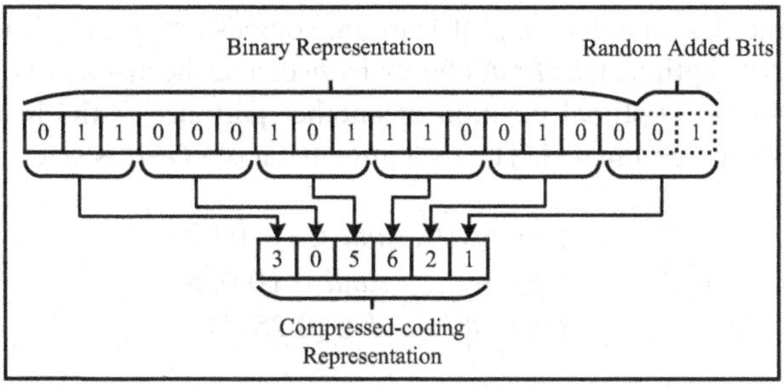

Fig. 1. The process of compressing binary representation into N-base representation.

3.2 Definitions Based on Compressed-Coding Representation

The Difference Between the Positions of Two Particles. The difference $\Delta(\boldsymbol{x}_1, \boldsymbol{x}_2)$ between the positions of two particles p_1 and p_2 is defined as the Hamming distance between their corresponding binary 0/1 strings, as shown in Eq. (4), where $\boldsymbol{x}_1$ and $\boldsymbol{x}_2$ are the positions of the two particles, x^d is the value of the d-th dimension of $\boldsymbol{x}$, function $h(x^d)$ is to get the binary strings corresponding to x^d.

$$x_1^d - x_2^d = \Delta\left(x_1^d, x_2^d\right) = HammingDistance\left(h\left(x_1^d\right), h\left(x_2^d\right)\right) \tag{4}$$

The Velocity of the Particle. The velocity of a particle is defined as the difference between two positions, as shown in Eq. (5). Since the value of Hamming distance is discrete, the value of the velocity v^d is also discrete. Hence, v^d can only take the value $\{0, 1, \ldots, \log_2 N\}$ under N-base compressed encoding.

$$v^d = \Delta\left(x_1^d, x_2^d\right) \tag{5}$$

The Addition Operation Between the Position and the Velocity. The addition operation between the position and the velocity is defined as selecting a position $\boldsymbol{x}'$ to re-place the original position $\boldsymbol{x}$, as shown in Eq. (6), where the value of each dimension x'^d should satisfy the equation $HammingDistance(h(x^d), h(x'^d)) = v^d$.

$$x^d + v^d = x'^d \tag{6}$$

3.3 Update Mechanism of Particles

Based on the above definitions, the velocity of the i-th particle p_i is updated as Eq. (7), where w_i is the inertia weight sampled randomly between 0.4 and 0.7, $c_1 = c_2 = 1$, r_1 and r_2 are a random number between 0 and 1, $\boldsymbol{cbest}_i$ is the chosen personal optimal position for p_i, $\boldsymbol{gbest}$ is the global best position in the swarm, and $[\cdot]$ is the rounding function. In addition, if the value of $\boldsymbol{v}_i$ is out of range $[0, \log_2 N]$, it should be modified to 0 or $\log_2 N$ accordingly.

$$\boldsymbol{v}_i = \left[w_i \boldsymbol{v}_i + c_1 r_1 (\boldsymbol{cbest}_i - \boldsymbol{x}_i) + c_2 r_2 (\boldsymbol{gbest} - \boldsymbol{x}_i)\right] \tag{7}$$

In order to increase the diversity of learning sources and prevent the particle from falling into the local optima, the $\boldsymbol{cbest_i}$ chosen by p_i can be the historical optimal position of itself, the historical optimal position of another particle, or the historical optimal position that has been eliminated. The d-th dimension of $\boldsymbol{cbest_i}$ is selected as

$$cbest_i^d = \begin{cases} archive_r^d, rand \in [0, 0.025) \\ pbest_{better}^d, rand \in [0.025, 0.25) \\ pbest_i^d, rand \in [0.25, 1] \end{cases} \tag{8}$$

where $\boldsymbol{pbest_i}$ is the historical optimal position of p_i, $\boldsymbol{pbest_{better}}$ is a historical optimal position chosen from two randomly selected particles with the tournament strategy, $\boldsymbol{archive_r}$ is a historical optimal position randomly selected from the archive which stores eliminated the optimal position.

The update equation for the position is shown in Eq. (9). In most cases, the particle jumps directly to the chosen optimal position $\boldsymbol{cbest_i}$, which can speed up the convergence rate. In the rest cases, the particle moves in the direction of the learned optimal position which is subject to the $\boldsymbol{cbest_i}$ and the $\boldsymbol{gbest}$ and can increase the diversity of direction and help the particle jump out of local optima.

$$x_i^d = \begin{cases} x_i^d + v_i^d, rand < 0.1 \\ cbest_i^d, rand \geq 0.1 \end{cases} \tag{9}$$

3.4 Local Search Strategy

For large-scale feature selection problems, a local search strategy based on the compressed-coding representation is proposed to reduce the search space and improve computational efficiency. The process of the local search strategy is described in Algorithm 1. The value of position x_i^d updates only when its corresponding $pbest_i^d$ is not zero. Otherwise, the value of x_i^d is set to 0 which is the same as the $pbest_i^d$.

With the local search strategy, some bits of the position are dynamically fixed to 0 and no longer updated, as shown in Fig. 2. In the process of searching for an optimal solution, each particle p_i only handles with the features represented by the bits whose values are not fixed in the $\boldsymbol{pbest_i}$ instead of all features. Thus, the actual length of the position is shortened and the search space for the particle is reduced. In addition, since the fixed bits in different particles are different, each particle can search in different feature subsets and the diversity of the swarm are retained.

Algorithm 1: Local Search Strategy

Input: The position x_i of particle p_i, the coding length D' after compression, the index of the particle i.

Output: The x_i updated by the local search strategy.

begin
  for $d = 1$ *to* D' **do**
    if ($pbest_i^d \neq 0$) **then**
      Update x_i^d with Eq. (9);
    else
      $x_i^d \leftarrow 0$;
    end
  end
  return x_i;
end

The particle may miss the global optimal solution because parts of the search space are discarded by the local search strategy. However, under the N-base compressed-coding representation, a value of 0 in $\boldsymbol{pbest_i}$ means that all features in the neighborhood represented by $pbest_i^d$ are not selected at the same time. Therefore, the probability of fixing a bit of x_i is reduced to $1/N$, which reduces the probability of blindly reducing the search space by the local search strategy.

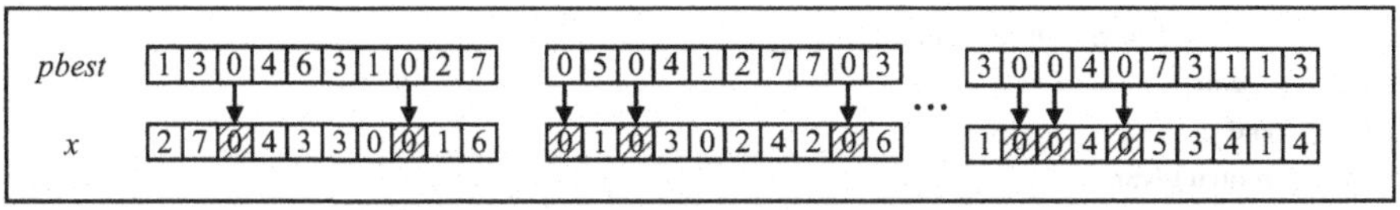

Fig. 2. Local search strategy (when $N = 8$).

3.5 Overall Framework of CCPSO

The overall framework of the proposed CCPSO is described in Algorithm 2. Before the swarm initialization, the symmetric uncertainty (SU) value between each feature and the classification label is obtained and all features are sorted in descending order according to the SU values. SU is a measure of correlation and can be used as a filter method for feature selection [14]. After the feature sorting, each feature and the features near it, i.e., features in the neighborhood, have a similar effect on the classification result, which is conducive to the search process because CCPSO also uses the information from the neighborhood for searching. Then, the length of particle representation D' after compression can be calculated according to the number of features D and the given N. In order to reduce the cost of computing the Hamming distance, an $N \times N$ table is constructed in advance, which stores the Hamming distance between any two binary strings represented by the N-base numbers.

Before evaluation, the particle needs to be decoded into a binary string to represent a solution of feature selection, in which the value 1 means that the corresponding feature is selected and the value 0 means that it is not selected. Then, the process of particles being updated and evaluated repeats until the terminal conditions are met.

Algorithm 2: CCPSO

Input: The maximum number of fitness evaluations MAX_FE, the size of the swarm P, the number of the features D, the base for coding compression N.

Output: The global optimal position $gbest$.

1. **begin**
2. Calculate the SU value between each feature and label;
3. Sort features according to the SU values;
4. $D' \leftarrow \left\lceil \frac{D}{\log_2 N} \right\rceil$;
5. Construct the $N \times N$ Hamming distance table;
6. Randomly initialize x and v of each particle;
7. **while** evaluations < MAX_FE **do**
8. **for** $i = 1$ *to* P **do**
9. Decode and evaluate x_i;
10. Update $pbest_i$;
11. **end**
12. Update $gbest$;
13. **for** $i = 1$ *to* P **do**
14. Update v_i with Eq. (7);
15. Update x_i with Algorithm 1
16. **end**
17. **end**
18. **return** $gbest$
19. **end**

In the worst case, the time complexity of CCPSO is $O(MAX_FE \times P \times D)$. However, because CCPSO uses the local search strategy to shorten the coding length, the actual time consumption of CCPSO is always less than that of the traditional PSOs, as shown in Sect. 4.

In addition, although CCPSO is proposed for large-scale feature selection problems, it can solve other binary discrete optimization problems without both the local search strategy and the feature sorting step designed especially for feature selection.

4 Experiments and Analysis

In this section, experiments for CCPSO and other PSO-based feature selection algorithms on data containing large-scale features are carried out to verify the effectiveness of the proposed CCPSO.

4.1 Datasets

The experiments used 6 open-access classification datasets[1] for feature selection, whose detailed information is listed in Table 1. All the used datasets contain large-scale features but a few samples, which leads to the difficulty of classification.

Table 1. Detailed information of datasets.

Index	Dataset	Feature Type	Samples	Features	Categories
1	Isolet	Continuous	1559	617	26
2	Madelon	Discrete	2000	500	2
3	COIL20	Continuous	1440	1024	20
4	WarpAR10P	Discrete	130	2400	10
5	Yale	Discrete	165	1024	15
6	Lung	Continuous	203	3312	5

4.2 Algorithms for Comparison and Parameter Settings

There are 4 PSO-based feature selection algorithms for comparison with CCPSO. The parameter settings of each algorithm are listed in Table 2. DBPSO, BBPSO-ACJ, BVDPSO, and CSO are all discrete binary PSOs that are suitable for solving feature selection problems.

Table 2. Parameter settings of algorithms.

Algorithm	Parameter Settings
DBPSO [8]	$P = 20$, the range of velocity: [-6,6], $c_1 = c_2 = 2.01$, $w = 1$.
BVDPSO [9]	$P = 20$, the range of w: [0.4,0.9], $c_1 = c_2 = 2$, selected threshold $\alpha = 0.5$.
BBPSO-ACJ [10]	$P = 20$, chaotic factor $z_0 = 0.13$, selected threshold $\lambda = 0.5$.
CSO [11]	$P = 100$, control factor $\phi = 0.1$, selected threshold $\lambda = 0.5$.
CCPSO	$P = 20$, archive size: 100, $c_1 = c_2 = 1$, the range of w: [0.4,0.7], the base used in compressed coding $N = 8$.

The maximum number of evaluations is set to 5000 for all algorithms. On each dataset, the 10-fold cross-validation method is used to divide samples into the training dataset and test dataset. Then, each algorithm runs 10 times on 10 groups of training data and test data divided by the same dataset and adopts the average results as the final results. In the training phase, particles also use the 10-fold cross-validation method to obtain evaluation fitness values. The *k*-nearest neighbor (*k*-NN) method is chosen as the

[1] The datasets can be downloaded from https://jundongl.github.io/scikit-feature/datasets.html.

classifier to calculate the classification accuracy values of the selected features in the experiments and k is set to be 5. When the accuracy values are the same, the particle with fewer features should perform better.

In addition, the Wilcoxon signed-rank test is employed to verify whether there is a significant difference between CCPSO and other compared algorithms, with a significance level of $\alpha = 0.05$. In the experimental statistical results, symbol "+" indicates that CCPSO is significantly superior to the compared algorithm, symbol "−" indicates that CCPSO is significantly inferior to the compared algorithm, and symbol "≈" indicates that there is no significant difference between CCPSO and the compared algorithm at the current significant level.

4.3 Experimental Results and Discussion

The average classification accuracy values on the test dataset (*Test_Acc*) of each algorithm on 6 datasets are shown in Table 3. The *Test_Acc* value of CCPSO on dataset Madelon is significantly superior to other compared algorithms. On other datasets, there is no significant difference between CCPSO and other compared algorithms on the *Test_Acc*.

Table 3. The *Test_Acc.* of algorithms on the 6 datasets.

Data	DBPSO	BBPSO-ACJ	BVDPSO	CSO	CCPSO
Isolet	0.866(≈)	0.862(≈)	0.870(≈)	0.870(≈)	**0.884**
Madelon	0.678(+)	0.684(+)	0.678(+)	0.682(+)	**0.786**
COIL20	0.904(≈)	**0.920(≈)**	0.918(≈)	0.910(≈)	0.906
WarpAR10P	0.554(≈)	0.531(≈)	0.523(≈)	0.523(≈)	**0.623**
Yale	**0.559(≈)**	0.512(≈)	0.553(≈)	0.518(≈)	**0.559**
Lung	0.900(≈)	**0.910(≈)**	**0.910(≈)**	0.905(≈)	0.895
+/-/≈	1/0/5	1/0/5	1/0/5	1/0/5	—

However, in terms of the number of features included in the found optimal solution (*Feature_Num*), CCPSO is significantly smaller than other algorithms on most datasets. The experimental results are shown in Table 4. On all the datasets, the *Feature_Num* of CCPSO are the smallest and much smaller than that of other compared algorithms.

Table 4. The *Feature_Num* of algorithms on the 6 datasets.

Data	DBPSO	BBPSO-ACJ	BVDPSO	CSO	CCPSO
Isolet	379.4(+)	255.6(+)	384.0(+)	384.0(+)	**106.4**
Madelon	303.9(+)	220.4(+)	320.8(+)	259.9(+)	**34.5**
COIL20	632.4(+)	207.9(+)	590.5(+)	404.2(+)	**79.6**
WarpAR10P	1468.1(+)	156.6(+)	1370.8(+)	893.7(+)	**26.7**
Yale	634.6(+)	188.4(+)	588.5(+)	314.8(+)	**60.0**
Lung	1982.7(+)	1325.2(+)	1875.3(+)	1781.4(+)	**178.8**
+/-/≈	6/0/0	6/0/0	6/0/0	6/0/0	——

The total running time for each algorithm on the 6 datasets (*Time*) is listed in Table 5. The *Time* of CCPSO is significantly less than DBPSO, CSO, BVDPSO, and BBPSO-ACJ. In general, when using a classifier to evaluate a particle, the smaller number of features contained in the solution, the less the evaluation time it needs. Because DBPSO, CSO, BVDPSO, and BBPSO-ACJ lack a mechanism to help them search in a smaller feature subset, their evaluations take more time than CCPSO. Such strength of CCPSO is more obvious in the later stage of the search process. Although CCPSO needs extra time to calculate the SU values, its *Time* is still much less than the DBPSO, CSO, BVDPSO, and BBPSO-ACJ.

Table 5. The *Time* of algorithms.

Algorithm	DBPSO	BBPSO-ACJ	BVDPSO	CSO	CCPSO
Time (min)	1246.02	933.25	1240.492	1256.85	**685.22**

5 Conclusion

This paper proposes a discrete binary PSO algorithm named compressed-coding PSO (CCPSO) for the large-scale feature selection problems. CCPSO adopts the N-base encoding method and treats the features in the same neighborhood as a whole for selection. Then, CCPSO designs the update mechanism for particles based on the Hamming distance and has a good explanation in the discrete space. For the large-scale features, CCPSO proposes a local search strategy to help particles search in a smaller feature subset to make good use of the computation resources. Experimental results show that CCPSO is promising in large-scale feature selection. It can avoid premature convergence and always select a feature subset that contains a small number of features but performs well on classification problems. The running time of CCPSO is also less than most compared algorithms.

Acknowledgments. This work was supported in part by the National Key Research and Development Program of China under Grant 2019YFB2102102, in part by the National Natural Science Foundations of China (NSFC) under Grants 62176094, 61822602, 61772207, and 61873097, in part by the Key-Area Research and Development of Guangdong Province under Grant 2020B010166002, in part by the Guangdong Natural Science Foundation Research Team under Grant 2018B030312003, and in part by the Guangdong-Hong Kong Joint Innovation Platform under Grant 2018B050502006.

References

1. Dash, M.: Feature selection via set cover. In: Proceedings 1997 IEEE Knowledge and Data Engineering Exchange Workshop, pp. 165–171. IEEE (1997)
2. Ladha, L., Deepa, T.: Feature selection methods and algorithms. Int. J. Comput. Sci. Eng. **3**, 1787–1797 (2011)
3. Chandrashekar, G., Sahin, F.: A survey on feature selection methods. Comput. Electr. Eng. **40**, 16–28 (2014)
4. Khalid, S., Khalil, T., Nasreen, S.: A survey of feature selection and feature extraction techniques in machine learning. In: 2014 Science and Information Conference, pp. 372–378. IEEE (2014)
5. Nguyen, B.H., Xue, B., Zhang, M.: A survey on swarm intelligence approaches to feature selection in data mining. Swarm Evol. Comput. **54**, 100663 (2020)
6. Xue, B., Zhang, M., Browne, W.N., Yao, X.: A survey on evolutionary computation approaches to feature selection. IEEE Trans. Evol. Comput. **20**, 606–626 (2016)
7. Kennedy, J., Eberhart, R.: Particle swarm optimization. In: Proceedings of ICNN 1995 - International Conference on Neural Networks, vol.4, pp. 1942–1948. IEEE (1995)
8. Kennedy, J., Eberhart, R.C.: A discrete binary version of the particle swarm algorithm. In: Computational Cybernetics and Simulation 1997 IEEE International Conference on Systems, Man, and Cybernetics, vol.5, pp. 4104–4108. IEEE (1997)
9. Shen, M., Zhan, Z.H., Chen, W., Gong, Y., Zhang, J., Li, Y.: Bi-velocity discrete particle swarm optimization and its application to multicast routing problem in communication networks. IEEE Trans. Industr. Electron. **61**, 7141–7151 (2014)
10. Qiu, C.: Bare bones particle swarm optimization with adaptive chaotic jump for feature selection in classification. Int. J. Comput. Intell. Syst. **11**, 1 (2018)
11. Gu, S., Cheng, R., Jin, Y.: Feature selection for high-dimensional classification using a competitive swarm optimizer. Soft. Comput. **22**(3), 811–822 (2016). https://doi.org/10.1007/s00500-016-2385-6
12. Tran, B., Xue, B., Zhang, M.: Variable-length particle swarm optimization for feature selection on high-dimensional classification. IEEE Trans. Evol. Comput. **23**, 473–487 (2019)
13. Song, X., Zhang, Y., Guo, Y., Sun, X., Wang, Y.: Variable-size cooperative coevolutionary particle swarm optimization for feature selection on high-dimensional data. IEEE Trans. Evol. Comput. **24**, 882–895 (2020)
14. Bommert, A., Sun, X., Bischl, B., Rahnenführer, J., Lang, M.: Benchmark for filter methods for feature selection in high-dimensional classification data. Comput. Stat. Data Anal. **143**, 106839 (2020)

An Attention-Based Multiobjective Optimization Evolutionary Algorithm for Community Detection in Attributed Networks

Xu Lin[1,2,3], Zhanhong Chen[1,2,3], Kun Guo[1,2,3](✉), and Yuzhong Chen[1,2,3]

[1] College of Computer and Data Science, Fuzhou University, Fuzhou 350108, China
{gukn,yzchen}@fzu.edu.cn

[2] Fujian Provincial Key Laboratory of Network Computing and Intelligence Information Processing, Fuzhou University, Fuzhou 350108, China

[3] Key Laboratory of Spatial Data Mining and Information Sharing, Ministry of Education, Fuzhou 350108, China

Abstract. Community detection is an important topic in complex network analysis which can explore valuable relationships in the networks, such as protein-protein interactions, advertisement recommendations, etc. Recently, the structure and attributes of a network are expected to be integrated to obtain a more accurate community division. But existing community detection algorithms based on multiobjective optimization evolutionary algorithms (MOEAs) for attributed networks have two common problems. First, their encoding strategies completely depend on the network structure, which limits their use of attribute information in search. Second, the calculation of the attribute objective function is time-consuming. In this paper, we propose a novel algorithm that combines the nodes' embedding vectors generated by a Skip-Gram model with an attention-based multiobjective optimization evolutionary algorithm to discover overlapping communities on networks with attributes. With the help of embedding vectors, the attention-based encoding strategy can overcome the problem of the limited searching capability of traditional MOEAs' encoding schemes that depend only on a network structure, and an attribute objective function based on embedding vectors is designed which can be calculated in linear time to improve the computational efficiency. The statistical results in artificial and real-world networks demonstrate the feasibility and effectiveness of the proposed method.

Keywords: Community detection · Multiobjective optimization · Attributed network · Attention-based encoding

1 Introduction

Many complex systems in the real world can be modeled as networks, such as biological networks [1], social networks [2], scientific collaboration networks [3].

Y. Sun et al. (Eds.): ChineseCSCW 2021, CCIS 1491, pp. 271–285, 2022.
https://doi.org/10.1007/978-981-19-4546-5_22

The goal of community detection is to divide all nodes in the network into a group of clusters such that nodes in the same cluster are densely connected in structure or similar in attributes. Community detection is a hot topic in complex network analysis, which can help us explore the deep relationships between nodes. In the past, many community algorithms consider only structure. However, many networks in the real world are attributed, and the community detection that combines structure and attributes is more widely used in the real world, such as user advertisement recommendations, public opinion analysis, etc. Therefore, we need to focus on structure and attributes at the same time when detecting communities.

Most existing community detection algorithms in attributed networks can only discover a single result. However, it is hard to distinguish which is more important between structure and attributes in the real world. Multiobjective optimization evolutionary algorithms can find the Pareto front (PF) composed of a set of contradictory objectives. Many MOEA-based algorithms have been proposed for community detection. However, to the best of our knowledge, only four of them consider attribute information when detecting communities. MOEA-SA [4] first considers the structure and attributes simultaneously by maximizing modularity [5] and attribute similarity to discover communities. The same objectives are also adopted in MOEA-SA_{OV} [6] proposed by Teng, and it expands MOEA-SA using a seed-expansion-based post-process to find the overlapping communities. Pizzuti et al. proposed MOGA-@Net [7] which uses a post-process of local merge method to merge communities. Sun proposed a graph neural network encoding method for the multiobjective evolutionary algorithm (CE-MOEA) [9] to discover communities in attributed networks. However, the existing MOEA-based community detection algorithms for attributed networks face two severe challenges. First, their search capability is limited by the network structure because they directly or indirectly use the adjacency encoding strategy [7] which encodes genes as structural neighbors of nodes. Second, the commonly used attribute objective function needs to traverse each node pair in all communities with a square computation complexity.

In this paper, we propose an attention-based multiobjective optimization for community detection in attributed networks (AMOCDA), which includes three stages. First, we design a node sampling method based on original attribute similarity to generate node sequences. The sequences are input to the Skip-Gram model [10] to learn attribute embedding vectors. The similarity matrix between nodes can be obtained through the embedding vectors. Second, we use NSGA2 [8] (a general framework of MOEA) to find the optimal center nodes. The community division obtained by ideal center nodes cannot dominate each other in the objectives of structure and attribute. Third, we integrate the attention-based encoding strategy into NSGA2 to find the optimal overlapping community structures. Instead of traditional adjacency encoding whose search capability is limited by the structure, each node's attention to the structure and attribute is encoded as a gene in the attention-based encoding strategy. The fusion similarity between nodes and center nodes can be denoted as a weighted sum of structure and attribute similarity. The overlapping community structure can be obtained through the fusion similarity. The main contributions of this paper are summarized as follows:

1. The attention-based encoding strategy can address the problem of structure limitation on the search capability of traditional MOEA-based algorithms.
2. The designed attribute objective function can be calculated in linear time to improve the efficiency of evolution.
3. The experiments on artificial and real-world networks were conducted to verify the superiority of our algorithm with respect to the baseline algorithms.

2 Preliminaries

2.1 Multiobjective Optimization

A multiobjective optimization problem (MOP) aims to optimize the multiple objectives at the same time [11], which can be stated as follows.

$$\min_{x \in \Omega} F(x) = \min[f_1(x), f_2(x), \ldots, f_m(x)] \tag{1}$$

Ω is the feasible space, m is the number of objectives. Given two vectors $a = \{a_1, a_2, \ldots a_n\}$ and $b = \{b_1, b_2, \ldots, b_n\}(a \neq b)$, a dominates b is denoted as $a \prec b$ if and only if $f_i(a) \leq f_i(b), i = \{1, 2, \ldots, m.\}$. a is called the Pareto optimal solution if there is no vector dominating a. All the Pareto optimal solutions constitute a Pareto front (PF).

2.2 Objective Functions

Extend Modularity (EQ) is a metric used to measure the quality of the discovered overlapping communities in network structure, which is defined as follows.

$$\mathrm{EQ} = \frac{1}{2m} \sum_i \sum_{v \in c_i, w \in c_i} \frac{1}{O_v O_w} (A_{vw} - \frac{k_v k_w}{2m}) \sigma(c_v, c_w) \tag{2}$$

where m is the number of edges, k_v is the degree of node v. O_v denote the number of communities which node v belongs to, $\sigma(c_v, c_w) = 1$ if nodes v and w belong to the same community, otherwise 0. $A_{vw} = 1$ if node v connects to w. The larger the value of EQ, the higher quality of the detected communities.

Within-Cluster Attribute Similarity (AS) is the most commonly used attribute objective function [7], which is as follows:

$$\mathrm{AS} = \frac{\sum_{k=1}^{c} \sum_{v_i, v_j \in C_k, i<j} 2s(a_i, a_j)}{\sum_{k=1}^{c} r_k (r_k - 1)} \tag{3}$$

where c is the number of clusters, r_k is the number of nodes in cluster k. $s(i, j)$ represents the similarity between nodes i and j and a_i means the attribute vector of node i. The larger the AS is, the more evident the division in the attribute. However, the AS needs to sum the attribute similarity between each pair of nodes within clusters, making the calculation complexity squared with the number of nodes. The cosine similarity is commonly used as the similarity metric, which is defined as follow.

$$s(a_i, a_j) = \frac{a_i \cdot a_j}{||a_i||||a_j||} \tag{4}$$

where a_i is the embedding vector of node i, $\cdot$ denotes inner product and $||\cdot||$ means L2-norm.

Within-Cluster Attribute Entropy (AE) is another attribute objective function [6]:

$$\mathrm{AE} = \sum_{k=1}^{c} \frac{r_k}{r} \sum_{a \in A} p_{ak} \log (p_{ak}) \tag{5}$$

where p_{ak} is the percentage of nodes in cluster k with attribute value a. A is the attribute vector of each node. c is the number of clusters and r_k and r denote the number of nodes in cluster k and the number of nodes in a network. The smaller the AE is, the more similar nodes in the detected communities are.

Within-Cluster Sum of Squared Errors (SSE) is the attribute objective function in our design, and it minimizes the within-cluster sum of squared errors based on the attribute embedding vectors. The definition of SSE is as follows.

$$\mathrm{SSE} = \sum_{i=1}^{c} \sum_{j=1}^{|c_i|} ||x_{ij} - \mu_i||_2^2 \tag{6}$$

where c is the number clusters, $|c_i|$ is the number of nodes in cluster c_i, x_{ij} denotes the vector of j-th node in i-th cluster. μ_i means the center vector of the cluster j. SSE can be calculated in near time. The smaller the SSE is, the more similar the nodes' attributes within the cluster are.

3 Problem Formulation

A community is a group of nodes which has dense connections in structure or high attribute similarity. The goal of community detection is to divide nodes in network into a set of communities $\{c_1, c_2, \ldots, c_K\} c_i \ neq c_j, \forall i \neq j, i, j \in \{1, 2, \cdots, k\}. V = \bigcup_{i=1}^{k} c_i, c_i \neq$. Therefore, the overlapping community detection problem in attributed networks can be modeled as the objectives of minimizing negative EQ and SSE, which are as follow.

$$\min \begin{cases} \text{-EQ} = -\frac{1}{2m} \sum_i \sum_{v \in c_i, w \in c_i} \frac{1}{O_i O_j} (A_{vw} - \frac{k_v k_w}{2m}) \sigma(c_v, c_w) \\ \mathrm{SSE} = \sum_{i=1}^{c} \sum_{j=1}^{|c_i|} ||x_{ij} - \mu_i||_2^2 \end{cases} \tag{7}$$

The larger the EQ is, the more density connections within all communities. The smaller the SSE is, the higher the attribute similarity among nodes within the same community.

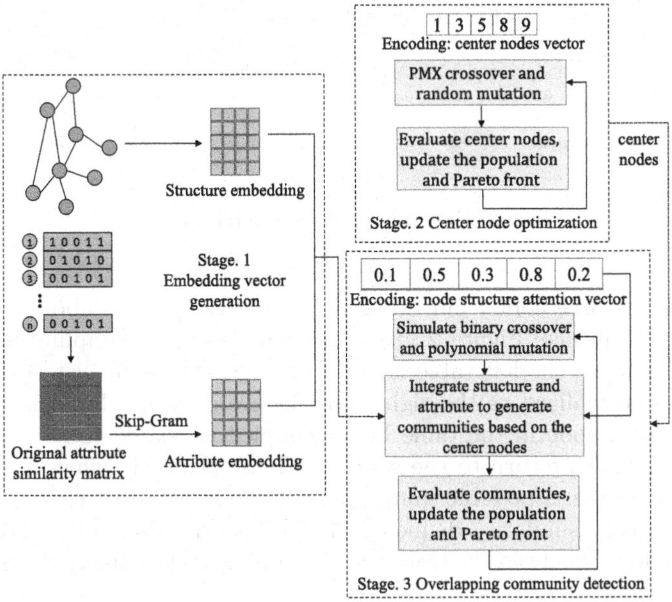

Fig. 1. Framework of AMOCDA

4 AMOCDA

AMOCDA is mainly composed of three stages, as shown in Fig. 1. In stage 1, We need to generate structure and attribute embedding vectors first, which is the basis for the subsequent processing. Stages 2 and 3 are both built on NSGA2 share the same optimization objectives defined in Eq. (7). In stage 2, our purpose is to optimize the center nodes. In stage 3, we integrate the structural information and attributes to detect the optimal overlapping community structures.

4.1 Embedding Vector Generation

We simply use the DeepWalk [12] algorithm to generate structure embedding vectors. A well-designed sampling method forces the attribute embedding vectors of nodes with high attribute similarity to be similar. First, we need to build a k-nearest nodes list KN_i for each node i through building a ball-tree [13] based on the original normalized attributes. The ball-tree can get each node's top-k nearest nodes in the complexity of $O(k \times \log n)$. Second, we build an alias table for each node i, and nodes in KN_i will be joined to the table according to their attribute similarity to node i. In this manner, we can sample a node with high similarity to node i in node i's alias table in const time. Intuitively, nodes with high similarity should frequently appear in the same window of a sequence. Based on this idea, we design the sampling method as follows: from a source node i, sample its attribute neighbor according to node i's alias table,

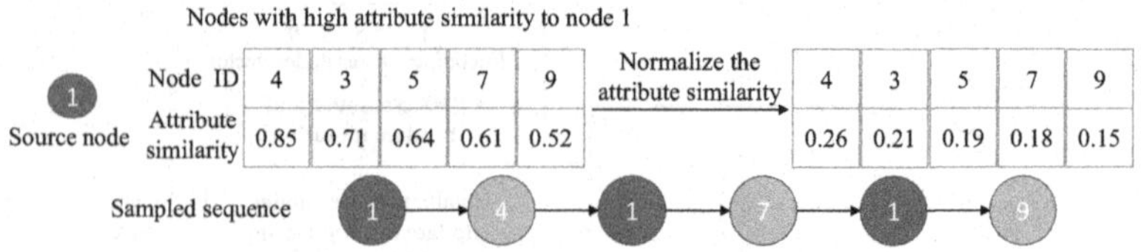

Fig. 2. Example of the sampling process

and return to source node i immediately. Repeat the process above to get node i's sampling sequence. Figure 2 gives an example of the sampling process. As shown in Figure 2, the left table is node 1's k-nearest nodes list KN_1, the list needs to be normalized as the right table before creating the alias table. The probability of a node in the table being sampled is related to its similarity to node 1. It needs to return to the source node immediately when a neighbor is sampled. Therefore, a possible sampling sequence is $1 \rightarrow 4 \rightarrow 1 \rightarrow 7 \rightarrow 1 \rightarrow 9$.

We use cosine similarity defined in Eq. (4) as the similarity metric. Based on the sampled sequences, we train the embedding vectors using the Skip-Gram model.

4.2 Center Node Optimization

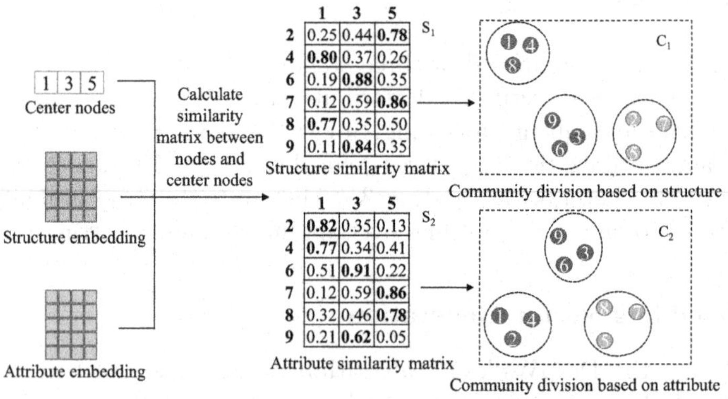

Fig. 3. Example of the center node decoding process

In this stage, our purpose is to obtain a set of center nodes that can further obtain excellent nonoverlapping community structures based on structure and attribute embedding vectors. We adopt the integer encoding and represent the ID of a center node as a gene. Each solution is sorted in ascending order to ensure that there are no duplicate solutions. Since the same center node cannot appear more than once in a solution, the partially mapped crossover (PMX) [14] is used as a crossover operator. The random mutation (RM) operator is adopted,

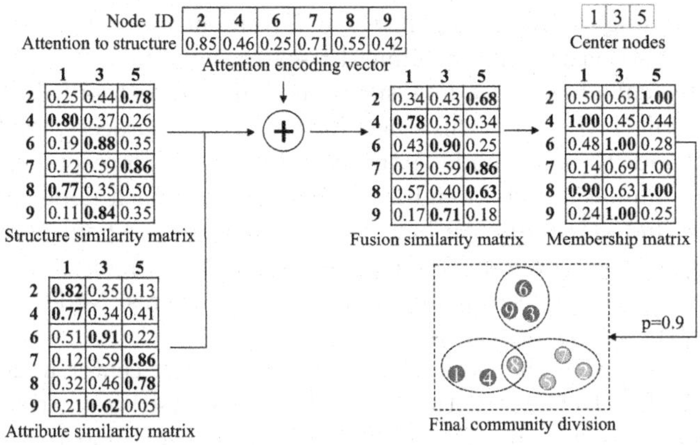

Fig. 4. Example of the attention vector decoding process

and each gene value has the probability of randomly selecting a node that is not in the current solution from the network as a new center node. The community structures are obtained by the decoding process and evaluated by Eq. (7). Figure 3 gives an example of the decoding process.

As shown in Fig. 3, we first calculate the similarity matrix between all nodes and center nodes (nodes 1, 3 and 5). The bold in the matrix means the maximum similarity with the center node. Structure similarity matrix S_1 and attribute similarity matrix S_2 can be obtained based on structure and attribute embedding vectors. We assign nodes to the center node with the highest similarity. For example, node 2 is assigned to the center node 1 because the similarity between node 2 and 1 is the highest (0.82, bold in the matrix) in S_2. In the above way, structure division C_1 and attribute division C_2 can be generated according to S_1 and S_2. C_1 is obtained based on the structure information and C_2 is based on the attribute information.

The two community divisions C_1 and C_2 are the inputs for structure and attribute objective function denoted in Eq. (7). The smaller the values of negative EQ and SSE, the more evident the structure-based and attribute-based community divisions are, which further demonstrates that the selected center nodes are accurate in both structure and attribute. We use NSGA2 [8] to optimize the center nodes.

4.3 Overlapping Community Detection

In this stage, our purpose is to integrate structure and attribute embedding vectors to find a set of overlapping community structures that are excellent both in objectives of structure and attribute.

Nodes in a network may pay different attention to the structure and attribute. Therefore, we encode each node i's attention to a network structure as a gene $g_i, g_i \in [0, 1]$, node i's attention to attribute can be denoted as $1-g_i$. Unlike using adjacency encoding indirectly or directly [6,7], our encoding strategy makes sure that a network structure will not limit the search capability.

We use the real integer encoding, simulated binary crossover (SBX) [15], polynomial mutation (PM) [16] in this stage. In the decoding process, the fusion similarity of each node to center nodes is the weighted sum of corresponding structure and attribute similarity. The weights are the values of each node's attention to the structure and attribute. We have an overlapping threshold parameter p to control the generated communities' overlapping degree. Figure 4 illustrates how to decode the attention vectors into community structures. Nodes 1,3 and 5 are still taken as the center nodes.

As shown in Fig. 4, the similarities of node 2 to the center node 1 are 0.25 and 0.82 according to the structure and attribute similarity matrix. The attention value to the structure of node 2 is 0.85, and the value to the attribute of node 2 is $1 - 0.85 = 0.15$. Then, the fusion similarity of node 2 to 1 is $0.25 * 0.85 + 0.82 * 0.15 \approx 0.34$. Similarly, the fusion similarities of all nodes to all center nodes can be calculated. After that, we normalize the similarity matrix to obtain a membership matrix. For each node i, the maximum similarity to all center nodes can be represented as $smax_i$, the similarity s_{ic} from node i to each center node c should be normalized as $s_{ic} = s_{ic}/smax_i$. The last step is to generate an overlapping community structure according to the membership matrix. Overlapping threshold p is set to 0.9 and node 8 in the membership matrix is analyzed for illustration, the normalized similarities of node 8 to center nodes 1, 3 and 5 are 0.9, 0.63, 1.00 respectively, node 8 can be assigned to two communities (center nodes 1 and 5) because the similarities between them are both greater than $p = 0.9$. Similarly, we can obtain each node's community assignment.

The generated community structure is evaluated according to Eq. (7). The smaller the values of negative EQ and SSE, the more evident our community structure both in structure and attribute. We still use NSGA2 to find the optimal attention vectors which can be decoded into the optimal overlapping community structures.

4.4 Pseudocode of AMOCDA

First, the two stages of MOEA are both built on an improved NSGA2 with modified crossover and mutation operators described in Algorithm 1. The tournament selection and fast nondominated sorting with crowding distance defined in NSGA2 are denoted as functions Selection() and NdSort(). Then, the overall procedure of AMOCDA is given in Algorithm 2.

The main stages of AMOCDA are summarized as follows: In stage 1, we generate structure and attribute embedding vectors. In stage 2, we search the accurate center nodes. In stage 3, we integrate structure and attribute to find the optimal overlapping community structures for each group of center nodes. Each subtask's results are joined to OC. Finally, the nondominated solutions in OC are returned.

Algorithm 1: Improved_NSGA2

Input: Population size p_s; Maximum generations gen; stage number sta;
structure and attribute embedding vectors V_{stru}, V_{attr}; center nodes cen;
Overlapping threshold p;

Output: Final population P;

1 $P \leftarrow$ Initialize p_s solutions;
2 **for** $g = 1$ *to gen* **do**
3 $parents \leftarrow$ Selection(P);
4 **if** $sta = 1$ **then**
5 $offpsring \leftarrow$ PMX$(parents)$;
6 $offspring \leftarrow$ RM$(offpsring)$;
7 $C_1, C_2 \leftarrow$ decode communities according to Fig. 3;
8 Evaluate C_1, C_2 according to Eq. (7);
9 **else**
10 $offpsring \leftarrow$ SBX$(parents)$;
11 $offspring \leftarrow$ PM$(offpsring)$;
12 $C \leftarrow$ decode overlapping communities based on V_{stru}, V_{attr}, cen and p according to Fig. 4;
13 Evaluate C according to Eq. (7);
14 Sort P by NdSort() and retain the best p_s solutions;
15 Return P;

Algorithm 2: AMOCDA

Input: Attributed Network $G = (V, E, A)$; Overlapping threshold p; Maximum
number of attribute neighbors k; Population sizes of two stages p_1, p_2;
Maximum generations of two stages g_1, g_2;

Output: Overlapping community structures $OC = \{c_1, c_2, \ldots, c_{p_n}\}$;

// STAGE 1: Embedding Vector Generation
1 $Kn \leftarrow$ ball-tree(A, k); // A is the attribute of network G
2 Generate V_{attr} based on Kn according to Fig. 2;
3 $V_{stru} \leftarrow$ DeepWalk(G);
// STAGE 2: Center Node Optimization
4 $cen \leftarrow$ Improved_NSGA2$(ps_1, gen_1, 1, V_{stru}, V_{attr}, null, p)$;
// STAGE 3: Overlapping Community Detection
5 $OC \leftarrow \emptyset$;
6 **for** $i = 1$ *to* $|cen|$ **do**
7 $subP \leftarrow$ Improved_NSGA2$(ps_2, gen_2, 2, vec_{stru}, vec_{attr}, cen_i, p)$;
8 $subC \leftarrow$ decode $subP$ according to Fig. 4;
9 $OC \leftarrow OC \cup subC$;
10 Remove all dominated solutions in OC;
11 Return OC;

4.5 Complexity Analysis

Let n be the number of nodes, m be the edges, f be the dimension of original attributes in the network. The dimension of embedding vectors is denoted as h, population sizes of two stages are p_1, p_2, maximum generations of the two stages are g_1 and g_2. The maximum number of attribute neighbors is k queried from the ball-tree. We analyze the complexity of the three stages of AMOCDA. In stage 1, the complexity of building ball-tree is $O(n \times f \times k \times \log n)$ and $k \ll n$. Building Alias table can be finished in $O(k \times n)$ and the complexity of DeepWalk is $O(m + n + n \times \log n)$. In stage 2, the main complexity is the calculation of EQ and SSE which can be calculated in $O(m)$ and $O(n \times h)$ respectively. SSE's complexity can be reduced to $O(n)$ because $h \ll n$ in a large network. Therefore, the total complexity in stage 2 is $O(p_1 \times g_1 \times (m+n))$. In stage 3, the complexity is $O(p_1 \times p_2 \times g_2 \times (m+n))$ because each group of center nodes obtained in stage 2 corresponds a subtask of stage 3. Therefore, the complexity of AMOCDA is $O(n \times f \times \log n + k \times n + m + n + n \times \log n + p_1 \times g_1 \times (m+n) + p_1 \times p_2 \times g_2 \times (m+n))$ which can be reduced to $O(n \times f \times \log n + p_1 \times p_2 \times g_2 \times (m+n))$.

5 Experiments

5.1 Datasets

Artificial Networks. We use LFR benchmark [17] to generate artificial networks whose parameters are described as follows: N is the number of nodes, k is the average node degree, k_{max} is the maximum node degree, c_{min} indicates the minimum community size, c_{max} denotes the maximum community size, μ is a mixing parameter, O_n means the number of overlapping nodes and O_m denotes the number of communities overlapping nodes belong to.

A larger μ indicates that the community structure of the network is ambiguous, and the attributes need to be considered to improve the accuracy of discovered communities. According to the real communities, the method proposed in [18] is used to generate attributes for all nodes for each network.

Two groups of artificial attributed networks are generated for experiments and their parameters are set as follow:

(1) D1 networks: $N = 1000$, $\mu = 0.1 - 0.7$ $O_n = 0.1$, $O_m = 2$;
(2) D2 networks: $N = 1000$, $\mu = 0.3$ $O_n = 0.1$, $O_m = 2 - 8$;

The other parameters of LFR are set by default: $k = 20$, $k_{max} = 50$, $c_{min} = 10$ and $c_{max} = 100$.

Real-World Networks. Cornell, Texas, Washington and Wisconsin are collected from WebKB [19] of the computer science departments in four American universities. Cora and Citeseer [19] are citation networks featuring scientific publications in different serval fields. Wiki [20] is a web page network and each edge represents the link relationship of the web pages. The detail of real-world networks is given in Table 1.

5.2 Baseline Algorithms

DeepWalk [12] samples sequences through random walking, and the sequences are input to the Skip-Gram model to learn embedding vectors. GEMSEC [21]

Table 1. Parameters of real-world attributed networks

Network	Number of nodes	Number of edges	Number of attributes	Communities
Cornell	195	286	1703	5
Texas	178	298	1703	5
Washington	230	417	1703	5
Wisconsin	265	479	1703	5
Cora	2708	5429	1433	7
Citeseer	3312	4732	3703	6
Wiki	2405	17981	4973	17

improves DeepWalk by considering the clustering objective to ensure nodes with more shared neighbors have similar representation vectors. ARGA and ARVGA [22] improve graph autoencoder and variational graph autoencoder [23] by adding an adversarial mechanism to enforce the embedding vectors match Gaussian distribution. EMOFM [24] is a two-stage MOEA that takes only structure into accounts for detecting overlapping communities. CE-MOEA [9] and MOEA-SA [4] are the state of art community detection algorithms based on MOEA that consider attributes. The embedding vectors learned by GEMSEC, ARGA, ARVGA are input to C-means [25] to obtain communities.

The parameters of all the baseline algorithms are set to the values recommended by their original papers. In AMOCDA, the maximum generations of two stages are set to 100, 50 respectively. The population sizes of the two stages are set to 20, 50 respectively.

5.3 Evaluation Metric

Overlapping normalized mutual information (ONMI) [26] is adopted to evaluate the overlapping community structure, which is as follows:

$$\mathrm{ONMI}(A,B) = 1 - \frac{1}{2}\left(\sum_{i}^{|A|}\frac{\mathrm{H}(A_i,B)}{|A|\mathrm{H}(A_i)} + \sum_{j}^{|B|}\frac{\mathrm{H}(B_j|A)}{|B|\mathrm{H}(B_j)}\right) \tag{8}$$

where $\mathrm{H}(A_i)$ is the entropy of the i-th community A_i, $\mathrm{H}(A_i|B)$ is the entropy of A_i with respect to B which is defined as follows:

$$\mathrm{H}(A_i|B) = \min_{l\in\{1,2,\ldots,|B|\}} \mathrm{H}(A_i|B_l) \tag{9}$$

The larger the value of ONMI, the higher an algorithm's accuracy.

5.4 Accuracy Experiment

Results on Artificial Networks are shown in Fig. 5 and 6. Figure 5 shows the accuracy of the algorithms on the D1 networks. Our accuracy is always

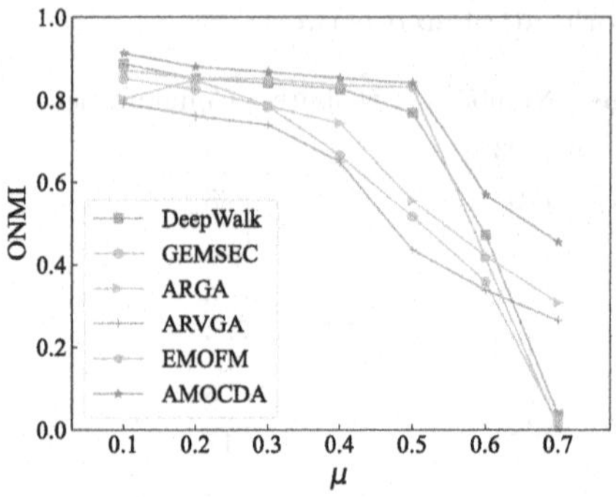

Fig. 5. Accuracy of the algorithms with varying values of μ

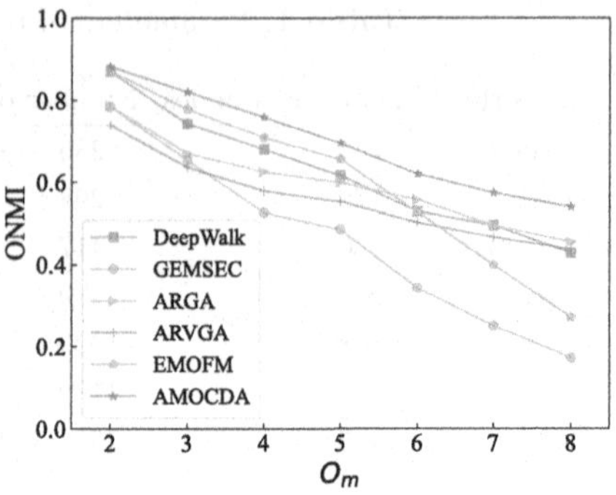

Fig. 6. Accuracy of the algorithms with varying values of O_m

higher than that of other algorithms in networks with different values of μ, which shows the attention-based encoding strategy can integrate structure and attribute well to improve the accuracy of discovered communities. Especially in networks with a high value of μ, an obvious community structure is hard to be detected using structure information alone. Therefore, the accuracy of DeepWalk, GEMSEC and EMOFM decreases sharply when $\mu \geq 0.6$ because they consider only network structure. ARGA and ARVGAs' accuracy drop more slowly when $\mu \geq 0.5$ because they use both structure and attribute information to discover communities.

Figure 6 shows the accuracy of the algorithms on the D2 networks. With the increase of O_m, the accuracy of all algorithms drops because the number of communities nodes belong to increase, making the community structure more difficult to identify. GEMSEC's performance decreases sharply when the value of $O_m \geq 5$ because its clustering objective may not work well on networks with highly overlapping communities. A similar phenomenon happens to EMOFM because its optimization objective limits the number of communities a node belongs to. AMOCDA is superior to other algorithms and its accuracy drops more slowly because of the threshold p-based overlapping communities decoding method and taking attribute into account through the attention-based encoding strategy.

Results on Real-World Networks are shown in Table 2. The slashes mean the data is inaccessible. In Cornell, Texas, Washington and Wisconsin, the structure information makes nearly no contribution to the real communities. Therefore, the structure-based algorithms DeepWalk, GEMSEC and EMOFM do not perform well in these networks. The same problem happens to ARGA and ARVGA because they cannot determine how important the attribute is in these networks when detecting communities. CE-MOEA and MOEA-SA can find diverse community divisions by optimizing the structure and attribute objectives. However, their encoding strategies are completely dependent on the structure,

Table 2. ONMI values of the algorithms on real-world networks

Network	Cornell	Texas	Washin	Wisco	Cora	Citeseer	Wiki
DeepWalk	0.0646	0.0495	0.0585	0.0867	0.3277	0.1425	0.0155
GEMSEC	0.0939	0.0465	0.0478	0.0766	0.2682	0.1346	0.0516
ARGA	0.0745	0.0759	0.0646	0.0631	0.3544	0.1886	0.1281
ARVGA	0.0834	0.0812	0.0516	0.0799	0.3421	0.2622	0.1072
EMOFM	0.0187	0.0343	0.0352	0.0229	0.0949	0.0385	0.0154
CE-MOEA	0.1760	0.1550	0.1860	0.1900	0.3980	0.3450	\
MOEA-SA	0.1320	0.1110	0.1390	0.1560	0.1180	0.1420	\
AMOCDA	**0.2588**	**0.1726**	**0.2820**	**0.2501**	**0.3991**	**0.3461**	**0.4057**

which limits their search capability. On the contrary, our AMOCDA performs the best in all networks because the attention-encoded strategy can simultaneously use structure and attribute information to discover optimal community structures.

5.5 Efficiency of SSE

The complexity of the calculation of SSE is O(n), where n is the number of nodes. The complexity of AS and AE are O(n^2) and O($n \times f$) according to Eq. (3) and (5), where f is the dimension of attributes.

Maximizing AS or minimizing AE can be also used as the attribute objective of AMOCDA to discover communities. We compare the running time of AMOCDA with different objectives in Table 3.

Table 3. Running time (seconds) with different objectives

Objective	Cornell	Texas	Washin	Wisco	Cora	Citeseer	Wiki
Maximizing AS	34.69	22.87	28.13	46.55	1475.88	2578.16	1690.35
Minimizing AE	464.83	447.31	557.43	640.39	6725.90	19210.80	20523.05
Minimizing SSE	**6.13**	**7.14**	**7.85**	**6.81**	**53.83**	**72.55**	**55.87**

As shown in Table 3, The efficiency of AMOCDA is significantly improved when minimizing SSE is used as the attribute objective. AS's efficiency decreases sharply in large-scale networks such as Cora, Citeseer because its complexity is $O(n^2)$. AE can only handle categorical attributes because it is defined based on entropy. The efficiency of minimizing AE is the lowest because of the large dimension of attributes in these real-world networks. In summary, AS and AE are not suitable objective functions in large-scale and high-dimensional attributed networks. Instead, minimizing SSE is a promising attribute objective for community detection in attributed networks based on MOEAs.

6 Conclusions

In this paper, we propose an attention-based multiobjective optimization for community detection in attributed networks. First, we design an attribute-similarity-based node sampling method to generate node sequences input to the Skip-Gram model to learn attribute embedding vectors. Second, with the help of the embedding vectors, the attention-based multiobjective optimization can integrate structure and attribute information to discover communities with high quality. Besides, an attribute objective function calculated in linear time is designed based on the embedding vectors to speed up the evolution process. In the future, we will integrate structure and attribute information tightly to improve the accuracy of detected communities further. Moreover, we attempt to expand this method to discover communities in heterogeneous networks.

Acknowledgements. This work was supported by the National Natural Science Foundation of China under Grant No. 61672159, No. 61672158, No. 61300104 and No. 62002063, the Fujian Collaborative Innovation Center for Big Data Applications in Governments, the Fujian Industry-Academy Cooperation Project under Grant No. 2017H6008 and No. 2018H6010, the Natural Science Foundation of Fujian Province under Grant No. 2018J07005, No. 2019J01835 and No. 2020J05112, the Fujian Provincial Department of Education under Grant No. JAT190026, the Fuzhou University under Grant 510872/GXRC-20016 and Haixi Government Big Data Application Cooperative Innovation Center.

References

1. Pizzuti, C., Rombo, S.E.: Algorithms and tools for protein-protein interaction networks clustering, with a special focus on population-based stochastic methods. Bioinformatics **30**(10), 1343–1352 (2014)
2. Newman, M.E.: The structure of scientific collaboration networks. In: The Structure and Dynamics of Networks. pp. 221–226. Princeton University Press, Princeton (2021)
3. Albert, R., Jeong, R., Barabási, A.-L.: Diameter of the world-wide web. Nature **401**(6749), 130–131 (1999)
4. Li, Z., Liu, J., Wu, K.: A multiobjective evolutionary algorithm based on structural and attribute similarities for community detection in attributed networks. IEEE Trans. Cybernet. **48**(7), 1963–1976 (2017)
5. Girvan, M., Newman, M.E.: Community structure in social and biological networks. Proc. Natl. Acad. Sci. **99**(12), 7821–7826 (2002)
6. Teng, X., Liu, J., Li, M.: Overlapping community detection in directed and undirected attributed networks using a multiobjective evolutionary algorithm. IEEE Trans. Cybernet. **51**(1), 138–150 (2019)
7. Pizzuti, C., Socievole, A.: Multiobjective optimization and local merge for clustering attributed graphs. IEEE Trans. Cybernet. **50**(12), 4997–5009 (2019)
8. Deb, K., Pratap, A., Agarwal, S., Meyarivan, T.: A fast and elitist multiobjective genetic algorithm: NSGA-II. IEEE Trans. Evol. Comput. **6**(2), 182–197 (2002)
9. Sun, J., Zheng, W., Zhang, Q., Xu, Z.: Graph neural network encoding for community detection in attribute networks. IEEE Trans. Cybernet. 1–14 (2021)

10. Mikolov, T., Chen, K., Corrado, G., Dean, J.: Efficient estimation of word representations in vector space. arXiv preprint arXiv:1301.3781 (2013)
11. Fonseca, C.M., Fleming, P.J.: Multiobjective optimization and multiple constraint handling with evolutionary algorithms. i. a unified formulation. IEEE Trans. Syst. Man Cybernet. Part A Syst. Hum. **28**(1), 26–37 (1998)
12. Perozzi, B., Al-Rfou, R., Skiena, S.: DeepWalk: online learning of social representations. In: Proceedings of the 20th ACM Sigkdd International Conference on Knowledge Discovery and Data Mining, pp. 701–710 (2014)
13. Kibriya, A.M., Frank, E.: An empirical comparison of exact nearest neighbour algorithms. In: Kok, J.N., Koronacki, J., Lopez de Mantaras, R., Matwin, S., Mladenič, D., Skowron, A. (eds.) PKDD 2007. LNCS (LNAI), vol. 4702, pp. 140–151. Springer, Heidelberg (2007). https://doi.org/10.1007/978-3-540-74976-9_16
14. Khan, I.H.: Assessing different crossover operators for travelling salesman problem. Int. J. Intell. Syst. Appl. **7**(11), 19–25 (2015)
15. Deb, K., Agrawal, R.B., et al.: Simulated binary crossover for continuous search space. Complex Syst. **9**(2), 115–148 (1995)
16. Zeng, G.Q., et al.: An improved multi-objective population-based extremal optimization algorithm with polynomial mutation. Inf. Sci. **330**, 49–73 (2016)
17. Lancichinetti, A., Fortunato, S., Radicchi, F.: Benchmark graphs for testing community detection algorithms. Phys. Rev. E **78**(4), 046110 (2008)
18. Huang, B., Wang, C., Wang, B.: NMPLA: uncovering overlapping communities in attributed networks via a multi-label propagation approach. Sensors **19**(2), 260 (2019)
19. Sen, P., Namata, G., Bilgic, M., Getoor, L., Galligher, B., Eliassi-Rad, T.: Collective classification in network data. AI Mag. **29**(3), 93–93 (2008)
20. Tang, L., Liu, H.: Relational learning via latent social dimensions. In: Proceedings of the 15th ACM SIGKDD International Conference on Knowledge Discovery and Data Mining, pp. 817–826 (2009)
21. Rozemberczki, B., Davies, R., Sarkar, R., Sutton, C.: GEMSEC: graph embedding with self clustering. In: Proceedings of the 2019 IEEE/ACM International Conference on Advances in Social Networks Analysis and Mining, pp. 65–72 (2019)
22. Pan, S., Hu, R., Fung, S.-F., Long, G., Jiang, J., Zhang, C.: Learning graph embedding with adversarial training methods. IEEE Trans. Cybernet. **50**(6), 2475–2487 (2019)
23. Kipf, T.N., Welling, M.: Variational graph auto-encoders. arXiv preprint arXiv:1611.07308 (2016)
24. Tian, Y., Yang, S., Zhang, X.: An evolutionary multiobjective optimization based fuzzy method for overlapping community detection. IEEE Trans. Fuzzy Syst. **28**(11), 2841–2855 (2019)
25. Bezdek, J.C., Ehrlich, R., Full, W.: FCM: the fuzzy c-means clustering algorithm. Comput. Geosci. **10**(2–3), 191–203 (1984)
26. McDaid, A.F., Greene, D., Hurley, N.: Normalized mutual information to evaluate overlapping community finding algorithms. arXiv preprint arXiv:1110.2515 (2011)

Kernel Subspace Possibilistic Fuzzy C-Means Algorithm Driven by Feature Weights

Yiming Tang[1,2(✉)], Zhifu Pan[1], Hongmang Li[1], and Lei Xi[1]

[1] Anhui Province Key Laboratory of Affective Computing and Advanced Intelligent Machine, School of Computer and Information, Hefei University of Technology, Hefei 230601, China
tym608@163.com

[2] Engineering Research Center of Safety Critical Industry Measure and Control Technology, Ministry of Education, Hefei University of Technology, Hefei 230601, China

Abstract. At present, one of the difficulties in the field of fuzzy clustering is the clustering analysis for high dimensional data. Most of the existing fuzzy clustering algorithms are sensitive to initialization, which are greatly affected by noise points and has weak adaptability to high-dimensional data. In order to solve these problems, a kernel space possibilistic fuzzy c-means clustering (KSPFCM for short) algorithm is proposed. Firstly, considering that the fuzzy possibilistic clustering algorithm can deal with the noise points better, the typicality matrix is introduced to weaken the constraint on the membership matrix. Secondly, to refine the granularity of clustering convergence, subspace clustering is introduced to assign each feature weight value to the data, and the feature weight value is obtained by adaptive collaborative iteration. Among them, a greater weight value are given for the important features of the data, which makes the feature weight allocation more reasonable. Thirdly, the Gaussian kernel distance is used as the distance measure between data points to optimize the sensitivity to the data set, and thus the KSPFCM algorithm is proposed. Finally, by comparing with several advanced clustering algorithms on the artificial data sets and UCI data sets in this field, the proposed KSPFCM algorithm performs better in the five clustering effectiveness indicators of ACC, EARI, NMI, CHI and XBI.

Keywords: Collaborative intelligence · Fuzzy clustering · Subspace · Possibilistic clustering · Kernel functions

1 Introduction

In fuzzy clustering, the fuzzy c-means (FCM) algorithm is the most commonly used method. Generally, FCM places equal importance on all feature weights of the data. With the development of research, it is found that each feature of the object has different effects on clustering. Therefore, the method of feature weights has become an important development direction.

The Weighted FCM (WFCM) algorithm [1] performed clustering by separating feature weighted values. The weighted Euclidean distance was used as the similarity index in WFCM. The improved versions such as the fuzzy weighted k-means (FWKM) and the

Y. Sun et al. (Eds.): ChineseCSCW 2021, CCIS 1491, pp. 286–300, 2022.
https://doi.org/10.1007/978-981-19-4546-5_23

fuzzy subspace clustering (FSC) algorithm have been proposed to overcome this weakness. In the objective function of FWKM [2], a constant was added when calculating the distance, which can effectively avoid the problems caused by the possible zero standard deviation of some attributes in AWA. Gan proposed the FSC algorithm [3], which used an objective function similar to FWKM. FSC also introduced a constant to avoid the problem of zero standard deviation. Unlike FWKM, the constant parameters introduced in the FSC algorithm were set manually, while constant parameters in FWKM were set through a predefined formula.

When performing clustering in high-dimensional space, the traditional clustering algorithm has some deficiencies. For example, these points may be far apart in a high-dimensional space, which are in the same cluster. For most traditional clustering algorithms, a key challenge is that clusters can reside in different subspaces. In many real-world problems, these subspaces are composed of different subsets of features. Frigui and Nasraoui [4] proposed a clustering and attribute identification (SCAD) algorithm that performed clustering and feature weighting simultaneously. It used continuous feature weights, thus provided a richer representation of feature correlation than feature selection. Later, Deng et al. [5] proposed the enhanced soft subspace clustering (ESSC), which combined the intra-class compactness and the separation of inter-cluster in the subspace. Yang and Nataliani [6] proposed a feature weight reduction fuzzy clustering algorithm (FRFCM), which calculated the weight of each feature and reduced the irrelevant feature weights.

From different viewpoint, a possibilistic clustering method (PCM) was proposed [7, 8]. The differences between PCM and the methods of existing clustering lie in that the result partition of data can be interpreted as possibilistic partition, while the membership value can be interpreted as the possibilistic degree of point extension. PCM can handle the problem of noise very well, but there is the problem of cluster center coincidence. Pal et al. [9] proposed the possibilistic fuzzy c-means (PFCM). PFCM generated membership and possibilistic value along with the updating of the point prototype or cluster center for each cluster. PFCM incorporated the possibilistic c-means (PCM) and fuzzy c-means (FCM), which avoided the problems of PCM and FCM. Tang et al. [10] proposed a possibilistic fuzzy clustering with high-density viewpoint algorithm (DVPFCM). By referring to the idea of generating cluster centers by finding density peak points in RLM [11], they proposed the HDCCI cluster center initialization algorithm, which overcame the sensitivity of previous algorithms to initial cluster centers.

Both fuzzy membership and possibilistic membership play an important role in clustering. Bahrampour et al. proposed a weighted and constrained possibilistic c-means clustering algorithm (WCPCM) [12]. WCPCM included both the segmentation of possibilistic time series and the weighting of local attribute, and allowed different weights to be assigned to different functions. Considering this imbalance between attributes, Shen et al. presented a fuzzy weighted kernel clustering algorithm (WFKCA) [13]. WFKCA performed clustering in the kernel feature space mapped by the Mercer kernel. Compared with the traditional hard clustering algorithm, WFKCA can generate the cluster center with numerical convergence.

At present, the problems of fuzzy clustering algorithm are mainly as follows:

1) Weak adaptability to high dimensions. With the rapid development of science and technology, the amount of data is more and more large and the dimension is higher and higher, which requires the clustering algorithm to deal with the ability of high-dimensional data. FCM, PFCM and DVPFCM lack special measures to deal with high-dimensional data. SCAD and FRFCM adopt the idea of subspace with different weights, which are relatively better. However, the existence of noise points lead to unstable feature weight distribution, and the robustness of the algorithm is weak.
2) The influence of noise points on clustering. Now the data are very complex, which have many noise points. So how to reduce the influence of noise points is an important problem to be solved.

To solve the above problems, a feature weight driven Kernel Subspace Possibilistic Fuzzy C-Means (KSPFCM) algorithm is proposed in this study. The ideas such as typicality matrix, subspace clustering and Gaussian kernel distance, are introduced to form an adaptive cooperative iterative strategy to obtain the feature weight value. The advantages of the proposed algorithm are verified by comparing with other advanced algorithms in six datasets.

2 Related Works

Suppose the data set is a set of n samples $X = \{x_j\}_{j=1}^{n}$. We try to break it down into c categories ($2 \leq c \leq n$), and obtain the cluster center set $V = \{v_i\}_{i=1}^{c}$. Each sample x_j and cluster center v_i are all l-dimensional data.

The objective function of the FCM algorithm was as follows.

$$J_{FCM} = \sum_{j=1}^{n}\sum_{i=1}^{c} u_{ij}^{m} d_{ij}^{2}. \tag{1}$$

Her u_{ij} represented fuzzy membership degree, whose value ranged from 0 to 1 and subjected to the constraint $\sum_{i=1}^{c} u_{ij} = 1, (j = 1, 2, \cdots, n)$. $d_{ij}^2 = \|x_j - v_i\|^2$ indicated the distance between the j-th point and the cluster center of the i-th class. And m denoted the weighted fuzzy factor, in which $m \in (1, +\infty)$.

Two versions of SCAD algorithms were established by Frigui and Nasraoui [4]. SCAD1 attempted to strike a balance between the two terms of a composite objective function, which introduced penalty terms to determine the optimal attribute correlation weights. In SCAD2, fuzzy weighted index was introduced to minimize the single term criterion. Their expressions were as follows.

$$J_{SCAD1} = \sum_{j=1}^{n}\sum_{i=1}^{c} u_{ij}^{m} \sum_{k=1}^{l} w_{ik} d_{ijk}^{2} + \sum_{i=1}^{c} \delta_i \sum_{k=1}^{l} w_{ik}^{2}, \tag{2}$$

$$J_{SCAD2} = \sum_{j=1}^{n}\sum_{i=1}^{c} u_{ij}^{m} \sum_{k=1}^{l} w_{ik}^{q} d_{ijk}^{2}. \tag{3}$$

Here $d_{ijk} = \left|x_{jk} - v_{ik}\right|$ indicated the distance between the k-th feature of j-th point and the k-th feature of the i-th cluster center. u_{ij} was the same as the one in FCM. q denoted the weighted fuzzy factor, and $q \in (1, +\infty)$. δ_i was the weighted constraint member, whose derived expression was:

$$\delta_i^{(t)} = K \frac{\sum_{j=1}^{n} (u_{ij}^{t-1})^m \sum_{k=1}^{l} w_{ik}^{t-1} d_{ijk}^{t-1}}{\sum_{k=1}^{l} (w_{ik}^{t-1})^2}. \tag{4}$$

Here K was a constant and superscript $t{-}1$ was the number of last iterations. They demonstrated that SCAD1 and SCAD2 had similar behavior and clustering results.

Recently, Tang et al. proposed the DVPFCM algorithm [10]. The specific objective function formula of DVPFCM was as follows.

$$J_{DVPFCM} = \sum_{j=1}^{n} \sum_{i=1}^{c} \left(au_{ij}^m + bt_{ij}^p\right) \left\|x_j - h_i\right\|^2 + \frac{\sigma^2}{m^2 c} \sum_{i=1}^{c} \sum_{j=1}^{n} \left(\varphi_j - t_{ij}\right)^p, \tag{5}$$

where the real cluster center was:

$$h_i = \begin{cases} v_i, \ i \neq q \\ x_d, \ i = q \end{cases}, \tag{6}$$

$$\sigma^2 = \frac{\sum_{k=1}^{N} \left\|x_k - \overline{x}\right\|^2}{N}, \ \overline{x} = \frac{\sum_{k=1}^{N} x_k}{N}, \tag{7}$$

$$\varphi_k = \frac{\sum_{j=1}^{N} \left\|x_j - x_k\right\|^2}{N} \quad (k = 1, \cdots, N). \tag{8}$$

Here m, p were fuzzy coefficient and typical matrix fuzzy coefficient respectively. σ^2 represented the distance of variance matrix. φ_k denoted the weight of each sample. DVPFCM introduced the parameters, which considered the compactness and isolation of the data set, as well as measured the contribution of each sample to clustering. With the help of the viewpoint and typicality values, it had relatively stronger robustness and noise resistance in the conceptual level of the algorithm.

The objective function of the FRFCM algorithm [5] was:

$$J_{FRFCM} = \sum_{j=1}^{n} \sum_{i=1}^{c} \sum_{k=1}^{l} u_{ij}^m \delta_k w_k (x_{jk} - v_{ik})^2 + \frac{n}{c} \sum_{k=1}^{l} (w_k \log \delta_k w_k), \tag{9}$$

where u_{ij} represented fuzzy membership degree. w_{ik} indicated the weight of the k-th feature and the cluster center of the i-th class. δ_k was the weight penalty term, which controlled function weights. Its formula was as follows:

$$\delta_k = \left(\frac{mean(x)}{\mathrm{var}(x)}\right)_k \tag{10}$$

FRFCM computed new weights for each feature by adding feature weighted entropy to its objective function. Then, the cluster center and fuzzy membership matrix were updated by these new weights during the iteration. FRFCM not only improved the performance of FCM, but also could select the important features by discarding the unimportant features. Therefore, this algorithm could automatically reduce the feature dimension and achieve a good clustering effect.

The objective function of PCM was as follows:

$$J_{PCM}=\sum_{i=1}^{C}\sum_{j=1}^{N}u_{ij}\left\|x_j-v_i\right\|^2+\sum_{i=1}^{C}\gamma_i\sum_{j=1}^{N}\left(u_{ij}\ln u_{ij}-u_{ij}\right), \tag{11}$$

where γ_i represented the penalty factor. The second binomial of (11) was for constraints u_{ij}. The update formulas for u_{ij} and v_i were as follows:

$$u_{ij}^{(iter)}=\exp\left(-\frac{\left\|x_j-v_i\right\|^2}{\gamma_i}\right), \tag{12}$$

$$v_i^{(iter+1)}=\frac{\sum_{j=1}^{N}u_{ij}^{(iter)}x_j}{\sum_{j=1}^{N}u_{ij}^{(iter)}}. \tag{13}$$

Here the parameter γ_i $(i=1,\cdots,C)$ needed to run FCM in advance, which generally set according to the results of FCM:

$$\gamma_i=K\frac{\sum_{j=1}^{N}u_{ij}^{(FCM)}\left\|x_j-v_i\right\|^2}{\sum_{j=1}^{N}u_{ij}^{(FCM)}}, i=1\cdots,C. \tag{14}$$

The PCM algorithm loosened the constraint on u_{ij},therefore it could handle noise data as a better way than FCM.

Pal et al. [9] proposed the PFCM algorithm to overcome the noise or outlier displayed in FCM. PFCM could eliminate the defect of overlapping clusters in PCM by introducing the typicality values matrix, which was updated along with the membership matrix. Its objective function was as follows:

$$J_{PFCM}=\sum_{i=1}^{C}\sum_{j=1}^{N}\left(au_{ij}^{m}+bt_{ij}^{p}\right)\left\|x_j-v_i\right\|^2+\sum_{i=1}^{C}\gamma_i\sum_{j=1}^{N}\left(1-t_{ij}\right)^p, \tag{15}$$

where u_{ij} represented fuzzy membership degree. t_{ij} was a typical component and $t_{ij}\leq 1.a$ and b were the relative importance parameters controlling the balance between typicality values and fuzzy membership. The PFCM algorithm was more robust than the FCM algorithm, but it was still sensitive to the initialization of cluster center. The calculation of γ_i depended on the FCM algorithm, so its operation was not simple enough.

3 The Proposed KSPFCM Algorithm

3.1 Objective Function

In this section, we propose a kernel space possibilistic fuzzy c-means clustering (KSPFCM) algorithm. Firstly, considering that fuzzy possibility clustering algorithm can deal with noise points better, a typicality values matrix is employed to weaken the constraints on the membership matrix. Then, in order to refine the granularity of clustering convergence, subspace clustering is introduced to give weight to each feature, and more weight is given to the important feature of clustering.

The proposed algorithm uses three parts to construct the objective function. In the first part, fuzzy feature weight, typicality values matrix and Gaussian kernel distance are introduced on the basis of FCM conventional objective function. The second part is the penalty term of the typicality matrix, which is used to guide the typicality values matrix to participate in the clustering process. The third part represents the weight entropy, which can guide the real-time iteration of the weight matrix in the process of clustering. Specifically, the objective function can be expressed as follows:

$$\begin{aligned} J= & \sum_{i=1}^{c}\sum_{j=1}^{n}(au_{ij}^{m}+bt_{ij}^{\eta})\sum_{k=1}^{d}w_{ik}\|\varphi(x_{jk})-\varphi(v_{ik})\|^2 \\ & +\delta\sum_{i=1}^{c}\sum_{j=1}^{n}\sum_{k=1}^{d}w_{ik}(1-t_{ij})^{\eta}+\xi\sum_{i=1}^{c}\sum_{k=1}^{d}w_{ik}\ln w_{ik}. \end{aligned} \tag{16}$$

Here c represents the number of clustering and n denotes the number of data in the set and each data has d features. u_{ij} is the membership matrix, and $u_{ij} \in [0, 1]$. w_{ik} indicates the weight of the k-th feature and the cluster center of the i-th class, in which $w_{ik} \in [0, 1][0, 1]$. t_{ij} is a typical component and $t_{ij} \leq 1$. There are restrictions as follows.

$$\sum_{i=1}^{c}u_{ij}=1, 1\leq i\leq c, 1\leq j\leq n, \tag{17}$$

$$\sum_{k=1}^{d}w_{ik}=1, 1\leq k\leq d. \tag{18}$$

Here δ and ξ are penalty factors for the second and third terms, respectively, β represents the variance of the data.

$$\|\varphi(x_{jk})-\varphi(v_{ik})\|^2 \tag{19}$$

denotes the Gaussian kernel feature distance between x_{jk} and v_{ik}. We have:

$$\|\varphi(x_{jk})-\varphi(v_{ik})\|^2=K(x_{jk},x_{jk})-2K(x_{jk},v_{ik})+K(v_{ik},v_{ik}), \tag{20}$$

then

$$\|\varphi(x_{jk})-\varphi(v_{ik})\|^2=2-2K(x_{jk},v_{ik}), \tag{21}$$

where

$$K(x,y)=\exp(\frac{-\|x-y\|^2}{\sigma^2}). \tag{22}$$

The formula is as follows (by the Lagrange multiplier method):

$$J' = J + \sum_{j=1}^{n} \lambda_j (1 - \sum_{i=1}^{c} u_{ij}) + \sum_{i=1}^{c} \gamma_i (1 - \sum_{k=1}^{d} w_{ik}). \tag{23}$$

The membership matrix is derived as follows. Let $\frac{\partial J'}{\partial u_{ij}} = 0$. (23) is transformed into:

$$mau_{ij}^{m-1} \sum_{k=1}^{d} w_{ik} \left\| \varphi(x_{jk}) - \varphi(v_{ik}) \right\|^2 - \lambda = 0. \tag{24}$$

It can be concluded that:

$$u_{ij} = (\frac{\lambda}{ma})^{\frac{1}{m-1}} \cdot (\sum_{k=1}^{d} w_{ik} \left\| \varphi(x_{jk}) - \varphi(v_{ik}) \right\|^2)^{\frac{-1}{m-1}}. \tag{25}$$

From (17), we can get:

$$\sum_{i=1}^{c} (\frac{\lambda}{ma})^{\frac{1}{m-1}} \cdot (\sum_{k=1}^{d} w_{ik} \left\| \varphi(x_{jk}) - \varphi(v_{ik}) \right\|^2)^{\frac{-1}{m-1}} = 1. \tag{26}$$

We have

$$(\frac{\lambda}{ma})^{\frac{1}{m-1}} = \frac{1}{\sum_{i=1}^{c} (\sum_{k=1}^{d} w_{ik} \left\| \varphi(x_{jk}) - \varphi(v_{ik}) \right\|^2)^{\frac{-1}{m-1}}}. \tag{27}$$

By substituting (27) into (25), we can get:

$$u_{ij} = \frac{(\sum_{k=1}^{d} w_{ik} \left\| \varphi(x_{jk}) - \varphi(v_{ik}) \right\|^2)^{\frac{-1}{m-1}}}{\sum_{i'=1}^{c} (\sum_{k=1}^{d} w_{i'k} \left\| \varphi(x_{jk}) - \varphi(v_{i'k}) \right\|^2)^{\frac{-1}{m-1}}}. \tag{28}$$

The typicality matrix is derived as follows. Let $\frac{\partial J'}{\partial t_{ij}} = 0$, (23) is transformed into:

$$\eta b t_{ij}^{\eta-1} \sum_{k=1}^{d} w_{ik} \left\| \varphi(x_{jk}) - \varphi(v_{ik}) \right\|^2 - \delta \eta \sum_{k=1}^{d} w_{ik} (1 - t_{ij})^{\eta-1} = 0. \tag{29}$$

According to (29), the following can be obtained:

$$t_{ij} = \frac{(\delta \sum_{k=1}^{d} w_{ik})^{\frac{1}{\eta-1}}}{(\delta \sum_{k=1}^{d} w_{ik})^{\frac{1}{\eta-1}} + (b \sum_{k=1}^{d} w_{ik} \left\| \varphi(x_{jk}) - \varphi(v_{ik}) \right\|^2)^{\frac{1}{\eta-1}}}. \tag{30}$$

The feature weight matrix is derived as follows. Let $\frac{\partial J'}{\partial w_{ik}} = 0$. One has

$$\sum_{j=1}^{n} (au_{ij}^m + bt_{ij}^\eta) \left\| \varphi(x_{jk}) - \varphi(v_{ik}) \right\|^2 + \delta \sum_{j=1}^{n} (1 - t_{ij})^\eta + \xi(1 + \ln w_{ik}) - \gamma = 0. \tag{31}$$

$$w_{ik} = \exp\left(\frac{\gamma - \sum_{j=1}^{n} (au_{ij}^m + bt_{ij}^\eta) \left\| \varphi(x_{jk}) - \varphi(v_{ik}) \right\|^2 - \delta \sum_{j=1}^{n} (1 - t_{ij})^\eta - \xi}{\xi} \right). \tag{32}$$

Because $\sum_{k=1}^{d} w_{ik} = 1$, we have

$$\sum_{k=1}^{d} \exp\left(\frac{\gamma - \sum_{j=1}^{n} (au_{ij}^m + bt_{ij}^\eta) \left\| \varphi(x_{jk}) - \varphi(v_{ik}) \right\|^2 - \delta \sum_{j=1}^{n} (1 - t_{ij})^\eta - \xi}{\xi} \right) = 1. \tag{33}$$

From (33), it can be deduced that:

$$\exp\left(\frac{\gamma - \delta \sum_{j=1}^{n} (1 - t_{ij})^\eta - \xi}{\xi} \right) = \frac{1}{\sum_{k=1}^{d} \exp(-\xi^{-1} \sum_{j=1}^{n} (au_{ij}^m + bt_{ij}^\eta) \left\| \varphi(x_{jk}) - \varphi(v_{ik}) \right\|^2)}. \tag{34}$$

By replacing (34) with (32), we obtain:

$$w_{ik} = \frac{\exp(-\xi^{-1} \sum_{j=1}^{n} (au_{ij}^m + bt_{ij}^\eta) \left\| \varphi(x_{jk}) - \varphi(v_{ik}) \right\|^2)}{\sum_{k'=1}^{d} \exp(-\xi^{-1} \sum_{j=1}^{n} (au_{ij}^m + bt_{ij}^\eta) \left\| \varphi(x_{jk'}) - \varphi(v_{ik'}) \right\|^2)}. \tag{35}$$

The clustering center matrix is derived as follows. Let $\frac{\partial J}{\partial v_{ik}} = 0$, by substituting (21) and (22), we get:

$$\frac{-4}{\sigma^2}\sum_{j=1}^{n}(au_{ij}^m + bt_{ij}^{\eta})w_{ik}\exp(\frac{-\left\|x_{jk} - v_{ik}\right\|^2}{\sigma^2})(x_{jk} - v_{ik}) = 0. \quad (36)$$

Then

$$v_{ik} = \frac{\sum_{j=1}^{n}(au_{ij}^m + bt_{ij}^{\eta})w_{ik}\exp(\frac{-\|x_{jk}-v_{ik}\|^2}{\sigma^2})x_{jk}}{\sum_{j=1}^{n}(au_{ij}^m + bt_{ij}^{\eta})w_{ik}\exp(\frac{-\|x_{jk}-v_{ik}\|^2}{\sigma^2})}. \quad (37)$$

The principle of the KSPFCM algorithm is all introduced.

3.2 Algorithm Operation Framework

The process of the KSPFCM algorithm is as follows (Table 1):

Table 1. The implementation process of the KSPFCM algorithm

Algorithm 1. The KSPFCM algorithm.

Input: The data set $X=\{x_j\}_{j=1}^n$ and cluster number c

Output: A membership matrix U, weights matrix W and cluster center matrix H.

```
procedure KSPFCM (Data X, Number c)
  Set the threshold ε and maximum number of iterations iM
    repeat
        iter = iter + 1;
        Update membership matrix U using (28);
        Update typicality values t_ik using (30);
        Update feature weight matrix W using (35);
        Update the clustering center H using (37);
    until ||U^(iter) - U^(iter-1)|| < ε and iter > iM ;
    return U^(iter), H^(iter), W^(iter);
end procedure
```

4 Experiment

The proposed KSPFCM algorithm is compared with several algorithms (including FCM, PFCM, KFCM, DVPFCM, SCAD and FRFCM). Experiment objects had two artificial data sets and four UCI machine learning data sets. The artificial data sets DATA1 and DATA2 are composed of points with Gaussian distribution, which are generated by the function make_blob() in Python's Scikit-Learn library. Both of the two data sets have the problem of interclass overlap and the data volume of DATA1 is larger than that of DATA2. The UCI data sets include Breast Cancer, Statlog, seeds, Wine data sets, which are frequently used in the field of machine learning.

There are mainly two types of clustering evaluation indexes: hard clustering validity index and soft clustering validity index. We use the superscript "(+)" to indicate that the indicator is the bigger the better, and the superscript "(−)" to show that the indicator is as small as possible. Here, five clustering evaluation indexes are adopted, namely Accuracy Rate (ACC), Normalized Information (NMI), EARI, and Calinski-Harabasz-Index (CHI), Xie-Ben-Index (XBI) [10]. The first three are hard clustering validity indexes, while the last two are soft ones. The results of clustering with the best performance are marked in bold. Table 2 provides the basic information of all the data sets to be used in the experiment.

Table 2. Information statistics of experimental data sets

	Name	Instances	Attributes	Classes
D1	DATA1	1000	2	7
D2	DATA2	150	2	3
D3	Wine	178	13	3
D4	Breast Cancer	569	30	2
D5	Statlog	2236	36	2
D6	Seeds	210	7	3

Figure 1 shows the clustering effect of each algorithm in DATA1. There are seven types of DATA1 reference clustering, and some data are easily divided into two categories, and there are too many categories.

The Gaussian kernel distance is not introduced into PFCM and FCM, and they are not sensitive to the data set, which leads to incorrect identification of the cluster center. The performance of KFCM algorithm is better. The same problem also occurs in the DVPFCM algorithm. As shown in f) and g) in Fig. 1, the introduction of feature weights in FRFCM and SCAD algorithm can effectively improve the accuracy of clustering, but it can also be seen that some data between the two class clusters are misclassified at the edge of noise data. The proposed KSPFCM algorithm combines the feature weights, possibility and data kernel of subspace, which integrates their respective advantages to get better clustering results.

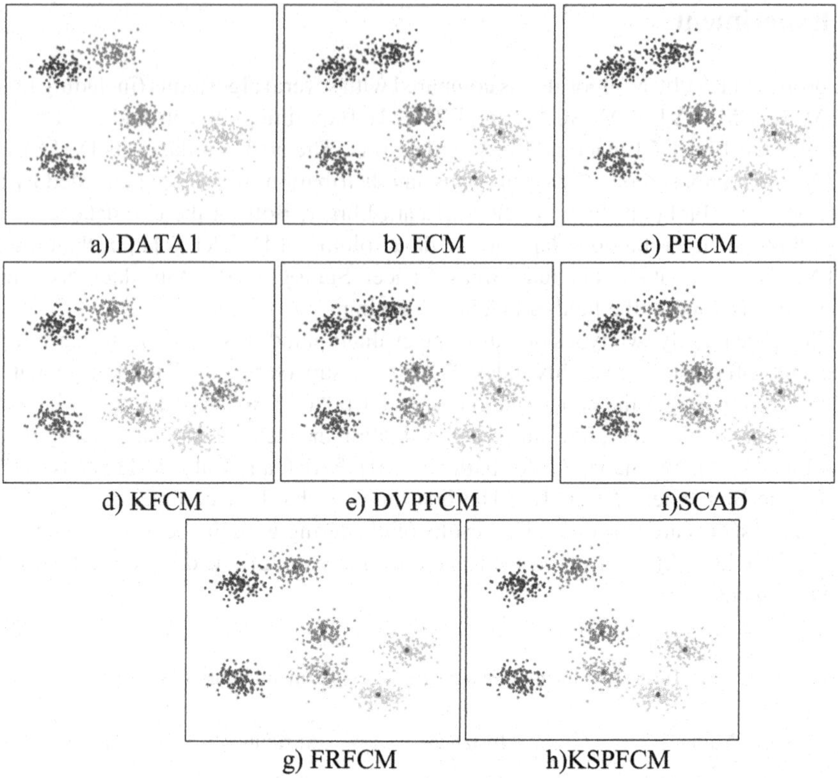

Fig. 1. Experimental effect diagram

For DATA1 data set, the specific data are shown in Table 3. From the clustering results of each index, the comparison of each algorithm is that: KSPFCM > FRFCM > SCAD > DVPFCM > KFCM > PFCM > FCM.

Table 3. Related algorithm clustering results in DATA1

	ACC	EARI	NMI	CHI	XBI
FCM	0.848	0.836	0.854	13.513	0.777
PFCM	0.849	0.900	0.858	13.881	0.630
KFCM	0.913	0.910	0.878	14.101	0.482
DVPFCM	0.928	0.936	0.895	14.282	0.458
SCAD	0.944	0.953	0.913	14.427	0.361
FRFCM	0.973	0.974	0.944	14.786	0.206
KSPFCM	**0.989**	**0.988**	**0.969**	**14.982**	**0.102**

Similar results were obtained for DATA2, Wine, Breast cancer, Statlog, and seeds data sets (see Table 4, 5, 6, 7 and 8). The proposed KSPFCM algorithm still achieved the best experimental results.

Table 4. Related algorithm clustering results in DATA2

	ACC	EARI	NMI	CHI	XBI
FCM	0.886	0.892	0.700	8.702	0.643
PFCM	0.900	0.901	0.714	10.194	0.470
KFCM	0.940	0.931	0.845	10.857	0.396
DVPFCM	0.953	0.939	0.861	11.639	0.321
SCAD	0.953	0.954	0.884	11.788	0.282
FRFCM	0.967	0.960	0.885	11.943	0.230
KSPFCM	**0.980**	**0.979**	**0.911**	**12.118**	**0.211**

Table 5. Related algorithm clustering results in wine

	ACC	EARI	NMI	CHI	XBI
FCM	0.770	0.744	0.579	7.521	3.243
PFCM	0.853	0.791	0.681	8.935	2.770
KFCM	0.876	0.833	0.726	10.748	1.860
DVPFCM	0.882	0.852	0.749	11.635	1.727
SCAD	0.932	0.906	0.807	13.230	1.375
FRFCM	0.943	0.934	0.876	13.911	1.207
KSPFCM	**0.966**	**0.990**	**0.884**	**14.844**	**1.118**

Table 6. Related algorithm clustering results in breast cancer

	ACC	EARI	NMI	CHI	XBI
FCM	0.776	0.524	0.440	47.919	1.095
PFCM	0.834	0.667	0.505	57.286	0.825
KFCM	0.884	0.760	0.531	61.211	0.428
DVPFCM	0.903	0.859	0.592	78.999	0.336
SCAD	0.919	0.870	0.597	82.496	0.305
FRFCM	0.926	0.880	0.610	85.655	0.292
KSPFCM	**0.936**	**0.884**	**0.644**	**90.144**	**0.286**

Table 7. Related algorithm clustering results in statlog

	ACC	EARI	NMI	CHI	XBI
FCM	0.869	0.716	0.559	218.662	0.567
PFCM	0.909	0.824	0.618	248.687	0.546
KFCM	0.930	0.871	0.668	298.394	0.387
DVPFCM	0.946	0.904	0.719	344.912	0.341
SCAD	0.956	0.924	0.763	393.673	0.318
FRFCM	0.964	0.931	0.799	400.146	0.312
KSPFCM	**0.966**	**0.939**	**0.801**	**401.460**	**0.235**

Table 8. Related algorithm clustering results in seeds

	ACC	EARI	NMI	CHI	XBI
FCM	0.819	0.751	0.581	13.626	0.598
PFCM	0.833	0.773	0.615	13.870	0.529
KFCM	0.847	0.786	0.634	14.051	0.466
DVPFCM	0.861	0.817	0.653	14.997	0.410
SCAD	0.871	0.829	0.665	16.061	0.301
FRFCM	0.895	0.857	0.675	16.534	0.281
KSPFCM	**0.900**	**0.859**	**0.683**	**16.714**	**0.247**

The advantages of the proposed algorithm are mainly reflected in the following aspects:

- It can be seen from the experimental results that the proposed KSPFCM algorithm shows the best performance of ACC, EARI, NMI, CHI and XBI on all six data sets. In general, the performance of KSPFCM is better than the other six comparison algorithms.
- By combining the advantages of feature weighted subspace, typicality values and kernel function, the KSPFCM algorithm is established. KSPFCM can effectively deal with complex data with high dimension and noise, and get better results.
- The processing of typicality value will bring a relatively stable performance result. The KSPFCM algorithm is less affected by noise points and has a better stable initialization center and convergence reference point. The weight processing of subspace can refine the convergence granularity, and give the corresponding weight according to the importance of each feature of each data point to the clustering process. This can optimize the clustering effect and efficiency to a certain extent. Kernel distance can map data points to kernel space, and using of Gaussian kernel distance can optimize the sensitivity of the algorithm to the data set. KSPFCM integrates the advantages of

the above techniques, and assigns a small weight to the noise points. So it can greatly reduce the impact of noise points and achieve a relatively ideal clustering effect.

5 Conclusion

In this study, a kernel space possibilistic fuzzy c-means clustering algorithm KSPFCM is proposed. Firstly, the idea of typicality matrix is introduced to weaken the constraints on the membership matrix. Secondly, subspace clustering is introduced, and the weight value of each feature is assigned to the data, which is obtained by adaptive cooperative iteration. Thirdly, the Gaussian kernel distance is used as the distance measure between data points to optimize the sensitivity of the data set, and thus the KSPFCM algorithm is established. According to the experimental analyses, the value of each index obtained by KSPFCM has the best performance, and KSPFCM has the highest ACC, EARI, NMI and CHI values, and the lowest XBI value. In general, our algorithm is superior in algorithm design, experimental results, index verification and so on.

In future research, considering the fundamental and core driving role of logical reasoning in the field of artificial intelligence, we will try to integrate the strategy of logical reasoning [14–17] with fuzzy clustering algorithm. Then we can form a new model of reasoning clustering, which is expected to bring new vitality and exploration direction to the field.

Acknowledgement. This work was supported by the National Key Research and Development Program of China (No. 2020YFC1523100) and the National Natural Science Foundation of China (Nos. 62176083, 61673156, 61877016, 61976078), the Fundamental Research Funds for the Central Universities of China (No. PA2021GDSK0092), the Natural Science Foundation of Anhui Province (Nos.1408085MKL15, 1508085QF129).

References

1. Wang, X., Wang, Y., Wang, L.: Improving fuzzy c-means clustering based on feature-weight learning. Pattern Recogn. Lett. **25**(10), 1123–1132 (2004)
2. Jing, L., Ng, M.K., Xu, J., et al.: Subspace clustering of text documents with feature weighting k-means algorithm. In: Ho, T.B., Cheung, D., Liu, H. (eds.) Pacific-Asia Conference on Knowledge Discovery and Data Mining. LNAI, vol. 3518 pp. 802–812. Springer, Berlin, Heidelberg (2005). https://doi.org/10.1007/11430919_94
3. Gan, G., Wu, J.: A convergence theorem for the fuzzy subspace clustering (FSC) algorithm. Pattern Recogn. **41**(6), 1939–1947 (2008)
4. Frigui, H., Nasraoui, O.: Unsupervised learning of prototypes and attribute weights. Pattern Recogn. **37**(3), 567–581 (2004)
5. Deng, Z., Choi, K.S., Chung, F.L., et al.: Enhanced soft subspace clustering integrating within-cluster and between-cluster information. Pattern Recogn. **43**(3), 767–781 (2010)
6. Yang, M.S., Nataliani, Y.: A feature-reduction fuzzy clustering algorithm based on feature-weighted entropy. IEEE Trans. Fuzzy Syst. **26**(2), 817–835 (2017)
7. Wu, C., Zhang, X.: A novel kernelized total Bregman divergence-driven possibilistic fuzzy clustering with multiple information constraints for image segmentation. IEEE Trans. Fuzzy Syst. **30**, 1624–1639 (2021). https://doi.org/10.1109/TFUZZ.2021.3063818

8. Timm, H., Borgelt, C., Döring, C., et al.: An extension to possibilistic fuzzy cluster analysis. Fuzzy Sets Syst. **147**(1), 3–16 (2004)
9. Pal, N.R., Pal, K., Keller, J.M., et al.: A possibilistic fuzzy c-means clustering algorithm. IEEE Trans. Fuzzy Syst. **13**(4), 517–530 (2005)
10. Tang, Y.M., Hu, X.H., Pedrycz, W., et al.: Possibilistic fuzzy clustering with high-density viewpoint. Neurocomputing **329**, 407–423 (2019)
11. Rodriguez, A., Laio, A.: Clustering by fast search and find of density peaks. Science **344**(6191), 1492–1496 (2014)
12. Bahrampour, S., Moshiri, B., Salahshoor, K.: Weighted and constrained possibilistic C-means clustering for online fault detection and isolation. Appl. Intell. **35**(2), 269–284 (2011)
13. Shen, H., Yang, J., Wang, S., et al.: Attribute weighted mercer kernel based fuzzy clustering algorithm for general non-spherical datasets. Soft. Comput. **10**(11), 1061–1073 (2006)
14. Tang, Y.M., Ren, F.J., Chen, Y.X.: Differently implicational α-universal triple I restriction method of (1, 2, 2) type. J. Syst. Eng. Electron. **23**(4), 560–573 (2012)
15. Tang, Y.M., Ren, F.J.: Universal triple I method for fuzzy reasoning and fuzzy controller. Iranian J. Fuzzy Syst. **10**(5), 1–24 (2013)
16. Tang, Y.M., Pedrycz, W.: Oscillation bound estimation of perturbations under Bandler-Kohout subproduct. IEEE Trans. Cybern. 1–14 (2021) https://doi.org/10.1109/TCYB.2020.3025793
17. Tang, Y.M., Pedrycz, W., Ren, F.J.: Granular symmetric implicational method. IEEE Trans. Emerg. Top. Comput. Intell. **6**, 710–723 (2021) https://doi.org/10.1109/TETCI.2021.3100597

Multi-loop Adaptive Differential Evolution for Large-Scale Expensive Optimization

Hong-Rui Wang, Yi Jiang(✉), Zhi-Hui Zhan(✉), and Jinghui Zhong

School of Computer Science and Engineering, South China University of Technology, Guangzhou 51006, China
vladimir_jiangyi@qq.com, zhanapollo@163.com

Abstract. Data-driven evolutionary algorithms (DDEAs) have shown promising performance in solving small- and medium-scale expensive optimization problems (EOPs) with low and medium dimensions. However, the performance of existing DDEAs is still not good enough for large-scale EOPs. To efficiently solve the large-scale EOPs, this paper proposes a new offline DDEA based on adaptive differential evolution (DE), called ADE-DDEA. To obtain a sufficiently accurate surrogate, ADE-DDEA introduces a Latin hypercube sampling strategy with standardization for collecting data and a grid searching based approach for training the surrogate. Moreover, ADE-DDEA employs a state-of-the-art adaptive DE (i.e., the jSO) as the optimizer and a multi-loop strategy to avoid trapping into local optima. In the experiment, this paper compares ADE-DDEA with the traditional algorithms on five commonly used test functions with different dimension scales. ADE-DDEA shows significant advantages on large-scale EOPs with only 10% computational budgets of traditional methods. Even if compared with the state-of-the-art DDEAs for large-scale EOPs, ADE-DDEA shows sufficient competitiveness. Furthermore, the experimental results also show the advantage of the algorithm in terms of running time consumption.

Keywords: Expensive optimization · Large-scale optimization · Data-driven evolutionary algorithms · Adaptive differential evolutionary · Surrogates · Grid search · Multi-loop strategy

1 Introduction

Evolutionary algorithms (EAs) received a lot of attention in the past decades. They have been applied to various optimization problems [1]. Traditional EAs include genetic algorithm (GA) [2], ant colony optimization (ACO) [3], particle swarm optimization (PSO) [4], and differential evolution (DE) [5]. For EOPs, the real function evaluation (FE) is usually computationally expensive, for example, a single evaluation of computational fluid dynamics (CFD) problem can take several minutes or even hours [6]. Therefore, existing EAs for EOPs usually combine with surrogates to reduce the number of FES. These algorithms are called data-driven evolutionary algorithms (DDEAs) [7], or surrogates-assisted evolutionary algorithms (SAEAs) [8]. Specifically, the surrogates

Y. Sun et al. (Eds.): ChineseCSCW 2021, CCIS 1491, pp. 301–315, 2022.
https://doi.org/10.1007/978-981-19-4546-5_24

are trained by data (i.e., evaluated solutions) and used to predict the fitness of the solution, thus replacing the real evaluation to drive the evolution of the optimizer. Through this way, the DDEAs can reduce the number of FEs and the time budget, which makes the algorithms perform well on EOPs.

In general, the existing DDEAs can be divided into two main categories, one is the online DDEA [9–11], which usually allocates some FEs to initialize and train the surrogates and then use the remaining FEs to support the iterations of the optimizer. It means that online DDEAs require the problem context to provide FEs during the optimization process. The other is offline DDEA [12, 13], which is suitable for offline scenarios where new evaluations are not available during the algorithm's optimization process. In this paper, our algorithm is based on the framework of offline DDEAs.

For the study of DDEAs, the choice of the surrogate is a crucial issue that can significantly affect the DDEAs' performance, especially on large-scale EOPs. Various models have been adopted as the surrogate such as Gaussian process (GP) [9], polynomial regression (PR) [14], artificial neural network (ANN) [15], and radial basis function neural network (RBFNN) [12]. Since the models are with different characteristics, their estimation performances are also different. Even the same model that adopts different training methods or settings of hyper-parameters can show different performance on estimation.

Recently, several well-performing DDEAs have been proposed for EOPs. Based on the GP, Liu et al. [9] proposed an online DDEA named GPEME. GPEME utilizes the computable prediction error of GP and proposes an evaluation criterion named lower confidence bound (LCB), which not only improves the algorithm's ability to find the best solution but also makes the model gradually improve its accuracy. Li [12] proposed a boosting data-driven evolutionary algorithm (BDDEA-LDG), adopts an ensemble RBFNN model and combines a strategy of local data generation (LDG). The experimental results verify that BDDEA-LDG is well-performing than most of the existing offline DDEAs. Wang et al. [11] proposed the evolutionary sampling assisted optimization (ESAO) to solve the large-scale EOPs, which employs DE as the optimizer and includes a global RBFNN and a local one. Empirical tests show that the ESAO performs well on EOPs with higher dimensions. Wei et al. [10] proposed a classifier-assisted level-based learning swarm optimizer (CA-LLSO), which uses a gradient boosting classifier (GBC) as the surrogate and employs a level-based PSO (LLSO) as the optimizer. CA-LLSO is one of the most advanced online DDEAs currently available to solve large-scale EOPs.

There are still some weaknesses in existing offline DDEAs: 1) Lack of sufficient accurate surrogates. Firstly, traditional DDEAs perform the training process on the original data from random sampling. However, it's not a sufficient way for problems with limited training data, especially for large-scale EOPs. Secondly, the hyper-parameters of the surrogate are user-defined. But in practical terms, it is hard to predict the optimal hyper-parameters with the lack of prior knowledge of the EOPs. 2) Ignoring the performance bottleneck of traditional optimizers. In most of the existing DDEAs, it's common that the optimizers used in the optimization process are traditional EAs [9, 11]. These traditional optimizers generally work well in simple problems with lower dimensions but are inefficient in large-scale problems.

To encounter the two weaknesses above, this paper proposes ADE-DDEA. To efficiently solve the large-scale EOPs, the main process of ADE-DDEA includes three parts, i.e., the data collection, the model management, and the optimization process. In the data collection, Latin hypercube sampling (LHS) [16] is employed to sample the data. Then standardization is used for preprocessing. In the modal management, ADE-DDEA firstly adopts a grid search method to find the optimal hyper-parameter settings for the surrogate (i.e., RBFNN) and then trains the RBFNN based on the collected data. Finally, ADE-DDEA adopts a jSO optimizer with a multi-loop strategy to search for the optimal solution of the EOPs. The improvements of ADE-DDEA can be summarized as flow:

1) For the data collection process, LHS can help to get uniformly distributed training data, which enables the surrogate to accurately reflect the landscape of the solution space of the large-scale EOP. To reduce the negative effects of the scale of data, the training data is standardized before the training process of the surrogate.
2) For model management, grid search is employed to determine the hyper-parameters of the RBFNN, which can improve the efficiency and accuracy of the surrogate.
3) To efficiently solve the large-scale EOPs, a state-of-the-art adaptive DE named jSO [17] is adopted as the optimizer. Also, the multi-loop strategy is utilized to avoid occasional bottlenecks during convergence. These improvements overcome the problems of traditional optimizers facing bottlenecks on larger-scale EOPs.

The rest of this paper is organized as follows. Section 2 describes the related work, including RBFNN and jSO; Sect. 3 describes the framework of ADE-DDEA; Sect. 4 gives experimental verification of the ADE-DDEA, including comparisons with the state-of-the-art algorithms in terms of solution fitness and running time; Sect. 5 draws the conclusion.

2 Related Work

2.1 Radial Basis Function Neural Network

Among existing DDEAs for large-scale EOPs, RBFNN [11, 12] is one of the commonly used models. Among different choices of the kernels for RBFNN, the gaussian radial basis function is applied in ADE-DDEA:

$$\mathrm{R}(\mathbf{x}, \mathbf{c}) = \exp(-\frac{\|\mathbf{x} - \mathbf{c}\|^2}{2\sigma^2}), \sigma > 0 \tag{1}$$

RBFNN can be represented as a three-layer structure of input-hidden-output layers. The input layer receives the input data with D decision variables. D is the number of dimensions of the optimization problem. The hidden layer has the size of k, where each unit represents a center selected in the hidden layer space. The output layer has only one unit, which outputs the weighted sum of the values of the hidden units. The weights are denoted as $w_1, w_2, \ldots, w_k$.

For an input vector $\mathbf{x}$, the prediction value of RBFNN can be expressed as

$$\mathrm{y}(\mathbf{x}) = \sum_{i=1}^{k} w_i R(\mathbf{x}, \mathbf{c}_i)$$

$$= \sum_{i=1}^{k} w_i \exp(-\frac{\|\mathbf{x} - \mathbf{c}_i\|^2}{2\sigma^2}), \sigma > 0 \quad (2)$$

The k centers of the hidden layer and the weights are variables to be learned in the RBFNN. The specific training method will be described in the model management section of ADE-DDEA (3.2).

2.2 jSO

DE is proposed by Price and Storn et al. in 1995 [5]. In the past decades, scholars have proposed many adaptive DE variants [18] to improve the optimizing ability. JADE [19] and SHADE [20] put up adaptive control strategies for parameters *F*, *CR*. L-SHADE [21] adds adaptive control of population size based on SHADE to further improve the algorithm's performance. jSO [17] is a high-performance DE variant developed from L-SHADE. On the CEC2017 single objective benchmark [22], jSO achieved 2nd place among multiple state-of-the-art algorithms.

The mutation strategy DE/current-to-pbest-w/1 is adopted in jSO, which is shown as

$$\mathbf{v}_{i,g} = \mathbf{x}_{i,g} + F_w(\mathbf{x}_{pbest,g} - \mathbf{x}_{i,g}) + F(\mathbf{x}_{r1,g} - \mathbf{x}_{r2,g}) \quad (3)$$

Compared with DE/current-to-best/1, the second part of the new strategy provides the main improvement. It takes the historical information to drive the evolution, which enhances the optimizing ability.

For the mutation parameter *F*, the crossover parameter *CR*, and the population size *Np*, jSO adaptively controls them via different strategies, which are respectively shown in Eqs. 4, 5, 6 as

$$F_i = Gaussion(mean_a(A_{i,F}), \sigma), \sigma > 0 \quad (4)$$

$$CR_i = Cauchy(mean_l(A_{i,CR}), \sigma), \ \sigma > 0 \quad (5)$$

$$Np_g = \max((Np_{\max} - Np_{\min}) * g/g_{\max} + Np_{\min}, Np_{\min}) \quad (6)$$

The fine-tuning of *F* and *CR* is based on their historical information. The new parameters are obtained by Gaussian and Cauchy perturbations with parameter σ setting to 0.1. The population size *Np* decreases linearly during the evolution until the minimum population size is reached ($Np_{max} = 100$, $Np_{min} = 4$). With such a parameter control strategy, the algorithm can achieve a better exploration-exploitation balance, resulting in the improvement of the search capability.

3 Proposed Algorithm

3.1 ADE-DDEA Framework

This section outlines the framework of ADE-DDEA. The main components of the proposed ADE-DDEA include the data collection, the model management, and the optimization process, which are shown in Fig. 1.

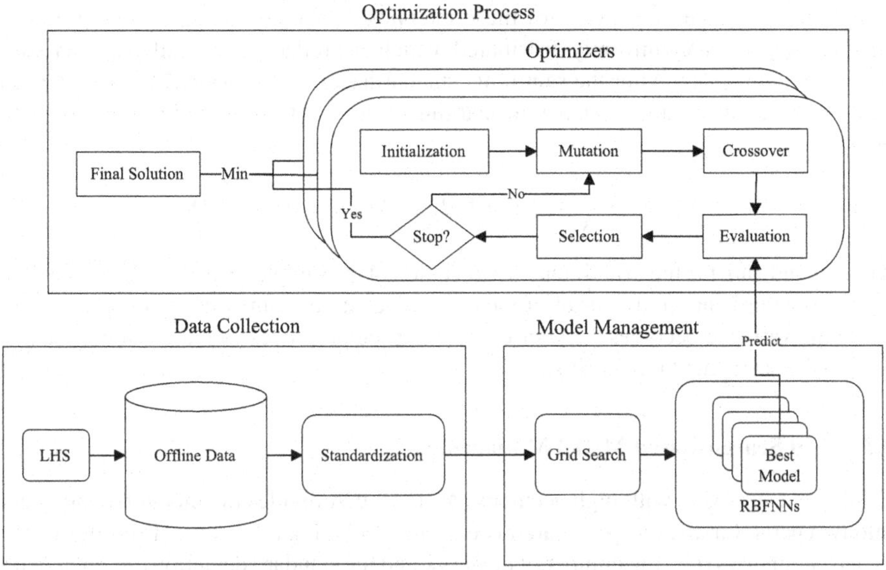

Fig. 1. ADE-DDEA framework

Step 1: Data sampling and preprocessing. In general, when solving optimization problems, we extract the objective function and the solution space from the problem. In ADE-DDEA, LHS is applied to randomly sample multiple points in the solution space. Then the sampled points are evaluated via the objective function to obtain corresponding fitness. Next, standardization is applied to preprocess the data (i.e., solutions and corresponding fitness values).

Step 2: Training of the surrogate. ADE-DDEA uses the grid search (Algorithm 1) to determine the optimal hyper-parameters of the surrogate and trains the surrogate with data collected in Step 1. The final trained surrogate is used to drive the evolutionary in Step 3.

Step 3: Optimization. ADE-DDEA uses jSO as the optimizer. It combines with the multi-loop strategy (Algorithm 2) to avoid trapping into local optima, aiming to find the optimal solution indicated by the surrogate, which is the final output of ADE-DDEA.

3.2 LHS-Based Data Collection

Under the constraints of large-scale EOPs, the number of FEs we can use is very small which is limited to 1000 in this paper. In offline DDEAs, the limited FEs are used to generate offline data before the optimizer works. The FEs cannot be required during the optimization process. To make full use of the FEs, ADE-DDEA performs the following processing.

To generate uniformly and widely distributed data, ADE-DDEA applies LHS [16] to sample data points from the solution space. LHS is a classical hierarchical sampling algorithm. It divides the sampling space into several continuous intervals with equal cumulative probabilities based on the probability distribution function. One random sample point is taken from each of these intervals to obtain the final sample set. The samples obtained are uniformly distributed, which can reflect the overall characteristics of the solution space. After the sampling, standardization [23], which is a widely used data preprocessing method in machine learning, is applied here. Its formula is expressed as

$$x_{i,d} = \frac{x_{i,d} - \mu}{s},\ i = 1, 2, ..., Np,\ d = 1, 2, ..., D \tag{7}$$

where μ and s are the mean and standard deviation of the sample set in the d-th dimension. By the standardization, the mean of the data values in the same dimension becomes 0, while the variance becomes 1. After completing the preprocessing, the training data is feed to the surrogate in the next step.

3.3 Grid Search-Based Model Management

To obtain a surrogate with high accuracy, ADE-DDEA divides the model management into two parts. Firstly, the grid search is executed to find out the optimal settings of the hyper-parameters (i.e., the number of centers k and the standard deviation σ). Then, with the optimal hyper-parameters, the training process of RBFNN is executed on the whole training data.

The RBFNN in ADE-DDEA requires two user-defined hyper-parameters. One is the number of centers k, which is also the number of nodes in the hidden layer. The other is the σ brought by the Gaussian radial basis function (Eq. 1). Both two hyper-parameters can affect the performance of the surrogate.

ADE-DDEA adopts grid search to find out the optimal settings of the two hyper-parameters mentioned above. Grid search is a simple but effective method for hyper-parameter optimization in situations where the training is not complex or time-consuming. This approach iterates through the candidate parameter combinations and measures the model performance by 5-fold validation and coefficient of determination [24]. When considering the hyper-parameter settings, ADE-DDEA uses *gamma* to denote the fraction of coefficient where σ is located ($gamma = 1/2\sigma^2$). In the experiments, the range of k is between 2 and 200, and *gamma* is between 0.01 and 100. The detailed process of grid search is shown in Algorithm 1.

After the grid search, RBFNN with the optimal hyper-parameter settings will be retrained on the whole training data. Its training process is described as follows:

Step 1: Calculate the clustering centers of sample points. K-means is a classical unsupervised learning algorithm for clustering tasks. It is employed to learn the clustering centers in the training process.

Step 2: Calculate the optimal weights with the least square method. The loss function of RBFNN is shown in Eq. 8. Compared to the gradient descent method, learning with the least square method is simple, straightforward, and efficient.

$$\mathrm{E} = \frac{1}{2}\sum_{i=1}^{Np}\sum_{j=1}^{k}(y_i - w_j R(\mathbf{x}_i, \mathbf{c}_j))^2 \tag{8}$$

Algorithm 1 Grid Search

```
Input: CP –a set of different combinations of candidate hyper-parameter;
       Fitness_train –the fitness corresponding to the individuals in the training data
Output: Model_best – the best model
Begin
Define the empty set Scores;
// Grid search
For each para_i in CP Do
    Score_i = 0;
    Randomly divide [X_train, Fitness_train] into 5 parts equally;
    For j=1:5 Do // Perform 5-fold verification
        Use [X_train, Y_train]_j as the validation set and the rest as the training set;
        Initialize the model model_ij using the parameter para_i;
        Train model_ij on the training set;
        Test model_ij and get the performance score as S_ij;
        Score_i = Score_i + S_ij;
    End For
    Scores = Scores ∪ (Score_i / 5); // record the score under 5-fold validation
End for
Find the hyper-parameter with best performance according to Scores, note as para_best;
// Training process
Retrain model with para_best on the whole training data, getting Model_best;
End
```

3.4 Multi-loop-Based Optimization Process

In the optimization process, traditional DDEAs usually employ simple EAs as the optimizers, which has insufficient performance for optimization on larger-scale problems reaching 50–300 dimensions. Therefore, ADE-DDEA applies a high-performance adaptive DE (i.e., jSO) as the optimizer.

The multi-loop strategy is used to overcome occasional bottlenecks during the optimization process. This strategy employs the jSO optimizer to perform multiple loops to find the optima of the trained RBFNN. For EAs which converge fast like jSO, it is easy to be trapped into local optima for problems above 100 dimensions, especially for problems with multiple peaks in the solution space. To avoid these occasional errors, a simple and intuitive approach is to employ a multi-loop strategy to let the optimizer repeat the search process and compare the results to get the best final solution. The pseudo-code is shown in Algorithm 2.

Algorithm 2 Multi-loop Strategy

Input: N_{op} – the number of optimizers; *Model* – the trained model; g_{max} – the maximum iteration number; *Np* – the initial population size
Output: $Solution_{best}$ – the final solution
Begin
$Fitness_{best}$=*MAX*;
For $i = 1{:}N_{op}$ **Do**
  Initialize $\boldsymbol{x}_g$ randomly, $g = 0$, $Fitness_g$=$Model(x_g)$; // Initialization
  While $g < g_{max}$ **Do**
    Execute mutation operation;
    Execute crossover operation;
    Execute greedy selection, get new $\boldsymbol{x}_g$ and fitness $Fitness_g$;
    Update $Fitness_{best}$, note the corresponding solution as $Solution_{best}$;
    $g = g + 1$;
    Update parameters; // (Equations 4, 5, 6)
  End while
End for
End

4 Experiment Result and Discussion

4.1 Experimental Settings

The experiment is performed on common test functions for EOPs: Ellipsoid, Rosenbrock, Ackley, Griewank, and Rastrigin [10–12]. The Ellipsoid problem is a unimodal function and the rest are multimodal functions while they all have the same optimal value of 0 as shown in Table 1.

Table 1. Test functions

Function	Optima	Domain	Note
Ellipsoid	0	[−5.12, 5.12]	Unimodal
Rosenbrock	0	[−2.048, 2.048]	Multimodal
Ackley	0	[−32.768, 32.768]	Multimodal
Griewank	0	[−600, 600]	Multimodal
Rastrigin	0	[−5, 5]	Multimodal

For brevity's sake, the test problems below are abbreviated in the form of problem type + dimension, for example, E20 denotes the Ellipsoid problem of dimension 20. To distinguish the Rosenbrock problem from the Rastrigin problem, the latter one is abbreviated as RA. The algorithms run on a platform of Windows 10/python 3.8, and the CPU is Intel Core i7-8700. To reduce statistical errors, all algorithms are tested 20 times independently on each problem and the average result is recorded.

4.2 Comparisons with the Traditional Algorithms

This section is comparisons with traditional EAs for large-scale EOPs. The algorithms to compare are random sampling, the classical DE/rand/1, and jSO. The FEs limitation for the latter two is set to 10000 in order to obtain valuable results. The initial population size *Np* is set to 100. The other parameters are set with reference to the theoretical section above.

Table 2. Comparisons between ADE-DDEA and traditional algorithms

Problem	ADE-DDEA	Random sample	DE/rand/1	jSO
E20	1.19E+0 ± 5.54E−1	8.81E+2 ± 1.17E+2(+)	2.19E+2 ± 3.81E+1(+)	**3.19E−4 ± 5.32E−4(−)**
E30	5.94E+0 ± 4.01E+0	2.20E+3 ± 2.27E+2(+)	9.24E+2 ± 1.73E+2(+)	**6.61E−2 ± 1.14E−1(−)**
E50	**1.52E+0 ± 2.31E+0**	7.02E+3 ± 5.49E+2(+)	4.30E+3 ± 5.00E+2(+)	3.09E+0 ± 1.29E+0(+)
E100	**1.32E+1 ± 3.58E+1**	3.29E+4 ± 1.90E+3(+)	2.40E+4 ± 1.75E+3(+)	1.37E+2 ± 3.02E+1(+)
E150	**1.04E+1 ± 7.58E+0**	7.81E+4 ± 3.33E+3(+)	6.03E+4 ± 4.77E+3(+)	6.41E+2 ± 1.17E+2(+)
E200	**3.43E+1 ± 1.04E+1**	1.44E+5 ± 3.16E+3(+)	1.10E+5 ± 9.00E+3(+)	1.63E+3 ± 2.08E+2(+)
E300	**3.55E+2 ± 8.38E+1**	3.36E+5 ± 7.76E+3(+)	2.60E+5 ± 2.51E+4(+)	5.78E+3 ± 4.53E+2(+)
R20	1.05E+2 ± 5.05E+0	3.16E+3 ± 6.94E+2(+)	7.61E+2 ± 1.33E+2(+)	**1.76E+1 ± 2.10E−1(−)**
R30	1.56E+2 ± 6.54E+0	6.50E+3 ± 8.16E+2(+)	2.53E+3 ± 3.36E+2(+)	**2.80E+1 ± 4.90E−1(−)**
R50	2.55E+2 ± 6.85E+0	1.32E+4 ± 1.31E+3(+)	7.15E+3 ± 8.79E+2(+)	**5.55E+1 ± 4.07E+0(−)**
R100	4.66E+2 ± 2.23E+1	3.28E+4 ± 2.15E+3(+)	2.13E+4 ± 1.90E+3(+)	**1.70E+2 ± 2.01E+1(−)**
R150	5.95E+2 ± 2.92E+1	5.22E+4 ± 2.61E+3(+)	3.80E+4 ± 4.58E+3(+)	**3.92E+2 ± 5.31E+1(−)**
R200	6.37E+2 ± 3.20E+1	7.41E+4 ± 3.14E+3(+)	5.38E+4 ± 5.37E+3(+)	**5.75E+2 ± 6.01E+1(−)**
R300	**6.72E+2 ± 4.28E+1**	1.17E+5 ± 5.07E+3(+)	7.93E+4 ± 9.05E+3(+)	1.08E+3 ± 8.81E+1(+)
A20	1.44E+0 ± 1.15E+0	2.04E+1 ± 2.00E−1(+)	1.78E+1 ± 6.66E−1(+)	**2.58E−2 ± 1.77E−2(−)**
A30	1.96E+0 ± 1.48E+0	2.06E+1 ± 1.46E−1(+)	1.93E+1 ± 3.86E−1(+)	**5.18E−1 ± 4.46E−1(−)**
A50	**2.13E+0 ± 1.46E+0**	2.08E+1 ± 8.66E−2(+)	2.01E+1 ± 2.45E−1(+)	2.80E+0 ± 6.42E−1(≈)
A100	**1.92E+0 ± 1.26E+0**	2.09E+1 ± 7.15E−2(+)	2.06E+1 ± 7.72E−2(+)	5.92E+0 ± 3.74E−1(+)
A150	**2.22E+0 ± 1.00E+0**	2.10E+1 ± 4.53E−2(+)	2.07E+1 ± 9.45E−2(+)	7.69E+0 ± 7.32E−1(+)
A200	**2.37E+0 ± 8.38E−1**	2.11E+1 ± 4.38E−2(+)	2.08E+1 ± 1.25E−1(+)	8.42E+0 ± 4.66E−1(+)
A300	**3.71E+0 ± 3.95E−1**	2.11E+1 ± 3.30E−2(+)	2.08E+1 ± 1.01E−1(+)	9.66E+0 ± 3.18E−1(+)
G20	4.59E−1 ± 1.15E−1	3.15E+2 ± 3.04E+1(+)	1.11E+2 ± 1.44E+1(+)	**3.37E−2 ± 2.72E−2(−)**
G30	8.26E−1 ± 1.34E−1	5.51E+2 ± 5.36E+1(+)	2.92E+2 ± 2.44E+1(+)	**7.41E−1 ± 1.92E−1(≈)**
G50	**1.01E+0 ± 2.09E−2**	1.04E+3 ± 6.12E+1(+)	6.67E+2 ± 6.14E+1(+)	1.50E+0 ± 1.10E−1(+)
G100	**1.20E+0 ± 4.06E−2**	2.29E+3 ± 1.32E+2(+)	1.76E+3 ± 1.24E+2(+)	1.23E+1 ± 2.97E+0(+)
G150	**1.28E+0 ± 1.85E−1**	3.67E+3 ± 1.27E+2(+)	2.88E+3 ± 2.52E+2(+)	3.68E+1 ± 7.50E+0(+)
G200	**1.79E+0 ± 2.11E−1**	5.09E+3 ± 8.86E+1(+)	4.00E+3 ± 3.43E+2(+)	7.60E+1 ± 1.14E+1(+)
G300	**8.67E+0 ± 1.09E+0**	7.85E+3 ± 2.16E+2(+)	5.89E+3 ± 4.86E+2(+)	1.57E+2 ± 1.06E+1(+)
RA20	**1.83E+1 ± 4.10E+1**	2.52E+2 ± 2.50E+1(+)	1.82E+2 ± 7.64E+0(+)	4.98E+1 ± 1.78E+1(+)
RA30	**3.06E+1 ± 4.18E+1**	4.11E+2 ± 2.38E+1(+)	3.19E+2 ± 1.73E+1(+)	1.11E+2 ± 2.16E+1(+)
RA50	**1.86E+1 ± 1.99E+1**	7.30E+2 ± 2.57E+1(+)	6.11E+2 ± 2.12E+1(+)	2.63E+2 ± 4.21E+1(+)
RA100	**4.42E+1 ± 4.20E+1**	1.58E+3 ± 4.99E+1(+)	1.40E+3 ± 2.96E+1(+)	6.02E+2 ± 2.98E+1(+)

(*continued*)

Table 2. (*continued*)

Problem	ADE-DDEA	Random sample	DE/rand/1	jSO
RA150	**4.40E+1 ± 5.29E+1**	2.43E+3 ± 4.21E+1(+)	2.22E+3 ± 5.50E+1(+)	9.97E+2 ± 1.38E+2(+)
RA200	**1.55E+2 ± 1.94E+2**	3.31E+3 ± 5.92E+1(+)	3.02E+3 ± 6.65E+1(+)	1.36E+3 ± 8.45E+1(+)
RA300	**3.74E+2 ± 1.28E+2**	5.07E+3 ± 6.73E+1(+)	4.63E+3 ± 1.26E+2(+)	1.97E+3 ± 2.18E+2(+)
+/≈/−	–	35/0/0	35/0/0	22/2/11

Table 2 shows the results of the comparison experiments between ADE-DDEA and the random sampling (1000 FEs), DE (10000 FEs), jSO (10000 FEs). Wilcoxon's rank-sum test is adopted to compare the experimental data at a significance level of 0.05. The notations +/≈/− in the last row represent the number of the results that ADE-DDEA is significantly better, similar, or worse.

From the experimental results overall, the ADE-DDEA outperforms the traditional EAs as well as the random sampling. Compared to jSO, ADE-DDEA performs worse on 11 problems, mainly on the lower dimensional problems. But on the other 22 problems, ADE-DDEA gets better results. This experiment demonstrates the great advantage of ADE-DDEA over traditional algorithms for large-scale EOPs.

4.3 Comparisons with Offline Data-Driven Evolutionary Algorithm

BDDEA-LDG [12] is one of the state-of-the-art offline DDEAs. It uses the same test function as in this paper. The comparison is mainly performed in 4 dimensions of 10, 30, 50, and 100. Only 11*D FEs are available. To set up a fair experiment, this section is under the same setting as the paper of BDDEA-LDG.

Table 3. Comparisons between ADE-DDEA and BDDEA-LDG

Problem	ADE-DDEA	BDDEA-LDG
E10	2.36E+00 ± 1.63E+00	**1.33E+00 ± 4.59E−01(−)**
E30	8.90E+00 ± 1.31E+01	**5.95E+00 ± 2.22E+00(≈)**
E50	**2.97E+00 ± 4.06E+00**	1.39E+01 ± 3.12E+00(+)
E100	**3.75E+00 ± 5.00E+00**	6.14E+01 ± 1.46E+01(+)
R10	7.11E+01 ± 1.87E+01	**3.69E+01 ± 8.73E+00(−)**
R30	1.73E+02 ± 1.38E+01	**6.65E+01 ± 6.36E+00(−)**
R50	2.66E+02 ± 2.10E+01	**9.69E+01 ± 5.70E+00(−)**
R100	4.76E+02 ± 1.94E+01	**2.06E+02 ± 2.47E+01(−)**
A10	**4.58E+00 ± 2.03E+00**	7.61E+00 ± 9.30E−01(+)
A30	**3.05E+00 ± 1.49E+00**	5.80E+00 ± 3.74E−01(+)
A50	**2.57E+00 ± 1.17E+00**	5.23E+00 ± 3.33E−01(+)

(*continued*)

Table 3. (*continued*)

Problem	ADE-DDEA	BDDEA-LDG
A100	**2.04E+00 ± 1.67E+00**	4.63E+00 ± 2.63E−01(+)
G10	**7.85E−01 ± 2.31E−01**	1.42E+00 ± 2.65E−01(+)
G30	**1.00E+00 ± 7.42E−02**	1.36E+00 ± 8.13E−02(+)
G50	**1.06E+00 ± 1.95E−02**	1.49E+00 ± 7.99E−02(+)
G100	**1.19E+00 ± 3.18E−02**	1.89E+00 ± 1.77E−01(+)
RA10	**2.19E+01 ± 2.62E+01**	7.16E+01 ± 1.28E+01(+)
RA30	**4.42E+01 ± 5.67E+01**	1.46E+02 ± 2.72E+01(+)
RA50	**4.04E+01 ± 4.76E+01**	1.90E+02 ± 3.17E+01(+)
RA100	**4.75E+01 ± 5.43E+01**	3.20E+02 ± 7.53E+01(+)
+/≈/−	–	14/1/5

Table 3 shows the experimental results of ADE-DDEA and BDDEA-LDG. From the overall 20 test problems, both the algorithms can get close to the global optima on most problems. BDDEA-LDG significantly outperforms ADE-DDEA on 5 problems which mainly are the problems of low dimensions and the Rosenbrock problems. It is reflected that possible underfit exists in the surrogates in ADE-DDEA. On the other 14 test functions, ADE-DDEA significantly outperforms BDDEA-LDG, demonstrating the superior performance of ADE-DDEA as an offline DDEA for large-scale EOPs.

4.4 Comparisons with Online Data-Driven Evolutionary Algorithm

In the field of large-scale EOPs, CA-LLSO [10] is one of the best online DDEAs, which uses a gradient boosting classifier (GBC) as the surrogate and a level-based PSO variant (LLSO) as the optimizer to achieve good optimization results with only 1000 FEs. In this section, ADE-DDEA is compared with CA-LLSO.

Table 4. Comparisons between ADE-DDEA and CA-LLSO

Problems	ADE-DDEA	CA-LLSO
E20	1.19E+00 ± 5.54E−01	**4.15E−01 ± 3.33E−01(−)**
E30	5.94E+00 ± 4.01E+00	**4.93E+00 ± 3.14E+00(≈)**
E50	**1.52E+00 ± 2.31E+00**	5.93E+01 ± 1.30E+01(+)
E100	**1.32E+01 ± 3.58E+01**	9.70E+02 ± 1.23E+02(+)
E150	**1.04E+01 ± 7.58E+00**	3.83E+03 ± 4.05E+02(+)
E200	**3.43E+01 ± 1.04E+01**	9.36E+03 ± 7.21E+02(+)

(*continued*)

Table 4. (*continued*)

Problems	ADE-DDEA	CA-LLSO
E300	**3.55E+02 ± 8.38E+01**	2.88E+04 ± 2.24E+03(+)
R20	1.05E+02 ± 5.05E+00	**1.87E+01 ± 8.17E−01(−)**
R30	1.56E+02 ± 6.54E+00	**3.46E+01 ± 4.63E+00(−)**
R50	2.55E+02 ± 6.85E+00	**9.24E+01 ± 8.99E+00(−)**
R100	4.66E+02 ± 2.23E+01	**4.57E+02 ± 2.38E+01(≈)**
R150	**5.95E+02 ± 2.92E+01**	1.09E+03 ± 1.24E+02(+)
R200	**6.37E+02 ± 3.20E+01**	1.88E+03 ± 1.20E+02(+)
R300	**6.72E+02 ± 4.28E+01**	3.83E+03 ± 2.10E+02(+)
A20	1.44E+00 ± 1.15E+00	**1.13E+00 ± 6.77E−01(≈)**
A30	**1.96E+00 ± 1.48E+00**	3.09E+00 ± 6.52E−01(+)
A50	**2.13E+00 ± 1.46E+00**	6.47E+00 ± 4.74E−01(+)
A100	**1.92E+00 ± 1.26E+00**	1.12E+01 ± 2.94E−01(+)
A150	**2.22E+00 ± 1.00E+00**	1.26E+01 ± 4.23E−01(+)
A200	**2.37E+00 ± 8.38E−01**	1.38E+01 ± 2.66E−01(+)
A300	**3.71E+00 ± 3.95E−01**	1.49E+01 ± 2.53E−01(+)
G20	**4.59E−01 ± 1.15E−01**	6.40E−01 ± 2.50E−01(+)
G30	**8.26E−01 ± 1.34E−01**	1.32E+00 ± 2.35E−01(+)
G50	**1.01E+00 ± 2.09E−02**	8.33E+00 ± 1.34E+00(+)
G100	**1.20E+00 ± 4.06E−02**	7.33E+01 ± 1.22E+01(+)
G150	**1.28E+00 ± 1.85E−01**	2.09E+02 ± 1.19E+01(+)
G200	**1.79E+00 ± 2.11E−01**	3.48E+02 ± 2.32E+01(+)
G300	**8.67E+00 ± 1.09E+00**	7.45E+02 ± 3.16E+01(+)
RA20	**1.83E+01 ± 4.10E+01**	6.93E+01 ± 2.33E+01(+)
RA30	**3.06E+01 ± 4.18E+01**	1.52E+02 ± 3.15E+01(+)
RA50	**1.86E+01 ± 1.99E+01**	3.56E+02 ± 1.53E+01(+)
RA100	**4.42E+01 ± 4.20E+01**	8.28E+02 ± 4.07E+01(+)
RA150	**4.40E+01 ± 5.29E+01**	1.35E+03 ± 3.85E+01(+)
RA200	**1.55E+02 ± 1.94E+02**	1.84E+03 ± 5.99E+01(+)
RA300	**3.74E+02 ± 1.28E+02**	2.90E+03 ± 5.03E+01(+)
+/≈/−	–	28/3/4

The results of the comparison experiments are presented in Table 4. From the overall experimental results, ADE-DDEA significantly outperforms CA-LLSO on 28 of the 35 problems, makes no difference on 3 problems, and behaves worse on the rest 4 test problems. This demonstrates that ADE-DDEA has greater performance on the experimental problems comparing with the state-of-the-art online DDEA.

4.5 Running Time Test

This section records the running time of ADE-DDEA. The algorithm for comparison is CA-LLSO, which can be run on the same platform and code environment (python 3.8), ensuring the fairness of the experiment. Since both the algorithms use the same number of FEs and consume the same time for the function evaluation part, the experiments here mainly consider the time consumed beside the FEs. The experiment ran on the Ellipsoid problem, whose actual time budget is negligible (1000 function evaluations take less than 0.01 s). The algorithms ran on the same platform three times independently to record the time consumed, and the results were averaged.

Table 5. Running time (second)

Dimension	Total	Training	Optimizing	CA-LLSO
20	**63.88**	34.86	29.01	83.47
30	**63.61**	35.06	28.54	97.57
50	**68.56**	40.75	28.81	236.39
100	**92.07**	64.25	27.82	390.94
150	**110.86**	82.81	28.06	549.43
200	**139.01**	110.74	28.26	712.88
300	**185.30**	155.46	29.84	1026.93

The experimental results are recorded in Table 5. The total time taken by ADE-DDEA ranges from about 1 min in 20 dimensions to 3 min in 300 dimensions, which is acceptable in terms of time and variation with dimensions. CA-LLSO takes longer time than ADE-DDEA in all dimensions due to the online mode. And it even takes more than 10 min for problems with dimensions more than 200, which is worse than ADE-DDEA. This demonstrates the excellent time complexity performance of ADE-DDEA. Of course, for an algorithm oriented to EOPs, the running time of the algorithm itself is often negligible comparing the real evaluation time in practical application.

5 Conclusion

In this paper, we propose a new algorithm ADE-DDEA for large-scale EOPs. To get an accurate surrogate, ADE-DDEA firstly uses LHS to get the training data that is uniformly distributed and then preprocesses the data by standardization. Secondly, ADE-DDEA utilizes the grid search approach to select the optimal hyper-parameters. To make full use of the surrogate and avoids the problem of falling into local optima, ADE-DDEA combines the jSO with the proposed multi-loop strategy for cooperative search in the optimization process. The experimental part shows that ADE-DDEA has an excellent performance in the field of large-scale EOPs.

Of course, the algorithm still has some shortcomings. Its optimizing ability is still inadequate on a few test functions and low-dimensional problems where a single model might be underfitting. These problems should be considered in the further research.

Acknowledgments. This work was supported in part by the National Key Research and Development Program of China under Grant 2019YFB2102102, in part by the National Natural Science Foundations of China (NSFC) under Grants 62176094, 61822602, 61772207, and 61873097, in part by the Key-Area Research and Development of Guangdong Province under Grant 2020B010166002, in part by the Guangdong Natural Science Foundation Research Team under Grant 2018B030312003 3, and in part by the Guangdong-Hong Kong Joint Innovation Platform under Grant 2018B050502006.

References

1. Fleming, P., Purshouse, R.: Evolutionary algorithms in control systems engineering: a survey. Control Eng. Pract. **10**(11), 1223–1241 (2002)
2. Whitley, D.: A genetic algorithm tutorial. Stat. Comput. **4**(2), 65–85 (1994). https://doi.org/10.1007/BF00175354
3. Dorigo, M., Christian, B.: Ant colony optimization theory: a survey. Theor. Comput. Sci. **344**(2), 243–278 (2005)
4. Kennedy, J., Eberhart, R.: Particle swarm optimization. In: Proceedings of ICNN 1995 - International Conference on Neural Networks, pp. 1942–1948. IEEE (1995)
5. Storn, R., Kenneth, P.: Differential evolution – a simple and efficient heuristic for global optimization over continuous spaces. J. Global Optim. **11**(4), 341–359 (1997). https://doi.org/10.1023/A:1008202821328
6. Jin, Y., Sendhoff, B.: A systems approach to evolutionary multiobjective structural optimization and beyond. IEEE Comput. Intell. Mag. **4**(3), 62–76 (2009)
7. Jin, Y., Wang, H., Chugh, T., Guo, D., Miettinen, K.: Data-driven evolutionary optimization: an overview and case studies. IEEE Trans. Evol. Comput. **23**(3), 442–458 (2019)
8. Jin, Y.: Surrogate-assisted evolutionary computation: recent advances and future challenges. Swarm Evol. Comput. **1**(2), 61–70 (2011)
9. Liu, B., Zhang, Q., Gielen, G.: A Gaussian process surrogate model assisted evolutionary algorithm for medium scale expensive optimization problems. IEEE Trans. Evol. Comput. **18**(2), 180–192 (2014)
10. Wei, F., et al.: A classifier-assisted level-based learning swarm optimizer for expensive optimization. IEEE Trans. Evol. Comput. **25**(2), 219–233 (2021)
11. Wang, X., Wang, G., Song, B., Wang, P., Wang, Y.: A novel evolutionary sampling assisted optimization method for high-dimensional expensive problems. IEEE Trans. Evol. Comput. **23**(5), 815–827 (2019)
12. Li, J., Zhan, Z., Wang, C., Jin, H., Zhang, J.: Boosting data-driven evolutionary algorithm with localized data generation. IEEE Trans. Evol. Comput. **24**(5), 923–937 (2020)
13. Wang, H., Jin, Y., Sun, C., Doherty, J.: Offline data-driven evolutionary optimization using selective surrogate ensembles. IEEE Trans. Evol. Comput. **23**(2), 203–216 (2019)

14. Zhou, Z., Ong, Y., Nguyen, M., Lim, D.: A study on polynomial regression and Gaussian process global surrogate model in hierarchical surrogate-assisted evolutionary algorithm. In: Proceedings of 2005 IEEE Conference on Evolutionary Computation, pp. 2832–2839. IEEE (2005)
15. Nessrine, A., Slim, B., Lamjed, B.: Steady state IBEA assisted by MLP neural networks for expensive multi-objective optimization problems. In: Proceedings of the 2014 Annual Conference on Genetic and Evolutionary Computation, pp. 581–588. ACM (2014)
16. Stein, M.: Large sample properties of simulations using Latin hypercube sampling. Technometrics **29**(2), 143–151 (1987)
17. Brest, J., Maučec, M., Bošković, B.: Single objective real-parameter optimization: algorithm jSO. In: Proceedings of 2017 IEEE Congress on Evolutionary Computation, pp. 1311–1318. IEEE (2017)
18. Das, S., Suganthan, P.: Differential evolution: a survey of the state-of-the-art. IEEE Trans. Evol. Comput. **15**(1), 27–54 (2011)
19. Zhang, J., Sanderson, A.: JADE: adaptive differential evolution with optional external archive. IEEE Trans. Evol. Comput. **13**(5), 945–958 (2009)
20. Tanabe, R., Fukunaga, A.: Success-history based parameter adaptation for differential evolution. In: Proceedings of 2013 IEEE Congress on Evolutionary Computation, pp. 71–78. IEEE (2013)
21. Tanabe, R., Fukunaga, A.: Improving the search performance of SHADE using linear population size reduction. In: Proceedings of 2014 IEEE Congress on Evolutionary Computation, pp, 1658–1665. IEEE (2014)
22. Awad, N., Ali, M., Liang, B., Suganthan, P.: Problem definitions and evaluation criteria for the CEC 2017 special session and competition on single objective bound constrained real-parameter numerical optimization. Technical report, Nanyang Technological University, Singapore (2016)
23. Shanker, M., Hu, M., Hung, M.: Effect of data standardization on neural network training. Omega **24**(4), 385–397 (1996)
24. Chicco, D., Warrens, M., Jurman, G.: The coefficient of determination R-squared is more informative than SMAPE, MAE, MAPE, MSE and RMSE in regression analysis evaluation. PeerJ Comput. Sci. **7**, e623 (2021)

Sentiment Analysis of Chinese Complex Long Sentences Based on Reinforcement Learning

Chaoli Zhang[1], Zhenjie Yu[1], Dazhen Lin[1], and Donglin Cao[1,2](✉)

[1] Artificial Intelligence Department, Xiamen University, Xiamen 361005, China
another@xmu.edu.cn

[2] The Key Laboratory of Cognitive Computing and Intelligent Information Processing of Fujian Education Institutions, WuYi University, Wuyishan 354300, China

Abstract. Sentiment Analysis is a hot topic of Natural Language Processing (NLP). There have been relatively good solutions to general sentiment analysis problems, but in the face of the complex long sentences and the change of sentence sentiments such as transition and progression, it is very difficult to effectively learn the sentiment changes of long sentences based on deep learning methods. So we propose an approach named Reinforcement Learning for Long Sentence Classification (RL4LSC), a method based on reinforcement learning, to automatically identify the sentiment transitions of sentences and output the local sentiment tendency of each specific location and give the intensity of the sentiment tendency. Experiment results show that RL4LSC not only outperforms the state-of-the-art methods, BiLSTM and TextCNN, but also outputs the sentiment change of each word in a sentence through Reinforcement Learning.

Keywords: Sentiment analysis · Reinforcement learning · Chinese complex long sentences

1 Introduction

Currently, the development of deep learning technology has greatly improved the effect of sentiment analysis task. At the same time, however, the sentiment analysis of Chinese complex long sentence can't be solved very well. Generally, there are two main difficulties in the sentiment analysis of Chinese complex long sentences. On the one hand, because of the length of long sentence, general classification algorithms can't capture the common features of the sentence with sentiment transition. On the another hand, at present, the state-of-the-art sentiment analysis methods of complex long sentence even consider the lexical structure information of complex long sentence, it is difficult to make full use of powerful learning ability of neural network. This is because many existing works rely on manual rules and pre-defined lexical structure analysis model to identify

Y. Sun et al. (Eds.): ChineseCSCW 2021, CCIS 1491, pp. 316–326, 2022.
https://doi.org/10.1007/978-981-19-4546-5_25

lexical structure, and do not combine the goal of lexical structure analysis and sentiment analysis closely. The problems above bring a great challenge to the sentiment analysis of Chinese complex long sentence. Generally, deep learning based methods for the sentiment classification model only focus on the sentence level sentiment, but the sentiment information or the sentiment tendency in words are not used. We suggest that the sentiment words of a complex long sentence can help the model learn the sentiment variation in a long sentence, understand the text and explain the predict result. Therefore, from the perspective of understanding the sentence meaning structure and capturing sentiment turn, we design a model to solve the sentiment analysis problem of Chinese complex long sentence. In this paper, our contributions are as follows:

(1) We propose a model based on Reinforcement Learning which combine the word level sentiment and the whole sentence level sentiment to predict the sentiment of Chinese complex long sentence.
(2) We can easily visualize the sentiment of a complex long sentence and obtain the interpretability of the predict results to use the method proposed by us.

2 Related Work

Traditional machine learning methods usually rely on sentiment dictionaries to provide the sentiment orientation information of the words [1]. There are some state-of-the-art sentiment dictionaries including HowNet Sentiment Dictionary [2], Student Testimonial and Derogatory Dictionary [3] and Testimonial and Derogatory Dictionary [4]. These works use the sentiment tendency of words, which is marked in the dictionary, as features. In the traditional machine learning methods [1,6–8] based methods, sentiment tendency of a word is used as features at the same time. The method processes the features to achieve the purpose of classification.

Currently, deep learning methods were used in sentiment analysis and achieved significant improvement. The Word2Vec [9] method obtains the vector representation of each word in a sentence by means of pre-training. By using the vector representation of words, the deep learning model can better understand the context between words and the overall sentence mean. Convolutional Neural Network [10] is used to extract sentence level semantic vector from word representation vector and predict the sentiment. Meanwhile, Recurrent Neural Network [11] is also an important method which combines context information to learn the overall semantics. Long-Short Term Memory Network [12] is an improved method of Recurrent Neural Network which introduces control gates to avoid gradient disappear. Gated Recurrent Unit [13] improves its performance [14] to discard useless control gates compared with LSTM. Bidirectional Long-Short Term Memory Network combines the information from back to front into the model. Hierarchical Recurrent Neural Network [15] cuts complex long sentences into short ones, extracts the sentence meaning information of each short sentence by using a recurrent neural network, and synthesizes the information of all sentences by using a recurrent neural network to get the overall information.

Transformer [16] and BERT integrate the full-text information by global self-attention mechanism. Since then, some models have been further improved on the basis of BERT [17–20]. Another part of the recent works introduce external knowledge to help the model make correct judgments [21,22].

Reinforcement learning is an important branch of machine learning. Reinforcement learning is mainly divided into Deep Q Network [23] and Actor Critic method [24]. Wiering et al. [25] modeled the text classification task as a sequence problem and used the Actor Critic algorithm to solve it. Chen et al. [26] used reinforcement learning method to analyze text sentiment at word level. In recent work, reinforcement learning method is also used to overcome the imbalance of data sets [27] in the field of sentiment analysis.

In the sentiment classification task of complex long sentences, we need to get the sentiment tendency of a sentence, or get the sentiment change tendency of the whole text for more in-depth data analysis. However, the deep learning based methods can not capture the structure information of a complex long sentence. In this paper, we propose RL4LSC which uses reinforcement learning to capture the structure information and model the sentiment change for Chinese complex long sentences.

3 Method

In this section, we give the problem definition of sentiment classification in complex long sentence in Sect. 3.1. We define the RL4LSC model and implementation detail in the Sect. 3.2.

3.1 Problem Definition

The problem or target can be decomposed into two sub-tasks:

Global Sentiment Classification. The RL4LSC predicts the sentiment tendency of the entire sentence.

Local Sentiment Classification. The RL4LSC predicts the sentiment tendency of each word in a sentence.

3.2 Our Approach

Our RL4LSC is shown in Fig. 1, which consists of four parts.

Pretreatment. Specially, we set the original Chinese character input as $x = [c_1, c_2, ..., c_l]$ and limit text length not to exceed 240. Our RL4LSC uses BERT as feature extractor and the word embedding sequence is obtained as $x^e = [e_1, e_2, e_3, ..., e_l]$.

State Coder. Sequence $x^e = [e_1, e_2, e_3, ..., e_l]$ is used as the input of the subsequent feature encoder. In order to recognize the words appearing in the sentiment dictionary, we need to operate word segmentation at the same time to get the

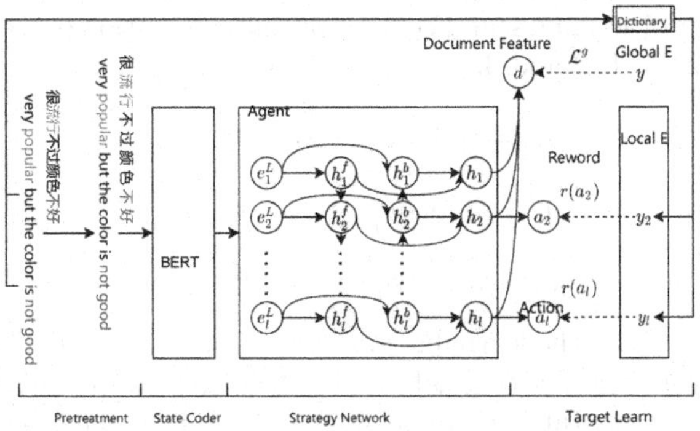

Fig. 1. Sentiment classification model of the long text based on Reinforcement Learning. The green part of the sentence is the positive words in the sentiment dictionary, and the red part is the negative words in the sentiment dictionary. Only the words appearing in the sentiment dictionary are used to predict the sentiment of words when model learns target. (Color figure online)

word sequence as $x^w = [w_1, w_2, w_3, ..., w_l]$.For every word w_i which appears in the sentiment dictionary whose details are shown in Table 1, we find out the word sequence of its corresponding position, and mark the words in the sequence with the same sentiment tendency y_i.

Strategy Network. The strategy network is used to make the model predict the sentiment tendency of sentences in every local position. The reinforcement learning algorithm based on policy gradient needs to define an agent, which inputs state and outputs action in the environment, obtains feedback and updates its own state. In the RL4LSC, the input of an agent is the output sequence of the feature encoder $[e_1, e_2, e_3, ..., e_l]$ and the output of an agent is a F-dimensional state sequence $[h_1, h_2, h_3, ..., h_l]$. Meanwhile, agents need to take corresponding actions $[a_1, a_2, a_3, ..., a_l]$ in every position of the sequence through the state sequence.

Table 1. Sentiment analysis dictionary data

Class	Number
Positive sentiment word	838
Positive comment word	3732
Negative sentiment word	1256
Negative comment word	3118
Sum	8944

The RL4LSC uses Bi-LSTM as the main agent and the memory c_i of LSTM is responsible for remembering the current state of the agent. Specially, for the input e_t^L of the position in a sentence, the specific calculation process of Bi-LSTM is shown in formula 1, 2 and 3.

$$i_t^f = \sigma(W_i^f h_{t-1}^f + v_i^f e_t^L + b_i^f) \tag{1}$$

$$f_t^f = \sigma(W_f^f h_{t-1}^f + v_i^f e_t^L + b_f^f) \tag{2}$$

$$o_t^f = \sigma(W_o^f h_{t-1}^f + v_o^f e_t^L + b_o^f) \tag{3}$$

The W^f,V^f and b^f are the learnable parameters of the model. The i^f,f^f and o^f are called input gate, forgetting gate and output gate respectively. The specific calculation method of state update is shown in the formula 4 and 5.

$$c_t^f = f_t^f \bullet c_{t-1}^f \bullet tanh(W_c^f h_{t-1}^f + V_c^f e_t^L + b_c^f) \tag{4}$$

$$h_t^f = o_t^f \bullet tanh(c_t^f) \tag{5}$$

The symbol • represents Hadamard plot. The h_t^f is the final output of the position t of a sentence. We merge the output h_i^f and h_i^b of the every position of the Bi-LSTM to obtain the final output in formula 6.

$$h_i = [h_i^f, h_i^b] \tag{6}$$

We use the formulas 7 and 8 to predict the sentiment tendency of the entire sentence. The d is the average of h_t. The W_c and b_c are the parameters of a linear layer.

$$d = \frac{1}{l}\sum_{t=1}^{l} h_t \tag{7}$$

$$G = W_c d + b_c \tag{8}$$

For every position in the input sequence, an agent outputs a sentiment action as its inference of the sentiment tendency of a sentence near this position. Intelligent sentiment action is determined by the output of the agent and the input at that time. The output action dimensions are three-dimensional, corresponding to positive sentiment, neutral sentiment and negative sentiment. The output value represents the positive and negative tendency of a word. We use linear transformation to get the intensity of every sentiment corresponding to every state like formula 9 and 10.

$$f_t = W_f h_t + b_t \tag{9}$$

$$p_{t,j} = \frac{f_{t,i}}{\sum_{j+1}^{C} f_{t,j}} \tag{10}$$

The W_f is a matrix to map states to every sentiment category. The action of strategy network taking position t by probability $\alpha_t \sim p_t$.

Target Learning. For reinforcement learning, we need to design the corresponding reward function. In this article, the reward function is divided into two parts, one part is the sentiment tendency of the whole sentence, and the other part is the sentiment tendency of the word level. In order to distinguish the difference between a sentence level sentiment and a word level sentiment, we design the formulas 11 and 12. In the formula 11, we designs an overall sentiment reward function r_g. For each word which has appeared in the sentiment dictionary, when the sentiment action taken at the corresponding position is the same as the tag sentiment y of the whole sentence, the $r_i^g(a_i)$ is 1, otherwise the $r_i^g(a_i)$ is 0.

$$r_i^g(a_i) = \begin{cases} 1 \; a_i = y \\ 0 \; a_i \neq y \end{cases} \tag{11}$$

$$r_i^l(a_i) = \begin{cases} 1 \; a_i = y_i \\ 0 \; a_i \neq y_i \end{cases} \tag{12}$$

We also designs a local sentiment reward function. For each word that has appeared in the sentiment dictionary, when the sentiment action taken at the corresponding position is the same as the tag sentiment in the dictionary, the $r_i^l(a_i)$ is 1, otherwise the $r_i^l(a_i)$ is 0. The reward function of these two parts use the parameter α to combine into the overall reward function like the formula 13.

$$r = r^l + \alpha r^g \tag{13}$$

Let θ denotes all the parameters in the network, and the outputs of sentiment action strategy is p_θ. The agent observes the reward r, so we can train the agent by the loss function 14 which minimizes the reward.

$$\ell^l(\theta) = -E_{\alpha \sim P_\theta}[r(a)] \tag{14}$$

The a is the sentiment action output by the strategy network in each step. The superscript l indicates that this is the loss function of the local sentiment target. We use REINFORCE [28] algorithm to count strategy gradient of the Reinforcement Learning. We use gradient descent algorithm to optimize each parameter of the RL4LSC and the θ is updated by the formulas 15 and 16.

$$\nabla_\theta \ell^l(\theta) = -E_{a \; p_\theta}[r(a_t)\nabla_\theta log p_\theta] \tag{15}$$

$$\theta = \theta + \eta^l \sum_i^B \sum_t^l r(a_{i,t})\nabla_\theta log p_\theta \tag{16}$$

4 Experiment

In this section, we first describe the experimental data.

WeiBoDa. WeiBoDa was extracted from the website named Sina Weibo, which contains 1900 records. it has 1531 positive records and 369 negative records, whose length is at least 150.

CommendDa. CommendDa was extracted from the websites including Douban, Amazon and Dianping, which contains 25000 records. It has 10000 positive records, 5000 neutral records and 10000 negative records.

The maximum length of text is set to 240 in RL4LSC. If the text length is greater than 240, we only keep the first two hundred characters. If the text length is less than 240, we use the [PAD] symbol to fill up to two hundred characters. The details of the WeiBoDa and the CommendDa are shown as Table 2 and 3.

Table 2. The details of the CommendDa

	Positive	Neural	Negative
Train set	6000	6000	3000
Validation set	2000	2000	1000
Test set	2000	2000	1000
Sum	10000	10000	5000

Table 3. The details of the WeiBoDa

	Positive	Negative
Train set	919	223
Validation set	306	73
Test set	306	73
Sum	1531	369

We use three evaluation metrics which include precision, recall and f1 to evaluate the effectiveness of RL4LSC. The calculation of precision, recall and f1 are shown in formulas 17, 18 and 19.

$$Precision_i = \frac{|TP|}{|TP \bigcup FP|} \tag{17}$$

$$Recall_i = \frac{|TP|}{|TP \bigcup FN|} \tag{18}$$

$$F1_i = \frac{2 \times Precision_i \times Recall_i}{Precision_i + Recall_i} \tag{19}$$

In order to test the effectiveness of the RL4LSC model, we conduct comprehensive experiments on multiple data sets. Firstly, we set the max length to 240 in a sentence and set the output dimension of the LSTM to 300. The adjustment ratio in the local sentiment target is fixed at 1. Table 4 and 5 show the comparison of the different models on the data set WeiBoDa and CommendDa. It can be seen that the RL4LSC, which takes into account the local sentiment information of a sentence, surpasses other models that use the lexical guide word embedding on the two data sets. On the Table 4, the precision and recall rate of RL4LSC surpasses TextCNN used lexical guide word embedding by nearly 0.01, and the F1 score exceeds 0.02.

Table 4. The results of the experiment on WeiBoDa. Comparison models all use word embedding vector guided by lexical method [30].

Model	Precision	Recall	F1
BiLSTM	0.8902	0.8010	0.8197
BiLSTM + Attention	0.7848	0.8024	0.7842
BiLSTM + Pooling	0.8478	0.7850	0.8132
DPCNN	0.8399	0.8007	0.8188
TextCNN	0.9055	0.8237	0.8321
RL4LSC	**0.9153**(+0.0098)	**0.8303**(+0.0066)	**0.8552**(+0.0231)

On the Table 5, the precision and recall rate of the RL4LSC surpass TextCNN about 0.01, which uses lexical guide word embedding, and the F1 score of the RL4LSC exceeds TextCNN nearly 0.01. The above experimental results fully illustrate the effectiveness of the RL4LSC model and the introduction of vocabulary sentiment information which has a significant improvement effect on the prediction performance of the model.

Table 5. The results of the experiment on the CommendDa. Comparison models all use word embedding vector guided by lexical method [30].

Model	Precision	Recall	F1
BiLSTM	0.8656	0.8374	0.8484
BiLSTM + Attention	0.8552	0.8668	0.8580
BiLSTM + Pooling	0.8694	0.8739	0.8694
DPCNN	0.8708	0.8692	0.8694
TextCNN	0.8848	0.8780	0.8810
RL4LSC	**0.8995**(+0.0147)	**0.8931**(+0.0151)	**0.8902**(+0.0092)

One of the advantages of the RL4LSC is that the sentiment tendency can be obtained at every word in a sentence. Specifically, the experiment in this section takes the sentiment strategy P of the strategy network model at every position of a sentence and takes the difference between the positive sentiment probability P_2 and the negative sentiment probability p_0 as the sentiment score of the position. Figure 2 shows the sentiment tendency diagram of some sentences, in which the color corresponding to each word in the sentence indicates the sentiment tendency predicted by the model. It can be seen from the figure that, while it obtains the overall sentiment information of the sentence, the RL4LSC has carried out an accurate sentiment analysis for each position in the complex long sentence. This shows that the RL4LSC can output the sentiment tendency of complex and long sentences while outputting the sentiment tendency of the

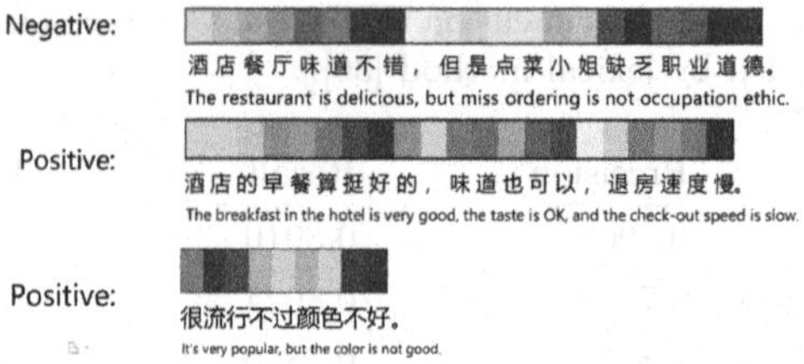

Fig. 2. The strategic network intercepts part of the content of the complex long sentence based on the sentiment tendency and sentiment strength output by each word position in the complex long sentence. Among them, red represents negative sentiments, green represents positive sentiments, the darker the color, the stronger the sentiment tendency, and the yellow represents the weaker sentiment tendency. (Color figure online)

entire sentence for further in-depth analysis. This property is very helpful for the analysis of complex long sentences, and can achieve more effective use of data.

paginationThe data given in the Fig. 3 shows that the learning rate of the local sentiment target and the global sentiment target needs to reach a good balance to achieve the best training effect. When it is too high or too low, the effect of the model will decrease, or even lower than the baseline model. This part of the experiment also plays a role in the ablation experiment. When the learning rate of the reinforcement learning equals zero, RL4LSC is not affected by the local sentiment of the single word, but only depends on the global sentiment feedback. At this time, the model is equivalent to a traditional supervised text sentiment classification model, which uses BERT pre-trained word vectors and bidirectional long-term short-term memory network for text classification. It can be found that the performance of the RL4LSC has dropped significantly at this time and is lower than the performance of the embedding vector model based on lexical guidance. The experiment results show that the performance

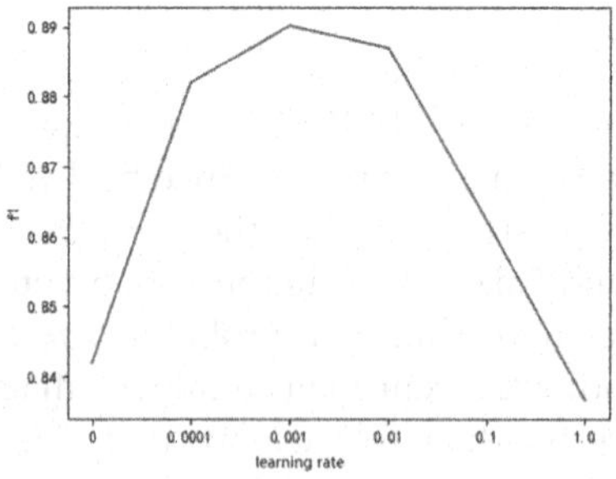

Fig. 3. The performance of RL4LSC when using different learning rates in the reinforcement learning part. F1 score is used as an indicator. The horizontal axis is the value of the learning rate of the reinforcement learning part, and the vertical axis is the F1.

improvement of the RL4LSC is closely related to its ability to recognize local sentiments. When this part of the function is stripped off, its best performance will not be achieved.

5 Conclusion

In this paper, we propose a sentiment classification algorithm named RL4LSC. By learning the whole sentence level sentiment tendency and the single word sentiment tendency which is given by the sentiment dictionary at the same time, RL4LSC tries to give an accurate overall sentiment category and predict the sentiment tendency of each local position at the same time. Through detailed comparative experiments, visualization experiments and ablation experiments, the design motivation and working mechanism of RL4LSC has been confirmed. Experiment results show that RL4LSC can predict the accurate sentiment tendency of each local position and recognize the sentiment change. Experiment results also show that the model can deal with different sentiment change structures and produce correct output when different sentiment sentences are combined .

Acknowledgement. This work is supported by the Nature Science Foundation of China (No. 62076210), the National Key Research and Development Program of China (No. 2018YFC0831402) and the Open Project Program of The Key Laboratory of Cognitive Computing and Intelligent Information Processing of Fujian Education Institutions, Wuyi University (No. KLCCIIP2020203).

References

1. Turney, P.D., Littman, M.L.: Measuring praise and criticism: inference of semantic orientation from association. ACM Trans. Inf. Syst. **21**(4), 315–346 (2003)
2. Zhendong, D.: HowNet released "sentiment analysis vocabulary (beta)"
3. Wei, Z., Jin, L., Xianzhen, G.: Dictionary of Students' Praise and Derogatory Meaning. Encyclopedia Press of China (2004)
4. Jilin, S., Yinggui, Z.: Dictionary of Commendatory Words. Sichuan Dictionary Press, Sichuan (2005)
5. Tsai, A.C.R., Wu, C.E., Tsai, R.T.H., et al.: Building a concept-level sentiment dictionary based on commonsense knowledge. IEEE Intell. Syst. **28**(2), 22–30 (2013)
6. Zhang, X., Zhao, J., LeCun, Y.: Character-level convolutional networks for text classification. Adv. Neural Inf. Process. Syst. **28**, 649–657 (2015)
7. Altman, N.S.: An introduction to kernel and nearest-neighbor nonparametric regression. Am. Stat. **46**(3), 175–185 (1992)
8. Cortes, C., Vapnik, V.: Support-vector networks. Mach. Learn. **20**(3), 273–297 (1995)
9. Mikolov, T., Sutskever, I., Chen, K., et al.: Distributed representations of words and phrases and their compositionality. In: Proceedings of the 26th International Conference on Neural Information Processing Systems, pp. 3111–3119 (2013)
10. Kim, Y.: Convolutional neural networks for sentence classification. In: Proceedings of the 2014 Conference on Empirical Methods in Natural Language Processing (EMNLP), pp. 1746–1751 (2014)

11. Elman, J.L.: Finding structure in time. Cogn. Sci. **14**(2), 179–211 (1990)
12. Hochreiter, S., Schmidhuber, J.: Long short-term memory. Neural Comput. **9**(8), 1735–1780 (1997)
13. Chung, J., Gulcehre, C., Cho, K., et al.: Empirical evaluation of gated recurrent neural networks on sequence modeling. arXiv preprint arXiv:1412.3555 (2014)
14. Tang, D., Qin, B., Liu, T.: Document modeling with gated recurrent neural network for sentiment classification. In: EMNLP, pp. 1422–1432 (2015)
15. Yang, Z., Yang, D., Dyer, C., et al.: Hierarchical attention networks for document classification. In: NAACL, pp. 1480–1489 (2016)
16. Vaswani, A., Shazeer, N., Parmar, N., et al.: Attention is all you need. In: Advances in Neural Information Processing Systems, pp. 5998–6008 (2016)
17. Liu, Y., Ott, M., Goyal, N., et al.: Roberta: a robustly optimized BERT pretraining approach. arXiv preprint arXiv:1907.11692 (2019)
18. Clark, K., Luong, M.T., Le, Q.V., et al.: Electra: Pre-training text encoders as discriminators rather than generators. arXiv preprint arXiv:2003.10555 (2020)
19. Yang, Z., Dai, Z., Yang, Y., et al.: XlNet: generalized autoregressive pretraining for language understanding. arXiv preprint arXiv:1906.08237 (2019)
20. Zhang, Z., Han, X., Liu, Z., et al.: ERNIE: enhanced language representation with informative entities. arXiv preprint arXiv:1905.07129 (2019)
21. Tian, H., Gao, C., Xiao, X., et al.: SKEP: sentiment knowledge enhanced pre-training for sentiment analysis. arXiv preprint arXiv:2005.05635 (2020)
22. Wang, K., Shen, W., Yang, Y., et al.: Relational graph attention network for aspect-based sentiment analysis. arXiv preprint arXiv:2004.12362 (2020)
23. Mnih, V., Kavukcuoglu, K., Silver, D., et al.: Playing Atari with deep reinforcement learning. arXiv preprint arXiv:1312.5602 (2013)
24. Konda, V.R., Tsitsiklis, J.N.: Actor-critic algorithms. In: Advances in Neural Information Processing Systems. Citeseer, pp. 1008–1014 (2000)
25. Wiering, M.A., van Hasselt, H., Pietersma, A.D., et al.: Reinforcement learning algorithms for solving classification problems. In: 2011 IEEE Symposium on Adaptive Dynamic Programming and Reinforcement Learning (ADPRL). IEEE, pp. 91–96 (2011)
26. Chen, R., Zhou, Y., Zhang, L., et al.: Word-level sentiment analysis with reinforcement learning. In: IOP Conference Series: Materials Science and Engineering, vol. 490, pp. 062–063. IOP Publishing (2019)
27. Lin, E., Chen, Q., Qi, X.: Deep reinforcement learning for imbalanced classification. Appl. Intell. **50,** 1–15 (2015)
28. Williams, R.J.: Simple statistical gradient-following algorithms for connectionist reinforcement learning. Mach. Learn. **8**(34), 229–256 (1992)
29. Cui, Y., Che, W., Liu, T., et al.: Pre-training with whole word masking for Chinese BERT. arXiv preprint arXiv:1906.08101 (2019)
30. Zhang, C., Lin, D., Cao, D., Li, S.: Grammar guided embedding based Chinese long text sentiment classification. Concurr. Comput. Pract. Exp. **33**, e6439 (2021). https://doi.org/10.1002/cpe.6439

CATS: A Cache Time-to-Live Setting Auto Adjustment Strategy for an Air Ticket Query Service

Chunhou Liu[1], Jian Cao[1(✉)], Yudong Tan[2], and Shiyou Qian[1]

[1] Department of Computer Science and Engineering, Shanghai Jiao Tong University, Shanghai, China
{oceans,cao-jian,qshiyou}@sjtu.edu.cn
[2] Ctrip.com, Shanghai, China
ydtan@Ctrip.com

Abstract. A cache is an efficient way to speed up the response of services, which can also be applied in air ticket query services. However, the time-to-live (TTL) setting is a challenging task for the caching mechanism especially when the validity periods of the records change with time, which is the case for the air tickets. In air ticket query services, the validity of air ticket information is verified when a user places the order. It provides a chance to adjust the initial TTLs. In this paper, we provide a *CA*che *T*ime-to-live setting auto adjustment *S*trategy (CATS) for air ticket query service based on the verification results during order placement. In addition, by considering the associations between cached records, CATS can also adjust the TTL settings for related cached records. Experiments are conducted to test and compare different implementations of CATS and the results show that CATS can maintain both the hit rates and verification success rates at a high level.

Keywords: Cache · Time-to-live setting · Air ticket query service · Deep reinforcement learning

1 Introduction

Currently, many online travel agencies (OTAs) [1] provide air ticket query services. As shown in Fig. 1, in order to book an air ticket, a customer needs to input the query conditions firstly. The query conditions consist of departure city, destination city, departure date, cabin, and number of passengers. After receiving this information, the ticket query engine sends the query conditions to the available ticketing platforms to query the available air tickets. Finally, the returned ticket quotation lists from each ticketing platform are collected, organized and returned to the customer. After the customer selects the ticket he prefers from the list, the ticket information is sent back to the related ticketing platforms to check if this quotation still exists which is known as quotation verification. The customer can order this ticket successfully only if the quotation verification

Y. Sun et al. (Eds.): ChineseCSCW 2021, CCIS 1491, pp. 327–341, 2022.
https://doi.org/10.1007/978-981-19-4546-5_26

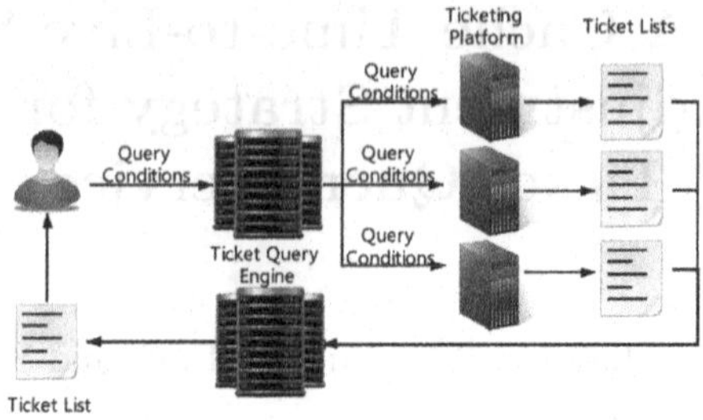

Fig. 1. The process of an air ticket query service

succeeds. Quotation verification is necessary since the availability of air tickets changes from time to time.

In the air ticket query service, when a query is received, the query engine first looks up the cache and the quotation list is returned from the cache if the key already exists. When the key is not found in the cache, the relevant records will be filled into the cache after obtaining the list of quotations from the ticketing platforms. This technique, which is often called a Web cache, has been widely applied in query engines. A key technique for a Web cache is to precisely set time-to-live (TTL) for each record. Improper TTL settings will cause problems for applications. TTL settings have already been a research topic for many years and many approaches have been proposed [2,3].

The good news is, in the quotation verification step, not only can the corresponding records be updated, it also provides some hints for updating the TTLs of other cached records because air ticket quotations are inherently associated in various forms. This fact can also be verified through the analysis of real-world air ticket data. We randomly select sets of cache keys, which includes the user's query condition. We collect the time points when the quotation list changes each day for the selected cache keys to observe their changed behavior patterns. The result is shown in Fig. 2. The x axis of the figure is the timeline. As we can see, the quotation list of every cache key changes frequently and the change time of the quotation lists is not the same. It can be observed that for some cache keys, the change points at the time of their corresponding air ticket quotations seem to be relevant.

Based on the fact that there is a chance of knowing the validity of the cached quotation list when a ticket order is placed, and the quotation adjustment occasions for some cache keys are relevant, we propose the idea of modifying the TTL settings for the cache keys when the quotation verification happens. The contributions of this work are as follows:

- We propose a *CA*che *T*ime-to-live setting auto adjustment *S*trategy (CATS) to maintain the validity of the cached quotation lists in the air ticket query service using deep reinforcement learning.
- We design approaches to measure the correspondences between the quotation lists and update the related quotation lists' TTL settings together.

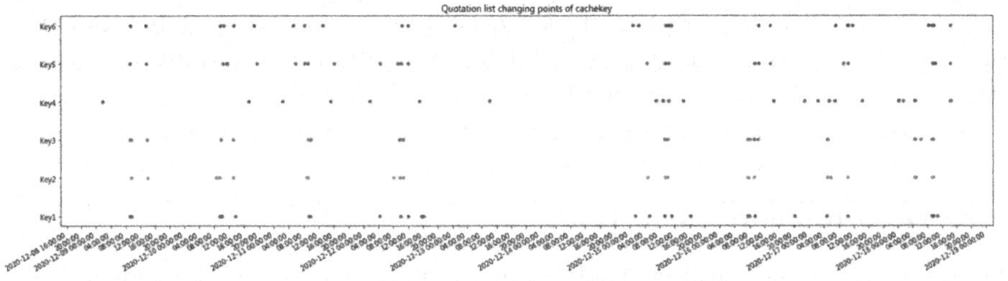

Fig. 2. Changing points in time of cache key's quotation list

– We perform extensive experiments on a real-world dataset and the experiment results prove our strategy achieves good performance.

2 Related Work

Our study is related to TTL settings for caches and deep reinforcement learning.

2.1 TTL Setting

Different from a conventional cache, a web cache aims to improve the performance of the web server, so inconsistency to some extent is tolerable which is called a weak consistency requirement. The weak consistency requirement introduces the concept of time-to-live (TTL).

We usually measure the performance of the TTL setting methods by *hit rate* and *consistency*. Hit rate measures the acceleration effect and it can be calculated by the fraction of queries which return results from the cache. Consistency measures the validation of the cache data and it can be calculated by the fraction of queries which return valid results from the cache. Hit rate and consistency are contradictory. A high hit rate means low consistency while high consistency means a low hit rate.

There are two conventional TTL methods, i.e., *the fixed TTL method* [4] and *the heuristic method* [5]. (1) *The fixed TTL method* always assigns the same TTL to every data item. This method ignores the distinction of data items which tends to lead to either a high hit rate and low consistency, or high consistency and low hit rate. (2) *The heuristic method* determines the TTL as a portion of the interval between the point of caching (*Now*) and the last point in time the original data was modified (*Last-Modified*). This method takes the characteristics of the time variant updating rate of the data item into consideration which is better than *the fixed TTL method*, but it is unable to take into consideration the differences between the different data items.

There is also *update-risk based TTL method* [2]. In this method, the updates of the data items are assumed to be independent and the number of updates of the data item is modeled as a Poisson process. This method works when the updates of data items are independent, however, in our problem, the data items are not updated independently. Ticket quotations are usually related and their updates are correlated. Therefore, modeling the number of updates of the data item is not an appropriate method.

In this paper, we apply a heuristic approach to set the initial TTLs.

2.2 Deep Reinforcement Learning

Deep reinforcement learning (DRL), a method combin- ing reinforcement learning (RL) and deep learning (DL), has developed rapidly in recent years. When AlphaGo [6] defeated Lee Sedol, deep reinforcement learning ushered in the spring of development. DRL has been used in many fields like recommendation [7–10], advertising [11,12], and games [13,14].

According to OpenAI spinning up documents [15], RL algorithms can be divided into Model-Free RL and Model-Based RL, based on whether the agent has access to (or learns) a model of the environment. Model-Free RL can further be divided into Policy Optimization and Q-Learning algorithms. Policy Optimization algorithms learn the policy $\pi_\theta(a|s)$ or $\pi_\theta(s)$ explicitly. Policy Gradient (PG) [16] and the Advantage Actor-Critic (A2C) algorithm [17] are two important branches in policy optimization with a discrete action space. The Deep Deterministic Policy Gradient (DDPG) algorithm [18] is another branch of policy optimization with a continuous action space. Q-learning learns an approximator $Q_\theta(s,a)$ for the optimal action value function $Q^*(s,a)$ The Deep Q-Network [19] and its expanding Double Q-learning [20] are important branches of Q-Learning.

In this paper, we use the PG, A2C and DDPG algorithms to train our agents to modify the TTL of the quotation list.

3 Problem Formulation and the Framework of CATS

3.1 Problem Formulation

For clarity and convenience, we first introduce the following notations:

- Query conditions (Q): Conditions input by user including: adult/child passenger number, departure date and departure city of flight, destination of flight and cabin type.
- Air Ticket (T): An air ticket consists of the flight number, cabin and passenger type, which can uniquely identify a seat type. Moreover, passenger type can be either adult or child. Airlines set different prices for different seat types.
- Cache Key (K): The cache key consists of query conditions and ticketing platform ID. It can uniquely identify a quotation list in a cache. In this paper, we also call the cache key the query key as it is constructed based on query conditions.
- Quotation List (L): A list of (ticket, price) pairs related to a certain ticketing platform.
- Cache (C): An in-memory key-value pair set. The query engine can get the quotation list given the cache key from the cache.

After a user submits a query at time t_i, a set of cache keys $\{K_{i_1}, K_{i_2}, ..., K_{i_{N_i}}\}$ are produced and sent to the cache to query the corresponding quotation lists, N_i is the number of ticketing platforms that will be queried, different query conditions have different ticketing platforms to query. If the key-value pair K_{i_p} is in the cache then L_{i_p} will be returned immediately from the cache. Otherwise, L_{i_p} will be queried from the related ticketing platform, then (K_{i_p}, L_{i_p}) is filled into the cache with a timestamp t'_{i_p} beyond which (K_{i_p}, L_{i_p}) will be removed from the cache, and L_{i_p} will be returned at last. If the customer wants to order tickets, then after a certain time period Δt_i, a set of (ticket, price) pairs will be selected from quotation lists $\{L_{i_1}, L_{i_2}, ..., L_{i_{N_i}}\}$ and then sent to the related ticketing platforms for verification which will check the existence of all these (ticket, price) pairs. If all (ticket, price) pairs in the selected set exist on the ticketing platforms, then the verification is considered a success. The target of the problem is to give an appropriate strategy to set timestamp t'_{i_p} so that we can maximize the number of quotation lists L_{i_p} immediately returned from the cache and maximize the success probability of verification. An example is shown in Fig. 3.

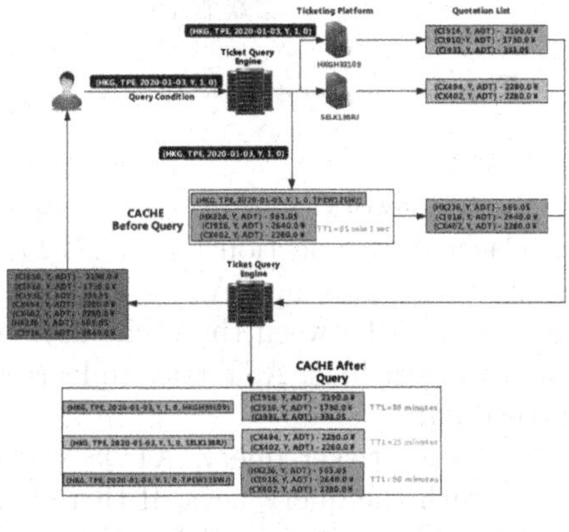

Fig. 3. A ticket query process example

The users' queries and the returned ticket quotation lists of each query are recorded in the log of the query service. The query log consists of following attributes: transaction id to identify user query, timestamp, query key. When the user initiates a query, a transaction id will be generated to identify the query. The timestamp when the user initiates the query will also be recorded. One transaction id corresponds to multiple query keys.

Since it is impossible to know how the quotation for the air ticket changes in real time, we construct the record of the quotation change of the ticket according to the returned result returned to the user's query. The ticket quotation change log consists of following attributes: query key, timestamp, ticket price list of the query key after changing.

Each verification record consists of following attributes: transaction id, query key, seat, price of the seat queried by user, timestamp. Verification records are sent to the ticketing platforms. The ticket platform checks whether the seat's price is the same as the queried price and returns the verification result.

3.2 The Framework for CATS

In this section, we describe the framework of CATS to set and adjust TTLs.

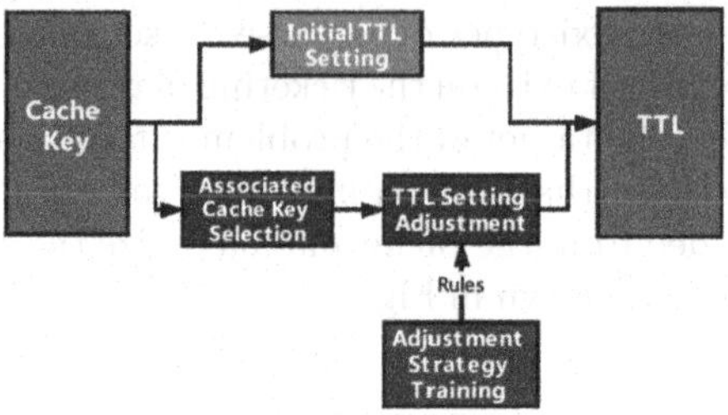

Fig. 4. The framework for CATS

As shown in Fig. 4, the framework contains components for Initial TTL Setting (ITS), Associated Cache Key Selection (ACK), TTL Setting Adjustment (TSA) and Adjustment Strategy Training (AST).

ACK decides the associations between the cache keys of the quotation lists in the cache based on some algorithms. AST tries to learn the TTL adjustment strategy from the historical data.

When a user submits an air ticket query, ATQS will search the cache by comparing the cache keys with the query keys. If there is a match, the cached quotation list will be returned immediately. When there is no matched one, the query will be sent to the ticketing platforms and the quotation lists are returned to the user. At the same time, the quotation lists will be saved in the cache and TTL will be attached to it by ITS firstly. When the user selects a ticket and decides to place an order, the ticket information is verified by querying the ticketing platforms. TSA is responsible for deciding how to update the TTLs of the associated quotation list records based on the rules learned by AST.

4 CATS: A Cache Time-to-Live Setting Auto Adjustment Strategy

CATS comprises three techniques, i.e., initial TTL setting, associated cache key selection and deep reinforcement learning based adjustment strategy learning.

4.1 Initial TTL Setting

When a quotation list is inserted into the cache, an initial TTL will be attached to it. Obviously, it is not appropriate to assign a fixed TTL for all the air ticket quotation lists and we should assign different TTLs for different air ticket quotation lists.

Predicting TTLs for an air ticket quotation list can be modeled as a machine learning problem if the true expiration time of the quotation list is available. Unfortunately, we do not know the exact expiration time since we will not know whether the cached records are still valid or not until they are verified. Therefore, we propose an approach to set the initial TTLs in a heuristic manner.

In this approach, instead of predicting the expiration time, we predict the possibility of verification since we have the verification records. For each query record, we build a sample for training. The features are described in Table 1 and the target is whether there is a verification record with the same query key within 24 h.

Table 1. Features to train the decision model

Feature name	Desc
departure_query_delta	Days between departure date and query date
query_weekday	Weekday of query date
departure_weekday	Weekday of depart date
query_hour	Hour of query timestamp
haschild	Whether the cache key has child passenger

This is a binary classification problem and we use the decision tree model to solve it. Specifically, the CART algorithm is adopted in our study. When the result is returned, it will be verified in 24 h, which means we need to set the TTL smaller. Furthermore, we use the rules listed in Table 2 to decide the TTLs. It reflects the relationships between the query frequency and the query hour considering the number of days between the departure date and query date. These heuristic rules have been verified in practice.

For the records that will not be verified in 24 h based on prediction, we set TTL to 18 h directly.

4.2 Associated Cache Key Selection

To determine the associated cache keys of the verified cache key, we propose two approaches.

1) *Key structure based association.* For the same query date, keys with the same departure date are often related to each other. Hence, we split the keys according to the departure date and keys with the same departure date are grouped.

Table 2. TTL rules when machine learning model predicts 1. Δ is the days between departure date and query date. H is the hours of query timestamp.

H (hours)	Δ (days)	TTL (minutes)
[0,7]	≤7	20
	[8,30]	30
	≥30	60
[8,17]	≤7	10
	[8,30]	15
	≥30	60
[18,23]	≤7	15
	[8,30]	25
	≥30	60

2) *Quotation list based association.* If the flight sets of two cache keys are very similar, there will be a high probability that their quotation lists will change simultaneously. Given two cache keys K_1 and K_2 and the flight sets F_1 and F_2 in their quotation lists, we use formula (1) to compute the similarity of K_1 and K_2.

$$sim = \frac{|F_1 \cap F_2|}{\sqrt{|F_1||F_2|}} \tag{1}$$

Cache keys whose similarity is greater than δ are considered to be associated with the verified cache key.

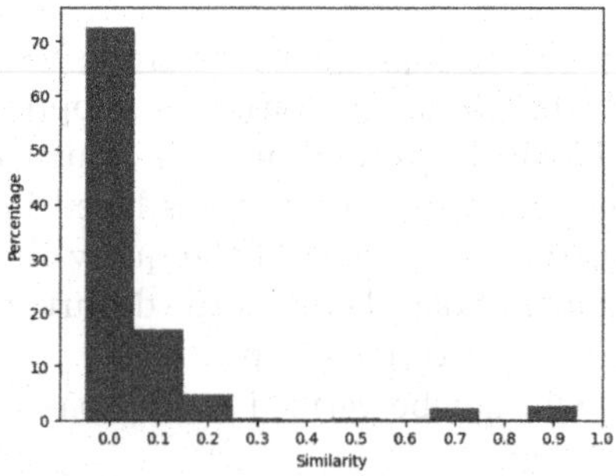

Fig. 5. Similarity distribution

We randomly select a set of candidate cache keys and compute their similarity with all cache keys, then we collect the similarity and the average number of cache keys. As shown in Fig. 5, the similarity of a cache key with all the cache keys is almost 0 and we therefore set δ to a very small number.

4.3 TTL Setting Adjustment Strategy Learning

For each associated cache key, we need to modify their TTLs. Our approach is based on reinforcement learning. Specifically, we use an agent to modify the TTL. Given the associated cache keys and their quotation list, the agent outputs the TTL adjustment value for each cache key.

The key problem is how to train the agent. To train the agent, we need to build an environment with which an agent should interact. When ticket verification occurs, the agent interacts with the environment and each verification is a time step.

We first determine how to represent the state of the environment. For a cache key and its quotation list, we can define a feature vector using the cache key and its quotation list and the state of this cache key is represented by the feature vector. Given the associated cache keys, we combine all the states of the associated cache keys as a matrix. Each row in the matrix is a cache key state vector. We regard this matrix as a batch of the cache key state. At each time step, the environment returns this matrix as its state.

Then we determine how to represent the reward at each time step. For each associated cache key, we count the number of queries and cache hits between the two verifications. We can use the number of queries, the cache hits and the verification result at the current time step to define the reward. For each associated cache key K, suppose the number of user queries is q, the number of cache hits is h, the verified key is K_v, and the verification result is $r \in \{-1, 1\}$. As our goal is to increase the hit rate while not increasing the verification failure rate, we need to give the agent a large penalty if verification failures occurs. Therefore we use Formula (2) to compute the reward of cache key K. If a verification failure happens, the agent will receive –1000 reward as penalty.

$$reward = \begin{cases} 0.001 * (2 * h - q), & K \neq K_v \\ 0.001 * (2 * h - q) + 1000 * r, & K = K_v \end{cases} \tag{2}$$

Based on the state and reward representation, we formulate the interaction between the environment and the agent when a cache key is verified. When a cache key is verified, the environment first uses the cache key association rules to extract associated cache keys $\{K_1, K_2, ..., K_n\}$. Then, for each associated cache key K_i, the environment builds a state vector $\mathbf{V_i}$ using its key structure and its quotation list. It also builds the reward r_i using formula (2). The environment then combines all the state vectors as a matrix $S = \{\mathbf{V_1}, \mathbf{V_2}, ..., \mathbf{V_n}\}$ and cache key reward as a vector $\mathbf{R} = \{r_1, r_2, ..., r_n\}$. Then the agent returns TTL modification amount vector $\mathbf{A} = \{\Delta_1, \Delta_2, ..., \Delta_n\}$ as the action. The environment accepts the action and modifies the TTLs of the associated cache keys. When the next cache key is verified, the environment again returns the state vectors and cache key rewards.

Another problem is how to update the agent's parameters. Because each verified cache key is different, their associated key set can be very different. The state matrix of the environment is also not aligned between two time steps. We can get the intersection set of the associated keys of two consequent time steps and use their state vectors to update the agent's parameters. If the intersection set is empty, we can consider it as the end of one episode. Suppose at time step T, the verified cache key is K_{v1} and its associated keys are $\{K_{i1}, K_{i2}, ..., K_{iN}\}$. At the same time, the reward returned by the environment can be one value from $\{r_{i1}, r_{i2}, ..., r_{iN}\}$ and the agent's action set is $\{a_{i1}, a_{i2}, ..., a_{iN}\}$. At time step $T+1$, the verified cache key is K_{v2} and its associated keys are $\{K_{j1}, K_{j2}, ..., K_{jM}\}$. The rewards returned by the environment can be one value of $\{r_{j1}, r_{j2}, ..., r_{jM}\}$ and the agent's action set is $\{a_{j1}, a_{j2}, ..., a_{jM}\}$. Then we use $\{K_1, K_2, ..., K_Q\}$, which is the intersection set of $\{K_{i1}, K_{i2}, ..., K_{iN}\}$ and $\{K_{j1}, K_{j2}, ..., K_{jM}\}$ as the keys to build the state at T and $T+1$ to train the agent. Their corresponding rewards and actions are also used to train the agent.

We use two algorithms to train different kinds of agents, i.e., PG (REINFORCE) [16], A2C [17] and DDPG [18].

5 Experiments

5.1 Dataset

We obtained the dataset from a large online trip agent. The dataset consists of two parts, i.e., the user query log and the ticket quotation change log. We collected the logs of route HKG-TPE between 2019-12-26 to 2019-01-01 from an OTA's database. There are a total 1735946 query logs. The logs between 2019-12-26 and 2019-12-30 are used to train the agent and the others are used to test the performance of the agent.

5.2 Verification and Evaluation

Query and Verification Simulator. We built a query and verification simulator for the air tickets to simulate the user's query and order placement behaviors. This simulator can also be used to train the agent. The working process of the simulator is event driven. The implementation of CATS can be denoted by a tuple (S, A, M, G), where S is the initial TTL setting approach, A is the associated cache key selection algorithm, M is the TTL adjustment strategy and G is the verification generator approach. Given a set of query logs and quotation change logs, this simulator will return the hit rate and verification success rate based on the given implementation of CATS.

Performance Evaluation. We evaluate the performance of an implementation of CATS in terms of cache hit rate and verification success rate. The verification success rate is defined as the ratio of the successful verification times to the total verification times, which is related to the profits of OTA so it is not supposed to decrease. The cache hit rate is the ratio of the number of queries hitting cache to the number of total queries. It should be as high as possible.

Verification Generator. Verifications are generated in terms of the real verification/query ratio r. We denote the verification generator with the verification/query ratio r as G_r. The generator first generates a random number $x \in (0, 1)$, then compares x and r. If x is smaller than r, then the generator randomly selects a ticket from the quotation list and returns it. The verification/query ratio in our dataset is 0.0087.

5.3 Initial TTL Setting Approach

The constant TTL setting approach sets the TTL of the cache key as a constant value from {10, 30, 60, 90} minutes. We denote the constant TTL setting approach with the constant value c as S_c. We run the simulator with the cache strategy (S_c, None, None, $G_{0.0087}$). The hit rate and verification success rate are shown in Table 3.

Table 3. Simulation results of CATS with only initial TTL setting approach applied

TTL settings	Hit rate	Verification success rate
S_5	65.91%	99.60%
S_{10}	73.07%	99.59%
S_{30}	82.25%	99.58%
S_{60}	86.37%	99.40%
S_{90}	88.62%	99.21%
S_{120}	89.74%	99.66%
S_{150}	90.72%	98.91%
S_{ML}	80.92%	99.71%

5.4 Associated Cache Key Selection and Agent Training Process

Key Structure Based Association. As shown in Table 4, at each query date, we group the cache keys with the same departure day into one group. For each group, we use an agent to decide how to adjust the TTLs. For two neighboring query dates, groups with the same Δ share one agent where Δ is the days between the query date and departure date. We denote this associated cache key selection approach as A_1. For example, on query date 2019-12-01, agent_2 is used to decide the TTL modification of the cache keys whose flight departure date is 2019-12-02. Then on query date 2019-12-02, agent_2 will be used to decide the TTL adjustment of the cache keys whose flights depart on 2019-12-03.

We use three reinforcement learning algorithms to train the agents, i.e., REINFORCE, A2C and DDPG respectively. For the agents in the REINFORCE and A2C algorithms, the representations of their actions are discrete and their actions are denoted as

Table 4. Key structure based association and related agents

Agent \ Departure / Query	2019-12-01	2019-12-02	2019-12-03	2019-12-04
2019-12-01	Agent 1	Agent 2	Agent 3	Agent 4
2019-12-02		Agent 1	Agent 2	Agent 3
2019-12-03			Agent 1	Agent 2
2019-12-04				Agent 1

$$\{-15, -10, -5, 0, 5, 10, 15, 20, 25, 30, 35, 40, 45, 50,\\ 55, 60, 65, 70, 75, 80, 85, 90\}.$$

For the agent in the DDPG algorithm, the representation of its action is continuous and its action space is $[-30, 90]$. The neural network used in all three algorithms has one hidden layer whose size is 100 (Table 5).

Table 5. Features used by the agent

Feature name	Desc
depart_query_delta	Days between departure date and query date
query_weekday	Weekday of query date
depart_weekday	Weekday of departure date
query_hour	Hour of query timestamp
haschild	Whether cache key has child passenger
verify_haschild	Whether verified cache key has child passenger
ttl_left	TTL left of cache key from verification timestamp
verify_result	Verification result

The simulation result using the cache strategy $(S_{ML}, A_1, M, G_{0.0087})$ is shown in Table 6. A comparison of the method S_{90}, S_{ML} and M_5 is also shown. S_{90} is $(S_{90}, None, None, G_{0.0087})$ cache strategy. S_{ML} is $(S_{ML}, None, None, G_{0.0087})$ cache strategy. M_5 is the cache strategy $(S_{ML}, A_1, M_5, G_{0.0087})$ which increases the TTL of the associated cache keys by 5 min when verification succeeds and decreases the TTL by 5 min when verification fails.

Quotation List Based Association. In this experiment, we use the REINFORCE, A2C and DDPG algorithms to train the agents. The parameters are the same as the algorithms in the key structure based association. The simulation result using the cache strategy $(S_{ML}, A_2, M, G_{0.0087})$ where A_2 is quotation list based association is shown in Table 7. A comparison of the methods S_{90},

Table 6. Experiment results with key structure based association

M	Hit rate	Verification success rate
REINFORCE	89.37%	98.02%
A2C	90.46%	96.63%
DDPG	86.15%	97.39%
S_{90}	88.62%	99.21%
S_{ML}	80.92%	99.71%
M_5	84.18%	99.66%

S_{ML} and M_5 is also shown. S_{90} is $(S_{90}, None, None, G_{0.0087})$ cache strategy. S_{ML} is $(S_{ML}, None, None, G_{0.0087})$ cache strategy. M_5 is the cache strategy $(S_{ML}, A_2, M_5, G_{0.0087})$ which increases the TTL of the associated cache keys by 5 min when verification succeeds and decreases the TTL by 5 min when verification fails.

Table 7. Experiment results with quotation list based association

M	Hit rate	Verification success rate
REINFORCE	97.51%	93.80%
A2C	91.09%	93.90%
DDPG	84.32%	95.16%
S_{90}	88.62%	99.21%
S_{ML}	80.92%	99.71%
M_5	92.90%	94.30%

6 Discussions and Conclusion

As shown in the Table 3, the hit rate increases and the verification success rate decreases as the TTL constantly increases. The results are consistent with our intuition. The longer the cache time, the higher the cache hit rates and the smaller the possibility that the verification may succeed. The hit rate of the machine learning-based initial TTL setting approach is about 80.92%, and its performance is similar to the constant TTL setting approach S_{30}.

A2C algorithm outperforms the REINFORCE and DDPG algorithms among the key structure based association methods. It is the most effective method to modify TTL. Its hit rate is 9.54% higher than S_{ML} methods, 1.84% higher than S_{90} and 6.28% higher than M_5.

The quotation list-based association method using the REINFORCE algorithm increases the hit rate by 16.59% compared with the S_{ML} method. It increases the hit rate by 8.89% compared with S_{90} and increases the hit rate by 4.61% compared with M_5.

Both the key structure-based and quotation list-based association methods improve the performance of the cache.

In the future, we will try other cache key association methods. We can use methods like collaborative filtering in recommender systems to explore the associations among the cache keys.

References

1. Koo, B., Mantin, B., O'Connor, P.: Online distribution of airline tickets: should airlines adopt a single or a multi-channel approach? Tour. Manag. **32**(1), 69–74 (2011). https://doi.org/10.1016/j.tourman.2009.11.008. https://www.sciencedirect.com/science/article/pii/0261517709002167
2. Lee, J.-J., Whang, K.-Y., Lee, B.S., Chang, J.-W.: An update-risk based approach to TTL estimation in web caching. In: Proceedings of the Third International Conference on Web Information Systems Engineering, WISE 2002, pp. 21–29 (2002). https://doi.org/10.1109/WISE.2002.1181640
3. Alici, S., Altingovde, I.S., Ozcan, R., Cambazoglu, B.B., Ulusoy, Ö.: Adaptive time-to-live strategies for query result caching in web search engines. In: Baeza-Yates, R., de Vries, A.P., Zaragoza, H., Cambazoglu, B.B., Murdock, V., Lempel, R., Silvestri, F. (eds.) ECIR 2012. LNCS, vol. 7224, pp. 401–412. Springer, Heidelberg (2012). https://doi.org/10.1007/978-3-642-28997-2_34
4. Disable DNS client-side caching on DNS clients (2021). https://docs.microsoft.com/en-us/windows-server/networking/dns/troubleshoot/disable-dns-client-side-caching
5. Danzig, P., et al.: A hierarchical internet object cache. In: Proceedings of the 1996 Usenix Technical Conference, pp. 153–163 (1995)
6. Silver, D., et al.: Mastering the game of go without human knowledge. Nature **550**, 354–359 (2017). https://doi.org/10.1038/nature24270
7. Chen, S.Y., Yu, Y., Da, Q., Tan, J., Huang, H.K., Tang, H.H.: Stabilizing reinforcement learning in dynamic environment with application to online recommendation, pp. 1187–1196. Association for Computing Machinery, New York (2018). https://doi.org/10.1145/3219819.3220122
8. Zheng, G., et al.: DRN: a deep reinforcement learning framework for news recommendation. In: International World Wide Web Conferences Steering Committee, Republic and Canton of Geneva, CHE, pp. 167–176 (2018). https://doi.org/10.1145/3178876.3185994
9. Wang, X., Wang, Y., Hsu, D., Wang, Y.: Exploration in interactive personalized music recommendation: a reinforcement learning approach. ACM Trans. Multimedia Comput. Commun. Appl. **11**(1), 1–22 (2014). https://doi.org/10.1145/2623372
10. Li, L., Chu, W., Langford, J., Schapire, R.E.: A contextual-bandit approach to personalized news article recommendation. In: Proceedings of the 19th International Conference on World Wide Web, WWW 2010, pp. 661–670. Association for Computing Machinery, New York (2010). https://doi.org/10.1145/1772690.1772758
11. Cai, H., et al.: Real-time bidding by reinforcement learning in display advertising. In: Proceedings of the Tenth ACM International Conference on Web Search and Data Mining, WSDM 2017, pp. 661–670. Association for Computing Machinery, New York (2017). https://doi.org/10.1145/3018661.3018702
12. Lou, K., Yang, Y., Wang, E., Liu, Z., Baker, T., Bashir, A.K.: Reinforcement learning based advertising strategy using crowdsensing vehicular data. IEEE Trans. Intell. Transp. Syst. **22**, 1–13 (2020). https://doi.org/10.1109/TITS.2020.2991029

13. Berner, C., et al.: Dota 2 with large scale deep reinforcement learning, arXiv:1912.06680 (2019)
14. Adamski, I., Adamski, R., Grel, T., Jędrych, A., Kaczmarek, K., Michalewski, H.: Distributed deep reinforcement learning: learn how to play atari games in 21 minutes. In: Yokota, R., Weiland, M., Keyes, D., Trinitis, C. (eds.) ISC High Performance 2018. LNCS, vol. 10876, pp. 370–388. Springer, Cham (2018). https://doi.org/10.1007/978-3-319-92040-5_19
15. Achiam, J.: Spinning Up in Deep Reinforcement Learning (2018)
16. Sutton, R.S., McAllester, D., Singh, S., Mansour, Y.: Policy gradient methods for reinforcement learning with function approximation. In: Proceedings of the 12th International Conference on Neural Information Processing Systems, NIPS 1999, pp. 1057–1063. MIT Press, Cambridge (1999)
17. Babaeizadeh, M., Frosio, I., Tyree, S., Clemons, J., Kautz, J.: Reinforcement learning through asynchronous advantage actor-critic on a GPU. arXiv:1611.06256 (2017)
18. Lillicrap, T.P., et al.: Continuous control with deep reinforcement learning. arXiv:1509.02971 (2019)
19. Mnih, V., et al.: Playing atari with deep reinforcement learning. arXiv:1312.5602 (2013)
20. Hasselt, H.: Double q-learning. In: Proceedings of the 23rd International Conference on Neural Information Processing Systems - Volume 2, NIPS 2010, pp. 2613–2621. Curran Associates Inc., Red Hook (2010)

Human-Machine Collaboration Based Named Entity Recognition

Zhuoli Ren, Zhiwen Yu(✉), Hui Wang, Liang Wang, and Jiaqi Liu

Northwestern Polytechnical University, Xi'an 710072, China
zhiwenyu@nwpu.edu.cn

Abstract. Named Entity Recognition (NER) is an important task in Natural Language Processing (NLP), and its main goal is to extract the required entities from a given text and label the entity type. Not only is an important research topic, but its identification quality and efficiency also have an important impact on follow-up tasks (such as machine translation, intelligent question answering system, etc.). Current research methods are primarily based on Deep Learning (DL) models. In practical applications, such models often rely on a large number of labeled data, which will show a certain limitation in applications in specific domains. At the same time, due to the high uncertainty of human language and the openness involving problems, the DL model does not reach the point of complete replacement of humanity. Human-machine collaboration refers to that in the changing environment, human and machines perform tasks alternately, so that the task can achieve the best performance with a small amount of human participation. In this paper, we propose a Human-Machine Collaboration based Named Entity Recognition (HMCNER) model by utilizing the complex cognitive reasoning ability of human beings and combining with existing DL model. The extensive experimental results show that our model can efficiently complete the NER task based on the existing research results, and have practical application.

Keywords: Human-machine collaboration · Named entity recognition · Deep learning · Natural language processing

1 Introduction

Text data is often lengthy, unstructured and of uneven quality, which makes it extremely difficult to obtain valuable information quickly and accurately. Faced with such a large scale of unstructured text filled with a lot of noise, how to use an automatic text processing technology to extract structured and valuable information has naturally become the top priority, so Named Entity Recognition (NER) technology arises at the moment. Text entity is usually divided into proprietary type entity and generic type entity. The entity of generic type generally includes three kinds: numerical expression, time expression and entity type. In particular, numeric expression contains a percentage value and a currency; Time expression contains a time and a date; The entity type contains the names of people, places, and organizations. In general, entities of a generic type can be used in

Y. Sun et al. (Eds.): ChineseCSCW 2021, CCIS 1491, pp. 342–355, 2022.
https://doi.org/10.1007/978-981-19-4546-5_27

any language and any type of text, while named entities of a proprietary type need to be defined in terms of a specific domain. For example, in the business field, the entities that usually need to be identified include products, product brands, product models, etc. In the military field, the identification of such entities as the names of military institutions, operations and weapons. In addition, for the entity of proprietary type, it also includes the entity type under a specific subdivision scene, such as identifying the specific person, location, song title or movie title in a specific text. In recent years, as Deep Learning (DL) began to show outperformance in computer vision, speech recognition and other fields, many researchers also began to use DL model to deal with NLP tasks including NER, and have made breakthrough progress. Like most NLP tasks, accurate entity identification depends on sufficient labelled samples. At present a lot of DL models have achieved good experimental results on different public data sets, but for a specific application and the actual scene, there is no publicly available data sets and idealized experimental environment. Or for a model that is migrated collectively from a common dataset, it performs and learns fewer effective features than it used to. In NLP, the characteristics of large scale, diversity and low value density of data pose obstacles to the utilization of data.

Faced with these problems, the traditional computing model may have been unable to meet the demand. Human-machine collaboration combines the strengths of human and machine, integrating the complex cognitive reasoning ability of human and the high-performance computing ability of computer groups to deal with complex tasks. In this way, it also brings new ideas for us to explore the NER method. Therefore, we aim to improve the accuracy and efficiency of NER by establishing a human-machine collaboration based model. The main contributions of this paper are:

- A Human-Machine Collaboration based Named Entity Recognition model (HMC-NER) is proposed. The overall framework of the model is composed of four modules, including data processing module, neural network module, human-machine collaboration module and prediction and evaluation module.
- Neural network module is designed based on Bi-LSTM, a neural network, and adds CRF layer to solve the constraint problem of predictive labels.
- In the human-machine collaboration module, the method of active learning is adopted. Considering the uncertainty measure for the problem of manual participation labeling, we implement and improve the various query strategies, such as RandomStrategy (RS), LeastConfidenceStrategy (LC), LeastTokenProbabilityStrategy (LTP), etc. And added the data pool update mode, can use manually generated data to update the data pool.
- An interactive NER operation interface is developed, based on pyqt5 and multi-threading technology.

2 Related Work

The early research on NER is mainly divided into rule-based methods and statistics-based methods. Yan Danhui et al. [1] made 152 rules when extracting the names of people, locations, institutions and other entities in Vietnamese. Institutional entities include political parties and social organizations, corporations and cultural and educational institutions, state power and administrative and judicial institutions. The rules systematically analyze the economic and political corpus of Vietnam and finally obtained the recall rates of the three entities were 79.3%, 77.4% and 74.3%. Other scholars have used rule-based methods to process Chinese text corpus. When extracting text entity for a January 2009 People's Daily review article, Zhou Kun et al. [2] formulated 9 matching rules for locations and 20 matching rules for person names, and achieved good results.

In recent years, DL has made a major breakthrough in the research of NER methods [3, 4]. Li et al. [5] divided DL based NER model into three sub-modules, namely input representation, context encoder and label decoder. At the same time, some researchers have made different processing on the model structure [6]. They tried to fully connect some features of the presentation layer directly with the tag decoding layer, or rebuild other network layers [7], and embedded them into the input layer and the coding layer, or between the coding layer and the decoding layer. In the absence of manual feature extraction, Collobert et al. [8] proposed a unified Deep Neural Network (DNN), which has achieved good results in NER task, semantic role annotation and other tasks. Similar to Collobert, Huang et al. [9] adopted a neural network framework of "word vector input + context semantic coding layer + CRF decoding layer", which is used to deal with the three-sequence labeling tasks of part of speech labeling, module analysis and NER task. Considering the good effect of Recurrent Neutral Network (RNN) in processing sequence marking tasks, Kuru et al. [10] chose a Bi-directional Long Short-Term Memory network (Bi-LSTM) to extract global text features. Through experiments on 8 different data sets, they have achieved good recognition results, and it is proved that the character-level labeling method is better than the sentence-level labeling method in dealing with sequence labeling. Nichols and Chiu [11] also selected a Bi-LSTM network to encode the input vector. The input vector not only splicing word vector and character feature vector, but also realized manual feature. For the processing of pre-trained word vectors, the author compared three methods including Senna [8], Word2vec [12] and Glove [13], and meanwhile proved that the 50-dimensional Senna word vector showed the best labeling effect.

Different from the single statistical learning method, some scholars have tried to combine statistical method with rule matching, taking into account both human cognitive ability and computer processing ability. Firstly, the entity extraction of text data is carried out by statistical method, and then the recognition results are corrected and filtered by manually formulated regular expressions [14]. The traditional machine learning model is to manually collect and label a large amount of data for the machine to learn, while the human-in-loop processing is to first-hand the data processed by the human to the machine, and then the machine will feedback the results to the human for proofreading, so as to achieve the effect of improving the accuracy. In 2019, Zhang et al. [15] proposed a NER model based on human-in-loop to solve the time allocation problem during data processing and model optimization. This model considers both manual regular expression construction and manual annotation, and the active learning method is added. An accurate entity extraction framework is built through three manual participations to reduce the time of data annotation. Similar to Zhang, Lihong [16] found that many entities appeared or arranged in specific patterns and could be recognized by regular expressions when extracting complex network text. Therefore, he first constructed or collected the existing rule set to identify a certain type of entity to establish weak labeling, pre-training the neural network, and then used human experts to label a small part of the text to optimize the neural network. Finally, the accuracy of the test effect on the data set for different entities reached 93.50%, 94.36% and 90.95% respectively. Sen Wan et al. [17] also used the idea of human-in-loop in a study on learning with a small sample. Existing active learning methods focus on the labeling budget in the model training phase, while their method uses a small number of samples to perform the labeling in the testing phase, those uncertain samples are handed over to human experts for active labeling in the next iteration and added to the trusted dataset. In the study of human participation, Ticiana et al. [18] made a further division. They split the human participants into two distinct roles: ordinary reviewer and data expert, and abandoned the annotation process using regular expressions. Data experts use existing NER models to identify, annotate and determine entity types. The common reviewer is involved in determining whether it is correct or whether the entity type needs to be updated, and finally the data expert is responsible for optimizing and iteratively updating the model.

3 Human-Machine Collaboration Based Named Entity Recognition Model

3.1 Overall Framework of HMCNER

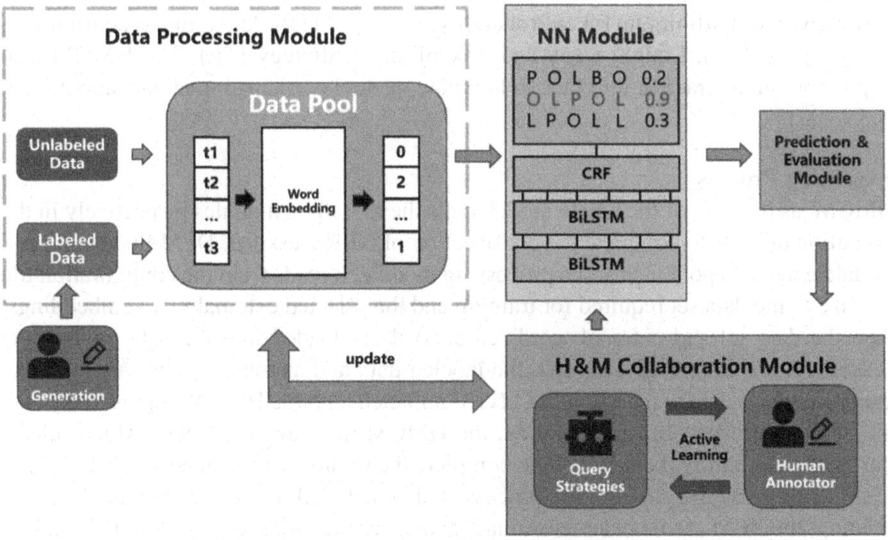

Fig. 1. Human-machine collaboration based named entity recognition model

The overall structure of the model is shown in Fig. 1. In terms of functions, the model is divided into four modules: Data Processing Module (DPM), Neutral Network Module

(NNM), Prediction and Evaluated Module (PEM) and Human-Machine Collaboration Module (HMCM).

Module Function

- The DPM includes loading the external embedding into the data pool and the mapping of data sets. The initial data set accepted by the model is all textual data. The purpose of word embedding is to convert them into data types that the model can use. It can convert words in the text into numeric vectors that are easy to process. The DPM also maintains a data pool that provides all data operations of the model. The data pool initially divides the text data into annotated data and unannotated data, and realizes several different data update methods, including the generation of data with human participation. The data pool remains functionally open to the other three modules.
- The NNM adopts the neural network of Bi-LSTM + CRF to select the data training model from the data pool.
- The PEM provides prediction and evaluation functions, which can be evaluated and predicted after each round of training to give the loss of training and the cost of human participation. The cost of human participation is also a key issue that the model needs to pay attention to. The PEM can give the reading cost of the machine and the labeling cost of human for each human-machine collaboration operation.
- In the HMCM, the method of active learning is applied. A variety of query strategies are implemented and improved considering the uncertainty measurement for manual participation annotation. Including RandomStrategy (RS), LeastConfidenceStrategy (LC), NormalizedLeastConfidenceStrategy (NLC), LeastTokenProbabilityStrategy (LTP), MinimumTokenProbabilityStrategy (MTP), MaximumTokenEntropyStrategy (MTE), LongStrategy and TokenEntropyStrategy (TE). The HMCM also provides an interactive interface to facilitate manual participation in data annotation.

Executing Process

HMCM, as the core of the whole model, calls the first three modules respectively in the execution process to complete the construction of NER classifier. DPM first create and initialize the data pool in the data processing module, it reads from the configuration file the size of the data set required for training and the selected external word embeddings, then the data set and external words embedded are loaded into the data pool of the model, the text data is divided into the labeled data and annotation data. At this time, the preliminary data preparation has been completed, and the HMCM begins to execute the iterative process. In each iteration, the HMCM first calls the NNM, which selects the labeled data from the data pool to complete the training of the standard Bi-LSTM + CRF neural network. An iteration process is also included inside the module. After the training, the PEM are invoked to evaluate and score the indicators in a single iteration. Next, the HMCM participates in the data update process. The module implements the active learning query strategy and gives data for manual participation and annotation. The results of each execution are timely updated to the data pool and added to the next iteration. During the whole iteration process, the data pool is kept open to the HMCM, which allows manual generation of data to update the data pool, and human can also select the unannotated data in the data pool for annotation. At the end of all iterations, the HMCM saves the last updated model and obtains a NER classifier with good effect. The classifier can complete entity type annotation and extraction according to the input text information.

3.2 Neutral Network Module Based on Bi-lSTM + CRF

The Bi-LSTM + CRF model combines Conditional Random Field (CRF) and Bi-directional Long and Short-Term Memory network (Bi-LSTM). The overall network structure of the model can be divided into three layers: Embedding layer, Bi-LSTM layer and CRF layer. The overall structure of the model is shown in Fig. 2:

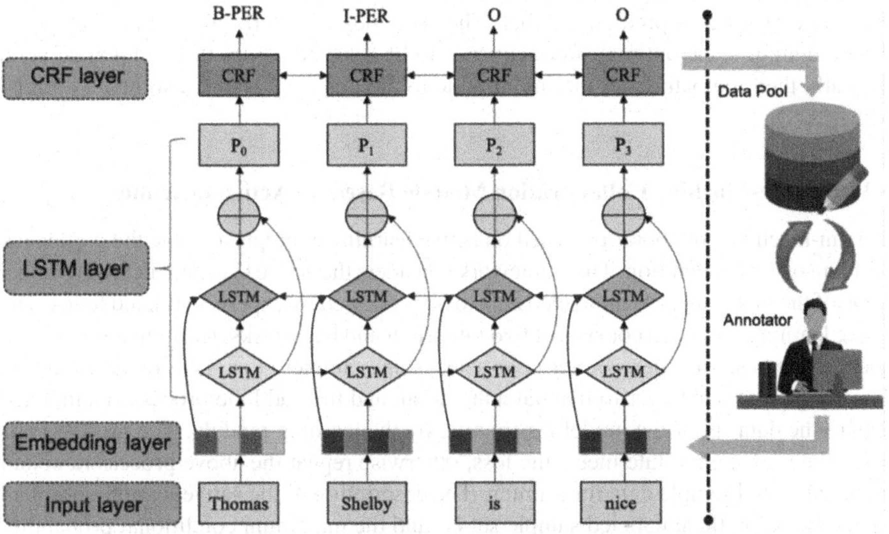

Fig. 2. The overall structure of Bi-LSTM + CRF network

CRF Layer

The CRF layer can normalize the output of the Bi-LSTM layer in the model to avoid unreasonable sequence. The model uses Viterbi algorithm to analyze the labeling sequence output by Bi-LSTM to find the optimal labeling sequence. For all probability transfer vectors o_t generated by Bi-LSTM, the CRF layer forms o_t and y_t tags into a conditional random field, that is, for a given $O = (o_1, o_2, ..., o_n)$, a maximized probability $P(Y|O)$ is found, where $Y = (y_1, y_2, ..., y_n)$ represents the correct labeling sequence. When the CRF layer is solving for this probability, let S_{y_{i-1},y_i} represent the maximum transition probability from label y_{i-1} to label y_i. If we set the tag sequence $Y = (y_1, y_2, ..., y_n)$ as the best labeled tag. Then the probability of the correct label sequence is shown in Eq. (1):

$$P(X, y) = \sum_{i=1}^{n} (S_{y_{i-1},y_i} + o_{iy_i}) \tag{1}$$

After the tag sequence is obtained, the softmax function is used to process the probability to obtain the corresponding conditional probability $P(y|X)$, as shown in Eq. (2):

$$P(y|X) = \frac{\exp(P(X, y))}{\sum_{y \in Y} \exp(P(X, y))} \tag{2}$$

where Y means that X contains all possible sequences of tags. During network training, the negative logarithm of $P(y|X)$ is used to select the loss function, as shown in Eq. (3):

$$loss = -\log(P(y|X)) = -P(X, y) + \log(\sum\nolimits_{y \in Y} \exp(P(X, y))) \tag{3}$$

During the training, the model is mainly trained to reduce the target loss function. In CRF layer, Viterbi algorithm can be used to find the most reasonable sequence from the whole O set as a prediction label. The core idea of Viterbi algorithm is dynamic programming. If the optimal state sequence to be selected passes through a node y_i on the path, then the path from the initial node to the node y_{i-1} must also be an optimal path.

3.3 Human-Machine Collaboration Module Based on Active Learning

Human-machine collaboration based on active learning attempts to solve the bottleneck problem of data annotation. The framework considers the active learning method to select some of the most valuable unlabeled data to be processed by experts in related fields. The active learning approach consists of two important and basic tasks: learning modules and query strategies. The query strategy can select some samples (1 or N) from the unlabeled data samples to hand over to manual annotation, and then add the processed annotated data to the data set of the model for training by the learning module. The process ends when the learning module meets the loss, otherwise repeat the above process to obtain more annotated sample data for training. The description of the active learning problem can be based on the unlabeled sample set U, and the maximum conditional probability is used to determine the object type T, as shown in Eq. (4):

$$T = \arg\max P(T|U, w) \tag{4}$$

where w is the weight of model parameters obtained by iteration on the data set through learning in the model. In each iteration, the importance of selected sample U is calculated and sorted, and experts in related fields involved in manual labeling only need to select data samples of high importance for labeling.

Iterative Process

Human-machine collaboration based on active learning can better process a lot of training data and select the sample points with high discrimination ability, which can reduce the amount of data and reduce the cost of manual labeling. Figure 3 illustrates a complete iteration.

The human-machine cooperation mode based on active learning can be expressed as $M = (C, L, U, H, Q)$. Where C represents entity extraction classifier (1 or N); L represents the data sample set that has been labeled; U represents the unlabeled data sample

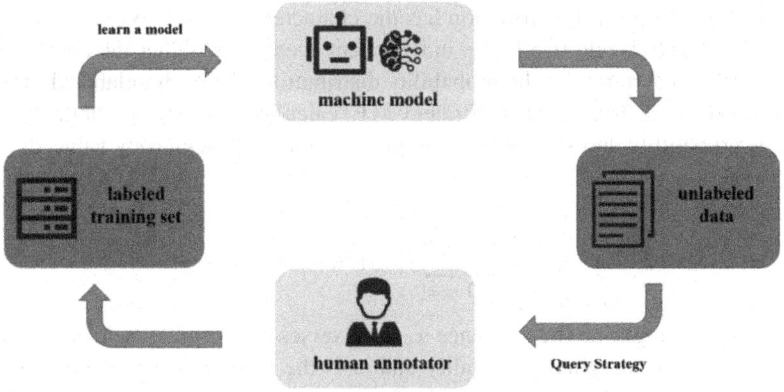

Fig. 3. Human-machine collaboration process based on active learning

set; H represents experts in related fields involved in manual labeling; Q represents the query strategy taken for the current iteration.

Human-Machine Query Strategy

The purpose of establishing human-machine query is to establish a set of query rules to judge the extent to which the addition of an unlabeled sample data to the training data set affects the generalization ability of the network model. Depending on the query strategy, the model learns on a small annotated sample and then uses the model to process the unannotated portion of the dataset. In this paper, the characteristics of text data are considered in the NER task, and the query strategy of uncertainty measurement is adopted. The algorithm uses a pool-based sampling method to select the data samples that are most useful for learning to be added to the growing training data set, i.e., the samples that the model classifier is least certain of. The simplest method is RandomStrategy (RS), which randomly selects data from the sample for annotation. From the perspective of sample space, data with large information content tend to be distributed near the boundary of model classifier, and LeastConfidenceStrategy (LC) is a relatively simple uncertainty strategy, as shown in Eq. (5):

$$\phi^{LC}(x) = 1 - P(y^*|x;\theta) \tag{5}$$

where y^* is the most likely annotated sequence, i.e., the Viterbi parse. For sequence labeling at the CRF layer, a posterior probability can be used to calculate this confidence. The measurement method of the minimum boundary uncertainty is the comparison between the best and the second-best uncertainties. If the probability of the most likely type is significantly different from that of the second likely type, then the model classifier will be more certain in determining this type, as shown in Eq. (6):

$$\phi^{M}(x) = -(P(y_1^*|x;\theta) - P(y_2^*|x;\theta)) \tag{6}$$

where y_1^* and y_2^* are the first and second best annotation sequences respectively, which can be calculated by using N-best algorithm in beam search respectively. Another information measurement method based on uncertainty is entropy. Shannon entropy is used in this model. Its uniform distribution has the characteristics of maximum uncertainty and the uncertainty is additive for an independent event. The higher the entropy value, the greater the uncertainty of the probability distribution. For each unlabeled sample in the training data set, TokenEntropyStrategy (TE) calculated the entropy of the predicted field type probability and selected the sample with the highest entropy value, as shown in Eq. (7):

$$\phi^{TE}(x) = -\frac{1}{T}\sum_{t=1}^{T}\sum_{m=1}^{M} P_{\theta}(y_t = m) \log P_{\theta}(y_t = m) \tag{7}$$

where T is the length of the sequence x, m traverses all possible field labels, where $P_{\theta}(y_t = m)$ is the marginal probability and m is the label at T in the sequence. For the CRF layer, forward propagation or backward propagation can be used to calculate these margins, and the total field entropy is usually normalized by the sequence length T to avoid querying longer sequences. But this method can be considered extended to MaximumTokenEntropyStrategy (MTE), as shown in Eq. (8):

$$\phi^{MTE}(x) = T \times \phi^{TE}(x) \tag{8}$$

The token-based query strategy treats the sequence of tokens as an isolated set of fields and evaluates uncertainty by summarizing the information about these fields. MinimumTokenProbabilityStrategy (MTP) choose the most amount of information field, regardless of the distribution of the CRF, this strategy of labels of the highest probability of field in low sampling, as shown in Eq. (9):

$$\phi^{MTP}(x) = 1 - \min_{i} \max_{j} \mathrm{P}(y_i = j | x_i; A) \tag{9}$$

where $P(y_i = j)$ is the probability that the j tag in the sequence is located at position i. Unlike MTP, LeastTokenProbabilityStrategy (LTP) considering the long and short sequences all have their own advantages, the two can complement each other, the strategy look for the long sequences with the highest probability, and demanded that the sequence of the local field also had a higher probability, as shown in Eq. (10):

$$\phi^{LTP}(x) = 1 - \min_{y_i^* \in y^*} P(y_i^* | x_i; A) \tag{10}$$

4 Experiment

4.1 Datasets

The dataset used in the experiment in this paper is the annotated corpus of People's Daily and the MSRA corpus used in the Chinese NER evaluation task of Microsoft Research. For these two kinds of data sets, this paper divides them into training set and test set when conducting experiments. Since the task studied in this paper contains unannotated data sets, in order to ensure the unity of data, part of the data sets was removed from the annotated processing in the experiment and divided into unannotated data sets. The statistics of corpus size and number of entities in the data set are shown in Table 1:

Table 1. Corpus size and entity number statistics

Corpus	#S	#T	#E	ASL	ASE	AEL
MSRA (train)	50658	2169879	3	42.83	1.47	3.23
MSRA (test)	4620	172590	3	37.35	1.33	3.25
People's Daily (train)	27350	409830	6	14.98	0.67	3.93
People's Daily (test)	6825	99616	6	14.59	0.67	3.87

where #S is the total number of sentences in the data set; #T is the number of characters in the data set; E the number of all entities; ASL is the average length of a sentence; ASE represents the average number of entities in each sentence; AEL represents the average length of each entity; The external word embedding in the data processing module of the model is the Chinese corpus of Wikipedia, which contains a total of 1.33 million words and sentences, about 438 million words, including the explanation and definition of various nouns, etc.

4.2 Contrast Experiments

The traditional method does not include human-machine collaboration. A separate model based on Bi-LSTM + CRF is selected here. Table 2 and Table 3 present the experimental results of human-machine collaboration methods with different query strategies and traditional methods on People's Daily dataset and MSRA dataset.

Table 2. Experimental results of different methods on the People's Daily dataset

Method	LOC-F1	ORG-F1	PER-F1	Entity-Level-F1
Bi-LSTM + CRF	**0.73**	**0.64**	**0.80**	**0.72**
Bi-LSTM + CRF + HMC (LC)	0.79	0.71	0.80	0.76
Bi-LSTM + CRF + HMC (LTP)	0.79	0.73	0.81	0.78
Bi-LSTM + CRF + HMC (MTP)	0.81	0.68	0.84	0.78
Bi-LSTM + CRF + HMC (MTE)	0.78	0.71	0.77	0.76
Bi-LSTM + CRF + HMC (LONG)	0.76	0.66	0.80	0.75

Bi-LSTM + CRF is the traditional method based on DL, Bi-LSTM + CRF + HMC is the method based on human-machine collaboration proposed in this paper, in brackets are the human-machine query strategies adopted. Human-machine collaboration improved by 4 to 6% compared to traditional approaches without human participation. For the accuracy of individual entity type, the improvement of human-machine collaboration on the PER type is not particularly outstanding, with only 1% to 2% improvement. However, for LOC entities and ORG entities, the HMCNER method has obvious advantages over the DL method, with 5% to 8% improvement respectively. This is because when dealing with the location entity or institution entity implied in the text sequence, people are more sensitive than machines. From the perspective of data volume, DL methods use all the training data sets during training and require strict annotation while the method based on human-machine collaboration only selects part of the data to participate in iteration and

Table 3. Experimental results of different methods on MSRA datasets

Method	LOC-F1	ORG-F1	PER-F1	Entity-Level-F1
Bi-LSTM + CRF	**0.78**	**0.71**	**0.85**	**0.78**
Bi-LSTM + CRF + HMC (LC)	0.85	0.74	0.83	0.81
Bi-LSTM + CRF + HMC (LTP)	0.86	0.76	0.84	0.83
Bi-LSTM + CRF + HMC (MTP)	0.85	0.75	0.85	0.82
Bi-LSTM + CRF + HMC (MTE)	0.84	0.74	0.84	0.81
Bi-LSTM + CRF + HMC (LONG)	0.85	0.76	0.84	0.82

does not require full labeling, thus achieving the same or even better recognition quality of the traditional method. In general, when aiming at practical problems, human-machine collaboration will have more excellent processing effect.

4.3 Comparison of Different Query Strategies

In addition to comparing with traditional DL methods, we also compare the performance of different human-machine query strategies on the two data sets in the experiment, as shown in Fig. 4 and 5:

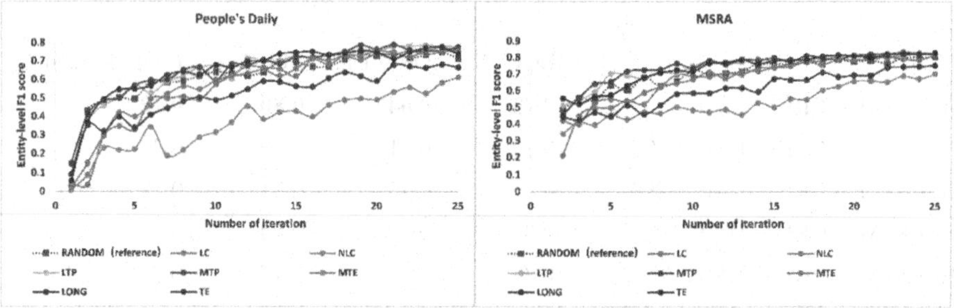

Fig. 4. Entity-level F1 value of different query policies on People's Daily and MSRA

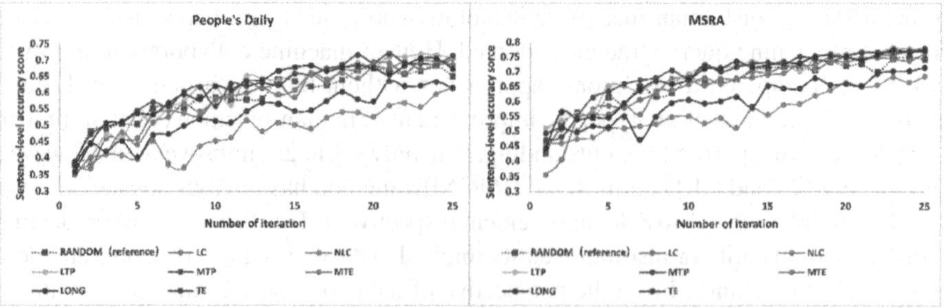

Fig. 5. Sentence-level accuracy of different query strategies on People's Daily and MSRA

As can be seen from the figure, if the RANDOM strategy is taken as the benchmark, except for TE and NLC, the other methods are better than the benchmark in terms of accuracy, both in the F1 value at the entity level and the sentence level, there is no obvious fluctuation and the convergence rate is good. NLC has some fluctuations in the accuracy of both entity level and sentence level during iteration, while TE is not as good as other query strategies in the final convergence result. From the perspective of performance, LTP has the best execution quality among different query strategies, with entity-level F1 and sentence-level accuracy on People's Daily data set reaching 0.78 and 0.71, respectively. The entity-level F1 and sentence-level accuracy of MSRA data set reached 0.83 and 0.78. Since the data volume of MSRA dataset is larger than that of People's Daily dataset, the performance of different query strategies on MSRA dataset is better than that of People's Daily dataset. From this point, we can also see the impact of the data volume on the model performance.

5 Human-Machine Collaboration Interactive Interface

For the human-machine cooperation module in the model, we developed a human-machine interactive interface to facilitate human participation in calculation. The interface is shown in Fig. 6:

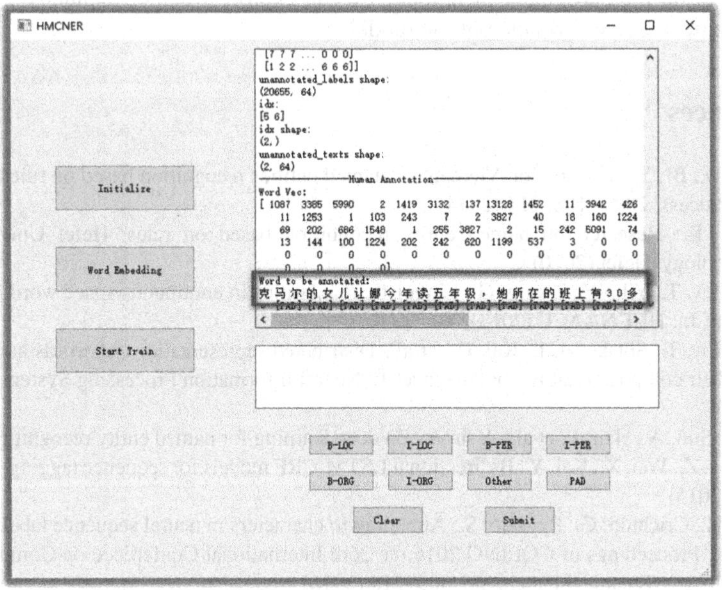

Fig. 6. HMC interactive interface

When the human-machine collaboration NER task is carried out, the overall framework can be initialized and the external word embedded can be loaded through the interface, and then the model training can be started. Human can modify parameters related to model construction, data sets participating in training and selection of human-machine query strategies through configuration files. During the training process, the current training information can be displayed in real time through the main window. In the human-machine cooperation stage, the main window of the interface will give statements that need manual annotation. At this time, users involved in calculation will make annotation for each entity according to their judgment. The corresponding operation is through buttons of different entities under the input window, as shown in Fig. 8. The human-machine collaboration interface provides an interactive window for users to participate in the collaboration, and can be integrated with the existing model framework to pass the annotated data to the input end of the model.

6 Conclusion and Future Work

For the task of NER, in this paper we propose a Human-Machine Collaboration based Named Entity Recognition (HMCNER) model. In the overall structure, we modularize and encapsulate the different functions, and propose a human-machine collaboration NER model. Through the study and analysis of the existing human-machine collaboration methods, the corresponding human-machine query strategy is designed. Through experimental tests, the HMCNER model achieves 5% to 7% improvement over the traditional DL approach, and uses less annotated data on this basis. Our future work will focus more on the participant of human, we can explore whether manually generated data can affect the performance of the model.

References

1. Yan, D., Bi, Y.: Research on Vietnamese named entities recognition based on rules. J. Chin. Inf. Process. **28**(5), 198–214 (2014)
2. Zhou, K.: Research on named entity recognition based on rules. Hefei University of Technology, Hefei (2010)
3. Mikolov, T., Yih, W., Zweig, G.: Linguistic regularities in continuous space word representations. In: HLT NAACL (2013)
4. Mikolov, T., Sutskever, I., Kai, C., et al.: Distributed representations of words and phrases and their compositionality. In: Advances in Neural Information Processing Systems, vol. 26 (2013)
5. Li, J., Sun, A., Han, J., et al.: A survey on deep learning for named entity recognition (2018)
6. Huang, Z., Wei, X., Kai, Y.: Bidirectional LSTM-CRF models for sequence tagging. Comput. Sci. (2015)
7. Rei, M., Crichton, G., Pyysalo, S.: Attending to characters in neural sequence labeling models. In: Proceedings of COLING 2016,the 26th International Conference on Computational Linguistics: Technical Papers, pp. 309–318 (2016)
8. Collobert, R., Weston, J., Bottou, L., et al.: Natural Language Processing (almost) from Scratch. J. Mach. Learn. Res. **12**(1), 2493–2537 (2011)
9. Huang, Z., Xu, W., Yu, K.: Bidirectional I STM-CRF models for sequence tagging (2015)
10. Kuru, O., Can, O., Yuret, D.: CharNER: character-level named entity recognition. In: 26th International Conference on Computational Linguistics, Osaka, Japan, 11–16 December 2016, pp. 911–921. Association for Computational Linguistics (2016)

11. Chiu, J., Nichols, E.: Named entity recognition with bidirectional LSTM-CNNs. Comput. Sci. (2015)
12. Mikolov, T., Sutskever, I., Chen, K., et al.: Distributed representations of words and phrases and their compositionality arXiv:1310.4546v1 [cs. CL], 16 October 2013
13. Pennington, J., Socher, R., Manning, C.: GloVe: global vectors for word representation. In: Conference on Empirical Methods in Natural Language Processing (2014)
14. He, Y., Luo, C., Hu, B.: A geographic named entity recognition method based on CRF and rules. Comput. Appl. Softw. **32**(1), 179–202 (2015)
15. Zhang, S., He, L., Dragut, E., et al.: How to invest my time: lessons from human-in-the-loop entity extraction. In: The 25th ACM SIGKDD International Conference. ACM (2019)
16. Zhang, S., He, L., Vucetic, S., et al.: Regular expression guided entity mention mining from noisy web data. In: EMNLP (2018)
17. Wan, S., Hou, Y., Bao, F., et al.: Human-in-the-loop low-shot learning. IEEE Trans. Neural Netw. Learn. Syst. **32**(7), 3287–3292 (2020)
18. da Silva, T.L.C., Magalhães, R.P., et al.: Improving named entity recognition using deep learning with human in the loop. In: Proceedings of the 22nd International Conference on Extending Database Technology, pp. 594–597. OpenProceedings.org, Lisbon (2019)

Cloud Manufacturing Workflow Scheduling with Learning and Forgetting Effects

Xiaoping Li[1], Jieqing Ye[1], Xia Zhu[1], Long Chen[1], and Xiaodong Zhang[2](✉)

[1] Southeast University, Nanjing 211189, China
[2] Nanjing Audit University, Nanjing 211815, China
zhangxd@nau.edu.cn

Abstract. How to schedule workflow tasks which are constrained by the workflow deadline to minimize the total cost is of great challenge in cloud manufacturing. The total cost is mainly determined by the production cost and the logistic cost. However, the production cost could change with the varying task processing times caused by learning and forgetting effects. The logistic cost depends on the allocated resources which are geographically distributed. The production and logistic costs could be conflicting when a task is executed on different service resources. In this paper, a learning-forgetting effect model is established for services. Two heuristic workflow scheduling algorithms based on task sequence and path clustering are proposed. The algorithmic components and parameters are statistically calibrated over a comprehensive set of random instances. The proposed algorithms are compared to a modified classical algorithm for similar problems. Experimental results show that the proposed algorithms outperform the compared one on average and the two proposals are suitable for different workflow scenarios in cloud manufacturing.

Keywords: Learning-forgetting effect · Workflow scheduling · Cloud manufacturing · Resourcing scheduling

1 Introduction

How to allocate manufacturing resources to minimize the total cost of production scheduling is one of the core issues of cloud manufacturing [1]. In addition to the production costs considered by traditional manufacturing systems, logistics costs for geographically distributed materials, equipment and manpower in the cloud manufacturing environment must also be considered. Production costs are directly related to the execution time of production tasks, and the learning and forgetting effects of workers will change production Task execution time [2,3], the learning effect will shorten the task processing time, and the forgetting effect will lengthen the task processing time. Production orders are also subject to the delivery date (deadline) constraints. This paper considers workflow task

Y. Sun et al. (Eds.): ChineseCSCW 2021, CCIS 1491, pp. 356–370, 2022.
https://doi.org/10.1007/978-981-19-4546-5_28

scheduling with deadline constraints in the cloud manufacturing environment, with the optimization goal of minimizing the total cost (the sum of logistics cost and production cost), and the distribution of manufacturing service resources is heterogeneous and has a learning forget effect. The problem under consideration is the NP-hard problem. The main challenges are as follows: (1) It is difficult to weigh the completion time of the workflow to meet the deadline and minimize the total cost. (2) How to ensure deadline constraints and minimize logistics costs. (3) How to reasonably allocate tasks with partial order constraints to different resources to minimize production cost is the key. This paper proposes a workflow scheduling system framework under cloud manufacturing environment. Based on the effect of learning and forgetting on task execution time, a learning and forgetting effect model of service resources is established. Two heuristic workflow scheduling algorithms based on task scheduling sequence adjustment and path clustering are proposed respectively.

2 Related Work

At present, cloud manufacturing tasks and resource scheduling, learning forgetting effect and cloud workflow scheduling have been researched accordingly.

The effects of learning and forgetting are widely present in the production environment [3]. Kuo et al. [4] studied the single machine scheduling problem with learning forgetting effect and gave a linear combination model. Yang et al. [5] studied the impact of learning and forgetting effects on the single-machine scheduling problem of job families, and constructed three task execution time models based on the task scheduling position, including no forgetting, complete forgetting and partial forgetting. Wu et al. [6] proposed a sequence-dependent generalized model of learning forgetting effects. This model assumes that learning and forgetting effects depend on the cumulative execution time and scheduling position of tasks.

Cloud workflow scheduling optimization is a research hotspot in recent years, and heuristic or meta-heuristic algorithms are often used to solve the problem. Commonly used list scheduling algorithms include HEFT algorithm [7], CPOP algorithm [7], DLS algorithm [8], etc. Cluster scheduling reduces the cost of task transmission by gathering multiple tasks, but at the expense of task parallelism [9], each cluster of the workflow is a subset of the workflow task set, executed on a separate resource, the key of cluster scheduling algorithm is how to balance maximization of parallelism and minimization of communication delay [10]. The copy scheduling algorithm is often used in combination with list scheduling and cluster scheduling. The basic idea is to copy the target task on the resource where the task is located, eliminate the transmission time between the two tasks, and try to make the task on the resource start as early as possible to shorten the completion time of the workflow [11,12]. However, the cloud workflow scheduling with learning forgetting effect considered in this paper has not been studied yet.

3 System Framework and Problem Description

3.1 System Framework

Combining the characteristics of the problem considered and the literature [13–15], this paper proposes a system framework as shown in Fig. 1. The framework mainly includes users, cloud manufacturing service platforms, and manufacturing service providers. The cloud manufacturing service platform mainly includes components such as resource managers, task managers, and schedulers. The specific operation process is as follows: a user submits a request to the cloud manufacturing service platform, and the task decomposer divides the request into multiple tasks, and establishes the partial order relationship constraints between tasks and constructs workflow application examples. The cloud manufacturing service platform receives the workflow application, the task manager estimates the relevant time attributes of the task, and divides the sub-deadline accordingly, and then generates task scheduling sequences or task clustering according to different scheduling strategies. The resource manager is responsible for monitoring manufacturing service resources, obtaining the set of available services and real-time availability. The scheduler assigns tasks to appropriate service processing, or adjusts the scheduling results according to optimization goals. The workflow application is executed according to the generated scheduling plan, and the platform returns the execution result to the user.

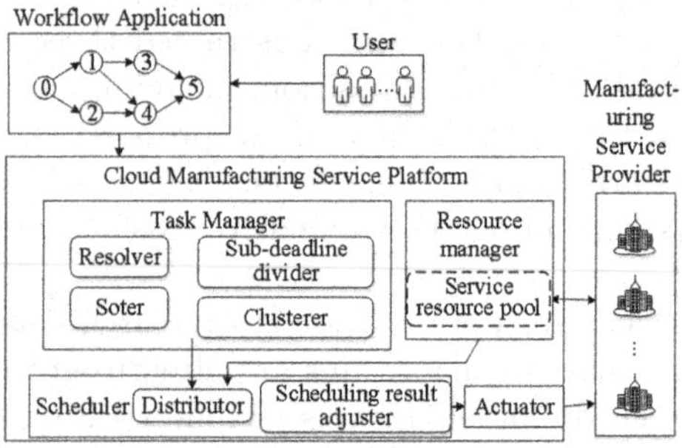

Fig. 1. Scheduling architecture for cloud manufacturing

3.2 Learning and Forgetting Effects Model

The learning and forgetting effects of service resources directly affect task execution time and production costs. The learning effect in the process of service execution task shown in Fig. 2 will reduce the execution time of the task according to a certain rule. Conversely, when the service is idle, it will produce a forgetting effect, resulting in the task execution time becoming longer according to a certain rule.

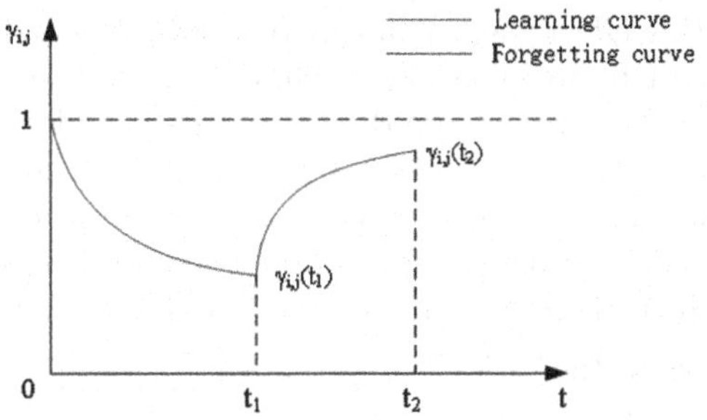

Fig. 2. Learning-forgetting effect model

Combining literature [2,5] and the characteristics of the problem under consideration, this paper constructs the following learning forgetting effect rate:

$$\gamma_{i,j}(t) = \begin{cases} (1+t)^{-\alpha_j}, t \in [0, t_1] \\ 1 - (1 - \gamma_{i,j}(t_1)) \cdot e^{-\beta_j \cdot (t - t_1)}, t \in (t_1, t_2] \end{cases} \tag{1}$$

$\gamma_{i,j}(t)$ represents the learning forgetting effect rate of service s_j at time t, and the corresponding actual execution time is $\gamma_{i,j}(t) \times T_{i,j}$. α_j and β_j are the learning effect coefficient and forgetting effect coefficient of service s_j. $(1 - \gamma_{i,j}(t_1))$ represents the level of learning of service s_j at t_1. The process of service s_j executing task v_i is in the time period $[0, t_1]$, and the idle time period after completion is $(t_1, t_2]$.

3.3 Problem Description

The following assumptions are made for the problems considered: (1) The deadline, topological structure, amount of tasks and workload of each task are all given in advance and are not changed in the scheduling execution. (2) Each task is executed by only one service, without considering task migration and without interruption. (3) The initial execution speed, unit time price, learning effect coefficient and forgetting effect coefficient of services do not change in the scheduling execution, and the logistics cost between services is given in advance, but there is no logistics cost within services. (4) One service executes only one task at a time, and one task executes only on one service at a time.

The deadline of workflow application $G = (V, E)$ is D, $V = \{v_0, v_1 ..., v_{n+1}\}$ represents the task set of G, v_0 and v_{n+1} represent the source node and sink node respectively, both of which are virtual nodes with processing time of 0. $E = \{(v_i, v_j) \mid v_i, v_j \in V\}$ represents the edge between workflow task set, $(v_i, v_i) \in$ E said task must be in the direct precursor v_i can begin, after the completion of W_i for v_i workload. There are m heterogeneous available services in the service resource pool $S = \{s_1, s_2, \ldots, s_m\}$, the initial speed of the service, the price per unit time, and the coefficient of learning and forgetting effects are different. The initial execution speed and unit time price of service S_j are ξ_j and r_i, and the learning and forgetting effect coefficients are α_j and β_j, respectively. The logistics time and logistics cost between service S_j and service s_K are respectively $LT_{j,k}$ and $LC_{j,k}$. φ_i^P and φ_i^S represent the direct precursor and direct successor task sets of V_i respectively. Decision variables $x_{i,j} \in \{0,1\}$ represents whether task v_i is assigned to the service s_j, If it is, then $x_{i,j} = 1$, otherwise $x_{i,j}$=0.

In this paper, the optimization of the target for total cost, namely, $\min C = \sum_{i=1}^{n} \left(C_i^l + C_i^e\right)$. The logistic cost of task v_j is equal to the sum of logistic cost of all its precursor tasks to the task $C_i^l = \sum_{v_p \in \varphi_i^P} \left(\sum_{j=1}^{m} \sum_{k=1}^{m} x_{p,k} \cdot x_{i,j} \cdot LC_{j,k}\right)$. The production cost of v_j is determined by its actual execution time and the unit time price of its service, which is $C_i^e = \sum_{j=1}^{m} x_{i,j} \cdot \lceil T_i^A \rceil \cdot r_j$. The actual execution time of v_j is determined by the initial execution time on the service and the learning forgetting effect value of the service at the actual start time of the task, that is, $T_i^A = \sum_{j=1}^{m} x_{i,j} \cdot T_{i,j} \cdot \gamma_{i,j}\left(AST_i\right)$. The initial service execution time of $T_{i,j} = \frac{W_i}{\xi_j}$. v_j cannot start until all its direct precursor tasks are completed, that is, $AST_i \geq \max_{v_p \in \varphi_i^P} AFT_p$. $AFT_i = AST_i + T_i^A$ indicates that it cannot be interrupted during its execution. Let $T = AFT_{n+1}$, then $T \leq D$. $\sum_{j=1}^{m} x_{p,j} \cdot x_{i,j} = 1$ means two tasks v_p and v_i are assigned to the same service for execution.

4 Task Sequence Adjustment Based Workflow Scheduling

Based on the idea of list Scheduling, a heuristic workflow Scheduling algorithm TSAS (Task Sequence Adjustment Based Workflow Scheduling) framework is proposed. Including task subdeadline division, scheduling sequence generation, service allocation, variable neighborhood search (scheduling result adjustment) and other algorithm components, as shown in Algorithm 1.

Algorithm 1. TSAS(Task Sequence Adjustment based workflow Scheduling)

Input: Workflow application G
    Deadline D
Output: The completion time of the workflow application G T
    The total cost C

```
begin
    Time parameter estimation;
    Division of task deadlines;
    Generate task scheduling sequence Q;
    while Q ≠ ∅ do
        Take out the first task v in Q;
        Assign services to task v;
    end while
    Calculate the total cost C;
    Calculate the completion time T;
    Variable neighborhood search;
    return C, T
```

4.1 Division of Task Sub-deadline

First obtain the sub-deadline of the task. If each task can be completed within its sub-deadline, the workflow can be guaranteed to be completed within the deadline. The sub-deadline is based on the earliest completion time of the task, and part of the floating time is allocated to it. Taking the fastest service can estimate the execution time of task $\widehat{e_l} = \frac{W_i}{\max\limits_{j=1,...m} \{\xi_j\}}$, the logistics time may be required between two tasks with partial order. When two tasks are assigned to the same service, the logistics time between them is zero, and the estimated logistics time is also assumed to be zero. Based on the estimated task execution time and logistics time, the earliest start time EST_i and the earliest completion time EFT_i can be calculated iteratively:

$$EST_i = \begin{cases} 0, & i = 0 \\ \max\limits_{v_p \in \varphi_i^P} \left(EST_p + \widehat{e_p}\right), & i \neq 0 \end{cases} \tag{2}$$

$$EFT_i = EST_i + \widehat{e_l} \tag{3}$$

The earliest completion time of the workflow is v_{n+1} earliest completion time EFT_{n+1}, because the service with the fastest execution speed estimates the task execution time initially, the possible floating time between the workflow.

Based on the earliest completion time, three types of workflow floating time FT are proposed according to different proportions:

- EFBS (Earliest Finish time based Sub-deadline): Divide FT according to the ratio of the earliest completion time of the task to the earliest completion time of the workflow, that is, $D_i = EFT_i + \frac{EFT_i}{EFT_{n+1}} \cdot FT$.
- Task node depth LDS (Level Depth based Sub-deadline): The task depth is determined by $l_i = \begin{cases} 0, i = 0 \\ \max\limits_{v_p \in \varphi_i^P} (l_p + 1), i \neq 0 \end{cases}$, divide FT according to the ratio of task depth and maximum workflow depth $l_{\max} = \max\limits_{i=1,...,n} \{l_i\}$, that is, $SD_i = EFT_i + \frac{l_i}{l_{\max}} \cdot FT$.
- *UpwardRank* method URS (Upward Rank based Sub-deadline): According to the average initial execution time of v_i on all services $\bar{T}_l = \frac{\sum_{j=1}^{m} T_{i,j}}{m}$ and service Average logistics time $\overline{LT} = \frac{\sum_{k=1}^{m}\sum_{j=1}^{m} LT_{j,k}}{m^2}$ calculate its *UpwardRank* value $\text{rank}_i^{up} = \begin{cases} \bar{T}_l, i = n+1 \\ \max\limits_{v_s \in \varphi_i^S} \left\{\text{rank}_s^{up} + \overline{LT}\right\} + \bar{T}_l, i \neq n+1 \end{cases}$, then $SD_i = EFT_i + \frac{\text{rank}_0^{up} - \text{rank}_i^{up}}{\text{rank}_0^{up}} \cdot FT$.

4.2 Scheduling Sequence Generation

According to $l_i = \begin{cases} 0, i = 0 \\ \max\limits_{v_p \in \varphi_i^P} (l_p + 1), i \neq 0 \end{cases}$ to divide the task hierarchy, low-level tasks take precedence over high-level tasks. Tasks at the same level can be executed in parallel, but their task priority methods have different definitions. This article proposes the following three priority scheduling sequence generation methods:

- MSF (Maximum Successors First): The workflow task scheduling sequence is sorted in non-ascending order according to the number of direct successor tasks $\left|\varphi_i^S\right|$ of task v_i.
- MFTF (Minimum Float Time First): According to the task floating time of the same level task $FT_i = LST_i - EST_i$, arranged in non-descending order to get the workflow task scheduling sequence.
- CPP (Critical Path based Priority): Calculate the $Up - downwardRank$ values of tasks in same level $l_i = \begin{cases} 0, i = 0 \\ \max\limits_{v_p \in \varphi_i^P} \left\{\text{rank}_p^{\text{down}} + \overline{T_p} + \overline{LT}\right\}, i \neq 0 \end{cases}$, the task scheduling sequence of workflow was obtained by non-ascending order of priority, that is, $priority_i = rank_i^{up} + rank_i^{down}$.

4.3 Service Assignment

Assign tasks that meet their deadlines for services. In order to minimize the total cost of workflow, the services that can meet the sub-deadline constraints and have the lowest total cost are preferred. If there is no service that can meet the subdeadline constraint of the task, the service with the earliest actual completion time of the task will be preferentially selected to avoid violating the deadline constraint of the subsequent task and even the whole workflow.

4.4 Variable Neighborhood Search

The above scheduling process produces the initial scheduling Q, which can be further optimized through variable neighborhood search. Divide the task into different depth task sets L_j $(j = 0, \ldots, l_{\max})$ according to the above levels, that is, $V = \bigcup_{j=0}^{l_{\max}} L_j$. Suppose there are k_max neighborhood structures, the k-th neighborhood structure generates neighborhood solution set N_k. The process of generating N_k is: randomly select a hierarchical task set (obviously the number of tasks cannot be less than 2), and randomly select two from the task set Tasks, exchange their positions in the scheduling sequence, and the above process is repeated —N_k— times. The search process starts from N_1. If the completion time exceeds the deadline constraint or the total cost is not optimized, then directly enter the next neighborhood structure search. If the completion time meets the deadline and the total cost is optimized, record this neighborhood solution and enter Search for the next neighborhood solution of the initial solution. Finally, the optimal solution of a total of $(k_{max}+1)$ solutions including the initial solution is obtained, and return. Let Q_{final} and C_{min} denote the final task scheduling sequence and its corresponding total workflow cost, respectively, and Q', C', and T' respectively denote the newly generated task scheduling sequence, the

Algorithm 2. TSAS(Task Scheduling Sequence Adjustment Algorithm)

Input: Workflow application G

Deadline D

Task scheduling sequence Q

The total workflow cost corresponding to Q G

Different depth of the task set L_j ($j = 0, \ldots, l_{\max}$)

Output: The total cost of the workflow after adjusting scheduling result C_{min}

1: **begin**
2: $Q_{final} \leftarrow Q$;
3: $C_{min} \leftarrow C$
4: **for** k \leftarrow 1 **to** k_{min} **do**
5: $Q' \leftarrow Q$;
6: **for** i \leftarrow 1 **to** k **do**
7: L_{random} \leftarrowRandomly select a meet set of $|L_j| \geq 2$;
8: Selected at random from the L_{random} two tasks v_a and v_b;
9: Exchange v_a and v_b position in Q';
10: **endfor**
11: **while** $Q \neq \varnothing$ **do**
12: Take out the first task v in Q;
13: Assign services to task v;
14: **end while**
15: Calculate the total cost C';
16: Calculate the completion time T';
17: **if**$(T' \leq D) \wedge (C' \leq C_{min})$ **then**
18: $Q_{final} \leftarrow Q'$;
19: $C_{min} \leftarrow C'$
20: **end** *if*
21: **end for**
22: **return** C_{min}

corresponding total workflow cost and completion time. The idea description is shown in Algorithm 2.

Variable neighborhood search performance is related to two key factors: k_{max} and exchange task of neighborhood solutions $|N_k|$, through successive logarithm increase exchange tasks, namely $|N_1| < \ldots < |N_k| < \ldots < |N_{k_{max}}|$. This article assumes that k_{max} is determined by the coefficient of μ and workflow task number n, namely $k_{max} = \mu \cdot n$, and set $|N_k| =$ k. Since the neighborhood solution N_k is generated by exchanging K for tasks, when K is small, the initial solution can be searched locally and the solution quality can be improved. However, when K is large, the task scheduling sequence tends to be randomly sorted more and more, making the quality of the neighborhood solution lower and lower and it is difficult to improve the solution quality. In this paper, the coefficient μ will be corrected in the experimental part.

5 Path Clustering Based Workflow Scheduling

By improving and extending the PCH algorithm [9], the path clustering workflow scheduling heuristic MPCH (Modified PCH) was proposed. Different from TSAS's overall consideration of total cost, MPCH algorithm optimizes the total cost of workflow from the perspective of reducing logistics cost and production cost, mainly including task sub-deadline division, task clustering and service allocation. The framework is shown in Algorithm 3.

Algorithm 3. MPCH(Modified Path Clustering Heuristic)

Input: Workflow application G
Deadline D
Output: The completion time of the workflow application G T
The total cost C

begin
  Division of task deadlines;
  Put all tasks into the unscheduled task set UTS;
  while $UTS \neq \varnothing$ **do**
    Call the task clustering algorithm to generate a task cluster CL for the tasks in UTS;
    Call the service allocation algorithm to allocate services for CL;
    $UTS \leftarrow UTS - CL$
  end while
  Calculate the total cost C;
  Calculate the completion time T;
  return C, T

5.1 Division of Task Sub-deadline

The MPCH algorithm sets the sub-deadline of the task as the latest completion time of the task, which is $LFT_i = \begin{cases} D, i = n+1 \\ \min_{v_s \in \varphi_i^S} \left(LFT_s - \widehat{e_s} \right), i \neq n+1 \end{cases}$, to ensure that the entire workflow application is completed within the deadline, the corresponding start time is $LST_i = LFT_i - \widehat{e_l}$.

5.2 Task Clustering

Task clustering selects several tasks from the unscheduled task set UTS as a whole, and the partial order constraint among tasks is considered in the process. To add task v_i to the cluster CL, any direct predecessor $v_p \in \phi_i^P$ has either been scheduled or is in the current cluster, otherwise v_i cannot be added to the CL. MPCH firstly selects v_f with the largest $UpwardRank$ value to join CL in UTS. Depth-priority traversal starts from v_f, and the direct successor with the largest priority value is selected to join CL in each case. The direct successor task must meet two conditions: (1) It has not been scheduled. (2) Other direct precursor tasks of this task have been scheduled. The $priority_i$ of task v_i is defined as the sum of $UpwardRank$ and $DownwardRank$, i.e. $priority_i = rank_i^{up} + rank_i^{down}$. The sub-deadline and completion time of task cluster CL are defined as the sub-deadline and completion time of the last task added to the cluster respectively. MPCH algorithm is described as Algorithm 4.

Algorithm 4. TSAS(Task Scheduling Sequence Adjustment Algorithm)

Input: Workflow application G
 Deadline D
 Unscheduled task set UTS
Output: A task cluster CL

1: **begin**
2: $CL \leftarrow \varnothing$;
3: $v_f \leftarrow$ The task with the largest $UpwardRank$ value in UTS;
4: $CL \leftarrow CL \cup \{v_f\}$
5: $v_{temp} \leftarrow v_f$;
6: **while** $\varphi_{temp}^{S} \neq \varnothing$ **do**
7: $child_{selected} \leftarrow NULL$;
8: $priority_{max} \leftarrow 0$;
9: Exchange **foreach** $v_s \in \varphi_{temp}^{S}$ **do**;
10: **if** $(v_s \in UTS) \wedge (UTS \cap (\varphi_s^{P} - \{v_{\text{temp}}\}) = \varnothing) \wedge (priority_s > priority_{\text{max}})$ **then**
11: $child_{selected} \leftarrow v_s$;
12: $priority_{max} \leftarrow priority_s$;
13: **end if**;
14: **end foreach**
15: **if** $child_{selected} = NULL$ **then**
16: **return** CL;
17: **end if**
18: **else**;
19: $CL \leftarrow CL \cup \{child_{selected}\}$;
20: $S' \leftarrow$ Get all services that meet the CL sub-deadline;
21: **if** $S' = \varnothing$ **then**
22: **return** $CL - \{child_{selected}\}$;
23: **end if**
24: **end else**
25: $v_{temp} \leftarrow child_{selected}$;
26: **end while**
27: **return** CL

5.3 Service Allocation

Service allocation of MPCH algorithm allocates services to each task cluster, and all tasks in the same cluster are assigned to the same service. Firstly, all the services that can meet the CL sub-deadline of task clustering are screened out as the candidate service set, and then these candidate services are assigned to CL in turn, and the service that can make the total cost of CL is selected as the distribution result of CL. If there is no service that can meet the CL sub-deadline, that is, the candidate service set is empty, select the service that can make the actual CL completion time earliest.

MPCH algorithm needs to go through the process of task clustering and service allocation, and has two advantages: (1) Clustering multiple workflow tasks and assigning them to the same service may sacrifice the parallelism between tasks and increase the risk of workflow completion beyond the deadline. But there is no parallelism between tasks in workflow serial structure. Therefore, MPCH performs linear clustering through depth-first traversal of the task clustering algorithm, and combines the tasks in the workflow serial structure into a cluster. In addition, several tasks with sequential partial order relationship can be directly assigned to the same service as a whole, which can avoid the logistics time and logistics cost between these tasks, and help to complete the workflow as soon as possible and minimize the total cost. (2) MPCH algorithm can ensure the continuous execution of task clustering on the service to a large extent, reduce the idle time in the cluster as much as possible, reduce the degradation effect of forgetting effect when the service is idle, give full play to the optimization effect of learning effect on task execution time, and effectively control the production cost of the task. When the number of serial structure tasks in workflow increases, the clustering scale of tasks obtained by MPCH algorithm increases, which is more conducive to optimizing logistics cost and production cost.

6 Experimental Results

In order to get the optimal combination of TSAS, parameter correction is given. Besides, TSAS and MPCH are compared with the classical algorithms on similar problems.

6.1 Experimental Enviroment

Using WorkflowSim [16] workflow simulation platform to simulate task scheduling in cloud manufacturing environment, all algorithms are written in Java language and run in Intel Core i5-9400F CPU @2.90 GHz with 8 GBytes of RAM.

At the task level [15], task number n was set at $\{50, 100, 150, 200, 250, 300\}$, and 10 workflow instances were randomly generated for each task number scenario. The deadline of workflow application is defined as $D = EFT_{n+1} \cdot \theta$, θ is the deadline urgency factor values $\{1.5, 1.6, 1.7, 1.8, 1.9\}$. Task workload follows uniform distribution $U(1, 30000)$. There were $6 \times 5 \times 10 = 300$ random workflow instances with 6 task numbers, 5 deadline factors and 10 instances per task number scenario.

At the service resource level [17], the number of services is 50, initial execution speed follows uniform distribution $U(600, 1200)$, price per unit time follows

$U(30, 60)$, and learning effect coefficients α and β follow $U(0.04, 0.06)$. Logistics time (h) follows $U(0, 10)$, and logistics cost is proportional to logistics time.

The multi-factor analysis of variance technology ANOVA is used to analyze the experimental results. Choose RPD (Relative Percentage Deviation) as the evaluation index. Suppose the solution obtained by the current algorithm is π, and the total workflow cost is $C(\pi)$. The optimal scheduling solution under different parameters or algorithms is π^*, and the minimum total cost is $C(\pi^*)$, then the total cost of the current algorithm is:

$$RPD = \frac{C(\pi) - C(\pi^*)}{C(\pi^*)} \times 100\% \quad (4)$$

6.2 Parameter Calibration

TSAS algorithm includes algorithm components and parameters: (1) Seed deadline division method EFBS, LDS, URS. (2) Task scheduling sequence generation method MSF, MFTF, CPP. (3) The maximum neighborhood structure quantitative coefficient $\pi = \{0, 0.01, 0.02, 0.03, 0.04, 0.05, 0.06, 0.07, 0.08, 0.09, 0.10, 0.11, 0.12\}$.

Figure 3(a) shows the comparison results of the three task subdeadline division rules. It can be seen from the figure that EFBS has the smallest RPD value. Figure 3(b) shows the comparison results of three different task scheduling sequence generation rules. It can be seen from the figure that the RPD values of MFTF is slightly lower than that of CPP. Figure 3(c) shows the corresponding results of different maximum neighborhood structure quantitative coefficients.

Based on the above analysis, TSAS will adopt EFBS, MFTF and set the coefficient $\mu = 0.11$.

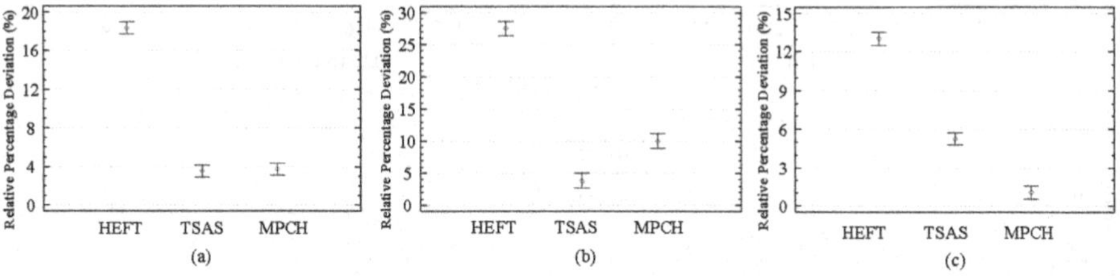

Fig. 3. Mean plots of the sub-deadline division methods, sequencing methods and values with 95.0% Tukey HSD confidence level intervals

6.3 Algorithms Comparison

This paper selects HEFT algorithm [7] for comparison, and adds learning forgetting effect in resource allocation stage to adapt to the problem under consideration.

In order to comprehensively compare the performance indicators of the algorithm, the RPD values of total cost, logistics cost and production cost were compared respectively in Fig. 4. Figure 4(a) shows the mean RPD chart of total cost of the three algorithms under different number of tasks and deadline coefficients. It can be seen that TSAS and MPCH have obvious advantages over HEFT, and TSAS is more suitable for workflow scheduling scenarios with fewer tasks and more loose deadlines, while MPCH is more suitable for workflow scheduling

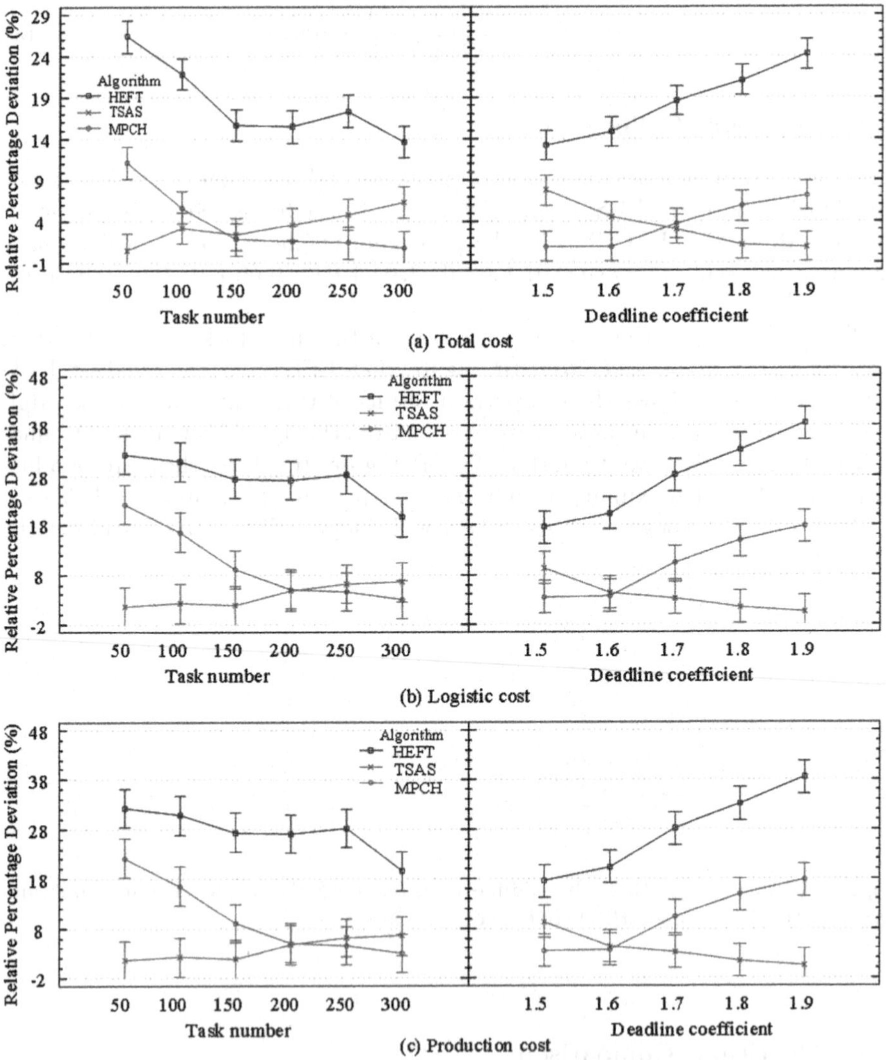

Fig. 4. Interaction plots of RPDs of different costs on the number of jobs, deadline levels with 95.0% Tukey HSD confidence level intervals

scenarios with more tasks and more urgent deadlines. As the number of tasks n increases, the total cost RPD of HEFT and MPCH generally decreases, while that of TSAS generally increases. Figure 4(b) shows the average RPD of the logistics costs of the three algorithms under different task numbers and deadline coefficients. It can be seen that the TSA algorithm has the best performance when the number of tasks is small and the deadline is relatively loose. Figure 4(c) shows the mean RPD of production cost of the three algorithms in different tasks and different deadline coefficients. It can be seen that MPCH performs better than TSAS and HEFT under most tasks and all deadline coefficients. As the number of tasks n increases, the RPD of HEFT and MPCH decreases, while the RPD of TSAS increases. With the increase of n, the probability of serial structure in workflow increases, and the number of tasks contained in serial structure also increases.

Based on the above results, the TSAS and MPCH algorithms proposed in this paper are close to each other in total cost performance, and both are obviously superior to the comparison algorithm. TSAS is more suitable for workflow scheduling scenarios with less tasks and loose deadlines. MPCH is more suitable for workflow scheduling scenarios with a large number of tasks and urgent deadlines.

7 Conclusion

This paper considers the workflow task scheduling problem with deadline constraint and learning and forgetting effects in cloud manufacturing environment, and analyzes two main factors of total cost: logistics cost and production cost, which contradict each other in cloud manufacturing environment. At the same time, the learning and forgetting effects of service resources is analyzed and the learning and forgetting effect model of service resources is established. Two heuristic algorithms, TSAS and MPCH, are proposed to minimize the total cost. A large number of experimental results show that TSAS is more suitable for workflow scheduling scenarios with fewer tasks and loose deadlines. MPCH is more suitable for workflow scheduling scenarios with a large number of tasks and urgent deadlines.

References

1. Ghomi, E.J., Rahmani, A.M., Qader, N.N.: Service load balancing, scheduling, and logistics optimization in cloud manufacturing by using genetic algorithm. Concurr. Comput. Pract. Exp. **31**(20), e5329 (2019)
2. Teyarachakul, S., Chand, S., Ward, J.: Effect of learning and forgetting on batch sizes. Prod. Oper. Manag. **20**(1), 116–128 (2011)
3. Xu, H., Li, X., Ruiz, R., Zhu, H.: Group scheduling with nonperiodical maintenance and deteriorating effects. IEEE Trans. Syst. Man Cybern. Syst. **51**(5), 2860–2872 (2021)

4. Kuo, W.H., Yang, D.L.: A note on due-date assignment and single-machine scheduling with deteriorating jobs and learning effects. J. Oper. Res. Soc. **62**(1), 206–210 (2011)
5. Yang, W.H., Chand, S.: Learning and forgetting effects on a group scheduling problem. Eur. J. Oper. Res. **187**(3), 1033–1044 (2008)
6. Wu, C.H., Lee, W.C., Lai, P.J., Wang, J.Y.: Some single-machine scheduling problems with elapsed-time-based and position-based learning and forgetting effects. Discret. Optim. **19**, 1–11 (2016)
7. Topcuoglu, H., Hariri, S., Wu, M.Y.: Performance-effective and low-complexity task scheduling for heterogeneous computing. IEEE Trans. Parallel Distrib. Syst. **13**(3), 260–274 (2002)
8. Sih, G., Lee, E.: A compile-time scheduling heuristic for interconnection-constrained heterogeneous processor architectures. IEEE Trans. Parallel Distrib. Syst. **4**(2), 175–187 (1993)
9. Bittencourt, L.F., Madeira, E.R.M.: Fulfilling task dependence gaps for workflow scheduling on grids, pp. 468–475 (2007)
10. Bittencourt, L.F., Madeira, E.R.M.: A performance-oriented adaptive scheduler for dependent tasks on grids. Concurr. Comput. Practi. Exp. **20**(9), 1029–1049 (2008)
11. Geng, X., Yu, L., Bao, J., Fu, G.: A task scheduling algorithm based on priority list and task duplication in cloud computing environment. Web Intell. **17**(2), 121–129 (2019)
12. Fan, Y., Wang, L., Chen, J., Jin, Z., Shi, L., Xu, J.: Multi-job associated task scheduling based on task duplication and insertion for cloud computing. In: Yu, D., Dressler, F., Yu, J. (eds.) Wireless Algorithms, Systems, and Applications, pp. 109–120 (2020)
13. He, W., Xu, L.: A state-of-the-art survey of cloud manufacturing. Int. J. Comput. Integr. Manuf. **28**(3), 239–250 (2015)
14. Dong, T., Xue, F., Xiao, C., Li, J.: Task scheduling based on deep reinforcement learning in a cloud manufacturing environment. Concurr. Comput. Pract. Exp. **32**(11), e5654 (2020)
15. Zhang, W., Xiao, J., Zhang, S., Lin, J., Feng, R.: A utility-aware multi-task scheduling method in cloud manufacturing using extended NSGA-II embedded with game theory. Int. J. Comput. Integr. Manuf. **34**(2), 175–194 (2021)
16. Chen, W., Deelman, E.: Workflowsim: a toolkit for simulating scientific workflows in distributed environments. In: 2012 IEEE 8th International Conference on E-Science, pp. 1–8 (2012)
17. Liu, Y., Xu, X., Zhang, L., Wang, L., Zhong, R.Y.: Workload-based multi-task scheduling in cloud manufacturing. Robot. Comput.-Integr. Manuf. **45**, 3–20 (2017)

Spatial-Temporal Graph Neural Network Framework with Multi-source Local and Global Information Fusion for Traffic Flow Forecasting

Yue-Xin Li[1], Jian-Yu Li[1(✉)], Zi-Jia Wang[2], and Zhi-Hui Zhan[1(✉)]

[1] School of Computer Science and Engineering, South China University of Technology, Guangzhou 510006, China
jianyulics@foxmail.com, zhanapollo@163.com

[2] School of Computer Science and Cyber Engineering, Guangzhou University, Guangzhou 510006, China

Abstract. As the increasing population is causing a large amount of traffic congestion nowadays, accurate traffic flow forecasting (TFF) has become increasingly significant for smart cities. While some recurrent neural network-based models have taken the spatial-temporal (ST) features of traffic flow data into account for TFF, they still treat the ST features from multi-source time-series data of each timestep separately, which may be inefficient to learn a general and robust representation with spatial correlation information for TFF. To address these issues, this paper proposes a Spatial-Temporal Graph Neural Network Framework (STGNNF) for TFF. This framework is based on the assumption that when a small range of adjacent temporal features of the multi-source time-series data is fused as the input, the model is still able to effectively learn meaningful representation and capture the time-series information. By doing so, the learned representation from the fused adjacent data can be more general and robust for TFF, because it considers the multi-source time-series data within a larger time scale. Moreover, three novel designs are proposed and integrated to further enhance the STGNNF, which are 1) a local ST unit for learning the local ST information from the fused adjacent multi-source time-series data; 2) a relevance evaluation module for paying more attention to the significant local ST information; and 3) a global ST unit for generating the global ST representation and information from local ST information with corresponding attentions. Experimental studies are conducted in three real-world traffic flow datasets, which indicate that STGNNF performs better than existing approaches and predicts reasonably when encountering anomalous data.

Keywords: Traffic flow forecasting · Spatial-temporal data · Graph neural network · Recurrent neural network · Attention mechanism

1 Introduction

The booming progress of urbanization has led to the continuous increase of people's travel demand [1]. Many traffic congestion problems are inevitably caused by the

Y. Sun et al. (Eds.): ChineseCSCW 2021, CCIS 1491, pp. 371–385, 2022.
https://doi.org/10.1007/978-981-19-4546-5_29

increasing traffic volume on urban roads, which greatly affect the livelihood level of citizens. How to make accurate traffic flow forecasting (TFF) and apply it to the decision-making of traffic dispersion control is a popular research direction in modern intelligent transportation systems.

Statistical methods are usually adopted in TFF. Historical average (HA) model regards the input traffic flow as a periodic process and adopts a weighted average to make predictions [2]. Autoregressive integrated moving average (ARIMA) is a model that transforms non-stationary time series into stationary time series [3], and then the dependent variables are regressed only to its lag value, the present value, and the lag value of the random error term. Vector auto-regression (VAR) forecasts the future traffic flow by linearly regressing the endogenous variables within the same sample period [4]. Another type of statistical method applied to TFF is statistical machine learning, and one of which is support vector regression (SVR) [5]. SVR applies support vector machine and linear kernel to perform linear regression for the traffic flow. One problem of these statistical methods is that their input sequence data should satisfy strict statistical conditions. For example, a smooth input sequence is required for ARIMA. Nevertheless, real-world traffic flow is highly complex and nonlinear, which makes it less likely for statistical methods to perform well.

Neural network (NN) models are powerful nonlinear fitting tools. Park et al. adopted a feed-forward NN (FNN) to predict the traffic flow, but the fully connected structure of FNN overlooks the relative positions in the time series [6]. As a special recurrent NN (RNN) variant, long short-term memory (LSTM) can process and predict important events with very long intervals and delays in time series [7]. Sutskever et al. designed an LSTM-based model with an encoder-decoder structure [8]. Similarly, Ma et al. proposed a simple LSTM network with a one-layer LSTM, a fully connected input layer, and an output layer [9]. They both benefit from the long-term and short-term temporal dependency learned from the LSTM units.

However, both statistical methods and NN methods mentioned above mainly consider the temporal information but fail to consider the spatial correlation of traffic flow. It is natural to observe that if traffic congestion happens on a certain road, the roads nearby are very likely to experience a similar increase in car volume. The past few years witnessed a remarkable growth in the number of works considering both spatial and temporal dependencies of traffic flow. On one hand, RNN-based models are modified to take spatial correlation of traffic flow into account, and are widely applied in spatial-temporal (ST) forecasting tasks including TFF [10, 11]. On the other hand, a spectral-based graph convolutional network (GCN) is proposed to process graph-structured data [12]. GCN receives a large amount of attention because of its simple structure and high expression ability. Yu et al. proposed an ST-based GCN, which utilizes convolution in both spatial and temporal domain and achieves fast training time [13]. Diao et al. improved STGCN by designing a graph Laplacian estimator to model the spatial dependency in a temporal dynamic way [14]. Other state-of-the-art models also apply graph neural network (GNN) variants, including graph attention networks [15–17], Graph Wavelets [18], in traffic forecasting-related tasks.

Based on the preliminary studies, we find that most RNN-based deep learning models treat the multi-source data of each timestep separately for TFF, which may be inefficient to learn general and robust representation (including local and global spatial correlation information) of the multi-source time-series data. Considering this, it is worth figuring out that "*Is it possible to learn a meaningful ST representation from a local perspective of spatially-correlated multi-source time-series data, rather than the dispersed perspective of data at different independent timestep?*". To address these issues, we start from the hypothesis that we can fuse a small range of adjacent temporal features, while the model is still able to effectively capture the time-series information locally and globally. By doing so, the ST representation and information learned by the model will be more general and robust, because that such ST representation can fuse knowledge and information from the multi-source time-series data within a larger time scale. Based on this, an ST deep learning framework named Spatial-Temporal Graph Neural Network Framework (STGNNF) is proposed in this paper with three novel designs, which are local ST-fusion unit, relevance evaluation module, and global ST-fusion unit. The STGNNF first adopts the local ST-fusion unit to fuse a certain range of the input sequence to generate local ST representations. After that, different local representations are utilized with corresponding attention given by the relevance evaluation module, and then they are mined globally via the global ST-fusion unit to generate higher-level features as global representations for TFF.

In summary, the main contributions of our work are:

- A novel ST deep learning framework called STGNNF with the local ST-fusion unit is proposed in this paper. As the local ST-fusion unit will force the model to learn ST representations from a local perspective of adjacent temporal features, the proposed STGNNF can obtain more general and robust local representations with spatial correlation information.
- A relevance evaluation module is further proposed to pay more attention to the more significant and relevant representations and information provided by local ST-fusion units, so as to improve the learning efficiency and effectiveness of the STGNNF.
- A global ST-fusion unit is proposed and integrated into the STGNNF to further mine the ST representations globally, which can result in a more powerful and robust high-level representation for TFF.

The experimental results reveal that the STGNNF achieves better performance than five existing approaches in three real-world traffic flow datasets. Furthermore, visualization of the prediction results shows that STGNNF can generate reasonable predictions when encountering anomalous inputs. Therefore, it is potential to learn a more meaningful and robust ST representation from a local perspective of multi-source time-series data for TTF and even other ST-based forecasting tasks.

2 Preliminaries

2.1 Problem Description

An intuitive method to abstract a traffic network is to convert it into a graph to utilize the spatial correlation within traffic flow. Here, we define the TFF problem as it is described in [13]. A traffic network can be defined as a graph $\mathcal{G} = (\mathcal{V}, \mathcal{E}, A)$, where $\mathcal{V}$ is the set of the traffic flow sensors in a certain area, $N = |\mathcal{V}|$ is the number of traffic flow sensors, $\mathcal{E}$ is the set of weighted edges which encode the connectivity of each traffic flow sensor pairs (e.g. the distances between every two sensors), and A is the weighted adjacency matrix of $\mathcal{G}$. All the traffic flow sensors are continuously generating a series of traffic flow observations.

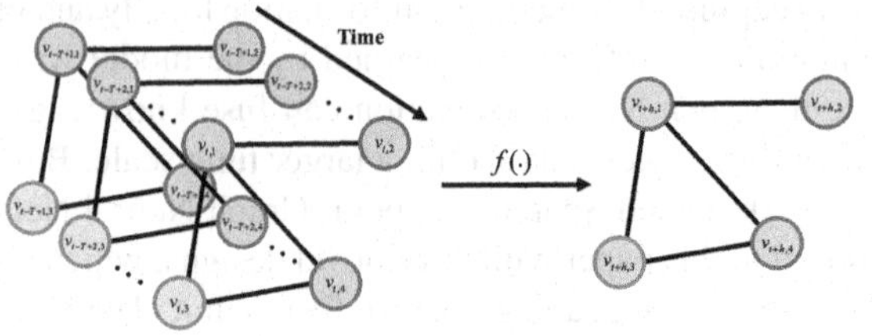

Fig. 1. An illustration of the TFF task. Here, the previous T traffic flow historical observations of four traffic flow sensors are utilized through a model f to forecast the traffic flow at the next h timestep.

Figure 1 illustrates the task of TFF. In a certain timestep t, we hope to use a prediction model $f(\cdot)$ to find the most likely traffic flow $\vec{v}_{t+h}$ in the future timestep $t + h$, according to the traffic flow data collected from the previous traffic flow sensors. The TFF problem can be therefore represented as:

$$\hat{\vec{v}}_{t+h} = \mathop{\arg\max}_{\vec{v}_{t+h}} \log P(\vec{v}_{t+h} | \vec{v}_{t-T+1}, \vec{v}_{t-T+2}, \ldots, \vec{v}_t) \tag{1}$$

2.2 Graph Convolutional Network

Denote the graph convolution operator as $*_\mathcal{G}$. The graph convolution of a graph signal $X \in \mathbb{R}^{N \times C}$ with a channel size of C is represented as:

$$\Omega *_\mathcal{G} X = \Omega(L)X = \Omega(U \Lambda U^\top)X = U\Omega(\Lambda)U^\top X \tag{2}$$

where U and Λ are the eigenvector matrix and the eigenvalue diagonal matrix of the normalized graph Laplacian matrix $L = I_N - D^{-1/2}AD^{-1/2}$, D is the degree matrix of the graph $\mathcal{G}$. The main purpose of graph convolution is to enhance or decay the graph signal component in the spectral domain. Hence, $\Omega(\Lambda)$ is designed as a frequency response function to fit the target signal. A Taylor polynomial can be adopted here to realize this goal:

$$\Omega *_\mathcal{G} X = U\left(\sum\nolimits_{i=0}^{O} \omega_i \tilde{\Lambda}^i\right)U^\top X \tag{3}$$

O represents the order of the Taylor polynomial, ω_i is the i-th coefficient of this polynomial, $\tilde{\Lambda} = 2\Lambda/\lambda_{\max} - I_N$ is rescaled eigenvalue matrix, and $\lambda_{\max}$ is the largest eigenvalue of L. In practice, the eigen-decomposition of L is time-consuming, especially

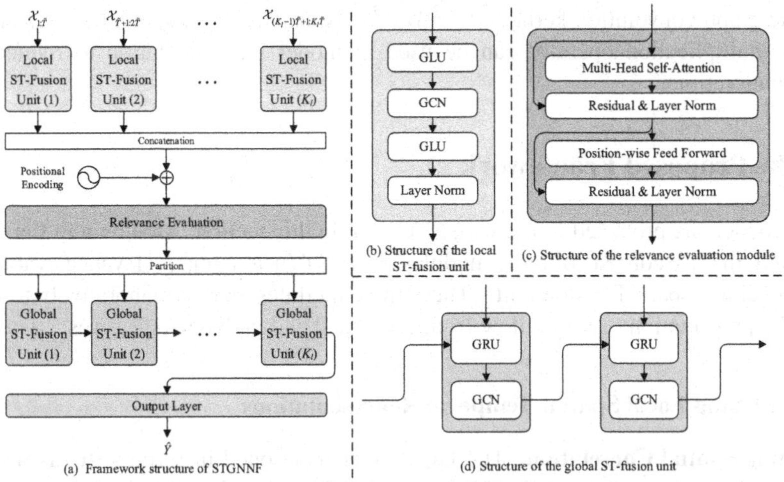

Fig. 2. Detailed framework of STGNNF. (a) is the framework structure of STGNNF, where its input traffic flow $\mathcal{X} \in \mathbb{R}^{T \times N \times F_{\text{in}}}$ is divided into K_l parts with each containing $\tilde{T}$ timesteps, and its output $\hat{Y} \in \mathbb{R}^{N \times F_{\text{out}}}$ contains a single timestep. (b), (c) and (d) illustrate the local ST-fusion unit, the relevance evaluation module, and the global ST-fusion unit, respectively.

in large graphs. Hence, we adopt a simple method to avoid using U and Λ. Consider restricting $O = 1$, then the graph convolution can be represented as follows:

$$\begin{aligned}\Omega *_{\mathcal{G}} X =& U\left(\omega_0 \tilde{\Lambda}^0 + \omega_0 \tilde{\Lambda}^1\right) U^\top X \\ =& U\left(\omega_0 I_N + \omega_0 \tilde{\Lambda}^1\right) U^\top X \\ =& (\omega_0 I_N + \omega_1 (2L/\lambda_{\max} - I_N))X \end{aligned} \tag{4}$$

Furthermore, we simplify formula (4) by assigning $\omega = \omega_0 = -\omega_1$ and $\lambda_{\max} = 2$. In fact, there is also no need to introduce ω to the graph convolution layer since the effect of ω will be ignored when incorporating trainable parameters in this layer. As a result, the graph convolution can be simplified as:

$$\begin{aligned}\Omega *_{\mathcal{G}} X =& \omega\left(I_N - \left(I_N - D^{-1/2} A D^{-1/2} - I_N\right)\right) X \\ =& \omega\left(I_N + D^{-1/2} A D^{-1/2}\right) X \\ =& \omega \tilde{D}^{-1/2} \tilde{A} \tilde{D}^{-1/2} X \\ =& \tilde{D}^{-1/2} \tilde{A} \tilde{D}^{-1/2} X \end{aligned} \tag{5}$$

where $\tilde{A} = A + I_N$ and $\tilde{D}_{ii} = \Sigma_{j=1}^N \tilde{A}_{ij}$. Eventually, an activation function ReLU$(\cdot)$ and a trainable parameter $W_{\mathcal{G}}$ are introduced to enhance the expression ability of the GCN layer as

$$\Omega *_{\mathcal{G}} X = \text{ReLU}\left(\tilde{D}^{-1/2} \tilde{A} \tilde{D}^{-1/2} X W_{\mathcal{G}}\right) \tag{6}$$

The graph convolution kernel $\tilde{D}^{-1/2}\tilde{A}\tilde{D}^{-1/2}$ is usually a sparse matrix, so a sparse matrix multiplication operator can be used in model implementation to reduce the computation time.

3 The Proposed Framework

We introduce the proposed framework STGNNF in this section. As shown in Fig. 2(a), STGNNF mainly consists of three modules, local ST-fusion units, relevance evaluation module, and global ST-fusion units. These three modules work collaboratively to learn the ST representation of traffic flow from both local and global perspectives.

3.1 Learning Local Spatial-Temporal Representations

Modeling Spatial Correlation. The GCN layer mentioned in formula (6) is used to model the spatial correlation of traffic flow, but with a minor modification. Suppose the input of the GCN layer is $\mathcal{Z} \in \mathbb{R}^{M \times N \times C_{\mathcal{G}}}$, M is the number of timesteps in $\mathcal{Z}$, $C_{\mathcal{G}}$ is the channel size of the GCN layer. The graph convolution operator should be therefore generalized for three-dimension graph signal input. Here, we simply apply the same graph convolution kernel to each timestep. In practice, the increasing number of layers may cause gradient explosion or vanishing. Therefore, a skip connection [19] is placed in the GCN layer. Then, the GCN layer mines the spatial features in the following way:

$$\Omega *_{\mathcal{G}} \mathcal{Z} = \mathrm{Concat}\left(\mathrm{ReLU}\left(\tilde{D}^{-1/2}\tilde{A}\tilde{D}^{-1/2}Z_m W_{\mathcal{G}} + Z_m\right)\right) \quad m = 1, 2, \ldots, M \tag{7}$$

where $Z_m \in \mathbb{R}^{N \times C_{\mathcal{G}}}$ represents the spatial features of the mth timestep in $\mathcal{Z}$.

Modeling Temporal Correlation. We adopt the gated linear unit (GLU) [20] to model the temporal correlation of traffic flow in the local ST-fusion unit. For an input $\mathcal{Y} \in \mathbb{R}^{M \times N \times C_{\mathcal{T}}}$, where $C_{\mathcal{T}}$ is the channel size of $\mathcal{Y}$, a GLU first adopts two one-dimension causal convolutions to $\mathcal{Y}$ for feature extraction. Both convolution kernels have the same kernel size K_t, and the convolution here will explore the K_t neighbors of each timestep. Denote the temporal convolution operator as $*_{\mathcal{T}}$, then the GLU generates an output $\Psi *_{\mathcal{T}} \mathcal{Y} \in \mathbb{R}^{(M-K_t+1) \times N \times C_{\mathcal{T}}}$ according to the following way:

$$\Psi *_{\mathcal{T}} \mathcal{Y} = \sigma(\Psi_a *_{\mathrm{1D}} \mathcal{Y}) \odot (\Psi_b *_{\mathrm{1D}} \mathcal{Y} + \mathrm{ALN}(\mathcal{Y})) \tag{8}$$

$\Psi = [\Psi_a, \Psi_b] \in \mathbb{R}^{2K_t \times C_{\mathcal{T}} \times C_{\mathcal{T}}}$ is the temporal convolution kernel, $\odot$ denotes dot product operation, $\sigma(\cdot)$ is the sigmoid activation function, and $*_{\mathrm{1D}}$ represents the one-dimension causal convolution operator. ALN($\cdot$) in (8) is a fully connected layer used for skip connection to avoid temporal channel inconsistency.

Local Spatial-Temporal Representation Fusion. To effectively fuse local ST features of the input traffic flow, we adopt the bottleneck structure proposed in [13]. Figure 2(b) illustrates the structure of a local ST-fusion unit, which stacks one GLU, one GCN layer, and another one GLU to learn local ST representation. A layer normalization is placed after the second GLU. Hence, the output L_{kl} of the kl-th local ST-fusion unit is computed by:

$$L_{kl} = \text{Layer Norm}\left(\Psi_2 *_{\mathcal{T}} \left(\Omega *_{\mathcal{G}} \left(\Psi_1 *_{\mathcal{T}} \mathcal{X}_{(kl-1)\tilde{T}+1:kl\tilde{T}}\right)\right)\right) \tag{9}$$

$\mathcal{X} \in \mathbb{R}^{T\times N\times F_{\text{in}}}$ is the traffic flow input, F_{in} is the number of input features. $\mathcal{X}$ is partitioned to K_l parts $\{\mathcal{X}_{1:\tilde{T}}, \mathcal{X}_{\tilde{T}+1:2\tilde{T}}, ..., \mathcal{X}_{(K_l-1)\tilde{T}+1:K_l\tilde{T}}\}$ as the input of each local ST-fusion unit, $\tilde{T} = T/K_l$ is the local fusion range. Normally, L_{kl} is expected to be a tensor with a temporal dimension size of 1, so $\tilde{T}$ is also equal to $2K_t - 1$. All the K_l local ST-fusion units are shared-weight to reduce the model complexity and enhance the generalization ability to each local part of input traffic flow. The local representations $\{L_1, L_2, ..., L_{K_l}\}$ are then concatenated to a single tensor $\mathcal{L} \in \mathbb{R}^{K_l\times N\times C_{\mathcal{T}}}$.

3.2 Relevance Evaluation for Local Representations

The local ST representations learned from local ST-fusion units may not have the same relevance and significance to the final prediction. Therefore, a relevance evaluation module is placed between local ST-fusion units and global ST-fusion units to control the amount of information flow and pay more attention to the significant local ST units. To attain this purpose, we place a Transformer encoder in the relevance evaluation module. A Transformer encoder mainly consists of a multi-head attention layer and a positional-wise feedforward layer [21], as shown in Fig. 2(c). Suppose there are nh attention heads, the attention mechanism then learns the temporal relevance for each sensor:

$$\begin{aligned}\text{Multihead}(\mathcal{L}[i]) =& \text{Concat}(\text{head}_1, \text{head}_2, ..., \text{head}_{nh})W_O \\ \text{where head}_j =& \text{Softmax}\left(\frac{(\mathcal{L}[i]W_{Qj})(\mathcal{L}[i]W_{Kj})^\top}{\sqrt{d_k}}\right)\mathcal{L}[i]W_{Vj} \quad j = 1, 2, ..., nh\end{aligned} \tag{10}$$

$\mathcal{L}[i]$ denotes the sequential representations of the i-th sensor in $\mathcal{L}$, d_k is the channel size in each attention head. Both the multi-head self-attention layer and positional-wise feed-forward layer are followed with a skip connection and a layer normalization in turn, as designed in the original Transformer. Note that the Transformer encoder cannot extract the relative position of local representations, so position encoding is added to the input of the Transformer encoder.

3.3 Learning Global Spatial-Temporal Representations

Similar to the local ST-fusion unit, the recurrent-structured global ST-fusion unit is used to learn the ST representations of traffic flow, but in a global perspective. The global ST-fusion unit is illustrated in Fig. 2(d), which is composed of two modules, one is a gated recurrent unit (GRU), and the other is a GCN layer. As a variant of LSTM, GRU can learn temporal dependency more efficiently since there are only two gates in each unit. We stack GRU and GCN layer in turn as the global ST-fusion unit to learn the global ST representations of traffic flow. For the kl-th global ST-fusion unit, GRU learns the temporal correlation as follows:

$$\begin{aligned}
R_{kl} &= \sigma\left(\tilde{L}_{kl}W_{R1} + H'_{kl-1}W_{R2} + B_R\right) \\
Z_{kl} &= \sigma\left(\tilde{L}_{kl}W_{Z1} + H'_{kl-1}W_{Z2} + B_Z\right) \\
\tilde{H}_{kl} &= \tanh\left(\tilde{L}_{kl}W_{\tilde{H}1} + \left(R_{kl} \odot H'_{kl-1}\right)W_{\tilde{H}2} + B_{\tilde{H}}\right) \\
H_{kl} &= (1 - Z_{kl}) \odot H'_{kl-1} + Z_{kl} \odot \tilde{H}_{kl}
\end{aligned} \tag{11}$$

where $\tilde{L}_{kl}$ is the kl-th output from the relevance evaluation module, and H'_{kl-1} is the output of the $(kl-1)$-th global ST-fusion unit. The following GCN layer learns the spatial correlation from the output of GRU:

$$H'_{kl} = \Omega *_{\mathcal{G}} H_{kl} \tag{12}$$

The output of the K_l-th global ST-fusion unit H'_{K_l} will go through a fully connected layer to generate the prediction $\hat{Y} \in \mathbb{R}^{N \times F_{\text{out}}}$, where F_{out} is the number of output features.

4 Experimental Studies

4.1 Datasets

Three commonly used traffic flow datasets are adopted. These three datasets are collections of data from three areas in California and show the aggregated traffic condition in thousands of 5-min slots [22, 23]. All the datasets are split into three parts, 70% is for training, 10% is for validation, and the rest 20% is for testing. A brief introduction of these three datasets is provided in Table 1.

Note that there are anomalous data in both METR-LA and PeMS-BAY datasets, which should be considered in the model training process. Here, we use a masked loss to address this issue. The masked loss first sets the anomalous elements in the loss tensor to zero, and then calculates the average of the rest elements for back propagation. In this way, the NN model learns from the correct error and ignores the anomalous ones.

Table 1. Statistical overview of METR-LA, PeMS-BAY and PeMS-D7(M) datasets

Dataset	#Sensors	#Edges	#Timesteps	Anomaly ratio
METR-LA	207	1722	34272	8.109%
PeMS-BAY	325	1515	52116	0.003%
PeMS-D7(M)	228	18890	12672	0

While the historical observations are used as training data, the distance between each sensor should also be utilized in the graph construction. We generate the weighted adjacency matrix A according to the method mentioned in [10]. Suppose the distance between sensor i and sensor j is dist(i, j), then A_{ij} in the is calculated as:

$$A_{ij} = \begin{cases} \exp\left(\text{dist}(i,j)^2/\sigma^2\right) & \text{if dist}(i,j) < \kappa \\ 0 & \text{otherwise} \end{cases} \quad i,j = 1,2,\ldots,N \tag{13}$$

Here, κ is set to 0.1 to mask the sensors that are too far from each other and control the sparsity of A.

4.2 Baselines, Settings, and Evaluation Metrics

Two statistical models and three NN-based models are adopted for comparison, which are:

- HA [2]: Historical average model views the traffic flow as a periodic process. For example, the traffic flow prediction at time interval 18:00–18:05 on the fourth Monday is the average of the traffic flow observation of the time interval on the first, second, and third Mondays.
- LSVR [5]: The linear support vector regression model with penalty term $C = 0.1$.
- FNN [6]: The feedforward NN model with two fully connected layers of 256 hidden units each.
- LSTM-NN [9]: An LSTM-based network with a fully connected input layer, a one-layer LSTM, and a fully connected output layer. The size of hidden units is 256.
- STGCN [13]: An ST deep learning model with convolution structure in spatial and temporal dependency modeling. The numbers of channels in the spatial and temporal convolution layer are set to 64 and 16, respectively.

For the proposed framework STGNNF, the channel size of all hidden layers is set to 128. The number of local ST-fusion unit and global ST-fusion unit K_l is both 4. K_t in the temporal convolution is set to 2. In the relevance evaluation module, the number of attention heads nh is 4, and the dropout rate is 0.1. We train STGNNF by minimizing the mean square error with RMSProp optimizer, and the batch size is 16. The initial learning rate is 0.1 with a decay rate of 0.7 after every 5 epochs. To reduce the risk of overfitting, an L2 regularization with penalty term (weight decay) 5e−7 is adopted. The training process is adaptively terminated by an early stop strategy, in which the patience is set to 20 epochs.

The experiment is conducted in three future time windows, which are 15 min, 30 min, and 60 min onward, to test the traffic flow prediction performance of the models. The prediction performance is measured by three commonly used evaluation metrics in prediction tasks, including mean absolute error (MAE), mean absolute percentage error (MAPE), and root mean square error (RMSE). The experimental results of the five baselines are reproduced in this paper.

4.3 Results and Discussion

Tables 2, 3, and 4 show the experimental results of all TFF models in three traffic flow datasets, respectively. The best results are both **bolded** and <u>underscored</u>.

Table 2. Experimental results of STGNNF and baselines in METR-LA dataset.

Time *h*	15 min			30 min			60 min		
Metrics	MAE	MAPE	RMSE	MAE	MAPE	RMSE	MAE	MAPE	RMSE
HA	8.78	26.68%	12.54	8.78	26.68%	12.54	8.78	26.68%	12.54
LSVR	3.44	8.11%	7.65	4.30	10.48%	9.78	5.67	14.25%	12.49
FNN	5.07	15.49%	8.38	5.82	18.11%	9.47	6.78	21.66%	10.80
LSTM-NN	3.18	8.89%	5.90	3.88	11.41%	7.18	4.97	15.33%	8.80
STGCN	2.89	7.74%	5.39	3.40	9.68%	6.32	4.00	11.82%	7.20
STGNNF	**2.76**	**7.27%**	**5.12**	**3.21**	**8.97%**	**6.02**	**3.69**	**10.76%**	**6.84**

Table 3. Experimental results of STGNNF and baselines in PeMS-BAY dataset.

Time	15 min			30 min			60 min		
Metrics	MAE	MAPE	RMSE	MAE	MAPE	RMSE	MAE	MAPE	RMSE
HA	4.97	12.36%	8.40	4.97	12.36%	8.40	4.97	12.36%	8.40
LSVR	1.69	3.58%	3.64	2.36	5.36%	5.35	3.36	8.29%	7.48
FNN	2.41	5.60%	4.49	3.07	7.61%	5.91	4.09	10.74%	7.71
LSTM-NN	1.66	3.66	3.45	2.38	5.78%	5.07	3.39	8.93%	6.92
STGCN	1.46	3.13%	2.91	1.89	4.33%	3.91	2.25	5.38%	4.60
STGNNF	**1.43**	**3.06%**	**2.87**	**1.80**	**4.05%**	**3.79**	**2.15**	**5.05%**	**4.51**

Table 4. Experimental results of STGNNF and baselines in PeMS-D7(M) dataset.

Time	15 min			30 min			60 min		
Metrics	MAE	MAPE	RMSE	MAE	MAPE	RMSE	MAE	MAPE	RMSE
HA	7.71	22.09%	11.36	7.71	22.09%	11.36	7.71	22.09%	11.36
LSVR	2.44	5.72%	4.60	3.45	8.56%	6.69	4.88	12.98%	9.22
FNN	3.45	9.01%	5.74	4.51	12.33%	7.44	6.18	17.61%	9.63
LSTM-NN	2.47	5.99%	4.51	3.59	9.40%	6.53	5.19	14.6%	8.89
STGCN	2.26	5.54%	4.06	3.09	7.96%	5.58	3.87	10.34%	6.81
STGNNF	**2.19**	**5.35%**	**4.02**	**2.92**	**7.50%**	**5.44**	**3.65**	**9.62%**	**6.68**

It is obvious that HA achieves the worst performance. HA generates the same results for all the three prediction time windows in each dataset, because it uses a fixed and long-period observation window. This restricts HA from capturing the short-term dynamic of the highly complex and nonlinear traffic flow. LSVR achieves approximately the same results as some NN-based models do in less challenging datasets, such as PeMS-BAY. It views the future prediction as the linear combination of the previous traffic flow observations, so it works well in smooth datasets. However, when facing more complex traffic flow in METR-LA, the performance gap between LSVR and NN-based models increases.

FNN does not generate promising prediction results as well. The fully connected structure in FNN makes it overlook the relative position in the traffic flow time-series. LSTM-NN, however, can better capture the sequential information with its unique recurrent structure. Compared to LSVR, LSTM-NN can achieve up to 29.54% improvement in RMSE. Meanwhile, the advantage of LSTM-NN is more evident in long-term prediction (e.g. 60 min) and more unstable datasets (e.g. METR-LA). These two situations often represent a larger difference in the historical observation and future observation.

When incorporating spatial features, the STGCN and STGNNF models perform far better than the other models without spatial correlation modeling. STGNNF generates the best prediction in all tasks under all evaluation metrics. For example, in the 30-min and 60-min prediction in METR-LA, STGNNF attains 8.97% and 7.33% improvement in MAPE compared to STGCN. The improvement is also observed in MAE, with a margin of 7.75% and 5.59% respectively. Similarly, STGNNF also achieves a 6.96% improvement in forecasting error under the MAPE metric. The superiority difference between STGNNF and other models is clearer in more challenging datasets.

Figure 3 shows the prediction results obtained by STGNNF and LSTM-NN when encountering anomalous traffic flow historical observation input. A stronger robustness of STGNNF can be observed in this figure.

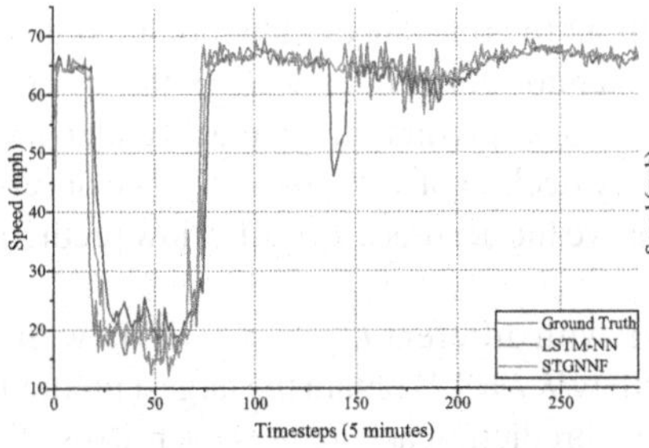

(a) STGNNF generates a smooth curve.

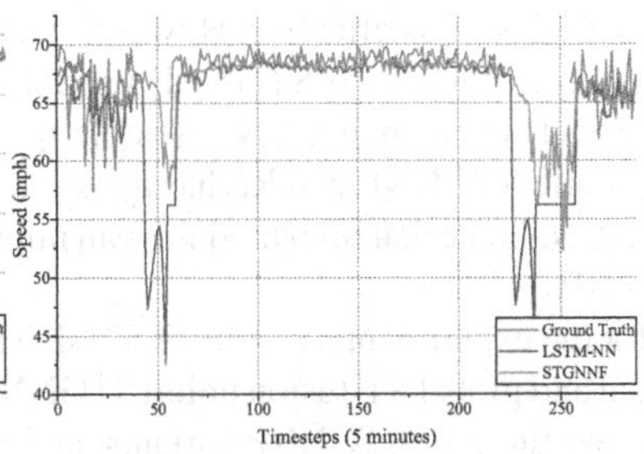

(b) STGNNF captures complex traffic flow variation.

Fig. 3. Forecasting results of LSTM-NN and STGNNF in a one-day duration (288 5-min timesteps). The parts with missing blue lines represent anomalous data.

The prediction results of STGNNF are more stable than those generated by LSTM-NN when receiving anomalous input. For example, in Fig. 3(a), the missing part should be a stable fluctuation, but not a sharp drop. The predicted traffic flow obtained by LSTM-NN is, however, an obvious decline, while STGNNF generates a smooth curve. The advantage of considering spatial features can be further illustrated in Fig. 3(b). Even though anomalous inputs last for almost 30 timesteps, STGNNF still captures the complex variation of the traffic flow by utilizing the information gathered from nearby sensors.

4.4 Ablation Studies

STGNNF is a framework with multiple modules inside. Ablation studies can be therefore conducted to verify whether these modules work. Meanwhile, STGNNF is proposed based on a local fusion hypothesis. To verify whether the local and global ST collaborative learning works, STGNNF with different fusion sizes (K_l) should be also investigated. Hence, we investigate five ablated variants of STGNNF:

- w/o RE: The relevance evaluation module is removed, and the model thus does not learn the relevance of the local ST representations.
- w/o GCN: The GCN layers within local and global ST-fusion units are removed, and the model could not utilize the spatial correlation of the traffic flow.
- w/$K_l = 1$ (complete fusion): The model fuses all the temporal features in a single local ST-fusion unit.
- w/$K_l = 2$ (local fusion with different fusion size): The model fuses local temporal features but with a larger local fusion range than the proposed one.
- w/$K_l = 12$ (no fusion): The local ST-fusion unit takes each timestep as its input, and does not fuse any temporal features.

Tables 5, 6, and 7 show the experimental results of STGNNF and its five variants. STGNNF with some components removed can also obtain better test results than those obtained by the five baseline models in almost all datasets. This proves the framework design of STGNNF is effective. However, without the relevance evaluation module and the GCN layer, these two STGNNF variants cannot perform as well as the complete STGNNF. STGNNF w/o GCN loses 0.5% to 4.0% prediction accuracy under MAE metrics, while STGNNF w/o RE has an accuracy decline of 1.4% to 4.8%. The observations above indicate that both modules can improve the accuracy of traffic flow prediction in STGNNF.

As for the experimental results of STGNNF with different K_l, the STGNNF with the most local and global ST-fusion units (STGNNF w/$K_l = 12$) obtain the largest prediction error among the four STGNNF variants, and its prediction accuracy is even worse than the baseline models in certain tasks. This shows that an over-complex structure weakens the expressiveness of the model. For the other extreme situation where all temporal features are fused in a single local ST-fusion unit (STGNNF w/$K_l = 1$), the local fusion works and improves the prediction performance, but is still inferior to the rest two variants with appropriate local fusion. The proposed STGNNF and STGNNF w/$K_l =$ 2 achieve similar test performance in all the three datasets, with STGNNF having a slight advantage. This shows that our local fusion strategy is not parameter sensitive. Considering that the parameter size increases with larger K_l, and the training time is also positively correlated with the parameter size in STGNNF, an appropriate local fusion range K_l (2 and 4 in our example) that achieves shorter training time and effective local and global ST cooperative learning, would be a cost-effective option in practice.

Table 5. Experimental results of STGNNF and its ablated variants in METR-LA dataset.

Time	15 min			30 min			60 min		
Metrics	MAE	MAPE	RMSE	MAE	MAPE	RMSE	MAE	MAPE	RMSE
w/o RE	2.90	7.59%	5.21	3.33	9.29%	6.11	3.79	11.15%	7.00
w/o GCN	2.79	7.34%	5.13	3.28	9.18%	6.09	3.88	11.47%	7.09
w/$K_l = 1$	2.85	7.59%	5.27	3.34	9.47%	6.27	4.02	11.99%	7.37
w/$K_l = 2$	2.81	7.37%	5.17	3.25	9.07%	6.09	3.73	10.90%	6.89
w/$K_l = 12$	2.86	7.54%	5.32	3.38	9.51%	6.26	4.43	12.95%	7.78
STGNNF	**2.76**	**7.27%**	**5.12**	**3.21**	**8.97%**	**6.02**	**3.69**	**10.76%**	**6.84**

Table 6. Experimental results of STGNNF and its ablated variants in PeMS-BAY dataset.

Time	15 min			30 min			60 min		
metrics	MAE	MAPE	RMSE	MAE	MAPE	RMSE	MAE	MAPE	RMSE
w/o RE	1.48	3.17%	2.90	1.87	4.27%	3.85	2.20	5.11%	4.55
w/o GCN	1.44	3.08%	2.89	1.86	4.21%	3.92	2.24	5.36%	4.71
w/$K_l = 1$	1.47	3.15%	2.95	1.90	4.34%	3.97	2.32	5.60%	4.79
w/$K_l = 2$	**1.42**	**3.05%**	**2.87**	1.81	4.07%	**3.79**	**2.15**	5.07%	**4.47**
w/$K_l = 12$	1.50	3.20%	3.00	1.95	4.48%	4.01	2.41	5.74%	4.85
STGNNF	1.43	3.06%	**2.87**	**1.80**	**4.05%**	**3.79**	**2.15**	**5.05%**	4.51

Table 7. Experimental results of STGNNF and its ablated variants in PeMS-D7(M) dataset.

Time	15 min			30 min			60 min		
metrics	MAE	MAPE	RMSE	MAE	MAPE	RMSE	MAE	MAPE	RMSE
w/o RE	2.22	5.47%	**4.02**	2.98	7.68%	**5.44**	3.77	10.07%	6.75
w/o GCN	2.20	5.37%	4.05	2.96	7.67%	5.53	3.72	9.88%	6.77
w/$K_l = 1$	2.24	5.50%	4.09	3.04	7.88%	5.58	3.89	10.25%	6.90
w/$K_l = 2$	2.20	5.38%	4.04	2.95	7.56%	5.49	3.67	**9.55%**	**6.62**
w/$K_l = 12$	2.68	6.77%	4.57	3.43	8.57%	6.00	4.97	13.08%	8.24
STGNNF	**2.19**	**5.35%**	**4.02**	**2.92**	**7.50%**	**5.44**	**3.65**	9.62%	6.68

5 Conclusion

In this paper, we propose an ST sequence forecasting-oriented deep learning model STGNNF for the TFF task, which is established on a motivation that the model can learn more meaningful and robust ST representation locally and globally for TFF by fusing a small range of adjacent temporal features of multi-source time-series data. Based on this, the STGNNF realizes local and global ST representation learning with its unique three-part structure, which includes the local ST-fusion units, the relevance evaluation module, and the global ST-fusion unit. To be more specific, all the local ST-fusion units are shared-weight, which adopt GCN and GLU to extract local ST features. The local ST representations are evaluated for their relevance to the prediction by a Transformer encoder, and then mined by several recurrent-structured global ST-fusion units. Experimental results demonstrate the effectiveness and robustness of the proposed STGNNF framework. Besides, there are many directions for future work, which includes applying STGNNF in other types of ST forecasting problem, implementing the local ST-fusion units in a distributed way, and designing more efficient network structure for the local and global ST-fusion units.

Acknowledgments. This work was supported in part by the National Key Research and Development Program of China under Grant 2019YFB2102102, in part by the National Natural Science Foundations of China (NSFC) under Grants 62176094, 61822602, 61772207, and 61873097, in part by the Key-Area Research and Development of Guangdong Province under Grant 2020B010166002, in part by the Guangdong Natural Science Foundation Research Team under Grant 2018B030312003 3, and in part by the Guangdong-Hong Kong Joint Innovation Platform under Grant 2018B050502006.

References

1. Shaikh, P.W., El-Abd, M., Khanafer, M., Gao, K.: A review on swarm intelligence and evolutionary algorithms for solving the traffic signal control problem. IEEE Trans. Intell. Transp. Syst. **23**(1), 48–63 (2020). https://doi.org/10.1109/TITS.2020.3014296
2. Liu, J., Guan, W.: A summary of traffic flow forecasting methods. J. Highw. Transp. Res. Dev. **21**(3), 82–85 (2004)
3. Hamed, M.M., Al-Masaeid, H.R., Said, Z.M.B.: Short-term prediction of traffic volume in urban arterials. J. Transp. Eng. **121**(3), 249–254 (1995)
4. Hamilton, J.D.: Time Series Analysis. Princeton University Press, Princeton (1994)
5. Wu, C.H., Ho, J.M., Lee, D.T.: Travel-time prediction with support vector regression. IEEE Trans. Intell. Transp. Syst. **5**(4), 276–281 (2004). https://doi.org/10.1109/TITS.2004.837813
6. Park, D., Rilett, L.R.: Forecasting freeway link travel times with a multilayer feedforward neural network. Comput.-Aided Civ. Infrastruct. Eng. **14**(5), 357–367 (1999)
7. Sundermeyer, M., Ney, H., Schlüter, R.: From feedforward to recurrent LSTM neural networks for language modeling. IEEE/ACM Trans. Audio Speech Lang. Process. **23**(3), 517–529 (2015). https://doi.org/10.1109/TASLP.2015.2400218
8. Sutskever, I., Vinyals, O., Le, Q.V.: Sequence to sequence learning with neural networks. In: Proceedings of the 28th Conference on Neural Information Processing Systems, Montreal, Canada (2014)
9. Ma, X., Tao, Z., Wang, Y., Yu, H., Wang, Y.: Long short-term memory neural network for traffic speed prediction using remote microwave sensor data. Transp. Res. Part C Emerg. Technol. **54**, 187–197 (2015)
10. Li, Y., Yu, R., Shahabi, C., Liu, Y.: Diffusion convolutional recurrent neural network: data-driven traffic forecasting. In: Proceedings of the 6th International Conference on Learning Representations, Vancouver, Canada (2017)
11. Shi, X., Chen, Z., Wang, H., Yeung, D.Y., Wong, W.K., Woo, W.C.: Convolutional LSTM network: a machine learning approach for precipitation nowcasting. In: Proceedings of the 29th Conference on Neural Information Processing Systems, Montreal, Canada, pp. 802–810 (2015)

12. Kipf, T.N., Welling, M.: Semi-supervised classification with graph convolutional networks. In: Proceedings of the 5th International Conference on Learning Representations, Toulon, France (2016)
13. Yu, B., Yin, H., Zhu, Z.: Spatio-temporal graph convolutional networks: a deep learning framework for traffic forecasting. In: Proceedings of the 26th International Joint Conference on Artificial Intelligence, Melbourne, Australia, pp. 3634–3640 (2017)
14. Diao, Z., Wang, X., Zhang, D., Liu, Y., Xie, K., He, S.: Dynamic spatial-temporal graph convolutional neural networks for traffic forecasting. In: Proceedings of the 33rd AAAI Conference on Artificial Intelligence, Hawaii, USA, pp. 890–897 (2019)
15. Park, C., et al.: ST-GRAT: a novel spatio-temporal graph attention networks for accurately forecasting dynamically changing road speed. In: Proceedings of the 29th ACM International Conference on Information and Knowledge Management. Virtual Conference, pp. 1215–1224 (2020)
16. Guo, S., Lin, Y., Feng, N., Song, C., Wan, H.: Attention based spatial-temporal graph convolutional networks for traffic flow forecasting. In: Proceedings of the 33rd AAAI Conference on Artificial Intelligence, Hawaii, USA, pp. 922–929, July 2019
17. Zhang, J., Shi, X., Xie, J., Ma, H., King, I., Yeung, D.Y.: GaAN: gated attention networks for learning on large and spatiotemporal graphs. arXiv preprint arXiv:1803.07294 (2018)
18. Wu, Z., Pan, S., Long, G., Jiang, J., Zhang, C.: Graph wavenet for deep spatial-temporal graph modeling. arXiv preprint arXiv:1906.00121 (2019)
19. He, K., Zhang, X., Ren, S., Sun, J.: Deep residual learning for image recognition. In: Proceedings of the 29th IEEE Conference on Computer Vision and Pattern Recognition, Las Vegas, USA, pp. 770–778 (2016)
20. Dauphin, Y.N., Fan, A., Auli, M., Grangier, D.: Language modeling with gated convolutional networks. In: Proceedings of the 34th International Conference on Machine Learning, Sydney, Australia, pp. 933–941 (2017)
21. Vaswani, A., et al.: Attention is all you need. In: Proceedings of the 31st Conference on Neural Information Processing Systems, Long Beach, USA (2017)
22. Chen, C., Petty, K., Skabardonis, A., Varaiya, P., Jia, Z.: Freeway performance measurement system: mining loop detector data. Transp. Res. Rec. **1748**(1), 96–102 (2001). https://doi.org/10.3141/1748-12
23. Jagadish, H.V., et al.: Big data and its technical challenges. Commun. ACM **57**(7), 86–94 (2014). https://doi.org/10.1145/2611567

A Quantum Evolutionary Algorithm and Its Application to Optimal Dynamic Investment in Market Microstructure Model

Yapeng Sun[1,2](✉) and Hui Peng[1]

[1] School of Computer Science and Engineering, Central South University, Hunan 410083 Changsha, China
yapengsun@csu.edu.cn

[2] School of Computer Science and Engineering, Hunan University of Science and Technology, Hunan 411201 Xiangtan, China

Abstract. Falling into local minimum and slow convergence are the drawbacks of traditional evolutionary algorithm in the process of function optimization. Combined with Quantum mechanism and intelligent optimization algorithm organically, the quantum evolution method can be introduced into the differential evolution algorithm in this paper. In this method, Probability amplitude of qubit can represent the real coding of chromosome and the updating of the chromosome position can be achieved by quantum mutation, quantum crossover and quantum selection operation. The two probability amplitudes of qubit are exchanged by quantum not-gate and the self-adaptive operator is introduced to improve the diversity of the population, which can prevent the premature convergence of the algorithm and improve the ability of the optimization algorithm to solve problems. Taking the function extremum problem as an example, the simulation results verify the effectiveness of the algorithm through this method. Finally, quantum differential evolution algorithm is used to estimate the market microstructure model and the asset allocation control problems caused by the model, So we can obtain the optimal structure and the implied excess demand and market liquidity. And furthermore we can use the estimated excess demand information rather than the forecast price to guide asset investment. The results of empirical analysis in financial investment practice show the effectiveness of the proposed method, and it achieves good results in the optimization of the model and obtain higher return on asset investment.

Keywords: Self-adaptive quantum differential evolution algorithm · Market microstructure model · Asset allocation

1 Introduction

In 1985, the first International Conference on genetic algorithm was held. In the past 30 years, the theoretical research on genetic algorithm was gradually deepening and its application scope was becoming more and more extensive, including artificial intelligence, neural network, operational research and so on. With the rapid improvement of

Y. Sun et al. (Eds.): ChineseCSCW 2021, CCIS 1491, pp. 386–396, 2022.
https://doi.org/10.1007/978-981-19-4546-5_30

computer computing performance, the ability to solve large-scale optimization problems has also been improved. Optimization problems have been widely used in production scheduling, engineering design management and other fields. But the complex numerical calculation problem requires a high level of mathematical modeling, which makes it quite difficult to solve the problem of complex engineering optimization. Therefore, with the progress of society, further research on the new optimization algorithm is needed. It is an important research direction to integrate different algorithms to solve different optimization problems. Each optimization algorithm has its advantages and disadvantages. It is possible to integrate two or more algorithms with complementary advantages, which may be more beneficial to solve the optimization problem better.

In 1996, Narayanan [1] and some other scholar first proposed quantum derived genetic algorithm, which improves the search efficiency of genetic algorithm by using the concept of quantum's multi-universe, and successfully solves TSP problem. It improves the efficiency of the algorithm by doing parallel search through multiple populations and the cross and rich diversity of the population.

In 2000, Han [2, 3] first introduced quantum coding and quantum gate into evolutionary algorithm, and he achieved the population updating by using rotary gate. In 2002, the algorithm was further developed. Population migration mechanism was introduced, which improved the ability of evolutionary algorithm to keep population diversity, and had fast convergence speed and global convergence ability. In 2009, Nodehi [4, 5] proposed a quantum evolutionary algorithm which uses function to dynamically change population size to keep population diversity. This algorithm avoids premature algorithm and accelerates convergence of algorithm.

In 2009, Gao Ying hui et al. [6, 7] took quantile as polar coordinate form and proposed a quantum genetic algorithm by using polar angle coding chromosome. By making use of the angle coding transformed quantum chromosome from complex pair to real number form, this algorithm simplified population updating operation and improved the efficiency of algorithm.

In addition, the fusion with differential evolution algorithm and the fusion of membrane computing are all aimed at avoiding premature convergence and improving convergence speed by using the global search performance of other evolutionary algorithms to jump out of local optimal solution. In 2014, Zhang Rui et al. [8] proposed a new quantum evolution algorithm, four-chain quantum-inspired evolutionary algorithm (FCQIEA), which is based on the study of the four gene chain coding method. In FCQIEA, chromosome is composed of four gene chains, which effectively expands searching space and improves the evolution rate. The optimization analysis of different parameters, including rotation angle and mutation probability, is also carried out.

2 A Self-adaptive Quantum Differential Evolution Algorithm

Considering the integration of quantum mechanism and differential evolution mechanism, the self-adaptive quantum differential evolution method proposed in this paper introduces quantum computing into differential evolution algorithm. In this method, Probability amplitude of quantum bits is used into real chromosome's coding, and the chromosome position is updated by quantum mutation, quantum crossover and quantum selection, The quantum not-gate is used to exchange the two probability amplitudes of qubits, and the self-adaptive operator is introduced to improve the diversity of the population, which can prevent the premature and convergence of the algorithm and improve the optimization algorithm's ability to solve problems.

2.1 Classical Quantum Genetic Algorithm

In the classical quantum genetic algorithm, the chromosome is represented by a qubit, a qubit is composed of $[\alpha, \beta]^T$, α and β represent the probability amplitude of state |0⟩ and |1⟩, which satisfies the normalization condition |α|2 + |β|2 = 1. A quantum chromosome can represent the superposition state of any solution in the solution space. The details are as follows [12]:

$$\begin{bmatrix} \alpha_1 \cdots \alpha_n \\ \beta_1 \cdots \beta_n \end{bmatrix} \tag{1}$$

Quantum genetic algorithm evolves according to quantum gate, which makes quantum population tend to the optimal solution. The commonly used quantum gates are revolving gate, XOR gate and Hadamard gate. The most widely used quantum revolving gate is the following quantum gate [12].

$$\begin{bmatrix} \alpha_i' \\ \beta_i' \end{bmatrix} = \begin{bmatrix} \cos\theta_i & -\sin\theta_i \\ \sin\theta_i & \cos\theta_i \end{bmatrix} \cdot \begin{bmatrix} \alpha_i \\ \beta_i \end{bmatrix} \tag{2}$$

Among them, $[\alpha_i, \beta_i]^T$ is the i-th qubit; $[\alpha_i', \beta_i']^T$ is the qubit after rotation; θ is the rotation angle, and its size is determined by the setting adjustment strategy. The revolving door can realize the transition between the States, which has high parallelism and can ensure the convergence of the algorithm.

2.2 Differential Evolution Algorithm

Differential evolution algorithm is a kind of population-based heuristic global search algorithm proposed by Storn and Price [13]. Because of its simple principle, less controlled parameters and strong robustness, it has been widely used in function optimization, data filtering, neural network learning and multi-objective optimization. Like other evolutionary algorithms, differential evolution also operates on the population of candidate solutions [14, 15]. Firstly, the population is initialized randomly in the solution space of the problem. X = (X1, X2, …, XN), N represents the population scale, and then the current population is mutated and crossed to produce an intermediate population, and the original population and the intermediate population are selected one-to-one by the selection operation based on greedy thought to produce a new generation of population. Although there are many different forms of differential evolution algorithm [16], most mathematicians choose DE/RAND/1/bin. The concrete operations of mutation, crossover and selection are following:

Mutation operation operation: randomly select one individual from the population as the base vector and the other two different individuals as the difference vector. The generation method is as follows:

$$v_i^{g+1} = x_{r1}^g + F(x_{r2}^g - x_{r3}^g) \tag{3}$$

Among them, r1, r2, r3 ∈ {1, 2, …, N}, and r1 ≠ r2 ≠ r3, N is the population scale. F ∈ [0,2], g is the current population. g + 1 is the next generation population.

Crossover operation: a new individual is generated by mixing the mutant individual with the predetermined parent individual according to certain rules.

$$u_{i,j}^{g+1} = \begin{cases} v_{i,j}^{g+1}, \; if \; (rand_j \le C_r \; or \; j = j_{rand}) \\ x_{i,j}^g, \; otherwise \end{cases} \tag{4}$$

Among them, j ∈ {1,2,…,D}, D is the dimension of the problem, randj is one of the random number between [0,1], jrand is one of the random integer selected from {1,2,…,D}, Cr is a cross factor, generally a random number between [0,1].

Selection operation: the selection operation adopts one-to-one greedy selection, and its principle of selection is that individuals with better adaptability would enter the next generation. The formula is as follows:

$$x_{i,j}^{g+1} = \begin{cases} u_i^{g+1}, \; if \; f(u_i^{g+1}) \le f(x_i^g) \\ x_{i,j}^g, \; otherwise \end{cases} \tag{5}$$

Among them, f(x) is the fitness function.

Through the above differential evolution's mutation, cross and selecting operation, the population will evolve to the next generation, and the final population will reach the optimal through repeated circular evolution.

2.3 Self-adaptive Quantum Differential Evolution Algorithm

Self-Adaptive Quantum Differential Evolution Algorithm (SAQDEA) is a search optimization algorithm combining quantum computing theory and differential evolution algorithm. In SAQDEA, the chromosome is composed of qubits, the qubits are encoded by the real numbers, the updating operation of quantum chromatin is realized by quantum revolving gate, and the chromosome is mutated by quantum not-gate, so that it can achieve the optimization of the goal Solution.

The composition and coding of quantum chromosome, quantum chromosome is composed of qubits which meet the requirements of normalizing condition. A qubit consists of a pair of corresponding states |0 > and the probability amplitudes of |1 > that are defined in a unit space, defining: $|\varphi\rangle = \alpha|0\rangle + \beta|1\rangle$ among them, α and β are a pair of complex numbers, called the probability amplitude of the qubit's corresponding state. $|\alpha|^2$ is the probability of quantum state collapsing to |0>, $|\beta|^2$ is the probability of quantum state collapsing to |1>, and satisfies the normalization condition, $|\alpha|^2 + |\beta|^2 = 1$.Therefore, qubit can also be described as $[\cos(\theta), \sin(\theta)]^T$.

In quantum difference evolution algorithm, the real number code is used for quantum chromosomes, and the coding method is as follows:

$$Q_{i,j} = \left[\begin{vmatrix} \cos(\theta_{i,1}) \\ \sin(\theta_{i,1}) \end{vmatrix} \begin{vmatrix} \cos(\theta_{i,2}) \\ \sin(\theta_{i,2}) \end{vmatrix} \begin{matrix} \wedge \\ \wedge \end{matrix} \begin{vmatrix} \cos(\theta_{i,D}) \\ \sin(\theta_{i,D}) \end{vmatrix} \right] \tag{6}$$

Among them, $\theta = 2\pi rand$, rand ∈ [0,1], i ∈ {1, 2, …, N}, j ∈ {1, 2, …, D}, D is the problem's dimension and N represents the population scale.

In the solution space transformation method of optimization problem and quantum differential evolution algorithm, the ergodic space of quantum is unit space I = [−1,1] in order to analyze the performance of quantum chromosome, it is necessary to map the variable of quantum chromosome from unit space to the solution space of optimization problem. Each quantum chromosome variable corresponds to an optimization variable of the optimization problem. Let's define the domain of the solution space variable $X_{i,j}$ of the optimization problem as $[a_j, b_j]$ and the qubit code as $\left[\cos(\theta_{i,j}), \sin(\theta_{i,j})\right]^T$. Then the corresponding solution space variables are:

$$\begin{bmatrix} X_{i,j}^0 \\ X_{i,j}^1 \end{bmatrix} = \begin{bmatrix} \frac{b_j - a_j}{2} & 0 \\ 0 & \frac{b_j - a_j}{2} \end{bmatrix} \begin{bmatrix} \cos(\theta_{i,j}) \\ \sin(\theta_{i,j}) \end{bmatrix} + \begin{bmatrix} \frac{b_j + a_j}{2} \\ \frac{b_j + a_j}{2} \end{bmatrix} \tag{7}$$

By simplifying the above formula, we can get the following results

$$\begin{bmatrix} X_{i,j}^0 \\ X_{i,j}^1 \end{bmatrix} = \frac{1}{2} \begin{bmatrix} 1 + \cos(\theta_{i,j}) 1 - \cos(\theta_{i,j}) \\ 1 + \sin(\theta_{i,j}) 1 - \sin(\theta_{i,j}) \end{bmatrix} \begin{bmatrix} b_j \\ a_j \end{bmatrix} \tag{8}$$

Among them, the quantum chromosome represented by cosine probability amplitude corresponds to $X_{i,j}^0$, and the quantum chromosome represented by sine probability amplitude corresponds to $X_{i,j}^1$.

When the quantum state is updating, the rotation angle of the quantum position is also adjusted, and the formula is as follows:

$$\Delta\theta_{ij}^g = \theta_{\min} + fit(\theta_{\max} - \theta_{\min}) rand_j \exp\left(\frac{gen}{\max gen}\right) \tag{9}$$

$$fit = \frac{fit_{gBest} - fit_i}{fit_{gBest}} \tag{10}$$

Among them, $\theta_{\min}$ is the minimum value 0.001 π of $\Delta\theta$ interval, $\theta_{\max}$ is the maximum value 0.05 π of $\Delta\theta$ interval, fitgBest is the adaptability of the whole optimal individual searched, fiti shows adaptability of the present individual, randij is the random number between [0,1]; gen is the current iteration times of population, and maxgen represents max iteration times of the limited population.

Quantum mutation's operation: corresponding to the standard differential evolution algorithm, a quantum's chromosome is chosen at random from quantum's population thorugh this method. It takes the quantum bit phase as a basis vector and quantum bit phase of the other two different quantum chromosomes as the difference vector. The generation method is as follows:

$$v_{i,j}^{g+1} = \theta_{r1,j}^{g} + F \cdot rand \cdot (\theta_{r2,j}^{g} - \theta_{r3,j}^{g}) \tag{11}$$

Among them, r1, r2, r3 ∈ {1,2..., N}, and r1 ≠ r2 ≠ r3, F ∈ [0,1] is a contraction factor, rand represents a random number between interval [0,1], g represents the current population, and g + 1 represents the next generation population.

In the basic differential evolution algorithm, the mutation operator often adopts constant, which is difficult to determine accurately. If the mutation rate is too large, the global optimal solution is low. If the mutation rate is small, the population diversity will decrease, and the phenomenon of "early maturity" is easy to appear. In this paper, a self-adaptive mutation operator is introduced. In this way, the mutation operator is 2F0 at the beginning, and the diversity can be maintained at the initial stage to prevent premature maturity. With the progress, the mutation operator decreases and finally changes to F0 to avoid the destruction of the optimal solution. The calculation method is as follows:

$$\varphi = \mathrm{e}^{1-\frac{G_m}{G_m+1-G}}, F = F_0 \times 2^{\varphi} \tag{12}$$

Among them, Gm is the maximum algebra, G is the current algebra, and e is the natural constant. In this way, the population can have better diversity in the early stage of evolution, and it is benificial to local fine search in the later stage of evolution, which can bring better results.

Quantum crossover operation: producing a new individual by combined the quantum mutation individual and the predetermined parent individual according to certain rules.

$$u_{i,j}^{g+1} = \begin{cases} v_{i,j}^{g+1}, \text{ if } (rand_j \le c_r \text{ or } j = j_{rand}) \\ x_{i,j}^{g}, \text{ otherwise} \end{cases} \tag{13}$$

Among them, j ∈ {1,2..., D}, D is the dimension of the problem, randj is a random number between [0,1], jrand is {1,2..., D}. Cr is a quantum crossover factor and is generally a random number in the interval [0, 1]. In this paper, a crossover operator of random range is designed as follows:

$$C_r = 0.5 \times [1 + rand(0, 1)] \tag{14}$$

In this way, the mean value of the crossover operator is 0.75, which can better maintain the diversity of the population.

Quantum selection operation: selection operation adopts one-to-one greedy selection. The principle of selection is that individuals with better fitness enter the next generation. It can be expressed as follows:

$$\theta_{i,j}^{g+1} = \begin{cases} u_{i,j}^{g+1}, \text{ if } f(u_{i,j}^{g+1}) \le f(\theta_{i,j}^{g}) \\ \theta_{i,j}^{gt}, \text{ otherwise} \end{cases} \tag{15}$$

$$\theta_{i,j}^{gt} = \theta_{i,j}^{g} + \Delta\theta_{ij}^{g} \tag{16}$$

Among them, f is the fitness function, the two new bits after the updating are:

$$Q_{i,j}^{g+1} = \left[\left|\begin{matrix}\cos(\theta_{i,1}^{g+1}) \\ \sin(\theta_{i,1}^{g+1})\end{matrix}\right| \begin{matrix}\cos(\theta_{i,2}^{g+1}) \\ \sin(\theta_{i,2}^{g+1})\end{matrix}\left| \begin{matrix}\wedge \\ \wedge\end{matrix} \right| \begin{matrix}\cos(\theta_{i,D}^{g+1}) \\ \sin(\theta_{i,D}^{g+1})\end{matrix}\right|\right] \tag{17}$$

It can be seen that by rotating the quantum phase angle, the position of two quantum chromosomes can be moved at the same time, which can speed up the convergence speed of the algorithm.

Mutation processing of quantum not-gate: make the mutation probability be Pm, if rand < Pm, randomly select several qubits in the quantum chromosome, and use the quantum not-gate to mutate the qubits, and the optimal position of its memory remains unchanged.

$$\begin{bmatrix} 01 \\ 10 \end{bmatrix}\begin{bmatrix} \cos(\theta_{ij}) \\ \sin(\theta_{ij}) \end{bmatrix} = \begin{bmatrix} \sin(\theta_{ij}) \\ \cos(\theta_{ij}) \end{bmatrix} = \begin{bmatrix} \cos(\pi/2 - \theta_{ij}) \\ \sin(\pi/2 - \theta_{ij}) \end{bmatrix} \tag{18}$$

2.4 Algorithm Steps

In a word, the implementation steps of the Self-Adaptive Quantum Differential Evolution Algorithm proposed in this paper are as follows:

Step 1. Population initialization: the initial population Q composed of N quantum chromosomes is generated according to formula (6); Take the mutation probability as PM and contraction factor as F.

Step 2. Solution space transformation and fitness calculation: according to formula (8), every quantum's chromosome Q is corresponding to a solution X in optimization problem, the fitness degree f (x) of each solution is calculated, and the global optimal solution is updated according to the greedy principle.

Step 3. Quantum differential operation: For every quantum's chromosome in population, the rotating angle of its position is calculated in the light of (9) and (10), the quantum mutation operation is performed according to (11) and (12), the quantum crossover operation is performed according to (13) and (14), and the quantum selection operation is performed according to (15) and (16).

Step 4. Each quantum chromosome is mutated by quantum not gate according to formula (18).

Step 5. Compare the calculation results: if the convergence condition is satisfied, the output result will end the program; if no, step 2 will be returned.

In the parameter optimization test of some common complex functions, good test results are obtained.

3 The Application of This Algorithm in Market Microstructure Model

Financial markets generally show some characteristics such as strong stochastic, nonlinear, jump, especially random fluctuations and so on. The time - varying fluctuation of financial time series can be expressed in two ways. One is to use a GARCH model with conditional heteroscedasticity. The other is to use the stochastic volatility model [21–23]. It will be discussed that we will use the algorithm in this paper to estimate the state and parameters of a kind of market microstructure model in the stochastic volatility model, and then apply the model into the investment decisions.The discrete-time microstructure model proposed by Peng Hui [24, 25] can be described as follows:

$$\begin{cases} P_k = P_{k-1} + \lambda_{k-1}\phi_{k-1} + \gamma_3\lambda_{k-1}\xi_{1,k} \\ \phi_k = \alpha_1 + \beta_1\phi_{k-1} + \gamma_1\xi_{2,k} \\ \log \lambda_k^2 = \alpha_2 + \beta_2 \log \lambda_{k-1}^2 + \gamma_2\xi_{3,k} \end{cases} \tag{19}$$

Among them, P_k, λ_k, ϕ_k represent the asset price, market liquidity respectively and excess demand at time K. $\xi_{1,k} \sim N(0,1)$, $\xi_{2,k} \sim N(0,1)$, $\xi_{3,k} \sim N(0,1)$ represent the processes of independent white noise; α_1, β_1, α_2, β_2, γ_1, γ_2 and γ_3 are constant parameters. In the model (1), ϕ_k is defined as $\phi_k = \phi_k^+ - \phi_k^-$, among them, ϕ_k^+ is immediate demand and ϕ_k^- is immediate supply. $\phi_k > 0$ implies that the market is undervalued, which will make the price up; $\phi_k < 0$ implies that the market is overvalued, which will bring the price down.

To evaluate the model by using Kalman Filtering and Maximum Likelihood Estimation, we should establish a state-space equation with observed variables. In model (19), the state-space equation can be easily obtained, regarding P_k and $\log(P_k - P_{k-1})^2$ as observational variable quantity, and Discrete-time microstructure state space can be written as [25]:

$$\begin{cases} \mathbf{X}_{k+1} = \mathbf{A}(\mathbf{X}_k \mid \boldsymbol{\theta})\mathbf{X}_k + \boldsymbol{\Omega}_k, \boldsymbol{\Omega}_k \ \square \ N(\mathbf{0},\mathbf{Q}_k) \\ \mathbf{Y}_k = \mathbf{C}(\mathbf{X}_k \mid \boldsymbol{\theta})\mathbf{X}_k + \boldsymbol{\Gamma}_k, \quad \boldsymbol{\Gamma}_k \ \square \ N(\mathbf{0},\mathbf{R}_k) \end{cases} \tag{20}$$

3.1 Model Parameter Estimation Based on the Self-adaptive Quantum Differential Evolution Algorithm

Kalman Filtering and Maximum Likelihood Estimation aim to estimate all the constant parameters from the model (20) and to use the observations in the model (20) to evaluate the state $X_{k|k-1} = E(X_k|Y_{k-1}, \cdots, Y_1)$, This is a non-linear filter problem, and Kalman Filtering and Maximum Likelihood Estimation Approach are ulitized to solve this problem [26]. Through minimizing the log likelihood equation, parameter $\theta*$ are given by [23]:

$$\boldsymbol{\theta}^* = \arg\min_{\theta} \sum_{k=1}^{N} \left\{ \log\left|\hat{\boldsymbol{\Psi}}_k(\boldsymbol{\theta})\right| + \hat{\boldsymbol{\Gamma}}_k(\boldsymbol{\theta})^T \hat{\boldsymbol{\Psi}}_k(\boldsymbol{\theta})^{-1}\hat{\boldsymbol{\Gamma}}_k(\boldsymbol{\theta}) \right\} + 2N\log 2\pi \tag{21}$$

For the optimization of Eq. (21), if the traditional gradient-based optimization method is used, it is easy to fall into the local optimal solution, so it may not get a good result. Therefore, we propose a search method which take the self-adaptive quantum differential evolution algorithm as a baseline to minimize the logarithmic likelihood function (21).

3.2 Application of Optimal Dynamic Investment

The daily closing price time series of Changjiang Industrial Stock in Hong Kong Stock (CJSY) Exchange from 2001-02-05 to 2004-12-03 is selected as the observation data for empirical analysis. Parameters and initial conditions of estimation in CJYS's time series in model (20) are as follows:

$\alpha_1 = -4.9513\text{e}{-05}$, $\beta_1 = 0.0492$, $\alpha_2 = -0.0689$,

$\beta_2 = -0.0610$, $\gamma_1 = 0.0560$, $\gamma_2 = 0.0979$,

$\gamma_3 = 1.3527$, $\delta = 0.1402$, $\varepsilon_1 = 0.0070$, $\varepsilon_2 = 1.0076$

$$X_{0|0} = \begin{pmatrix} 462.35 \\ -0.6995 \\ -0.1470 \end{pmatrix}, S_0 = \begin{pmatrix} 1.50\ 0\ 0 \\ 0\ 1.54\ 0 \\ 0\ 0\ 0.03 \end{pmatrix} \times 10^{-4}.$$

Using the estimated excess demand information and asset allocation strategy obtained above, the dynamic asset allocation control of Changjiang Industrial Stock time series is carried out. Figure 1 present a dynamic changing process of the whole assets of the test data in Changjiang Industrial Stock with the control of asset allocation strategy. The blue curve is the changing process in total assets without asset allocation controlling strategy (fixed to 100 shares), and the black curve is the changing process of the whole assets with the controlling of asset allocation strategy under the Nelder-Mead

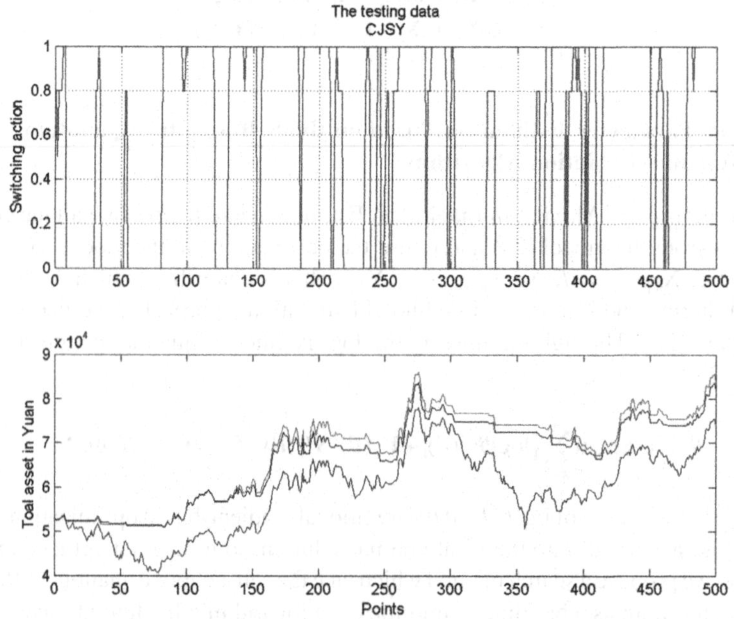

Fig. 1. Asset allocation control results of CJSY testing data

optimization method [24], The red curve is the change process of total assets with the control of asset allocation strategy optimized by SAQDEA method in this paper.

You can see that the optimization dynamic investment application of market microstructure asset estimated by self-adaptive quantum evolution algorithm Quantum differential evolution algorithm can obtain higher total assets than the total assets obtained under the original Nelder-Mead method [24] and without control.

4 Conclusion

Combined with quantum mechanism and evolutionary algorithm, this paper puts forward a self-adaptive real-coded quantum evolutionary algorithm. It introduced the self-adaptive mutation operator and crossover random operator under the framework of two strategies of quantum and differential evolution, so that in the early stages of evolution it can make the population have a better diversity, and in the later stages of the evolution it is advantageous to the local fine search. The algorithm it makes the algorithm search the optimal solution quickly and carefully in the solution space. The comparative analysis of the numerical optimization of the test function proves its effectiveness. In the microstructure model proposed by Iino, Ozaki, Peng Hui et al., the self-adaptive quantum differential evolution algorithm discussed in this passage is used to optimize the discrete time microstructure model, and the process of excess demand and market liquidity is estimated based on Kanlman Filter. It takes the information of excessive demand as the determinant of whether the market is undervalued or overvalued, the optimal dynamic asset allocation is made on the basis of the excessive demand. The threshold parameters in asset allocation strategy are also estimated by the self-adaptive quantum differential evolution algorithm. The investment application proves the effectiveness of the modeling and optimization method.

References

1. Narayanan, A., Moore, M.: Quantum-inspired genetic algorithm. In: Proceedings of IEEE International Conference on Evolutionary Computation, pp. 61–66. IEEE Press, Piscataway, NJ (1996)
2. Han, K.H., Jong, H.K.: Quantum-inspired evolutionary algorithm for a class of combination optimization. IEEE Trans. Evol. Comput. **6**(6), 580–593 (2002)
3. Alba, E., Dorronsoro, B.: The exploration/exploitation tradeoff in dynamic cellular genetic algorithms. IEEE Trans. Evol. Comput. **9**(2), 126–142 (2005)
4. Mikki, S.M., Kishk, A.A.: Quantum particle swarm optimization for electromagnetics. IEEE Trans. Antennas Propag. **54**(10), 2764–2775 (2006)
5. Nodehi, S., Tayarani, M., Mahmoudi, F.: A novel functional sized population quantum evolutionary algorithm for fractal image compression. In: 14th International CSI Computer Conference. CSICC 2009, pp. 564–569. Tehran (2009)
6. Gao, Y.-H., Shen, Z.-K.: An angle-coding chromosome quantum genetic algorithm. Comput. Eng. Sci. **31**(3) (2009)
7. Cai, Y., Zhang, M., Cai, H.: A hybrid chaotic quantum evolutionary algorithm. 2010 IEEE International Conference on Intelligent Computing and Intelligent Systems (ICIS), PP. 771–776. Xiamen (2010)

8. Zhang, R., Wang, Z., Zhang, H.: Quantum-inspired evolutionary algorithm for continuous space optimization based on multiple chains encoding method of quantum bits. Math. Probl. Eng. **9** (2014)
9. Yu, Z., Zhang, Z., Fang, W., Liu, W.: A variable-angle-distance quantum evolutionary algorithm for 2D HP model. In: 4th International Conference. ICCCS 2018, pp. 323–333. Haikou, China (2018)
10. Jing, J.J., Guan, S., Mu, X.: Dynamic Assignment Model of Terminal Distribution Task Based on Improved Quantum Evolution Algorithm. Big Data Analytics for Cyber-Physical System in Smart City, pp. 359–367 (2019)
11. Tayarani-Najaran, M.-H.: Novel operators for quantum evolutionary algorithm in solving timetabling problem. Evol. Intell. 560–578 (2020)
12. Moore, M.P., Narayanan, A.: Quantum-inspired computing. Department of Computer Science, University of Exeter, Exter EX44PT, UK (1995)
13. Storn, R., Price, K.: Differential evolution-asimple and efficient heuristic for global optimization over continuous spaces. J. Global Optim. **11**(4), 341–359 (1997)
14. Abbass, H.A.: The self-adaptive Pareto differential evolution. In: Proceedings of the 2002 Congress on Evolutionary Computation (CEC2002), vol. 1, pp. 831–836. IEEE Service Center, New York (2002)
15. Qin, A.K., Huang, V.L., Suganthan, P.N.: Differential evolution algorithm with strategy adaptation for global numerical optimization. IEEE Trans. Evol. Comput. **13** (2009)
16. Babu, B.V., Jehan, M.M.L.: Differential evolution for multi-objective optimization. In: Proceedings of the 2003 Congress on Evolutionary Computation, pp. 2696–2703. IEEE Press, Canberra (2003)
17. Dorigo, M., Maniezzo, V., Colorni, A.: Ant system: optimization by a colony of cooperating agents. IEEE Trans Syst. Man Cybern. Part B **26**(1), 29–41 (1996)
18. Dong, W.: Research and application based on differential evolution algorithm. Sci. Technol. Eng. **9**(22), 6673–6676 (2009)
19. Yang, L.H.: Genetic algorithm based on function optimization. Software Guide **8**(2), 44–46 (2009)
20. Fei, Z.Z.: Novel improved quantum genetic algorithm. Comput. Eng. **36**(6), 181–183 (2010).
21. Bouchaud, J.P., Cont, R.: A Langevin approach to stock market fluctuations and crashes. Eur. Phys. J. B-Condensed Matter Complex Syst. **6**(4), 543–550 (1998)
22. Iino, M., Ozaki, T.: A nonlinear model for financial dynamics. In: Proceeding of the International Symposium on Frontiers of Time Series Modeling, pp. 334–335. The Institute of Statistical Mathematics, Tokyo Japan (2000)
23. Peng, H., Ozaki, T., Haggan-Ozaki, V.: Modeling and asset allocation for financial markets based on a discrete time microstructure model. Euro. Phys. J. B-Condensed Matter Complex Syst. **31**(2), 285–293 (2003)
24. Peng, H., Tamura, Y., Gui, W., Ozaki, T.: Modeling and asset allocation for financial markets based on a stochastic volatility microstructure model. Int. J. Syst. Sci. **36**(6), 315–327 (2005)
25. Peng, H., Kitagawa, G., Tamura, Y., et al.: Detection of low-frequency large-amplitude jump in financial time series. In: Proceeding of the 46th IEEE Conference on Decision and Control, pp. 4944–4949. New Orleans, LA, USA (2007)
26. Haykin, S.: Kalman Filtering and Neural Networks. Adaptive and Learning Systems for Signal Processing, Communications and Control. Wiley, New York (2001)

Domain-Specific Collaborative Applications

A Novel Method of Multi-sensor Information Fusion Based on Comprehensive Conflict Measurement

Kaiyi Zhao[1], Li Li[2], Zeqiu Chen[1], Ruizhi Sun[1(✉)], and Gang Yuan[1(✉)]

[1] College of Information and Electrical Engineering, China Agricultural University, Beijing 100083, China
{zhaokaiyi1204,chenzq,sunruizhi,yuangang}@cau.edu.cn

[2] Computer School, Beijing Information Science and Technology University, Beijing 100101, China
lili_2018@cau.edu.cn

Abstract. The Internet of things expands the ability of human beings to perceive the surrounding environment, bringing a great challenge to the multi-sensor data processing. Evidence theory, one of the most effective processing technologies, is commonly employed in the multi-sensor information fusion. However, many counter-intuitive results of multi-sensor data fusion may be obtained when fused evidence is highly conflicting. In this study, a new comprehensive method for calculating the entropy of each evidence is proposed, with the goal of improving information volume measurement. In addition, a conflict measure method of multi-sensor evidence is introduced, which can calculate the weighted average evidence, by synthesizing vector space and evidence distribution. Finally, the pre-processed body of evidences have been merged based on the evidence theory. The proposed multi-sensor fusion approach based on comprehensive conflict measurement produces a more credible fusion outcome compared to other approaches, according to experimental results.

Keywords: Evidence theory · Conflict · Entropy · Vector space

1 Introduction

It is widely accepted in the Internet of Things age that multi-sensor information fusion can provide a more precise and dependable target state than a single sensor. The sensing terminals of the multi-sensor system contains different types of sensors and the same type of sensors with different observation angles. Due to the fact that the sensing system can describe precise state, consistent estimation and complete real-time evaluation of the observation object, by fusing the redundant and complementary information obtained from multiple sensors, the use of multi-sensor information fusion technology is gaining popularity in a variety of sectors, including military, robotics, navigation, medical diagnosis,

Y. Sun et al. (Eds.): ChineseCSCW 2021, CCIS 1491, pp. 399–408, 2022.
https://doi.org/10.1007/978-981-19-4546-5_31

and environmental monitoring, etc. However, there is still an issue, i.e., how to deal with data that is in conflict, resulting in counter-intuitive fusion results.

Nowadays, a variety of strategies have been suggested to solve the issue such as probability theory, possibility theory, evidence theory, fuzzy set, rough set, Bayesian reasoning. As one of the effective fusion theories, evidence theory, whose full name is Dempster-Shafer evidence theory, has already been improved and applied in many scenarios. Aiming at the shortcomings of evidence theory, there are two main improvement ideas to avoid generating counter-intuitive results when highly conflicting evidences are fused. The first way is to modify the evidence's combination rule, such as model of transferable belief [6], Bayesian approximation [8] and Dubois's combination rule [1]. Another way is to preprocess the evidence, such as Deng's weighted average method [10], Zhang's cosine theorem-based method [12], Yuan's entropy-based approach [11], the belief divergence-based approach of Xiao [9] and Zhao's improved evidence fusion algorithm [13,14]. Although the methods based on modifying combination rules have good performance, especially for some specific conflict scenarios, they are difficult to deal with the conflict caused by raw data. Therefore, the latter is a more effective improvement strategy. Although these methods have achieved good performance in avoiding the impact of conflict evidence and obtaining credible fusion result, there are still some things that could be done better.

A novel multi-sensor fusion strategy based on thorough conflict measurement is proposed in this research. First, a comprehensive method is developed to determine the information volume in a piece of evidence to satisfy different discernment frameworks of evidence theory. Then, considering multiple factors of evidence weight, including the information volume, the distribution of evidence and the angle of evidence in vector space, we propose a comprehensive evidence weight measurement. Finally, based on the comprehensive weighting, the weighted average evidence will be obtained, and the fusion result will be obtained by using DS theory. To put the proposed method to the test, a multi-sensor information fusion example of fault diagnosis is employed in the comparative experiment, and the results of the fusion are compared to those of other methods. What's more, the conclusion is proved that the proposed approach can produce more trustworthy fusion results.

The remainder of this article is structured as follows. Section 2 begins with some preliminaries on evidence theory. Section 3 describes in detail the proposed method. Section 4 is dedicated to validating the proposed method and discussing the comparative experimental results. Section 5 summarizes the paper's conclusion and future work.

2 Preliminaries

Evidence theory, also known as Dempster-Shafer evidence theory, was developed in the 1960s by mathematician A.P. Dempster, who applied upper and lower limit probability to address a multi-valued mapping issue. The concept of belief function was then introduced by G. Shafer in order to establish a set of "evidence" and "combination" to deal with the mathematical method of uncertainty reasoning, namely DS evidence theory.

2.1 Discernment Framework

The discernment framework Ω is a set that isn't empty, whose elements are mutually exclusive and form a complete event set. Ω is defined as follows:

$$\Omega = \{e_1, e_2, e_3, ..., e_n\} \tag{1}$$

Here, $e_i(i \in [1, n])$ is the atomic event which may occur in the closed-world hypothesis. n is the quantity of possible events. The power set 2^Ω of the discernment framework Ω has the following definition:

$$2^\Omega = \{\emptyset, \{e_1\}, \{e_2\}, ..., \{e_n\}, ..., \{e_1, e_2, ...\}, ..., \Omega\} \tag{2}$$

Here, $\emptyset$ is an empty set, which means that all events will not happen, and 2^n is the number of subsets contained by the power set 2^Ω.

2.2 Assignment of Basic Probabilities

Assignment of basic probabilities (BPA), also known as mass function, is widely employed to represent uncertain information. Assignment of basic probabilities $m(A)$ is the mapping of power set 2^Ω on interval [0,1]. Its definition is as follows:

$$m(y) : 2^\Omega \rightarrow [0, 1] \tag{3}$$

Here, $m(y)$ is the value of mass function of subset $y(y \subseteq 2^\Omega)$ and $\sum_{y \subseteq \Omega} m(y) = 1 (m(\emptyset) = 0)$. If $m(y) > 0$, y will be referred to as the focal element.

2.3 Dempster's Combination Rule

Two distinct mass functions, m_a and m_b, can be fused by using Dempster's fusion rule. The definition of fusion rule has the following definition:

$$m(z) = (m_a \oplus m_b)(z) = \frac{1}{1-K} \sum_{x \cap y = z} m_a(x) m_b(y) \tag{4}$$

Here, the normalization factor, denoted by K, is as follows defined:

$$K = \sum_{x \cap y = \emptyset} m_a(x) m_b(y) \tag{5}$$

3 The New Method of Multi-sensor Information Fusion

In this section, a novel method of multi-sensor fusion based on comprehensive conflict measurement will be introduced in detail. As shown in the flowchart of Fig. 1, further explanation will be divided into three modules.

1) Section 3.1: Considering the complexity of the closed-world hypothesis in evidence theory, a comprehensive information volume measure method is proposed for different discernment framework.
2) Section 3.2: To develop a comprehensive weight of evidence, the distribution of the body of evidence, the angle of evidences in vector space, and the information volume of each evidence are combined.
3) Section 3.3: The weighted average evidence will be obtained based on the weight of evidence, and then it will be merged to generate the fusion result using Dempster's fusion rule.

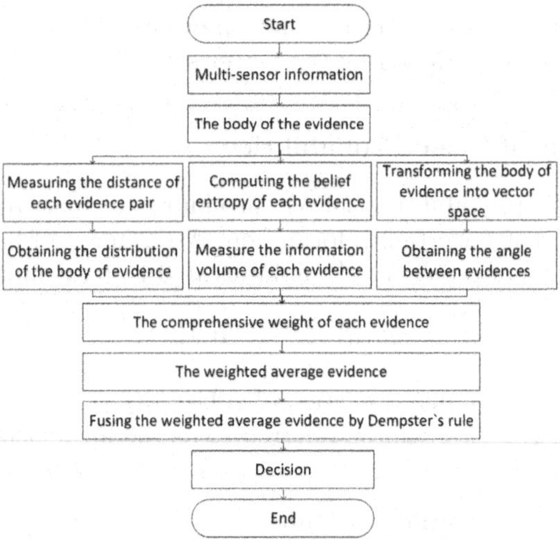

Fig. 1. Flow chart of the proposed multi-sensor information fusion approach

3.1 New Belief Entropy

Evidence theory is an uncertain reasoning strategy based on the closed-world hypothesis. In its discernment framework, the uncertainty information includes not only mass function, but also the framework of discernment's cardinal number and the hypothesis set of uncertainty. Therefore, we not only unify the form of belief entropy calculation methods in literatures [3–5, 7], and also define a new belief entropy. The unified form of computing belief entropy is given below.

$$E(m) = -\sum_{y \subseteq \Omega} m(y) log_2 (\frac{m(y)}{2^{|y|} - 1} e^{f(y,\Omega)}) \tag{6}$$

Here, e is the natural logarithm. $f(y, \Omega)$ is the uncertainty information measurement function about y and Ω. In this work, the proposed comprehensive measurement approach of uncertain data is as follows.

$$f(y) = \sum_{x \subseteq \Omega, x \neq y} \frac{|y \cap x|}{|y \cup x|(2^{|\Omega|} - 1)} \tag{7}$$

Here, $|y \cap x|$ is the intersection's cardinality of y and x. $|y \cup x|$ is the union's cardinality of y and x. $|\Omega|$ is the cardinality of discernment framework.

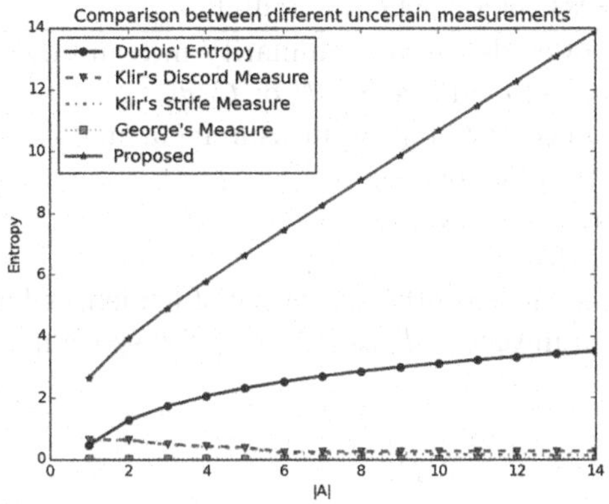

Fig. 2. Comparison of the proposed method to other unreliable measurements

Example: assuming that the discernment framework is complete and mutually exclusive, expressed as $\Omega = \{e_1, e_2, e_3, ..., e_{15}\}$, the basic probability assignment of an evidence will be as follows:

$$\begin{cases} m(\{e_3, e_4, e_5\}) = 0.05, \\ m(\{e_6\}) = 0.05, \\ m(A) = 0.8, \\ m(\Omega) = 0.1 \end{cases} \tag{8}$$

Here, A is a variable and $A \subseteq 2^{\Omega}$. The atomic events contained in A gradually increase from e_1 to e_{15}, such as $A = \{e_1\}, A = \{e_1, e_2\}, A = \{e_1, e_2, e_3\}$ and $A = \{e_1, e_2, e_3, e_4, ..., e_i\}, i \in [1, 15]$. When A changes, the calculation results of different evidence entropy are illustrated in Fig. 2. As shown in Fig. 2, the horizontal axis represents the cardinal number of A, and the vertical axis represents the corresponding entropy value. Based on the results of various evidence entropy calculations in Fig. 2, as can be seen, the values of the evidence entropies by our proposed algorithm will gradually increase with the increase of cardinality of A, which indicates that the proposed algorithm outperforms other algorithms in terms of evidence uncertainty.

3.2 Generating Evidences Weight

In this section, the distribution distance of the body of these evidence, the information volume of evidences and the angle between these evidences in the vector space will constitute the joined weight of the evidences. Based on the distribution distance and vector angle of evidence, the pseudo-code of calculating the weight factor of evidence is shown in Algorithm 1. In this input of Algorithm 1, similarity measure method d represents the method based on evidence distribution distance. Its definition is shown in Eq. 9. Here, $m_{1,2}$ is the distribution distance measure among m_1 and m_2 [13].

Algorithm 1: Assess the evidence's credibility.

Data: The body of evidence, m_i; Similarity measure method, d or v
Result: Credibility of evidence, Crd^d or Crd^v

Initialize the evidence distribution measurement matrix, $DMM_{n \times n}$ (n denotes the number of evidence);
for $i = 1 \rightarrow n$ **do**
  for $j = 1 \rightarrow n$ **do**
    $DMM_{i,j} \leftarrow$ Measure the similarity of evidences based on distribution measure, d (Eq. 9) or vector space measure, v (Eq. 11);
  end
end
Initialize support vector, SUP_n;
for $i = 1 \rightarrow n$ **do**
  $SUP_i = \frac{n-1}{\sum_{j=1, j \neq i}^{n} DMM_{i,j}}$
end
Initialize credibility vector, $Crd_n^{d\ or\ v}$;
for $i = 1 \rightarrow n$ **do**
  $Crd_i^{d\ or\ v} = \frac{SUP_i}{\sum_{k=1}^{n} SUP_k}$
end
return $Crd_i^{d\ or\ v}$

$$d_{1,2} = \sqrt{\frac{[\sum_i m_1(A_i) log \sqrt{\frac{2m_1(A_i)^2}{m_1(A_i)^2 + m_2(A_i)^2}}]^2 + [\sum_i m_2(A_i) log \sqrt{\frac{2m_2(A_i)^2}{m_1(A_i)^2 + m_2(A_i)^2}}]^2}{2}} \tag{9}$$

Another similarity measure between evidences is based on vector space, expressed as v. The main definitions are shown in Eq. 10 and Eq. 11. Equation 10 is used to transform the basic probability assignment function m into a vector m_v, where e represents the atomic hypothesis and A is a subset of 2^{Ω}. In short, this transformation is to evenly distribute the probability of a set of atomic hypotheses to each atomic hypothesis, so that the basic probability assignment of evidences can be stated in vector form.

$$m_v(e) = \sum_{e \in A \subseteq \Omega} \frac{m(A)}{|A|} \tag{10}$$

After the evidence m_1 is transformed into vector form m_{v_1}, the similarity measure between evidences is based on the inner product of vectors. Its definition is demonstrated in Eq. 11, where $|m_{v_1}|$ and $|m_{v_2}|$ represent the norm of vector m_{v_1} and m_{v_2} respectively.

$$v_{1,2} = 1 - \frac{m_{v_1} \cdot m_{v_2}}{|m_{v_1}||m_{v_2}|} \tag{11}$$

Based on the above two similarity measures, Algorithm 1 can output the credibility of evidence Crd^d and Crd^v, which are also the input of Algorithm 2. The pseudo-code of the evidence weight generation method is demonstrated in Algorithm 2. First, the developed belief entropy will be applied to determine each piece of evidence's information volume. Then, the normalized information volume is joined with the credibility Crd^d and Crd^v to form a comprehensive measure of evidence uncertainty. After normalization, each piece of evidence's weight is calculated.

Algorithm 2: Generate evidence weight

Data: The body of evidence, m_i; Credibility of evidence, Crd^d and Crd^v
Result: Weight of evidence, W
Initialize information volume of evidence, IV_n;
for $i = 1 \to n$ **do**
    $IV_i = e^{E(m_i)}$ //Determine the evidence's information volume by using Eq. 6 and Eq. 7;
end
Initialize evidence weight vector, W_n;
for $i = 1 \to n$ **do**
    $W_i = Crd_i^d \times Crd_i^v \times \frac{IV_i}{\sum_{k=1}^{n} IV_k}$ //Crd_i^d and Crd_i^v are obtained from Algorithm 1;
end
$W_i = \frac{W_i}{\sum_{k=1}^{n} W_k}$;
return W

3.3 Evidences Fusion

Based on the weight of evidence, the weighted average evidence is obtained after preprocessing the body of evidence. Using Dempster's fusion rule, the final combination result is calculated by combining this processed evidences. The pseudo-code of this process is demonstrated in Algorithm 3 .

Algorithm 3: Fusing the body of evidence

Data: The body of evidence, m_i; Weight of evidence, W
Result: Fusion result, m_{fusion}
Initialize weighted average evidence, WAE;
$WAE = \sum_{i=1}^{n} W_i \times m_i, i \in [1, n]$;
$m_{fusion} \leftarrow$ Combine WAE by Dempster with $(n-1)$ times. ;
return m_{fusion}

4 Experiment and Analysis

4.1 Example for Fault Diagnosis

The empirical data of fault diagnosis is shown in Table 1. In the discernment framework $\Omega = \{E_1, E_2, E_3\}$, $\{E_1\}$, $\{E_2\}$, $\{E_2, E_3\}$ and $\{E_1, E_2, E_3\}$ are the possible hypotheses. These evidences (m_1, m_2 and m_3) comes from sensors (S_1, S_2 and S_3) respectively. Furthermore, two parameters (the sufficiency index $\mu(m)$, the importance index $\nu(m)$) involved in this application are shown in Table 2. They will be joined to form the static reliability SR, which is defined as $SR_i = \mu_i \times \nu_i$. The static reliability SR needs to be multiplied by the weight W of evidence before normalization, and the normalized result is the final weight.

Table 1. BPAs of multi-sensor information fusion

BPA	$\{E_1\}$	$\{E_2\}$	$\{E_2, E_3\}$	$\{E_1, E_2, E_3\}$
$m_1(\bullet)$	0.41	0.29	0.30	0.00
$m_2(\bullet)$	0.00	0.90	0.10	0.00
$m_3(\bullet)$	0.58	0.07	0.00	0.35

Table 2. The index of μ, ν

Parameter	m_1	m_2	m_3
μ	1.00	0.60	1.00
ν	1.00	0.34	1.00

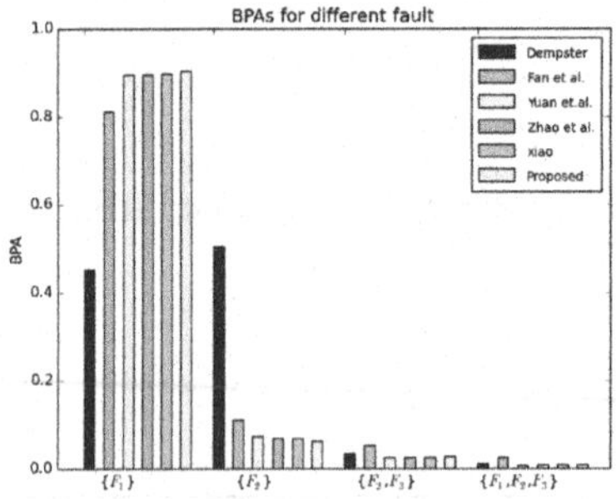

Fig. 3. Comparison of BPAs produced by various methods for all hypotheses

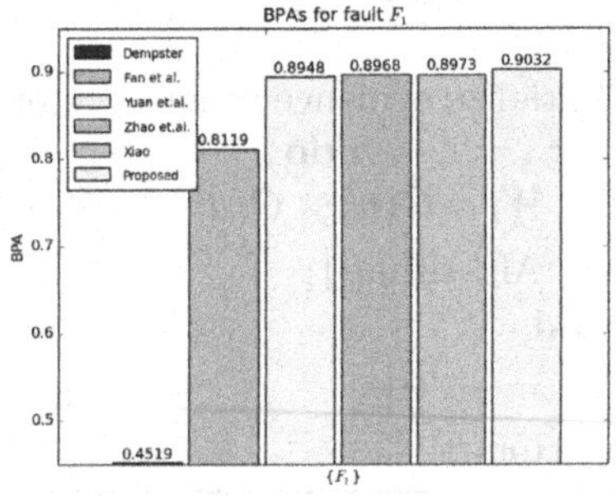

Fig. 4. Comparison of BPAs produced by various methods for $\{E_1\}$

4.2 Discussion and Analysis

The methods by Dempster, Fan et al. [2], Yuan et al. [11], Zhao et al. [13], and Xiao [9], are also employed in the experiment. As shown in Table 3, the first row is the set of possible faults, the other rows are the outcomes of various methods' experiments, and the final column is the corresponding faults. In addition, we have visualized the data of Table 3 in Fig. 3 and Fig. 4. The horizontal axis in two figures represents a possible hypothesis, and the vertical axis represents the BPA of different methods in the corresponding hypothesis. Following a thorough and reasonable analysis, the following conclusions are reached:

Table 3. Comparison of fusion results from various fault diagnosis methods

BPA	$\{E_1\}$	$\{E_2\}$	$\{E_2, E_3\}$	$\{E_1, E_2, E_3\}$	Fault
Dempster	0.4519	0.5048	0.0336	0.0096	E_2
Fan et al. [2]	0.8119	0.1096	0.0526	0.0259	E_1
Yuan et al. [11]	0.8948	0.0739	0.0241	0.0072	E_1
Zhao et al. [13]	0.8968	0.0692	0.0257	0.0083	E_1
Xiao [9]	0.8973	0.0688	0.0254	0.0080	E_1
Proposed	0.9032	0.0622	0.0261	0.0085	E_1

1) Using Dempster's fusion rule to directly fuse evidence, the counter-intuitive conclusion is generated, which means that the diagnosis is greatly affected by the conflict evidence and leads to the wrong conclusion E_2.
2) Except Dempster's combination rule, other methods can avoid the occurrence of abnormal results when conflict evidence exists. The correct fault E_1 is accurately diagnosed, and the credibility of the diagnosis result is increased.
3) The proposed method can diagnose the correct fault E_1. What's more, the proposed method has higher credibility of the diagnosis result than other methods with the credibility of 90.32%, more than 0.59% higher than others.

All in all, the proposed method for multi-sensor data fusion based on comprehensive conflict measurement performs better than alternative methods. This method eliminates the flaw of Dempster's fusion rule, and avoids the occurrence of the counter-intuitive results when conflict evidence exists. It also can obtains higher credibility than other methods.

5 Conclusion and Future Work

The following are the contributions of this paper: 1) an effective belief entropy is proposed to improve the measurement of information volume. 2) Considering the distribution distance measure of evidence, the angle between evidences in vector space and the improved information volume, a comprehensive conflict measurement method is proposed to generate evidence weight. 3) Based on comprehensive evidence weight, a method for combining data from multiple sensors is proposed. In the comparative experiments of multi-sensor fault diagnosis application, the proposed method can not only diagnose the correct fault, but also achieve higher credibility than other methods. As a result, we can see that our proposed approach outperforms other algorithms.

Acknowledgments. This study was supported by National Development and Reform Commission integrated data service system infrastructure platform construction project (JZNYYY001) and Application of collaborative precision positioning service for mass users (2016YFB0501805-1).

References

1. Dubois, D., Prade, H.: Consonant approximation of belief functions. Int. J. Approx. Reason. **4**(5–6), 419–449 (1990). https://doi.org/10.1016/0888-613X(90)90015-T
2. Fan, F., Zuo, M.: Fault diagnosis of machines based on d-s evidence theory. part 1: D-s evidence theory and its improvement. Pattern Recogn. Lett. **27**, 366–376 (2006). https://doi.org/10.1016/j.patrec.2005.08.025
3. Florea, M., Jousselme, A.L., Grenier, D., Bosse, E.: An unified approach to the fusion of imperfect data? In: Proceedings of SPIE - The International Society for Optical Engineering, vol. 4731 (2002). https://doi.org/10.1117/12.458372
4. George, T., Pal, N.: Quantification of conflict in dempster-shafer framework: a new approach. Int. J. General Syst. **24**, 407–423 (1996). https://doi.org/10.1080/03081079608945130
5. Pal, N.R., Bezdek, J.C., Hemasinha, R.: Uncertainty measures for evidential reasoning I: a review. Int. J. Approx. Reason. **7**(3), 165–183 (1992). https://doi.org/10.1016/0888-613X(92)90009-O
6. Smets, P.: The combination of evidence in the transferable belief model. IEEE Trans. Pattern Anal. Mach. Intell. **12**(5), 447–458 (1990). https://doi.org/10.1109/34.55104
7. Tang, Y., Zhou, D., Xu, S., He, Z.: A weighted belief entropy-based uncertainty measure for multi-sensor data fusion. Sensors **17**, 928 (2017). https://doi.org/10.3390/s17040928
8. Voorbraak, F.: On the justification of dempster's rule of combination. Artif. Intell. **48**(2), 171–197 (1991). https://doi.org/10.1016/0004-3702(91)90060-W
9. Xiao, F.: Multi-sensor data fusion based on the belief divergence measure of evidences and the belief entropy. Inf. Fusion **46**, 23–32 (2019). https://doi.org/10.1016/j.inffus.2018.04.003
10. Yong, D., WenKang, S., ZhenFu, Z., Qi, L.: Combining belief functions based on distance of evidence. Decis. Support Syst. **38**(3), 489–493 (2004). https://doi.org/10.1016/j.dss.2004.04.015
11. Yuan, K., Xiao, F., Fei, L., Kang, B., Deng, Y.: Conflict management based on belief function entropy in sensor fusion. SpringerPlus **5**(1), 1–12 (2016). https://doi.org/10.1186/s40064-016-2205-6
12. Zhang, Z., Liu, T., Chen, D., Zhang, W.: Novel algorithm for identifying and fusing conflicting data in wireless sensor networks. Sensors **14**, 9562–9581 (2014). https://doi.org/10.3390/s140609562
13. Zhao, K., Sun, R., Li, L., Hou, M., Yuan, G., Sun, R.: An improved evidence fusion algorithm in multi-sensor systems. Appl. Intell. **51**(11), 7614–7624 (2021). https://doi.org/10.1007/s10489-021-02279-5
14. Zhao, K., Sun, R., Li, L., Hou, M., Yuan, G., Sun, R.: An optimal evidential data fusion algorithm based on the new divergence measure of basic probability assignment. Soft Comput. **25**(17), 11449–11457 (2021). https://doi.org/10.1007/s00500-021-06040-5

Research on the Structure and Key Algorithms of Smart Gloves Oriented to Middle School Experimental Scene Perception

Hongyue Wang[1,2], Xin Meng[1,2], and Zhiquan Feng[1,2](✉)

[1] College of Information Science and Engineering, University of Jinan, Jinan 250022, China
1536748981@qq.com

[2] Shandong Provincial Key Laboratory of Network Environment Intelligent Computing Technology, University of Jinan, Jinan 250022, China

Abstract. The existing virtual experiment platform mainly uses virtual reality technology or animation technology to assist students in experimental teaching, but it lacks the standardized supervision of users' experimental behaviors. To address the above problems, this paper designs a prototype smart glove application for middle school experimental scenarios and proposes a scene perception algorithm based on the smart glove, so as to obtain the user's experimental behavior more accurately. Based on the perception of the experimental scene, this paper also proposes a multimodal fusion of intelligent navigation interaction paradigm to obtain the user's experimental intention, thus allowing students to conduct exploratory experiments on a virtual experimental platform with targeted guidance and monitoring of user behavior. Experiments show that the smart glove designed in this paper can sense the relative relationship between experimental equipment and objects in the scene in real time. Based on the user's experimental behavior, the smart glove can also infer the operator's experimental intent and provide timely feedback and guidance on the user's experimental behavior.

Keywords: Virtual experiment platform · Smart gloves · Scene perception · Intention inference

1 Introduction

Experimental teaching is an important part of secondary school teaching, but in practice there are problems such as the existence of dangerous experimental supplies for operation and irregularities in experimental operations. With the development of Internet technology, the virtual experiment platform has solved these problems. However, there are still some defects in the existing virtual experiment platform. On the one hand, the virtual experiment platform tends to use animation to present the experimental process. On the other hand, most virtual experiment platforms lack the monitoring of users' experimental behaviors.

In order to solve the above problems, this paper designs a smart glove that can be used for experimental teaching in secondary schools and also has the ability of field

Y. Sun et al. (Eds.): ChineseCSCW 2021, CCIS 1491, pp. 409–423, 2022.
https://doi.org/10.1007/978-981-19-4546-5_32

perception. The smart glove can sense the information of objects in the experimental scene and their corresponding position relationship in real time. Students can operate the real experimental apparatus on the virtual experimental platform to conduct experiments. Based on the field perception, this paper also presents an interactive example of intelligent navigation, which can synthesize the information of speech, vision and sensors used to infer the user's experimental intention and provide feedback and guidance to the user.

2 Related Work

The development of information technology has provided a broad platform for virtual labs. Experimental teaching through the use of virtual laboratories has the following advantages: 1. Virtual laboratories can save the cost of experiments and allow students to conduct more types of experiments for schools with insufficient experimental funds; 2. The use of virtual laboratories can better ensure the safety of students; 3. Traditional laboratories require teachers to spend time on equipment setup and maintenance.

In recent years, with the continuous development of Internet technology, virtual laboratories have become a research hotspot for scholars at home and abroad. Sotomayor-Moriano J [1] enable students to conduct experiments in a real environment through a Web browser, and can design and practice controls in an interactive virtual laboratory. Khulood Aljuhani [2] have developed a virtual laboratory platform based on the Web. Users can use the mouse to perform experiments in the virtual laboratory individually and perform multiple experiments as needed. It can not only enhances the flexibility of teaching technology, but also deepens students' understanding of experimental phenomena. Web-based platforms can only immerse students in the learning experience to a limited extent. In order to improve immersion, Ioannis Doumanis [3] uses game mechanics and game design thinking to design a multi-mode immersive teaching environment. Experiments show that the platform can better improve students' academic performance and subjective experience. Dongfeng Liu [4] also used computer simulation technology to design a low-cost virtual laboratory. Compared with the above methods, this virtual laboratory allows students to assemble instruments and use their own assembled instruments to perform physical experiments, so it can help students understand the scientific process better. Although the above virtual laboratory design methods have achieved good results, the attractiveness of the virtual learning environment is relatively weak due to the operation of the mouse and keyboard.

In response to the problems of insufficient experimental funds and lack of experimental equipment in some middle schools, Francisco Torres [5] built a virtual laboratory on the Unity platform, allowing students to interact with experimental equipment on the virtual platform and design experiments based on learning topics. Diana Bogusevschi [6] uses virtual reality technology to teach water cycle experiments in order to save experimental costs. Students can conduct experiments in accordance with the guidelines of the program, which greatly enhances students' interest in learning and deepens students' understanding of water cycle experiments. Augmented reality technology (AR) can increase the user's immersion, so many researches also focus on augmented reality technology. For example, Joanne Yip [7] applied AR video to students' learning process to help students understand space-related knowledge. Mustafa Fidan [8] integrated

AR technology into the teaching process of physics and invited 91 students to conduct experiments. The experimental results show that with the assistance of AR technology, students' learning attitudes are more active and their academic performance is improved.

The above research schemes have proved that virtual experimental teaching is feasible in teaching work. It can not only enhance students' interest in learning, help students understand knowledge, but also make up for the shortcomings in traditional experimental teaching. Lowell M [9] has further confirmed this point by comparing traditional teaching methods and virtual experimental teaching methods. They selected 50 students to use traditional multimedia presentation methods and virtual assisted teaching methods using VR equipment for chemistry teaching, and tested two groups of users. The final score shows that the performance of students who use virtual assisted teaching is significantly higher than that of students who use traditional methods. Also using two different teaching methods, Sarah Sullivan [10] asked students to conduct pulley experiments. The results proved that using virtual experiments can be more beneficial to deepen students' understanding of scientific concepts.

Whether using a web browser or using virtual reality technology, most studies tend to use a single channel to interact with users, and the process of human-computer interaction is often accompanied by the collaborative work of multiple channels. For example, Sidenmark [11] proposed in the study of the user's gaze that the user's gaze is often accompanied by the coordinated operation of the eyes, head and body. Therefore, it is very important to treat the line of sight as a coordinated operation of multiple modalities. Using multiple channels as input in the human-computer interaction process not only improves the efficiency of human-computer interaction, but also enables more flexible and free communication. In the design of the car driving user interface, Jingun Jung [12] combines touch and voice to solve the problem of low control efficiency caused by only using voice for input in some aspects, and enhance the user experience.In the AR environment, Ismail A W [13] allows users to interact with virtual objects in two ways: voice commands and gestures, making user operations more natural. The advantages of using multi-channel interaction are more prominent in robot application scenarios. Deng Yongda [14] proposed the use of gestures and voice commands to control the robot to make the interaction process more natural. It also integrates the data of gestures and voice channels. TingHan [15] proved that the result of multi-channel fusion is better than the result of using only a single channel.

In summary, although the virtual experiment platform has shown excellent results in teaching results, there are still shortcomings. In actual experimental teaching, the standardization of experimental procedures is also very important, which puts forward new requirements for the virtual experimental platform, that is, the virtual experimental platform should have the ability to perceive and understand the user's experimental scene.To this end, this paper designs a smart glove with the ability to perceive the scene, which can perceive the object information and the corresponding position relationship in the experimental scene in real time. On the basis of scene perception, this paper also proposes an intelligent navigational interaction paradigm based on multi-modal fusion to infer the user's experimental intention, so as to give the user corresponding feedback and guidance during the experiment. Finally, the user can complete the experimental operation under the guidance of smart gloves.

3 Scene Perception Algorithm Based on Smart Gloves

Scene perception technology allows smart gloves to understand the environment like a human. When smart gloves perform scene perception, they can use the camera to detect experimental objects and thus understand the experimental scene. In secondary school experiment scenarios, when users operate experimental equipment with smart gloves, they often cannot obtain a complete image containing the experimental object, so it is difficult to identify and locate the experimental equipment. To address the above problems, this paper proposes an algorithm for perceiving and locating experimental objects in specific scenes based on smart gloves, so as to obtain information about the experimental objects operated by users and their location relationships with other objects in real time.

3.1 Smart Glove Structure Design

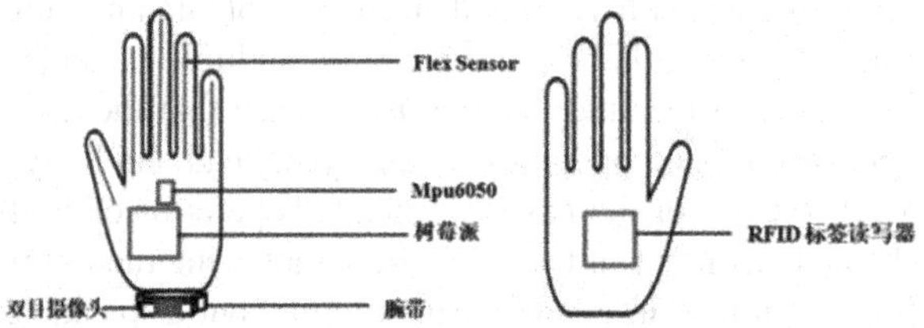

Fig. 1. Hardware structure design of the palm of smart glove

The hardware structure design of the smart glove is shown in Fig. 1. The structure of the smart glove is divided into several parts: 1. We use the curvature sensor to obtain the change of the user's finger curvature; 2. The Mpu6050 sensor is small in size and can directly obtain the three-axis acceleration, angular velocity, and angle of the user during movement. Therefore, it is used to restore the posture of the user's hand; 3. As the functional module of the smart glove, the Raspberry Pi is mainly responsible for processing various sensor data; 4. In the palm of the smart glove, we place a small RFID tag to read and write The smart glove can obtain real-time information about the object currently being operated by the user's hand; The data transmission mode of the smart glove designed in this paper adopts wireless transmission, so that users can conduct experiments more conveniently.

3.2 Target Detection System Based on YOLOv3

In the process of experimenting, due to the limitation of experimental space and other factors, smart gloves sometimes cannot capture the complete image of the experimental article. Therefore, this article uses a combination of different colors to mark the experimental article. Considering that the smart gloves designed in this article will ultimately need to be applied to middle school experimental scenes, when performing target detection, the target detection algorithm is required to ensure high recognition rate while pursuing real-time performance. In order to achieve faster and better identification of experimental objects, this article uses the YOLOv3 network [16] to detect objects in the experimental scene. First, we use binocular cameras to collect experimental scene data of experimental item tags from different perspectives and distances. In the process of data collection, in order to ensure that smart gloves can realize real-time scene perception in different experimental situations, we use LabelImg tool to label the collected pictures, and send the labeling information as training samples to the YOLOv3 network model After training in YOLOv3, the experimental item detection model FC based on YOLOv3 was finally obtained. Figure 2 shows the target detection process of the YOLOv3 network.

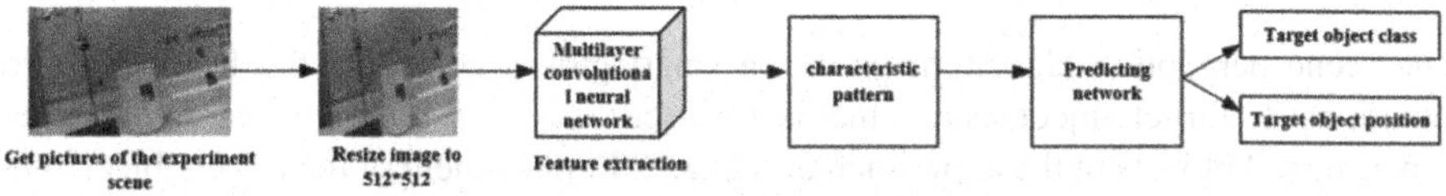

Fig. 2. Schematic diagram of YOLOv3 target detection process

3.3 Smart Glove Movement Track Acquisition

In the process of the user's experiment, the smart glove needs to obtain the user's hand movement trajectory and map it to the virtual experiment platform built in Unity in real time, so as to lay the foundation for the smart glove to better perceive the experimental scene and track the user's experimental behavior. This paper uses the open source ORB-SLAM2 system [17] to realize the perception of the user's movement trajectory by smart gloves. The schematic diagram of ORB-SLAM2 system obtaining the user's hand movement trajectory is shown in Fig. 3:

Fig. 3. Smart glove's perception of the user's hand trajectory

After obtaining the movement trajectory of the user's hand, we can use the formula (1) to process the coordinate information according to the coordinate mapping relationship between the virtual scene and the camera position.

$$\begin{bmatrix} Pos_x \\ Pos_y \\ Pos_z \end{bmatrix} = k \times \begin{bmatrix} U_x \\ U_y \\ U_z \end{bmatrix} \tag{1}$$

Among them, (Pos_x, Pos_y, Pos_z) is the position coordinate of the smart glove obtained by the ORBSLAM2 system.(U_x, U_y, U_z) is the three-dimensional position of the smart glove mapped to the virtual environment. k is the scale factor for coordinate conversion.

3.4 Scene Perception Algorithm Based on Smart Gloves

The scene perception algorithm based on smart gloves considers the following two situations: 1. Target object search, that is, the user uses smart gloves to search for target experimental objects in the experimental scene; 2. Replacement of the target object, that is, the user has an experimental object in his hand and needs to perform an operation on another target object. This paper use the SGBM (Semi-global Block Matching) algorithm to obtain the depth information of the target object. Combining the position information of the target object obtained by target detection, the identification and positioning of the experimental object is realized, and the obtained information is transferred to the Unity platform. During the user's experiment, this article sets the target object set E. Each time an experimental operation is performed, the target object E operated by the user will be dynamically updated. The specific steps of the Scene Perception Algorithm Based on Glove (Scene Perception Algorithm Based on Glove, hereinafter referred to as SPABG) are as follows:

Algorithm 1: Scene Perception Algorithm Based on Smart Gloves (SPABG Algorithm)

Input: experimental scene image pig captured by binocular camera, sensor information O^h.

Output: target object information set E voice prompt V, scene response.

1. Obtain images of experimental scenes pig;
2. Use ORBSLAM2 algorithm to obtain current smart glove location information $Oh(x_h, y_h, z_h)$ and output Oh to Unity platform.
3. Use the target detection model FC to detect the experimental objects on pig, and store the name and location of the detected target object in E_n, E_p;
4. Determine whether E_n is empty, if E_n is empty, return to step 1; If E_n is not empty, then obtain the three-dimensional coordinates of E_p and store it in $E_w(x, y, z)$;
5. Pass E_n and E_w into the Unity platform, and use formula (2) to process E_w to obtain the coordinate E_u in the virtual scene;

$$\begin{bmatrix} E_{ux} \\ E_{uy} \\ E_{uz} \end{bmatrix} = r \times \begin{bmatrix} E_{wx} \\ E_{wy} \\ E_{wz} \end{bmatrix} + B \tag{2}$$

Among them, r is the scale factor of coordinate conversion, and B is the position correction matrix from the real environment to the virtual environment.

6. Determine whether the current user operating object set O^h is empty.

(1) If O^h is empty, perform the formula (3) operation on Oh and E_u to obtain the distance d between the two in real time. If the value of d keeps decreasing, output a voice prompt c V_1 to the user and return to step 1;

$$d = \sqrt{(x_h - E_{ux})^2 + (y_h - E_{uy})^2 + (z_h - E_{uz})^2} \tag{3}$$

(2) If O^h is not empty and E is empty, then O^h is processed, the target object name O^n corresponding to O^h is queried, and O^n and Oh are stored in the target object set E, output E and voice prompt V_2 and display the corresponding target object model in the virtual scene, return to step 1;

(3) If O^h is not empty and E is not empty, then:

①Execute formula (3) operation on O^h and E_u, and obtain the distance d between the two in real time;
②If d satisfies $d \leq \xi$ (ξ is the threshold for judging whether the target object is maneuverable), the corresponding target object model is displayed in the virtual scene, and the current target object name E_n and target object position E_u are stored in E ,output E and voice prompt V_3, and return to step 1.

In the SPABG algorithm, the sensor information O^h is the result obtained by the RFID tag reader placed on the palm of the smart glove; V_1 is "currently you are approaching E_n"; V_2 is "currently you have selected O^n"; V_3 is "currently you have selected E_n .

4 Intelligent Navigational Interaction Paradigm Based on Scene Perception

This chapter will introduce the intelligent navigational interaction paradigm based on scene perception proposed in this article. It processes information from different channels to infer the user's experimental intention and guide the user on the experimental operation. The intention understanding here refers to the fusion of visual data, sensor data and voice data from the smart glove for specific application scenarios and context-based interaction scenarios, so as to infer the user's experimental intent.

4.1 Overall Framework

We constructed an overall framework for the navigational interaction paradigm of smart gloves based on multi-modal fusion intention understanding (Fig. 4). The overall process can be divided into three levels: the input layer, the interaction layer, and the presentation layer. In the input layer, smart gloves obtain data from voice, sensors, and visual channels through interactive devices such as microphones and cameras. In the interaction layer, the smart glove first extracts the semantics of the data from the three channels. When processing the data of the voice channel, this article uses Baidu Voice to recognize and analyze the user's voice instructions. This paper proposes a user intention understanding strategy based on intention screening, which integrates information from various channels to obtain the user's experimental intention. According to the different experimental intentions of the user, combined with the set experimental library, the user's experimental behavior is judged, and finally the user's experimental intention, scene response, voice prompt and other information are output. The output result of the interactive layer will finally be presented in the interactive interface in the presentation layer.

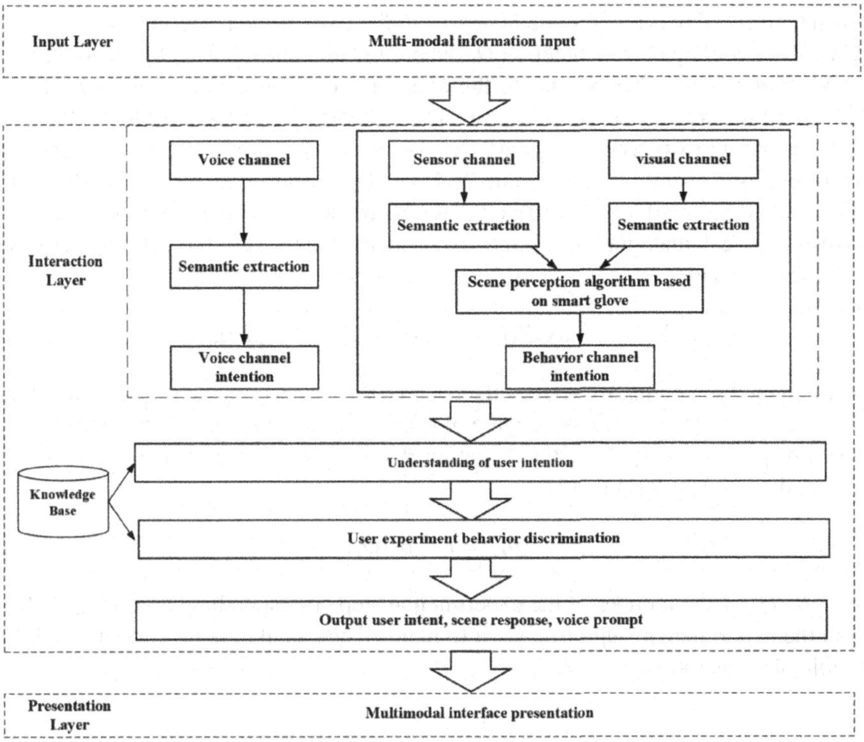

Fig. 4. The overall framework of multi-modal intelligent navigation interaction paradigm based on scene perception.

4.2 User Intent Understanding

In this paper, the process of inferring the user's most likely intention is defined as the problem of intention screening, and the uncertainty of the user's experimental intention is modeled as the possibility of different categories. We define the intent screening problem as a classification task. In the case of a given experimental operation by the user, the smart glove infers the experimental target from the set of possible experimental targets I.

We have pre-established an experiment library for the interaction process between smart gloves and users, which stores the experiment categories and the steps corresponding to each experiment. The set of experiment goals is set to $I = \{I_1, I_2, I_3, \ldots .I_n\}$, and the different experiment categories are set to I_n. We use Baidu Voice to recognize and analyze user commands'. For the voice command T acquired by the voice channel, after lexical analysis, the voice channel intention $T_i\{T_{s_i}, T_{ni}\}$ is obtained, where T_{s_i} and T_{n_i} are the actions and target objects contained in the voice command, respectively.For the data set Q from the sensor channel and the data pig from the vision channel, we integrate the obtained sensor processing results and the target object set E obtained using the SPABG method to obtain the integrated result $G_i\{G_{s_i}, G_{ni}\}$. Among them, G_{s_i} and G_{n_i} are the actions performed by the user and the names of the target objects operated on respectively. After that, the intentions from the two channels are matched to obtain the user's current operation intention O_i, where i is the time label set by the system.

When users conduct experiments, the order of operations is often consistent. Therefore, when we screen user intentions, in addition to using the information in the experiment library, we also need to combine the context information set $\delta\{O_1, O_2 ... O_{i-1}\}$ of the current user operation. Each value in δ is independent of each other. In the t time period, when the smart glove obtains the user's operation intention O_i, it will add O_i to δ. We need to calculate the most likely experimental target H of the current user based on the set δ, namely:

$$P(I_k|\delta) = \max\{P(I_1|\delta), P(I_2|\delta), P(I_j|\delta), ...P(I_n|\delta)\} \tag{4}$$

In the intention screening, we set the offset degree ϑ for each possible experimental target I_n, which is used to calculate the degree of offset of each value in δ in the experimental step corresponding to I_n. Then the deviation ϑ_{n_i} of the experimental operation O_i in I_n can be calculated by formula (5):

$$\vartheta_{n_i} = i - \beta_n[O_i] \tag{5}$$

where $\beta_n[O_i]$ is the number of the experimental step corresponding to O_i in I_n. If O_i is not in the experimental step of I_n, set it to blank. The calculation process of $P(I_n|\delta)$ in formula (4) is as follows:

$$P(I_n|\delta) = \frac{\alpha_n - \sum \vartheta_{ni}}{\alpha_n} \times 100\% \tag{6}$$

$$\alpha_n = \frac{[N(I_n)]^2 - 1}{2} \tag{7}$$

Among them, α_n is the maximum deviation degree of each experiment, and $N(I_n)$ is the total number of experimental steps in each experiment. For the finally obtained $P(I_k|\delta)$, it is necessary to make a confidence judgment. If $P(I_k|\delta)$ is greater than the intention determination threshold Θ, the user's current most likely experimental target is determined to be I_k, otherwise the intention screening state will continue to be maintained.

4.3 Navigational Interactive Algorithm Based on Scene Perception

After obtaining the user's experimental intent, the smart glove will determine the user's behavior based on the rules in the knowledge base, and output corresponding voice feedback on the user's experimental behavior to guide the user to complete the experiment in a standardized manner. As shown in the navigational interactive algorithm (Navigational Interactive Algorithm, hereinafter referred to as NIA algorithm) based on multi-modal fusion intention understanding:

Algorithm 2: Navigational Interactive Algorithm Based on Multi-modal Fusion Intention Understanding (NIA Algorithm)

Input: experimental scene image pig, sensor information set Q, voice command T;

Output: user experiment intention, scene response combined with a, voice prompt;

1. Obtain information from each channel and perform preprocessing;
2. Use the SPABG Algorithm to process pig, get the smart glove's own position information set Oh, and the target object information set E;
3. Pass Oh to the Unity platform;
4. Integrate Q and E to obtain the integration result $G_i\{G_{si}, G_{ni}\}$ of the visual channel and the sensing channel;
5. Determine whether T is empty. If it is not empty, call Baidu Voice API to analyze T and obtain the current voice channel intention $T_i\{T_{si}, T_{ni}\}$;
6. Use the multi-modal intent matching method to match $G_i\{G_{si}, G_{ni}\}$ and $V_i\{V_{si}, V_{ni}\}$:

(1) If the multi-modal intention matching fails, the voice prompt Y_1 will be output to ask the user whether to continue the hand operation. If the user confirms that the hand behavior is correct, save $G_i\{G_{si}, G_{ni}\}$ as the user's operation intention O_i into the experimental behavior set δ, and output O_i; otherwise, keep T_{ni} and return to step 1;

(2) If the multi-modal intention matching is successful, the user's operation intention O_i will be output, and O_i will be stored in the experimental behavior set δ.

7. Determine whether the experiment target I_m is empty:

(1)If I_m is empty:

① Combined with the experimental target set $I = \{I_1, I_2, I_3, ...I_n\}$, use formula (5), formula (6) and formula (7) to filter δ by intention to obtain the calculation result $P(I_n \mid \delta)$;

② Let $P(I_k \mid \delta) = max(P(I_n \mid \delta))$, determine whether $P(I_k \mid \delta)$ is greater than the intention determination threshold Θ;

③ If $P(I_k \mid \delta) > \Theta$, the user's current most likely experimental target is determined to be I_k, and a voice prompt Y_2 is output to the user to confirm to the user whether the experimental intention is correct:

a) If the user confirms that I_k is wrong, output voice prompt Y_3, return to step 1, and update the experimental target set $I = \{I_1, I_2, I_3, \ldots I_n\}$;

b) If the user confirms that I_k is correct, set $I_m = I_k$ to end the intent screening process.

8. If I_m is not empty, query the rule set $R\{r_1, r_2, r_3..r_n\}$ corresponding to I_m from the experiment library, and judge user behavior according to the corresponding rules in $R\{r_1, r_2, r_3..r_n\}$. Then output the scene response set $a\{a_0, a_1, a_2, \ldots, a_n\}$ and the corresponding navigation prompt according to the user behavior judgment result until the end of the experiment;

In the NIA algorithm, Y_1 indicates that the current hand behavior is inconsistent with the voice command, whether to continue the experimental operation; Y_2 indicates whether the current experimental target is guessed to be I_k is correct; Y_3 indicates that you continue to perform the experimental operation.

5 Experiment and Analysis

Experimental hardware environment: CPU: i7-8750H.

Experimental software environment: Win10 64bit + Unity2018.3.8.

5.1 Feasibility Verification of Smart Gloves

In order to verify the effectiveness of the smart gloves designed in this article, this article selects one typical experiments in middle school experimental teaching for testing. The user wears gloves to verify whether the intelligent navigational interaction paradigm

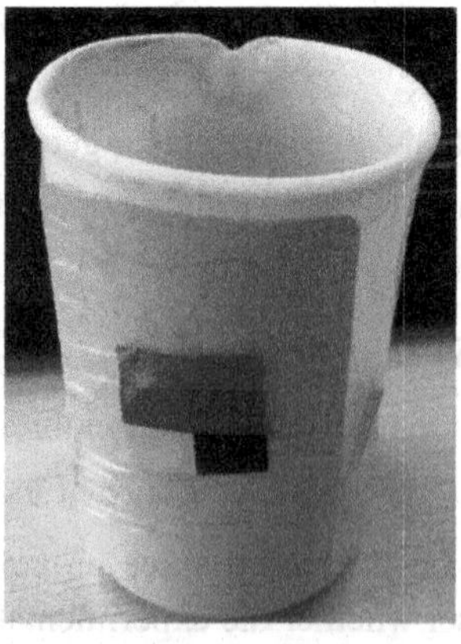

Fig. 5. Experimental equipment diagram

based on scene perception proposed in this paper can realize the perception of the experimental scene. In this paper, 3D printing technology is used to make the experimental supplies according to the size of the experimental supplies used in the actual experiments, and a label representing the category of the experimental supplies is set on the outside of the experimental mold. Some experimental equipment is shown in Fig. 5.

5.2 Experiment: Explore the Experimental Process of Concentrated Sulfuric Acid Dilution Experiment

The scene shown in Fig. 6 is a scene where users conduct experiments in a chemical experiment platform. Figure a shows that the user wears smart gloves to select experimental items. The items in the red boxes in Fig. 6b and Fig. 6c are the experimental reagents and instruments selected by the user; By judging the user's operating behavior, the smart glove speculates that the user wants to do a concentrated sulfuric acid dilution experiment. If the user confirms that the experiment intention is correct, the name of the experiment currently in progress and the steps of the experiment will appear on the screen (the information marked in the green box in Fig. 6d). At the same time, the smart glove recognizes that the reagent currently held by the user's hand is an aqueous solution by identifying the user's operating behavior. The smart glove reminds the user that if the experiment operation is continued, there will be danger. The information marked in the yellow box in the picture e is that the user injected water into the concentrated sulfuric acid solution, and the two reacted violently. The information marked in the green box in the figure f is the user's experimental results. The system also uses voice to explain the user's wrong operation and prompts the user to retry the experiment.

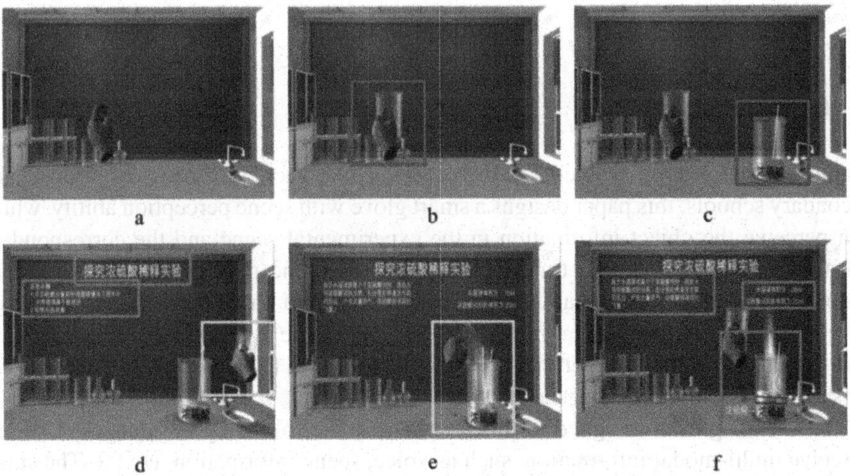

Fig. 6. Concentrated sulfuric acid dilution experiment diagram (wrong operation). (Color figure online)

As is shown in Fig. 7, after the user chooses to re-experiment, he will re-select experimental reagents (the information in the red box in Fig. 7b). The information marked in the yellow box in Fig. 7c is that the user pours the concentrated sulfuric acid solution in front of the aqueous beaker. Figure 7d shows that due to the user's dumping position is too high (information marked in the yellow box), the concentrated sulfuric acid solution splashed, causing corrosion of the desktop (information marked in the green box). Under the guidance of the smart glove, the user finally conducts the concentrated sulfuric acid dilution experiment at the correct experimental location, and uses a glass rod to continuously stir.

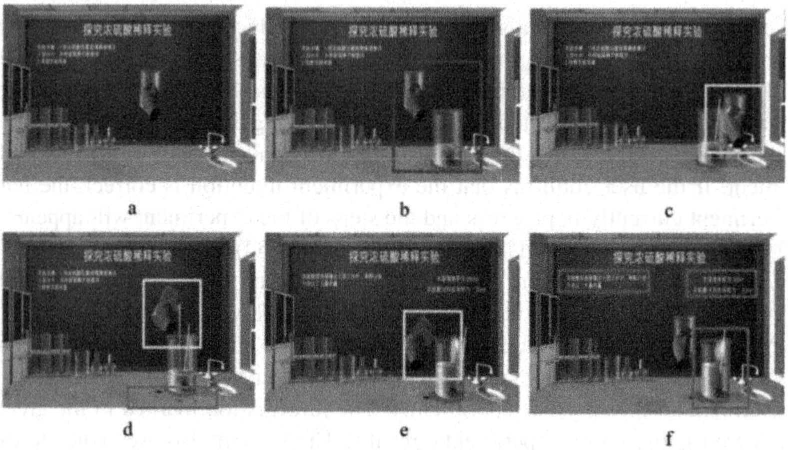

Fig. 7. Concentrated sulfuric acid dilution experiment diagram (right operation). (Color figure online)

6 Conclusion

Aiming at the existing problems in the experimental teaching process of primary and secondary schools, this paper designs a smart glove with scene perception ability, which can perceive the object information in the experimental scene and the corresponding position relationship in real time. On the basis of scene perception, this paper also proposes an intelligent navigational interaction paradigm based on multi-modal fusion to infer the user's experimental intention, so as to give the user corresponding feedback and guidance during the experiment, so that the user is in the smart glove Complete the experimental operation under the guidance.

The smart gloves designed in this article have the following advantages: 1. It can perceive multi-modal information, such as voice, scene information, etc.; 2. The smart glove kit combines human, machine, and material, allowing students to operate real experimental objects, which can improve students' experimental immersion and practical ability; 3. The smart glove kit designed in this paper can monitor and guide the user's behavior, and to a certain extent solve the problem that the teacher cannot guide every student in the classroom.

Acknowledgment. This paper is supported by the National Key R&D Program of China (No. 2018YFB1004901), and the Independent Innovation' Team Project of Jinan City (No. 2019GXRC013).

References

1. Mur-Artal, R., Tardós, J.D.: ORB-SLAM2: an open-source SLAM system for monocular, stereo, and RGB-D cameras. IEEE Trans. Robot. (2017)
2. Redmon, J., Farhadi, A.: YOLOv3: An Incremental Improvement. arXiv e-prints (2018)
3. Han, T., Kennington, C., Schlangen, D.: Placing objects in gesture space: toward real-time understanding of spatial descriptions. In: AAAI conference of Artificial Intelligence (2018)
4. Yongda, D., Fang, L., Huang, X.: Research on multimodal human-robot interaction based on speech and gesture. Comput. Electr. Eng. **72**, 443–454 (2018)
5. Ismail, A.W., Billinghurst, M., Sunar, M.S., Yusof, C.S.: Designing an augmented reality multimodal interface for 6DOF manipulation techniques. In: Arai, K., Kapoor, S., Bhatia, R. (eds.) IntelliSys. AISC, vol. 868, pp. 309–322. Springer, Cham (2019). https://doi.org/10.1007/978-3-030-01054-6_22
6. Jung, J., et al.: Voice+Tactile: augmenting in-vehicle voice user interface with tactile touchpad interaction voice user interface; tactile feedback touchpad; in-vehicle user interface. In: 2020 CHI Conference on Human Factors in Computing Systems (CHI 2020) (2020)
7. Sidenmark, L., Gellersen, H.: Eye, head and torso coordination during gaze shifts in virtual reality. ACM Trans. Comput. Hum. Interact. **27**(1), 1–40 (2019)
8. Sullivan, S., et al.: Middle school students' learning of mechanics concepts through engagement in different sequences of physical and virtual experiments. Int. J. Sci. Educ.
9. Gabunilas, L., et al.: Utilizing Portable Virtual Reality in Teaching Chemistry (2018)
10. Fidan, M., Tuncel, M.: Integrating augmented reality into problem based learning: the effects on learning achievement and attitude in physics education. Comput. Educ. **142**, 103635.1-1036351.9 (2019)
11. Yip, J., et al.: Improving quality of teaching and learning in classes by using augmented reality video. Comput. Educ. **128**, 88–101 (2018)
12. Salinas, P., Pulido, R.: Visualization of conics through augmented reality. Procedia Comput. Sci. **75**, 147–150 (2015)
13. Carlos, C.A., et al.: An approach of training virtual environment for teaching electro-pneumatic systems - ScienceDirect. IFAC-PapersOnLine **52**(9), 278–284 (2019)
14. Liu, D., et al.: Integration of virtual labs into science E-learning. Procedia Comput. Sci. **75**(2015), 95–102 (2015)
15. Hodges, G.W., et al.: An exploratory study of blending the virtual world and the laboratory experience in secondary chemistry classrooms. Comput. Educ. **122**, 179–193 (2018)
16. Aljuhani, K., Sonbul, M., Althabiti, M., Meccawy, M.: Creating a Virtual Science Lab (VSL): the adoption of virtual labs in Saudi schools. Smart Learn. Environ. **5**(1), 1–13 (2018). https://doi.org/10.1186/s40561-018-0067-9
17. Sotomayor-Moriano, J., Pérez, G., Soto, M.: A Virtual laboratory environment for control design of a multivariable process. IFAC-PapersOnLine **52**(9), 15–20 (2019)

Minimum-Energy Computation Offloading in Mobile Edge Computing with Hybrid PSO-DE Algorithm

Xiao Zhang[1], Wenan Tan[1,2](✉), Xin Zhou[1], Xiaojuan Cai[1], Weinan Niu[1], and Panwang Xu[2]

[1] College of Computer Science and Technology, Nanjing University of Aeronautics and Astronautics, Nanjing 211106, Jiangsu, China
wtan@foxmail.com

[2] School of Computer and Information Engineering, Shanghai Polytechnic University, Shanghai 201209, China

Abstract. With the advent of the 5G era, mobile devices (MDs) have gradually become an irreplaceable part of people's lives. More and more users use MDs to handle some intensive tasks. However, such tasks cannot be processed efficiently as these MDs' operating memory and computing power are limited, which may result in high energy consumption and thus lower users' quality of experience (i.e., perceived service quality). Therefore, how to improve the computational offloading strategy for users with satisfactory service quality is a major challenge. Motivated by this challenge, this paper formally models this computation offloading problem in mobile edge computing for the minimum energy consumption calculation under the time delay constraint, which exploits the penalty function to maintain the balance between the delay and energy consumption. To minimize the energy of computation offloading, we propose a cooperative approach with joint consideration of particle swarm optimization and differential evolution (PSO-DE). Through extensive experiments, we demonstrate that the proposed scheme can obtain lower energy consumption.

Keywords: Computation offloading · Mobile edge computing · Particle swarm optimization · Mobile devices · Differential evolution

1 Introduction

With the rise of 5G networks and the continuous development of wireless networks, mobile devices (MDs) have gradually become an irreplaceable part of people's lives. Meanwhile, according to the continuous improvement of people's life needs, a large number of high-quality services and applications have been spawned, such as smart homes, VR, face recognition, fingerprint recognition, and other applications. This application would result in high energy consumption and poor equipment performance [1]. However, it is impossible to perform such tasks efficiently, due to the limited storage space and computing power of mobile terminal equipment [2]. Although the emergence

Y. Sun et al. (Eds.): ChineseCSCW 2021, CCIS 1491, pp. 424–436, 2022.
https://doi.org/10.1007/978-981-19-4546-5_33

of Mobile Cloud Computing (MCC) [3] can provide equipment with insufficient storage space and computing power to handle complex calculations and high storage capabilities, it still has some shortcomings: MCC uses centralized data processing, that is, each task must be transmitted from the MDs to the remote cloud through a remote network. When the amount of tasks continues to increase, because the cloud server is far away from the terminal device, a series of problems such as data loss, high energy consumption, and network delay are prone to occur during data transmission. These problems will seriously affect the user experience.

To further reduce system energy consumption and time delay, improve user experience quality, etc., the introduction of mobile edge computing (MEC) [4]. Mobile edge computing is a further optimization of cloud computing: Adopting a reasonable computation offloading strategy to decentralize computing storage and computing resources to the edge of the network close to mobile devices [3] is conducive to solving the problems of high latency, high energy consumption, network delay, data leakage and other problems caused by centralized cloud computing. At the same time, the calculation and storage pressure of the MDs is relieved, and the service life of the equipment is prolonged. In recent years, computation offloading has become a research hotspot in the field of mobile edge computing. Since 2014, many researchers have begun to study it and have achieved many research results. Computation offloading mainly includes two aspects: offloading decisions and resource allocation. Among them, the offloading decision mainly studies how to divide the tasks generated by the MDs and offload some tasks to the MEC server for execution by measuring the benefits generated by the strategy. That is, how to reasonably allocate the limited MEC server resources to each task is a very critical problem. Therefore, it is very necessary to propose an efficient and reasonable computation offloading strategy.

Luo et al. [5] mainly addressed the problems of high time delay and high energy consumption in industrial production lines and uses particle swarm optimization (PSOA) to solve the problem of the optimal offloading strategy for minimizing time delay under energy consumption constraints. Liu et al. [6] used the Markov decision process to deal with the problem of minimizing power-constrained delay and proposes an efficient one-dimensional search algorithm to find the optimal task scheduling strategy. Liu et.al [7] used population diversity-binary particle swarm optimization (PD-PSO) to find the optimal decision combination under the minimization of energy consumption for intensive task offloading. About the optimization problem of task offloading and resource allocation, Yan et al. [8] used an adaptive genetic algorithm to continuously adjust the offloading decision, and optimize the system overhead in the process of task offloading. Mao et al. [9] and Ulukus et al. [10] mainly focused on the scenario of computation offloading on a single MD, setting time intervals and calculating the cost of task offloading in each time interval to determine whether offloading was required. Chen et al. [11] transformed the task offloading decision problem into a multi-user game problem and proved that an efficient computation offloading strategy can be designed through Nash equilibrium, to obtain the smallest delay.

At present, the most extensive research is to take time delay as the main optimization goal, often neglecting that excessive energy consumption will also affect the performance and service life of the MDs, and also affect the user experience. In this paper, we will investigate the MEC system that includes a multi-user, single MEC server. The resources of a single MEC server are limited, so how to reduce the total energy consumption of task execution through reasonable task offloading strategies and resource allocation techniques is the key to this paper. The main contributions of this paper are as follows.

1) We formally model this computation offloading problem in mobile edge computing for the minimum energy consumption calculation under the time delay constraint, which exploits the penalty function to tradeoff the delay and energy consumption.
2) We propose a computational offloading strategy of the PSO-DE algorithm which is aimed to solve the complexity of the combination of multi-task computation offloading decisions and optimization goals. Also, we can use the PSO-DE algorithm to solve the above computational model and obtain the best task offloading strategy. This algorithm introduces DE to increase the diversity of offloading strategy combinations and improve the accuracy of finding the optimal offloading strategy by improving operations such as mutation and crossover.
3) Simulation experiments are carried out under different time delay constraints, task data volume, and user tasks. The experimental results show that the computation offloading strategy of PSO-DE is better than other offloading schemes.

2 System Model

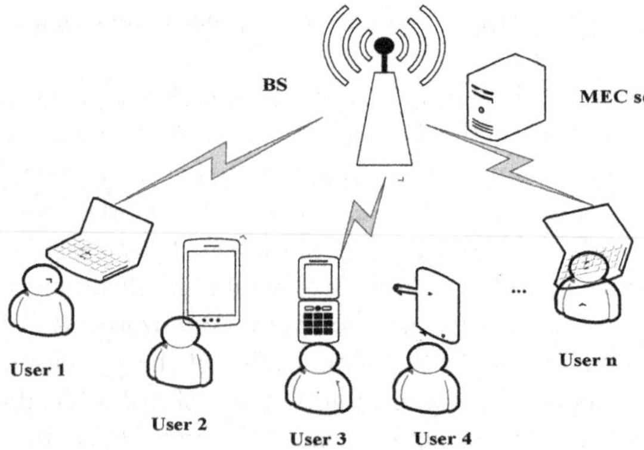

Fig. 1. MEC system model

This paper considers a MEC system composed of multiple MDs and a base station (BS) (see Fig. 1). MDs can be expressed as $U = \{1, 2, \ldots, n\}$. Each user has a task and the task of user i can be denoted as $Task_i = \{D_i, c_i, T_i^{max}\}$, where D_i is the amount of data required for $Task_i$, c_i is the number of CPU cycles required to calculate each byte, and $Task_i^{max}$ is denoted as the maximum time delay that each user can tolerate. S is defined as a combination of offloading decisions made up of n tasks, where $S = \{s_1, s_2, \ldots, s_n\}, n \in U$. There are 2 possibilities for the offloading decision method for each task. If $s_i = 0$, it means the task i is locally executed on its device. If $s_i = 1$, it means that the task i will be offloaded to the MEC server for execution. Note: When task offloading occurs, this paper only considers the processing by a MEC server, and does not consider part of the offloading problem.

2.1 Local Computing Model

When the user task i is locally executed on its device, we have $s_i = 0$. Note: we assume that the MD has enough computing power and storage space to process tasks. Let C_i and T_i^{local} be the number of CPU cycles and the computational time of the task in the local device, which can be respectively defined as

$$C_i = D_i c_i \tag{1}$$

$$T_i^{local} = \frac{C_i}{f_i^{local}} \tag{2}$$

where f_i^{local}, $F_{i,max}^{local}$ are defined as the computational capability and maximum computational capability of the MD.

The energy consumption to complete the task in the local device can be defined as

$$E_i^{local} = k(f_i^{local})^2 C_i \tag{3}$$

where $k = 10^{-26}$, and it is a constant related to the chip structure of the MDs [12].

2.2 Edge Computing Model

The storage space and computational capability of MDs are not enough to efficiently process some tasks with complex calculations and high data storage, so some tasks need to be offloaded to the MEC server for processing. When the user chooses to offload the task i to the MEC for execution, we have $s_i = 1$.

The calculation of the time required for the completion of this task in the MEC server mainly includes two aspects: $T_{i,trans}^{MEC}$ and $T_{i,commit}^{MEC}$ [13].

$T_{i,trans}^{MEC}$ is the time required to transmit task data from the MD i to the MEC server, which is denoted as

$$T_{i,trans}^{MEC} = \frac{D_i}{W log_2(1 + \frac{P_i(l_i)^{-\sigma}}{WN_0})} \tag{4}$$

where $R_i = W log_2(1 + \frac{P_i(l_i)^{-\sigma}}{WN_0})$ represents the transmission rate from the MD i to BS [14]. W is the channel bandwidth between the MDs and BS. P_i is denoted as the transmit power of the MD i. $(l_i)^{-\sigma}$ represents the channel gain between the MD i and the BS, l_i is the distance between the MD i and the BS and σ is the path loss factor.

$T_{i,commit}^{MEC}$ is the time to process this task on the MEC server, which is defined as

$$T_{i,commit}^{MEC} = \frac{C_i}{f_i^{MEC}} \tag{5}$$

The computational time of the task i in the MEC server can be defined as

$$T_i^{MEC} = T_{i,trans}^{MEC} + T_{i,commit}^{MEC} \tag{6}$$

Similarly, offloading tasks to the MEC server will also produce energy consumption, which is mainly reflected in two parts: $E_{i,trans}^{MEC}$ and $E_{i,commit}^{MEC}$.

$E_{i,trans}^{MEC}$ is the energy consumption to transmit task data from the MD i to the MEC server, which is denoted as

$$E_{i,trans}^{MEC} = \frac{P_i D_i}{W log_2(1 + \frac{P_i (l_i)^{-\sigma}}{WN_0})} \tag{7}$$

$E_{i,commit}^{MEC}$ is the energy consumption to process this task on the MEC server, which is represented as [14]

$$E_{i,commit}^{MEC} = D_i q_i \tag{8}$$

where q_i is the energy consumption by the MEC server to process each bit of data.

The total energy consumption when this task is offloaded to the MEC serve can be defined as

$$E_i^{MEC} = E_{i,trans}^{MEC} + E_{i,commit}^{MEC} \tag{9}$$

2.3 Problem Formulation

Computation offloading is to solve the shortage of computing resources and insufficient energy efficiency of the MDs. It can optimize the performance of the equipment and provide users with the best quality service. This paper is mainly aimed at establishing a model in a computationally intensive application task scenario. Due to the limited resources of the MEC server, intensive task offloading will cause problems such as high latency, high energy consumption, and even reduced performance of the MEC server and MDs. The problem of high energy consumption may deplete the battery energy of the MD, which may cause subsequent task offloading to fail to complete. The goal of this paper's optimization is how to provide users with high-quality services while minimizing the total energy consumption of task execution. To avoid the phenomenon that low energy consumption is exchanged for high time delay, a penalty function is introduced [5]. If the task execution time exceeds the maximum time delay that the user can tolerate, the penalty function is used to increase the total energy consumption of the offloading strategy. Considering the multi-objective constraint problem, the optimization objective of computation offloading can be formulated as

$$\min_{s} \sum\nolimits_{i=1}^{n} E_i + \varphi * \sum\nolimits_{i=1}^{n} (T_i - T_{max}) \tag{10}$$

Subject to

$$E_i = \{ \begin{matrix} E_i^{local}, \ s_i = 0 \\ E_i^{MEC}, \ s_i = 1 \end{matrix} \tag{11}$$

$$0 \le f_i^{local} \le F_{i,max}^{local} \tag{12}$$

$$\sum\nolimits_{i=1}^{n} f_i^{MEC} \le F_{max}^{MEC} \tag{13}$$

$$T_i \le T_i^{max}, T_i = \{ \begin{matrix} T_i^{local}, \ s_i = 0 \\ T_i^{MEC}, \ s_i = 1 \end{matrix} \tag{14}$$

where $S = \{s_1, s_2, \ldots, s_n\}$ is a combination of task offloading strategies in the search for minimizing energy consumption and φ is the coefficient of the penalty function. Constraint (11) represents that the energy consumption of task i performed on the MEC server or the MDs. Constraint (12) ensures that the computational capability of the MDs in processing tasks cannot exceed its maximum computational capability. Constraint (13) states that the total computational capability of all tasks on the MEC server cannot exceed the maximum computational capability that the server can withstand. Constraint (14) indicates that the time required to complete each task does not exceed the user's maximum tolerable delay.

3 Approach Design

In the previous chapter, a multi-user MEC system model is constructed. By comparing the energy consumption of tasks at different locations, it is decided whether the task is either executed on the MDs or the MEC server and finally, the optimal offloading decision is found. As the amount of tasks continues to increase, the calculation process is too complicated and the number of combinations of offloading strategies increases exponentially. It is almost impossible to find the best offloading strategy directly through the enumeration method. The advantage of the heuristic algorithm is that it is more efficient than blind search. If a heuristic algorithm is meticulously improved, the optimal solution to an optimization problem can be obtained in a short time. In this paper, we propose a cooperative approach with joint consideration of the PSO-DE algorithm to minimize the energy of computation offloading. Since in the later stage of population evolution, all individuals in the PSO algorithm will move toward the optimal solution, which will cause the population diversity to decrease and fall into a local optimum. Therefore, the combination of mutation and crossover operations in the DE algorithm with PSO can enhance the diversity of the population and makes up for the low accuracy of the later optimization of the PSO algorithm.

3.1 Particle Swarm Optimization

The core idea of PSO comes from the behavior of imitating a flock of birds searching for food in an unknown space [15].

Suppose that in an N-dimensional search space, P particles are randomly generated as the initial population $X^0 = \{x_1, x_2, \ldots, x_M\}, x \in P$. The position of any particle i in the population can be expressed as $x_i = \{x_{i1}, x_{i2}, \ldots, x_{iN}\}$. The velocity of the particle can be expressed as $v_i = \{v_{i1}, v_{i2}, \ldots, v_{iN}\}$. The best position of the particle in the current search process, that is, the best individual $p_{besti} = \{p_{i1}, p_{i2}, \ldots, p_{iN}\}$. The best position of the particle in the entire population, that is, the global best $g_{best} = \{g_{b1}, g_{b2}, \ldots, g_{bN}\}$. During each iteration, the particle will update its position by tracking two extreme values (p_{besti}, g_{best}), so the formulas for the particle's velocity and position can be defined as

$$v_{ij}^t = w * v_{ij}^{t-1} + c1 * rand * \left(p_{ij} - x_{ij}^{t-1}\right) + c2 * rand * (g_{bj} - x_{ij}^{t-1}) \tag{15}$$

$$x_{ij}^t = x_{ij}^{t-1} + v_{ij}^{t-1} \tag{16}$$

where t is the number of current iterations, w is the inertia weighting factor, and $w \geq 0.c1$, $c2$ are learning factors, and $rand$ is a random number from [0, 1].

To avoid the premature phenomenon of particle swarm algorithm in the early search process, the linear weight reduction method [16] is introduced to avoid premature convergence in the early stage and fall into the local optimal solution.

$$w = w_{max} - \frac{t * (w_{max} - w_{min})}{t_{max}} \tag{17}$$

where w_{max}, w_{min} are the maximum and minimum inertia weights respectively. t, t_{max} are the current number of iterations and the maximum number of iterations respectively.

3.2 Differential Evolution

Storm et al. first proposed the DE algorithm in 1995. It is an efficient global optimization algorithm. The DE algorithm updates the population by performing operations such as mutation, crossover, and selection on the individuals according to the difference information between the individuals in the initial population [17]. In the iterative process, it retains the elite group by the rule of "survival of the fittest" and guides the entire optimization process to gradually approach the optimal solution.

Mutation Operation. To balance the global and local optimization capabilities of the population, and improved mutation strategy is proposed. Combining the global optimal individual and the random individual in the population to form the basis vector provides an accurate search direction for the individual and also improves the convergence speed. To prevent premature convergence and other phenomena, the mutation factor F is changed to an adaptive mutation factor. In the early stage of population evolution, the value of F is very large. At this time, the population needs to expand to find the global optimal solution, which is beneficial to improve global searchability. As the number of iterations continues to increase, F gradually approaches F_0, which is beneficial to refine the search range and enhance local optimization capabilities. Individual x_i^t performs mutation operation to generate a new individual m_i^t based on the following formula:

$$\mu = e^{1-\frac{1}{1+\frac{1-t}{t_{max}}}} \tag{18}$$

$$F = F_0 * 2^{\mu} \tag{19}$$

$$m_i^t = \left(\alpha g_{best}^t + \beta x_{r1}^t\right) + F * (x_{r2}^t - x_{r3}^t) \tag{20}$$

where $\alpha, \beta \epsilon [0, 1]$ and $\alpha + \beta = 1.i \neq r1 \neq r2 \neq r3$ and $i, r1, r2, r3 \in [1, P] \cap \mathbb{Z}$. F_0 is mutation operator and $F \in [F_0, 2F_0]$.

Crossover Operation. To effectively enhance the global optimization capability and increase the diversity of the population, the new crossover individual u_i^t is generated by the individual x_i^t in the current population and the mutated individual m_i^t.

$$u_{ij}^t = \{ \begin{matrix} m_{ij}^t, & if\ rand = CR\, or\, j = j_{rand}, \\ x_{ij}^t, & otherwise. \end{matrix} \tag{21}$$

where $j \in \{1, 2, \ldots, n\}, j_{rand}$ is a random integer within the range $[1, n]$, and CR is the crossover rate, which is a specific random number from [0, 1].

Selection Operation. DE algorithm adopts the idea of the greedy algorithm, which calculates the fitness value of the original population individual X^t and the population individual U^t that undergoes mutation and crossover operations. Select the first P individuals with better fitness values to form the elite population X^{t+1} as the parent of the next iteration and update the global optimal value and optimal solution.

3.3 The Task Offloading Strategy of the PSO-DE Algorithm

Coding Mode. This paper uses binary coding mode to describe the task offloading decision. Suppose there are currently k tasks, that is, there are a total of 2^k task offloading strategies. $S = \{s_1, s_2, \ldots, s_k\}$ represents one of the task offloading schemes (that is a particle). The problem of finding the optimal task offloading strategy is transformed into a problem of finding the vector S optimal solution. s_i represents the position where task i is executed, and $s_i \in \{0, 1\}$. Table 1 shows the relationship between the particle foraging process and the task offloading strategy.

Fitness Function. Each particle represents a feasible solution for the current task offloading, and the degree of the task offloading strategy is measured by calculating the fitness value of each particle. The optimization problem in this paper is to minimize

Table 1. The relationship between particle foraging process and task offloading strategy

Particle foraging process	Task offloading strategy
Individual particle	A task offloading strategy
Individual particle dimensions	Number of user tasks
Population of particles	Different task offloading strategies
The best position of the particles	The best strategy for task offloading
Particle fitness value	Optimization effect of task offloading strategy

the energy consumed by the task under the constraint of the user's maximum tolerance time, so the fitness value of the particle is mainly affected by two factors, the delay, and energy consumption of the processing task. The greater the energy consumption to complete the task, the worse the optimization effect; the smaller the energy consumption, the better the optimization effect. The fitness function is defined as

$$fitness = \sum_{i=1}^{n} E_i + \varphi * \sum_{i=1}^{n} (T_i - T_{max}) \tag{22}$$

3.4 The Task Offloading Process of the PSO-DE Algorithm

This paper proposes the application of the PSO-DE algorithm to the optimal solution problem of task offloading strategy. The specific steps of the algorithm are as follows.

Step1: Randomly generate a population X^0 according to the individual particle's dimension N, particle code, population size P, etc. Set relevant parameters of the PSO-DE algorithm, like $c1$, $c2$, t_{max}, F_0, CR, w_{max}, w_{min}.
Step2: Calculate the fitness value of each particle i according to formula (22) and record the global best position g_{best} and its corresponding fitness value. (Note: The best p_{besti} for each particle is the initial position of the particle).
Step3: Update the velocity and position of each dimension of particle i according to formulas (15)–(17), and check the boundaries of the velocity and position of each dimension of the particle.
Step4: Perform a mutation operation on the particle individual X^t in the population according to formula (18)–(20) and check the boundaries of each dimension of the new particle individual. Finally, the population M^t is formed.
Step5: Perform a crossover operation of individual X^t and M^t of the current population according to formula (21) and check the boundaries of each dimension of the new particle individual. Finally, the population U^t is formed and the fitness of each particle of the population is calculated.
Step6: Sort the fitness value of each particle in the population X^t and U^t in descending order and select the first P individuals with lower fitness values as the initial population for the next iteration X^{t+1}. Update the best individual p_{besti}^{t+1} and the global best g_{best}^{t+1} and their fitness values respectively.

Step7: Determine whether the end condition is met. If not satisfied, go to step 3 and repeat steps 3–7. Otherwise, exit the loop and directly output the best task offloading strategy and the corresponding fitness value.

4 Experimental Results

In this section, we use simulation experiments to verify the performance of our proposed algorithm. We use Matlab2016a software for simulation. In simulations, we assume that the coverage area is an area with a radius of 100m centered on EMC and base stations. We set the particle swarm size $P = 30$, the maximum number of iterations $t_{max} = 200$, crossover probability $CR = 0.9$, variation factor $F_0 = 0.8$, $w_{max} = 0.9$, $w_{min} = 0.4$, $c1$, and $c2 = 1.5$. We assume that the data size D_i of each task is ranging from 0.5 to 3MB.The number of CPU cycles required for each byte of each task c_i is randomly generated from 500 to 1000 cycles. Computational capability and transmission power of the MD are generated from [0.5,1] GHz and [500, 600] mw. We set path loss factor $\sigma = 4$, $W = 4$ MHz, and $N_0 = 10^{-11}$ mw/Hz [16]. Also, we set $f_i^{MEC} = 4$ GHz, $q_i = 10^{-6}$ J/bit, $T_i^{max} = 1$ s.

Compare the offloading strategy of the PSO-DE algorithm proposed in this paper with the local offloading strategy (all-local), MEC offloading strategy (all-MEC), and other algorithms like PSOA [5], LSWPSO [16], and DE.

Figure 2 shows that the relationship between the size of the task data and the average total energy consumption of the task. Due to the limitation of the computational capability of the MDs, when the amount of tasks continues to increase, the equipment will produce more energy consumption, so some tasks are more suitable to be offloaded to the MEC server for processing. The average energy consumption of offloading strategy of the PSO-DE algorithm proposed in this paper is much lower than the all-local and all-EMC offloading strategy. When the data size of each task is 1MB, compared with all-local, all-EMC, DE, PSOA and LSWPSO, and DE, the average energy consumption generated by the offloading strategy based on the PSO-DE algorithm is reduced by 54.09%, 26.08%, 14.05%, 11.80% and 9.7% respectively.

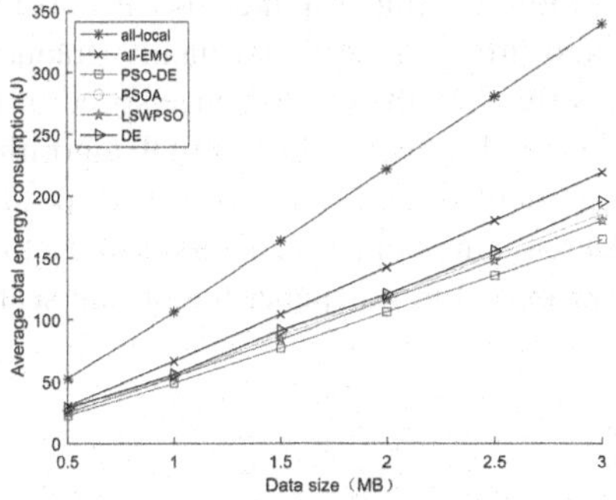

Fig. 2. The relationship between the data size of each task and the average total energy consumption

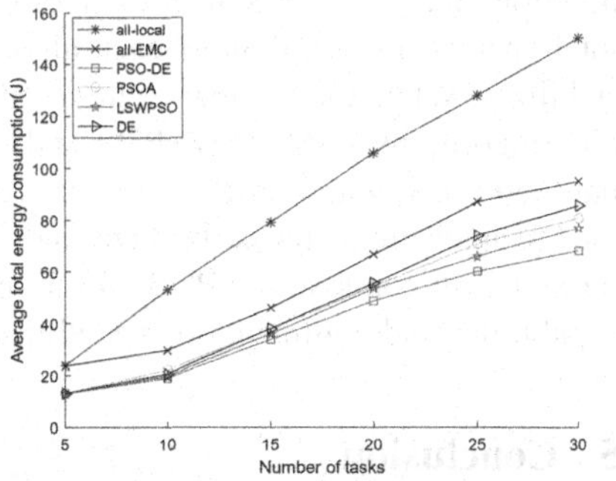

Fig. 3. The relationship between the number of tasks and the average total energy consumption of task

Figure 3 reflects the energy consumption of tasks when the number of tasks is different. As the number of tasks continues to increase, the average total energy consumption for executing tasks is also increasing. The average total energy consumption of all-local is still much higher than other offloading strategies. When the number of tasks is less than 15, the average total energy consumption of offloading strategy of the PSO-DE is not very obvious compared with the offloading schemes of other algorithms. But when the number of tasks is greater than 15, the optimization effect of the PSO-DE and other algorithms is gradually obvious, indicating that the algorithm is more suitable for solving the problem of multi-task offloading strategy optimization.

Figure 4 describes the change in the average total energy consumption of tasks under different time constraints. As the time constraint becomes larger, the average total energy consumption of various offloading strategies gradually slows down, and finally gradually stabilizes. Although the optimization effect of the three strategies of LSWPSO, DE, and PSO-DE is not obvious, the effect of the PSO-DE algorithm is still slightly better than other algorithms.

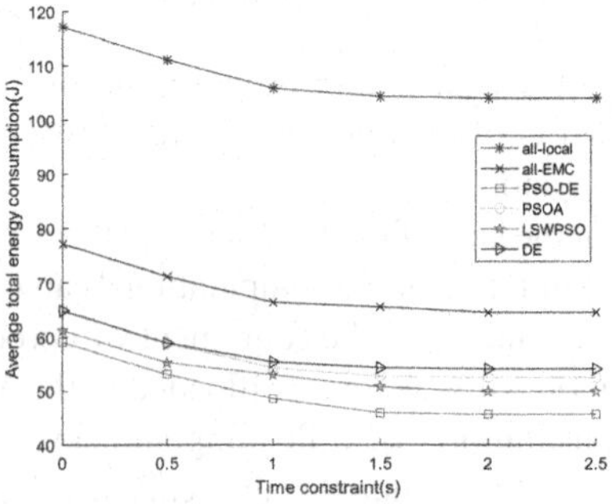

Fig. 4. The relationship between the time constraint and the average total energy consumption of the task

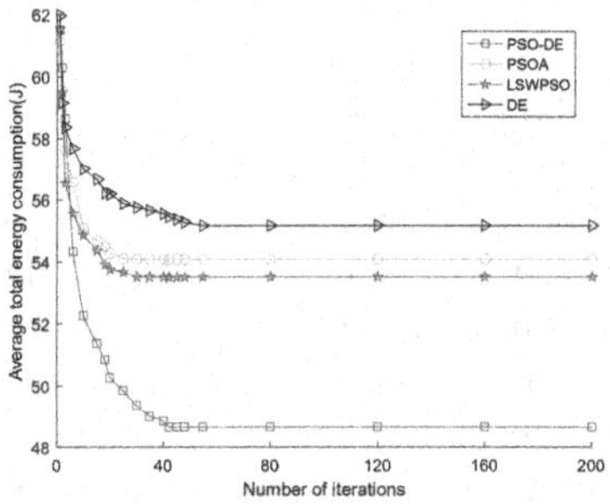

Fig. 5. Convergence analysis of various algorithms under different iteration times

Figure 5 describes the convergence analysis of various algorithms under different iteration times. As the number of algorithm iterations continues to increase, the average total energy consumption of each algorithm first drops rapidly, and finally gradually stabilizes. When the number of iterations is less than 20, the convergence speed of the three algorithms, PSOA, LWSPSO, and DE, is higher than that of the PSO-DE algorithm, but their optimization effects are not ideal. In particular, the fast convergence speed of the DE algorithm in the early stage leads to a decrease in population diversity and a local optimum. In contrast, the PSO-DE algorithm proposed in this paper has strong search capabilities and optimization capabilities.

5 Conclusion

In this paper, we study the problem of minimizing energy consumption in the process of multi-user offloading tasks to MDs or a MEC server and propose a multi-user and single

MEC server computation offloading model that comprehensively considers time delay and energy consumption. To prevent the problem of time-to-energy consumption during task offloading, a penalty function is used to maintain the balance between time delay and energy consumption. And we propose an offloading strategy based on the PSO-DE. The algorithm converts the problem of finding the best offloading strategy into a process of particle foraging and introduces operations such as mutation, crossover, and selection in DE to increase the diversity of offloading strategies. Simulation experiment results show that the optimization effect of the offloading strategy of the PSO-DE proposed in this paper is better than other offloading strategies.

Acknowledgements. The paper is supported in part by the National Natural Science Foundation of China under Grant (No. 61672022 and No. U1904186), Key Disciplines of Master Program of Electronic Information of Shanghai Polytechnic University.

References

1. Zhang, J., et al.: Joint offloading and resource allocation optimization for mobile edge computing. In: GLOBECOM 2017 - 2017 IEEE Global Communications Conference, Singapore, pp. 1–6 (2017)
2. Lu, W., Gong, Y., Liu, X., Wu, J., Peng, H.: Collaborative energy and information transfer in green wireless sensor networks for smart cities. IEEE Trans. Industr. Inf. **14**(4), 1585–1593 (2018)
3. Baraki, H., Jahl, A., Jakob, S., et al.: Optimizing application for mobile cloud computing through MOCCAA. J. Grid Comput. **17**(4), 651–676 (2019). https://doi.org/10.1007/s10723-019-09492-0
4. Hu, T.C., Patel, M., Sabella, D., et al.: Mobile edge computing-a key technology towards 5G. ETSI White Paper. **11**(11), 1–16 (2015)
5. Luo, B., Yu, B.: Computation offloading strategy based on particle swarm optimization in mobile edge computing. Comput. Appl. **40**(08), 2293–2298 (2020)
6. Liu, J., Mao, Y., Zhang, J., Letaief, K.B.: Delay-optimal computation task scheduling for mobile-edge computing systems. In: 2016 IEEE International Symposium on Information Theory (ISIT), pp. 1451–1455 (2016)
7. Liu, X.X.: Research on Computation Offloading and Energy Efficiency Optimization Based on Mobile Edge Computing. Lanzhou University of Technology (2020)
8. Yan, W.: Research on Computation Offloading and Load Balancing Algorithms in Mobile Edge Computing Network. Chongqing University of Posts and Telecommunications (2020)
9. Mao, Y., Zhang, J., Letaief, K.B.: Dynamic computation offloading for mobile-edge computing with energy harvesting devices. IEEE J. Sel. Areas Commun. **34**(12), 3590–3605 (2016)
10. Ulukus, S., et al.: Energy harvesting wireless communications: a review of recent advances. IEEE J. Sel. Areas Commun. **33**(3), 360–381 (2015)
11. Chen, X., Jiao, L., Li, W., Fu, X.: Efficient multi-user computation offloading for mobile-edge cloud computing. IEEE/ACM Trans. Network. **24**(5), 2795–2808 (2016)
12. Zhang, J., Xia, W., Yan, F., et al.: Joint computation offloading and resource allocation optimization in heterogeneous networks with mobile edge computing. IEEE Access. **6**, 19327–19337 (2018)
13. Dong, S.Q., Li, H.L., et al.: Review of research on computation offloading strategies in mobile edge computing. Comput. Sci. **46**(11), 32–40 (2019)

14. Deng, X.M.: Research on Task Offloading and Resource Allocation Algorithm Based on Mobile Edge Computing. Hunan Normal University (2020)
15. Zhao, Q., Li, C.: Two-Stage multi-swarm particle swarm optimizer for unconstrained and constrained global optimization. IEEE Access. **8**, 24905–124927 (2020)
16. Cui, Y.S.: Research on Resource Optimization Methods to Minimize Time Delay in Mobile Edge Networks. Nanjing University of Posts and Telecommunications (2020)
17. Goudos, S.K., Deruyck, M., Plets, D., et al.: Optimization of power consumption in wireless access networks using Differential Evolution with eigenvector based crossover operator. In: 2016 10th European Conference on Antennas and Propagation (EuCAP), Davos, Switzerland, pp. 1–4 (2016)

A Semi-supervised Video Object Segmentation Method Based on Adaptive Memory Module

Shaohua Yang, Zhiming Luo(✉), Donglin Cao, Dazhen Lin, Songzhi Su, and Shaozi Li

Department of Artificial Intelligence, Xiamen University, Xiamen, China
{zhiming.luo,another,dzlin,ssz,szlig}@xmu.edu.cn

Abstract. Video object segmentation has becoming a hot research topic in the computer vision society, with a wide range of applications, such as autonomous driving, video editing, and video surveillance. However, due to the complexity of video data, video object segmentation still faces challenges like occlusion, object appearance changes, and similar objects. Previous methods mainly tackle this task by using the memory module, but the computation cost will linearly increase along with the length of the video. To deal with the issue of the previous memory-based method, we proposed a cascaded semi-supervised video object framework with an adaptive memory module. In addition, we use a cascaded instance tracker to find the object and reduce the image resolutions, and we further use a boundary estimation branch to improve the accuracy. Experimental results on several benchmarks demonstrate the effectiveness and efficiency of our proposed method.

Keywords: Video object segmentation · Memory module · Boundary prediction

1 Introduction

With the development of technology, video data are increased vastly in our daily life. The main goal of the semi-supervised video object segmentation task is to segment the objects from the videos by only providing the annotations from the first frame. Semi-supervised video object segmentation has become a hot research topic in the computer vision society, with many applications, such as autonomous driving, video editing, and video surveillance. However, due to the complexity of video data, video object segmentation still faces challenges like occlusion, object appearance changes, and similar objects.

Early semi-supervised video object segmentation methods firstly use hand-extracted features to construct Spatio-temporal maps, such as the histogram of directional gradient (HOG) [16] or optical flow [22]. They then use probability graphical models [5,18,26] to predict the result of each frame. Caelles et al. [1]

Y. Sun et al. (Eds.): ChineseCSCW 2021, CCIS 1491, pp. 437–450, 2022.
https://doi.org/10.1007/978-981-19-4546-5_34

firstly proposed an online learning method OSVOS for this task. The OSVOS will firstly fine-tune the model based on the first frame of a new testing video. After that, several imporved version have proposed, such as OnAVOS [24], OSVOS-S [11]. Luiten et al. [10] proposed the PREMVOS, which combines optical flow, re-identification network (ReID), semantic segmentation and online learning, and can significantly improve the performance.

Due to the strong temporal continuity between adjacent video frames, the semi-supervised video object segmentation task can be regarded as adjusting the mask of the previous frame to the current frame. MaskTrack [14], VPN [6], RGMP [12], AGAME [7] and other models predict the segmentation result of the current frame by concatenating the output mask of the previous frame. Unlike the propagation-based method, the appearance matching-based methods mainly focus on computing the appearance similarity of the target in different frames. SiamMask [25] model also uses the siamese network structure, but the difference is that the model uses the first frame as a template frame for matching, in addition to image-level matching. PLM [21] and PM L [2] model mainly uses the similarity between pixels to predict. VideoMatch [4] model can simultaneously perform similarity matching on the foreground and background to obtain the foreground image and the background image. In addition, methods such as FEELVOS [23] and CFBI [32] perform a global matching on the first frame while also using similar characteristics between consecutive frames to make a local match on the previous frame.

Seoung et al. [13] proposed the STM model uses the memory mechanism. The STM uses a memory module to store the information of the past frame, and experiments showed that the memory module could significantly improve performance. Li et al. proposed the GC [9] model based on the STM, which uses a global context module to prevent the memory overflow and other problems with a continuous concatenation of frames and improve the speed of the model's prediction on video data. Meanwhile, Seong et al. [20] argued that STM is a non-local calculation, and the target tends to only appear in some surrounding positions in the past frame. They proposed an improved model named KMN by introducing the Gaussian kernel as a probability distribution map to alleviate the non-local calculation issue in STM. Although, these methods can improve the segmentation performance, but they still suffer a issue that the memory usage and time cost will increase linearly along with the video length.

To deal with the previous issue, we propose a cascaded semi-supervised video object segmentation method based on an adaptive memory module. This method uses an adaptive memory module to avoid the problem of linear growth. At the same time, a cascaded object tracking network is proposed to provide a more accurate prior object area for subsequent memory segmentation models. In addition, because the boundary pixels of the object and the pixels within the object have different prediction difficulties and unbalanced distribution, a boundary prediction branch is proposed to predict the boundary of the object to enhance the results of the model prediction. Experimental results on several benchmark datasets also demonstrate the effectiveness and efficiency of our proposed method.

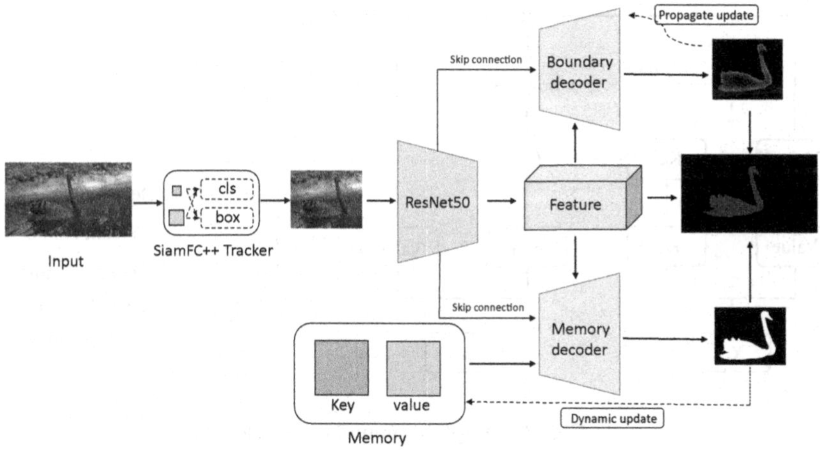

Fig. 1. The framework of our proposed model for semi-supervised video object segmentation.

2 Cascade Model Based on Adaptive Memory Module

The overall framework of our proposed model is shown in Fig. 1, which mainly contains three parts: 1) Cascaded Target Tracker, 2) Adaptive Memory Module, and 3) Boundary Prediction Branch. As shown in Fig. 1, we first input the current frame into the Cascaded Target Tracker to locate the target, then we cut the target out from the input frame. After that, the ResNet-50 [3] is used to the image feature. Then, we feed the feature into the Adaptive Memory Module to estimate the object's foreground mask and update the memory. The Memory Module stores the information from previous frames. Additionally, a boundary prediction branch is added to enhance the performance of boundary estimation. Finally, we combine the results from the memory module and the boundary branch to obtain the final video object segmentation.

2.1 Cascade Target Tracker

In order to accurately find the approximate position of the target object, we use the SiamFC++ [31] to be the target tracker in this study. For improving the efficiency of the tracker, we leverage the shallow AlexNet [8] as the backbone network of SiamFC++, instead of using a deep residual network.

However, even a fully trained target tracker cannot guarantee that it can predict a complete target when facing various scenarios. To ensure that the obtained bounding box containing the entire target, we will expand the target area obtained by the target tracker. Assuming the bounding box from the tracker is $[x_1, y_2, x_2, y_2]$ with a certainty score of S, we then use S to calculate the

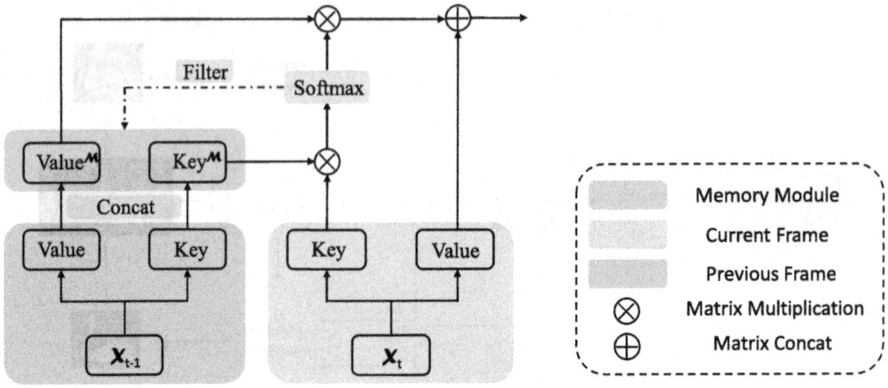

Fig. 2. Adaptive memory module

padding factor *Padding* to extent the object area. As we known, a smaller score S means a large uncertainty of the tracking result, and it is preferred to use a large expanding factor. Therefore, we compute the padding factor *Padding* by

$$Padding = \alpha + \left(e^{1-S} - 1\right) * \beta, \tag{1}$$

where α represents the basic distance that needs to be expanded, and $\left(e^{1-S} - 1\right) * \beta$ represents adding an exponential smoothing to the score, and β is the expansion weight. When the score S is higher and tends to 1, the final padding *Padding* will tend to 0, and vice versa.

In addition, due to the inconsistent aspect ratio of the target frame, it is necessary to expand the width and height to different degrees. The following Eq. (2) represents the required expanded aspect ratio *Scale*:

$$Scale = 2 * e^{w/h-1}, \tag{2}$$

where w and h represent the width and height of the prediction target box, respectively. After obtaining the padding factor and the extended aspect ratio, the new interception coordinates can be calculated based on the tracking results of the target tracker. The calculation formula is as shown in (3):

$$\begin{aligned} \hat{x}_1 &= \max(0, x_1 - Padding * Scale) \\ \hat{y}_1 &= \max(0, y_1 - Padding) \\ \hat{x}_2 &= \min(x_2 + Padding * Scale, W) \\ \hat{y}_2 &= \min(y_2 + Padding, H) \end{aligned} \tag{3}$$

2.2 Adaptive Memory Module

After obtaining the cropped target image, we then perform a more accurate segmentation. Our proposed adaptive memory module is with a similar structure to the STM [13]. The main difference is that STM simply concatenates each frame in the memory module, while ours use an adaptive filtering mechanism to improve the STM. The main computation process our proposed adaptive memory module is shown in Fig. 2.

First, the current and previous frames are encoded into a key-value pair by the corresponding feature encoder. Since the previous frame has the most significant similarity to the current frame, the previous frame will be added to the memory module by default. Then the Key of the memory module and the Key of the current frame are multiplied to obtain the similarity matrix, followed by the Softmax function to generate a weight matrix. Then we multiply the normalized similarity matrix with the Value matrix of the memory module and then sum them together. The value matrix of the current frame is concatenated to obtain the final result and sent to the subsequent decoder.

Meanwhile, the memory modules are filtered according to the normalized weight matrix to fix the size of the memory modules and enable the memory modules to be updated adaptively over time. Since the normalized weight matrix represents the similarity between each pixel in the memory module and each pixel in the current frame, pixels with lower similarity generally correspond to background noise pixels, which are difficult or unable to provide helpful information. Therefore, a certain threshold is selected to filter the pixels with low similarity to achieve the adaptive update of the memory module. This filtering mechanism can significantly improve the model's efficiency without affecting the model's accuracy, and the calculation cost will not increase linearly with time. The update process of the adaptive memory module after processing each frame is illustrated in the Algorithm 1.

Algorithm 1: Adaptive memory module update algorithm

Input : Key matrix of the current frame K_t; Key matrix of the previous frame K_{t-1};
Key matrix of the memory module K_m and Value matrix V_m;
Fixed threshold of memory module $thres$;

Output: Key matrix in memory module after update K_m and Value matrix V_m;

$K \leftarrow [K_m, K_{t-1}]; V \leftarrow [V_m, V_{t-1}]$

$S_{im} \leftarrow Softmax(K^T * K_t)$

if $len(K) > thresh$ **then**

  $S_{im} \leftarrow Sum(S_{im}, dim = 1)$

  $index \leftarrow Sort(S_{im})$

  $index \leftarrow index[: thres]$

  $K_m \leftarrow K[index]; V_m \leftarrow V[index]$

end

else

  $K_m \leftarrow K; V_m \leftarrow V$

end

return K_m, V_m

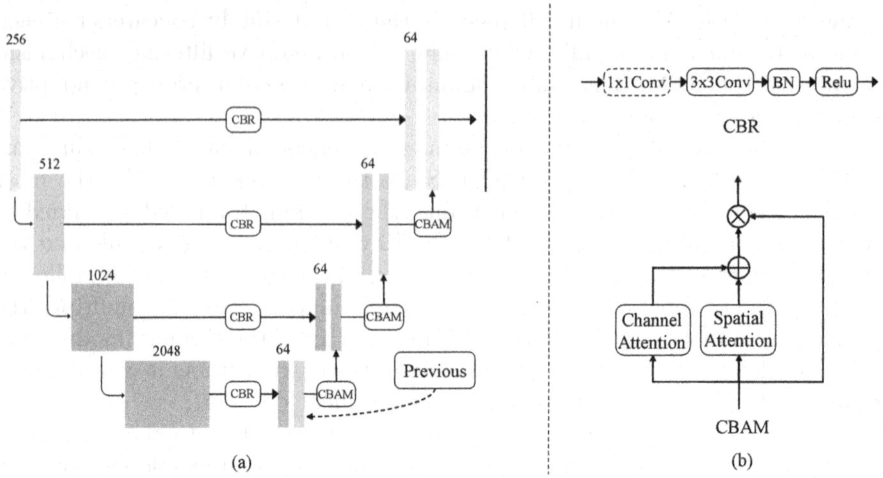

Fig. 3. The architecture of the boundary prediction branch

2.3 Boundary Prediction Branch

Although the model based on the adaptive memory module can produce good results, the matching mechanism still processes each pixel separately. The boundary pixels have a considerable distribution difference compared to the internal pixels, mainly those closer to the boundary. Therefore, to further improve the performance of the entire model, we also add a boundary prediction branch to predict the boundary of the target as an auxiliary prediction output to help the memory module improve the model's prediction accuracy. Figure 3(a) is the architecture of the boundary prediction branch proposed in this study, which adopts a similar structure to U-Net [19].

In order to reduce the number of parameters and speed up the prediction, the number of channels of the four-stage feature is first down-sampled to 64. Then we start up-sampling from the last stage and concatenate the features of the previous frame as the enhanced feature so that the information of the past frame can be better utilized. In addition, a parallel CBAM [29] attention module will be used to process the features. Its structure is shown in Fig. 3(b). The channel attention and spatial attention are processed in parallel. After being added, the original features are multiplied.

In order to predict the boundary image of the target, it is necessary to convert the original label mask of the target into a boundary image for training. We leverage the boundary expansion strategy used in LDF [28] and assign a new label to each foreground pixel according to the minimum distance from the background. For pixels closer to the background, the greater the difficulty of prediction due to background noise interference, the higher the value it will be. Figure 4 shows some newly generated boundary label images, where (a) is the input images, (b) is the original label masks, and (c) is the generated boundary

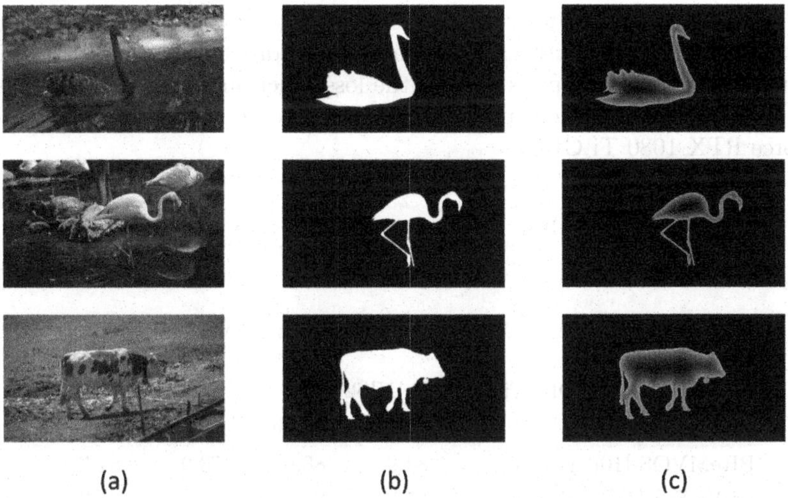

Fig. 4. Generated boundary labels.

labels. It can be seen that compared to the pure boundary image, the distribution of the front background is much more balanced, and it has a larger pixel value for the pixels that are more difficult to classify.

3 Experimental Results and Analysis

3.1 Dataset

To evaluate the performance of our proposed method, we conduct experiments on three semi-supervised video object segmentation datasets, i.e., DAVIS [15,17] and YouTube VOS [30]. Notice that the DAVIS dataset contains two different versions 2016 and 2017, that corresponded to single-object annotation [15] and multi-object annotations [17], respectively. The **DAVIS2016** [15] contains 50 videos with 3455 labeled frames, of which 30 videos are used as the training set, and the remaining 20 videos are used as the validation set. The **DAVIS2017** [17] divides the single object in the video into multiple objects for labeling and expands the number of videos to 150, of which 60 are used as training sets. **YouTube VOS** [30] is a multi-object semi-supervised video object segmentation dataset, and it is also the largest semi-supervised video object segmentation dataset to date. A total of 4453 video clips are included, of which 3471 video clips are used as training sets, and each video is also a short video clip of 3–6 s. To evaluate the performance, we use the official evaluation metrics from the DAVIS dataset: regional similarity $\mathcal{J}$ and contour accuracy $\mathcal{F}$.

3.2 Experimental Settings

In the training phase, we resize all the images into a resolution of 240 × 432 for the DAVIS [15,17] and YouTube VOS [30] video dataset. We train the whole model with the SGD optimizer with a learning rate of 0.01. The weight decay is set to 1e-6 to avoid over-fitting. For each video, 8 consecutive frames are selected as input, and cross entropy is used as the loss function to train 100 epochs. All the experiments are implemented with PyTorch toolbox and run on a NVIDIA GeForce RTX 1080 Ti GPU.

3.3 Analysis of Results

Table 1. The experimental results on the DAVIS dataset.

Method	OL	Time(s)	DAVIS2016		DAVIS2017	
			$\mathcal{J}$ Mean	$\mathcal{F}$ Mean	$\mathcal{J}$ Mean	$\mathcal{F}$ Mean
PReMVOS [10]	✓	38	84.9	88.6	73.9	81.7
OSVOS-S [11]	✓	4.5	85.6	87.5	64.7	71.3
OnAVOS [24]	✓	13	86.1	84.9	64.5	71.2
FEELVOS [23]	-	0.45	81.1	82.2	69.1	74.0
RGMP [12]	-	0.13	81.5	82.0	64.8	68.6
AGAME [7]	-	0.07	81.5	82.2	67.2	72.7
RANet [27]	-	0.03	85.5	85.4	63.2	68.2
CFBI [32]	-	0.18	88.3	90.5	79.1	84.6
STM [13]	-	0.16	88.7	90.1	79.2	84.3
GC [9]	-	0.04	87.6	85.7	69.3	73.5
KMN [20]	-	0.12	89.5	91.5	80.0	85.6
Ours	-	0.07	88.7	90.0	79.4	84.0

We report the results on the DAVIS dataset in Table 1, where OL indicates whether to use online learning or not. First, comparing the results on the DAVIS2016 single-object dataset, we can observe that the memory mechanism-based models have better advantages in both accuracy and efficiency. Our method can reach 88.7% on $\mathcal{J}$ Mean and 90.0% on $\mathcal{F}$ Mean, and the processing speed only needs 0.07s per frame.

The GC [9] proposed by Yu Li et al. also deals with the linear growth of memory in STM [13]. Their method uses a fixed-size global context module to store memory information and update during each frame. However, it is just use a simple weight addition when updating, our method will perform a adaptively update according to the similarity of each pixel, which can better adapt to the change of the target appearance. Compared with GC [9], our method can obtain 1.1% higher in $\mathcal{J}$ Mean and 4.3% higher in $\mathcal{F}$ Mean. The KMN [20] believe that STM is a global calculation, but the target usually only appears locally in the video. Therefore, the KMN model adopt a local matching based on the Gaussian distribution to improve the accuracy of STM. Although the KMN is 0.8% higher in $\mathcal{J}$ Mean than our method, it still stitches the results of each frame into the memory module, which still suffer a linear increase in memory and computing costs over time and cannot be applied on long videos.

When processing the multi-object dataset, each object is tracked and segmented separately. The segmentation results of multiple objects are combined using the Softmax normalization function. From the Table, we can find that our method can achieve good results. It can reach 79.4% on $\mathcal{J}$ Mean and 84.0% on $\mathcal{F}$ Mean, which also surpasses most methods. Although some methods can have slightly better performance than ours, our method uses a fixed memory size to achieve better efficiency.

3.4 Ablation Study

In order to verify the effectiveness of each module in the proposed model, an ablation experiment was performed on the DAVIS2016 dataset, and $\mathcal{J}$ Mean and time consumption were selected as evaluation metrics. From the experimental results in the Table 2, it can be seen that the adaptive memory network based only on filtering reaches 87.4% on $\mathcal{J}$ Mean, which is better than most existing methods. After adding the cascaded network for tracking to segmentation, not only the accuracy is improved by 0.9%, but also the speed is faster by 0.02 s per frame. It can be seen from the FPS that there is still a significant improvement effect. In addition, after adding the boundary branch, the accuracy of the model is further improved by 0.4%.

Table 2. Results of ablation experiments on the DAVIS2016 dataset.

	$\mathcal{J}$ Mean	Time(s)	FPS
Adaptive memory network	87.4	0.06	17
+Cascade network	88.3	0.04	24
+Boundary branch	88.7	0.07	14

Then further analyze the computation cost of each module in our model, we report the computation time of each module in Table 3. From the results, it can be seen that the proportion of time occupied by the target tracker is very small, accounting for only about 6% of the time of the entire algorithm. At the same time, the target tracker can cut the image into a smaller region of interest, and the time consumption in the subsequent segmentation step will be reduced. Therefore, it can be seen that the cascade network proposed in this study is very effective, increasing the accuracy of the model and improving the computational efficiency.

3.5 Visualization of Segmentation Results

Finally, to show the model's output more intuitively, we visualized some prediction results of our model in this section. Figure 5 shows the visualization results

Table 3. Time performance analysis of each module in our model.

	Target tracker	Memory module	Boundary branch	In total
Time(s)	0.0037	0.039	0.024	0.067

Fig. 5. The segmentation results on the DAVIS2016 single object dataset.

on the DAVIS2016 single object dataset. It can be seen that our model can segment the object more accurately. In the first row, when the camel moves to the middle of the video, another camel with a similar appearance appeared, and our model can still accurately focus on the correct object without object drift phenomenon. In the second row, not only does the appearance of the target change greatly due to the rapid movement, but the background also changes significantly with the camera's movement, but our model also can still accurately identify the details of the object. A similar result can be observed in the third row. Even if the person is in a complex motion, our model can still correctly estimate the body parts.

Figure 6 shows the visualization results of our model on a multi-object dataset. In the first row, the dog marked in green occulted the dog marked in red in the middle frame, and when the dog marked in red appears again, our model can find it and segment it accurately. As can be seen from the following two rows, even if multiple objects are in contact, we can still distinguish different targets and perform the segmentation.

Figure 7 shows the evaluation result of each video in the DAVIS2016 dataset. Overall, the $\mathcal{J}$ Mean of most videos can reach higher than 90% on $\mathcal{J}$ Mean, except three videos are around 70%. To further examine the reason for the poor prediction of our model, the prediction outputs of these three videos are compared with the ground truth label in Fig. 8. In Fig. 8, the left side represents the ground-truth label of the video data, and the right side is the predicted output of our model. When only examining the overall segmentation, we can find that our model has accurately segmented the target in the video. Therefore, we zoom in and observe some of the details.

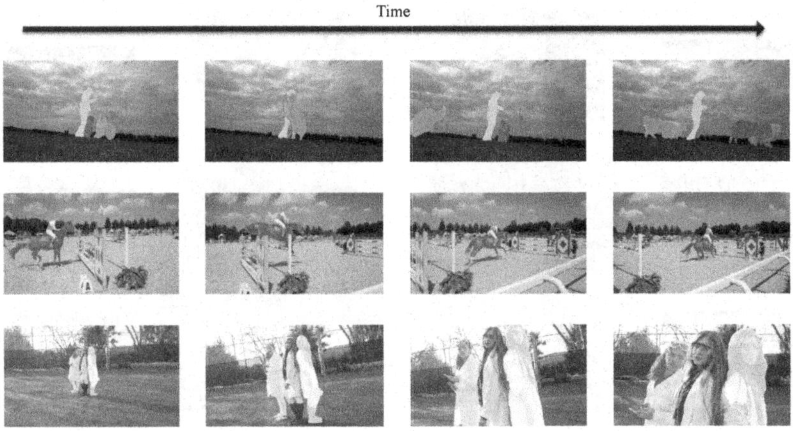

Fig. 6. The segmentation results on the DAVIS2017 multi-object dataset.

In the first row, the target is occluded by tree branches. Because the small tree branches occlude the object and separate it into multiple parts, even if it is observed with the naked eye, it is necessary to magnify the image before carefully dividing the branches and the object. However, in deep learning methods, images are often down-sampled and then feature-processed. Therefore, it is inevitable that some detailed information will be lost after down-sampling. By examining the second and third rows, it can be seen that the model has been able to segment people out better. However, after comparing with the ground-truth label, it is found that the lower accuracy mainly comes from the missed scene. That is, the line that needs to be accurately divided cannot be marked. These small lines will also become blurred after down-sampling to make it difficult to distinguish from the background, but the existing backbone models are often accompanied by down-sampling. For example, ResNet50 will down-sample the image by 32 times. If you want to down-sample such a large, it isn't easy to find a line with the size of only a few pixels in the original image. Therefore, the focus of subsequent research is

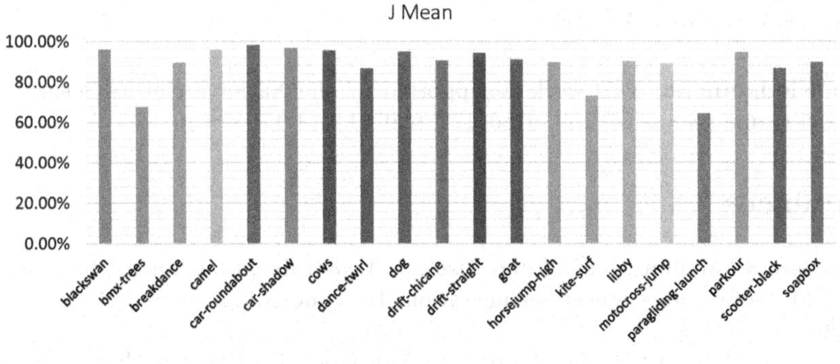

Fig. 7. The $\mathcal{J}$ values of each video in the DAVIS2016.

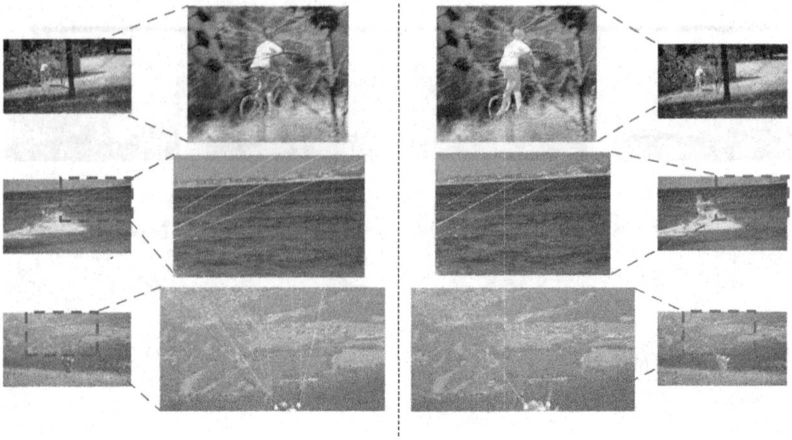

Fig. 8. The video data with poor segmentation results of our model.

how to avoid the loss of detailed information caused by image down-sampling and better segment the small foreground objects in the image.

4 Conclusion

This study proposes an adaptive memory module to deal with the linear computational cost explosion of STM in long videos by using the fixed-size memory module. In addition, a cascaded network from tracking to segmentation is used, which helps to eliminate the influence of background noise and interference and reduces the image resolution and the amount of calculation for subsequent segmentation modules. At the same time, a further boundary prediction branch is added to improve the model's accuracy. Unlike the simple prediction of the target boundary, the boundary pixels are expanded inward to avoid the imbalance between pixels. Finally, the effectiveness of the model is verified on the DAVIS dataset. The model in this article can achieve similar results with STM while achieving faster processing speed and will not increase memory consumption and computational cost over time.

Acknowledgement. This work is supported by the National Nature Science Foundation of China (No. 61876159, 61806172, 62076116, U1705286).

References

1. Caelles, S., Maninis, K.K., Pont-Tuset, J., Leal-Taixé, L., Cremers, D., Van Gool, L.: One-shot video object segmentation. In: Proceedings of CVPR, pp. 222–230 (2017)
2. Chen, Y., Pont-Tuset, J., Montes, A., Van Gool, L.: Blazingly fast video object segmentation with pixel-wise metric learning. In: Proceedings of CVPR, pp. 1189–1198 (2018)

3. He, K., Zhang, X., Ren, S., Sun, J.: Deep residual learning for image recognition. In: Proceedings of CVPR, pp. 770–778 (2016)
4. Hu, Y.T., Huang, J.B., Schwing, A.G.: VideoMatch: matching based video object segmentation. In: Proceedings of ECCV, pp. 54–70 (2018)
5. Jain, S.D., Grauman, K.: Supervoxel-consistent foreground propagation in video. In: Fleet, D., Pajdla, T., Schiele, B., Tuytelaars, T. (eds.) ECCV 2014. LNCS, vol. 8692, pp. 656–671. Springer, Cham (2014). https://doi.org/10.1007/978-3-319-10593-2_43
6. Jampani, V., Gadde, R., Gehler, P.V.: Video propagation networks. In: Proceeding of CVPR, pp. 451–461 (2017)
7. Johnander, J., Danelljan, M., Brissman, E., Khan, F.S., Felsberg, M.: A generative appearance model for end-to-end video object segmentation. In: Proceedings of CVPR, pp. 8953–8962 (2019)
8. Krizhevsky, A., Sutskever, I., Hinton, G.E.: ImageNet classification with deep convolutional neural networks. Proc. NeurIPS **25**, 1097–1105 (2012)
9. Li, Yu., Shen, Z., Shan, Y.: Fast video object segmentation using the global context module. In: Vedaldi, A., Bischof, H., Brox, T., Frahm, J.-M. (eds.) ECCV 2020. LNCS, vol. 12355, pp. 735–750. Springer, Cham (2020). https://doi.org/10.1007/978-3-030-58607-2_43
10. Luiten, J., Voigtlaender, P., Leibe, B.: PReMVOS: proposal-generation, refinement and merging for video object segmentation. In: Jawahar, C.V., Li, H., Mori, G., Schindler, K. (eds.) ACCV 2018. LNCS, vol. 11364, pp. 565–580. Springer, Cham (2019). https://doi.org/10.1007/978-3-030-20870-7_35
11. Maninis, K.K., et al.: Video object segmentation without temporal information. IEEE TPAMI **41**(6), 1515–1530 (2018)
12. Oh, S.W., Lee, J.Y., Sunkavalli, K., Kim, S.J.: Fast video object segmentation by reference-guided mask propagation. In: Proceedings of CVPR, pp. 7376–7385 (2018)
13. Oh, S.W., Lee, J.Y., Xu, N., Kim, S.J.: Video object segmentation using space-time memory networks. In: Proceedings of ICCV, pp. 9226–9235 (2019)
14. Perazzi, F., Khoreva, A., Benenson, R., Schiele, B., Sorkine-Hornung, A.: Learning video object segmentation from static images. In: Proceedings of CVPR, pp. 2663–2672 (2017)
15. Perazzi, F., Pont-Tuset, J., McWilliams, B., Van Gool, L., Gross, M., Sorkine-Hornung, A.: A benchmark dataset and evaluation methodology for video object segmentation. In: Proceedings of CVPR, pp. 724–732 (2016)
16. Perazzi, F., Wang, O., Gross, M., Sorkine-Hornung, A.: Fully connected object proposals for video segmentation. In: Proceedings of ICCV, pp. 3227–3234 (2015)
17. Pont-Tuset, J., Perazzi, F., Caelles, S., Arbeláez, P., Sorkine-Hornung, A., Van Gool, L.: The 2017 DAVIS challenge on video object segmentation. arXiv:1704.00675 (2017)
18. Ren, X., Malik, J.: Tracking as repeated figure/ground segmentation. In: Proceedings of CVPR, pp. 1–8 (2007)
19. Ronneberger, O., Fischer, P., Brox, T.: U-net: convolutional networks for biomedical image segmentation. In: Proceedings of MICCAI, pp. 234–241 (2015)
20. Seong, H., Hyun, J., Kim, E.: Kernelized memory network for video object segmentation. In: Vedaldi, A., Bischof, H., Brox, T., Frahm, J.-M. (eds.) ECCV 2020. LNCS, vol. 12367, pp. 629–645. Springer, Cham (2020). https://doi.org/10.1007/978-3-030-58542-6_38

21. Shin Yoon, J., Rameau, F., Kim, J., Lee, S., Shin, S., So Kweon, I.: Pixel-level matching for video object segmentation using convolutional neural networks. In: Proceedings of ICCV, pp. 2167–2176 (2017)
22. Tsai, Y.H., Yang, M.H., Black, M.J.: Video segmentation via object flow. In: Proceedings of CVPR, pp. 3899–3908 (2016)
23. Voigtlaender, P., Chai, Y., Schroff, F., Adam, H., Leibe, B., Chen, L.C.: FEELVOS: fast end-to-end embedding learning for video object segmentation. In: Proceedings of CVPR, pp. 9481–9490 (2019)
24. Voigtlaender, P., Leibe, B.: Online adaptation of convolutional neural networks for video object segmentation. arXiv preprint arXiv:1706.09364 (2017)
25. Wang, Q., Zhang, L., Bertinetto, L., Hu, W., Torr, P.H.: Fast online object tracking and segmentation: a unifying approach. In: Proceedings of CVPR, pp. 1328–1338 (2019)
26. Wang, Z., et al.: Understanding human activities in videos: a joint action and interaction learning approach. Neurocomputing **321**, 216–226 (2018)
27. Wang, Z., Xu, J., Liu, L., Zhu, F., Shao, L.: RANeT: ranking attention network for fast video object segmentation. In: Proceedings of CVPR, pp. 3978–3987 (2019)
28. Wei, J., Wang, S., Wu, Z., Su, C., Huang, Q., Tian, Q.: Label decoupling framework for salient object detection. In: Proceedings of CVPR, pp. 13025–13034 (2020)
29. Woo, S., Park, J., Lee, J.-Y., Kweon, I.S.: CBAM: convolutional block attention module. In: Ferrari, V., Hebert, M., Sminchisescu, C., Weiss, Y. (eds.) ECCV 2018. LNCS, vol. 11211, pp. 3–19. Springer, Cham (2018). https://doi.org/10.1007/978-3-030-01234-2_1
30. Xu, N., Yang, L., Fan, Y., Yang, J., Yue, D., Liang, Y., Price, B., Cohen, S., Huang, T.: YouTube-VOS: sequence-to-sequence video object segmentation. In: Ferrari, V., Hebert, M., Sminchisescu, C., Weiss, Y. (eds.) ECCV 2018. LNCS, vol. 11209, pp. 603–619. Springer, Cham (2018). https://doi.org/10.1007/978-3-030-01228-1_36
31. Xu, Y., Wang, Z., Li, Z., Yuan, Y., Yu, G.: SiamFC++: towards robust and accurate visual tracking with target estimation guidelines. In: Proceedings of AAAI, vol. 34, pp. 12549–12556 (2020)
32. Yang, Z., Wei, Y., Yang, Y.: Collaborative video object segmentation by foreground-background integration. In: Proceedings of ECCV, pp. 332–348 (2020)

An Improved SSD-Based Gastric Cancer Detection Method

Minggui Liu, Zhiming Luo(✉), Donglin Cao, Dazhen Lin, Songzhi Su, and Shaozi Li

Department of Artificial Intelligent, Xiamen University, Xiamen, China
{zhiming.luo,another,dzlin,ssz,szlig}@xmu.edu.cn

Abstract. Gastric cancer is one of the malignant cancers with a very high fatal rate, and early detection plays an essential role in the treatment and improves the five-year 5-year survival rate. In this study, we an improved gastric cancer detection method in endoscopy image based on SSD (Single Shot MultiBox Detector). Our methods mainly aim to deal with the insufficient fusion of different semantic feature maps and the existence of semantic gaps during fusion in the SSD detector. To achieve these goals, we leverage a recurrent feature pyramid network, a multi-layer feature fusion module, and an auxiliary lesion segmentation branch. The experimental results on the gastric cancer dataset collected from the First Affiliated Hospital of Xiamen University show that the improved SSD algorithm can improve the mAP metric by 5.9% compared with the original SSD algorithm to reach 56%.

Keywords: Deep learning · Gastric cancer detection · SSD · Feature fusion

1 Introduction

According to data released by the China Cancer Center in 2018 [2], 500,000 people died of gastric cancer in 2014. However, the detection level of gastric cancer in China is far lower than those in developed countries, such as Japan and South Korea. In Japan, the 5-year survival rate of patients with early gastric cancer after active treatment can exceed 90% [5]. Therefore, it is with essential needs to develop early detection methods for gastric cancer.

Gastric endoscopy is the most effective device to detect gastric cancer. However, the morphological characteristics of gastric cancer, especially early gastric cancer, are very insignificant in gastric endoscopy images. The diagnosis of early gastric cancer depends on identifying the small changes in the color of the mucosa and the abnormality of the lower blood vessels under the mucosa. Besides, each patient needs to take hours during the whole endoscopy diagnosis, and then the endoscopist will check them one by one to see if there is any malignant tumor or cancer. It is a severe challenge to endoscopists and may lead to missed or incorrect diagnosis. Therefore, it is of great significance to develop an algorithm that can assist endoscopic doctors in the diagnosis of gastric cancer.

Y. Sun et al. (Eds.): ChineseCSCW 2021, CCIS 1491, pp. 451–459, 2022.
https://doi.org/10.1007/978-981-19-4546-5_35

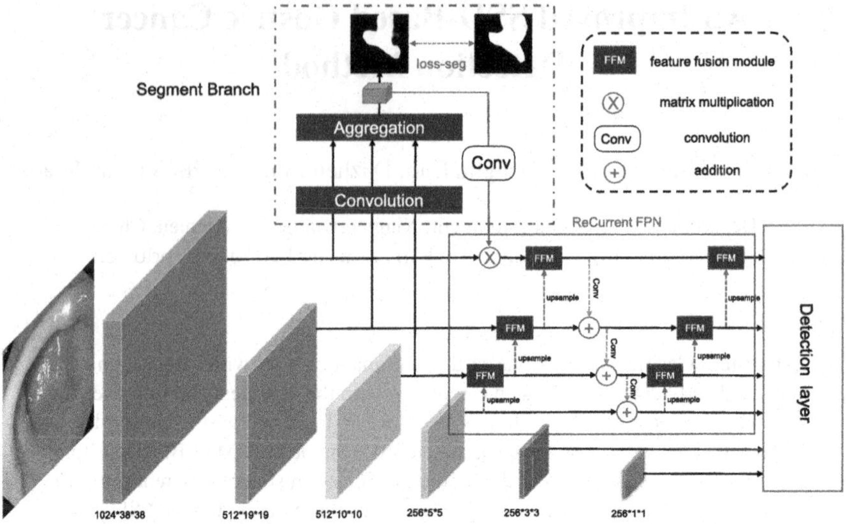

Fig. 1. The overall network architecture of our improved SSD Model.

Recently, with the development of deep learning, the clinical assistant diagnosis and treatment involving artificial intelligence provide a new direction for disease diagnosis. Many revolutionary algorithms and models in artificial intelligence have gradually been applied to clinical applications. Such as the diagnosis system of artificial intelligence skin cancer that can reach the expert level proposed by Stanford University [3], the artificial intelligence system for detecting lymph node metastasis of breast cancer [11], and the artificial intelligence system for polyp recognition [13] and cancer recognition [4] under digestive endoscopy.

In this study, we also mainly focus on gastric cancer detection in the endoscopy images. To deal with the challenge of small tumor detection, we developed an improved SSD detection framework [7] for this task. Our framework contains a multi-scale feature fusion module to leverage features from high layers to increase the feature discrimination in lower layers. Besides, we also leverage a multi-task learning framework by combining the lesion segmentation to assist the detection further. Experimental results on a dataset collected from the First Affiliated Hospital of Xiamen University demonstrate the effectiveness of our proposed method.

2 The Proposed Method

The overall structure of our improved SSD model is shown in the Fig. 1. Compared with the original SSD framework, we add a Recurrent Feature Pyramid Networks to promote the integration of different semantic features, and a segmentation branch to assist the detection of small lesions.

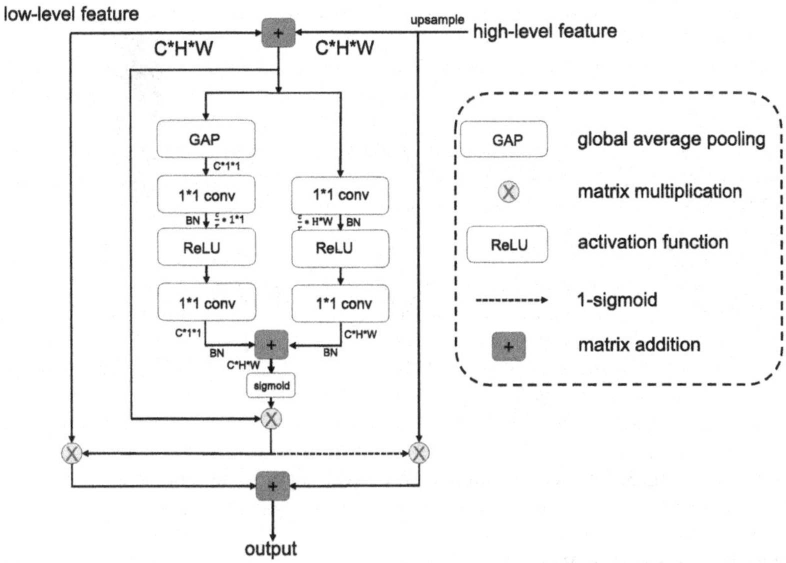

Fig. 2. The computation process of our proposed feature fusion module.

2.1 The Recurrent FPN

When labeling gastric cancer lesions, doctors do not directly mark the lesion area at a glance but need to look carefully and repeatedly to identify the lesion area accurately. To mimic this process, we first use a recurrent FPN network structure [9] as shown in the left part of Fig. 1. In the recurrent pyramid network, a feedback connection is used to transport the features obtained from the previous FPN to the feature extraction (bottom-up) backbone network on the left again. Instead of using the features obtained by FPN directly on the detection layer. This idea is similar to the Cascade RCNN [1] using more selected samples for training. The recurrent feature pyramid improves the more powerful expressive ability of FPN.

2.2 The Feature Fusion Module

In the original SSD, there is no connection between feature maps of different sizes, so the texture and color information of low-level features and semantic information of high-level features cannot be fully integrated. Therefore, in this study, we propose a novel Feature Fusion Module (FFM) for feature fusion as shown in Fig. 2. The feature fusion module is similar to the idea in ParseNet [8], that combines the local and global features of the feature maps of different layers of CNN and integrates multi-scale and multi-semantic spatial sum Channel characteristics. In the FFM, we mainly adopt a dual-branch attention module to fuse the features from low-level and high-level. The detailed computation flow of the FFM can be found in Fig. 2.

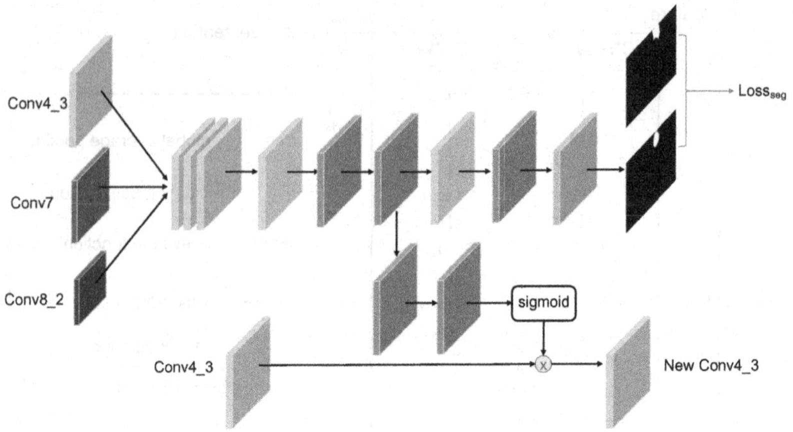

Fig. 3. The network architecture of the segmentation branch.

2.3 The Segmentation Branch

Although the original SSD framework uses six different scale features to detect targets of different sizes, low-level feature maps contain more shallow information such as texture and color, lacking semantic information. To deal with this issue, we add a semantic segmentation branch into the detection framework to increase the feature discrimination in shallow layers. The network architecture of the segmentation branch is shown in Fig. 3. In order to reduce the number of parameters to achieve real-time gastric cancer recognition, we only use the features from Conv4_3, Conv7, Conv8_2.

The segmentation branch is then integrated into Conv4_3, and the semantic information is added to it to assist the object detection in this layer. In other words, the semantic feature map is used to activate the original low-level detection feature map by pixel-by-pixel multiplication, denoted as:

$$Conv4\_3^{new} = Conv4\_3 \odot Attention_{seg}. \tag{1}$$

2.4 Loss Function

In the original SSD, there are two loss functions, i.e., L_{cls} and L_{reg}, corresponding to the classification and bounding box regression. However, for our gastric cancer detection task, we suffer a severe imbalance data issue between the lesion and normal area. To deal with this issue, we further adopt the Focal loss [6] into the L_{cls}, denoted as:

$$L_{cls} = \begin{cases} -\alpha\,(1-\hat{y})^{\gamma}\log(\hat{y}), & y=1 \\ -\,(1-\alpha)\,\hat{y}^{\gamma}\log(1-\hat{y}), & y=0 \end{cases} \tag{2}$$

where γ is used to adjust the rate of weight reduction of simple samples, and α is used to balance the ratio between positive and negative samples. The γ and α are set to 2 and 0.25 in this study, respectively. The L_{reg} is implemented by the L1 loss as the same as SSD.

For the segmentation branch, we adopt the weighted cross-entropy loss and IoU loss for training, denoted as:

$$L_{seg} = L_{IoU}^{w} + L_{BCE}^{w}. \tag{3}$$

The final loss function for our whole network is a multi-task loss function which combines the L_{cls} and L_{seg},

$$L_{all} = \lambda L_{seg} + (L_{cls} + L_{reg}), \tag{4}$$

where λ balances the influence between L_{seg} and L_{reg}, and is set to 0.1.

3 Experiments

3.1 Dataset

The endoscopic images used in the study are collected in the First Affiliated Hospital of Xiamen University. The whole dataset contains 646 gastric cancer images from 73 patients. Two endoscopic doctors annotated the images by using the LabelMe toolbox. The training and testing split used in this study is shown in Table 1.

Table 1. The training and testing split.

	# Patients	# Images	# BBox
Dataset	73	646	733
Training Set	63	560	629
Testing Set	10	86	104

3.2 Experimental Setup

We implement our model by using the PyTorch toolbox, and conduct experiments on a GTX 1080Ti GPU. All the input images are resized to 300 × 300, and the model is trained by the SGD optimizer for a total of 12,000 iterations with an initial learning of 3e–4. The batch size is set to 16, and a variety of data augmentation methods have been used, such as random rotation, random flip, random color adjustment. The mean average precision (mAP), precision and recall are used to evaluate the detection, and the mIoU and mDice are used to evaluate the segmentation results.

3.3 Experimental Results

The experimental results are shown in Table 2. For the original SSD model, we can find that the mAP metrics for both VGG16 and ResNet-50 backbone are around 0.5. The mAP for the YOLO-v3 is only 0.478, which is lower than the SSD-based methods. Besides, we also compute the mIoU and mDice for the segmentation model U-Net, which are 0.478 and 0.563, respectively. After adding the segmentation branch and recurrent FPN and feature fusion mentioned in this paper, we can observe that the detection accuracy mAP is increased to 0.560, which is about 6% higher than the original SSD. Besides, we can find that the mIoU and mDice are improved in our model compared with U-Net [12]. These results suggest that the multi-task learning network is helpful for the detection of gastric cancer when considering the detection and segmentation tasks simultaneously.

Table 2. The comparison of our method with other different methods.

Method	mAP	Precision	Recall	mIoU	mDice
SSD (VGG16) [7]	0.505	0.421	0.536	*	*
SSD (ResNet50) [7]	0.502	0.437	0.542	*	*
YOLO-V3 [10]	0.478	0.418	0.523	*	*
U-Net [12]	*	*	*	0.478	0.563
Ours	**0.560**	**0.512**	**0.603**	**0.493**	**0.610**

In addition, we also conduct an ablation study to verify the effectiveness of each part in our proposed network. As shown in Table 3, we can find adding the segmentation branch, FPN, and Recurrent FPN individually can increase the performance overall the baseline model. By comparing the results of FPN and Recurrent FPN, we can find that our proposed Recurrent FPN can outperform the FPN. Finally, after adding both segmentation branch and Recurrent FPN, the mAP will further increase to 0.560. These results suggest the mutual benefits of the segmentation branch and the proposed Recurrent FPN.

Table 3. Ablation experiments

Method	mAP	Precision	Recall
Baseline	0.502	0.437	0.542
+Seg branch	0.526	0.458	0.563
+FPN	0.514	0.449	0.552
+Recurrent FPN	0.547	0.481	0.586
+Seg branch & Recurrent FPN	**0.560**	**0.512**	**0.610**

3.4 Visual Analysis

In order to intuitively show the effectiveness of the proposed method, this paper selects several representative test set images to do visual analysis. The visualization results of our improved SSD and the original SSD are shown in Fig. 4. Columns 1 and 2 are the ground-truth labels of gastric cancer images and gastric cancer locations, respectively. Column 3 is the results obtained by the original SSD, and columns 4 and 5 are the results obtained by the segmentation and detection branches of our improved SSD. It can be

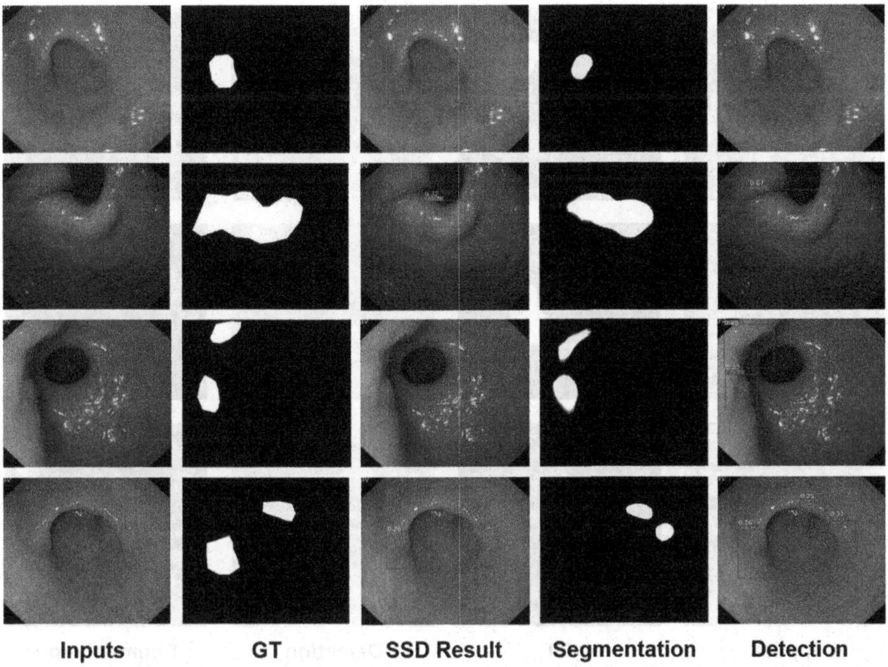

Fig. 4. Some detection and segmentation results obtained by the SSD and our model.

seen that the smaller cancer lesion areas were missed in the original SSD detection. Such as gastric cancer lesions in rows 1, 3, and 4 cannot be accurately identified in the original SSD but can be accurately in the segmentation branch and the final detection in our model. In addition, as shown in the first row, the gastric cancer area detected by the original SSD is much smaller than that of the real lesion and cannot accurately frame the entire gastric cancer lesion. However, the method proposed in this study is more accurate in detecting the lesion area, which can almost identify the whole gastric cancer lesion and has higher confidence than that of the original SSD.

In addition, we also visualized some failure cases of our model in Fig. 5. It can be found that these relatively poor results mainly appear in those areas with very similar textures to normal areas. For example, gastric cancer and normal areas in the first row are very similar and have very similar appearance characteristics. There are also missed areas, such as the second row and third row, which are some early gastric cancers, and their appearance is very inconspicuous. Even experienced gastro endoscopy doctors can hardly distinguish them, and they need to use tools such as magnifying endoscopy to achieve accurate identification.

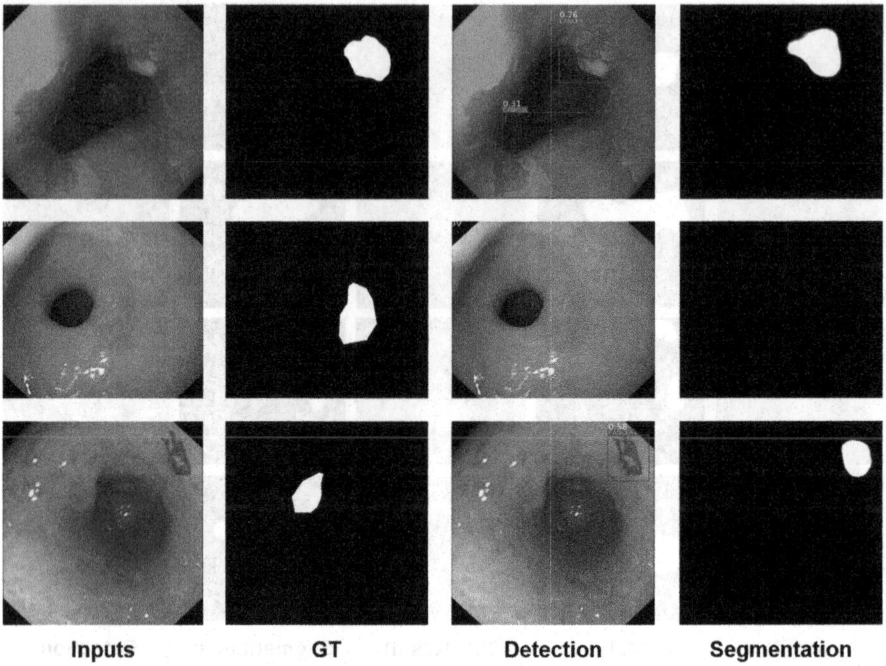

Fig. 5. Some failure cases produced by our model.

4 Conclusion

This study proposes an improved SSD-based gastric cancer detection method. Compared with the original SSD detector, we use a recurrent feature pyramid network (RFPN) to improve the feature discrimination of FPN. In addition, we further adopt a dual-branch feature fusion model, one of which focuses on global semantic information and the other on local semantic information. Finally, to address the lack of semantic information in the lower feature map of SSD, this paper proposes a novel small target detection method by fusing semantic supervision information. A semantic segmentation branch is added to the SSD, and its semantic information is added to the first part of the SSD. Experiments show that the accuracy of the improved SSD detector on the gastric cancer dataset of Xiamen First Hospital is much better than that of ordinary SSD detectors and other detectors.

Acknowledgement. This work is supported by the National Nature Science Foundation of China (No. 61876159, 61806172, 62076116, U1705286).

References

1. Cai, Z., Vasconcelos, N.: Cascade R-CNN: delving into high quality object detection. In: Proceedings of the IEEE Conference on Computer Vision and Pattern Recognition, pp. 6154–6162 (2018)
2. Chen, W., et al.: Cancer incidence and mortality in China, 2014. Chinese J. Cancer Res. **30**(1), 1 (2018)
3. Esteva, A., et al.: Dermatologist-level classification of skin cancer with deep neural networks. Nature **542**(7639), 115–118 (2017)
4. Horie, Y., et al.: Diagnostic outcomes of esophageal cancer by artificial intelligence using convolutional neural networks. Gastrointest. Endosc. **89**(1), 25–32 (2019)
5. Katai, H., et al.: Five-year survival analysis of surgically resected gastric cancer cases in Japan: a retrospective analysis of more than 100,000 patients from the nationwide registry of the Japanese gastric cancer association (2001–2007). Gastric Cancer **21**(1), 144–154 (2018)
6. Lin, T.Y., Goyal, P., Girshick, R., He, K., Dollár, P.: Focal loss for dense object detection. In: Proceedings of the IEEE International Conference on Computer Vision, pp. 2980–2988 (2017)
7. Liu, W., et al.: SSD: single shot multibox detector. In: Leibe, B., Matas, J., Sebe, N., Welling, M. (eds.) ECCV 2016. LNCS, vol. 9905, pp. 21–37. Springer, Cham (2016). https://doi.org/10.1007/978-3-319-46448-0_2
8. Liu, W., Rabinovich, A., Berg, A.C.: ParseNet: Looking wider to see better. arXiv preprint arXiv:1506.04579 (2015)
9. Qiao, S., Chen, L.C., Yuille, A.: DetectoRS: detecting objects with recursive feature pyramid and switchable Atrous convolution. In: Proceedings of the IEEE/CVF Conference on Computer Vision and Pattern Recognition, pp. 10213–10224 (2021)
10. Redmon, J., Farhadi, A.: Yolov3: an incremental improvement. arXiv preprint arXiv:1804.02767 (2018)
11. Rodríguez-Ruiz, A., Krupinski, E., Mordang, J.J., Schilling, K., Heywang-Köbrunner, S.H., Sechopoulos, I., Mann, R.M.: Detection of breast cancer with mammography: effect of an artificial intelligence support system. Radiology **290**(2), 305–314 (2019)
12. Ronneberger, O., Fischer, P., Brox, T.: U-Net: convolutional networks for biomedical image segmentation. In: Navab, N., Hornegger, J., Wells, W.M., Frangi, A.F. (eds.) MICCAI 2015. LNCS, vol. 9351, pp. 234–241. Springer, Cham (2015). https://doi.org/10.1007/978-3-319-24574-4_28
13. Wickstrøm, K., Kampffmeyer, M., Jenssen, R.: Uncertainty modeling and interpretability in convolutional neural networks for polyp segmentation. In: 2018 IEEE 28th International Workshop on Machine Learning for Signal Processing (MLSP), pp. 1–6. IEEE (2018)

Attention and Multi-granied Feature Learning for Baggage Re-identification

Huangbin Wu, Zhiming Luo(✉), Donglin Cao, Dazhen Lin, Songzhi Su, and Shaozi Li

Department of Artificial Intelligence, Xiamen University, Xiamen, China
wuhuangbin@stu.xmu.edu.cn,
{zhiming.luo,another,dzlin,ssz,szlig}@xmu.edu.cn

Abstract. The current baggage re-identification methods only consider the global coarse-grained features while ignoring the fine-grained features. To deal with this issue, we proposed a simple and efficient multi-granularity feature learning based on attention mechanisms for this task. First, we introduce the global context attention mechanism into the backbone network to improve global features. Then, we use the batch feature dropbox module to learn local fine-grained features with context information combined with global coarse-grained feature learning. Our method achieved 84.6% Rank-1 and 82.5% mAP on the public dataset, which verified the performance of baggage re-identification can be improved by global context information and multi-granularity feature learning.

Keywords: Baggage re-identification · Attention mechanisms · Multi-grained feature learning

1 Introduction

The mainstream method of baggage tracking and identification in the airport is based on radio frequency identification technology. Radio frequency identification technology can identify and track baggage without additional manual operations and locate and investigate suspicious baggage smuggled by customs quickly and improve the customs clearance rate of passengers. However, this technology has the following shortcomings due to the reliance on radio frequency tag identification. (1) The radiofrequency tag may fall or be torn off by some passengers deliberately during transmission. (2) The radiofrequency tag must be marked by humans or some equipment, which will cause additional costs and may affect the customs clearance rate. (3) Some baggage or devices with metal materials may interfere with the detection signal of the radio frequency tag, which may lead to false negatives. The industry is considering using other technologies, and baggage re-identification technology has attracted attention.

With the inspiration of Person Re-Identification method, some vision based baggage re-identification have been proposed by different researchers, such as the MSN [13] and [5]. However, these methods only focus on the difference between

Y. Sun et al. (Eds.): ChineseCSCW 2021, CCIS 1491, pp. 460–472, 2022.
https://doi.org/10.1007/978-981-19-4546-5_36

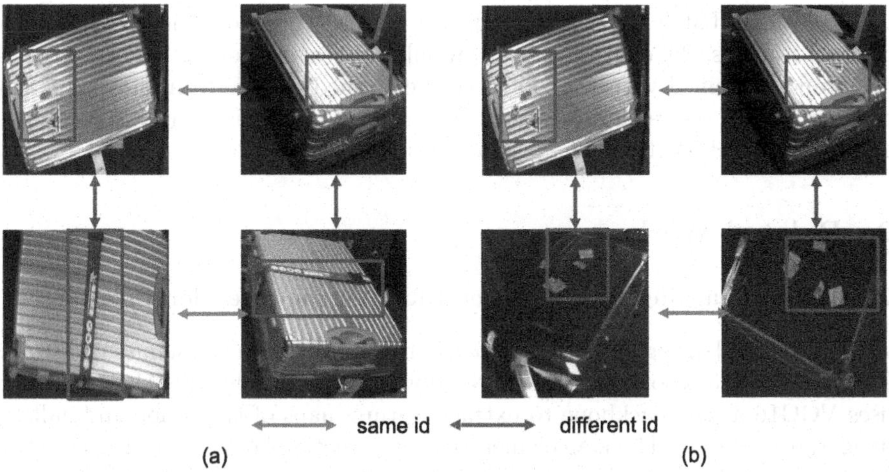

Fig. 1. Fine-grained feature and context of the baggage.

probe image and the images in the gallery collection, and largely ignored the fine-grained characteristics of the baggage. Besides, these methods are based on the siamese network which only uses the weak label information (only considers the relationship between the two samples), but not the identity label of the baggage re-identification data set.

As shown in Fig. 1-(a), some common styles of baggage are very similar and can not be distinguished if some fine-grained features are not considered. Fine-grained features focus on objects (baggage with different identities) belonging to multiple subcategories of the same category (baggage). In addition, the smalle and larger intra-class differences in pose, scale, and rotation is caused by the highly similar subcategories, which determined that a single global coarse-grained feature is difficult to identify of baggage images.

On the other hand, we argue that fine-grained features have a certain meaning only under the overall context information. For example, two baggage have similar cartoon stickers (as shown in Fig. 1-(b)), and they are not the same baggage since they are in different colors. In the absence of context, only relying on fine-grained features will result in a higher similarity between the two baggage images during retrieval (that is, the ranking in the retrieval ranking will become relatively high). Therefore, instead of only considering the fine-grained local features, we also need to consider the more general global information. In this study, we will introduce a global attention mechanism to learn contextual information. This mechanism can learn global context information through long-range modeling to enhance the feature expression of the backbone.

After considering the above-mentioned aspects, this study proposes a baggage re-identification method of multi-granularity feature learning based on the attention mechanism. This method integrates with ResNet-50 by introducing a Global Context (GC) attention mechanism [1]. Based on the features of context information, a batch feature dropbox module is proposed to learn local fine-grained features. That is, the local granularity feature context information is given and combined with the global coarse-grained feature to improve the discriminability of the retrieval feature. Our method can achieve an 84.6% Rank-1 and 82.5% mAP on the public baggage re-identification data set MVB.

2 Related Work

2.1 Deep Learning-Based Method for Baggage Re-identification

At present, the baggage re-identification is mainly based on the siamese network. Zhang et al. [13] proposed the MSN network. Specifically, the MSN network uses VGG16 as the backbone to extract feature maps of the probe and gallery images, respectively. Then, an element-wise subtraction layer is performed on the feature maps of the two branches, and the output is fed to the fully connected layer for binary classification. The classification part of the network predicts the possibility of whether the probe image and the gallery image are from the same identity. In the training phase, the MSN mainly aims to reduce the cross-entropy loss function of the two classifications. The purpose of element-wise subtraction is to suppress similar features at the same position on the feature map while enhancing the different features and preserving spatial information. In the same way, Mazzeo et al. [5] tried ResNet-50 and SENET and other classic image classification networks as backbone networks to build siamese networks. Different from the MSN network that uses an element-wise subtraction operation, it uses a square layer. The square layer operation is defined as:

$$f_s = (f_1 - f_2)^2 . \tag{1}$$

where, f_1 and f_2 are the feature maps extracted by the backbone network for the two input images. The utilization of a deeper backbone network improves the accuracy by nearly 20% compared to the MSN network.

We can find that the current baggage re-identification methods have the following shortcomings. (1) These methods consider the difference between the probe image and the gallery image, but not the characteristics of the baggage image, which makes it challenging to make full use of the information in the baggage image and improve the performance of the baggage re-identification. (2) The methods based on the siamese network only use the weak label information (that is, they only consider the relationship between the two samples), but not the baggage to re-identify the identity label of the dataset. (3) Single-task training is insufficient to improve the performance of baggage re-identification.

2.2 Multi-grained Feature Learning

Wang et al. [8] proposed the Multiple Granularity Network (MGN) for person re-identification. The MGN network introduced a multi-branch operation from res_conv4-3 to res_conv5-3 in ResNet. The pooling was used at different granularities for extracting coarse-grained to fine-grained feature vectors in each branch. Notice that the parameters of each branch are not shared. In [9], researchers proposed a multi-granularity learning method based on receptive fields to represent multi-granularity local features of different scales comprehensively. Unlike other methods, this method performs local division on the intermediate representation to manipulate the range of the receptive field, instead of performing the division method on the input image or output feature, so this method can enhance the position representation while maintaining proper local correlation.

2.3 Attention Mechanism

The attention mechanism can focus on the most informative input signals and has been effectively used in various tasks, including natural language processing, semantic segmentation, and image description. Vaswani et al. [7] first proposed the self-attention mechanism to learn the global dependency between the input and output sequence, which calculates the position response by paying attention to all positions in the sequence. Hu et al. [3] proposed the "Squeeze-And-Excitation" (SE) module, which can modeling the interdependence between different channels by using a soft self-attention and re-weighting the channel responses. Woo et al. [11] proposed a module called CBAM that integrates space and channel attention mechanisms inspired by the SE module. Wang et al. [10] proposed a non-local block (Non-local Block). The local is based on the receptive field (for example, the receptive field of the convolution operation is usually the size of its convolution kernel) in the non-local block. Non-local means that the range of the receptive field is not limited to the convolution operation. The Non-local process is defined as:

$$y_i = \frac{1}{C(x)} \sum_{\forall_j} f(x_i, x_j)\, g(x_j). \tag{2}$$

where, x_i and x_j are the feature vectors at a certain spatial position of the input feature map (the dimension is the same as the number of channels of the input feature map). $f(x_i, x_j)$ is the similarity function between x_i and x_j. $g(x_j)$ is a mapping function of 1, which is usually realized by the convolution operation of the convolution kernel 1×1, $\frac{1}{C(x)}$ is the normalization coefficient. For $f(x_i, x_j)$, it can be implemented in many different forms. The most commonly used form in the field of computer vision is Embedded Gaussian. The form of the embedded Gaussian function is:

$$f(x_i, x_j) = e^{\theta(x_i)^T \phi(x_j)}. \tag{3}$$

That is, the Gaussian function is mapped to the embedding space and then the similarity is calculated.

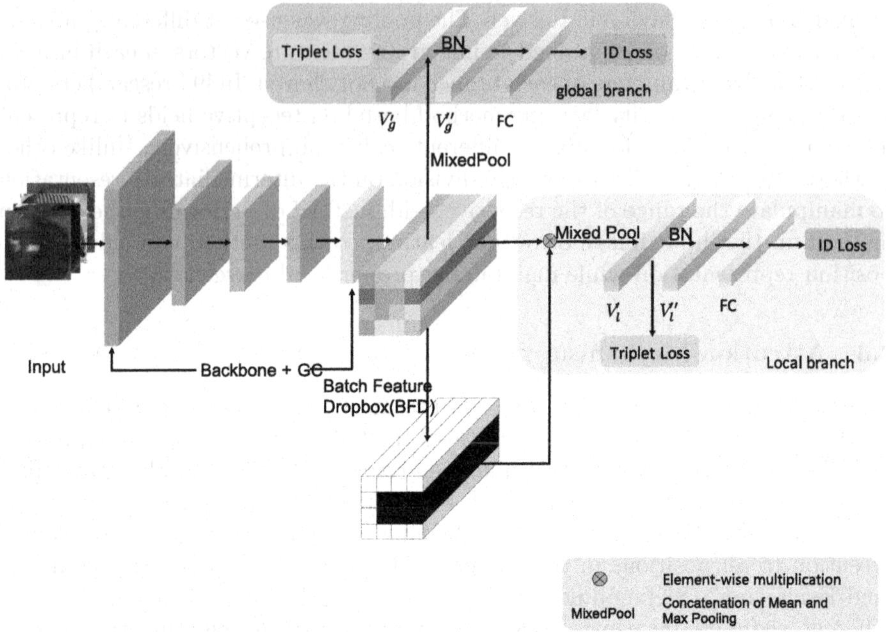

Fig. 2. The Pipeline of the proposed AMG for baggage re-identification.

3 Proposed Method

The overall network structure of our proposed AMG model is shown in Fig. 2. Our AMG model mainly contains three modules: the backbone network with global context information, the global coarse-grained feature learning branch, and the local fine-grained feature learning branch. To learning more discriminative local features, we introduce a batch feature dropbox process into the local branch. In the following section, we will describe the computation details of each module.

3.1 The Backbone Network with Global Context

The AMG network introduces the Global Context (GC) [1] module to learn the global context information. Because of the low computational complexity and the ability to model global contextual attention of the GC module, this study will introduce the GC module to the baggage re-identification and propose the combination of the GC module and the backbone network ResNet-50. Specifically, the AMG network first passes the feature map through the original ResNet convolution module, and then feeds the output to the GC module. Due to the characteristics of the attention mechanism, the GC module only needs a single feature map as input. Figure 3 is a schematic diagram of the combination of the third convolutional layer of ResNet50 and the GC module. The AMG network

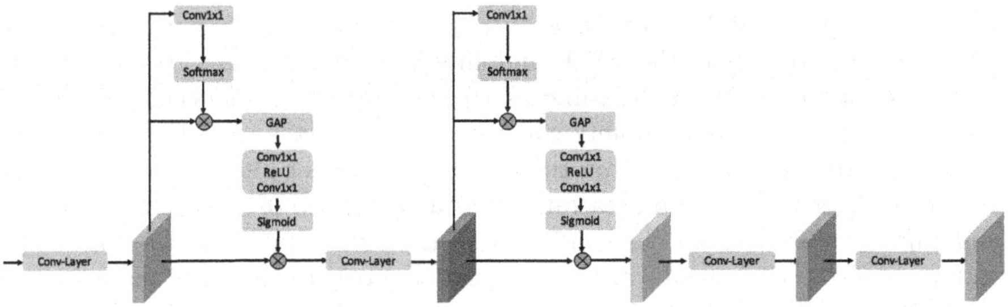

Fig. 3. The diagram of integrating the GC module in to the ResNet50-Layer3

embeds the GC module into ResNet-50, and pays more attention to global context information when enhancing network learning features, thereby enriching the discriminative power of features.

3.2 The Global Coarse-Grained Feature Learning Branch

As shown in Fig. 2, the AMG network obtains a feature map of size $b \times c \times h \times w$ after the backbone network with GC, denoted as S. Then the feature map undergoes a hybrid pooling operation to obtain tensor V_g. Hybrid pooling is a simple pooling operation, which is obtained by splicing along the channel dimension after maximum and average pooling operation on the input tensor. The operation can be expressed as:

$$V_g = Concat\left(GMP\left(S\right), GAP\left(S\right)\right). \tag{4}$$

Then we flatten the tensor to the size of $b \times (2 \times c)$, and denote this tensor as $V_g^{'}$. The feature vector $V_g^{'}$ will be used for the training of the triplet loss function, and then fed to a batch normalization layer (BN) to obtain the feature vector $V_g^{''}$. According to the analysis in [4], the batch normalization layer can smooth the feature distribution in the embedding space. The batch-normalized output feature vector $V_g^{''}$ is sent to the Softmax layer. The number of neurons in this layer is the number of identities (categories) of the baggage, and the output of the Softmax layer is used for the training of the identity loss function (ID Loss).

3.3 The Local Fine-Grained Feature Learning Branch

For another core branch, the AMG network uses it to learn fine-grained features, which is called the local fine-grained feature learning branch. This branch leverage the Batch Feature Dropbox (BFD) module to assist the feature learning. The BFD randomly generates a rectangular area on the feature map S and sets the values in the rectangular area to 0, forcing the network to use the remaining information to learn more discriminative local features.

Algorithm 1 describes the detail of the proposed BFM module. In brief, the input baggage image is obtained by integrating the GC module and the integrated network of ResNet-50 to obtain a feature map S with the size of $b \times c \times h \times w$. And then, the BFD randomly generates a mask, denoted as M. The shape of the mask is the same as the feature map, and their values are 1. A rectangular area is randomly generated on the Mask, and the area of the rectangular area is random within the range of the upper limit a_h and the lower limit a_l of the given original area ratio. The aspect ratio of the rectangle is also randomly generated under the conditions of the given upper limit r_2 and lower limit r_1. After the elements in the rectangular area are set to 0 as described above, the Mask and the feature map S are multiplied element by element to obtain a new feature map S^*. What needs to be explained here is that the neural network training uses batch (Batch) input images, so the batch loss module applies the same mask to the same batch input. That is the elements at the same position of each $c \times h \times w$ tensor are the same. The subsequent operations of the output new feature map S^* are the same as the global coarse-grained feature learning branch. After the hybrid pooling operation and dimensional compression, the feature vector is obtained and then used for the training of the triple loss function. In addition, the tensor is also subsequently fed to a batch normalization layer to obtain a new feature vector, which is used in the Softmax layer to train the identity loss function.

Algorithm 1: Batch Feature Dropbox Algorithm

Input : the size $B \times C \times H \times W$ of S; the area of S as:A; the area ratio from a_l to a_h; the aspect ratio from r_1 and r_2;
Output: S^*

```
if Model is training then
    while True do
        A_d ← Rand(a_l, a_h) × S;   r_d ← Rand(r_1, r_2);
        H_d ← sqrt(A_d × r_d);   W_d ← sqrt(A_d / r_d);
        x_d ← Rand(0, H);   y_d ← Rand(0, W);
        if x_d + H_d ≤ W and y_d + W_d ≤ H then
            M ← Ones(B, C, H, W);
            M[:, :, x_d : x_d + H_d, y_d : y_d + W_d] ← 0;
            S* ← S × M;
            return S*;
        end
    end
else
    S* ← S;
    return S*;
end
```

Discussion: The local fine-grained feature learning branch can set the original main focus area to 0 by random batch feature discarding during training, which can force the remaining part of the feature map to participate in the backpropagation. It should be noted that the batch feature loss module is not the same as the Batch DropBlock in the BDB network [2] in the person re-identification network. The differences are:

(1) The generation rules of the rectangular area are different. In this paper, the generation area of the batch feature loss module is randomly generated under the conditions of the upper and lower limits of the given aspect ratio, not a rectangular area with a fixed aspect ratio. The Batch DropBlock in the BDB network has the aspect ratio fixed in advance, and the rectangular area generated each time only differs in position. By doing so, our generation rules can increase the diversity of the generated rectangular area.
(2) The original intention of Batch DropBlock applied in the BDB network is to erase the features of the same position of pedestrians in the same batch, which is equivalent to introducing prior information of pedestrian structure. The "batch" used in the batch feature discarding module proposed in this paper does not cover the same parts of the baggage (baggage does not have inherent constraints similar to pedestrians walking upright) but only improves the execution efficiency of discarding. Compared to generating a Mask for each bag image, the same batch input generates a Mask with higher operating efficiency.

3.4 Loss Function

For both the global branch and the local branch, we use the triplet loss and ID classification loss for training. The final loss function is the combination of the two branches, denoted as follows:

$$Loss = L_{global}^{ce} + L_{global}^{tri} + L_{local}^{ce} + L_{local}^{tri} \tag{5}$$

where L^{ce} is cross-entropy loss function, and L^{tri} is the triplet loss function.

4 Experiment

4.1 Dataset

To evaluate the performance of our proposed method, we conduct experiments on the baggage re-identification data set MVB [13]. The MVB contains 4,519 different baggage identities (categories) and 22,660 labeled images. The training set contains 20,176 baggage images from 4,019 baggage identities, while the probe set of the test set has 1052 images from 500 identities, and the gallery set includes 1,432 images and 500 identities.

4.2 Experiment Settings

We implemented the proposed AMG network by using the PyTorch deep learning toolbox. In the training phase, we randomly cropped the input image to the size of 256 × 256, and applied random horizontal flipping, random vertical flipping, and random erasing [14] for data argumentation. For each training batch, we randomly sampled 32 identities, with each has 4 images. The area of the Mask rectangular is randomly selected from [0.25, 0.75], and the aspect ratio is randomly generated from [0.3, 1.3]. We trained the AMG by using the Adam optimizer for 250 epochs on 2×1080Ti. In the testing phase, we concatenated the features from the two branches for computing the similarity based on the Euclidean distance.

4.3 Experiment Results

Due to there are very little researches about baggage re-identification, we further include some typical person re-identification methods for comparison. PCB and MGN networks are classic horizontally divided feature maps to extract local features in person re-identification. It can be seen from Table 1 that MGN's Rank-1 is only 57.8%, and mAP is only 56.6%. PCB is better than MGN, but the Rank-1 is only 64.4%, and the mAP is 65.5%. This is because the postures of baggage images are quite different, and local features cannot be extracted by horizontal division like pedestrian images, which causes the failure of methods like PCB in the task of re-identification of baggage. BDB is similar to the model proposed in this study and achieved 78.5% of Rank-1 and 78.0% of mAP. But the effect of BDB is not as good as the AMG network because BDB does not incorporate global context information. The methods proposed by MSN and Mazzeo P. L. have only two baggage re-identification tasks, and the method in this paper is far ahead of them.

Table 1. Comparison with state-of-the-art object Re-ID methods on the MVB dataset.

	Method	Rank-1	mAP
Person Re-ID	PCB [6]	64.4%	65.5%
	MGN [8]	57.8%	56.6%
	BDB [2]	78.5%	78.0%
	Strong baseline [4]	75.9%	73.6%
	OSNet [15]	72.6%	69.1%
	RGSC [12]	74.5%	74.4%
Baggage Re-ID	MSN [13]	50.2%	51.8%
	Mazzeo et al. [5]	64.8%	61.7%
	AMG	**84.6%**	**82.5%**

4.4 Ablation Studies

In order to explore the effects of each module of the AMG network, ablation experiment was conducted in this section.

The Effectiveness of the Global Context: First, to explore the integration effects of our proposed global-context-based attention mechanism, we compared it with the CBAM, SE, Non-local. The results are shown in Table 2. It can be seen that after integrating ResNet-50 with the attention mechanism, the performance indicators of bag re-identification have improved in different degrees. The result of integrating our proposed GC module into ResNet-50 is better than that of using the non-local module and the SE module alone. This result suggests that the global context information and the interdependence between channels can mutually promote feature learning.

Table 2. The effect of different attention on the ResNet-50.

	Rank-1	mAP
Baseline	75.9%	73.6%
Baseline + Non-local [10]	77.3%	77.5%
Baseline + SE [3]	79.4%	78.6%
Baseline + CBAM [11]	77.6%	76.8%
Baseline + GC [1]	80.4%	79.9%

The Effectiveness of the Global and Local Branch: In this part, we train two different models, each containing the global branch or the local branch, to evaluate their effectiveness. As shown in Table 3, we can find that the effect of the local fine-grained feature learning branch is higher than that of the global-grained feature learning branch. This is mainly because the proposed fine-grained feature eliminates a certain ambiguity under the global attention mechanism condition and improves the feature's discrimination. On the other aspect, we can observe the mutual benefits of considering these two branches jointly.

Table 3. The effectiveness of the global and local branch

	Rank-1	mAP
Global branch	81.4%	79.8%
Local branch	82.9%	81.2%
AMG	84.6%	82.5%

The Generalization of the GC and Local Branch: We further integrate the proposed global context learning and local branch into other person re-identification methods. As shown in Table 4, we can observe a significant boost in both Rank-1 and mAP compared with the original PCB, MGN, and OSNet. This experiment shows that local fine-grained features based on contextual information can further improve its performance in general methods and prove the Generalization ability of the proposed method in this study.

Table 4. GC Block + Local Branch on different methods

	Rank-1	mAP
PCB	64.4%	65.5
PCB + GC + Local Branch	69.1%	70.1%
MGN	57.8%	56.5%
MGN + GC + Local Branch	60.9%	59.2%
OSNet	72.6%	69.1%
OSNet + GC + Local Branch	73.5%	73.2%

4.5 Visual Analysis

Visual analysis is conducted to explore the actual retrieval effect of the AMG network in this paper. Figure 4 shows the top 10 images corresponding to the sorting results of the 8 probe images (the leftmost column) on the baggage re-identification MVB dataset of the AMG network. The green frame represents the same baggage identity as the probe image, but the red frame is different.

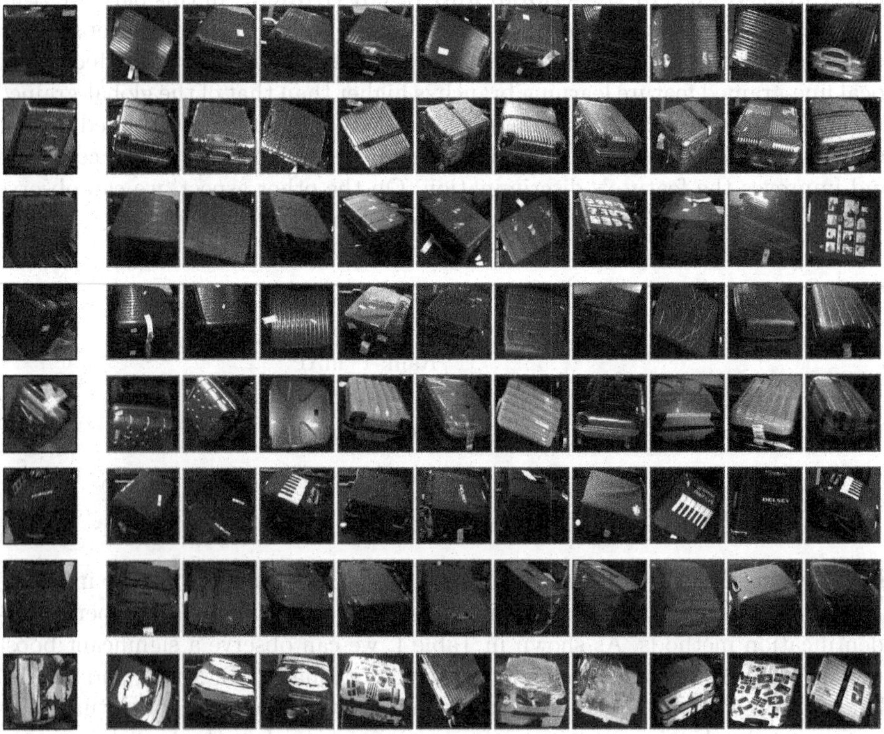

Fig. 4. The Top-10 ranking list of the proposed AMG model. (Color figurte online)

In general, we can find that the AMG network can sort the similar baggage in the front, which can help us to filter out some similar baggage images as candidates (ranking results are higher) even when the viewing angle changes significantly.

5 Conclusion

Since the current baggage re-identification methods ignore the fine-grained features and are more complex, this paper proposes a simple and efficient baggage re-identification method based on multi-grained feature learning and the attention mechanism. Our method combines multi-granularity feature learning and global attention mechanism to improve the performance of baggage re-identification and then proposes a multi-granularity feature learning network AMG based on the attention mechanism. The AMG network only uses the global attention module and simple multi-granularity branch structure for multi-task learning (without additional tag information). It obtains efficient features for the retrieval of baggage re-identification. Extensive experiments on the AMG network on the baggage re-identification MVB dataset proved the effectiveness of the multi-granular feature learning and attention mechanism, and finally achieved 84.6% of Rank-1 and 82.5% of mAP on the MVB dataset, which is far ahead of the currently published baggage re-identification method.

Acknowledgement. This work is supported by the National Nature Science Foundation of China (No. 61876159, 61806172, 62076116, U1705286).

References

1. Cao, Y., Xu, J., Lin, S., Wei, F., Hu, H.: GCNet: non-local networks meet squeeze-excitation networks and beyond. In: Proceedings of the IEEE/CVF International Conference on Computer Vision Workshops (2019)
2. Dai, Z., Chen, M., Gu, X., Zhu, S., Tan, P.: Batch dropblock network for person re-identification and beyond. In: Proceedings of the IEEE/CVF International Conference on Computer Vision, pp. 3691–3701 (2019)
3. Hu, J., Shen, L., Sun, G.: Squeeze-and-excitation networks. In: Proceedings of the IEEE Conference on Computer Vision and Pattern Recognition, pp. 7132–7141 (2018)
4. Luo, H., et al.: A strong baseline and batch normalization neck for deep person re-identification. IEEE Trans. Multimed. **22**(10), 2597–2609 (2019)
5. Mazzeo, P.L., Libetta, C., Spagnolo, P., Distante, C.: A Siamese neural network for non-invasive baggage re-identification. J. Imaging **6**(11), 126 (2020)
6. Sun, Y., Zheng, L., Yang, Y., Tian, Q., Wang, S.: Beyond part models: person retrieval with refined part pooling (and a strong convolutional baseline). In: Ferrari, V., Hebert, M., Sminchisescu, C., Weiss, Y. (eds.) ECCV 2018. LNCS, vol. 11208, pp. 501–518. Springer, Cham (2018). https://doi.org/10.1007/978-3-030-01225-0_30
7. Vaswani, A., et al.: Attention is all you need. In: Advances in Neural Information Processing Systems, pp. 5998–6008 (2017)

8. Wang, G., Yuan, Y., Chen, X., Li, J., Zhou, X.: Learning discriminative features with multiple granularities for person re-identification. In: Proceedings of the 26th ACM International Conference on Multimedia, pp. 274–282 (2018)
9. Wang, G., Yuan, Y., Li, J., Ge, S., Zhou, X.: Receptive multi-granularity representation for person re-identification. IEEE Trans. Image Process. **29**, 6096–6109 (2020)
10. Wang, X., Girshick, R., Gupta, A., He, K.: Non-local neural networks. In: Proceedings of the IEEE Conference On Computer Vision and Pattern Recognition, pp. 7794–7803 (2018)
11. Woo, S., Park, J., Lee, J.-Y., Kweon, I.S.: CBAM: convolutional block attention module. In: Ferrari, V., Hebert, M., Sminchisescu, C., Weiss, Y. (eds.) ECCV 2018. LNCS, vol. 11211, pp. 3–19. Springer, Cham (2018). https://doi.org/10.1007/978-3-030-01234-2_1
12. Zhang, Z., Lan, C., Zeng, W., Jin, X., Chen, Z.: Relation-aware global attention for person re-identification. In: Proceedings of the IEEE/CVF Conference On Computer Vision and Pattern Recognition, pp. 3186–3195 (2020)
13. Zhang, Z., Li, D., Wu, J., Sun, Y., Zhang, L.: MVB: a large-scale dataset for baggage re-identification and merged Siamese networks (2019)
14. Zhong, Z., Zheng, L., Kang, G., Li, S., Yang, Y.: Random erasing data augmentation. In: Proceedings of the AAAI Conference on Artificial Intelligence, pp. 13001–13008 (2020)
15. Zhou, K., Yang, Y., Cavallaro, A., Xiang, T.: Omni-scale feature learning for person re-identification. In: Proceedings of the IEEE/CVF International Conference on Computer Vision, pp. 3702–3712 (2019)

Legal Judgement Prediction of Sentence Commutation with Multi-document Information

Yao Chi, Peng Zhang(✉), Fangye Wang, Tun Lu, and Ning Gu

School of Computer Science, Fudan University, Shanghai, China
{19210240168,zhangpeng,fywang18,lutun,ninggu}@fudan.edu.cn

Abstract. Legal judgment prediction is a task that automatically predicts the outcome of court judgments. The sentence prediction contained in it aims to predict the range of the sentence based on past textual information, providing reference comments for relevant departments. Since previous related researches mainly focused on criminal cases, they did not pay attention to penalty change activities, for example, commutation cases. The main difficulty is that the amount of direct information in commutation cases is less than that in criminal cases. Based on the actual process of commutation, this paper proposes a method of commutation prediction with multi-document information, by expanding the information in the commutation documents. We collect criminal documents related to commutation cases and integrate them into a knowledge base. Then, based on hierarchical attention networks for document classification, we design a multi-document commutation model with dynamic context vectors. Indirect information, such as criminal documents, can generate document vectors that are more relevant to specific commutation prediction tasks based on direct information, such as commutation documents. The experimental results prove that this method can combine the vector features of multiple documents to better predict the sentence of commutation.

Keywords: Legal judgment prediction · Sentence commutation prediction · Multi-document classification · Attention

1 Introduction

Sentence commutation is one of the activities of penalty execution changes. It is a litigation mechanism that is initiated by the criminal himself, the prison provides evidence of whether the criminal can be commuted, the procuratorial organ implements legal supervision and the people's court judges. As the final link of criminal proceedings, penalty execution bears the task of punishing, educating, and reforming criminals, and how its effectiveness is directly related to the realization of the ultimate goal of criminal proceedings [1].

Supported by National Key Research and Development Project (No. 2018YFC0832303).

Y. Sun et al. (Eds.): ChineseCSCW 2021, CCIS 1491, pp. 473–487, 2022.
https://doi.org/10.1007/978-981-19-4546-5_37

China has focused on the process of investigation, prosecution and trial while neglecting the execution for a long time, making the execution of penalty the weakest link in the construction of the legal system [1]. At the same time, there are certain structural flaws in the execution of penalties in China. Compared with the openness and transparency in the criminal trial process, the commutation trial adopts a more secret method in practice. The supervision of penalty enforcement authorities and courts have limited reference materials for judging penalty changes [2].

At present, judicial materials are usually in the form of text documents. Natural language processing has achieved remarkable results in the practice of the judicial field, and the main application is legal judgment prediction. The legal judgment prediction is based on the textual information described by the facts of the case and aims to predict the outcome of the judgment. Natural language processing models can assist in real legal judgments. Judges can use the results predicted by the model as a reference for judgments, which reduces the cost of judgments, improves fairness, and begins to serve as an important auxiliary tool for judicial judgments. However, the legal judgment prediction mainly focuses on the criminal cases, ignoring penalty change activities, for example, commutation cases. If we can collect and extract the data needed for penalty execution changes, and apply the natural language processing model to the sentence commutation prediction, the commutation prediction results given by the model can help improve the last link of criminal litigation and contribute to the construction of the legal system.

Compared with the more complete information on criminal trial documents, the content of current commutation trial documents is not sufficient. The documents which can be publicly obtained mostly are the "Commutation Criminal Verdict". They only mention the direct information when the penalty execution changed, that is, it only contains the crime, the original sentence, the previous changes of the sentence, and the performance of the reform. In the actual commutation trial process, according to the "Provisions on the Working Procedures for Prisons to Propose Commutations and Paroles", when the prison districts or sub-districts propose commutation, the main textual material that should be submitted is the "Commutation (Parole) Review Form", which does not only contain direct information such as crime, original sentence, the previous changes of sentence, the performance of the reform, as well indirect text information not mentioned in the "Commutation Criminal Verdict", such as the defendant's personal information and the criminal facts. At the same time, the main materials that the prison should submit to the court for commutation are the "Proposal for commutation" and the copy of the final judgments. "Proposal for commutation" has the same format and content as "Commutation Criminal Verdict", and they only contain direct information on commutation, while the final judgments attach indirect information. It can be seen that the commutation judgment should not only be based on the crime, the original sentence, the previous changes of the sentence, and the performance of the reform, but also on the criminal facts at the time, and more importantly, on specific legal provisions. This is a judicial process that combines multiple information. It is obvious that the amount of information is not sufficient to predict the commutation only through the document content of "Commutation Criminal Verdict". It is necessary to find the content of the relevant criminal document to provide sufficient information for predicting.

By studying the content of the "Commutation Criminal Verdict", we found that the case number of the original criminal judgment is generally mentioned, and the relevant specific criminal facts can be inquired through the case number, to obtain more specific and rich data information. The information obtained through the above process is multi-document text information, and the content of criminal documents related to commutation is indirect information, which itself does not serve for commutation. The amount of indirect information is larger than that of direct information, and it is complex. It is necessary to extract some of the most relevant information for the specific task of predicting the sentence of commutation to predict more accurately. In the actual process of commutation sentence, it also needs to extract indirect information related to the current commutation task, and combine it with direct information to better predict the sentence of commutation.

To sum up, a model that can effectively combine the key content of the commutation document, the criminal judgment document, and the legal provisions will be in line with the actual commutation trial process, and the commutation results obtained by the model will be more precise. The main contributions of the commutation prediction method with multi-document information are summarized as follows:

1. Extract the direct document information of the commutation document and the indirect document information of the related criminal document.
2. Design a commutation prediction model, based on the direct document information of the commutation document, use the attention mechanism to combine the indirect document information related to this specific commutation task in a many-to-one way.
3. The experimental results show that this method can improve the effect of commutation sentence prediction, which is more matched with the logic of commutation sentences in reality.

2 Related Work

Legal Judgment Prediction is a classic legal task in deep learning, which aims to predict the outcome of the judgment based on the facts of the case.

Most of the legal judgment prediction tasks in deep learning use the text classification model framework. In the abstract, the legal judgment prediction task is a classification task, what needs to be predicted is the result of judgment. The main focus is how to optimize the text classification model framework based on the specific task, we summarize two optimization methods in past research as follows.

Some research integrates multiple data sources, such as facts, defense requests, clauses, to optimize the interaction of data. Luo et al. [3] predict the charges for criminal cases based on the law articles, extract the representation vector of the crime facts through the article encoder, and input the criminal fact vector into the law article extractor to find the most relevant k law articles. However, the structure of the model only considers the crime facts and law articles and uses the attention mechanism to extract the information about the crime facts from law articles, and the data interaction is relatively simple. Long et al. [4] refer to the reading comprehension model architecture, and actually use the attention mechanism. They calculate the attention in pairs and selects useful factual text descriptions to produce more relevant plaintiffs' pleas and law articles, and then more accurately predict the binary classification problem of whether to accept the defense request. The model integrates the factual text information into the plaintiffs' pleas and law articles and adds more information to make the prediction more accurate. Although the model takes multiple crimes situation into account, it uses binary classification, and the number of combined document information is also less, and the data interaction is relatively simple.

Some research expands to multi-task and optimizes the interaction of multi-task. Zhong H et al. [5] propose that the subtasks of predicting legal articles, crimes, fines, and sentences are not independent. They transformed the dependency between these subtasks into a directed acyclic graph (DAG) and proposed a topology multi-task learning framework, TopJudge, which contains multiple subtasks and DAG dependencies for decision prediction. In fact, for a single task, it adds information about the results of other tasks, making the prediction more accurate. It can be seen that, compared to the method of calculating attention in pairs, the multi-task interaction model can make the prediction of the model more accurate through a more complex data interaction process.

In summary, it can be seen that the current mainstream legal judgment prediction model optimizes and improves the model by adding more information. Researchers can add information through the vector generation process in the model or can associate multiple tasks to add information through the whole process, these improvements are in line with the process of manual judgment, and have good model interpretability. However, the current legal judgment prediction tasks:

1. They merely predict criminal cases, which cannot meet the complex and diverse needs of court criminal justice activities. There are activities of penalty execution changes such as commutation and parole. At the same time, combined with the actual sentencing process, legal judgments such as commutation can also learn from the current research way of legal judgment prediction tasks, and combine more text information to predict the commutation sentence.
2. For the single-task prediction model, the number of document inputs is usually no less than 3, and most text information interactions use paired attention interaction mechanisms. Based on the actual process of commutation sentences, we combine multiple document information to have many-to-one attention interaction, to extract effective document information vectors.

Therefore, we propose a commutation prediction method that combines multi-document information. Firstly, jointly collect criminal documents related to commutation, and integrate them into a knowledge base containing commutation documents, criminal documents, and legal provisions. Secondly, based on the hierarchical attention network of document classification, we design a multi-document commutation prediction model. This model uses dynamic context vectors, referring to the actual process of commutation sentence, criminal documents and other indirect documents can generate the document vector that is more relevant to the specific task of commutation.

3 Prediction of Sentence Commutation Combined with Multi-document Information

The main innovations of the commutation sentence prediction method combined with multi-document information are as follows. We construct a new commutation sentence knowledge base, which not only contains the direct information of the commutation document but also contains the indirect information of the criminal document related to the commutation document, and extract it into multiple document information, including the crime (Crime), the previous changes of the sentence (Judge), the performance of the reform (Performance), the criminal facts at the time (Fact), specific legal provisions (Article). According to the actual process of commutation sentence, We use dynamic context vectors based on the hierarchical attention network of document classification, so that indirect document information can generate deeper vector representations based on direct document information, and effectively combine multiple documents to predict sentence of commutation.

3.1 Commutation Knowledge Base

The construction of the knowledge base for commutation is to search for public legal documents through the Tianyancha website. The ultimate source of legal documents from Tianyancha is the China Judgment Document website. "The Provisions of the Supreme People's Court on the Issuance of Judicial Documents on the Internet by the People's Courts" clarify that the Supreme Court has established the China Judgment Document website on the Internet to uniformly publish the effective judgment documents of the people's courts.

The construction process of the commutation knowledge base is shown in the Fig. 1:

Collect Related Documents. We collect the public "Commutation Criminal Verdict" as the direct document information source, and search for the corresponding original criminal judgment as the indirect information source of the documents.

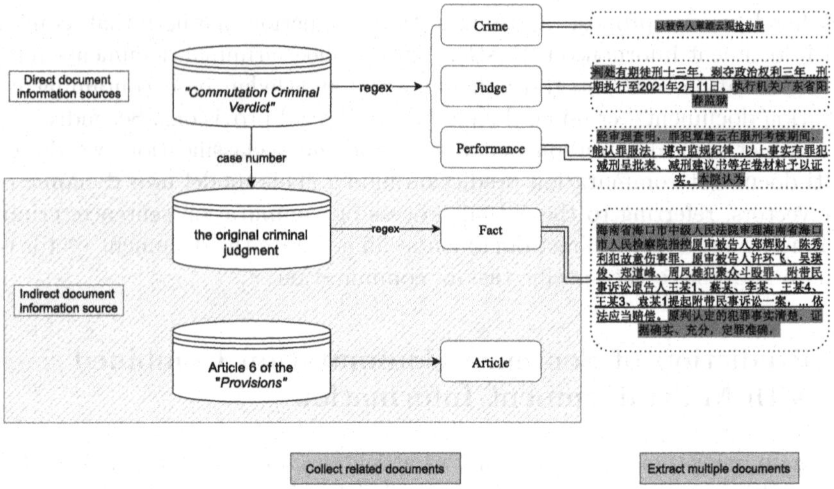

Fig. 1. Commutation knowledge base

The steps to collect related documents are as follows: obtain a public "Commutation Criminal Verdict" as a direct document information source; extract the case numbers of relevant criminal judgment through regular matching; search for the public original criminal judgment through case number, and use it as an indirect document information source.

Extract Multiple Documents. According to the main material submitted at the time of commutation -"Commutation (Parole) Review Form", comparing it with the content of the documents collected, the "Commutation Criminal Verdict" is extracted and divided into the crime (Crime), the original sentence (Judge), and the performance of the reform (Performance); the original criminal judgment can be extracted into the criminal facts (Fact); most of the "Commutation Criminal Verdict" only refer to Article 6 of the "Provisions of the Supreme People's Court on the Specific Application of Law in Handling Commutation and Parole Cases" which is the main basis for commutation sentence, and take this document as the legal basis (Article).

Since the document has a certain format, we can use regular expressions to extract the corresponding document by writing rules. Extract from the commutation document and the corresponding criminal judgment document to obtain the multi-document data required by the model. For example, the crime is generally referred to as "the defendant commits"; the original sentence generally starts with "sentence" and ends with "executive agency"; the performance of reform generally starts with "ascertained by trial, in the period of sentence evaluation the criminal" and ends with "this court thinks"; the criminal facts generally begin with "The People's Procuratorate charges" and the end with "the criminal facts ascertained by the original verdict".

3.2 The Multi-document Commutation Sentence Prediction Model

The main part of the multi-document commutation sentence prediction model is the Text Encoder, as shown in Fig. 2. There are three types of Text Encoders in this article, they are Static Text Encoder, Crime Encoder, and Dynamic Text Encoder. The function of the Text Encoder is to input the crime (Crime), the original sentence (Judge), the performance of the reform (Performance), the criminal facts (Fact), and the specific legal article (Article). The corresponding encoder generates the encoded document vector-d_{crime}, d_{judge}, $d_{performance}$, d_{fact}, $d_{article}$.

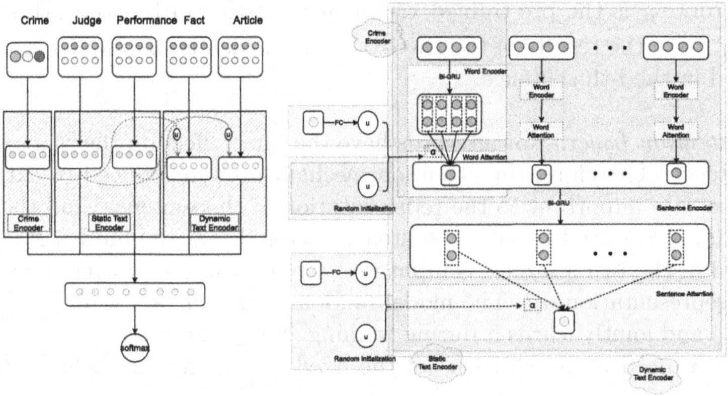

Fig. 2. Multi-document commutation sentence prediction model

Static Text Encoder. Static Text Encoder adopts the Hierarchical Attention Networks for Document Classification [6], shown as the orange part on the right side of Fig. 2. The Judge documents and Performance documents will be generated by the Static Text Encoder to generate the representation vector, in which the global level Context Vectors is used to select the informative words and sentences. Static Text Encoder consists of several layers: Word Encoder Layer; Word Attention Layer; Sentence Encoder Layer; Sentence Attention Layer.

The specific explanation of each part is as follows:

Suppose that a document has L sentences, $sentence_i$ represents the i-th sentence, the i-th sentence contains T_i words, and $word_{it}(i \in [1, L], t \in [1, T_i])$ represents the t-th word in the i-th sentence. Static Text Encoder can map the original textual document to the vector representation.

Word Encoder Layer. To preprocess the sentence, the embedding matrix can be used to convert the word into a word vector, and then the Bi-GRU layer can be used to obtain the contextual representation of the word. Among them, the encoding part can introduce BERT pre-training, so that the model can transfer and learn the information of other text, optimize the representation degree of some words, and further improve the accuracy of the model.

For the i-th sentence, the process of Word Encoder is expressed as follows:

$$x_{it} = W_{we} word_{it}, t \in [1, T_i] \tag{1}$$

$$\overrightarrow{h_{it}} = \overrightarrow{GRU}(x_{it}), t \in [1, T_i] \tag{2}$$

$$\overleftarrow{h_{it}} = \overleftarrow{GRU}(x_{it}), t \in [T_i, 1] \tag{3}$$

Among them, $word_{it}$ is the one-hot vector of the t-th word in the i-th sentence, the word length of the i-th sentence is T_i, and W_{we} represents the embedding vector. x_{it} is the pre-trained vector of the t-th word in the i-th sentence. $\overrightarrow{h_{it}}$ and $\overleftarrow{h_{it}}$ are the results of the Bi-GRU layer, which is the hidden state of the t-th word in the i-th sentence.

Word Attention Layer. Not all words have the same effect on the representation of a sentence. Therefore, the attention mechanism is introduced to extract the words that are important to the representation of the sentence, and these word vectors are aggregated to form a sentence vector. First, the hidden state of the t-th word in the i-th sentence is input into a fully connected layer to obtain the learned representation u_it. The model randomly initializes a word-level context vector μ_w and jointly learns it during training. The context vector μ_w is regarded as the "advanced representation" of the fixed query, that is, "which are useful words".

The specific process is expressed by the formula as follows:

$$u_{it} = tanh(W_{wa} h_{it} + b_{wa}) \tag{4}$$

$$\alpha = \frac{exp(u_{it}^T \mu_w)}{\sum_t exp(u_{it}^T \mu_w)} \tag{5}$$

$$s_i = \sum_{t=1}^{t=T_i} \alpha_{it} h_{it} \tag{6}$$

Among them, W_{wa} and b_{wa} are the weight parameters and bias parameters of the fully connected layer, respectively; h_{it}, mentioned in the Word Encoder section above, is the hidden state of the t-th word in the i-th sentence obtained by the bi-GRU layer; u_{it} represents the representation of the t-th word in the i-th sentence obtained by the fully connected layer. μ_w represents the word-level context vector, and α_{it} represents the weight of the t-th word in all T_i words in the i-th sentence. s_i represents the vector representation of the i-th sentence obtained by weighting and summing T_i word vectors in the i-th sentence.

Sentence Encoder Layer. Sentence Encoder Layer and Word Encoder Layer adopt a similar method. Taking the calculated representation vectors of L sentences as input to the Bi-GRU layer to obtain the context representation of each sentence. The specific process is expressed as follows:

$$\overrightarrow{h_l} = \overrightarrow{GRU}(s_i), i \in [1, L] \tag{7}$$

$$\overleftarrow{h_l} = \overleftarrow{GRU}(s_i), i \in [L, 1] \tag{8}$$

Among them, s_i is the vector representation of the i-th sentence calculated above; $\overrightarrow{h_l}$ and $\overleftarrow{h_l}$ are the results of the bidirectional GRU layer, representing the hidden state of the i-th sentence.

Sentence Attention Layer. Sentence Attention Layer and Word Attention Layer use similar methods. Firstly, through a fully connected layer, and then the model uses the sentence context vector u_s to calculate the weight of the i-th sentence in the document, and finally the document vector d is obtained, which sums up all the information of the sentence in the document.

The specific process is expressed by the formula as follows:

$$u_i = \tanh(W_{sa}h_i + b_{sa}) \tag{9}$$

$$\alpha_i = \frac{\exp(u_i^T \mu_s)}{\sum_t \exp(u_i^T \mu_s)} \tag{10}$$

$$d = \sum_{i=1}^{i=L} \alpha_{it} h_i \tag{11}$$

Among them, W_{sa} and b_{sa} are the weight parameters and bias parameters of the fully connected layer, respectively; h_i, mentioned in the Sentence Encoder section above, is the hidden state of the i-th sentence obtained by the bi-GRU layer; u_i represents the vector representation of the i-th sentence obtained by a fully connected layer. μ_s represents the sentence-level context vector, and α_i represents the weight of the i-th sentence in all L sentences in the entire document. d represents the document vector representation by weighting and summing all L sentence vectors of the entire document.

d_{judge} and $d_{performance}$ are the document vectors generated by the above Static Text Encoder, representing the Judge documents and the Performance documents.

Crime Encoder. Crime Encoder shown as the purple part on the right side of Fig. 2. The crime is a limited and discrete entity data. The model treats a crime as a word, and also uses a one-hot vector to represent the crime. We learn from the text encoder to encode the crime into a vector form and input it into the Crime Encoder. Crime Encoder draws on the word-level structure of the Hierarchical Attention Networks for Document Classification [6], and the sentence-level encoding result represents the Crime vector d_{crime}.

Dynamic Text Encoder. The Dynamic Text Encoder which encodes the Fact and Article also draws on the Hierarchical Attention Networks for Document Classification [6], shown as the yellow part on the right side of Fig. 2. However, due to the Indirectness of the Fact document and Article document. For the specific task of predicting the commutation sentence, only part of the text information can play a key role. It can refer to Crime, Judge, Performance documents that are more related to this specific task to extract key information from the Fact and Article.

To effectively combine the related information of all documents and realize multi-document learning, the Dynamic Text Encoder adopts a special process: receiving the encoding results of Crime, Judge, Performance, relying on the dynamic context vectors of the modified HAN model, embedded in the Fact and Article encoding to get the vector which is specialized for the specific task of commutation.

Transform the context vectors μ_w and μ_s in the Static Text Encoder. They are not randomly initialized during training but are represented by the vectors of the relevant source documents, which are learned through training by a fully connected layer. The abstract dynamic context vector generation process is formulated as follows:

$$\mu_w = W_w d + b_w \tag{12}$$

$$\mu_s = W_s d + b_s \tag{13}$$

Among them, d represents the source document encoded vector that needs to be referred to, μ_w and μ_s represent the context vector at the word and sentence level respectively; W_w and b_w are the weight parameter and the bias parameter of the fully connected layer at the word level, respectively; W_s and b_s are the weight parameter and the bias parameter of the fully connected layer at the sentence level, respectively.

In practice, extracting Fact related information generally needs to be combined with Crime's key information to get more accurate information, so the context vectors of Fact require Crime's representation vector d_crime; In practice, the relevant information of Articles generally needs to be combined with the key information of Judge and Performance. Therefore, The context vectors of the Article need Judge's representation vector d_{judge} and Performance's representation vector $d_{performance}$.

The specific formula of the context vector combined with other document information is as follows:

$$u_{w_{fact}} = W_{wa} d_{crime} + b_{wa} \tag{14}$$

$$u_{s_{fact}} = W_{sa} d_{crime} + b_{sa} \tag{15}$$

$$u_{w_{article}} = W_{wa_1} d_{judge} + W_{wa_2} d_{performance} + b_{wa} \tag{16}$$

$$u_{s_{article}} = W_{sa_1} d_{judge} + W_{wa_2} d_{performance} + b_{sa} \tag{17}$$

Among them, d_{crime}, d_{judge}, and $d_{performance}$ are the document encoded vectors of the Crime document, the Judge document, the Performance document obtained by the Static Text Encoder. $\mu_{w_{fact}}$ and $\mu_{w_{article}}$ are the word-level context vectors of the Crime document and the Article document, respectively; $u_{s_{fact}}$ and $u_{s_{article}}$ are the sentence-level context vectors of the Crime document and the Article document, respectively.

The context vectors of the Fact and the Article in the Dynamic Text Encoder are not directly initialized randomly but learned through the combination of the Crime, the Judge, and the Performance. The model can correlate and extract criminal facts and article information, and generate document encoded vectors that are more relevant to the commutation task-d_{fact}, $d_{article}$.

The Distribution of Sentence Commutation. Finally, these encoded document vectors d are concatenated, and a SoftMax classifier is used to predict the distribution of sentence commutation.

$$d = concat(d_{crime}, d_{judge}, d_{performance}, d_{fact}, d_{article}) \quad (18)$$

$$p = softmax(W_c d + b_c) \quad (19)$$

Among them, $d.$ represents the encoded vector obtained by the Text Encoder, d represents the multi-document vector needed to predict the commutation of sentence, and W_c and b_c are the weight parameters and bias parameters of the fully connected layer.

Using Categorical Cross-Entropy as the training loss:

$$CE(x) = -\sum_{i=1}^{C} y_i \log f_i(x) \quad (20)$$

Among them, x represents the input sample, C is the total number of commutation categories to be classified, y_i is the real commutation label of the i-th data, and $log f_i(x)$ is the predicted commutation label of the i-th data. By minimizing the Categorical Cross-Entropy Loss and training the model parameters, a model can predict the distribution of the sentence commutation.

4 Experiment and Analysis

4.1 DataSet

In order to verify the effectiveness of the commutation prediction method with multi-document information, multiple sets of comparisons are set up on the commutation knowledge database.

We have collected 19,571 original "Commutation Criminal Verdict", including 8,663 original criminal judgments. After regular matching, the Crime, Judge, Performance, Fact were extracted, 19,253 pieces of direct information on commutation were screened out, of which 7,336 pieces of indirect information on commutation were included. After data cleaning, blank and invalid data were deleted, and 18,953 pieces of direct information data and 8,663 pieces of indirect data were obtained.

The division of labels is shown in the following table. The data is divided into four categories, namely, sentence commutation of fewer than 3 months, sentence commutation of 4–7 months, sentence commutation of 8–12 months, and special. According to the approximate ratio of 9:1, the experimental data set is divided into the training set and validation set, as shown in the following Table 1.

Table 1. DataSet

Label	Total	Training set	Validation set
Low (0–3)	2439	2199	240
Middle (4–7)	10499	9431	1068
High (8–12)	4321	3889	432
Special	1694	1539	155
	18953	17058	1895

4.2 Benchmark Models

The TextCNN model applies the convolutional neural network to natural language processing and inputs the vector representation of the text into the convolutional neural network to extract deeper representations. It is a classic text classification model and is used in classification tasks in legal judgment prediction, and gets excellent results. We use the model parameters of [7].

The DPCNN model [8] also uses the convolutional neural network model to deepen the number of CNN layers and extract deeper representations.

The TextRNN model uses neural recurrent networks to solve the text classification problem, adopts the architecture of the literature [9], uses bidirectional LSTM to encode the text representation, and obtains a deeper representation of the text.

The ATT-TextRNN model [10] introduces an attention mechanism based on the TextRNN model, adds an Attention layer to the bidirectional LSTM layer, learns a weighted text representation vector, and encodes a deeper representation.

The ATT-RCNN model [11] flexibly combines the advantages of CNN and RNN, adding a pooling layer to the two-way LSTM layer to learn a deeper semantic representation.

The Transformer model [12] uses Transformer's encoder to encode text. The encoder uses a multi-head attention mechanism to encode a deeper representation.

4.3 Parameter Settings

For the experimental control models, since their design is for a single document, we spliced multi-document data into a single document and input it into these models. Except for the parameter settings mentioned in Sect. 4.3, the other parameters of all models are shown in the Table 2.

Table 2. Parameters table

Parameter	Value
Optimizer	Adam
Batch size	128
Dropout	0,5
Learning rate	0.001 (exponential decay, gamma = 0.9)
Pad size	32
Size of filters	2,3,4
Number of filters	256
Number of hidden state	128

Our model (Dynamic-HANConcat) counts the distribution of Crimes and finds that most of the data has only one crime, and the length of 3 crimes can cover most of the data, so the vector number of crimes is set to 3; respectively count the sentence length and word length of the Judge, Performance and Fact documents, sort the lengths from small to large, and take the length occupying 80% as the length of the document vector of the model. The sentence length of the Judge documents is 5 and the word length is 10; the sentence length of the Performance documents is 6 and the word length is 10; the sentence length of the Fact documents is 8 and the word length is 33.

4.4 Evaluation

We use sklearn classification evaluation report indicators: Accuracy, Precision calculated using macro average, Recall, and F1 value as evaluation indicators.

4.5 Analysis of Results

To verify the effectiveness of this method on the knowledge database dataset, Our model (Dynamic-HANConcat) is compared with the existing 6 benchmark models. The experimental results are shown in the Table 3.

As can be seen from the Table 3, the four indicators of our model, Dynamic-HANConcat, exceed all benchmark models. In addition to our model, the model with excellent classification performance is TextRCNN. Compared with this model, the Accuracy, Macro Precision, Macro Recall, and Macro F1 of Dynamic-HANConcat have increased by 4.30%, 10.56%, 8.75%, 9.04%, respectively. The experimental results show that our method has obvious advantages in the task of predicting sentence commutation.

Table 3. Experimental results

Model	Accuracy/%	Macro_Precision/%	Macro_Recall/%	Macro_F1/%
TextCNN	65.91	60.11	52.01	54.97
DPCNN	64.8	61.32	52.56	54.94
TextRNN	64.17	58.19	49.53	52.41
TextRCNN	67.39	62.86	51.85	55.45
Att-TextRNN	66.33	62.77	52.55	55.8
Transformer	62.11	55.26	48.78	51.04
Dynamic-HANConcat	70.29	69.5	56.39	60.46

Classification Performance Analysis of Each Commutation Category. To prove that our model, Dynamic-HANConcat, can effectively improve the classification performance of a single commutation category, Dynamic-HANConcat and the best-performing TextRCNN in the benchmark models are compared in each category. We use Precision, Recall, and F1 as the evaluation indicators. The results are shown in the Fig. 3.

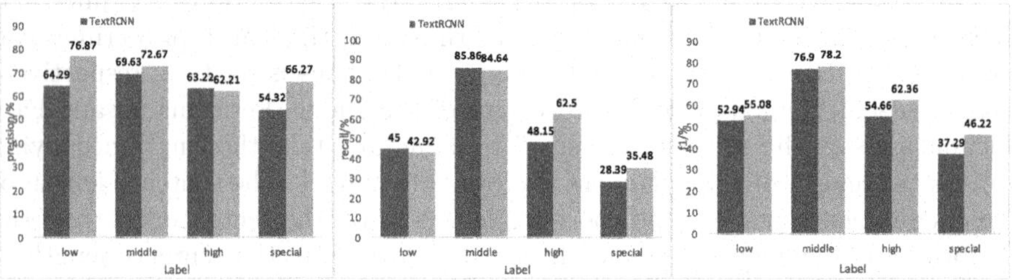

Fig. 3. Comparison of each commutation category

It can be seen that the Precision of Dynamic-HANConcat is higher than that of TextRCNN, except that the category of high. And the category of low is much higher than TextRCNN. At the same time, in terms of the Recall, our model is higher than TextRCNN except for low and medium categories. And the category of high is much higher than TextRCNN. Our model improves the Precision of the low commutation category, but slightly loses the Recall, and improves the Recall of the high commutation category, but slightly loses the Precision. Due to the task of predicting the sentence commutation, Precision is more important in practice. Our model mainly improves the Precision of each category, which proves that the model is more accurate and effective in practice. It can also be seen from the F1 value that the Dynamic-HANConcat model has a certain improvement in each category compared with the TextRCNN model.

5 Summary

Aiming at the task of sentence commutation, we propose a method of predicting the sentence of commutation combined with multi-document information.

We not only collect and construct a commutation knowledge base but also construct a multi-document classification model that conforms to the actual commutation process. The experimental results show that our model, compared with other benchmark models, has a certain improvement, and can provide related personnel with suggestions for the sentence of commutation. Our method may have some limitations and shortcomings. Pre-training is not added in the experiment so that our model can't obtain certain language knowledge before training. There is no structured semantic analysis in our model, it may just learns the shallow language representation. At present, the transfer of knowledge in the same or different fields is a hot and difficult point in legal judgment prediction. In the next step, we want to carry out research on the transfer of legal knowledge and combine the knowledge graph or other methods to optimize the method of prediction, so that the method is more in line with the actual judging process.

References

1. Yang, G.Z.: Lun JianXing JiaShi JianDu [On the Supervision of Commutation and Parole]. Zhongguo xingshifa zazhi (5), 80–85 (1999)
2. Cheng, Y.S.: ZhongGuo JianXing, JiaShi Chengxu Zhi Tantao [Review of China's commutation and parole procedures]. FaShang Yanjiu (2), 32–40 (2007)
3. Luo, B., Feng, Y., Xu, J., et al.: Learning to predict charges for criminal cases with legal basis. arXiv preprint arXiv:1707.09168 (2017)
4. Long, S., Tu, C., Liu, Z., Sun, M.: Automatic judgment prediction via legal reading comprehension. In: Sun, M., Huang, X., Ji, H., Liu, Z., Liu, Y. (eds.) CCL 2019. LNCS (LNAI), vol. 11856, pp. 558–572. Springer, Cham (2019). https://doi.org/10.1007/978-3-030-32381-3_45
5. Zhong, H., et al.: Legal judgment prediction via topological learning. In: Proceedings of the 2018 Conference on Empirical Methods in Natural Language Processing (2018)
6. Yang, Z., et al.: Hierarchical attention networks for document classification. In: Proceedings of the 2016 Conference of the North American chapter of the Association for Computational Linguistics: Human Language Technologies (2016)
7. Kim, Y.: Convolutional Neural Networks for Sentence Classification. Eprint Arxiv (2014)
8. Johnson, R., Zhang, T.: Deep pyramid convolutional neural networks for text categorization. In: Proceedings of the 55th Annual Meeting of the Association for Computational Linguistics (Volume 1: Long Papers), pp. 562–570 (2017)
9. Liu, P., Qiu, X., Huang, X.: Recurrent neural network for text classification with multi-task learning. arXiv preprint arXiv:1605.05101 (2016)
10. Zhou, P., et al.: Attention-based bidirectional long short-term memory networks for relation classification. In: Proceedings of the 54th Annual Meeting of the Association for Computational Linguistics (Volume 2: Short Papers) (2016)
11. Lai, S., Xu, L., Liu, K., et al.: Recurrent convolutional neural networks for text classification. In: Proceedings of the AAAI Conference on Artificial Intelligence, vol. 29, no. 1 (2015)
12. Vaswani, A., Shazeer, N., Parmar, N., et al.: Attention is all you need. arXiv preprint arXiv:1706.03762 (2017)

Understanding Expert Knowledge for Chinese Essay Grading

Xiaoyue Liu[1], Yi Xie[1,2], Tao Yang[1], and Yuqing Sun[1,3](✉)

[1] School of Software, Shandong University, Jinan, China
sun_yuqing@sdu.edu.cn
[2] School of Computer Science and Technology, Shandong University, Qingdao, China
[3] Engineering Research Center of Digital Media Technology, Ministry of Education, Shandong University, Jinan, China

Abstract. Essay grading is an important issue in natural language processing. There are two challenges for Chinese essay grading, namely the subjectivity of expert grading standards and the lack of fine-grained labeled data. In this paper, we propose an automatic Chinese essay grading method based on multi-aspect expert knowledge. We introduce essay grading expert rules to turn the existing standards into indexes, such as 'The Essay Grading Standards for College Entrance Examination' and 'The Chinese Curriculum Standards for Compulsory Education'. Based on the expert rules, we propose different encoders to learn multiple essay features in three aspects, namely the topic consistency, structure rationality and linguistics proficiency. An essay is graded by unifying the three grades in different aspects. Experimental results on two real datasets show the effectiveness of our method. We also analysis the influence of each aspect on the essay grading results. The experiment on the material essay grading dataset shows the practicability of our model in general exam scenarios.

Keywords: Essay grading · Multiple aspects · Expert knowledge

1 Introduction

Essays are the logical organization of texts based on fixed topics and the students' ideas. Compared with manual essay grading, many existing automated essay grading models have the advantages of low cost, high efficiency, systematic and unified grading standards, and freedom from the subjectivity of evaluation experts. Therefore, educational institutions gradually introduce automated essay grading models to replace part or all of the manual grading in some essay examination scenarios.

Chinese essay grading has specific challenges compared to traditional English essay grading tasks. The first challenge is the subjectivity of expert grading standards. Existing expert standards for Chinese essay grading are mainly divided into two types: the first type is the instructional standards in the teaching scenarios, such as 'The Chinese Curriculum Standards for Compulsory Education' [1], which are focus on cultivating the writing abilities of students with different cognitive levels in different education grades;

Y. Sun et al. (Eds.): ChineseCSCW 2021, CCIS 1491, pp. 488–501, 2022.
https://doi.org/10.1007/978-981-19-4546-5_38

another type is the instructional standards for essay evaluation experts in the examination scenarios, such as 'The Essay Grading Standards for College Entrance Examination' [2]. In the above two kinds of standards, teachers are instructed to grade essays by combining the standards with their own subjective judgements, such as 'A low grade essay always be far off the point, a normal grade essay should keep to the point, while a high-grade essay's point should be profound'. However, it difficult for experts to quantify essays in a uniform way according to such standards.

Another challenge is the lack of fine-grained labeled datasets. Existing Chinese essay grading datasets always contain essay texts and overall grades for full marked or excellent essays, lack of essays with various grades in different cognitive levels. Some datasets have the topic or category labels of essays, while few datasets have the grading comments given by experts. It is difficult for automated essay grading models to learn interpretability features from multiple aspects of essays.

To tackle the above challenges, we propose a Chinese essay grading method based on multi-aspect expert knowledge. The contributions of this paper are listed below:

(1) We introduce Chinese essay grading expert rules that integrates existing expert standards. The multi-aspect expert knowledge is proposed to grade the topic consistency, structure rationality and linguistics proficiency.
(2) We propose the joint multi-aspect essay feature encoders based on pre-trained language models. The encoders are adopted to represent the essay topic, structure, and linguistics, respectively. The multi-aspect essay grades are calculated based on these representations.
(3) We combine the multi-aspect essay grades with the attention mechanism [20], and integrate them into an overall grade for each essay.
(4) The method is verified against real datasets and the experimental results show that it outperforms other methods on the Chinese essay grading task. We also analysis the influence of each aspect on the essay grading results. The experiment on the material essay grading dataset shows the practicability of our model in general exam scenarios.

The rest of this paper is organized as follows. Section 2 presents the related works. Section 3 introduces existing expert essay grading standards and the datasets. Section 4 presents the Chinese essay grading method based on multi-aspect expert knowledge. Section 5 evaluates our model on real datasets. We conclude our paper in Sect. 6.

2 Related Work

The classical automatic essay grading works mainly use machine learning methods to analyze the intrinsic essay features and predict the English essay grades. in 1966, Ellis Page [3] developed the first automatic essay grading system, which uses surface features such as the number of words in the essay to make judgments, and does not involve the semantic part of the essay. It can perform batch review, which greatly improves the efficiency of essay grading. In the 1990s, the essay grading system added features such as vocabulary, grammar, syntax, and semantic similarity to the essay content, such as

Intelligent Essay Assessor [4] and Electronic Essay Rater [5] etc. In recent years, machine learning has been gradually applied to essay grading tasks. In 2006, Rudner developed a essay grading system IntelliMetricTM [6], which extracting features from multiple aspects such as grammar, syntax, text content, etc., greatly improves the consistency with manual review, and can review essays in multiple languages. Some works use the Naive Bayes method to merge the nearest neighbor classification and other statistical methods to convert the essay scoring problem into a text classification problem, such as [7–9] etc.

Recently, many essay grading works adopt deep learning methods. Dasgupta et al. [10] chose to consider the representation vectors of words and sentences, and use the convolutional neural network of the attention-pooling mechanism on the word vectors to extract the internal relationship between the essay contents. Dong et al. [11] construct a hierarchical convolutional neural network review model to examine essay sentence structure and article structure. Wang et al. [12] used an enhanced model framework combined with the second weighted Kappa coefficient to review the essay. Tay et al. [13] proposed an improved model for the LSTM structure. By modeling the hidden state at different time steps, they improved the memory problem that exists when using recurrent neural networks such as RNN and LSTM to process long texts. Alikaniotis et al. [14] mainly consider the influence of vocabulary in the essay. They generate special word representations by learning the contribution of specific vocabulary to the essay score, thereby improving the effect of the model. Jin et al. [15] proposed a two-stage deep neural network model. The first stage uses data under non-current topics to train a shallow model, and the second stage is an end-to-end model for scoring.

However, the current related works mainly focuses on English essays. The study of Chinese essay grading tools has theoretical significance and application value for in-depth exploration.

3 Quantifying Expert Knowledge for Essay Grading

3.1 The Expert Standards for Essay Grading

We first present a few existing expert standards for essay grading. In practice, there are a few standards for professionals to grade essay, which represent the expert knowledge on essays. We choose two authoritative standards: (1) "The Chinese Curriculum Standards for Compulsory Education" officially issued by the Ministry of Education in 2018. This framework is to guide cultivating the writing ability of students in primary and middle school. We list some key points in Table 1. (2) "The Essay Grading Standards for College Entrance Examination" officially issued by the Examination Institute. We list some key points in Table 2.

3.2 The Proposed Metrics Based on Expert Standards

In this Section, we propose a set of quantified metrics based on these standards that cover three aspects of topic, structure, and linguistics. Based on the above authoritative standards on essay grading, we propose the unified metrics that cover three aspects of an essay:

Table 1. Some key points of The Chinese Curriculum Standards for Compulsory Education.

Student grade	Education goals
1–2	• Cultivate interest in writing and observation skills
3–4	• Cultivate interest in writing • Able to communicate in short letters and notes • Accumulate and use language materials, use novel words and sentences
5–6	• Able to write simple documentary essays and imaginative essays, with specific content and sincere emotions • Able to segment reasonably on demand • Fluent sentences, correct writing
7–9	• Use reasonable expressions according to needs. Reasonably arrange the order and details of content, and express your meaning clearly. Enrich the content using association and imagination • Enrich content in narrative writing; clear in expository writing; well-founded in argumentative writing; able to do practical writing according to daily needs

Table 2. Some key points of The Chinese essay grading standards for 2019 college entrance examination.

Basic level	Advanced level
Fit the topic	The topic is profound; Going deep into essence through phenomena, revealing the inner relations of things; the viewpoints are enlightening
Fit the essay type requirements	The essay is rich in content. The argument is substantial, vivid and connotative
Sincere emotions, healthy thoughts, fluent language and intact structure	The essay is full of literary talent. It is appropriate in expression, flexible in sentence structure, good at using rhetorical skills, expressive in sentences
Rich in content and clear topic	The essay is innovative. The viewpoints and examples are novel, the ideas are new and clever, the reasonings and imaginations are unique

(1) Linguistics proficiency. It considers the fluency and rationality of sentences in an essay. It reflects whether the writing follows the usual usage of language. This metric can be quantified on different levels, namely sentence level and document level.
(2) Topic consistency. It judges whether the essay is related to the given topic and whether there is always only one definite topic.
(3) Structure rationality. It reflects the author's logical thinking and the ability to organize materials. Taking argumentative essays as example, its common structure is to

give the argument at the beginning, gradually introduce materials and examples to prove the argument, and summarize at the end.

3.3 The Dataset of Essay Grading on Primary and Middle School

The existing essay grading datasets have some shortcomings. Many publicly available Chinese essay datasets only include excellent essays, and lack of those at different levels. In addition, these datasets usually only include attributes such as essay score and topic, lack of diversified attributes such as essay classification and student grade, which are helpful for grading essay. We address these by crawling the essays with multiple attributes from http://www.leleketang.com/zuowen/ to generate the dataset of essay grading on **p**rimary **a**nd **m**iddle school (PAM for short).

We collected essay data from grade 1 to grade 12. The metadata crawled includes: the title; the essay content; the essay classification, which is used to describe the style and content of the essay, and can represent the topic to a certain extent, such as narration, writing of people, writing of scenery and so on; the student grade; excellent words and sentences; the essay grade, including four grades of excellent, good, medium and poor. In order to ensure the uniformity of the essay grade in the dataset, we refer to the mapping method proposed by [16]. This method regards the student grade as the essay grade if the essay is marked medium, adds one to the student grade as the essay grade if the essay is marked good, and adds two if marked excellent, as shown in Fig. 1(a). The distribution of essays in each grade after the mapping method is shown in Fig. 1(b).

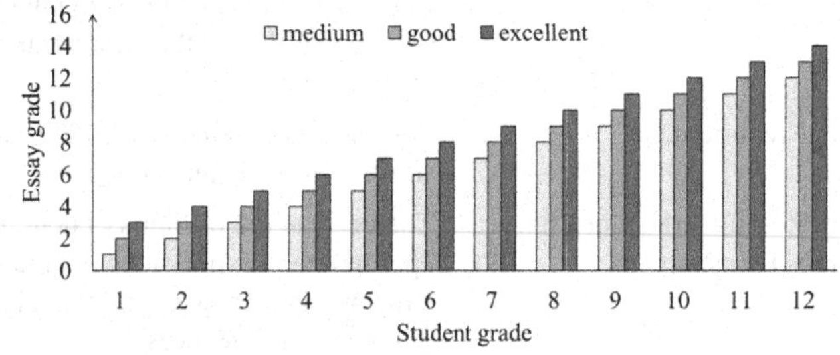

(a) Mapping relationship between student grades and essay grades.

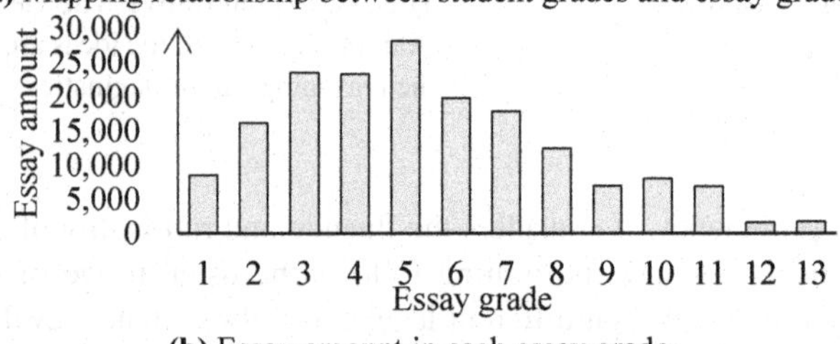

(b) Essay amount in each essay grade.

Fig. 1. PAM dataset statistics.

3.4 Linguistics Indexes and Topic Features for Essay Grading

We adopt linguistics indexes to grade essays in the linguistics aspect. We first analyze the correlation between each index and the essay grade. Then we select several indexes from the candidates as the essay grading features in the linguistics aspect, which are more correlated with the essay grades. The candidate linguistic indexes are introduced from L2SAC [17], as shown in Table 3. Different from the grading object in [17], the research subject in this paper is Chinese essay, therefore, some index definitions are different from the original meanings, such as T-unit [18].

Table 3. Linguistics index definitions and calculation methods.

Index	Definition	Calculation method
Sent	Sentence number	The sentence number in an essay
Clause	Clause number	The clause number in an essay
MLS (MLT)	Average sentence length at word level	Word/sentence number
MLC	Average clause length at word level	Word/T-unit number
C/S (T/S)	Average clause number in sentences	Clause/sentence number
CT/T	Average T-unit complexity in T-units	T-unit complexity/number
CN/C	Average compound noun number in clauses	Compound noun/clause number
VP/T	Average verb number in T-units	Verb/T-unit number
MLCC	Average clause length at character level	Character/clause number
MLSC (MLTC)	Average sentence length at character level	Character/sentence number

Table 4. Performance comparison of different essay grading models on PAM dataset.

Model	QWK	SCC	PCC
ATT + CNN + Bi-LSTM (Ours)	**0.7503**	**0.7324**	**0.7742**
ATT + CNN + GRU	0.6379	0.6319	0.6691
ATT + Bi-LSTM	0.7199	0.7068	0.7445
CNN + Bi-LSTM	0.5095	0.5952	0.6216
ATT + CNN	0.6419	0.6341	0.6825
Bi-LSTM	0.7120	0.6972	0.6972
Bert	0.6152	0.6506	0.6629

We calculate the above indexes on the PAM dataset, and verify the Pearson, Spearman and Kendall correlation coefficients [19] between the index values and essay grades, respectively. The results are shown in Fig. 2.

Table 5. Performance comparison of different essay grading models on EGC dataset.

Model	QWK	SCC	PCC
ATT + CNN + Bi-LSTM (Ours)	**0.6339**	**0.6265**	0.6606
ATT + CNN + GRU	0.6265	0.5151	**0.6817**
ATT + Bi-LSTM	0.6067	0.5122	0.6675
CNN + Bi-LSTM	0.6129	0.4649	0.6510
Bi-LSTM	0.6042	0.4820	0.6586

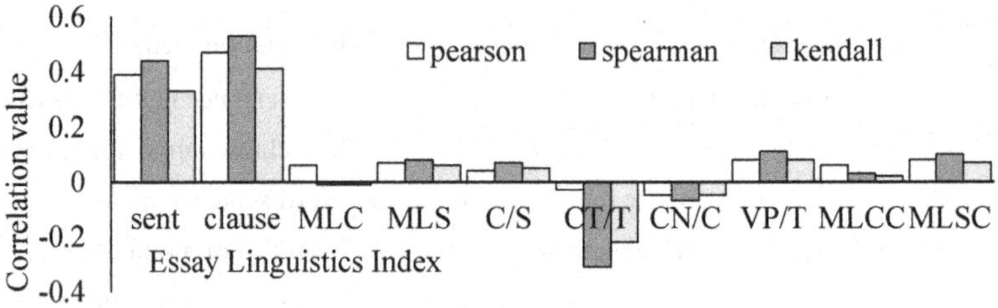

Fig. 2. Correlation coefficients between linguistics indexes and grades in PAM dataset.

Then we choose the indexes with high correlation coefficients and consistent positive and negative values as the indexes of the quantification method, including sent, clause, MLS, CT/T and MLSC. The calculation formula is:

$$\hat{y}_{e_i} = \alpha_1 sent + \alpha_2 clause + \alpha_3 MLS + \alpha_4 (CT/T) + \alpha_5 MLSC \quad (1)$$

Among them, $\hat{y}_{e_i}$ is the quantitative score calculated using multiple indexes. α is the weight corresponding to each index, equals to its corresponding Spearman correlation coefficient. In detail, $\alpha_1 = 0.448$, $\alpha_2 = 0.534$, $\alpha_3 = 0.102$, $\alpha_4 = -0.315$, $\alpha_5 = 0.114$.

Considering the essay grading in topic aspect, we train a neural network model to predicate the grades based on the topic features, as shown in Fig. 3. In order to obtain the vector representing the topic features of the essay, we use the LDA topic model to train the distribution of the essay in the implicit topic space, and use the distribution as the input of the neural network model, and finally gets the topic score of the essay after activation of the ReLU function.

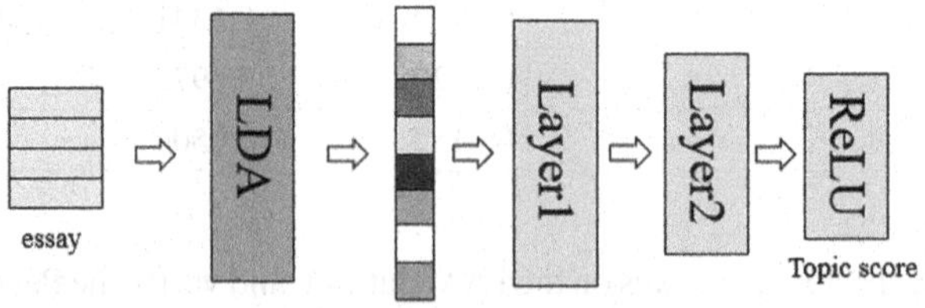

Fig. 3. Topic aspect features based essay grading model.

When the number of labeled essay is limited, we can use the linguistics indexes and topic model mentioned above to calculate the score of the unlabeled essay, thus obtain more labeled data for training the multi-aspect essay grading model, which we will introduce next.

4 The Chinese Essay Grading Method Based on Expert Knowledge

We propose a grading model based on the metrics mentioned in Sect. 3.2, shown in Fig. 4, which is divided into three parts: topic, structure, and linguistics, represented by the yellow, orange and green parts respectively. We will introduce them in detail in the following.

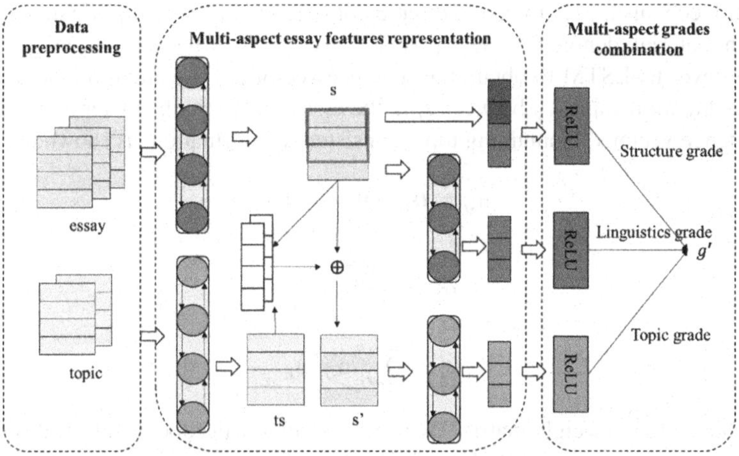

Fig. 4. The essay grading model based on multi-aspect expert knowledge.

4.1 The Topic Part of Essay Grading Model

Considering that the pretrained word vector contains abundant semantic and syntactic information, which is beneficial to the model. We introduce the pretrained vector to generate the lookup table $W^{|V|\times d}$ in the embedding layer of the sentence encoder, where |V| is the size of vocabulary V, d is the embedding dimension. The input is an essay $x = s_1, s_2, \ldots, s_{n_{sent}}$, where s_i represents the i-th sentence of the essay, n_{sent} is the number of sentences. s_i can be represented as a sequence of word embeddings $\boldsymbol{e}_1, \boldsymbol{e}_2, \ldots, \boldsymbol{e}_{n_{word}}$, where $\boldsymbol{e}_k$ represents the embedding of the k-th word in the sentence, n_{word} is the number of words in s_i.

We use the bidirectional long and short-term memory network (Bi-LSTM [20]) as the text encoder, obtain the sentence and document vectors constructing the sentence-level and document-level Bi-LSTM respectively. The word sequence passed through the embedding layer, enters a forward and a backward LSTM layer respectively to obtain hidden states $\overrightarrow{\boldsymbol{h}}_i$ and $\overleftarrow{\boldsymbol{h}}_i$. Combine them to get the hidden state $\boldsymbol{h}_i$ of the i-th word in the sentence. For the j-th sentence, we use the hidden state $\boldsymbol{h}^j_{last}$ of the last word in the sentence as the sentence vector, denoted as $\boldsymbol{s}_j$,s shown in formulas (2–4).

$$\boldsymbol{h}^i_j = \overline{LSTM}\ (\boldsymbol{h}^j_{i-1}, e^j_i) \tag{2}$$

$$\boldsymbol{h}^i_j = LSTM\,(\boldsymbol{h}^j_{i-1}, e^j_i) \tag{3}$$

$$s_j = \boldsymbol{h}^j_{last} = \overrightarrow{h}^j_{last} \cdot \overleftarrow{h}^j_{last} \tag{4}$$

In many cases, based on a given text material, students should choose a topic within the scope of the material and write an essay developed closely around the topic. We adopt attention mechanism [21] to take the topic consistency into account. First, we process the given material, denoted as t $= ts_1, ts_2, \ldots, ts_{n_{sent}}, ts_j = w_1, w_2, \ldots, w_{n_{word}}$. We use sentence-level Bi-LSTM to obtain the sentence vector $\boldsymbol{ts}_j$, use attention mechanism to calculate attention value w_{ij} between $\boldsymbol{s}_i$ in the essay and $\boldsymbol{ts}_j$ in the material, finally get a new sentence vector $\boldsymbol{s'}_i$ containing topic consistency information, as shown in (5)–(7).

$$w_{ij} = \boldsymbol{ts}_j \cdot (\boldsymbol{W}_t \cdot \boldsymbol{s}_i + b) \tag{5}$$

$$\alpha_{ij} = \frac{\exp(w_{ij})}{\sum_{k=1}^{n} w_{ik}} \tag{6}$$

$$s'_i = \sum\nolimits_i^n \alpha_{ij} \cdot s_i \tag{7}$$

In which, $\boldsymbol{W}_t$ is a weight matrix. We use $\boldsymbol{s'}_i$ as input to the document-level Bi-LSTM, obtain the essay vector $\boldsymbol{d}$, use $ReLU$ to predict the topic consistency score at the document level, as shown in (8):

$$g_t = ReLU(\boldsymbol{d}) \tag{8}$$

4.2 The Structure Part of Easy Model

The structure of an excellent essay should be clear and structured, especially argumentative essay, which should be able to put forward and gradually prove their point of view. Inspired by the paper [22], we use convolutional neural network (CNN) to extract the structure rationality on sentence level. Let $\boldsymbol{s}_i \in \mathbb{R}^{k_{sent}}$ denote each sentence embedding of the essay. All the embeddings are concatenated together to generate a 2D tensor $\boldsymbol{s}_{1:n_{sent}}$ of shape $n_{sent} \times k_{sent}$, n_{sent} denotes the number of sentences in the essay. We select different convolution kernel size $n_{ks} \in \{2, 3, 7\}$, use $\boldsymbol{W}_{ks} \in \mathbb{R}^{n_{ks} \times k_{sent}}$ denotes convolution kernel. The convolution formula is shown in (9):

$$c^j_i = f_i\left(\mathbf{W}^j_{ks} \cdot s_{i:i+n_{ks}-1} + b\right) \tag{9}$$

where j represents the index of convolution kernel, c_i^j represents the i-th element of the 1D tensor obtained by convolution of $s_{1:n_{sent}}$ using the j-th convolution kernel, $i \in [1, n_{sent} - n_{ks} + 1]$. We perform the maximum pooling operation on all c^j, get a vector v_{sent} representing structure rationality, and use $ReLU$ function to get the structure rationality score g_s, as shown in (10), W_s is the weight matrix, and b is the bias.

$$g_s = ReLU(\boldsymbol{W}_s \cdot \boldsymbol{v}_{sent} + b) \tag{10}$$

4.3 The Linguistics Part of Essay Grading Model

The linguistics expression of the essay is also important to essay grading, which can reflect the student's ability of choice of words and building of sentences. we introduce the linguistics part, which is used to evaluate the essay in terms of linguistics expression.

We mentioned in Sect. 4.1, we obtained sentence vector $\boldsymbol{s}_j$ encoded by the sentence-level Bi-LSTM. In this part, $\boldsymbol{s}_j$ is directly input into a document-level Bi-LSTM, and the linguistics expression vector $\boldsymbol{d}'$ is obtained. We use formula (11) to calculate the linguistics score:

$$g_e = ReLU\left(\boldsymbol{d}'\right) \tag{11}$$

In addition, we introduce the interpretability algorithm proposed in the paper [16] to extract excellent words and sentences in the essay, as shown in formula (12).

$$\mathrm{P}\left(r^j_{m_j} = 1 | \boldsymbol{h}^j_{m_j}, \alpha^j_{m_j}, s_j, \beta_j, \boldsymbol{d}\right) = \sigma(\boldsymbol{W}_1 \boldsymbol{h}^j_{m_j} + w_2 \alpha^j_{m_j} + \boldsymbol{h}^{j\,T}_{m_j} \boldsymbol{W}_3 s_j + w_4 \beta_j + \boldsymbol{s}_j^T \boldsymbol{W}_5 \boldsymbol{d} + b) \tag{12}$$

For a sentence s_j, m_j is the word index with the largest attention value in s_j, $\alpha^j_{m_j}$ is the corresponding attention value, $\boldsymbol{h}^j_{m_j}$ is the word's hidden state. β_j is the attention value calculated between s_j and the essay, $\boldsymbol{s}_j$ is the sentence vector. $\boldsymbol{d}$ is essay vector. $\boldsymbol{W}_1 \boldsymbol{h}^j_{m_j}$ denotes word content information. $w_2 \alpha^j_{m_j} + \boldsymbol{h}^{j\,T}_{m_j} \boldsymbol{W}_3 \boldsymbol{h}_j$ denotes the importance of word for s_j. $w_4 \beta_j + \boldsymbol{h}_j^T \boldsymbol{W}_5 \mathbf{d}$ denotes the importance of s_j for the essay. Judge whether the word or sentence is excellent from the importance of it to the essay, r_i^j denotes whether the i-th word in s_j is extracted or not.

4.4 Multi-aspect Essay Grading and Optimization Objective

Given an essay x, the output of the model is a set of scores $g = \{g_t, g_s, g_e, g'\}$, g_t represents the topic consistency score, g_s represents the structure rationality score, g_e represents the linguistics proficiency score, g' represents the final score. After scoring from three aspects respectively, we get the g' by combine them linearly as shown in formula (13).

$$g' = \alpha_1 g_t + \alpha_2 g_s + \alpha_3 g_e + b \tag{13}$$

In terms of the loss function, the final loss function is the sum of the cross-entropy loss of excellent words and sentences extraction and the mean square error loss of the score, as shown in formula (14).

$$J(\theta) = \text{CrossEntropy}\left(r, r'\right) + \text{MSE}(g, g') \tag{14}$$

5 Experiments

5.1 The Dataset of Essay Grading on College and Experimental Settings

In addition to the PAM dataset mentioned in Sect. 3.3, we also conduct experiments on the same cognitive level Chinese essay grading dataset from some college (EGC for short). The dataset contains the essay attributes and the grading information, gives material and requires students to write essays according to the material. The EGC dataset contains 49,642 essays, and the scope of the grades is [0,14]. The essay grade distribution is shown in Fig. 5. There is no essay with the score of 13.5 or 14, and the highest is 13. The average grade in EGC is 9.28, and the variance is 5.80.

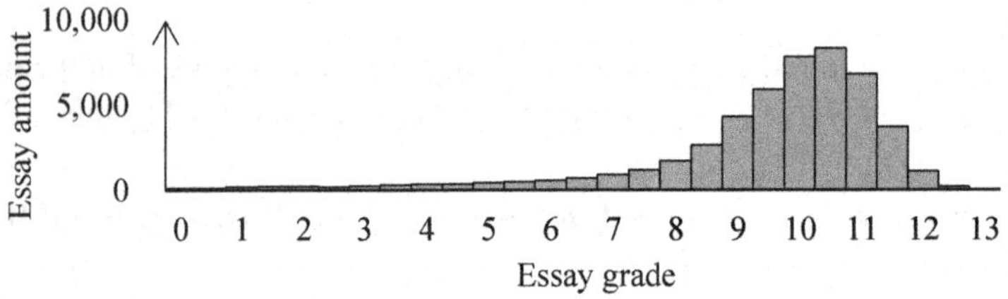

Fig. 5. The EGC dataset statistics.

We set both the maximum number of sentences and the maximum number of words to 50, fill the insufficient part with 0 and cut off the excess part of the sentence. As for the training parameters, the number of epochs is set to 15, the number of batches is set to 32, both the dimension of the sentence vector and the essay vector are 64.

5.2 Experimental Results and Analysis

We conduct experiments on PAM and EGC dataset. The model's name is a collection of encoders' short names. Variation models are used for ablation study by removing or changing some encoders. Bi-LSTM and Bert [23] are adopted as baselines. We use metrics of Quadratic Weighted Kappa (QWK for short) [24], Spearman's correlation coefficient (SCC for short) and Pearson's correlation coefficient (PCC for short). The results are shown in Table 3 and Table 4 below.

Because most of the essays in PAM dataset come from students' daily writing exercises, there are no materials given. So, we use essay's title as the topic-related material. The results shown in Table 3 indicate that our method has achieved the best results on

PAM dataset. Moreover, removing any part will cause a degradation of performance, because the model structure designed in Sect. 4 are based on the expert knowledge. Also, it can be seen that the most important parts of the model are the linguistics and topic part. We guess the reason is that, the CNN used in structure part pays more attention to the consistency of sentences. However, in reality, experts pay more attention to whether the context can be logically connected. It can't extract logical relations well.

We also conduct experiments on EGC dataset to explore whether our model can be applied to exam scenarios, the results are shown in Table 4. Since there is no information about excellent words and sentences in EGC dataset, the first term of loss function in formula (14) is abandoned. It can be seen that the performance of the model significantly reduced, but our method is still the best. According to the above results, we find that our model can be used in exam scenarios (Table 6).

Table 6. Performance comparison of using given material to learn topic features on EGC dataset.

Model	QWK	SCC	PCC
ATT + CNN + Bi-LSTM (Ours)	**0.6171**	0.4756	0.6584
ATT + CNN + GRU	0.6309	**0.4948**	**0.6783**
ATT + Bi-LSTM	0.5365	0.4671	0.4671
CNN + Bi-LSTM	0.5390	0.4858	0.6311
Bi-LSTM	0.6099	0.4910	0.6628

We continue to conduct experiments on EGC dataset using the given material as input to the topic part rather than the essay's title, the results are shown in Table 5. Comparing Table 5 and Table 4, we found that using text materials as the topic consistency content is slightly worse than using the title. The possible reason may be that, the given material usually contains multiple implicit topics. Students often focus on a certain topic when writing. Therefore, integrating the whole material into the text vector may cause the essay has poor correlations with other topics, cause the poor topic consistency score. In addition, the material in EGC dataset is classical Chinese, some words are not included in the pretrained dictionary. So, some features are lost when encoding the material.

6 Conclusion

Based on expert knowledge, we integrate existing essay grading standards, propose metrics from three aspects: topic, structure, and linguistics. Based on these metrics, we first give a quantification grading method using a set of indexes and topic model for low resource situation. Second, we propose a multi-aspect essay grading model. The model uses Bi-LSTM as encoder to generate text vectors, and extracts features from topic, structure and linguistics to grading the essay. We designed complete experiments to verify the effectiveness of our model on PAM and EGC dataset. In addition, we designed experiments to analyze the influence of different topic materials.

References

1. Ministry of Education the People's Republic of China: Compulsory Education Chinese Curriculum Standard. People's Education Press, Beijing (2011). ISBN: 9787303133178
2. General College Admissions Unified National Examination Outline in 2019. Higher Education Press, National Education Examination Authority (2018)
3. Page, E.B.: Grading essays by computer: progress report. In: Proceedings of the Invitational Conference on Testing Problems (1967)
4. Foltz, P.W., Laham, D., Landauer, T.K.: The intelligent essay assessor: applications to educational technology. Interact. Multim. Electr. J. Comput. Enhan. Learn. **1**(2), 939–944 (1999)
5. Burstein, J.: The E-rater® scoring engine: automated essay scoring with natural language processing. In: Shermis, M.D., Burstein, J. (eds.) Automated Essay Scoring: A Cross-Disciplinary Perspective, pp. 113–121. Lawrence Erlbaum Associates, Mahwah (2003)
6. Rudner, L.M.: An evaluation of the IntelliMetric essay scoring system. J. Technol. Learn. Assess. **4**(4), 3–21 (2006)
7. Rudner, L.M., Liang, T.: Automated essay scoring using Bayes' theorem. J. Technol. Learn. Assess. **1**(2), 1–22 (2002)
8. Larkey, L S.: A text categorization approach to automated essay grading. Automated Essay Scoring: A Cross-Disciplinary Perspective, 55–70 (2002)
9. Larkey L.S.: Automatic essay grading using text categorization techniques. In: 21st Annual International ACM SIGIR Conference on Research and Development in Information Retrieval, pp. 90–95. ACM, Melbourne (1998)
10. Dasgupta, T., Naskar, A., Dey, L., et al.: Augmenting textual qualitative features in deep convolution recurrent neural network for automatic essay scoring. In: 5th Meeting of the Association for Computational Linguistics, pp. 93–102. ACM, Melbourne (2018)
11. Dong, F., Zhang, Y., Yang, J.: Attention-based recurrent convolutional neural network for automatic essay scoring. In: 21st Conference on Computational Natural Language Learning, pp. 153–162. Association for Computational Linguistics, Vancouver (2017)
12. Wang, Y., Wei, Z., Zhou, Y., Huang, X.: Automatic essay scoring incorporating rating schema via reinforcement learning. In: Proceedings of the 2018 Conference on Empirical Methods in Natural Language Processing, pp. 791–797. Association for Computational Linguistics, Brussels (2018)
13. Tay, Y., Phan, M.C., Tuan, L.A., et al.: SkipFlow: incorporating neural coherence features for end-to-end automatic text scoring. In: Thirty-Second AAAI Conference on Artificial Intelligence, pp. 5948–5955. AAAI Press, New Orleans (2018)
14. Alikaniotis, D., Yannakoudakis, H., Rei, M., et al.: Automatic text scoring using neural networks. In: the 54th Annual Meeting of the Association for Computational Linguistics, pp. 715–725. The Association for Computer Linguistics, Berlin (2016)
15. Jin, C., He, B., Hui, K., et al.: TDNN: a two-stage deep neural network for prompt-independent automated essay scoring. In: 56th Annual Meeting of the Association for Computational Linguistics, pp. 1088–1097. The Association for Computer Linguistics, Melbourne (2018)
16. Yifei, G.: Explainable essay grading method based on expert knowledge. Shandong University (2020)
17. Lu, X.: Automatic measurement of syntactic complexity in child language acquisition. Int. J. Corpus Linguist. **14**(1), 3–28 (2009)
18. Na, H.: A corpus-based study on the syntactic features of primary school students' compositions. Shanghai Normal University (2014)
19. Jäntschi, L., et al.: Pearson versus Spearman, Kendall's Tau correlation analysis on structure-activity relationships of biologic active compounds (2005)

20. Hochreiter, S., Schmidhuber, J.: Long Short-Term Memory. Neural Comput. **9**(8), 1735–1780 (1997)
21. Wang, Yequan, et al. "Attention-Based LSTM for Aspect-Level Sentiment Classification." Proceedings of the 2016 Conference on Empirical Methods in Natural Language Processing, 2016, pp. 606–615
22. Kim Y.: Convolutional neural networks for sentence classification[C]. In: Empirical Methods in Natural Language Processing, pp. 1746–1751. The Association for Computer Linguistics, Doha (2014)
23. Devlin J, Chang M W, Lee K, et al. Bert: Pre-training of deep bidirectional transformers for language understanding[J]. arXiv preprint arXiv:1810.04805, 2018
24. Cohen, J.: Weighted Kappa: Nominal Scale Agreement Provision for Scaled Disagreement or Partial Credit. Psychol. Bull. **70**(4), 213–220 (1968)

Autonomous Navigation System for Indoor Mobile Robots Based on a Multi-sensor Fusion Technology

Hongcheng Wang[1], Niansheng Chen[1(✉)], Dingyu Yang[2], and Guangyu Fan[1]

[1] School of Electronic Information Engineering, Shanghai Dianji University, Shanghai, China
chenns@sdju.edu.cn
[2] Alibaba Group, Shanghai, China

Abstract. Map construction and path planning are two critical problems for an autonomous navigation system. One traditional map construction method is to construct a 2D grid map based on LiDAR, but this method has some limits. It easily ignores 3D information which affects the accuracy of navigation. Another one is visual SLAM techniques, such as ORB-SLAM2 and S-PTAM algorithms, which can recognize 3D objects. But the visual methods perform not well because of light changes. Some conventional path planning algorithms, such as TEB and DWA, are proposed for auto-navigation. However, those algorithms are likely to go to a stalemate due to local optimum, or have the problems of collision caused by sudden speed changes in constrained environments. In order to address these issues, this paper proposes a multi-sensor fusion method for map construction and autonomous navigation. Firstly, the fusion model combines RGB-D, lidar laser, and inertial measurement unit (IMU) to construct 2D grid maps and 3D color point cloud maps in real-time. Next, we present an improved local planning algorithm (Opt_TEB) to solve the velocity mutation problem, enabling the robot to get a collision-free path. We implemented the whole system based on the ROS framework, which is a wide used an open-source robot operating system. The map construction and path planning algorithms are running on the robot, while the visualization and control modules are deployed on a back-end server. The experimental results illustrate that the multi-sensor fusion algorithm is able to conform to the original map more than the 2D grid map. Furthermore, our improved algorithm Opt_TEB performs smoothly and has no collision with obstacles in 30 trials. The navigation speed is improved by 4.2% and 11.5% compared to TEB and DWA, respectively.

Keywords: Mobile robot · RTABMAP · Sensor fusion · Path planning

1 Introduction

Mobile robots have been developed and widely applied in various applications, such as indoor transportation logistics [1], shopping guide [2], and so on. With the help of high computing power and robust sensors, a robot can quickly construct an identifiable

Y. Sun et al. (Eds.): ChineseCSCW 2021, CCIS 1491, pp. 502–517, 2022.
https://doi.org/10.1007/978-981-19-4546-5_39

map in a complex indoor environment. It continuously receives real-time sensor data from multiple devices, processes the data timely, and makes a reasonable decision [3]. For example, the robot needs to identify moving obstacles on its path, and determine to change to a new router to avoid them in a short time. We can find that there existing two key technologies for autonomous robot navigation: map construction and navigation algorithms.

There are two main types of simultaneous localization and mapping techniques: LiDAR and Visual SLAM. Laser lidar is to construct a 2D grid map using laser [4–6], but the 2D method is relatively single and might ignore some information. Another technique uses visual SLAM [4, 5] to identify and construct maps. ORB-SLAM2 [7] and S-PTAM [8] are graph-based SLAM methods that use loop closure detection and graph optimization to construct a sparse feature graph. However, they cannot produce a dense point cloud map and build an accurate map. DVO-SLAM [9] uses the luminosity and depth on all pixels of the RGB-D image to produce a dense 3D point cloud map. This method is susceptible to go further with the target due to the inability to determine the current locus in terms of local vision, making it challenging to adjust the position shift caused by prolonged navigation.

Path planning is one of the significant control aspects of the robot, which mainly includes global path planning and local path planning [10–13]. The established path planning algorithms are Dijkstra [14], A* [15]. D*, where the Dijkstra algorithm is defaultly used in the navigation planner (Navfn) in the ROS [16, 17] platform for global navigation. DWA [13] and TEB [18] algorithms are proposed for local path planning in some works. We find that the DWA algorithm might fall into local optimum and incur oscillation problems. The robot with the TEB algorithm needs to run backwardness when the target point is not aligned with its orientation. In this case, the robot is prone to sudden speed changes causing collisions.

To tackle the problems of existing technologies in map construction and path planning. This paper proposes a multi-sensor fusion and autonomous navigation system for mobile robots. The system combines RGB-D, radar-laser, and inertial measurement unit (IMU) data to build 2D raster maps and 3D color point cloud maps in real-time, improving map recognizability and robustness. A local path planning algorithm is developed to solve the backward velocity mutation problem, enabling the robot to run a collision-free path. Finally, a distributed architecture system based on the ROS framework [18, 19] has been implemented, and the mapping algorithm and navigation algorithm are deployed on the robot. The visualization module is remotely deployed on a back-end server.

The main contributions of this paper are listed as follows:

(1) A multi-sensor fusion method is proposed for map construction, which integrates RGB-D, Radar-Laser, and Inertial measurement unit (IMU) data to build a refined real-time map instead of single sensor.
(2) We present a local path planning algorithm (Opt_TEB) to solve the velocity abruptness problem. It combines angular and linear velocities to plan a collision-free path;
(3) The whole system is implemented based on the ROS platform. The experimental results shows that the map build our multi-sensor fusion method conforms to the original map more than the 2D grid map. In addition, a 3D point cloud map is not

limited by the flatness of a 2D map, so that the 3D features beyond 2D can be clearly shown in the map;

(4) We evaluate our system with existing navigation algorithms. Our improved navigation algorithm (Opt_TEB) has a significantly lower chance of oscillation and has no collision with obstacles in 30 trials. Moreover, the navigation speed is improved by 11.5% on average compared to DWA and 4.2% on average compared to TEB.

The organization of this paper is as follows. Section 1 introduces the background and significance of the study. Section 2 investigates the advantages and disadvantages of existing map construction algorithms and navigation algorithms. The details of the map construction algorithm and navigation algorithm are presented in Sect. 3. Sections 4 and 5 introduce the robot's hardware and software configurations.

We evaluate the efficiency and accuracy of the algorithm in a multidimensional experimental comparison in Sect. 6. Section 7 summarizes the work of the paper.

2 Related Work

2.1 Map Construction

Simultaneous localization and mapping (SLAM) technology of robots has made some achievements. there are two major slam systems: Laser-based slam [4–6] and Vision-based slam [7–9].

LiDAR-based SLAM scans the space environment to get the point cloud data by matching the data to generate a map. It dynamicly calculates the motion distance and attitude for localization. Grisettiet al. in 2007 [5] proposed the gmapping SLAM, which is a popular method and regarded as the default SLAM technique for ROS. The disadvantage of this technique is that it uses a large number of particle filters to estimate the robot's trajectory, thus a larger quantity of computational resources has been comsumed. The Hector SLAM [4] proposed by Kohlbrecher et al. in 2011 is capable of creating 2D raster maps in real-time using 2D LiDAR and needs less computational resources. Apart from this, this slam method also uses IMU to estimate the robot's poses. However, this algorithm degrades the performance of laser scan matching in complex environments. Karto SLAM [6] was proposed by Vincent et al. in 2010 and Lago SLAM [19] was proposed by Carlone et al. in 2012. Both graph optimization-based SLAM methods utilize the mean value of the graph to represent the map, and each node in the map is a location point of the robot trajectory and a sensor measurement data set. When a loop closure is detected, the location of the sub-map is re-optimized to reduce the prediction errors brought by sensor noise. In contrast to Hector SLAM, both algorithms [6, 19] are more robust in a complex environments.

Visual SLAM is one of the most used SLAM technologies, which can be done using monocular cameras, but monocular SLAM has a scale drift problem. Studies have demonstrated that the problem can be solved by using RGB-D cameras. The Maplab SLAM [11] was proposed by Schneider et al. in 2018 and VINS-Mono SLAM [12] was proposed by Yi et al. in 2017. Both visual-inertial map-based SLAM systems provide visual maps only using IMU and camera. ORB-SLAM2 [7] was proposed by Tard os in 2017 and it is a SLAM method based on image feature extraction. This method is used depth information to synthesize stereo coordinates by an RGB-D camera. The RANSAC + PNP [13] method is used to estimate motion transformation. This method constructs a sparse feature map by utilizing loop closure detection and graphical optimization. But it cannot export a dense point cloud map and construct an accurate map. Moreover, all the above visual SALM methods are implemented based on the assumption of no occlusion, which is not fit in a real scenario. To address this problem, RGB-D-SLAM-V2 [13] was proposed by Endres et al. in 2014, using external ranging methods for motion estimation. Note that, ROS packages (such as the robot positioning package) can be used for sensor fusion (using Extended Kalman Filtering, EKF) of multiple range sources to obtain more reliable ranges. In this paper, we improve the robustness of the robot by multi-sensor fusion RGBD-SLAM-V2, which can generate 3D occupancy grid maps and 3D dense point cloud maps.

2.2 Path Planning

Path planning is one of the significant control aspects of the robot, which mainly includes global path planning and local path planning [10–13].

Global path planning is responsible for finding a collision-free optimal path from the starting point to the end point in a well-constructed global map, which generally does not work well to dynamic avoid obstacles. One of the representative global path planning algorithms is the A* algorithm [13], which uses a direct search algorithm to get a shortest path. The disadvantage of this algorithm is that the state recalculation and the valuation ranking cause it to occupy a large amount of computing memory. The D* algorithm, which works similarly to A*, is also applied to robot global path planning. The D* algorithm is also known as dynamic A*, but it incorporates over linear interpolation planning to make its planned paths smoother and needs fewer memory resources.

Local path planning modifies the global path for dynamic obstacle avoidance by adjusting the path with real-time updates. One representative local path planning algorithm is the dynamic window approach [20], which simulates the robot's trajectory in the following phase by sampling the space [v,w]. The artificial potential field method [21] is also commonly used in the robot's local path planning. The disadvantages of this method are that when the gravitational part is not proportional to the distance between the robot and the target point position, it may lead to the collision of the robot with the obstacle. The graph optimization-based TEB algorithm [18] was proposed by Rosmann et al., which is applicable to complete or incomplete constrained machine movers [7]. These algorithms are subject to the situation where sudden changes in velocity can produce impact oscillations on the robot without constraints on acceleration, leading to a problem where the robot falls into a local optimum solution.

3 Architecture

The multi-sensor fusion autonomous navigation system proposed in this paper can be classified into two phases: map construction and navigation.

3.1 Map Construction Algorithm

In this paper, the mapping algorithm uses the improved RTAB_MAP [22] of RGBD-SLAM [23], and the process model is shown in Fig. 1.

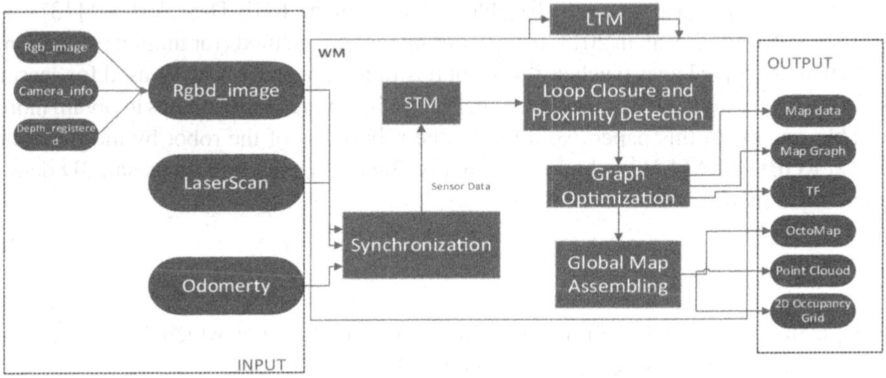

Fig. 1. RTAB-Map construction algorithm

Input: There are three ROS node topics (ROS Topic [16]) for the input of RTAB-MAP: (i) Depth information from an RGB-D camera. Since the Astar pro depth camera used in the experiment cannot provide both color (rgb-image) and depth images (rgbd-image), the RGB images need to be provided separately through the USB Video Cameras (UVC) and then the RGB image topics are remapped. At the same time, camera distortion parameter calibration (camera_info) incorporating the depth image to get the depth data format. Finally, wrapping it as /camera/depth_registered/image_raw topic. (ii) Using LiDAR scanned maps to obtain raster map message formats and wrapping them into/scan topics. (iii).

The quaternion message format of the robot pose obtained from the position inertial odometer (IMU) of the robot base is wrapped in the /mobile_base/sensors/imu_data topic.

Map construction: The sensor information is synchronized by practical calibration and fed into the Short Memory Module [23] (STM). After receiving the data, the STM module will create a node to remember the sensor's raw data for other modules (such as for loop closure and proximity detection of locus points).

The memory of RTAB was divided into Working Memory (WM) and Long Term Memory (LTM). The STM updates the weight of the locus by observing the similarity of consecutive images in time. When the number of locus reaches a particular value, the locus with the longest storage time will be moved to WM Working Memory (WM) to detect the locus's closed-loop hypothesis in space. When the number of locus points in WM exceeds a certain memory threshold "Rtabmap/MemoryThr," the locus points are transferred to LTM (Long Term Memory) according to the rule "High weight < Low weight < Long storage time", so that these transferred locus points do not participate in the next closed-loop detection operation. The extracted localization points are subjected to graph optimization, which propagates the computational error to the whole graph to reduce the odometry drift. The octomap (3D occupied grid), the point cloud data, and the 2D grid map are updated globally as the optimization process proceeds. The global map is eventually assembled through graphical optimization. According to the back-end optimization results, the global map is "assembled" on the local grid map information before the map is corrected.

Output: The graph-optimized part of the output contains map data with compressed sensor data and graphs, alongside with Map Graph without any data; The TF transform part (/map→/odom) is used to output the odometer correction for robot positioning in the map frame; The output of the global map assembly part is OctoMap (3D occupied grid map), dense point cloud and 2D occupied grid map.

3.2 Navigation Algorithm

The process of path planning can be divided into global path planning and local path planning. A path search is carried out in the previously created 3D point cloud map in global path planning. The local path planner avoids obstacles not present in the a priori map and performs local obstacle avoidance without affecting the global path. In this paper, the existing TEB algorithm is improved (Opt_TEB algorithm) to control the velocity mutation problem by jointly constraining the angular and linear velocity.

The Navfn planner method is used in global path planning, using the Dijkstra algorithm. The Dijkstra algorithm used breadth-first search to solve the shortest path problem, and the algorithm ultimately obtains a shortest-path tree.

Dijkstra's algorithm uses a greedy strategy:

Initially, define an array (dis) to reserve for each vertex T the shortest path from s to v found so far. When starting the search, the path weight of the starting point s is assigned as d[s] = 0. Set the dis[m] of the vertex S that can reach the boundary directly to w(s,m), assuming that the vertex S points that are indirectly earned or unreachable are infinite. The algorithm starts with the vertex set T having only the source point s. The next step selects the minimum value from the dis array as the shortest path value from the source point s to the minimum vertex and adds it to the set T. When the first vertex is added, determine whether the newly added vertex can reach other vertices and determine whether the path length through the vertex to other points is shorter than the path length directly to the source point. If true, the value of the vertex in dis is replaced. Eventually, the minimum value is found from dis, and the above process is repeated until all vertices of the graph are included in T. The pseudo code for the evolution is shown as follows.

Algorithm 1 Djikstra

```
function dijkstra(s, m)
dis[s] ← 0
create vertex set Q
for each vertex T in m do
    dist[T] ← INFINITY
    prev[T] ← UNDEFINED
    if T ≠ s then
        Q.add − with − priority(T, dis[T])
        while Q is not empty do
            u ← Q.extract − min()
        end while
    end if
end for
for for each unvisited neighbour T of u do
    alt ← dist[u] + length(u, T)
    if altdist[T] then
        dis[T] ← alt
        prev[T] ← u
        Q.decrease − priority(T, alt)
        return dist[], prev[]
    end if
end for
end function
```

In terms of the local path planning algorithm, we have improved the existing TEB algorithm [3] (Opt_TEB algorithm) by changing the backward phenomenon to in-situ rotation to control it in a narrow space to avoid collisions.

The original TEB algorithm is a segmented row of the global path planner output result, where each small segment has its own endpoint, and that direction always points to its next pose. The canonical "Elastic-Band" [18] is described by a sequence of n robot poses [18] poses $X_i = (x_i, y_i, \beta_i)^T$, where x_i, y_i represent the robot position, β_i represent Global robot orientation. This sequence can be expressed as $Q = \{X_i\}_{i=0...n}$. In this method, the kinematic time between points is defined to display the trajectory's kinematic information, called "Timed-Elastic-Band". The TEB algorithm adds a time interval sequence $\tau = \{\Delta T_i\}_{i=0...n-1}$. In the TEB algorithm, each time interval represents the time required for the robot to switch from the current pose to the next pose in sequence Q. Consequently, TEB consists of the above two sequences $B = (Q, \tau)$.

The ultimate goal of TEB is to perform path planning, as in Eq. (1) and (2):

$$f(B) = \sum_k f_k(B) \tag{1}$$

$$B^* = arg\,\min_B f(B) \tag{2}$$

where f(B) represents the global objective function, a weighted sum considering various constraints; B^* represents the optimized TEB sequence, which is the path we need for local planning.

Nevertheless, the original TEB algorithm does not consider the constraints on the robot's forward velocity and angular velocity, which may lead to sudden changes in the robot's velocity to generate oscillations, as shown in Fig. 2.

Fig. 2. An example of TEB obstacle avoidance trajectory

Therefore, we propose a joint robot forward velocity and angular velocity constraint, The expressions for the velocity and acceleration of the robot are presented as follows.

Linear velocity:

$$v_i \approx \frac{1}{\Delta T_i}\begin{pmatrix} x_{i+1} - x_i \\ y_{i+1} - y_i \end{pmatrix} \tag{3}$$

Angular velocity:

$$w_i \approx \frac{\theta_{i+1} - \theta_i}{\Delta T_i} \tag{4}$$

Linear acceleration:

$$a_i \approx \frac{2(v_{i+1} - v_i)}{\Delta T_i + \Delta T_{i+1}} \tag{5}$$

Angular acceleration:

$$\alpha_i = \frac{2(w_{i+1} - w_i)}{(\Delta T_i + \Delta T_{i+1})} \tag{6}$$

The maximum forward linear velocity and angular velocity constraints are combined as follows:

$$v(k) = \frac{v_{max}}{1 + \beta|k|^{\mu}} \quad \beta > 0 \ \mu > 0 \tag{7}$$

where $k = w_i/v_i$ represents the curvature value of the point, β and μ are variable values. The specific values of β and μ can be adjusted according to the actual situation. In the experiment, β is 0.2, μ is 2. The improved robot motion trajectory is shown in Fig. 3.

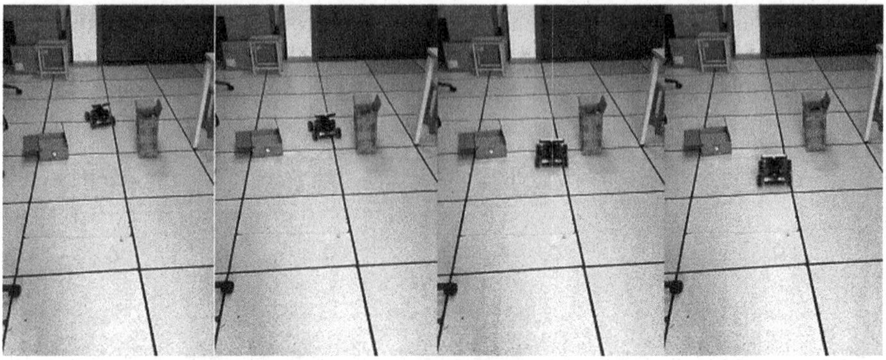

Fig. 3. An example of Opt_TEB obstacle avoidance trajectory

The optimized TEB algorithm (Opt_TEB) considers the joint constraint of angular velocity and linear velocity to control the sudden change of velocity, thus avoiding the vibration of the robot, which leads to the loosening of the sensor and the damage of the trolley. In the actual experiment, we used an omnidirectional moving robot and the max_vel_x_backwords parameter to 0/ms^{-1} so that its backward movement becomes in-situ rotation, thus reducing the impact of oscillation.

4 Experimental Setup

4.1 Hardware Configuration

Robot Configurations: Our experiment employs a omnidirectional robot, including four mecanum wheels with each connected to a geared motor. It uses an STM32 development board as the driver board for the whole robot. We supply some components for power and network connection: a 6 V 6000 mAh battery, and a router for wireless connection between the host computer and the car. The robot is also equipped with Astar pro depth camera and Silan PRLIDAR_A1 16 Hz LIDAR. The backend server could config RVIZ for remote observation and controllor.

LIDAR Configurations: In the experiment, we use Silan PRLIDAR_A1 LIDAR, which has a measurement radius of 0.12 m–35 m, a sampling frequency of 8K, a scanning frequency of 16 Hz, an angular resolution of $\leq 1°$, a ranging accuracy of 2 cm, and a scanning range of 360°. This lidar can meet our indoor navigation.

Camera Configurations: We use Astar pro depth camera for depth image acquisition; the depth range of this camera is 0.6m-8m, power consumption is 2.5 w max, peak current is less than 500 mA, color map resolution supports up to 1280 × 720@30 FPS, depth map resolution supports up to 1280 × 1024@FPS, accuracy is ±1–3 mm@1 m 1 m, the transmission delay is 30–45 ms.

Robot Control Unit: We use Nvidia Jetson Nano as an on-board microcomputer with equipped NVIDIA Maxwell architecture GPU, which has 128 NVIDIA CUDA cores. The CPU model is ARM Cortex-A57 MPCore CPU, and 4 GB of 64-bit LPDDR4 memory, and the size of storage is 16 GB flash memory. We config the Nano in Ubuntu envoriment and ROS platform to execute our experiments' map construction and navigation algorithm.

Driver Board: We use Hibot driver board as the chassis driver, which includes a six-axis IMU attitude module, motor drive interface, Laser lidar interface, battery input interface, power switch interface, STM32 controller, charger input interface, 5 V USB interface, and upper computer communication module.4.2 Software Configuration.

4.2 Software Configuration

Operating System: Our system is running on the Ubuntu 18.04, a desktop application-based Linux operating system that provides a robust, feature-rich computing environment.

ROS Platform: ROS is an acronym for Robot Operating System, a highly flexible software architecture for writing robot software programs. It provides the services expected of an operating system, including inter-process messaging, underlying device control, and management of available packages. This framework combines loosely coupled components together and provides a general communication architecture. The platform provides the tools and library functions for easily acquiring, compiling, modification, and running. The main goal of ROS is to provide open-source packages to support robotics research and development. It is a distributed framework packaged in packages and feature packs that can be easily shared.

4.3 Experimental Environment

Our experiment is running in a confined and complex laboratory. Carton obstacles are simulated to distinguish the original static map; Fig. 4 shows the experimental environment where the map will be constructed.

Fig. 4. Experimental environment

5 System Implementation

5.1 Map Construction

The original map is built without any obstacles in our experiment. When starting the robot, we can control the robot with the help of wireless network. Some othe control nodes are launched from the start scripts, which contains the lidar sensor, IMU sensor, and odometer, and Astar pro depth camera. The map fusion algorithm then is executed to process data and construct the map. After that, we can see the map remotely through RVIZ. In this process, we apply a robot handle to slowly scan the room with the speed of 0.3 m/s, 0.3 m/s, and 0.4 m/s. Finally, a whole map can be generated for our next navigation.

5.2 Navigation

Due to the narrow environment of the laboratory, the space left for the robot to avoid obstacles is relatively tiny. We change the expansion coefficient of obstacles to 0.1. After several navigation testings, we set the kinematics parameters of the robot, as shown in Table 1. To distinguish the original maps, we use cardboard boxes as barriers placed in the laboratory. After using RTAB-MAP SLAM to construct the map, the handle topic is paused or closed, and the navigation command is opened at the robot side when all declarations are not completed by default. To better view the global and local paths during navigation, we added two path display types in Rviz to show global path planning and local path planning, respectively.

The whole navigation planning framework is designed based on the ROS system. We can control the robot behavior using the move_base package (such as forward, backward, turn around, etc.). The navigation combine global and local navigation together to accomplish the task. The whole framework is shown in Fig. 5. When move_base receives a request to a target point from the user, move_base calls the Navfn planner for global

Table 1. Robot kinematic parameters

Constraint parameters	Numeric value
Max_vel_x/($m \cdot s^{-1}$)	0.25
Max_vel_x_back/($m \cdot s^{-1}$)	0
Max_vel_y/($m \cdot s^{-1}$)	0
Max_vel_theta/($rad \cdot s^{-1}$) Acc_lim_x/($m \cdot s^{-2}$)	0.63 0.5
Acc_lim_theta/($rad \cdot s^{-2}$)	0.7

planning. While the local path planning, the move_base module will call our improved algorithm Opt_TEB to reduce the chance of collision. The laser lidar is responsible for detecting obstacle information. The odometer IMU information is used for localization. The recovery behaviors mode is triggered when global and local planning fails or when anomalous trapped behavior occurs.

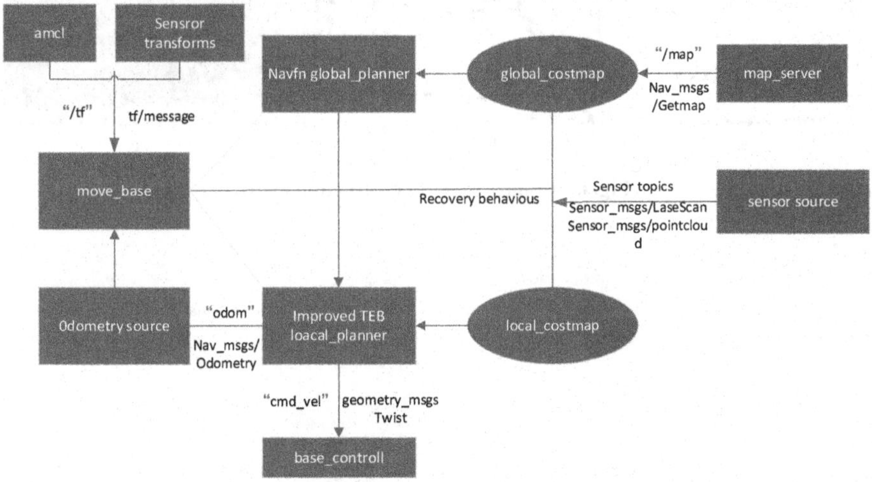

Fig. 5. Motion planning framework

6 Experimental Results

The whole experimental results are evaluated on the ROS framework. We compare the performance between different constructing map algorithms on boundary analysis and trajectory fitting. Then we evaluate the runtime of navigation algorithms based on different contructed maps. Last but least, we analysis the navigation efficiency on different number of obstacles in the map, and compare the number of collisions in the navigation stage.

6.1 Boundary and Trajectory Fitting Analysis of Constructing Maps

In our experiments, we compare the mapping boundaries of Karto SLAM [16], which only uses lidar for mapping, and RTAB-SLAM [21], which uses multi-sensor fusion. The RTAB-SLAM algorithm mainly matches by locating points, then estimates camera motion, and finally reduces the error by closed-loop detection.

The comparison results are shown in Fig. 6(a) for RTAB-SLAM and (b) for Karto SLAM, which shows that the use of the RTAB-SLAM algorithm reduces the map matching error, and the boundaries are more clear. Figure 6(c) is a 3D point cloud map combining camera and Lidar, which solves the limitation of 2D map with a single plane and shows the 3D features beyond 2D.

In addition to performing the see figure edge comparison, the trajectory coordinates of the two algorithms were extracted for comparison with the real trajectory coordinates in our experiment. The results illustrate that Karto's turning has a clear estimation error in Fig. 7. We can also find that the map of RTAB is more conform to the original map than that of Karto.

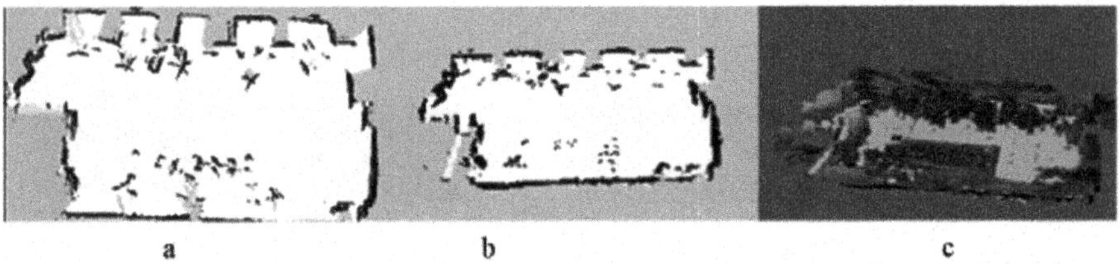

Fig. 6. Comparison of construction maps

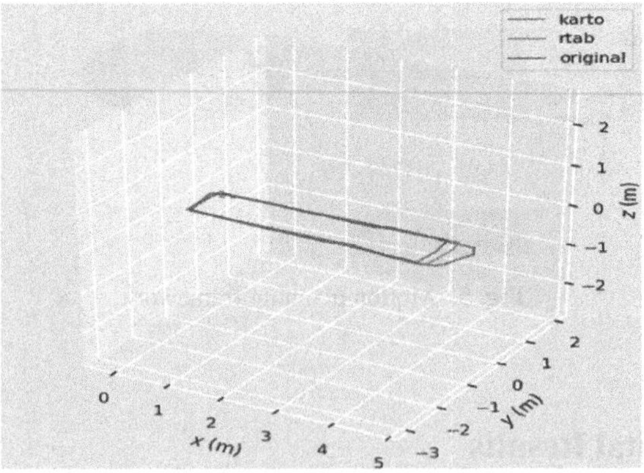

Fig. 7. Motion track comparison

6.2 Navigation Algorithm Analysis

We conducted the experiments to evaluate the algorithm efficiency. We compare the runtime of two navigation algorithms (TEB and DWA) with same start point and end point.

The experiment was divided into two phases (Half of Map, and Whole) according to the navigation distance of the target points. In the first phase, we randomly select ten points as our navigation targets among the half of our map. This procedure is repeated to test their navigation time. The second phase is executed in the same process except the whole map. We can find that the TEB algorithm reaches the target point more quickly in the map created by the RTAB algorithm and also sees a little more fluctuation in the operational efficiency of the randomly selected points in the second stage in Fig. 8.

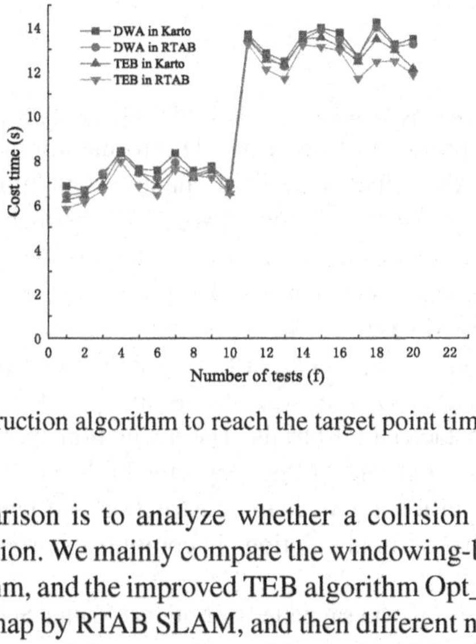

Fig. 8. Map construction algorithm to reach the target point time without obstacles

The second comparison is to analyze whether a collision occurs after setting an obstacle during navigation. We mainly compare the windowing-based local path planner DWA, the TEB algorithm, and the improved TEB algorithm Opt_TEB. The map is based on a well-built global map by RTAB SLAM, and then different numbers of obstacles are set to test the performance of the obstacle avoidance algorithm.

The number of testing is set to 6 * 5 times, one obstacle was placed every 60 cm in the whole global map created by RTAB SLAM, and a total of 1–6 obstacles were placed in the environment. Each test was conducted five times: 0 collisions for DWA, TEB, and Opt_TEB in environments with 1 to 3 obstacles placed, one collision for DWA in environments with four obstacles placed, two collisions for DWA, and one collision for TEB in environments with five obstacles placed; Two collisions occurred in DWA, and two collisions occurred in TEB in the environment where six obstacles were placed. Overall, the DWA algorithm was subjected to 5 obvious shocks with a shock probability of 1/6, and the TEB algorithm was subjected to 3 obvious shocks with a shock probability of 1/10. The Opt_TEB algorithm does not collide with the robot during navigation, and the motion trajectory is smooth.

Figure 9 shows the average time to reach the target point for the three algorithms in environments with different obstacles. The results show an average 11.5% improvement in navigation speed compared to DWA and an average 4.2% improvement over TEB.

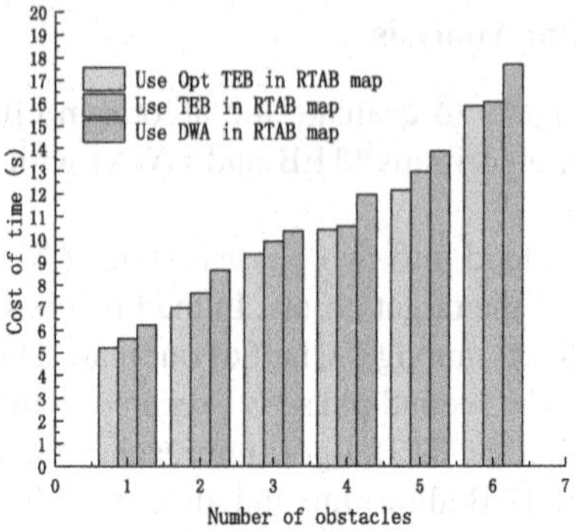

Fig. 9. Comparison of algorithm times

7 Conclusion

This paper proposes a multi-sensor fusion method for map construction and autonomous navigation to solve the problem of ignoring 3D information in LiDAR SLAM, or the limitation of visual SLAM affected by light changes. Our model combines RGB-D, lidar laser, and inertial measurement unit (IMU) to construct 2D grid maps and 3D color point cloud maps in real-time. In order to get a collision-free path, we present an improved local planning algorithm (Opt_TEB) to solve the velocity mutation problem. Our system is implemented based on the ROS framework and the experimental results illustrate that the multi-sensor fusion algorithm is able to conform to the original map more than the 2D grid map. Our improved algorithm Opt_TEB performs smoothly and has no collision with obstacles in 30 trials. The navigation speed is improved by 4.2% and 11.5% compared to TEB and DWA, respectively. Next we plan to use binocular cameras to improve the efficiency of map construction and neural networks solve the problem of local or global optimal solutions in complex environments.

Acknowledgements. This work was supported by National Natural Science Foundation of China (no. 61702320).

References

1. Wang, P., Wang, Y., Wang, X., Liu, Y., Zhang, J.: An intelligent actuator of an indoor logistics system based on multi-sensor fusion. Actuators **10**, 120 (2021)
2. Song, S., Baba, J., Nakanishi, J., Yoshikawa, Y., Ishiguro, H.: Teleoperated robot sells toothbrush in a shopping mall: a field study. In: Extended Abstracts of the 2021 CHI Conference on Human Factors in Computing Systems, pp. 1–6. Association for Computing Machinery, New York, NY, USA (2021)
3. Makris, S.: Synthesis of data from multiple sensors and wearables for human–robot collaboration. In: Cooperating Robots for Flexible Manufacturing. Springer Series in Advanced Manufacturing. pp. 321—338. Springer, Cham (2021). https://doi.org/10.1007/978-3-030-51591-1_17

4. Zhang, X., Fang, Z., Lu, Z., Xiao, J., Cheng, X., Zhang, X.: 3D reconstruction of weak feature indoor scenes based on hector SLAM and floorplan generation. In: IEEE 7th International Conference on Virtual Reality, pp. 117–126. IEEE, China (2021)
5. Fan, X., Wang, Y., Zhang, Z.: An evaluation of Lidar-based 2D SLAM techniques with an exploration mode. J. Phys. **1905**, 012021 (2021)
6. Liu, B., Guan, Z., Li, B., Wen, G., Zhao, Y.: Research on SLAM algorithm and navigation of mobile robot based on ROS. In: 2021 IEEE International Conference on Mechatronics and Automation, pp. 119–124. IEEE, Takamatsu (2021)
7. Diao, Y., Cen, R., Xue, F., Su, X.: ORB-SLAM2S: a fast ORB-SLAM2 system with sparse optical flow tracking. In: 13th International Conference on Advanced Computational Intelligence, pp. 160–165. IEEE, Wanzhou (2010)
8. Pire, T., Fischer, T., Castro, G., De Cristóforis, P., Civera, J., Berlles, J.J.: S-ptam: stereo parallel tracking and mapping. Robot. Auton. Syst. **93**, 27–42 (2017)
9. Babu, B. W., Kim, S., Yan, Z., Ren, L.: σ-dvo: sensor noise model meets dense visual odometry. In: 2016 IEEE International Symposium on Mixed and Augmented Reality, pp. 18–26 (2016)
10. Luo, M., Hou, X., Yang, J.: Surface optimal path planning using an extended Dijkstra algorithm. IEEE Access **8**, 147827–147838 (2016)
11. Liu, Z., Liu, H., Lu, Z., Zeng, Q.: A dynamic fusion pathfinding algorithm using delaunay triangulation and improved A-Star for mobile robots. IEEE Access **9,** 20602–20621 (2021)
12. Stentz, A.: Optimal and efficient path planning for partially known environments. In: Hebert, M.H., Thorpe, C., Stentz, A. (eds.) Intelligent Unmanned Ground Vehicles. The Springer International Series in Engineering and Computer Science, vol 388, pp. 203–220. Springer, Boston (1997). https://doi.org/10.1007/978-1-4615-6325-9_11
13. Endres, F., Hess, J., Sturm, J., Cremers, D., Burgard, W.: 3-D mapping with an RGB-D camera. IEEE Trans. Robot. **30**, 177–187 (2013)
14. Akir, E., Ulukan, Z., Acarman, T.: Hortest fuzzy hamiltonian cycle on transportation network using minimum vertex degree and time-dependent dijkstra's algorithm. In: 16th IFAC Symposium on Control in Transportation Systems CTS 2021, vol. 54, pp. 348–353. IFAC-PapersOnLine, Lille (2021)
15. Tang, G., Tang, C., Claramunt, C., Hu, X., Zhou, P.: Geometric A-star algorithm: an improved A-star Algorithm for AGV path planning in a port environment. IEEE Access **99,** 1 (2021)
16. Newman, W.S.: A Systematic Approach to Learning Robot Programming with ROS, 1st edn. Chapman and Hall/CRC, New York (2017)
17. Crick, C., Jay, G., Osentoski, S., Pitzer, B., Jenkins, O.C.: Rosbridge: ROS for non-ROS users. In: Christensen, H.I., Khatib, O. (eds.) Robotics Research. STAR, vol. 100, pp. 493–504. Springer, Cham (2017). https://doi.org/10.1007/978-3-319-29363-9_28
18. Rosmann, C., Feiten, W., Wosch, T., Hoffmann, F., Bertram, T.: Efficient trajectory optimization using a sparse model. In: 2013 European Conference on Mobile Robots, pp. 25–27. IEEE, Barcelona (2014)
19. Carlone, L., Aragues, R., Castellanos, J.A., Bona, B.: A linear approximation for graph-based simultaneous localization and mapping. Robot. Sci. Syst. **VII** (2014)
20. Chang, L., Shan, L., Jiang, C., Dai, Y.: Reinforcement based mobile robot path planning with improved dynamic window approach in unknown environment. Auton. Robots **33**, 268–304 (2020)
21. Cho, J.H., Pae, D.S., Lim, M.T., Kang, T.K.: A real-time obstacle avoidance method for autonomous vehicles using an obstacle-dependent gaussian potential field. J. Adv. Transp. **2018**, 1–15 (2018)
22. Bampis, K., Amanatiadis, A.: Fast loop-closure detection using visual-word-vectors from image sequences. Int. J. Robot. Res. **37**, 62–82 (2018)
23. Li, S., Lee, D.: RGB-D SLAM in dynamic environments using static point weighting. IEEE Robot. Autom. Lett. **99**, 2263–2270 (2017)

Inertial Sensor-Based Upper Limb Rehabilitation Auxiliary Equipment and Upper Limb Functional Rehabilitation Evaluation

Shanshan Wang, Jun Liao, Zirui Yong, Xiaohu Li, and Li Liu(✉)

School of Big Data and Software Engineering, Chongqing University, Chongqing 401331, China
dcsliuli@cqu.edu.cn

Abstract. Stroke patients in rehabilitation period often encounter problems such as high training cost and weak self supervision. We proposed a rehabilitation evaluation method of upper limb function based on wearable inertial sensor data acquisition auxiliary equipmen, which aims to realize the self-monitoring and evaluation of rehabilitation of patients in the middle and late stage of upper limb function rehabilitation. We have used three inertial sensing units MPU6050 to make wearable upper limb rehabilitation training auxiliary equipment, which can collect the motion data of stroke patients in rehabilitation period during daily rehabilitation training. Combined with lindmark upper limb rehabilitation scale, we collected eight hand gesture data for upper limb rehabilitation exercise evaluation. For the original data, quaternion data and Euler angle data, we established upper limb rehabilitation training action evaluation models based on libsvm, multi-layer LSTM and cnn-lstm neural network respectively to evaluate the rehabilitation status of patients. The results show that CNN LSTM model has the best performance, with the recognition accuracy of 99.67%, followed by multi-layer LSTM, and the model recognition accuracy of 97.00%. The work of this paper will provide a reference for patients in the middle and later rehabilitation stage of upper limb after stroke to realize their own supervised rehabilitation training and recovery state evaluation.

Keywords: Inertial sensors · Wearable devices · Upper limb rehabilitation training and assessment

1 Introduction

Stroke, also known as apoplexy, is an acute cerebrovascular disease that often occurs in middle-aged and elderly people. It is accompanied by high mortality and high disability and has become one of the main diseases that endanger human health in today's society. Due to the large range of the cerebral cortex mapped by the upper limb motor control, the rehabilitation treatment and

Y. Sun et al. (Eds.): ChineseCSCW 2021, CCIS 1491, pp. 518–528, 2022.
https://doi.org/10.1007/978-981-19-4546-5_40

rehabilitation assessment of the upper limb motor function have become a key problem to be solved urgently after stroke. Medical research has shown that the upper limb rehabilitation training of post-stroke patients can not only effectively improve the patient's condition, but hand and upper limb rehabilitation also plays a vital role in the rehabilitation of other diseases. The standardized training program given by the doctor is combined with regular follow-up visits. The assessment helps to restore the normal movement of upper limbs quickly. However, the current post-stroke rehabilitation training system has excessive time and resource costs, weak self-supervision, and high hospital dependence, which lead to prolonged rehabilitation and low efficiency. Therefore, the development of a low-cost, high-efficiency upper-limb rehabilitation system for patients in the recovery phase of stroke has become increasingly important. Unreasonable rehabilitation training without the guidance of professional doctors will not only produce unsatisfactory recovery effect, but also aggravate the condition: Patients with hand injury may have complications such as scar, tissue adhesion, joint stiffness and so on; Stroke patients may cause symptoms such as hand nerve paralysis and dyskinesia [1].

The existing rehabilitation assessment mainly focuses on the following four aspects: assessment of the severity of brain damage; motor function assessment; balance function assessment; and assessment of activities of daily living [13]. We mainly focuses on the upper limb motor function assessment in motor function assessment. According to the Lindmark upper limb motor function assessment method [5], the eight single-arm motor function recovery actions in this article are determined as Table 1.

2 Upper Limb Rehabilitation Data Collection Equipment

The wearable device that collects upper limb movement data in this article is composed of a main control module (Arduino) and a six-axis inertial sensor (MPU6050). The connection part is made of a 6 cm wide polyester elastic band, which transmits movement gestures through a serial port like terminal The signal data is stored in the terminal. MPU6050 is a space motion sensor chip that can obtain current three-axis acceleration components and three-axis rotation angular velocity, with a rated working voltage of 5 V and a rated current of 3.5 mA. The chip has a built-in data processing sub-module DMP, which uses the I2C bus communication protocol and the Wire library to realize the communication between the Arduino main control module and the MPU6050. The $MPU6050$ embeds the chip's registers to read and write data. The experimental data is stored in the 14-byte registers from $0x3B$ to $0x48$. The data will be dynamically updated in real time and the update frequency can reach 1000 Hz. Each data occupies 2 bytes. The MPU6050 chip has its own coordinate system: make the chip face itself and rotate the text on its surface to the correct angle. At this time, with the center of the chip as the origin, the X axis is horizontal to the right, the Y axis is vertically upward, and the Z axis points to itself. The specific structure of the upper limb wearable exercise data collection device is shown in Fig. 1.

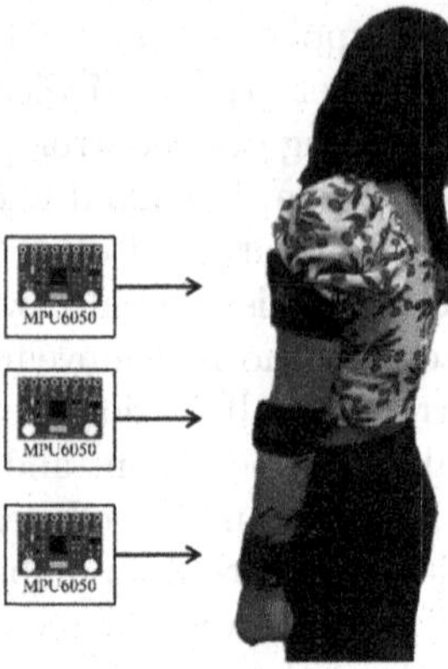

Fig. 1. Our upper limb rehabilitation data collection equipment.

3 Rehabilitation Assessment Method

Stroke is a common neurological disease. After the onset, patients often have half-body motor dysfunction is one of its important clinical features, which will greatly affect the daily life of patients, in order to determine the degree of motor function damage in stroke patients and The degree of recovery in the later period, and provides standards for the later recovery of motor training and active recovery training. A unified standard and recognized effective motor function evaluation method will provide an important basis for patient rehabilitation training. The reliability and validity of these sports training rehabilitation evaluation standards should be Is reliable [6]. There are different evaluation standards for patients in different recovery periods, including early, middle and late stages, and different professional evaluation standards for different rehabilitation parts, such as upper limbs, lower limbs, and back.

3.1 Eight Rehabilitation Assessment Motions Based on Lindmark Scale

Lindmark upper extremity motor function assessment is a complete set of comprehensive assessment methods for patients' motor function [5,12], revised on the basis of the Fugle-Meyer Assessment Scale (FMA) [2]. It mainly includes seven aspects: active movement, rapid rotation movement, posture transfer and walking, balance function, sensation, passive movement and pain. This article mainly discusses the upper limb motor function assessment in motor function examination.

Based on the evaluation criteria for upper limb rehabilitation in the Lindmark Motor Function Rating Scale [5], this article has determined the eight upper limb rehabilitation actions in this experiment, as illustrated in Table 1.

Table 1. Eight rehabilitation assessment motions.

Abbreviation	Gesture	Description
HTM	Hand touch mouth	Bend your elbows, suppose your forearms, your hands can touch your lips
HTN	Hand touch Back of neck	Shoulder Abduction, Elbow Bend, Forearm Pronation
SF	Shoulder flexion	Shoulder forward 180°, elbow extension
SA	Shoulder abduction	180 shoulder abduction, elbow extension
TTOK	Touch the opposite knee joint	Touch the outer side of the contralateral knee joint, shoulder adduction, internal rotation, elbow extension, and forearm pronation
FS	Forearm supination	Forearm supination 80°–90°
FP	Forearm pronation	Forearm pronation 80–90
TTW	Touch the waist	Bend your elbows and place the back of your hands on the same waist

When performing upper limb rehabilitation training movement check, you need to sit on a bed or a chair, wear a wearable upper limb movement data collection device, perform the specified movement and repeat it many times. The collected movement data will be passed through the serial port at 115200 baud rate 14 Hz. The sampling frequency is stored as a CSV data file.

3.2 Quaternion Expression

In this experiment, we perform data preprocessing, filtering and smoothing, and signal segmentation to obtain the quaternion after the original data obtained by the inertial sensor. The quaternion can well integrate the object space information represented by the accelerometer and the gyroscope and transform it into a more concise form of expression. It contains four elements, expressed as:

$$\mathbf{q}(q_0, q_1, q_2, q_3) = q_0 + q_1\mathbf{i} + q_2\mathbf{j} + q_3\mathbf{k}, \tag{1}$$

among them, **i**, **j**, **k** are imaginary number units, and they are required to obey the following algorithm:

$$\mathbf{ii} = \mathbf{jj} = \mathbf{kk} = -1; \mathbf{ij} = -\mathbf{ji}, \mathbf{jk} = -\mathbf{kj}, \mathbf{ki} = -\mathbf{ik}; \mathbf{ij} = \mathbf{k}, \mathbf{jk} = \mathbf{i}, \mathbf{ki} = \mathbf{j}. \tag{2}$$

The Runge-Kutta method [10,11] is used to update the quaternion, and the update formula is as follows:

$$\mathbf{q_{n+1}} = \mathbf{q_n} + \frac{1}{2}\begin{bmatrix} 0 & -g_{(n+1)x} & -g_{(n+1)y} & -g_{(n+1)z} \\ -g_{(n+1)x} & 0 & -g_{(n+1)z} & -g_{(n+1)y} \\ -g_{(n+1)y} & -g_{(n+1)z} & 0 & -g_{(n+1)x} \\ -g_{(n+1)z} & -g_{(n+1)y} & -g_{(n+1)x} & 0 \end{bmatrix}\mathbf{q_n}, \tag{3}$$

where g is the value obtained by the gyroscope. Bring the quaternion representation of upper limb movements into classification models to classify and recognize eight upper limb rehabilitation training movements.

4 Experiment

We selected eight adult college students aged 22–25, including four males and four females. Before the experiment, we recorded the one arm real person front video and 3D simulation animation video tutorial of the upper limb rehabilitation action used in the experiment in advance. 15 min before the experiment, inform the purpose and process of the experiment, and then play the tutorial video to make the volunteers familiar with the action. After the volunteers watched the eight upper limb single arm action teaching videos, let the volunteers face the computer and sit on the side, and put their hands on the hammer naturally to make them in the initial sitting position of the acquisition experiment. After that, the volunteers were shown a single action repetition video and asked to simulate and follow each action twice, with a total of eight groups of actions. After the simulation training, the volunteers rest for 5–10 min to relax the arm muscles again. Before the start of the formal experiment, we will wear the experimental upper limb wearable motion data acquisition device for the volunteers, open the data serial port, let the volunteers swing their upper limbs at will, and monitor whether the data transmission is normal. After confirming that the wearable equipment, data acquisition equipment and volunteers are ready, raise their hands and open the serial port to receive data. Volunteers follow the rehabilitation training actions played by computer video, 19–22 times for each action, a total of eight groups of actions. Among them, six volunteers use their right hands and two volunteers use their left hands. The sensing action data collected through the serial port will be stored as a CSV format file according to the volunteer serial number and action tag name. The whole experiment process of a single person lasts about 30 min. Volunteers wear the acquisition device to perform SA action, as shown in Fig. 2.

Fig. 2. Rehabilitation training motion SA.

5 Gesture Recognition

5.1 Data Preprocessing

The median filter [7] is used to smooth the data and remove abnormal points. The inertial sensor data fusion algorithm performs Mahony complementary filtering on the data according to the characteristics of inertial sensor data [8], but this does not ensure the smoothness of the data, and ignores the noise of bending sensor data. In order to solve this problem, the gravity acceleration is eliminated by subtracting the average value of the sampling acceleration from each data point to obtain the acceleration generated by the movement of the upper limb. The next step is to smooth the high-frequency noise by using the moving average filter. By measuring the same data source for many times, the multi-point set average method is used to obtain the data. The reasonable estimation is the moving average filter [9], and the filtering expression is as follows:

$$f[n] = \frac{1}{2M+1} \sum_{m=-M}^{M} f_r[n+m], \tag{4}$$

Which $f_r[n]$ refers to the n-th point of the data sample and M is the window size which is often set from 3 to 7 in this work.

5.2 Temporal Data Segmentation

The purpose of temporal data segmentation is to identify the beginning and end of each upper limb rehabilitation action. Continuous sensor data can be divided into individual upper limb action sequence intervals. A segmentation scheme of timing data is as shown in Fig 3, which shows the action HTM information. When no action is made, the upper limb sensing data is relatively stable. On the contrary, when an action is made, the sensing data will change greatly. Set the preprocessed attitude data sequence $\mathbf{P} = < \mathbf{p}_1, \mathbf{p}_2, ..\mathbf{p}_t, ..\mathbf{p}_n >$. Define $d[n]$ as the Euclidean distance between $\mathbf{P}[n]$ and $\mathbf{P}[n-1]$. The $d[n]$ of the action interval is much larger than the $d[n]$ without action. This conclusion can be used to segment the beginning and end of the action of time series data.

5.3 Build the Classifier

LibSVM. Different from the traditional SVM classifier, LibSVM is a set of support vector machine library developed by Taiwanese professor Lin Zhiren. It has an SVM library with fast calculation speed, easy expansion and convenient parameter adjustment. Different from the other two network models used in this article, LibSVM needs to process upper limb motion sensing data into lib format data, because the experimental data set extracted in this experiment is a time series data set. Therefore, we consider converting the original outs after data preprocessing and action segmentation into quaternion and Euler angle data, and then converting the three-dimensional format to two-dimensional to perform

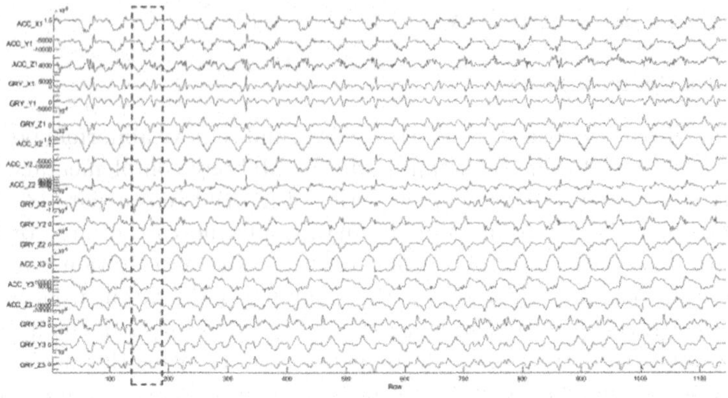

Fig. 3. Motion HTM raw attitude signal.

the conversion of the lib data format, and finally bring the data into the LibSVM classification Model. Use the grid tuning tool to optimize the parameters c and g. The principle is network traversal. In this experiment, the optimal parameters are obtained when $c = 2.0$ and $g = 0.001953$.

Multi-layer LSTM. LSTM is a variant time series model based on RNN network, it can obtain information in the time domain well [4,14]. In this experiment, we constructed single-layer, double-layer, four-layer, and six-layer LSTM networks to learn eight upper limb rehabilitation exercises.

CNN-LSTM. Considering the time-series information stored in the original data, this paper will combine traditional convolutional neural network (CNN) and long-short-term memory neural network (LSTM) to process upper limb motion sensing data [3,15]. Among them, the convolutional layer performs feature extraction, and the LSTM layer learns time series to achieve simultaneous processing of timing information and feature extraction of original data in a network. The CNN-LSTM network structure used in this paper to process the upper limb rehabilitation training sensor data is shown in Fig. 4.

As shown in Fig. 4, feed the collected upper limb single arm rehabilitation training action data to the array in numpy. The array dimension is (sample_size, time_step, features). After inputting the data, we use the one-dimensional convolution kernel moving on the sequence to construct the convolution layer. The convolution kernel in the sequence can act as a filter in training. In many CNN architectures, the greater the depth of the level, the more the number of filters. Each convolution operation is followed by a pooling layer to reduce the length of the sequence. In the experiment, we use a convolution layer and a pooling layer to process the original data and transmit it to the LSTM layer to learn the information between time series.

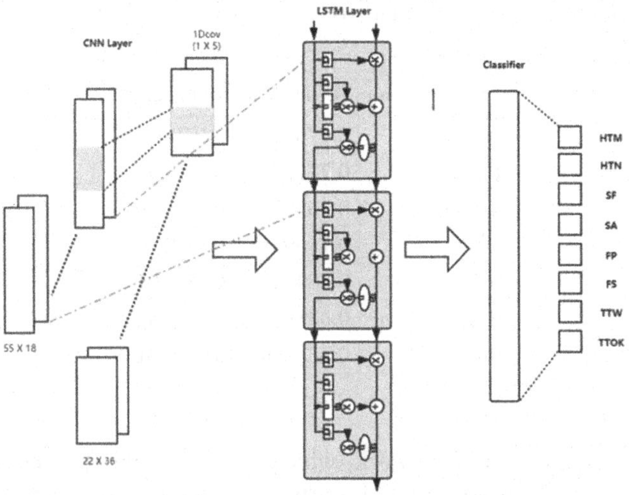

Fig. 4. CNN-LSTM network structure.

The performance of quaternion and Euler angle on libsvm is that the average recognition accuracy is about 70%. In order to analyze why the performance of the classifier is affected, we re process the original data into lib format data and feed it into the libsvm classifier with the same parameters. The results show that the performance of the original data on libsvm is much lower than that after processing the data into quaternions and Euler angles. It can be seen that quaternion and Euler angle can capture important information features of motion attitude and are better than the original accelerometer and gyroscope data set. However, because libsvm classifier can well learn the time correlation information hidden in time series, it does not perform well on the original data set without quaternion and Euler angle feature extraction.

Considering the time series characteristics of the above training action data, we built single-layer, double-layer, four layer and six layer LSTM networks. Compared with each classifiers' results, the performance of upper limb training action data in different layers of LSTM is almost the same, and the average recognition accuracy is about 97%, which is significantly higher than that in libsvm classifier. The final performance of LSTM with different layers used in this experiment is shown in Table 2. The effect of LSTM learning time series data is very good. It can be seen from the results that the recognition accuracy of LSTM networks with different layers for upper limb training recovery action is stable at about 97%. Compared with single-layer LSTM, the performance of six-layer LSTM is only improved by less than 0.1%. The performance of upper limb sensing data set on six-layer LSTM is shown in Fig. 5(a). Therefore, cnn-lstm network does not pay close attention to the characteristics of data sets in time series. At the same time, CNN convolution layer can automatically extract the most basic features of data sets and combine them into high-level and abstract features, and

Table 2. Performance of upper limb recovery training on different layers of LSTM network model.

LSTM layers	Batch loss	Accuracy
1	0.776494	0.970066
2	0.777375	0.970199
3	0.694999	0.970199
4	0.719958	0.973510
5	0.684645	0.976821
6	0.688868	0.980132
6	0.753726	0.976821

then feed them into LSTM network, which can better learn general statistical features and time series features. Figure 6 shows the performance of upper limb training motion sensing data set on CNN-LSTM model. The average recognition accuracy on the test set is 99.00% and the highest recognition accuracy is 99.67%.

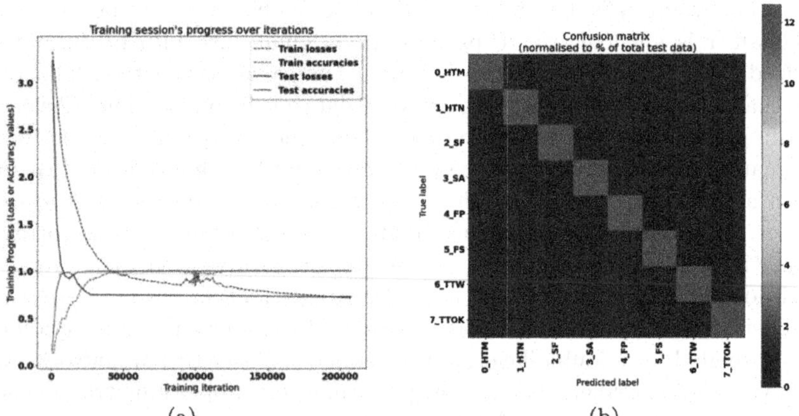

(a) (b)

Fig. 5. (a) Recognition accuracy of six layer LSTM network on test set; (b) Confusion matrix.

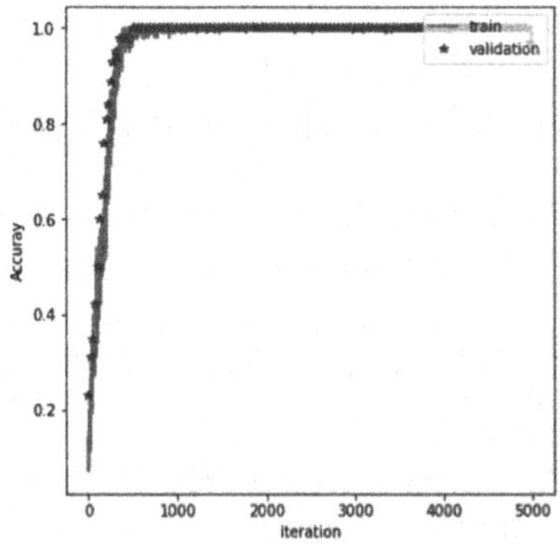

(a)

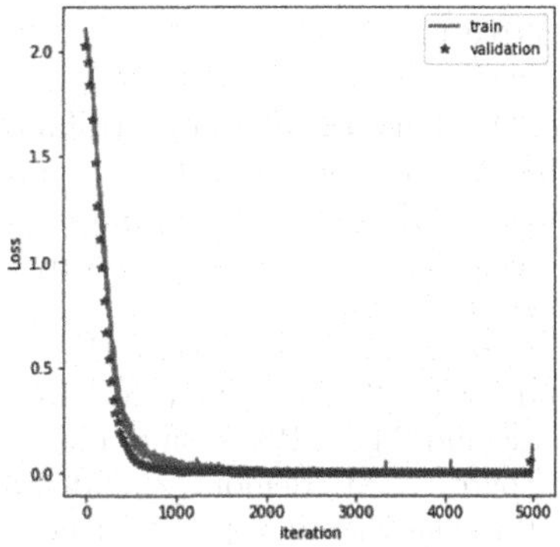

(b)

Fig. 6. (a) The accuracy of the CNN-LSTM model on the validation set; (b) Loss curve.

6 Conclusion

This paper presents a rehabilitation evaluation method of upper limb function based on inertial sensor data acquisition equipment, which aims to realize the self supervision and rehabilitation grade evaluation of patients in the middle and late rehabilitation stage of upper limb function. The upper limb wearable rehabilitation training data acquisition device is made of three inertial sensing units MPU6050, which can collect the motion data of patients during daily rehabilitation training. Combined with the lindmark upper limb rehabilitation evaluation scale, through the self collected eight kinds of upper limb rehabilitation movement evaluation gesture data, data preprocessing, filtering and smoothing, signal segmentation and other steps are carried out. For the original data, quaternion data and Euler angle data, the upper limb rehabilitation training movement evaluation models based on libsvm, multi-layer LSTM and cnn-lstm neural network are established respectively, Grade evaluation of patients' rehabilitation status. The results show that cnn-lstm model performs best, and the recognition accuracy is about 99.67%. Multi-layer LSTM performs second, and the model recognition accuracy is about 97%. Our follow-up work will continue to pay attention to the patients in the middle and late stage of rehabilitation after stroke, understand their rehabilitation training needs and rehabilitation schemes, continue to improve the upper limb rehabilitation movement data acquisition hardware equipment proposed in this paper, improve the wearable comfort of patients, and continue to improve the self-monitoring and evaluation scheme of rehabilitation training according to the needs of patients' rehabilitation training, Improve the recognition accuracy and real-time performance of the recognition model.

Acknowledgement. This work was supported by grants from the National Natural Science Foundation of China (Grant No. 61977012), the Central Universities in China (Grant No. 2021CDJYGRH011).

References

1. Bo, Q.: Home rehabilitation training system based on data glove. Master's thesis, Qingdao University (2014)
2. Duncan, P.W., Propst, M., Nelson, S.G.: Reliability of the Fugl-Meyer assessment of sensorimotor recovery following cerebrovascular accident. Phys. Ther. **63**(10), 1606–1610 (1983)
3. Kim, H.J., Lee, J.S., Park, J.H.: Dynamic hand gesture recognition using a CNN model with 3D receptive fields. In: 2008 International Conference on Neural Networks and Signal Processing, pp. 14–19. IEEE (2008)
4. Lefebvre, G., Berlemont, S., Mamalet, F., Garcia, C.: BLSTM-RNN based 3D gesture classification. In: Mladenov, V., Koprinkova-Hristova, P., Palm, G., Villa, A.E.P., Appollini, B., Kasabov, N. (eds.) ICANN 2013. LNCS, vol. 8131, pp. 381–388. Springer, Heidelberg (2013). https://doi.org/10.1007/978-3-642-40728-4_48
5. Lindmark, B., Hamrin, E.: Evaluation of functional capacity after stroke as a basis for active intervention. Presentation of a modified chart for motor capacity assessment and its reliability. Scand. J. Rehabil. Med. **20**(3), 103–109 (1988)
6. Nordin, N., Xie, S.Q., Wünsche, B.: Assessment of movement quality in robot-assisted upper limb rehabilitation after stroke: a review. J. Neuroeng. Rehabil. **11**(1), 1–23 (2014). https://doi.org/10.1186/1743-0003-11-137
7. Phillips, R.D., Blinn, C.E., Watson, L.T., Wynne, R.H.: An adaptive noise-filtering algorithm for AVIRIS data with implications for classification accuracy. IEEE Trans. Geosci. Remote Sens. **47**(9), 3168–3179 (2009)
8. Tian, H.L., Sun, Y.Q., Liu, H.P.: 3D motion trajectory recovery based on improved Mahony complementary filtering algorithm. Transducer Microsyst. Technol. **20**(1), 41–47 (2018)
9. Wu, X., Mao, X., Chen, L., Xue, Y.: Trajectory-based view-invariant hand gesture recognition by fusing shape and orientation. IET Comput. Vis. **9**(6), 797–805 (2015)
10. Xiayun Li, C.C.: Solving nonliner equations by using Runge-Kutta method. Math. Theory Appl. **28**(2), 62–65 (2008)
11. Xu, M.Y., Li, J.l., Zhang, D.C.: Analysis of the error result from single step of Runge-Kutta for the Euler equation with quaternion method. J. Air Force Eng. Univ. **2**, 37–49 (2002)
12. Yan, T.: Modern Rehabilitation Technology. Anhui Science and Technology Press (1994)
13. Effects of scalp acupuncture combined with rehabilitation training on motor function and activities of daily living in patients with spastic stage after stroke. Chin. Rehabil. **30**(2), 120–131 (2015)
14. Zebin, T., Sperrin, M., Peek, N., Casson, A.J.: Human activity recognition from inertial sensor time-series using batch normalized deep LSTM recurrent networks. In: 2018 40th Annual International Conference of the IEEE Engineering in Medicine and Biology Society (EMBC), pp. 1–4. IEEE (2018)
15. Zhang, L., Zhu, G., Shen, P., Song, J., Afaq Shah, S., Bennamoun, M.: Learning spatiotemporal features using 3dcnn and convolutional LSTM for gesture recognition. In: Proceedings of the IEEE International Conference on Computer Vision Workshops, pp. 3120–3128 (2017)

An Improved Ant Colony Algorithm for Vehicle Routing Problem with Workload Balance

Yaohuiqiong Fang and Jingjing Li(✉)

School of Computer Science, South China Normal University, Guangzhou 510631, China
lijingjing@scnu.edu.cn

Abstract. This paper studies a bi-objective vehicle routing problem considering both travel cost and workload balance. Different from the existing research, the workload balance is calculated by workload variance and average value. We propose an improved multi-objective ant colony algorithm (MO-ACOTC) to eliminate distorted solutions and use a new global pheromone update strategy. The algorithm also designs a travel constraint mechanism to dynamically control the workload for each vehicle. The experimental results on traditional and revised instances show that the algorithm can obtain satisfactory solutions.

Keywords: Vehicle routing problems · Workload balancing · Ant colony algorithm

1 Introduction

Vehicle routing problem (VRP) is one of the most important fields in transportation systems. The solution to this problem is to determine the route of vehicle distribution according to the target requirements [11]. For solving the problem, there are many algorithms proposed to reduce cost and improve customer satisfaction.

The fairness between vehicles is a key issue in VRP. The benefits of achieving fairness are three fold: 1) as to deliverers, reducing overtime and ensuring each driver is treated equally and fairly. 2) as to logistics company, saving the shipping cost and improving the service quality. 3) as to customers, improving user experience. However, the general VRP only consider the maximization of platform benefits, rarely consider the workload distribution among different deliverers, and it is difficult to meet the general demand of performance bonus balance [3]. Unfairness directly affects employee benefits and morale, and indirectly affects company revenue and service quality.

In recent years, fairness-related topics have gradually been discussed by researchers. Study [6] by Halvorsen-Weare and Savelsbergh proposes four

Supported by the Key Project of Science and Technology Innovation 2030 supported by the Ministry of Science and Technology of China (Grant No. 2018AAA0101300).

Y. Sun et al. (Eds.): ChineseCSCW 2021, CCIS 1491, pp. 529–540, 2022.
https://doi.org/10.1007/978-981-19-4546-5_41

different models that comprehensively explore the classification and characteristics of "fairness" in VRP. Different papers have different ways to quantify the fairness. In most papers, the VRP's fairness is defined as the balance of the length of routes (travel cost) between vehicles. Y. Sun et al. [13] modeled the problem as a bi-objective optimization problem (VRP with routing balance, VRPRB), in which route balance is to minimize the difference between the longest and the shortest route lengths among vehicles. For solving this problem, [7] proposed a multi-start method based on two search spaces.

Balancing the capacity or load of vehicles can increase the utilization rate of vehicles. Green VRP considers load and the fuel consumption directly related to load and distance in the paper [12]. Paper [8] proposed a fairness model and designed a meta heuristic algorithm considering load fairness.

In the logistics systems, the performance of employees is generally related to workload [15]. The workload often not only refers to the transportation time and service time [14], but also includes quantifiable information such as the weight and quantity of goods that affect the distribution progress of the deliveryman [9]. This paper addresses a VRP with workload balance (VRPWB), which minimizes both travel cost and workload balance. An improved ant colony algorithm called Multi-objective Ant Colony Algorithm with Travel Constraints (MO-ACOTC) is designed to solve VRPWB. MO-ACOTC adds a travel constraint to the ant routing process to ensure workload balance, and proposes the elimination method of distorted solution. In addition, the global pheromone update strategy is improved to speed up the convergence of MO-ACOTC.

The remaining sections are organized as follows. Section 2 presents problem formulation. Section 3 proposes the algorithm for the problem. Section 4 presents experimental results. Finally, Sect. 5 presents the conclusion.

2 Problem Formulation

We define VRPWB on a complete undirected graph $G = \langle N, E \rangle$, where vertex set $N = \{0, 1, 2, \cdots, n\}$ consists of depot 0 and n customers, $E = \{(i, j) \mid i, j \in N\}$ is the edge set. The travel cost of each edge (i, j) is represented by c_{ij}, and each customer $i \in N \setminus 0$ is associated with a demand d_i. The demand of depot is assumed as $d_0 = 0$.

The logistics company has a driver crew and their vehicle collection V, with m vehicles. Each vehicle corresponds to a driver, which has the same upper capacity limit C^v. The mathematical formulation and constraints for VRPWB are defined as follows

$$(minf_1(s), minf_2(s)) \tag{1}$$

$$\sum_{i \in N} x_{ij}^v = y_j^v, \quad \forall v \in V, \forall j \in N, j \neq i \tag{2}$$

$$\sum_{j \in N} x_{ij}^v = y_i^v, \quad \forall v \in V, \forall i \in N, i \neq j \tag{3}$$

$$\sum_{i,j \in N} x_{ij}^{v} \geq 1, \quad \forall v \in V, \forall i, j \in N, i \neq j \tag{4}$$

$$\sum_{v \in V} y_{i}^{v} = 1, \quad \forall i = 1, \cdots, n \tag{5}$$

$$\sum_{v \in V} y_{0}^{v} = m \tag{6}$$

$$\sum_{i \in N} \left(y_{i}^{v} d_{i}\right) \leq C^{v}, \quad \forall v \in V \tag{7}$$

$$\begin{aligned} & u_{i}^{v} - u_{j}^{v} + C^{v} x_{ij}^{v} \leq C^{v} - d_{j}, \\ & \forall i, j \in N \backslash \{0\}, i \neq j, v \in V, d_{i} + d_{j} \leq C^{v} \end{aligned} \tag{8}$$

$$d_{i} \leq u_{i}^{v} \leq C^{v}, \quad \forall i \in N \backslash \{0\}, v \in V \tag{9}$$

Formula (1) shows the optimization objectives of the VRPWB model. The objective functions $f_1(s)$ and $f_2(s)$ are defined by the travel cost and workload balance indicator, respectively. The constraints (2) along with (3), indicate that each node obeys flow conservation constraints. If vehicle v enters node i, then it must depart from node i. Where x_{ij}^{v} is binary variable equal to 1 if vehicle v can travel from i to j directly, and 0, otherwise. And y_{i}^{v} is a binary variable which takes value of 1 if vehicle v serves customer i. Constraint (4) ensures that each vehicle has at least one customer. Constraint (5) ensures that each customer only served by one vehicle. Constraint (6) ensures that all vehicles must depart from the same depot. Constraint (7) ensures that the total delivery demand of the nodes in each route should not exceed the vehicle capacity. Subtour elimination is given in (8) and (9) which are proposed by [10].

For the two objective functions of formula (1), the first objective function can be written as:

$$f_1 = \sum_{i \in N} \sum_{j \in N} \sum_{v \in V} c_{ij} x_{ij}^{v} \tag{10}$$

To represent the second objective function, this paper uses b_v to represent the driver v's workload, as shown in formula (11). The workload of driver v is defined as the weighted sum of the travel costs and load of all orders he has completed.

$$b^{v} = \sum_{i \in N} \left(y_{i}^{v} \left(\alpha d_{i} + \beta \sum_{j \in N} \left(c_{ij} \sum_{v \in V} x_{ij}^{v} \right) \right) \right) \tag{11}$$

In the paper [6], variance b^{Varia} is minimized to achieve fairness, as shown in formula (12). The formula controls the difference of workload of each driver in a smaller range.

$$f_{2}^{-}(s) = b^{Varia} = \frac{\sum_{v \in V} \left(b^{v} - \bar{b}\right)^{2}}{m} \tag{12}$$

Minimizing variance may result in falling into a local optimal solution, that is, a solution with a great overall workload. In this paper, we introduce average workload $\bar{b}$ to control the overall workload for second objective. Therefore, the second objective function is shown in formula (13), where the workload balance is consisted of the workload variance and average workload, the γ and δ is weight.

$$f_2(s) = \gamma b^{Varia} + \delta \bar{b} \tag{13}$$

3 Multi-objective Ant Colony Optimization Algorithm

The main procedure of MO-ACOTC is given in Algorithm 1, in which a set of Pareto optimal solutions is updated by modifying the concentration of pheromone. The entire inner loop (line 4–16) shows the process of solutions construction. The ant uses the pheromone updating rule and travel constraint mechanism in the program **CNN**($Point_i$) to select the next customer node.

Algorithm 1. MO-ACOTC

Require: N
Ensure: The Pareto solution set P
1: initialize P and the pheromone trails on each arc;
2: **for** $r \leftarrow 0$ to R **do**
3: $S_P \leftarrow$ greedy algorithm gets the initial solution;
4: **for** $a \leftarrow 0$ to n_k (number of ants) **do**
5: $S^a \leftarrow$ depot 0, $ri \leftarrow 0$, $Demand^a_{ri} \leftarrow 0$;
6: **repeat**
7: **if** ($Point_j \leftarrow$ **CNN** ($Point_i$))==depot 0 **then**
8: r_i++;
9: **end if**
10: $S^a \leftarrow S^a \bigcup Point_j$, $Point_i \leftarrow Point_j$, $Demand^a_{ri} += d_{Point_j}$;
11: update tabu list and update the local pheromone according to equation (14);
12: **until** ($N \subseteq S^a$)
13: $P' \leftarrow$ **update** (S^a, P');
14: **end for**
15: $P \leftarrow$ **update** (P', P);
16: **if** P doesn't change after $R0$ iterations **then**
17: Break;
18: **end if**
19: eliminating cross-paths in the extreme solution on the two objectives;
20: update the global pheromone according to equation (16);
21: **end for**

There are n_k ants at the depot. The path of each ant represents a feasible solution. The ant departs from the depot, visits some customer nodes and returns to the depot. Each ant can go in and go out the depot some rounds. The number of rounds an ant needs to perform is equal to the number of vehicles. That is, an ant completes traversing all customers in set N and builds a tabu list, forming a route that represents a solution S^a. The path visited by the ant in a round ri corresponds to the path traveled by a vehicle v. The ants produce a set of Pareto solution P' in each iteration, and update the Pareto optimal solution set P according to P' at the end of this iteration.

3.1 Eliminating Cross-paths

As shown in Fig. 1(a), for balancing the workload of each vehicle, a driver may lift the workload by detouring. The solution is not the desired workload balancing effect, thereby is called a "distorted solution". For avoiding the distorted solution, we design a method to eliminate the cross-paths.

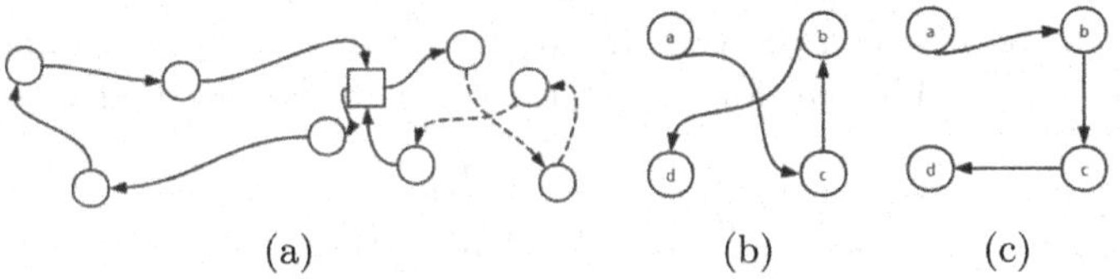

Fig. 1. Distorted solution (a), initial path (b) and uncrossed path (c).

The specific rules for eliminating crosspoint are as follows: assuming that the current routing edge intersects or is collinear with an edge in the previous tabu list. The starting node of the current edge and the ending node of the intersecting edge are exchanged. For example, suppose that the path from node a to d in the tabu list order $[a, c, b, d]$ is shown in Fig. 1(b). Edges (a, c) and (b, d) are determined to be crossed, then the tabu list is reset to cancel the crossing. The reset tabu list is $[a, b, c, d]$, as shown in Fig. 1(c).

3.2 Improved Pheromone Update Rules

Pheromones on the route are updated locally according to formula (14).

$$phe_{ij} = Vp \times phe_{ij} + (1 - Vp) \tag{14}$$

Among them, Vp is the pheromone volatilization parameter, and the phe_0 is computed by:

$$phe_0 = \frac{1}{n \times cost_{NN}} \tag{15}$$

The $cost_{NN}$ is the total travel costs of all vehicles obtained by the nearest neighbor heuristic algorithm (NN) [1], which is fixed. Ant k updates the pheromone locally whenever it moves from the node $Point_i$ to the next node $Point_j$ (line 11 of Algorithm 1).

After all ants build their routes, the algorithm updates the pheromones globally to enhance the pheromone on the optimal solution of the two objectives in P. The volatilization rules are as follows:

$$phe_{ij} = \begin{cases} Vp\left(phe_{ij} + \frac{Kp}{\overline{cost_P}}\right), if\ (i,j) \in \left\{S_{min\{f_1(s)\}}, S_{min\{f_2(s)\}}\right\} \\ Vp \times phe_{ij} + (1 - Vp)\frac{Kp}{\overline{cost_P}}, \\ \quad if\ (i,j) \in P\backslash\left\{S_{min\{f_1(s)\}}, S_{min\{f_2(s)\}}\right\} \\ Vp \times phe_{ij}, \quad otherwise \end{cases} \tag{16}$$

where Vp and Kp are parameters, and $\overline{cost_P}$ is the average total path length in the Pareto optimal solution set. Different from the traditional way of strengthening the solution path of the whole Pareto optimal solution set [2], in this paper we enhance the pheromone on the optimal solution path satisfying the first objective and the second objective in the current Pareto optimal solution set, and evaporate the pheromone according to Vp on the non Pareto optimal solution path. The path pheromone concentration of other Pareto optimal solutions is set to be between the two. In addition, we set a upper bound $Maxpha$ and a lower bound $Minpha$ for the pheromone phe_{ij} on each edge (i, j).

$$Maxphe = \frac{Kp}{(1 - Vp) \times \overline{cost_P}} \tag{17}$$

$$Minphe = \frac{Maxphe}{2n} \tag{18}$$

3.3 Route Search with Traffic Constraints

The travel constraint mechanism is divided into two parts. First, the workload indicator $doub^k_{ri}$ for the driver represented by the ants in the current round ri is defined. This indicator is determined by the driver's current workload $nowBk^k_{ri}$ and the average workload $avBk$ of the most balanced solution in the current P, as shown in formula (19)–(21):

$$doub^k_{ri} = \frac{nowBk^k_{ri}}{avBk} \tag{19}$$

$$nowBk^k_{ri} = b^v \tag{20}$$

$$avBk = \frac{\sum_{x \in N\backslash\{0\}} (\alpha d_x) + \beta cost_{f_2}}{m} \tag{21}$$

Second, when $doub^k_{ri}$ is less than ε, ants can choose the next node through the visibility Tp_{ij} from the current node to other nodes. At the same time, the mechanism prevents the ant from returning to the depot when the $doub^k_{ri}$ is lower than ζ.

$$Tp_{ij} = phe^{K1}_{ij} \times \left(\frac{K3}{c_{ij}}\right)^{K2} \tag{22}$$

Tp_{ij} is calculated as shown in formula (22), where $K1$, $K2$, and $K3$ are constant parameters.

When $doub_{ri}^{k}$ is greater than ε, the ants can be forced to return to the depot with probability. If the $doub_{ri}^{k}$ is less than 1, which means that the workload of the vehicle represented by the ant is less than the average workload $avBk$, the ant returns to the depot with a small probability ε_1. Otherwise, the ant returns with a higher probability ε_2. The pseudocode of route search with traffic constraints is shown in Algorithm 2.

Algorithm 2. CNN($Point_i$)

Input: the previous node $Point_i$
Output: the next node $Point_j$
1: initialize $doub_{ri}^{k}$, $nowBk_{ri}^{k}$ and $avBk$ according to equation (19), (20) and (21)
2: **if** $Demand_{ri}^{k} == C^{v}$ **then**
3: return depot 0;
4: **end if**
5: **if** $doub_{ri}^{k} > \varepsilon$ and $doub_{ri}^{k} \leq 1$ **then**
6: **if** $Random_1 < \varepsilon_1 doub_{ri}^{k}$ **then**
7: return depot 0;
8: **end if**
9: **else if** $doub_{ri}^{k} > 1$ **then**
10: **if** $Random_2 < \varepsilon_2 doub_{ri}^{k}$ **then**
11: return depot 0;
12: **end if**
13: **end if**
14: **if** $doub_{ri}^{k} > \zeta$ **then**
15: **if** $Random_3 \leq \zeta_1$ **then**
16: return the node with the highest visibility Tp_{ij} in N;
17: **else**
18: return the node randomly selected by roulette in N;
19: **end if**
20: **else**
21: return the node randomly selected by roulette in $N \setminus \{0\}$;
22: **end if**

4 Experimental Results

We implement the experiments in C++ on a PC (INTEL i7-8750H CPU 2.20 GHz with 16 GB RAM). We execute the algorithm 10 times per instance and compute the average runtime. All experimental test data sets are derived from the instances of Christofides et al. [4,5]. These instance names consist of $X - nnum1 - knum2$. The $num1$ is the number of customers, $num2$ is the number of vehicles, K is the identifier, X is the "E" for instance from [4] and the "M" for instance from [5].

When calculating $f_2(s)$, the workload variance b^{Varia} is on the same order of magnitude as the average workload \bar{b}. Therefore, unless otherwise specified, the weights α, β, γ, and δ for all test datasets in this experiment are all 1. For the basic parameters of MO-ACOTC, the range of values of each parameter will be determined by referring to the relevant literature. Instance E-n101-k8 of [4] are taken as test example. By calculating the average number of iterations required to reach an approximate optimal solution, the best results are obtained when $Vp = 0.8$, $Kp = K3 = 1or100$ (the value is determined by the size of the sample space node), $K1 = 2$, and $K2 = 5$. Through observation on the test instances, we assign $\varepsilon = 0.7$, $\varepsilon_1 = 0.3$, $\varepsilon_2 = 0.7$, $\zeta = 0.85$ and $\zeta_1 = 0.5$ to the return mechanism.

Since the algorithm for the multi-objective problems should satisfy both convergence and diversity, we use two metrics to evaluate the performance of the algorithm. Inverted generational distance (IGD) is an indicator to quantify the convergence and diversity of the nondominated solutions obtained. The smaller value of the IGD means the solution set obtained is denser and closer to the true Pareto front. Hypervolume (HV) takes into consideration the degree of accuracy and diversity of the solutions produced by the algorithm. The greater value of the HV means the more closeness of the solutions to the Pareto-optimal front.

We validate the effectiveness of the eliminating cross-paths method in avoiding distorted solutions, and discusses how to enhance the pheromones on the path. Next, the performance of the proposed algorithm is verified.

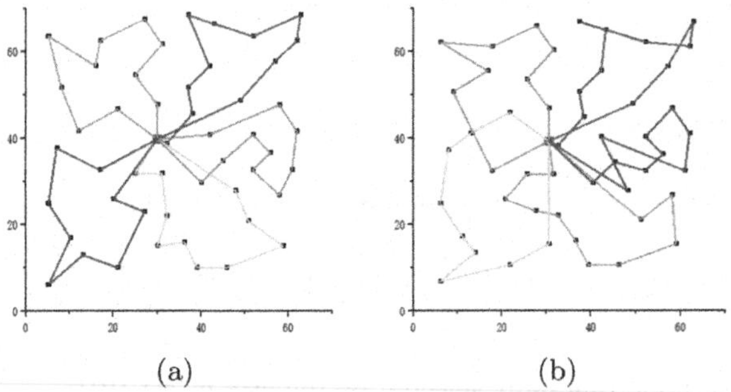

Fig. 2. The most balanced solution obtained by MO-ACOTC (a) and ACO (b).

As shown in Fig. 2, an example of the balanced routes obtained by MO-ACOTC and ACO without eliminating cross-paths method on instance E-n51-k5 [4]. This instance contains 5 vehicles, and the routes in the same color belong to the same vehicle. From Fig. 2(b), we can find that many routes take detours, thereby there are many crossing points on the routes. In Fig. 2(a), there is no cross path for each vehicle, indicating that the balance is not achieved by detouring. Therefore, it can be concluded that the eliminating cross-paths method adopted in MO-ACOTC can effectively the avoid distorted solutions.

We attempt to discuss two global pheromone updating methods to determine the best way to enhance pheromones. 1) Increase the path of the entire Pareto solution set; 2) Maintain the pheromones of other non-dominated solution paths while mainly increasing the pheromones of paths in the optimal solutions of $f_1(s)$ and $f_2(s)$.

The algorithms with the above two global pheromone updating methods are carried out 10 times on the instance E-n101-k8 in the same running time. According to the distribution of all Pareto solutions obtained by the two methods shown in Fig. 3 (a), the first method was able to converge better in the obtained nondominated front. However, the proposed method was able to maintain a better spread of solutions and converge closer to the true Pareto-optimal front. Their respective Pareto-optimal front are shown in Fig. 3(b). It can be seen that the Pareto-optimal front of the proposed method are at the lower left of the Pareto-optimal front of the first method, which means that both of these objectives are getting better solutions. One possible reason for this is that when the size of the Pareto solution set obtained by the algorithm increases, in the first method, the effect of global pheromone updating is weaken because there are too many paths to be enhanced in the solution. Therefore, compared with the traditional methods, the proposed algorithm ensures diversity and speeds up the convergence.

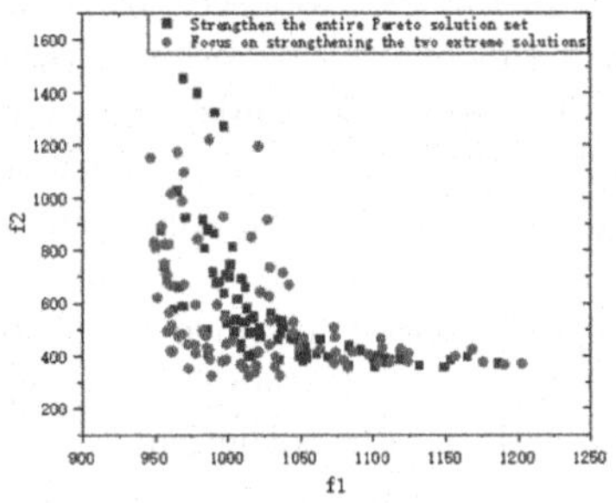

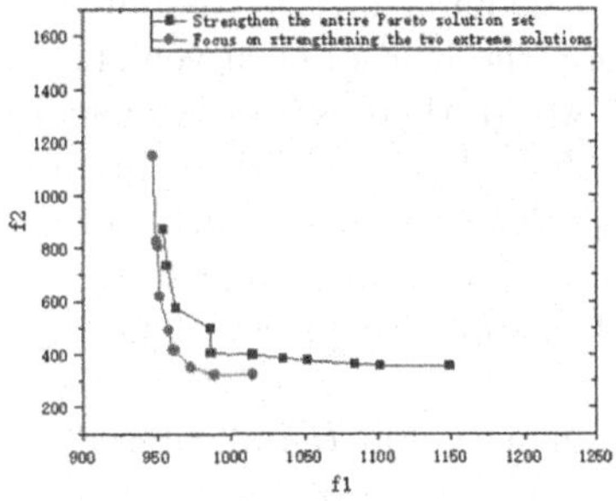

Fig. 3. (a) All Pareto solution sets. (b) The Pareto-optimal front.

Furthermore, we compare MO-ACOTC with the traditional ACO and the algorithm (MO-ACO) proposed by Chen Xiqiong et al. [2].

As shown in Table 1, on average, the *IGD* of MO-ACOTC is 46.4% and 45.6% lower than that of other algorithms, and the *HV* is 31.2% and 29.8% higher than that of other algorithms. In summary, MO-ACOTC significantly outperforms other algorithms in all the instances. Figure 4(a) shows the comparison of the Pareto-optimal front obtained by MO-ACOTC with that obtained by ACO and MO-ACO on the selected instance E-n101-k8 over 10 runs. It can be seen that MO-ACOTC can greatly push the ACO's front toward left and bottom directions, which means that two objectives get significantly improved. We also notice that the extent of the approximated Pareto front by MO-ACOTC is greater than that by ACO and MO-ACO. The above results show that MO-ACOTC can accelerate the convergence and improve the diversity.

Table 1. Performance comparison of three algorithms on 7 instances

Instance	IDG			HV		
	ACO	MO-ACO	MO-ACOTC	ACO	MO-ACO	MO-ACOTC
E-n51-k5	0.177	0.190	**0.136**	0.748	0.740	**0.815**
E-n76-k10	0.417	0.410	**0.155**	0.375	0.417	**0.717**
E-n101-k8	0.353	0.336	**0.102**	0.573	0.590	**0.886**
M-n101-k10	0.061	0.058	**0.056**	0.786	0.785	**0.788**
M-n121-k7	0.350	0.312	**0.148**	0.419	0.449	**0.679**
M-n151-k12	0.313	0.311	**0.170**	0.482	0.495	**0.650**
M-n200-k17	0.355	0.377	**0.316**	0.542	0.491	**0.619**
AVERAGE	0.289	0.285	**0.155**	0.561	0.567	**0.736**

It is to be noted that, the capacity of all vehicles is always very close to the total demand of the customers in the instances proposed by [4] and [5]. Therefore, the load of each vehicle is almost full before delivering. However, in the real world, there is another usual situation where the loads of most vehicles are less than their capacities, only a few vehicles are fully loaded. This scenario can easily lead to unfair workload arrangements for drivers. According to this situation, we modified the instances that the vehicle capacity is expanded to 1.5 times the original capacity. The format of the revised instance is the original name appended by $num3H$, where $num3$ indicates the number of expanded vehicle capacity and H indicates the previous data is hypothetical.

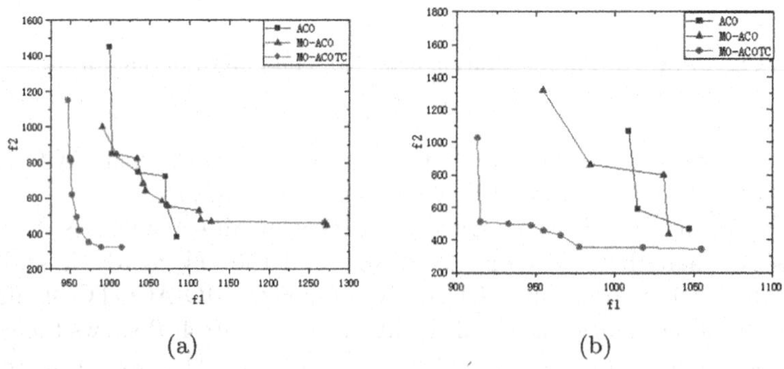

Fig. 4. The Pareto-optimal front obtained by MO-ACOTC, ACO and MO-ACO on instances E-n101-k8 (a) and E-n101-k8-300H (b).

Table 2. Performance comparison of three algorithms on 7 revised instances

Instance	IDG			HV		
	ACO	MO-ACO	MO-ACOTC	ACO	MO-ACO	MO-ACOTC
E-n51-k5-240H	0.364	0.446	**0.106**	0.612	0.517	**0.910**
E-n76-k10-210H	0.485	0.477	**0.196**	0.374	0.392	**0.771**
E-n101-k8-300H	0.415	0.394	**0.125**	0.393	0.429	**0.789**
M-n101-k10-300H	0.130	0.115	**0.075**	0.560	0.587	**0.746**
M-n121-k7-300H	0.408	0.355	**0.086**	0.278	0.312	**0.694**
M-n151-k12-300H	0.397	0.343	**0.200**	0.490	0.519	**0.616**
M-n200-k17-300H	0.343	0.339	**0.244**	0.451	0.468	**0.572**
AVERAGE	0.363	0.353	**0.147**	0.451	0.461	**0.728**

Table 2 shows the IGD and HV values of the three algorithms on the revised instances. We can find that MO-ACOTC obtains the best value on all instances. Compared with Table 1, the gap of the HV and IGD values between the ACO/MO-ACO and MO-ACOTC is greater. Figure 4(b) shows that both ACO and MO-ACO get stuck at different local Pareto-optimal sets, and the convergence and ability to find a diverse set of solutions are still better with MO-ACOTC. Therefore, it can be concluded that MO-ACOTC is more stable when dealing with instances with different sizes of vehicle capacity, which reflects strong robustness.

5 Conclusion

This paper presents a new vehicle routing problem with workload balancing. Which considers vehicle capacity and travel constraints while minimizing total travel cost and workload balance. The workload balance is composed of the workload variance and average value of workload. For solving the problem, we propose a multi-objective ant colony algorithm with traffic constraints. The algorithm uses a new global pheromone update strategy to accelerate the convergence and applies a method to avoid distorted solutions. In the route search, the travel constraint mechanism is proposed to a ensure fair workload for all drivers. The experiment results verify the validity of the new pheromone update strategy and the distorted resolution method. The comparison experiments shows MO-ACOTC performs better than other algorithms on traditional in terms of IGD and HV. The superiority of MO-ACOTC over other algorithms on revised instances is more obvious than on real-world instances.

References

1. Barán, B., Schaerer, M.: A multiobjective ant colony system for vehicle routing problem with time windows. In: Applied Informatics, pp. 97–102 (2003)

2. Chen, X., Hu, D.: An improved ant colony algorithm for multi-objective vehicle routing problem with simultaneous pickup and delivery. Control Theory Appl. **35**(09), 1347–1356 (2018)
3. Chiang, W.C., Cheng, C.Y.: Considering the performance bonus balance in the vehicle routing problem with soft time windows. Procedia Manufact. **11**, 2156–2163 (2017)
4. Christofides, N., Eilon, S.: An algorithm for the vehicle-dispatching problem. J. Oper. Res. Soc. **20**, 309–318 (1969)
5. Christofides, N.: The vehicle routing problem. Comb. Optim. **40**, 315–338 (1979)
6. Halvorsen-Weare, E.E., Savelsbergh, M.W.: The bi-objective mixed capacitated general routing problem with different route balance criteria. Eur. J. Oper. Res. **251**(2), 451–465 (2016)
7. Lacomme, P., Prins, C., Prodhon, C., Ren, L.: A multi-start split based path relinking (MSSPR) approach for the vehicle routing problem with route balancing. Eng. Appl. Artif. Intell. **38**, 237–251 (2015)
8. Londono, J., Rendon, R., Ocampo, E.: Iterated local search multi-objective methodology for the green vehicle routing problem considering workload equity with a private fleet and a common carrier. Int. J. Ind. Eng. Comput. **12**(1), 115–130 (2021)
9. Mancini, S., Gansterer, M., Hartl, R.F.: The collaborative consistent vehicle routing problem with workload balance. Eur. J. Oper. Res. **293**(3), 955–965 (2021)
10. Miller, C.E., Tucker, A.W., Zemlin, R.A.: Integer programming formulation of traveling salesman problems. J. ACM **7**(4), 326–329 (1960)
11. Reihaneh, M., Ghoniem, A.: A branch-cut-and-price algorithm for the generalized vehicle routing problem. J. Oper. Res. Soc. **69**(2), 307–318 (2018)
12. Saka, O.C., Gürel, S., Woensel, T.V.: Using cost change estimates in a local search heuristic for the pollution routing problem. OR Spectrum **39**(2), 557–587 (2016). https://doi.org/10.1007/s00291-016-0464-9
13. Sun, Y., Liang, Y., Zhang, Z., Wang, J.: M-NSGA-II: a memetic algorithm for vehicle routing problem with route balancing. In: International Conference on Industrial Engineering and Other Applications of Applied Intelligent Systems, Arras, France, pp. 61–71, June 2017
14. Wang, J., Zhou, Y., Wang, Y., Zhang, J., Chen, C.P., Zheng, Z.: Multiobjective vehicle routing problems with simultaneous delivery and pickup and time windows: formulation, instances, and algorithms. IEEE Trans. Cybern. **46**(3), 582–594 (2015)
15. Worku, Z.: A study of employee perceptions about performance appraisal at transnet engineering, South Africa. J. Appl. Bus. Res. **35**(5), 145–156 (2019)

Cooperative Localization for Human Pose Estimation

Zifan Chen[1], Xin Qin[2], Chao Yang[3], and Li Zhang[1(✉)]

[1] Center for Data Science, Peking University, Beijing 100080, China
{czifan,zhangli_pku}@pku.edu.cn
[2] Zhejiang University, Hangzhou 310058, China
xinqin@zju.edu.cn
[3] College of Computer Science and Electronic Engineering, Hunan University, Changsha 410082, China
yangchaoedu@hnu.edu.cn

Abstract. The existing methods for human pose estimation are needed to predict either dense heatmap, which requires more complex model architecture, or to execute long-distance regression, which makes the model unable to achieve good performance. This work proposes an accurate and efficient deep learning framework for human pose estimation called cooperative localization. It uses a sparse heatmap to find the keypoint's approximate location while two short-distance offsetmaps obtain its precise coordinates. To realize the framework, we construct two types of cooperative localization networks: CLNet-ResNet and CLNet-Hourglass. We evaluate the networks on three benchmark datasets: the Leeds Sports Pose dataset, the MPII Human Pose dataset, and the COCO keypoints detection dataset. Experimental results show that our framework consistently improves the average precision of their plain counterparts. The CLNet-ResNet50 outperforms SimpleBaseline by 1.14% with about 1/2 GFLOPs, and the CLNet-Hourglass outperforms the original stacked-hourglass by 4.45% on COCO.

Keywords: Human pose estimation · Cooperative localization · Deep learning

1 Introduction

Human pose estimation, predicting a person's body part or joint positions from an image or a video, is fundamental in computer vision with plenty of applications in human-computer interaction, action recognition, and other practical tasks. Recently, deep neural networks have surpassed the previous methods based on hand-crafted features by significantly improving the prediction accuracy in human pose estimation [14,17,24,25].

Supported by the Grants under Beijing Natural Science Foundation (Z180001), the National Natural Science Foundation of China (NSFC) under Grants 12090022, 11831002, and 81801778.

Y. Sun et al. (Eds.): ChineseCSCW 2021, CCIS 1491, pp. 541–552, 2022.
https://doi.org/10.1007/978-981-19-4546-5_42

The human pose estimation based on deep learning can be divided into regression-based and heatmap-based methods. The regression-based method can predict the coordinates of keypoints in an end-to-end fashion but may sacrifice prediction accuracy due to possible information loss of the long-distance regression [4,18,24]. The heatmap-based method predicts the probability of different keypoints on specific pixels and forms a heatmap to present the probabilities [12,20–23,26], which usually produces higher prediction accuracy but requires more computational resources. There are also a handful of studies that have attempted to combine the two types of methods, but they often fail to achieve satisfactory accuracy because they just stack the two types of methods to produce an over-complex model which is difficult to train [19].

In this work, we decouple the complex and high-dimensional task of keypoint detection into two simpler and cooperative low-dimensional tasks: to detect an approximate location of the keypoints with a low-resolution heatmap (called sparse heatmap) and to find the accurate keypoint coordinates using short-distance regression from the approximate location. Rather than stacking the models [19], we propose a cooperative localization (CL) framework that learns two simpler objectives simultaneously in a multi-task learning paradigm. Such two simple objectives have proved to be suitable for neural networks to learn rather than a complex one [9].

The main contributions can be summarized as follows: 1) We propose a CL framework to decouple the high-dimensional task of keypoint detection into two cooperative low-dimensional tasks and train them in a multi-task learning manner. 2) The proposed CL framework is easy to implement and can readily replace the detection head networks of the existing models. 3) We evaluate the CLNets on three benchmark datasets, the results show that the CLNets achieve start-of-the-art performance and prove the rationality of framework design by sufficient ablation experiments.

2 Related Work

Early studies of human pose estimation have limited practical applications, primarily because they rely heavily on hand-crafted features [27]. Most recent works are based on deep learning and can be roughly divided into regression-based and heatmap-based methods. There are also some works attempting to combine these two ideas for better performance.

Regression-Based Method. The first human pose estimation based on deep learning, DeepPose [24], proposes a cascaded deep neural network to extract information evenly from the whole image to regress the coordinates of the keypoints. Carreira et al. [4] use a self-correcting model to expand the expression ability of hierarchical feature extractors. Sun et al. [18] use bones to reparameterize the pose representation and joint connection structure to encode the long-range interactions in the specific posture. Although these methods improve the regression accuracy, they may suffer from information loss due to the long-distance regression.

Heatmap-Based Method. Shortly after DeepPose was published, Tompson et al. [22] use heatmaps to represent the probabilities of the keypoints in different locations. The stacked Hourglass architecture proposed by Newell et al. [12] uses repeated encode-decode structures with multiple supervision on intermediate heatmaps to improve the accuracy of the final prediction results. Many models [8, 20, 21, 26] continuously improve the performance of the classic stacked Hourglass network. Xiao et al. [25] propose a simple but effective baseline methods, named SimpleBaseline. Chen et al. [5] use a two-stage strategy to further optimize the model for difficult samples. Sun et al. [17] maintain the high resolution of the model by training multi-resolution subnetworks. Although these models have good performance, learning dense heatmaps requires a complex network architecture and high computational costs.

Composite Method. A handful of works are also introduced to combine the regression-based and heatmap-based methods to overcome the aforementioned shortcomings. Sun et al. [19] estimate the positions of keypoints as the integrals of all positions in the heatmaps to preserve the end-to-end differentiability. Papandreou et al. [14] solve a binary classification problem for each position, and all the positive locations need to predict offsets towards the keypoints. However, these methods fail to achieve good performance because they just stack the heatmap-based method and the regression-based method and do not explore the cooperative framework for them.

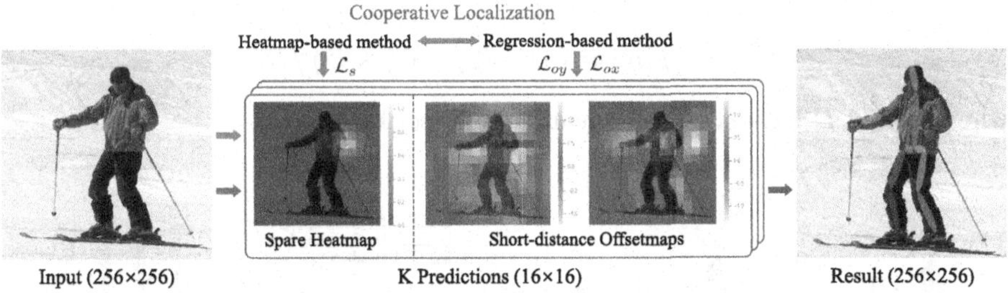

Fig. 1. Illustration of cooperative localization framework. In the box of the K prediction maps, red represents a positive number, and blue represents a negative number. The brighter the color, the greater the absolute value. In addition, the red and blue arrows indicate training and inference, respectively. (Color figure online)

3 Proposed Method

3.1 Cooperative Localization

As shown in Fig. 1, the cooperative localization framework uses a sparse heatmap to find an approximate position meanwhile two corresponding offsetmaps to carry out short-distance regression.

Suppose the original image size is $W \times H$, the number of keypoints is K, and the sizes of sparse heatmaps and short-distance offsetmaps are $W' \times H'$. There are the following relationships: $W' = \lfloor W/D \rfloor$ and $H' = \lfloor H/D \rfloor$, where D is the down-sampling stride. Thus, each location in sparse heatmaps or short-distance offsetmaps corresponds to a patch of the original image with $D \times D$ size.

Sparse Heatmap. For K keypoints, there are K sparse heatmaps, $\{S_1, S_2, ..., S_K\}$. Suppose the ground truth location of the kth keypoint in the original image is defined as $g^k = (g_x^k, g_y^k), g_x^k \in \{1...W\}, g_y^k \in \{1...H\}$. The value at $p' = (p'_x, p'_y), p'_x \in \{1...W'\}, p'_y \in \{1...H'\}$ in S_k is defined as,

$$S_k(p') = exp\left(\frac{-\|t(p') - g^k\|_2}{2\sigma^2}\right), \tag{1}$$

where $t(p')$ translates the location $p' = (p'_x, p'_y)$ in S_k to the center coordinates of the corresponding patch in the original image, which can be expressed as,

$$t(p') = \left((p'_x - C) \times D, (p'_y - C) \times D\right), \tag{2}$$

where C is a deviation constant, set to 0.5.

Short-Distance Offsetmaps. For K keypoints, there are $2K$ offsetmaps, where the first K ($\{O_1, O_2, ..., O_K\}$) and the last K offsetmaps ($\{O_{K+1}, O_{K+2}, ..., O_{2K}\}$) predict y-offsets and x-offsets, respectively. Similarly, for the ground truth location g^k, the value at $p' = (p'_x, p'_y)$ in O_k and O_{K+k} can be defined as,

$$\begin{cases} O_k(p') &= \left(g_y^k - (p'_y - C) \times D\right)/D, \\ O_{K+k}(p') &= \left(g_x^k - (p'_x - C) \times D\right)/D, \end{cases} \tag{3}$$

where C and D have the same meaning as described above.

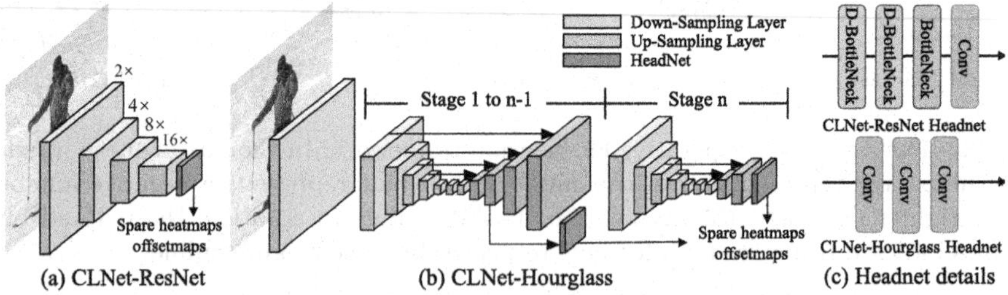

Fig. 2. Illustration of CLNet-ResNet and CLNet-Hourglass. "D-BottleNeck" stands for the dilated bottleneck in [10].

3.2 Network Design

We construct two networks to examine the effectiveness and generalizability of our proposed cooperative localization (CL) framework: CLNet-ResNet and CLNet-Hourglass.

CLNet-ResNet uses ResNet's first four feature extraction stages [6] as its network backbone, as shown in Fig. 2(a). Inspired by Detnet [10], we sequentially add two dilated bottleneck layers, one bottleneck layer, and one convolutional layer to build the head subnetwork in CLNet-ResNet.

CLNet-Hourglass uses the classic stacked Hourglass [12] as its network backbone. As shown in Fig. 2(b), CLNet-Hourglass removes some up-sampling layers in the final stage and generates the predictions with appropriate resolution through the head subnetwork in each stage. The head subnetwork consists of three convolutional layers in series.

3.3 Loss Function Design

For sparse heatmap, let S_k and $\hat{S}_k$ be the kth ground truth target and the kth keypoint prediction, respectively. The loss could be defined as

$$\mathcal{L}_s = \frac{1}{K}\sum_{k=1}^{K} f(S_k, \hat{S}_k),$$

where $f(\cdot)$ is the mean square error loss.

In our cooperative localization framework, offsetmaps only need to learn short-distance regression within a general region provided by sparse heatmaps, and its loss function can be expressed as follows,

$$\begin{cases} \mathcal{L}_{oy} = \frac{1}{K}\sum_{k=1}^{K}\left(\frac{1}{N_\Omega}\sum_{p'\in\Omega} g(O_k(g'), \hat{O}_k(g'))\right), \\ \mathcal{L}_{ox} = \frac{1}{K}\sum_{k=1}^{K}\left(\frac{1}{N_\Omega}\sum_{p'\in\Omega} g(O_{K+k}(g'), \hat{O}_{K+k}(g'))\right), \end{cases} \tag{4}$$

where Ω indicates $S_k(p') \geq \tau$ with using threshold τ to control the range of regression. $g(\cdot)$ represents the smooth L1 loss. Note that the region may contain the approximate location of the keypoint and the location around it, which allows short-regression from adjacent approximate locations to improve the robustness of the model.

The overall loss function is

$$\mathcal{L} = \omega_s\mathcal{L}_s + \omega_o(\mathcal{L}_{oy} + \mathcal{L}_{ox}), \tag{5}$$

where ω_s and ω_o are the weights of two cooperative tasks, respectively.

3.4 Inference

There are three steps to parse sparse heatmaps and short-distance offsetmaps into 2d coordinates vector. For the kth keypoint, 1) the locations with high activation value ($\geq \tau$) in $\hat{S}_k$ are selected, and their center points are used as the initial locations of regression. 2) The values of $\hat{O}_k$ and $\hat{O}_{K+k}$ in the corresponding locations are used as y-offset and x-offset to obtain the kth keypoint's coordinates. 3) The predicted coordinates are weighted average according to their activation values on $\hat{S}_k$ to obtain a final predicted coordinate about the kth keypoint.

4 Experiments

4.1 Experimental Setup

Datasets. LSP and its extended training set provide 11k training images and 1k test images [7], and MPII [1] provides around 25k images with 40K person instances for single-person. MS COCO dataset [11] requires localization of multi-person keypoints in the wild. COCO train2017 set includes 120K images and 150K person instances, while val2017 set and test-dev2017 set include 5K images with 6K person instances and 20K images, respectively.

Evaluation Protocol. We use the Percentage of Correct Keypoints (PCK) [1] as the evaluation metric for single-person human pose estimation. The normalized distance is torso size for LSP while a fraction of the head size (referred to as PCKh) for MPII. For the MS COCO dataset, object keypoint similarity (OKS) based mAP is used as an evaluation metric.

Table 1. Comparisons of results on COCO val2017.

Method	Backbone	Pretrain	Input size	GFLOPs	val2017					
					AP	AP^{50}	AP^{75}	AP^{M}	AP^{L}	AR
Hourglass [12]	8 stacked hourglass	N	256 × 192	14.3	71.9	91.0	80.0	69.3	77.1	77.5
CPN [5]	ResNet50	Y	256 × 192	6.2	69.2	88.0	76.2	65.8	75.6	-
SimpleBaseline [25]	ResNet50	Y	256 × 192	8.9	70.4	88.6	78.3	67.1	77.2	76.3
HRNet [17]	HRNet-W48	Y	256 × 192	14.6	**75.1**	90.6	82.2	71.5	81.8	80.4
Cai et al. [3]	RSN50	N	256 × 192	6.4	74.7	91.4	81.5	71.0	80.2	80.0
CLNet-ResNet	ResNet50	Y	256 × 192	**4.2**	71.2	88.8	78.5	67.4	77.8	78.2
CLNet-Hourglass	8 stacked hourglass	N	256 × 192	26.5	**75.1**	89.4	81.8	71.7	81.6	82.0
CPN [5]	ResNet-Inception	Y	384 × 288	-	72.2	89.2	78.6	68.1	79.3	-
SimpleBaseline [25]	ResNet152	Y	384 × 288	35.6	74.3	89.6	81.1	70.5	81.6	79.7
HRNet [17]	HRNet-W32	Y	384 × 288	16.0	75.8	90.6	82.5	72.0	82.7	80.9
HRNet [17]	HRNet-W48	Y	384 × 288	32.9	76.3	90.8	82.9	72.3	83.4	81.2
CLNet-ResNet	ResNet50	Y	384 × 288	**9.5**	73.4	89.1	79.9	69.4	80.0	79.7
CLNet-ResNet	ResNet101	Y	384 × 288	17.7	74.2	89.3	80.5	70.2	81.0	80.5
CLNet-ResNet	ResNet152	Y	384 × 288	25.9	74.9	89.7	81.4	70.9	81.9	81.1
CLNet-Hourglass	8 stacked hourglass	N	384 × 256	52.9	**76.5**	89.8	82.8	72.9	82.9	82.6

Implementation Details. The size of the input image is 256 × 256 for LSP and MPII by convention. The input size for COCO varies among experiments. The standard deviation σ in sparse heatmaps is 16, and the threshold τ is 0.6. The loss weight of ω_s and ω_o is 0.5 and 2, respectively. Training data are augmented by shearing, scaling, rotation, flipping as reported in [12,21,25]. The networks are trained using PyTorch [16]. We optimize the models via Adam [13] with a batch size of 128 for 140 epochs. The learning rate is initialized as 1×10^{-3} and then dropped by a factor of 10 at the 90th and 120th epochs for CLNet-ResNet. For CLNet-Hourglass, we follow the same hyper-parameters and settings in [12]. For top-down multi-person human pose estimation in COCO, we use the same detector as SimpleBaseline [25] and HRNet [17].

Table 2. Comparisons of results on COCO test-dev2017 set.

Method	Backbone	Pretrain	Input size	GFLOPs	test-dev2017					
					AP	AP^{50}	AP^{75}	AP^{M}	AP^{L}	AR
G-RMI [14]	ResNet101	Y	353 × 257	57.0	64.9	85.5	71.3	62.3	70.0	69.7
CPN [5]	ResNet-Inception	Y	384 × 288	-	72.1	91.4	80.0	68.7	77.2	78.5
SimpleBaseline [25]	ResNet152	Y	384 × 288	35.6	73.7	91.9	82.8	71.3	80.0	79.0
HRNet [17]	HRNet-W32	Y	384 × 288	**16.0**	74.9	92.5	82.8	71.3	80.9	80.1
HRNet [17]	HRNet-W48	Y	384 × 288	32.9	75.5	92.5	83.3	71.9	81.5	80.5
CLNet-ResNet	ResNet152	Y	384 × 288	25.9	74.1	91.5	81.5	70.4	80.1	80.3
CLNet-Hourglass	8 stacked hourglass	N	384 × 256	52.9	**75.8**	91.7	83.2	72.4	81.4	82.0

4.2 Comparison with State-of-the-Art Methods

Results on COCO. As shown in Table 1, on the COCO val2017 set, CLNet-ResNet50 achieves a 71.2 AP score with the input size 256×192, and outperforms SimpleBaseline-ResNet50 by 1.14% with near 1/2 FLOPs. CLNet-Hourglass, trained from scratch, achieves a 75.1 AP score and obtains 3.2 points improvement compared with the original Hourglass. As for the input size 384 × 288, CLNet-ResNet outperforms SimpleBaseline and CLNet-Hourglass outperforms the HRNet while original Hourglass is not as good as other methods. As shown in Table 2, on test-dev 2017 set, CLNet-ResNet152 outperforms SimpleBaseline-ResNet152 0.4 points. CLNet-Hourglass outperforms all other methods with a 75.8 AP score.

Table 3. Comparisons of results on the MPII test set. "*" means using multi-scale image pyramids as input.

	Head	Sho.	Elb.	Wri.	Hip	Knee	Ank.	PCKh@0.5
Tompson et al. [23]	95.8	90.3	80.5	74.3	77.6	69.7	62.8	79.6
Carreira et al. [4]	95.7	91.7	81.7	72.4	82.8	73.2	66.4	81.3
Newell et al. [12]	98.2	96.3	91.2	87.1	90.1	87.4	83.6	90.9
Yang et al.* [26]	98.5	96.7	92.5	88.7	91.1	88.6	86.0	92.0
Ke et al.* [8]	98.5	96.8	92.7	88.4	90.6	89.4	86.3	92.1
Tang et al.* [21]	98.4	96.9	92.6	88.7	91.8	89.4	86.2	92.3
Xiao et al. [25]	98.5	96.6	91.9	87.6	91.1	88.1	84.1	91.5
Sekii [15]	97.9	95.3	89.1	83.5	87.9	82.7	76.2	88.1
Zhang et al. [28]	98.3	96.4	91.5	87.4	90.9	87.1	83.7	91.1
Sun et al. [17]	98.6	96.9	92.8	89.0	91.5	89.0	85.7	92.3
Tang et al.* [20]	98.7	97.1	93.1	89.4	91.9	90.1	86.7	**92.7**
Artacho et al. [2]	-	-	-	-	-	-	-	**92.7**
CLNet-ResNet50	98.2	95.9	90.5	85.9	90.4	86.6	82.0	90.4
CLNet-Hourglass	98.4	96.6	92.4	88.4	90.9	89.4	84.8	91.9

Table 4. Comparisons of complexity. FPS are calculated with batch size one, while FPS' are calculated using full GPU memory. "*" means using multi-scale image pyramids.

	Param	FLOPs	FPS	FPS'	PCKh@0.5
8-stacked Hourglass, ECCV'16 [12]	26M	55G	20	70	90.9
PyraNet, ICCV'17* [26]	28M	46G	6	40	92.0
SimpleBaseline, ECCV'18 [25]	69M	23G	60	202	91.5
PPN, ECCV'18 [15]	16M	6G	**388**	**728**	88.1
HRNet, CVPR'19 [17]	64M	21G	29	283	92.3
FPD, CVPR'19 [28]	**3M**	9G	40	250	91.1
UniPose, CVPR'20 [2]	47M	15G	41	210	**92.7**
CLNet-ResNet50	13.5M	**5.6G**	136	571	90.4

Results on MPII. Table 3 shows our results on the MPII test. Furthermore, we compare the complexity of CLNet-ResNet50 and the most popular methods on the MPII test set in Table 4. We measure the speed and latency by float-point operations (FLOPs) and frames-per-second (FPS). As shown in Table 4, FPD [28] has much fewer FLOPs than SimpleBaseline [25] but is slower, and has comparable FLOPs with PPN [15] but is much slower. Our method achieves an excellent trade-off between efficiency and effectiveness. Our CLNet-ResNet50 is approximately two times slower than PPN but has higher accuracy, while it has comparable accuracy but surpasses the others in terms of FPS by a large margin. Figure 3 shows the visualization of CLNet-ResNet50 on the MPII test set.

Table 5. Comparisons of results on the LSP test set. "*" means using multi-scale image pyramids as input.

	Head	Sho.	Elb.	Wri.	Hip.	Knee	Ank.	PCK@0.2
Tompson et al. [23]	90.6	79.2	67.9	63.4	69.5	71.0	64.2	72.3
Yang et al.* [26]	98.3	94.5	92.2	88.9	94.4	95.0	93.7	93.9
Tang et al.* [21]	97.5	95.0	92.5	90.1	93.7	95.2	94.2	94.0
Tang et al.* [20]	**98.6**	95.4	93.3	89.8	94.3	95.7	**94.4**	94.5
Artacho et al. [2]	-	-	-	-	-	-	-	94.5
CLNet-ResNet50	**98.6**	95.2	94.1	92.5	95.5	95.2	93.1	94.9
CLNet-Hourglass	98.5	**96.3**	**95.4**	**94.6**	**96.7**	**96.0**	94.3	**96.0**

Results on LSP. Table 5 shows the results of CLNets and the most popular methods on the LSP test set. Our results outperform the previous state-of-the-art methods.

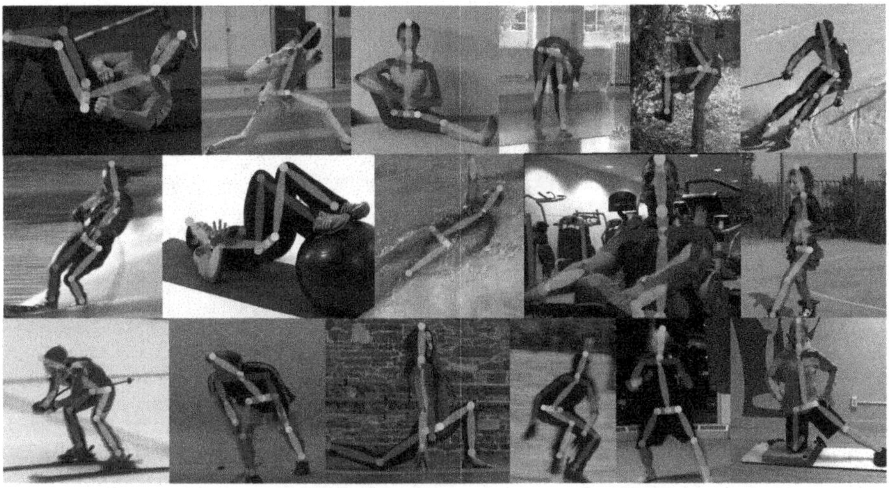

Fig. 3. The random qualitative results on MPII test set.

Table 6. Comparisons of results on the LSP test set with different down-sampling stride D.

Stride D	Heatmap size	Params	PCK@0.2
4	64×64	16.8M	92.2
8	32×32	15.7M	93.9
16	16×16	**13.4M**	**94.9**
32	8×8	28.9M	93.4

4.3 Ablation Study

Influence of the Down-Sampling Stride. Different down-sampling stride D adjusts the range of short-distance regression and the model's complexity, significantly influencing the results. We therefore test different values of D. As shown in Table 6, the 8×8 heatmap has the most parameters because of the vast channel numbers in the last stage, while 16×16 heatmap achieves the best results with the fewest parameters.

Influence of Loss Function. We compare the results of using our loss function with the results of two other loss functions. The first calculates the MSE loss on offsetmaps where the corresponding position in the heatmap is the peak and keeps the heatmap loss the same as traditional Gaussian heatmap loss with a 93.2 score. The second is the loss function used in G-RMI [14], which uses a binary classification method to find approximate locations and calculates their offset with a 93.7 score. Our loss function helps the models achieve the best score of 94.9.

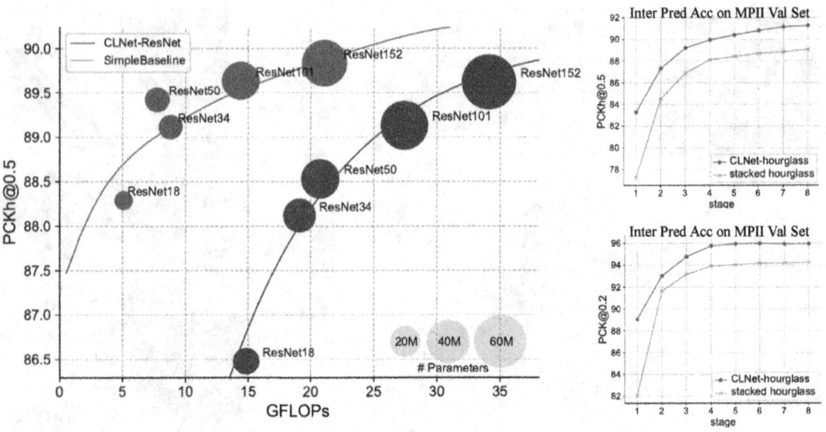

(a) CLNet-ResNet vs. SimpleBaseline (b) CLNet-Hourglass vs. Stacked Hourglass

Fig. 4. Comparisons of accuracy at different stages of the network on our CLNet-hourglass and stacked hourglass network on MPII validation set (left) and LSP test set (right).

Cost-Effectiveness Analysis. As shown in Fig. 4(a), we test different backbone networks in design. The performance continues to improve as the network deepens. SimpleBaseline is a baseline for effectiveness and efficiency verification of CLNet-ResNet due to the most similar architecture. CLNet-ResNet outperforms the SimpleBaseline in all backbones. Using the same backbone, CLNet-ResNet has fewer GFLOPs and parameters than SimpleBaselines because our networks do not have any up-sampling layer and the last stage with vast channels in ResNet. The gap goes from 0.2% to 1.8% when the backbone changes from ResNet152 to ResNet18. It demonstrates that our method can use the features more efficiently.

Generalization. Our method can also be used in other popular models. We conduct our generalization experiments by embedding CLNet into the stacked hourglass network, named CLNet-Hourglass, which improves performance by about 2% on two commonly used single-person pose estimation benchmarks, as shown in Fig. 4(b). Especially, CLNet-Hourglass surpasses the original stacked hourglass network on the first stage by a large margin (relative 8.5% on MPII validation set and 8.0% on LSP test set), confirming our method can use features more effectively.

5 Conclusion

In this paper, we have proposed an effective framework for human pose estimation called cooperative localization (CL), which uses low-resolution heatmaps and its corresponding offsetmaps to regress the precise coordinates of the keypoint. Besides, we design the loss function to allow the model to use non-local information to regress the keypoint. In addition, we have constructed two types of CL networks named CLNet-ResNet and CLNet-Hourglass. With fewer parameters than their plain counterparts, CLNets have achieved better average precision on three standard benchmark datasets. Experimental results prove the effectiveness and generality of our framework. We believe that our framework can improve most of the heatmap-based methods, including many recently proposed models [8,20,21,26]. In future work, we expect to optimize the CL framework and design a more elegant and powerful network.

References

1. Andriluka, M., Pishchulin, L., Gehler, P., Schiele, B.: 2D human pose estimation: new benchmark and state of the art analysis. In: The IEEE Conference on Computer Vision and Pattern Recognition (CVPR), June 2014
2. Artacho, B., Savakis, A.: Unipose: unified human pose estimation in single images and videos. In: Proceedings of the IEEE/CVF Conference on Computer Vision and Pattern Recognition, pp. 7035–7044 (2020)
3. Cai, Y., et al.: Learning delicate local representations for multi-person pose estimation. In: Vedaldi, A., Bischof, H., Brox, T., Frahm, J.-M. (eds.) ECCV 2020. LNCS, vol. 12348, pp. 455–472. Springer, Cham (2020). https://doi.org/10.1007/978-3-030-58580-8_27
4. Carreira, J., Agrawal, P., Fragkiadaki, K., Malik, J.: Human pose estimation with iterative error feedback. In: Proceedings of the IEEE Conference on Computer Vision and Pattern Recognition, pp. 4733–4742 (2016)
5. Chen, Y., Wang, Z., Peng, Y., Zhang, Z., Yu, G., Sun, J.: Cascaded pyramid network for multi-person pose estimation. In: Proceedings of the IEEE Conference on Computer Vision and Pattern Recognition, pp. 7103–7112 (2018)
6. He, K., Zhang, X., Ren, S., Sun, J.: Deep residual learning for image recognition. In: Proceedings of the IEEE Conference on Computer Vision and Pattern Recognition, pp. 770–778 (2016)
7. Johnson, S., Everingham, M.: Clustered pose and nonlinear appearance models for human pose estimation. In: Proceedings of the British Machine Vision Conference (2010). https://doi.org/10.5244/C.24.12
8. Ke, L., Chang, M.C., Qi, H., Lyu, S.: Multi-scale structure-aware network for human pose estimation. In: The European Conference on Computer Vision (ECCV), September 2018
9. Ke, Z., et al.: Is a green screen really necessary for real-time human matting? arXiv preprint arXiv:2011.11961 (2020)
10. Li, Z., Peng, C., Yu, G., Zhang, X., Deng, Y., Sun, J.: Detnet: design backbone for object detection. In: The European Conference on Computer Vision (ECCV), September 2018
11. Lin, T.-Y., et al.: Microsoft COCO: common objects in context. In: Fleet, D., Pajdla, T., Schiele, B., Tuytelaars, T. (eds.) ECCV 2014. LNCS, vol. 8693, pp. 740–755. Springer, Cham (2014). https://doi.org/10.1007/978-3-319-10602-1_48
12. Newell, A., Yang, K., Deng, J.: Stacked hourglass networks for human pose estimation. In: Leibe, B., Matas, J., Sebe, N., Welling, M. (eds.) ECCV 2016. LNCS, vol. 9912, pp. 483–499. Springer, Cham (2016). https://doi.org/10.1007/978-3-319-46484-8_29

13. Kingma, D.P., Ba, J.: Adam: a method for stochastic optimization (2015)
14. Papandreou, G., et al.: Towards accurate multi-person pose estimation in the wild. In: The IEEE Conference on Computer Vision and Pattern Recognition (CVPR), July 2017
15. Sekii, T.: Pose proposal networks. In: Proceedings of the European Conference on Computer Vision (ECCV), pp. 342–357 (2018)
16. Steiner, B., et al.: Pytorch: an imperative style, high-performance deep learning library. In: Advances in Neural Information Processing Systems 32 (2019)
17. Sun, K., Xiao, B., Liu, D., Wang, J.: Deep high-resolution representation learning for human pose estimation. In: The IEEE Conference on Computer Vision and Pattern Recognition (CVPR), June 2019
18. Sun, X., Shang, J., Liang, S., Wei, Y.: Compositional human pose regression. In: Proceedings of the IEEE International Conference on Computer Vision, pp. 2602–2611 (2017)
19. Sun, X., Xiao, B., Wei, F., Liang, S., Wei, Y.: Integral human pose regression. In: The European Conference on Computer Vision (ECCV), September 2018
20. Tang, J., Aksoy, Y., Oztireli, C., Gross, M., Aydin, T.O.: Learning-based sampling for natural image matting. In: The IEEE Conference on Computer Vision and Pattern Recognition (CVPR), June 2019
21. Tang, W., Yu, P., Wu, Y.: Deeply learned compositional models for human pose estimation. In: The European Conference on Computer Vision (ECCV), September 2018
22. Tompson, J., Goroshin, R., Jain, A., LeCun, Y., Bregler, C.: Efficient object localization using convolutional networks. In: The IEEE Conference on Computer Vision and Pattern Recognition (CVPR), June 2015
23. Tompson, J.J., Jain, A., LeCun, Y., Bregler, C.: Joint training of a convolutional network and a graphical model for human pose estimation. In: Advances in Neural Information Processing Systems, pp. 1799–1807 (2014)
24. Toshev, A., Szegedy, C.: Deeppose: human pose estimation via deep neural networks. In: Proceedings of the IEEE Conference on Computer Vision and Pattern Recognition, pp. 1653–1660 (2014)
25. Xiao, B., Wu, H., Wei, Y.: Simple baselines for human pose estimation and tracking. In: Proceedings of the European Conference on Computer Vision (ECCV), pp. 466–481 (2018)
26. Yang, W., Li, S., Ouyang, W., Li, H., Wang, X.: Learning feature pyramids for human pose estimation. In: The IEEE International Conference on Computer Vision (ICCV), October 2017
27. Yang, Y., Ramanan, D.: Articulated human detection with flexible mixtures of parts. IEEE Trans. Pattern Anal. Mach. Intell. **35**(12), 2878–2890 (2012)
28. Zhang, F., Zhu, X., Ye, M.: Fast human pose estimation. In: The IEEE Conference on Computer Vision and Pattern Recognition (CVPR), June 2019

The Image-Based Automatic Detection Method for Cutter Ring Edge Wear of Shield Machine

Wen Bo[1], Fengyuan Li[2], Xiaofeng Cai[1], and Changyou Zhang[1](✉)

[1] Laboratory of Parallel Software and Computational Science, Institute of Software, Chinese Academy of Sciences, Beijing, People's Republic of China
changyou@iscas.ac.cn

[2] State Key Laboratory of Shield Machine and Boring Technology, Zhengzhou 450001, People's Republic of China

Abstract. In order to satisfy the intelligent requirements of industrial systems and assist in automatic recognition of cutter wear, this paper proposes an image-based automatic detection method for cutter ring edge wear of shield machine. The paper mainly studies: (1) Preprocess the original cutter images, the pixel image is generated by graying and thresholding methods, using the gray characteristics to suppress background, it has only two gray values; (2) Based on DBSCAN clustering algorithm, the optimization of cutter ring edge clusters is realized, and the edge pixel clusters are retained; (3) An ring edge extraction method based on structural constraints is proposed, the internal pixels are removed by orthogonal bidirectional projection, we obtained the preliminary image edge extraction results; (4) The circular edge of cutter-image is obtained by remaining pixels polynomial fitting based on polar coordinates. Finally, through the reference the actual size of cutter, the actual radius error is less than 3%. The experimental results show that this method can automatically and accurately detect the actual cutter wear of shield machine, and it provides an effective solution for the intelligent detection of cutter wear.

Keywords: Image processing · Shield machine · Cutter ring edge · Wear detection · Automation

1 Introduction

In recent years, China's modern transportation industry and manufacturing industry have developed rapidly. As a large-scale construction equipment, shield machine is used in the construction of subway or tunnel and other large-scale underground projects. It is known as "underground dragon". The shield machine cutter is the main tool for cutting the working face during tunneling. The research shows that the daily maintenance and replacement time of the cutter accounts for 1/3 of the time cost [1]. Recording accurately the level of cutter wear, on the one hand, reduce the vicious chain reaction of overload operation and the degree of cutter wear [2], on the other hand, reduce the tool change time and improve the project progress. Therefore, the research on cutter wear prediction is one of the important tasks to ensure the efficient operation of shield machine.

Y. Sun et al. (Eds.): ChineseCSCW 2021, CCIS 1491, pp. 553–562, 2022.
https://doi.org/10.1007/978-981-19-4546-5_43

The main types of cutter wear detection technologies: Sensor based detection technology and vision-based detection technology. In the wear prediction and analysis model, the CSM model proposed by Rostami [3] in his doctoral thesis is the most widely used. Zhu Yingwei [4] and others analyzed the advantages and disadvantages of limit detection technologies such as metal limit detection, hydraulic detection and gas detection and ultrasonic continuous detection technology. Among them, ultrasonic wear detection can provide real-time data. Huang Tao [5] et al. monitored the wear state of shield machine scraper in real time through the change of resistance value in the wear sensing module. Zheng Wei [6, 7] and others proposed an on-line monitoring method of TBM cutter ring wear based on eddy current sensor. Li Hongbo [8] et al. used adaptive filtering shield cutter noise signals judge different wear degrees. Liu Zhaowei [9, 10] et al. proposed to realize real-time monitoring of tool wear based on ultrasonic detection and wireless communication tech-nology. Cui Fengsheng [11] and others designed a new wear detection system for EPB shield machine, which can monitor the cutter wear in real time by combining the resistance strain with the ultimate stress deformation of the tool. Zhang Ning [12] made a visual study on shield cutter wear and measured the ultrasonic transmission rate through the ultrasonic image of cutter, to judge the wear information. Yang Yu [13] put forward the wear prediction of shield cutter image for subsea tunnel and predicted wear speed by establishing the CAI values of wear rate and delay corrosion. Bai Yingqian [14] and others built a shield cutter load sensitivity model through AMESim, established a visual study of that, and monitored the working state of different geological conditions. Shi Zhenming [15] and others combined drilling television and close-range photogrammetry technology to detect tool wear through 3D modeling of images.

In this paper, we deeply studied the calculation method of cutter wear based on computer vision. According to the characteristics of complex image background in construction scene, gray and threshold segmentation algorithms are used to separate complex back-ground and extract target pixels, density-based clustering method is used to optimize pixel clusters, to further determining cutter wear edge pixels. We proposed a method based on structural knowledge constraint correction and orthogonal projection pixel optimization to obtain accurate edge pixels, and the final wear is calculated based on polynomial fitting. The method proposed in this paper can not only satisfies intelligent requirements of underground industrial scene system, but also has the advantages of high accuracy and fast calculation, which expands ideas for improving the efficiency of engineering.

2 Pixel Cluster Extraction of Original Cutter Image

The image data is collected by mobile phone and uploaded to the system. The system needs to preprocess for the original image data of shield machine cutter, extract pixel clusters, separate the image background and highlight the image edge by graying and thresholding methods.

The image data used in this paper mainly come from the field collection of site scenes, which are the front view images of shield machine cutter. Image dataset is shown in Fig. 1.

The original image is RGB color image. Because human eyes are most sensitive to green, this paper uses the weighted average method to gray the original image. A reasonable gray image can be obtained by weighted average of RGB three components. The weighted average formula (2-1) is as follows:

$$f(i,j) = w_1 * R(i,j) + w_2 * G(i,j) + w_3 * B(i,j) \tag{2-1}$$

Each pixel is grayed, where f(i, j) is the grayscale value of the point with coordinate (i, j) in the two-dimensional picture, and R (i, j), G (i, j), B (i, j) are the values of the point with coordinate (i, j) on the three components of R, G and B, w_1, w_2, w_3 are adopted respectively of 0.3, 0.59 and 0.11, and the results are good. After the above graying processing of the original image, a grayscale image as shown in Fig. 2. is obtained, and the grayscale value of each pixel of the grayscale image is between 0 and 255.

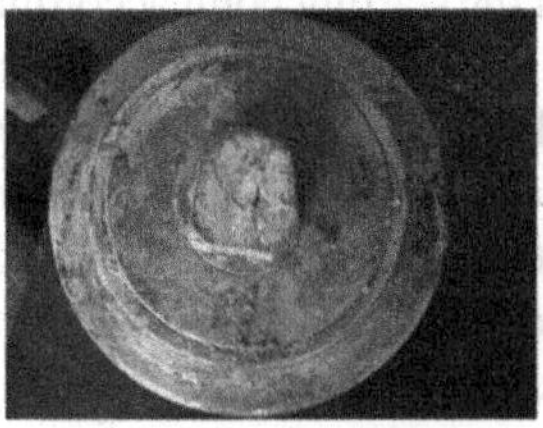

Fig. 1. Original image of shield machine

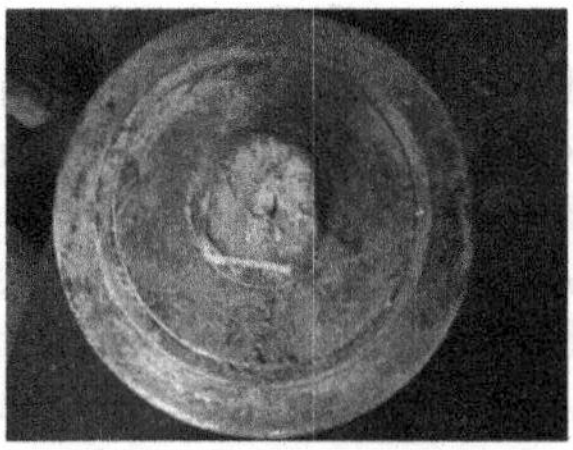

Fig. 2. Cutter gray image.

Fig. 3. Cutter thresholding cutter image

In this paper, Otsu algorithm is selected for threshold segmentation of image. This algorithm has strong adaptability and stability for the complex and changeable lighting and background conditions of underground construction scene.

The steps of thresholding the gray image are as follows: (1) Calculate the normalized gray histogram of the original image of the accessory to represent the distribution probability of each gray level in the histogram; (2) Determine the initial threshold and calculate the probability of pixel division to the target and background respectively; (3) Calculate the average gray value and of the pixels in the target and background class; (4) Calculate the average gray value of the whole accessory image; (5) Calculate the inter class variance based on the current threshold division; (6) Iteratively calculate the threshold so that the variance between classes reaches the maximum here. The formula is shown in (2-2) (2-3) (2-4) (2-5):

$$P_1 = \sum_{i=0}^{j} p_i, P_2 = \sum_{i=j+1}^{L} p_i \tag{2-2}$$

$$G_1 = \sum_{i=0}^{j} ip_i/P_1, G_2 = \sum_{i=j+1}^{L} ip_i/P_2 \tag{2-3}$$

$$G_0 = P_1G_1 + P_2G_2 = \sum_{i=0}^{L-1} ip_i \tag{2-4}$$

$$\sigma_B^2 = P_1(G_1 - G_0)^2 + P_2(G_2 - G_0)^2 \tag{2-5}$$

M_1 and M_2: Target and background gray; P_k: Pixel partition probability; G_0, G_1, G_2: Pixel average gray value, M_1 and M_2: Gray value of the area; σ_B^2: variance between image classes. According to the above process, the thresholding operation by Otsu algorithm, and the results are shown in Fig. 3.

The thresholding method still has some background interference, which needs to be combined with the other methods to complete the cutter edge extraction process.

3 Cluster Optimization Based on DBSCAN

Shield machine cutter ring edge has continuous characteristics. K-means and other algorithms cannot distinguish well. In this paper, DBSCAN density clustering algorithm is used to process threshold images. The specific operation process is as follows:

(1) Reading the gray information of all pixel points in the image and generating the pixel coordinate set P of all edge points; (2) Randomly select the starting point according to the set ε Neighborhood and density threshold MinPts, judge that the point belongs to core point, boundary point or outlier, and delete it if it is outlier; (3) The above judgment is also performed on the remaining pixels in turn; (4) If the distance between the core points is less than MinPts, the two core points are connected together to form several groups of pixel clusters; (5) The boundary point is assigned to the pixel cluster closest to its core point; (6) According to the above rules, the final clustering result C is formed by continuous iteration.

Two key parameters of DBSCAN algorithm: neighborhood ε and density threshold MinPts. The results of different parameter combinations, it is found that the regularity is shown in Table 1.

Table 1. Parameter setting regularity of DBSCAN algorithm

Key parameter	Larger	Larger
ε Neighborhood	The pixel clusters of clustering results contain noise	The data cannot be clustered normally
Threshold MinPts	The data cannot be clustered normally	The data cannot be clustered normally

By trying different parameter combinations and comparing the clustering effect on the data set, we finally chose $\varepsilon = 5$, $MinPts = 8$. By trying different parameter combinations and comparing the clustering effect on the data set, we finally chose. It is found that the noise ratio of clustering results is 0.20%, which belongs to the normal range. If the noise ratio high, the parameter combination needs to be readjusted. In the final clustering result, pixel clusters $C = \{cluster\ 1, cluster\ 2 \ldots cluster\ n\}$, $n = 469$, as shown in Fig. 4.

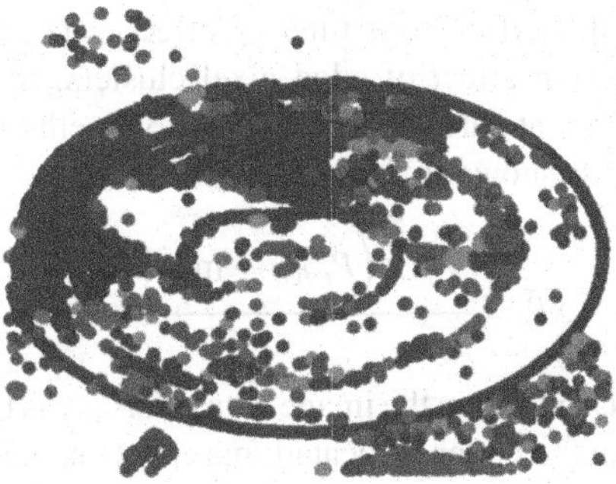

Fig. 4. DBSCAN clustering results

4 Cutter Image Ring Edge Extraction

Cluster optimization based on structural knowledge constraints, structural knowledge refers to the physical parameters of the object. For shield machine cutter, it includes the knowledge such as size parameters and shape features. Firstly, the total number of pixels P in each pixel cluster is calculated_ Count and the maximum coordinate spans Δ X and Δ Y in the X and Y directions. The data of the two dimensions are normalized by using the dispersion standardization formulas (4-1) and (4-2).

$$\Delta X^* = \frac{x - x_{min}}{x_{max} - x_{min}} \tag{4-1}$$

$$\Delta Y^* = \frac{y - y_{min}}{y_{max} - y_{min}} \tag{4-2}$$

In order to eliminate the interference of sparse clusters and reduce the computational complexity, this paper only retains the number of pixels P_{count} the top 5 pixel clusters participate in subsequent calculations, and the reserved results are recorded as C1: C1 = {Cluster2, Cluster237, Cluster353, Cluster130, Cluster59}, The number of pixels in each pixel cluster is 36484, 1421, 616, 483, 437. Calculate the maximum coordinate span in the X and Y directions for the five pixel clusters in C1 are ΔXandΔY, S:S $= \{(\Delta X_1, \Delta Y_1), (\Delta X_2, \Delta Y_2), (\Delta X_3, \Delta Y_3), (\Delta X_4, \Delta Y_4), (\Delta X_5, \Delta Y_5)\}$. Normalize the data brought into C1 and S respectively. The pixel number and pixel coordinate span data are recorded as C1* and S*, and calculate the edge possibility score *P* of the object according to formula (4-3).

$$P = q\omega_1 \cdot P^*_{count} \cdot + \cdot q\omega_2 \cdot \frac{(\Delta X^* + \Delta Y^*)}{2} \tag{4-3}$$

where *P* represents the possibility score of edge, and the greater the value of *P*, the greater the probability that the pixel cluster contains the edge of the target object; $q\omega_1$ is the design weight of pixel quantity dimension, $q\omega_2$ is the weight of pixel coordinate span, condition $\omega_1 + \omega_2 = 1$; $P_{count}{}^*$ and ΔX^*, ΔY^* are normalized pixel number information and pixel span information.

Set the evaluation index ΔP of edge filtering effect. The greater the difference ΔP, the better the discrimination effect of edge pixel clusters. Select the optimal weight combination under the current data set. The calculation method of the average different ΔP of the whole data set is shown in formula (4-4).

$$\overline{\Delta P} = \frac{\sum_{i=1}^{m}\left(P_{edge} - \max_{n}\{P_{bg}\}\right)}{m} \tag{4-4}$$

where m is the number of samples in the image data set; P_{edge} is the edge possibility score of the pixel cluster where the cutter is located; $\max_{n}\{P_{bg}\}$ is the cluster with the highest possibility score among the background pixel clusters. Using the formula to calculate the fitting edge data set, the experimental comparison results are $q\omega_1 = 0.68, q\omega_2 = 0.32$, $\overline{\Delta P}$ reaches the maximum value. The change trend of the difference $\overline{\Delta P}$ is shown in Fig. 5, which achieves the best edge pixel cluster filtering effect on the whole sample data set.

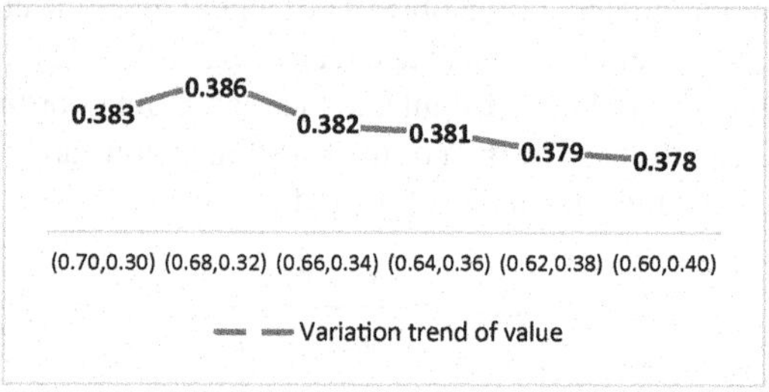

Fig. 5. Variation trend of value

Score is P_{edge}:$P_{edge} = \{P_{Cluster2}, P_{Cluster237}, P_{Cluster353}, P_{Cluster130}, P_{Cluster59}\}$:{0.903, 0.176, 0.034, 0.027, 0.023}, cluster 2 as an edge cluster containing object edge information, obtains the following result diagram, as shown in Fig. 6.

Fig. 6. Cutter image ring edge extraction.

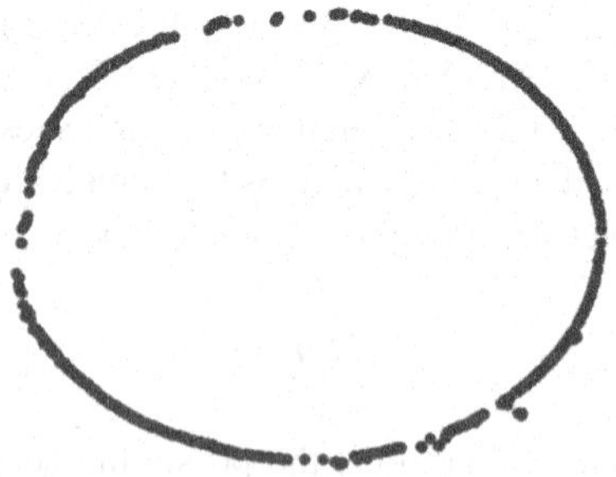

Fig. 7. Orthogonal bidirectional projection.

We basically eliminate the external pixel noise points and achieve a result more in line with the cutter vision, but we need to further extract the ring edge.

There are still many non-edge pixels in the image. We use the closed characteristics of the image and learn from the concept of orthogonality in linear algebra for noise filtering. It is preferred that the pixel clusters are projected respectively in two orthogonal directions. The image edge extraction results are shown in Fig. 7. The result diagram show that we have the initial conditions for cutter wear calculation now.

5 Calculation of Cutter Ring Edge Wear

This paper studies the calculation method of wear based on cutter structure: polynomial fitting based on polar coordinates. (1) The polar coordinate system is established, and the average coordinate in the set is calculated by formula (5-1) to represent the actual center point O_r. Where, n = 2766:

$$O_r = (\overline{x}, \overline{y}) = \frac{\sum_i^n (x_i, y_i)}{n} \tag{5-1}$$

Calculated actual center point O_r $(\overline{x}, \overline{y}) = (515.3344, 624.1562)$, the polar coordinate set $\overrightarrow{P}$ of each edge point is obtained, and we chose the polynomial fitting method to construct the coordinate set about the angle ω and the polynomial function of edge distance d, it is shown in the following formula (5-2):

$$L(\omega, K) = k_0 + k_1\omega + k_2\omega^2 + \cdots + k_M\omega^M = \sum_{j=0}^{M} k_j\omega^j \tag{5-2}$$

The fitting results of different M has polynomials of different order. When M is set large, it will show an over fitting tendency to the edge data. Calculate the distance from each edge point to the center point O_r, calculate the average distance a as the correction benchmark, construct the correction formula, and obtain the corrected actual edge distance D'. Angle ω_i and edge distance d_i, as shown in Fig. 8.

For the edge point set $\overrightarrow{P}$, take the edge distance data set $\overrightarrow{P}_d = \{d_1, d_2, \ldots, d_i, \ldots, d_n\}$, and calculate the average edge distance a as the correction benchmark by using formula (5-3).

$$A = \frac{\sum_{i=1}^n d_i}{n} \tag{5-3}$$

According to the constructed edge distance correction formula (5-4), (5-5), the change trend of edge distance sinusoidal function caused by the change of edge shape is eliminated:

$$\Delta Y_i = d_i - L(\omega_i, K) \tag{5-4}$$

$$d_i' = A + \Delta Y_i \tag{5-5}$$

This paper tests the angles brought by M values of different orders ω_i, the result of the relationship with the edge distance d_i is shown in Fig. 9.

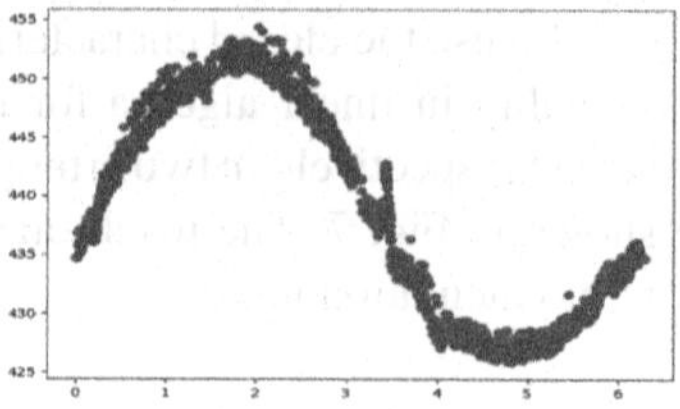

Fig. 8. Angle ω_i and edge distance d_i

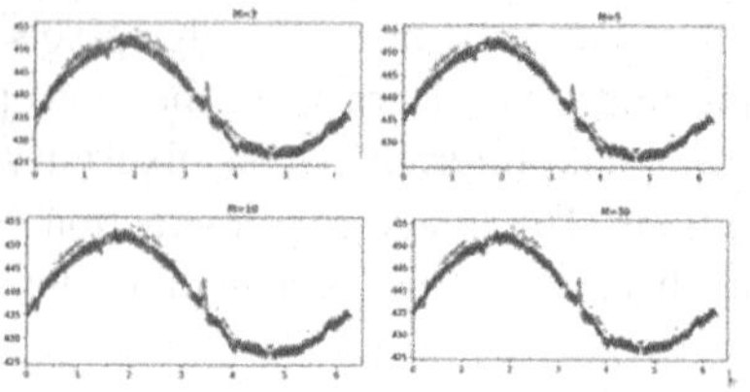

Fig. 9. Angle under different M ω_i And edge distance d_i

From the results, when M = 30, it will show the tendency of over fitting the edge data. In this paper, the edge distance function $L_{10}(\omega, K)$ with polynomial order M = 10 is selected for the correction of subsequent edge distance data. The data is approximate to the standard circle. The average edge distance a calculated by formula (5–3) is the edge, and the pixel radius is A = 441.89. In the original image of the tool selected in this paper, by determining the feature that there is no wear inside the image, combined with the manufacturing size information, and using formula 5–6, the proportional relationship R between the pixel length and the physical length in the image is calculated:

$$r = \frac{\overline{l_p}}{l_{design}} \tag{5-6}$$

In actual construction, the feature of no wear inside the shield machine tool image is covered by mud. Therefore, to accurately extract the edge and calculate the wear amount. We developed a method to place a circle with a known radius on the image as a reference, as shown in Fig. 10.

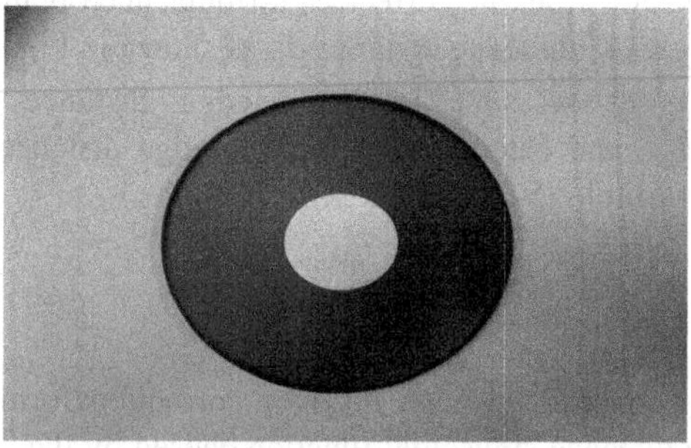

Fig. 10. Reference simulation diagram

Take the edge distance $\overrightarrow{P}'_d$ to the corrected edge point set $\overrightarrow{P}'_d$. According to the proportional relationship R between the pixel length and the physical length, the ring edge diameter of the object is calculated, the actual ring edge diameter is 8.85 cm, and the pixel error rate is 2.49%. If the wear radius error of the cutter corresponding to the actual radius of 28.33 cm (17 in.) is 0.71 cm, which is less than 3% of the engineering consumption error.

6 Summary and Prospect

In this paper, an automatic detection method of shield machine cutter ring edge wear based on image processing is proposed. we analyzed from the shield machine tool image wear system, the cluster optimization method based on DBSCAN, the pixel cluster optimization method based on structure knowledge are designed to effectively preserve the cutter edge pixels; An orthogonal projection method is designed to preserve the image edge pixel information; The image-based cutter wear detection of shield machine is completed. The method proposed in this paper can automatically and accurately detect the actual wear of shield machine tools, then provide an effective solution for the intelligent detection of accessories in underground industrial scene.

In the next stage, we will focus on how to monitor the wear of shield machine cutter in real time. Among them, the research on intelligent and real-time tool wear early warning method is the focus of our future research.

Thanks. Thank the review experts for their valuable comments and modification suggestions. This paper is supported by the national key R & D Program (2018YFB1701403) and the open fund of State Key Laboratory of Shield Machine and Boring Technology (SKLST-2019-K05).

References

1. Xiyang, W.: Tool damage in shield tunneling and its maintenance. Equipment Manag. Maintenance **06**, 59–61 (2021)
2. Xuanyu, L., Ziwen, W., Cheng, S., Yudong, W., Qiumei C.: Overview of research progress on mechanical fault diagnosis of shield machine. Control Engineering, pp. 1–8 [2021–06–21] https://doi.org/10.14107/j.cnki.kzgc. Twenty million two hundred thousand nine hundred and two
3. Rostami, J.: Development of a force estimation model for rock fragmentation with disc cutters through theoretical modeling and physical measurement of crushed zone pressure, Colorado School of Mines, Colorado (1997)
4. Yingwei, Z., Libo, Z., Hongtao, Z.: Research on tool wear detection technology of new shield machine. Constr. Tech. 1 (2014)
5. Tao, H., Quansheng, L., Xing, H., Xiaoping, Z., Xinjing, L.: Research and development of scraper wear real-time monitoring system and indoor verification test. Tunnel Construction (Chinese and English) (2018) (S2)
6. Wei, Z., Haiming, Z., Hao, L., Qing, T., Biao, S., Yimin, X.: On line monitoring system for TBM hob ring wear. Instrum. Technol. Sens. 2 (2015)
7. Jianfang, L.: Experimental research on real-time wear monitoring system of disc hob. Mech. Eng. 11 (2016)
8. Hongxia, Z.: Research on wear detection technology of shield hob. Shijiazhuang Railway University (2015)
9. Hongbo, L., Jianjun, Z., Zhufeng, W.: Vibration and impact. New Shield Tool Detect Technol. 20 (2014)
10. Ruihu, L., Guanghui, W., Tao, L.: Research on new ultrasonic shield tool wear detection system. Constr. Mechanization 09 (2015)
11. Zhaowei, L., Baiquan, W., Wei, S.: Research on wireless detection system of shield cutter wear based on ultrasonic. Tunnel Constr. (Chinese and English) 11 (2017)

12. Fuxing, C., Tong, S., Shanghai, C., Haoyuan, Q., da, J.: Research on tool wear detection system of new earth pressure balance shield machine. J. Jiangsu Constr. Vocat. Tech. Coll. 01 (2018)
13. Ning, Z.: Visual research on tool wear detection of shield machine. Shijiazhuang Railway University (2013)
14. Yang, Y.: Prediction of shield hob wear in sea crossing section of Xiamen rail transit line 3. Tunnel Constr. **38**(A01), 182–187 (2018)
15. Yingqian, B., Panke, G., Rui, R.: Simulation of shield cutter head load sensing system based on AMESim. Hydraul. Pneumatic **09**, 56–62 (2019)
16. Zhenming, S., Liu, L., Shenggong, G., et al.: Research and application of visual detection system for shield machine front cabin equipment. Highw.. Traffic Sci. Technol. **1**, 109–116 (2019)

Reinforcement Learning-Based Computation Offloading Approach in VEC

Kai Lin, Bing Lin(✉), and Xun Shao

College of Physics and Energy, Fujian Normal University, Fuzhou 350117, China
wheellx@163.com

Abstract. Intelligent and Connected Vehicles (ICV) can effectively improve driving safety and traffic efficiency. With the national approach of energy conservation and emission reduction continuously promoting, Electric vehicles (EV) have become the main body of the next generation ICV. For the limited computing capacity and endurance of EV, it cannot meet the high computational requirements of in-vehicle intelligent applications. Therefore, it is a great challenge to design a appropriate offloading approach to reduce failure rate of vehicular applications and energy consumption of offloading, while considering inter-dependencies of applications, position change of vehicles and computing power of collaborative vehicles. In this paper, ICV computation offloading model is formulated as Markov Decision Process (MDP). A computing offloading approach based on Reinforcement Learning (RL) is proposed, which adopts Q-Learning based on Simulated Annealing (SA-QL) to optimize failure rate of vehicular applications and energy consumption of offloading. The simulated results show that the proposed approach can reduces the failure rate of vehicular applications and energy consumption of offloading.

Keywords: Vehicular edge computing · Mobility · Reinforcement learning · Intelligent and Connected Vehicles

1 Introduction

In recent years, there are increasing tendency of traffic accidents, which pose great threat to driving safety. With the increase of automobile ownership, a lot of vehicle exhaust has caused serious pollution to environment. Moreover, people no longer regard vehicles as a simple travel tools, and begin to pursue the intelligence of vehicles.

To provide more safe and intelligent driving experience, vehicles are gradually becoming intelligent terminals, called Intelligent and Connected Vehicles (ICV). ICV integrates modern communication and network technology. Through information sharing with collaborative vehicles [25], it can perceive real-time road condition. This can significantly improve driving safety, and bring great convenience to travel [10].

Y. Sun et al. (Eds.): ChineseCSCW 2021, CCIS 1491, pp. 563–576, 2022.
https://doi.org/10.1007/978-981-19-4546-5_44

With the national approach of energy conservation and emission reduction continuously promoting, new energy technology has developed rapidly, which widely applied in many fields. Electric vehicles (EV) adopt new energy technology. Therefore, these advantages make EV become the main body of the next generation ICV [18].

The development of ICV has spawned the emergence of these vehicular applications, such as autonomous driving [7], virtual reality gaming [29], etc. These applications require high-performance computing resources, the computing capability of ICV may not satisfy the requirements of these applications.

To overcome above challenges, the paradigm of computation offloading has been widely applied. The computation offloading in traditional cloud computing platform [1] is a popular technology. Through offloading computation tasks to the cloud computing center, the computing burden of vehicles can be effectively improved. However, it will cause serious task transmission delay [13], which cannot satisfy the latency requirements of in-vehicle applications [14].

Vehicular Edge Computing (VEC) is a new paradigm to solve above shortcomings. Roadside Units (RSU) deploy with Mobile Edge Computing (MEC) servers. Therefore, in-vehicle applications can either be processed by On-Board Units (OBU), or offloaded to RSUs [20]. In addition, it can also be offloaded to cooperative vehicles for processing. This can significantly shorten the completion time of applications, and reduce the energy consumption of application processing [24].

Due to the high cost for deploying RSUs with wired network on expressways and rural roads, it is not commercially feasible [2]. Through powering RSUs with solar energy, it can greatly reduce the cost for deploying RSUs [3]. However, this poses a challenge to the endurance of RSUs. To improve the endurance of RSUs, energy consumption optimization for RSUs should be considered.

Recently, the offloading problems for ICV are studied in many works. These researches have cooperative vehicleeral drawbacks. They seldom considered the dynamic offloading method, which considers vehicle position change in different time-slots [26]. Few of them considered the offloading approach for dependent tasks (i.e., there is no data dependency among tasks, thus they have not specific execution sequence) [4,11]. The computing resource of cooperative vehicles is neglected in most of researches [5,28].

For the above neglected research contents, this study establishes a computation offloading model for ICV, considering the task dependency, vehicle mobility and the computing capacity of different computing resources. An computation offloading approach based on Q-Learning is proposed. To satisfy the requirements of application service and improve the endurance of ICV and RSU, Reinforcement Learning (RL) algorithm is adopted to optimize failure rate of vehicular applications and energy consumption of offloading for ICV application. The contributions of our study are as follows:

- A model for offloading of ICV applications is established in VEC. Computation tasks can be either processed in local, or offloaded to service nodes.

- The computation offloading problem for ICV is first modeled as a RL problem. And then we propose a computation offloading approach based on RL for ICV.
- The experiments are based on the real vehicle trajectory. Simulation results show that the proposed approach can reduce the application offload failure rate and the total energy consumption. Based on the real vehicle trajectory, simulation results show that the proposed offloading approach can reduce the offloading failure rate of vehicular applications and energy consumption of ICV.

The rest of this paper is organized as follows. Section 2 establishes system model for ICV applications. Section 3 defines the computation offloading problem for ICV applications. Section 4 proposes the computation offloading approach based on RL. Section 5 shows the details of experiment parameters, and discuss the results of experiments. Section 6 sums up this paper and discusses the future of our work.

2 System Model

2.1 Network Model

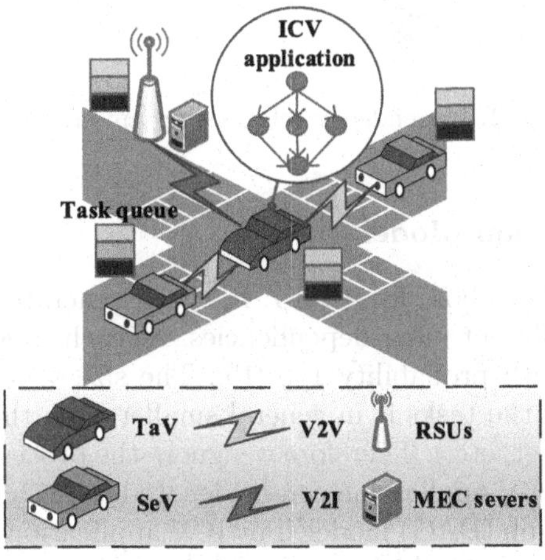

Fig. 1. Network model.

The network model is shown in Fig. 1. We consider a scenario c, which contains RSU, request vehicle and cooperative Vehicle [22]. cooperative Vehicles and RSUs are called as Service Nodes (SN) [19]. The details of network in this scenario are as follows.

- Request vehicle: Request vehicle is equipped with On-Board Unit (OBU). request vehicle will generate applications, which can be processed locally. After application decomposition, computation tasks can be either offloaded to RSUs, or offloaded to cooperative vehicles for execution.

- Cooperative vehicle: There are n cooperative vehicles equipped with OBU. Its computing capacity is the same as request vehicle. It first receives applications from request vehicle, and then processes them. The communication radius of cooperative vehicle is r^v.
- RSU: m RSUs are connected with MEC servers through wired connection [27]. The communication range of RSUs are r^s. It has stronger computing capacity than vehicles.
- Task queue: All the entities are equipped with task queues. Task queues on request vehicle is denoted as $\boldsymbol{Q}^t$. Task queues on SNs is expressed as $\boldsymbol{Q}^{SeN} = \{\boldsymbol{Q}^s, \boldsymbol{Q}^r\}$, where $\boldsymbol{Q}^s$ is the task queues on cooperative vehicles, $\boldsymbol{Q}^r$ is the task queues on RSUs.

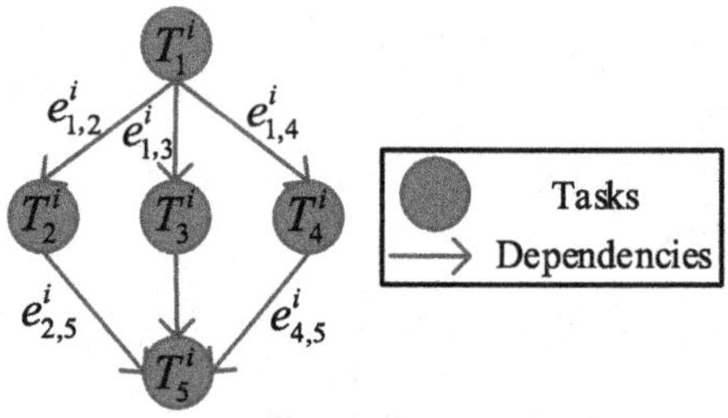

Fig. 2. Dependency relationship among tasks.

2.2 ICV Application Model

There are s time-slots, whose length is t. ICV can generate g types of in-vehicle applications with different inner-dependencies. At each time slot, these applications is generated with probability $1/g$ [15]. The size of return result (such as object label, etc.) of the tasks is in general smaller than the task data (such as program code, data set, etc.). Therefore we ignore the process of return result [9]. As shown in Fig. 2, ICV application can be denoted as $\boldsymbol{A}_i = \{\boldsymbol{G}_i, l_i\}$. $\boldsymbol{G}_i$ denotes Directed Acyclic Graph (DAG) modeled by ICV applications, and l_i is delay constraint for i-th application, which represents the number of tolerance time-slots. $\boldsymbol{G}_i$ can be expressed as $\boldsymbol{G}_i = \langle \boldsymbol{N}_i, \boldsymbol{E}_i \rangle$, the set of tasks can be expressed as $\boldsymbol{N}_i = \{\boldsymbol{T}_1^i, \boldsymbol{T}_2^i, ..., \boldsymbol{T}_{|\boldsymbol{N}_i|}^i\}$, and the set of directed edges can be expressed as $\boldsymbol{E}_i = \{e_{u,v}^i | \Psi(e_{u,v}^i) = 1\}$. $\Psi(e_{u,v}^i) = 1$ represents a directed edge $\boldsymbol{T}_u^i \rightarrow \boldsymbol{T}_v^i$, and $\Psi(e_{u,v}^i) = 0$ represents no edge between $\boldsymbol{T}_u^i$ and $\boldsymbol{T}_v^i$. $\boldsymbol{T}_u^i$ is the direct predecessor task of $\boldsymbol{T}_v^i$, and $\boldsymbol{T}_u^i$ should be completed before $\boldsymbol{T}_v^i$. $\boldsymbol{R}_v^i = \{\boldsymbol{T}_u^i | \Psi(e_{u,v}^i) = 1\}$ is denoted as the set of direct predecessors of $\boldsymbol{T}_v^i$. $\boldsymbol{T}_v^i$ meets the execution condition when all tasks in $\boldsymbol{R}_v^i$ have been completed. Moreover, tasks can be further expressed as $\boldsymbol{T}_u^i \triangleq \{u, Depth(\boldsymbol{T}_u^i), d_u^i\}(u \in \{1, 2, ..., |\boldsymbol{N}_i|\}$, where u is the task index, task depth can be expressed as $Depth(\boldsymbol{T}_u^i)$, which is defined by Eq. (1), d_u^i is the data size of $\boldsymbol{T}_u^i$.

$$Depth(\boldsymbol{T}_u^i) = \begin{cases} 0, \boldsymbol{R}_u^i = \emptyset \\ 1 + max(Depth(\boldsymbol{R}_u^i)), otherwise \end{cases} \tag{1}$$

2.3 Communication Model

Due to the position change of vehicles, the data transmission rate between request vehicle and SNs will change. request vehicle communicate with SNs through LTE-V2X protocol [6]. Channel bandwidth is defined as B, transmission power of request vehicle can be expressed as p_t, channel fading coefficient as h, χ is denoted as Gaussian white noise power and path loss exponent is expressed as ϖ, $\varPhi_i^j$ is denoted as the Euclidean distance between request vehicle and j-th SN. According to Shannon theory, the data transmission rate between request vehicle and the j-th SN can be expressed as

$$\tau_i^j = B\log_2(1 + \frac{|h|^2 p_t}{\chi(\varPhi_i^j)^{\varpi}}) \tag{2}$$

The amount of task data transmitted can be expressed as

$$\eta_i^j = \begin{cases} t \cdot \tau_i^j, \varPhi_i^j \leq r^s \\ 0, \varPhi_i^j > r^s \end{cases} \tag{3}$$

Moreover, the energy consumption of data transmission can be expressed as

$$\delta_{i,j}^t = \begin{cases} t \cdot p_t, \varPhi_i^j \leq r^s \\ 0, \varPhi_i^j > r^s \end{cases} \tag{4}$$

2.4 Computation Model

Local Computing For local computing, the energy consumption of vehicle is given by

$$\delta_l = \kappa_t (f_t)^3 \cdot t \tag{5}$$

where κ_t is computation energy efficiency coefficient of vehicle [17], and f_t is the computing capacity of request vehicle.

The data size of task to be processed at one time-slot is given by

$$d_l = \frac{f_t \cdot t}{c} \tag{6}$$

where c is CPU cycles required to complete per bit data.

SNs computing For SNs computing, the energy consumption of SNs is given by

$$\delta_s = \kappa_s (f_s)^3 \cdot t \tag{7}$$

where κ_s denotes computation energy efficiency coefficient of SNs [17]. $f_s = \{f_r, f_v\}$ denotes the processing capability of SNs, where $\{f_r$ is the processing capability of RSU and $\{f_v$ is the processing capability of cooperative vehicles.

The data size of task to be processed at one time-slot is given by

$$d_s = \frac{f_s \cdot t}{c} \tag{8}$$

3 Problem Formulation

To satisfy requirements of application and improve the endurance of ICV and RSU, there are two optimization objectives should be considered.

We define $\mathbf{A} = \{a_i\}, \mathbf{B} = \{b_i^j\}, \mathbf{X} = \{x_i^j\}$ as the decision variable for local computing decision, SNs computing decision and SNs processing decision.

3.1 Offloading Failure Rate

Two cases will cause application offloading failure:

1. The distance between request vehicle and SNs is out of communication range during data transmission.
2. The offloading delay of application exceeds its delay constraint.

We first define the set of offloading failure applications at i-th time-slot as $\boldsymbol{F_i} = \{f_1, f_2..., f_{|\boldsymbol{F_i}|}\}$, $\Theta(f_i)$ denotes the remaining data size of f_i. And then the penalty of offloading failure can be expressed as

$$penalty_i = \sum_{j=1}^{|\boldsymbol{F_i}|} \Theta(f_i) \tag{9}$$

3.2 Energy Consumption

The energy consumption is caused by local computing, SNs computing and communication. Therefore, the total energy consumption at i-th time-slot is given by

$$energy_i = \delta_i^l + \delta_i^{as} + \delta_i^c \tag{10}$$

where $\delta_i^l = a_i \delta_l$ denotes energy consumption of local computing, $\delta_i^{as} = \sum_{j=1}^{m+n} b_i^j \delta_s$ denotes energy consumption of SNs computing, $\delta_i^c = \sum_{j=1}^{m+n} x_i^j \delta_{i,j}^t$ denotes energy consumption of communication.

3.3 Optimization Objective

α is denoted as the coefficient for failure rate of vehicular applications, β is denoted as the coefficient for energy consumption of offloading, and $\alpha + \beta = 1$.

$$\begin{aligned} &\underset{\mathbf{A,B,X}}{\textbf{Min}} \ \sum_{i=1}^{t} [\alpha \cdot penalty_i + \beta \cdot energy_i] \\ &\textbf{s.t.} \ \sum_{j=1}^{m} a_i b_i^j = 0 \end{aligned} \tag{11}$$

4 Computation Offloading Approach Based on Reinforcement Learning

4.1 MDP Model

The following include four elements, and the MDP model for ICV can be expressed as following.

- **Agent**:Request vehicle
- **State space**:We define the state space as $S_i = \{P_i, T_i\}$ at i-th time slot, where $P_i = \{x_i^t, y_i^t\}$ is the position of request vehicle. $T_i = \{\eta_i^1, \eta_i^2, ..., \eta_i^{n+m}\}$ denotes the amount of task data transmitted.
- **Action space** : Action space can be expressed as $A_i = \{LC_i, SC_i^j, RC_i^j\}$ at i-th time slot, where LC_i indicates local computing, $SC_i^j = \{sc_i^1, sc_i^2, ..., sc_i^n\}$ represents whether tasks are offloaded to cooperative vehicle i and $RC_i^j = \{or_i^1, or_i^2, ..., or_i^m\}$ represents whether tasks are offloaded to RSU i.
- **Reward function**:The reward is given by $R_i = 1/(\alpha \cdot penalty_i + \beta \cdot energy_i)$ at k-th time slot.

4.2 SA-QL Algorithm

Value function is optimized through $<S_i, A_i, R_i, S_i'>$, where state is expressed as S_i, action is expressed as A_i, reward is expressed as R_i, and S_i' represents the state observed at next time-slot [12].

The value function can be updated as follows:

$$Q(S_i, A_i) = Q(S_i, A_i) + \alpha[R_i + \gamma \max_{A_i'} Q(S_i', A_i') - Q(S_i, A_i)] \tag{12}$$

where learning rate is expressed as α. discount factor is expressed as $\gamma \in [0, 1]$, which indicates discount of long-term rewards. $\max_{A_i'} Q(S_i', A_i')$ denotes the maximum Q-value of next state.

We design the computation offloading approach through combining Q-learning with Simulated Annealing (SA). Furthermore, Q-Learning is used to optimize approach, and SA [8] is combined with Q-Learning, cooling approach of SA can be given by:

$$T_e = \theta^e T_0 \tag{13}$$

initial temperature is denoted as T_0 , cooling coefficient can be expressed as θ, and the number of episode is denoted as e.

SA-QL-based computation offloading approach for ICV is shown in Algorithm 1.

5 Simulation Results and Analysis

5.1 Parameter Setting

Simulation environment is operating system of Windows 10, and proposed approach is carried out by Python language. Real vehicle trajectory is considered [16]. The communication range of the vehicle is 130 m. The communication range of RSU is 300 m. After cooperative vehicleeral parameter adjustments, the best effect of joint optimization is achieved, and we set α to 0.6 and β to 0.4. ICVs will generate six types of ICV applications. The slot length is 100 ms.

5.2 Comparative Algorithms and Strategies

To compare the impact of different methods for task processing, we designed three comparative strategies. **Approach 1** is our proposed approach. **Approach 2** considers local computing. **Approach 3** considers local computing and RSU offloading. **Approach 4** considers local computing and cooperative vehicles offloading. These strategies are optimized by SA-QL algorithm.

To validate the feasibility of SA-QL for ICV offloading approach, Sarsa [21], Sarsa(λ) [23], Q(λ) [23] are chosen as comparative algorithms. These algorithms selects actions through SA approach, and adopts the task processing methods of **Approach 1**.

5.3 Results and Discussion

Convergence of SA-QL Algorithm. The average reward of SA-QL and comparative algorithms in every 10 episodes is shown in Fig. 3, which indicates that reward of SA-QL converges around 100th episodes, and reward is about 958 with little fluctuate. After 200 episodes of training, SA-QL algorithm has only small fluctuations, which proves the feasibility of SA-QL for ICV computation offloading approach.

We name average offloading failure rate of applications as **AOFR**. **AOFR** in every 20 episodes is shown in Fig. 4. With the number of episodes increasing, **AOFR** of all algorithms decreases. Around the 120th round, the offloading failure rate trained by the SA-QL algorithm is about 3% with little fluctuate. Compared with SA-QL algorithm and Q-learning(λ) algorithm, Sarsa and Sarsa(λ) can optimize **AOFR** to a lower level. On-line learning approach has better performance for optimizing the **AOFR**. The possible reason is that the value function of on-line learning approach is updated through the samples generated by the current approach, which makes it converges faster.

Algorithm 1: SA-QL based computation offloading approach

Input: parameters of VEC network
Output: Optimized computation offloading approach

for $e \leftarrow 1$ *to* $e_{\max}$ **do**
  Initialize the VEC network parameters;
  Update T_e according to Eq. (13);
  for $i \leftarrow 1$ *to* s **do**
    Applications of request vehicle is first generated with probability of $1/g$ for each application type, and then all tasks are stored in $\boldsymbol{Q}^t$;
    Get the coordinates of request vehicle P_i according to data set of vehicle trajectory and the coordinates of SNs;
    Calculate T_i according to Eq. (3), obtain $S_i = P_i \cup T_i$;
    if $\boldsymbol{Q}(\mathbf{0})^t$ *have not completed* **then**
      $A_i = A_{i-1}$;
      if *the distance between request vehicle and SNs is out of communication range during data transmission* **then**
        Delete all tasks which have depedency with $\boldsymbol{Q}(\mathbf{0})^t$ from queues of request vehicle and SNs ;
      end
    else
      Take the random number r follow the uniform distribution on the $[0, 1]$ interval, select the random action A_r and select the best action $A_b = \arg\max_{A_i} Q(S_i, A_i)$;
      if $r < exp\{[Q(S_k, A_r) - Q(S_k, A_k)]/T_e\}$ **then**
        $A_i = A_r$
      else
        $A_i = A_b$
      end
    end
    Check whether the tasks at the head of $\boldsymbol{Q}^t$, $\boldsymbol{Q}^{SeN}$ meets the execution conditions;
    Execute A_i, SNs process task, update VEC network parameters, obtain S_i';
    Calculate $penalty_i$ according to Eq. (9) and $energy_i$ according to Eq. (10), get R_i;
    Update value function according to Eq. (12) through $< S_i, A_i, R_i, S_{i+1} >$;
  end
end

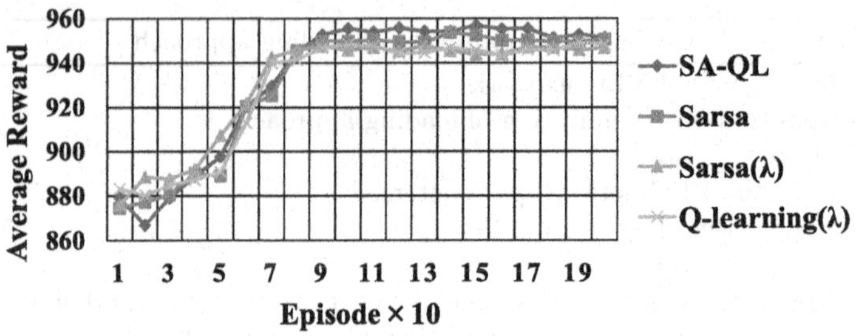

Fig. 3. The average reward of SA-QL and comparative algorithms in every 10 episodes.

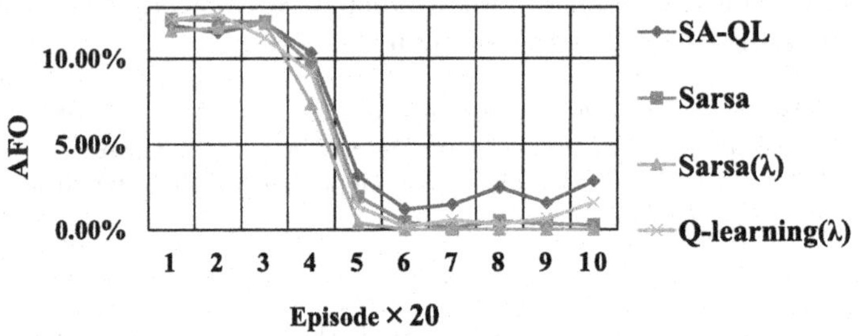

Fig. 4. The **AOFR** in every 20 episodes.

We name average energy consumption of offloading as **AEC**. Figure 5 shows the **AEC** in every 20 episodes, which indicates that with episodes increasing, the **AEC** of SA-QL and comparative algorithms decreases. Compared with Fig. 6, for the setting of weight coefficients are more inclined to **AOFR**, the **AEC** has slower convergence, and the **AOFR** converges faster in the process of approach optimization. Compared with TD(0) algorithms, the **AEC** of TD(λ) can be reduced to lower level in 200-th round, this is because the eligibility trace matrix is introduced into TD(λ), and the multi-step updating approach is adopted, thus the convergence speed can be accelerated.

Performance Difference of Comparative Strategies. Figure 6 shows **AOFR** of different strategies under the change of data size. As data size increases, **AOFR** of strategies increase. When the data size is 14, **Approach 3** and **Approach 4** reach a higher level than **Approach 1** and **Approach 2**. This is because when the task data varies from 4 to 14, local computing can meet the delay constraint of applications. **Approach 1** has a variety of offloading methods, and **Approach 2** only have local computing, the processing capacity of vehicles is able to complete these applications, thus offloading failure rate is lower. **Approach 3** and **Approach 4** have SNs computing method, offloading process needs certain communication time. In the case of small data size,

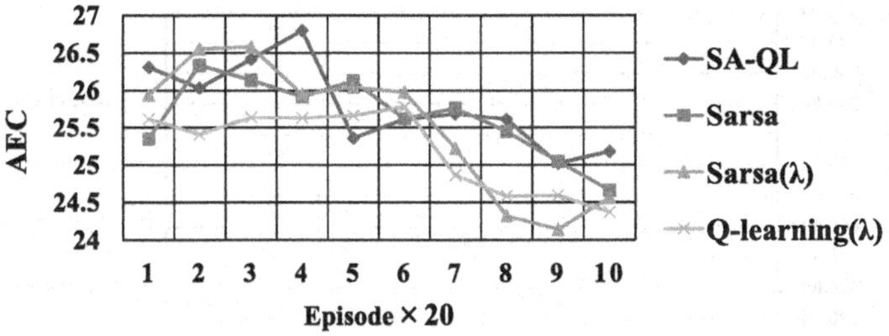

Fig. 5. The **AEC** in every 20 episodes.

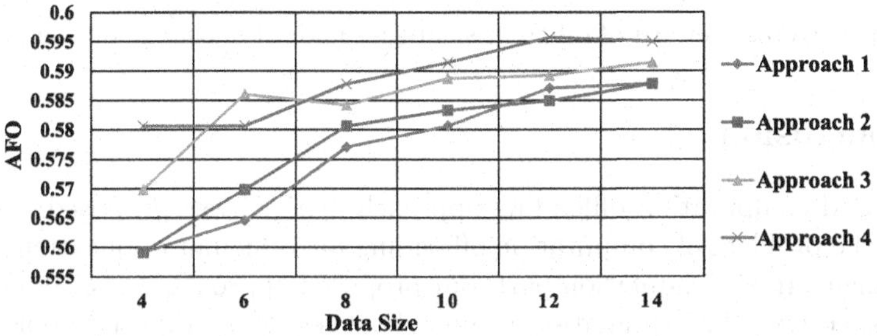

Fig. 6. The **AOFR** of different strategies under the change of data size.

long communication time may cause the completion time of ICV application to exceed its delay constraint, thus average offloading failure rate will be higher.

The average reward of different strategies under the change of tolerance time is shown in Fig. 7. Compared with other strategies, the average reward obtained by **Approach 1** can reach a higher level under the change of tolerance time [4, 16]. When the tolerance time-slot increases, except **Approach 3**, the rewards increases. One possible reason is that as tolerance time increases, offloading failure rate of applications decreases, thus the reward value increases. The reason for the decrease of reward in **Approach 3** may be that as tolerance time increases, most applications can be completed locally within delay constraints, and the punishment of offloading failure is lower. However, in **Approach 3**, the applications can be offloaded to RSU for processing, which will cause high cost of computation and communication.

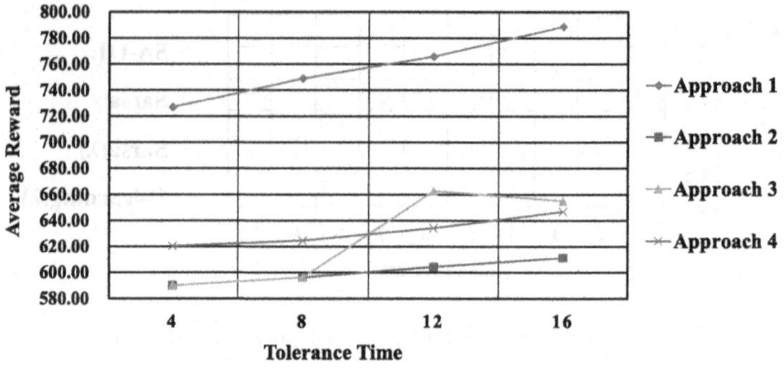

Fig. 7. The average reward of different strategies under the change of tolerance time.

6 Conclusion

A RL-based computation offloading approach in VEC was proposed. Its goal is to solve the problem of computation offloading for vehicular applications in VEC environment. In the simulation part, our proposed approach was evaluated from two perspectives. The simulation results show that our proposed approach can reduce the offloading failure rate of vehicular applications and energy consumption of offloading.

In the future, we will combine SA-QL algorithm with deep learning technology for approach optimization. In addition, we will design cache-assisted secure computing offloading approach in VEC environment.

References

1. Adiththan, A., Ramesh, S., Samii, S.: Cloud-assisted control of ground vehicles using adaptive computation offloading techniques. In: 2018 Design, Automation Test in Europe Conference Exhibition (DATE). pp. 589–592 (2018). https://doi.org/10.23919/DATE.2018.8342076
2. Azimifar, M., Todd, T.D., Khezrian, A., Karakostas, G.: Vehicle-to-vehicle forwarding in green roadside infrastructure. IEEE Trans. Veh. Technol. **65**(2), 780–795 (2016). https://doi.org/10.1109/TVT.2015.2402177
3. Bondok, A.H., Lee, W., Kim, T.: Efficient scheduling for VANET considering renewable energy. In: 2020 22nd International Conference on Advanced Communication Technology (ICACT), pp. 217–221 (2020). https://doi.org/10.23919/ICACT48636.2020.9061360
4. Dai, P., et al.: Multi-armed bandit learning for computation-intensive services in MEC-empowered vehicular networks. IEEE Trans. Veh. Technol. **69**(7), 7821–7834 (2020). https://doi.org/10.1109/TVT.2020.2991641
5. Dai, Y., Xu, D., Maharjan, S., Zhang, Y.: Joint load balancing and offloading in vehicular edge computing and networks. IEEE Internet Things J. **6**(3), 4377–4387 (2019). https://doi.org/10.1109/JIOT.2018.2876298
6. Dong, P., Wang, X., Rodrigues, J.: Deep reinforcement learning for vehicular edge computing: an intelligent offloading system. ACM Trans. Intell. Syst. Technol. **10** (2019). https://doi.org/10.1145/3317572

7. Feng, J., Liu, Z., Wu, C., Ji, Y.: AVE: autonomous vehicular edge computing framework with ACO-based scheduling. IEEE Trans. Veh. Technol. **66**(12), 10660–10675 (2017). https://doi.org/10.1109/TVT.2017.2714704
8. Guo, M., Wang, Y., Sun, H., Liu, Y.: Research on q-learning algorithm based on metropolis criterion. J. Comput. Res. Dev. **39**(6), 684–688 (2002). https://doi.org/10.1007/s11769-002-0038-4
9. Hou, X., et al.: Reliable computation offloading for edge-computing-enabled software-defined IoV. IEEE Internet Things J. **7**(8), 7097–7111 (2020). https://doi.org/10.1109/JIOT.2020.2982292
10. Hu, B., Li, J.: An edge computing framework for powertrain control system optimization of intelligent and connected vehicles based on curiosity-driven deep reinforcement learning. IEEE Trans. Ind. Electron. **68**(8), 7652–7661 (2021). https://doi.org/10.1109/TIE.2020.3007100
11. Ke, H., Wang, J., Deng, L., Ge, Y., Wang, H.: Deep reinforcement learning-based adaptive computation offloading for MEC in heterogeneous vehicular networks. IEEE Trans. Veh. Technol. **69**(7), 7916–7929 (2020). https://doi.org/10.1109/TVT.2020.2993849
12. Li, J., Xiao, Z., Li, P.: Discrete-time multi-player games based on off-policy q-learning. IEEE Access **7**, 134647–134659 (2019). https://doi.org/10.1109/ACCESS.2019.2939384
13. Li, X., Dang, Y., Aazam, M., Peng, X., Chen, T., Chen, C.: Energy-efficient computation offloading in vehicular edge cloud computing. IEEE Access **8**, 37632–37644 (2020). https://doi.org/10.1109/ACCESS.2020.2975310
14. Liu, L., Chen, C., Pei, Q., Maharjan, S., Zhang, Y.: Vehicular edge computing and networking: a survey. Mob. Netw. Appl. **26**(3), 1145–1168 (2021)
15. Luo, Q., Li, C., Luan, T.H., Shi, W.: Collaborative data scheduling for vehicular edge computing via deep reinforcement learning. IEEE Internet Things J. **7**(10), 9637–9650 (2020). https://doi.org/10.1109/JIOT.2020.2983660
16. Lèbre, M.A., Le Mouël, F., Ménard, E.: Microscopic vehicular mobility trace of Europarc roundabout, Creteil, France (2015)
17. Mao, Y., Zhang, J., Song, S.H., Letaief, K.B.: Power-delay tradeoff in multi-user mobile-edge computing systems. In: 2016 IEEE Global Communications Conference (GLOBECOM), pp. 1–6 (2016). DOI: https://doi.org/10.1109/GLOCOM.2016.7842160
18. Meng, B., Yang, F., Liu, J., Wang, Y.: A survey of brake-by-wire system for intelligent connected electric vehicles. IEEE Access **8**, 225424–225436 (2020). https://doi.org/10.1109/ACCESS.2020.3040184
19. Qin, Y., Huang, D., Zhang, X.: Vehicloud: Cloud computing facilitating routing in vehicular networks. In: 2012 IEEE 11th International Conference on Trust, Security and Privacy in Computing and Communications, pp. 1438–1445 (2012). DOI: https://doi.org/10.1109/TrustCom.2012.16
20. Raza Naqvi, S.S., Wang, S., Ahmed, M., Anwar, M.: A survey on vehicular edge computing: architecture, applications, technical issues, and future directions. Wirel. Commun. Mob. Comput. **2019**, 1–19 (2019). https://doi.org/10.1155/2019/3159762
21. Speck, C., Bucci, D.J.: Distributed UAV swarm formation control via object-focused, multi-objective sarsa. In: 2018 Annual American Control Conference (ACC), pp. 6596–6601. IEEE (2018)

22. Sun, Y., Song, J., Zhou, S., Guo, X., Niu, Z.: Task replication for vehicular edge computing: a combinatorial multi-armed bandit based approach. In: 2018 IEEE Global Communications Conference (GLOBECOM), pp. 1–7 (2018). https://doi.org/10.1109/GLOCOM.2018.8647564
23. Sutton, R.S.: Learning to predict by the methods of temporal differences. Mach. Learn. **3**(1), 9–44 (1988)
24. Wang, J., Feng, D., Zhang, S., Tang, J., Quek, T.Q.S.: Computation offloading for mobile edge computing enabled vehicular networks. IEEE Access **7**, 62624–62632 (2019). https://doi.org/10.1109/ACCESS.2019.2915959
25. Xiaoping, D., Dongxin, L., Shen, L., Qiqige, W., Wenbo, C.: Coordinated control algorithm at non-recurrent freeway bottlenecks for intelligent and connected vehicles. IEEE Access **8**, 51621–51633 (2020). https://doi.org/10.1109/ACCESS.2020.2980626
26. Xu, X., Zhang, X., Liu, X., Jiang, J., Qi, L., Bhuiyan, M.Z.A.: Adaptive computation offloading with edge for 5g-envisioned internet of connected vehicles. IEEE Trans. Intell. Transp. Syst. **22**(8), 5213–5222 (2021). https://doi.org/10.1109/TITS.2020.2982186
27. Zeng, F., Chen, Q., Meng, L., Wu, J.: Volunteer assisted collaborative offloading and resource allocation in vehicular edge computing. IEEE Trans. Intell. Transp. Syst. **22**(6), 3247–3257 (2021). https://doi.org/10.1109/TITS.2020.2980422
28. Zhan, W., et al.: Deep-reinforcement-learning-based offloading scheduling for vehicular edge computing. IEEE Internet Things J. **7**(6), 5449–5465 (2020). https://doi.org/10.1109/JIOT.2020.2978830
29. Zhao, J., Li, Q., Gong, Y., Zhang, K.: Computation offloading and resource allocation for cloud assisted mobile edge computing in vehicular networks. IEEE Trans. Veh. Technol. **68**(8), 7944–7956 (2019). https://doi.org/10.1109/TVT.2019.2917890

A Survey on Learning Path Recommendation

Fengjun Zhu[1,2], Yiping Wen[1,2(✉)], and Qi Fu[1,2]

[1] School of Computer Science and Engineering, Hunan University of Science and Technology, Xiangtan, China
ypwen81@gmail.com

[2] Key Laboratory of Knowledge Processing and Networked Manufacturing, Hunan University of Science and Technology, Xiangtan, China

Abstract. With the popularization of online learning, a wide range of learning activities have occurred and produced a huge amount of related data. A learning path consists of a set of learning activities that help users achieve particular learning goals. Learning path recommendation is important in smart education applications, which can provide suitable learning resource sequences for large-scale online learners, reduce the impact of information overload on learners, and help learners realize learning goals more quickly. Besides, it is necessary to apply popular technologies such as data mining, machine learning, optimization, knowledge graph and user profile in the domain of learning path recommendation to effectively handle related personalizing learning path parameter problems. So far, a variety of learning path recommendation methods have been proposed, which can be conducted in two ways: 1) single learner-oriented recommendation and 2) grouped learners-oriented recommendation. This paper presents an overview of these methods and analyzes future research directions of learning path recommendation.

Keywords: Learning path · Learning resource · Recommendation system

1 Introduction

The COVID-19 that broke out in early 2020 accelerated the reformation process of "Internet + education", and the number of online learning users is rapidly increasing. As a by-product of the process of large-scale online teaching activities, the learning platform has accumulated a large number of relevant learning behavior data related to learners' learning behaviors from login to exit. Technological and pedagogical innovations are redefining learning. Online learning promotes the convergence of technology and pedagogical innovation. The main advantages of online learning include availability, reduced cost, improved collaboration, enhanced flexibility (learners learn at their own convenience), etc. On the other hand, information overload and knowledge fragmentation are two major challenges facing human learning in the 21st century. It is difficult for learners to find appropriate learning resources on the Internet. Many learning resource recommendation systems do not fully consider learners' learning purpose, time limitation, knowledge backgrounds, etc. The recommended learning resources are

Y. Sun et al. (Eds.): ChineseCSCW 2021, CCIS 1491, pp. 577–589, 2022.
https://doi.org/10.1007/978-981-19-4546-5_45

not suitable for learners, which increases the difficulty of learning for learners, causes learning difficulties for learners, and slows down their learning process.

Learning path recommendation helps learners select more appropriate learning resources and organize them into learning paths suitable for learners according to their personalized learning needs. Learning Path recommendations will help learners have a better online learning experience. In this paper, focusing on the two mainstream directions of the learning path is recommended: single learner-oriented recommendation and grouped learners-oriented recommendation. This paper introduces the relevant terms involved in learning path recommendation and learners' personalized parameters, analyzes the difficulties and development directions of learning path recommendation, and provides a reference for the study of recommended learning path recommendation.

2 Terminology

We refer to a modular content hierarchy [24], which is proposed by Duval & Hodgins. We propose a modular content hierarchy for some of the main terms in the learning path recommendation research, as shown in Fig. 1. The modular content hierarchy introduces the relationship between learning resources. According to the different relationships of learning resources, the modular content hierarchy is abstracted into four levels: subject, learning unit, learning topic, learning object.

2.1 Subject

Subject is the most informative level. For example, a course such as Python programming language can be viewed as a subject. Multiple courses can be represented as directed graphs. In these graphs, the vertices indicate the learning topics or the learning objects, and directed edges represent the prerequisite relations among the vertices [23].

2.2 Learning Unit

Each subject consists of some learning units, each learning unit covers a unique concept. Each learning unit covers one or more learning topics. For example, in the Python programming language, the learning units include data types, arrays, loops, functions, etc. In some researches, the learning units might be referred to as "learning chapters".

2.3 Learning Topic

In each lesson, learners study at least one learning topic. For example, the learning unit on "loops" in Python programming language covers two learning topics: "for loops" and "while loops".

2.4 Learning Object

A learning object is the smallest unit of learning content that is reusable and constructed around a certain learning goal [21, 22]. Learning objects can be presented in many different forms, such as tests, an audio, a video, a text file, etc. In some researches, learning objects might be referred to as "learning materials" or "knowledge units".

Learning path can be understood as the sequence of the above contents (learning objects, learning topics, etc.) [25, 26], and there is a certain learning sequence relationship between these contents. Learning path recommendation is to generate learning paths that satisfy learners' preferences and learning goals. The main goal of learning path personalization is to generate a learning path that meets the preferences and requirements of the learners [41]. The way to identify learners' characteristics and requirements is to apply personalization parameters.

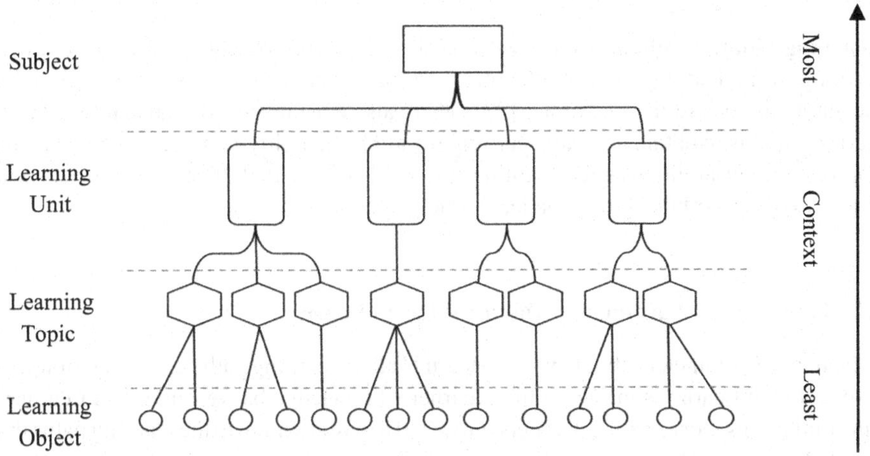

Fig. 1. Content hierarchy for learning path recommendation

3 Personalization Parameters

Personalized parameters are critical for generating personalized learning paths. Learners' personalization parameters are used to describe learners' characteristics and learning requirements, such as learning style, knowledge background, etc. According to the needs of learning path recommendation researches, we divide these parameters into three categories: "why to learn", "what to learn" and "how to learn", as shown in Fig. 2.

It is worth noting that some of the personalization parameters are dynamic, such as master ability and learning style. These values may change during the learning process. Some parameters may not be identified in advance, such as learning style, knowledge background. These parameters only are identified when learners learn through online learning platforms. It is necessary to update learners' information based on personalized parameters modeling regularly [22, 35].

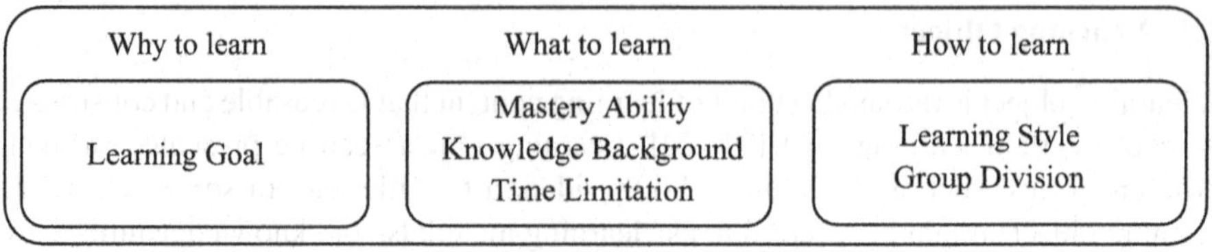

Fig. 2. Classification of personalization parameters

3.1 Personalization Parameters About "Why to Learn"

Personalization parameters about "why to learn?" can be denoted as the learning goal. The differences between learners are reflected in the personalization parameters about "why to learn". For example, a learner's goal is to master the Python programming language in two months.

Learning Goal. It refers to the level that learners hope to achieve after a period of learning. If the learning goal of a learner is to maximize his score, it is considered that the learner is a score-driven learner [23]. There also exist reward-driven learners whose learning goal is to obtain a certain learning reward [32], ability-driven learners who take improving their abilities as the learning goals [21, 33], and skills-driven learners who aim to master a certain skill in the least time [21].

3.2 Personalized Parameters About "What to Learn"

Personalized parameters about "what to learn?" allow learning path personalization with respect to the Learner's master ability, learner's knowledge background, and Learner's time limitations. For example, learners only need to pay attention to the learning paths that match their knowledge background, mastery ability, and time limitation after determining their learning goals.

Mastery Ability. Mastery ability indicates learners' mastery of the knowledge and skills required for a specific course or task [28]. This is a dynamic parameter that might change during the learning process.

Knowledge Background. This refers to the knowledge reserve of users before they accept the recommendation of the learning path. A good knowledge reserve can help learners better understand new knowledge. Knowledge background can be divided into objective knowledge background and subjective knowledge background. The objective knowledge background refers to the course grades or predicted scores of the course. Subjective knowledge background refers to learners' judgment on their current knowledge level reserve based on their judgment [13, 31].

Time Limitation. This refers to the time that learners can spend to achieve learning goals [23, 27]. If learners choose a learning path to achieve a certain learning goal, they usually need to spend a certain amount of time, and the length of time is usually fixed.

Learners may not have enough time to follow an entire learning path due to various reasons such as poor time management, inability to multi-task at the same time, and so on. Hence, The information provided by the "time limit" personalization parameter is used to generate a learning path that satisfies the learner's time limitation.

3.3 Personalized Parameters About "How to Learn"

Personalized parameters about "How to Learn" are used to describe the individual differences of learners as the manner that they deal with learning ways, including learners' learning styles, and group division. For example, a learner who plans to learn the Python programming language expects his learning materials to be in Chinese, and he also hopes to learn cooperatively in the form of a group so that he can communicate with other learners in the learning process.

Learning Style. This is an important parameter that indicates how a learner learns [22]. According to individual learning style preferences, learners can be divided into four categories: active-reflective learners, Sensing-intuitive learners, visual-verbal learners, and sequential-global learners [29, 30].

Group Division. Collaborative Learning is a learning strategy that learners form study groups and learn in groups. In the context of collaborative learning, learners are divided into study groups, in which learners with similar learning interests are normally in the same study group. Recommend similar or identical learning paths to members of the same group. Group division requires obtaining learners' preferences, alleviating preference conflicts among group members, and making the learning path recommendation results satisfy the preferences of all group members as much as possible [34].

4 Methods of Learning Path Recommendation

4.1 Single Learner-Oriented Recommendation

Methods Based on Learner Characteristics. This kind of research mainly applies the methods of data mining, machine learning, and optimization. This kind of research generates a personalized learning path according to the learning behavior and characteristics of learners in the learning process. Lin et al. [2] used the hybrid decision tree method to provide learning path recommendations for learners with different learning abilities and characteristics. Their personalized innovative learning system integrates personalized learning and game-based learning into a personalized learning plan. Based on the learner model and knowledge model, Zhao et al. [3] dynamically matched and restructured learning resources through association rule mining technology, and then realized personalized learning path recommendations. Aleksandra et al. [4] proposed a personalized learning path recommendation method based on social tags and sequential pattern mining. The method collects labels about learning resources entered by learners, then these tags are rated and used to recommend sequences of learning resources. Cheng

[5] applied ant colony optimization algorithm to generate learning path recommendation results. However, these methods do not consider the learning efficiency of learners who follow the learning path recommendation results. In order to further improve the quality of recommendation, Zhou et al. [6] proposed a full-path learning recommendation model. In this model, learners are clustered based on their feature similarity, and then learners' learning paths and learning effects are predicted by Long-Short Term Memory. Finally, a personalized learning path suitable for learners is recommended according to the prediction learning effects.

Methods Based on the Internal Relationships Between Learning Resources. This kind of research mainly uses ontology, semantic chain network, knowledge graph, and other technologies to generate recommendation results by analyzing semantic or cognitive relations among learning resources involved in learning paths. For example, Huang et al. [9] constructed the ontology-based context model and subject domain ontology library and elaborated the adaptive learning path recommendation mechanism and its implementation process based on context awareness. Yang et al. [10] proposed a learning path recommendation tool suitable for learners' learning style bias by using the semantic link network technology. Wan et al. [7] used mixed concept maps to establish the relationship between learners and learning resources, described recommendation as a constraint satisfaction problem, and applied the immune algorithm to obtain recommendation results. Zhu et al. [8] verified that learners have different preferences for learning paths in different learning scenarios, and they proposed a multi-constraint learning path recommendation algorithm based on a knowledge map. Guillaume Durand et al. [11] established a learning path recommendation model that can describe the ability dependency relationship between learning resources based on graph theory. However, these methods are not considering the diversity of the relationships between the learning resources. In order to better generate diversified learning paths that satisfy different learning needs, Shi et al. [12] used the knowledge graph to represent six main semantic connections between learning resources and proposed an interpretable and reusable learning path recommendation model based on the multidimensional knowledge graph.

4.2 Grouped Learners-Oriented Recommendation

In the domain of recommendation research, group recommendation methods are usually divided into two categories: recommendation by mixed model and recommendation by mixed recommendation results [34], which are illustrated in Fig. 3 and Fig. 4 respectively. The former kind of method is to aggregate user preferences into group preferences and then provide recommendation services to group learners. The more similar the learners' preferences in the group, the better the group recommendation effect. The latter kind of method normally takes each learner's personalized recommendation list and merges all the lists into the same list as the group recommendation results.

In order to satisfy the needs of learning paths recommendation for group learners rather than individual learners in practical applications, researchers have made active explorations, but only a few research results have been obtained. In the field of online learning, group learners usually refer to learners with similar learning interests. The

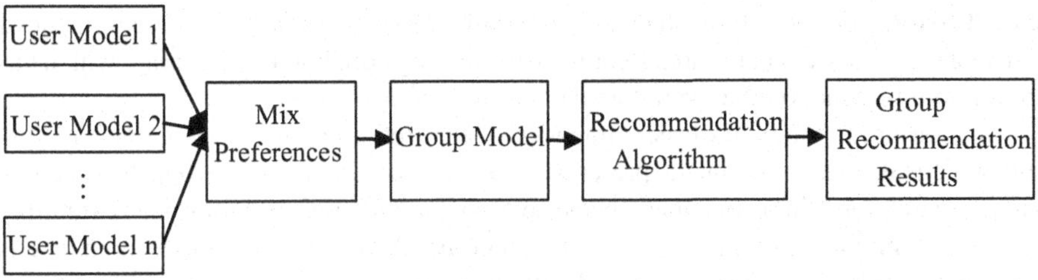

Fig. 3. Group recommendation by mixed models

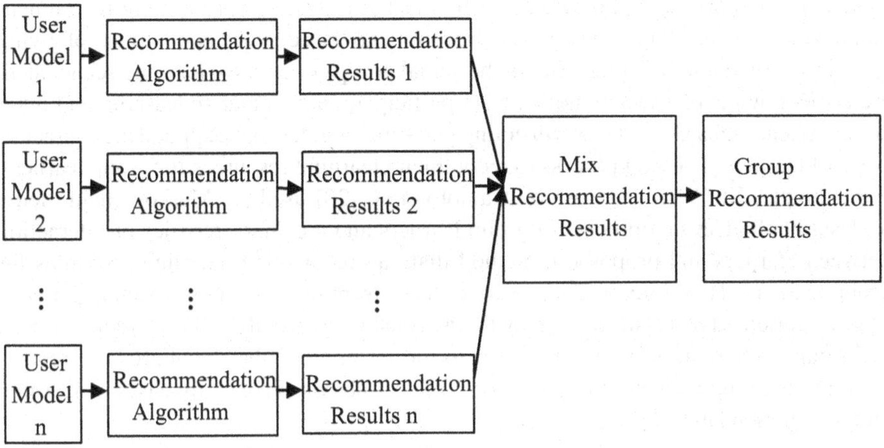

Fig. 4. Group recommendation by mixed recommendation results

explicit attributes of learners on learning resources and the implicit attributes of accessing resources, such as learning time and learning frequency, are often used together to calculate the similarity between learners [14]. Xie et al. [13] proposed a group learning path recommendation framework based on user profile to help each learner in the group efficiently learn the needed new knowledge within the time limitation, and to enable the whole group to acquire all the knowledge needed to complete the group learning task on the whole. This method considers learners' knowledge background, learning preference, and group learning task. However, the computational complexity of this method is relatively high, and it is difficult to ensure its recommendation performance when the relevant data of learners is too sparse. Because of these deficiencies, Zhu et al. [14] used the data and knowledge graph in the learner's learning history log to firstly represent the knowledge point learning of learners in different periods as personalized learning to generate a network, and then conducted cluster analysis on these personalized learning to generate a network. In this way, the group learning generation network reflecting the common characteristics of the learning group is generated. Finally, the recommendation results are generated based on the preferences of the learning group for different types of learning paths in different learning situations. However, these methods do not take into account the differences in learning behaviors of learners when they learn different courses and finish different learning tasks, and whether the recommended learning resources and paths are effective in promoting collaborative learning, which has an important impact on the overall actual learning effect of the group.

In addition, in the field of recommender system research, group recommender system, which takes into account the preferences of each user in the same group, has become a hot research topic in recent years, because of the application scenarios where multiple users watch movies, catering and tourism in a group. A large number of research results have been obtained [15–19]. Compared with the recommended method for a single user, grouped user-oriented methods recommended to consider the emotional contagion and consistency (i.e., the various user satisfaction degree can be a profound impact on others, users express opinions will influence each other) affect the performance of recommendation and other social phenomenon and recommend the accuracy and fairness of giving attention to two or more things. But in the actual group cooperative learning scene, there are also a few people who do not actively participate in cooperative learning and other similar phenomena. And, it is worth noting that some scholars have applied the characteristics of learners' learning process to recommend learning resources for group learners. For example, Xin Wan and Toshio Okamoto et al. [20] used the Markov chain model to describe the learning process of group learners and the characteristics of interaction between learners and proposed a method that can recommend learning resources for group learners. Therefore, it is necessary to learn from the existing research experience of group-oriented recommendation methods, consider and analyze the characteristics of the group collaborative learning process, to further improve the actual effect of recommending learning paths to group learners. Table 1 shows some study cases of learning path recommendations.

Table 1. Summarizing some methods of learning path recommendation

Single learner-oriented recommendation	Methods based on learner characteristics	Lin, C., et al. (2013) [2]
		Zhao, X., et al. (2016) [3]
		Klašnja-Milićević, A., et al. (2018) [4]
		Cheng, Y. (2011) [5]
		Zhou, Y., et al. (2018) [6]
	Methods based on the relationships between learning resources	Wan, S., et al. (2016) [7]
		Zhu, H., et al. (2018) [8]
		Huang, Z., et al. (2015) [9]
		Yang, J., et al. (2013) [10]
		Durand, G., et al. (2013) [11]
		Shi, D., et al. (2020) [12]
Grouped learners-oriented recommendation		Xie, H., et al. (2017) [13]
		Zhu, H., et al. (2018) [14]

5 Future Research Directions

At present, the number of research on single learner-oriented recommendation methods is more than that of group-oriented recommendation methods. In recent years, a lot of progress has been made in the research and application of learning path recommendation methods. However, many of the methods proposed by researchers still have a set of limitations and challenges with regard to these methods and these problems have led to some very significant consequences. Introducing these challenges will help researchers make breakthroughs in the current study and achieve the desired results. Not only are there several difficulties with learning path recommendation methods that we mentioned regarding learning path personalization, but there are also some pressing issues that need to be addressed. We summarized the difficulties and development directions of the following learning path recommendation:

5.1 Time Limitation

If learners cannot devote enough time to follow the learning path to learn, it will be difficult to achieve their original learning goals. For various reasons, learners spend less time learning than they expect to spend in learning. There are many reasons for this situation, the most notable part of which is: improper time management, laziness, multitasking, etc. When learners do not have enough time to study, learners are faced with two questions: can the outcome of the learning justify the time spent by learners; what are learners can learn from the learning path that they want to follow in limited time? In many studies [27, 36], the study time of the course is usually specified by experts, and the duration is the same for all learners. Antonio Garrido et al. [37] considered learners' learning background, learning environment, and time available for learning, and generated personalized learning path recommendations for learners to help learners better achieve their learning goals.

5.2 Updating Learners' Profile

The learner's master ability and the time available to reach the learning goal may change during the learning process. Sometimes the learner's knowledge background cannot be accurately identified. Therefore, taking into account the changes that may occur to the learner during the learning process, the user's configuration file should be updateable. Updating the learner's configuration file also has the following problems: how to determine under which circumstances the learner's configuration file should be updated; what information needs to be updated in the learner's configuration file. It is a difficult task to determine the updating time. It is because updating learners' profiles and frequently evaluating learners is time-consuming and sometimes unnecessary. But delaying updating learners' profiles may result in the recommendation of learning resources that are not suitable for learners, thus increasing learners' knowledge fragmentation and wasting learners' time. Do the updated learners' profiles have the same importance when generating recommendations? Is there a ranking (weight) among them? How to check the validity of updated learners' information.

5.3 Designing Course Map

In the current research, the design of the curriculum map is usually done manually by the teacher, which requires a lot of manpower and material resources and cannot be changed. It means that each learner who takes this course uses the same course map, and more importantly, the course map is teacher-centered [42]. The teacher-centered course map is not suitable for all learners because of the differences in learning goals, knowledge backgrounds, and other personalized learning parameters. Therefore, it is necessary to construct a course map from the learners' perspectives. Yu et al. [1] divided the classification and annotation of learning object concepts into two processes. First, for each curriculum concept, a pre-trained word embedding was used to calculate its most likely category. Then the three annotators in the corresponding field are required to mark whether the concept belongs to this category. For the concept category pair marked as "not belonging", select the previous sibling category as the new candidate, and put the refreshed pair in the annotation again Pool. This process effectively reduces the number of invalid comments. Although this reduces part of the manual operation, it may still cause the learning goals that learners want to achieve cannot be matched with the designed course map, thereby reducing the efficiency of learning path recommendation.

5.4 Learner Privacy and Information Security

Preference sharing and learner interaction are conducive to the improvement of the accuracy of group learning path recommendations. But at the same time, it also brings a lot of learner privacy and information security issues. At present, there are relatively little researches on the privacy issues of group recommendation [38, 39]. And there are situations where different groups have different requirements for privacy protection.

5.5 Interpretability and Validity of Group Recommendation Results

A Reasonable explanation of the group learning path recommendation results helps learners to better understand the recommendation mechanism and the preferences of other members in the group, it is easier to accept the recommendation results of the learning path, and enhance the learning effect [40]. Currently, offline evaluation methods are mainly used to measure the effectiveness of group learning path recommendation results. The more similar the learning characteristics of the learners in the group, the more effective the group recommendation will be.

6 Conclusion

In summary, learning path recommendation is a research hotspot in recent years, and a large number of research results have been obtained. In recent years, the methods for single learner-oriented recommendation have been extensively researched in depth, and the research is relatively mature. grouped learners-oriented recommendation research results are relatively few, and there is still room for improvement in the effectiveness of recommendation results.

In this paper, we have introduced the two mainstream directions of current learning path recommendation methods, and clearly explained the related terminology that will be involved in learning path recommendation methods. Finally, combined with recent research work, the future development direction of learning path recommendation research is introduced.

Acknowledgement. This work was supported by the Natural Science Foundation of China (No. 62177014, 6177219), National Key R&D Program of China (No. 2018YFB1702600), and Research Foundation of Hunan Provincial Education Department of China (No. 20B222, 19A174, HNJG-2020-0488).

References

1. Yu, J., Luo, G., Xiao, T., Zhong, Q., Wang, Y., Feng, W., et al.: MOOCCube: a large-scale data repository for NLP applications in MOOCs. In: Proceedings of the 58th Annual Meeting of the Association for Computational Linguistics, pp. 3135–3142 (2020)
2. Lin, C., Yeh, Y., Yu, H., Chang, R.I.: Data mining for providing a personalized learning path in creativity: an application of decision trees. Comput. Educ. **68**, 199–210 (2013)
3. Zhao, X., Cen, L.: Research on personalized learning path recommendation of adaptive learning system oriented to user needs. Chinese J. ICT Educ. **21**, 28–31 (2016)
4. Klasnja-Milicevic, A., Vesin, B., Ivanovic, M.: Social tagging strategy for enhancing e-learning experience. Comput. Educ. **118**, 166–181 (2018)
5. Cheng, Y.: A method of swarm intelligence-based learning path recommendation for online learning. J. Syst. Manag. **20**(02), 232–237 (2011)
6. Zhou, Y., Huang, C., Hu, Q., Zhu, J., Tang, Y.: Personalized learning full-path recommendation model based on LSTM neural networks. Inf. Sci. **444**, 135–152 (2018)
7. Wan, S., Niu, Z.: A learner oriented learning recommendation approach based on mixed concept mapping and immune algorithm. Knowl. Based Syst. **103**, 28–40 (2016)
8. Zhu, H., Tian, F., Wu, K., Shah, N., Chen, Y., Ni, Y., et al.: A multi-constraint learning path recommendation algorithm based on knowledge map. Knowl. Based Syst. **143**, 102–114 (2018)
9. Huang, Z., Zhao, C., Huang, X., Wan, L., Chen, Z.: Research on adaptive learning path recommendation based on situational awareness. Electr. Educ. Res. **36**(05), 77–84 (2015)
10. Yang, J., Zhang, Y., Huang, Z., Liu, H., Huang, X.: Smap: a dynamic learning path recommendation tool that can adapt the Felder-Silverman learning style model. Dist. Educ. China **05**, 77–86 (2013)
11. Durand, G., Belacel, N., LaPlante, F.: Graph theory based model for learning path recommendation. Inf. Sci. **251**, 10–21 (2013)
12. Shi, D., Wang, T., Xing, H., Xu, H.: A learning path recommendation model based on a multidimensional knowledge graph framework for e-learning. Knowl. Based Syst. **195**, 105618 (2020)
13. Xie, H., Zou, D., Wang, F., Wong, T., Rao, Y., Wang, S.: Discover learning path for group users: a profile-based approach. Neurocomputing **254**, 59–70 (2017)
14. Zhu, H., Ni, Y., Feng, T., Pei, F., Yan, C., Zheng, Q.: A group-oriented recommendation algorithm based on similarities of personal learning generative networks. IEEE Access **6**, 42729–42739 (2018)
15. Jeong, H., Kim, M.: HGGC: A hybrid group recommendation model considering group cohesion. Expert Syst. Appl. **136**, 73–82 (2019)

16. Feng, S., Zhang, H., Wang, L., Liu, L., Xu, Y.: Detecting the latent associations hidden in multi-source information for better group recommendation. Knowl. Based Syst. **171**, 56–68 (2019)
17. Wang, X., Liu, Y., Lu, J., Xiong, F., Zhang, G.: TruGRC: trust-aware group recommendation with virtual coordinators. Futur. Gener. Comput. Syst. **94**, 224–236 (2019)
18. Xiao, Y., Pei, Q., Yao, L., Yu, S., Bai, L., Wang, X.: An enhanced probabilistic fairness-aware group recommendation by incorporating social activeness. J. Netw. Comput. Appl. **156**, 102579 (2020)
19. Qin, D., Zhou, X., Chen, L., Huang, G., Zhang, Y.: Dynamic connection-based social group recommendation. IEEE Trans. Knowl. Data Eng. **32**(3), 453–467 (2020)
20. Xin, W., Okamoto, T.: Utilizing learning process to improve recommender system for group learning support. Neural Comput. Appl. **20**(5), 611–621 (2009)
21. Belacel, N., Durand, G., Laplante, F.: A binary integer programming model for global optimization of learning path discovery. In: Proceedings of the 7th International Conference on Educational Data Mining (2014)
22. Dharani, B., Geetha, T.: Adaptive learning path generation using colored petri nets based on behavioral aspects. In: 2013 International Conference on Recent Trends in Information Technology (ICRTIT), pp. 459–465. IEEE, India (2013)
23. Nabizadeh, A., Jorge, A., Leal, J.: Rutico: recommending successful learning paths under time constraints. In: Adjunct Publication of the 25th Conference on User Modeling, Adaptation and Personalization, pp. 153–158. ACM, New York (2017)
24. Duval, E., Hodgins, W.: A LOM research agenda. In: The Twelfth International World Wide Web Conference (WWW2003), pp. 1–10. ACM, Budapest, Hungary (2003)
25. Muhammad, A., Zhou, Q., Beydoun, G., Xu, D., Shen, J.: Learning path adaptation in online learning systems. In: 2016 IEEE 20th International Conference on Computer Supported Cooperative Work in Design (CSCWD), pp. 421–426. IEEE, Nanchang, China (2016)
26. Adorni, G., Koceva, F.: Educational concept maps for personalized learning path generation. In: AI* IA 2016 Advances In Artificial Intelligence, pp. 135–148. Springer, Hobart, TAS, Australia (2016)
27. Zhan, L., Papaemmanouil, O., Koutrika, G.: Coursenavigator: Interactive learning path exploration. In: Proceedings of the Third International Workshop on Exploratory Search in Databases and the Web, pp. 6–11. ACM, Chengdu, China (2016)
28. McGaghie, W., Issenberg, S., Barsuk, J., Wayne, D.: A critical review of simulation-based mastery learning with translational outcomes. Med. Educ. **48**, 375–385 (2014)
29. Essalmi, F., Ayed, L., Jemni, M., Graf, S.: A fully personalization strategy of e-learning scenarios. Comput. Hum. Behav. **26**, 581–591 (2010)
30. Klašnja-Milicěvic, A., Vesin, B., Ivanovic, M., Budimac, Z.: E-learning personalization based on hybrid recommendation strategy and learning style identification. Comput. Educ. **56**, 885–899 (2011)
31. Feng, X., Xie, H., Peng, Y., Chen, W., Sun, H.: Groupized learning path discovery based on member profile. In: Luo, X., Cao, Y., Yang, B., Liu, J., Ye, F. (eds.) ICWL 2010. LNCS, vol. 6537, pp. 301–310. Springer, Heidelberg (2011). https://doi.org/10.1007/978-3-642-20539-2_32
32. Durand, G., Laplante, F., Kop, R.: A learning design recommendation system based on markov decision processes. In: KDD- 2011: 17th ACM SIGKDD Conference on Knowledge Discovery and Data Mining (2011)
33. Chi, Y.: Developing curriculum sequencing for managing multiple texts in e-learning system. In Proceedings of international conference on engineering education, pp. 1–8 (2010)
34. Zhang, Y., Du, Y., Meng, X.: Research on group recommender systems and their applications. Chinese J. Comput. **39**(04), 745–764 (2016)

35. Iglesias, J., Angelov, P., Ledezma, A., Sanchis, A.: Creating evolving user behavior profiles automatically. IEEE Trans. Knowl. Data Eng. **24**, 854–867 (2012)
36. Xu, J., Xing, T., Schaar, M.: Personalized course sequence recommendations. IEEE Trans. Signal Process. **64**, 5340–5352 (2016)
37. Garrido, A., Onaindia, E.: Assembling learning objects for personalized learning: an AI planning perspective. IEEE Intell. Syst. **28**, 64–73 (2013)
38. Masthoff, J., Gatt, A.: In pursuit of satisfaction and the prevention of embarrassment: affective state in group recommender systems. User Model. User-Adap. Inter. **16**(3/4), 281–319 (2006)
39. Shang, S., Hui, Y., Hui, P., Cuff, P., Kulkarni, S.: Beyond personalization and anonymity: towards a group-based recommender system. In: Proceedings of the 29th Annual ACM Symposium on Applied Computing, pp. 266–273 (2014)
40. Masthoff, J.: Group Recommender Systems: Combining Individual Models. Recommender Systems Handbook, pp. 677–702. Springer, Boston (2011)
41. Nabizadeh, A.H., Leal, J.P., Rafsanjani, H.N., Shah, R.R.: Learning path personalization and recommendation methods: a survey of the state-of-the-art. Expert Syst. Appl. **159**, 113596 (2020)
42. Railean, E.A.: Teacher-centered versus learner-centered design of screen. In: User Interface Design of Digital Textbooks. LNET, pp. 59–80. Springer, Singapore (2017). https://doi.org/10.1007/978-981-10-2456-6_4

Olfactory Psychological Computation and Olfactory Environment for Human-Machine Collaboration

Weihui Dai[1(✉)], Liu Liu[1], Meilin Li[2], Gaoyang Zhang[1], Qiyun Xue[1], and Lijuan Song[3(✉)]

[1] School of Management, Fudan University, Shanghai 200433, China
{whdai,17307130345,18307100089,18307100104}@fudan.edu.cn
[2] School of Education, Shanghai Jianqiao University, Shanghai 201306, China
[3] School of Humanities and Management Sciences, Southwest Medical University, Luzhou 646000, China
slj@swmu.edu.cn

Abstract. In the environment of human-machine collaboration, human brain is susceptible to physical fatigue and various psychological factors. Olfaction plays special roles in regulating human psychological states, and can be applied to improve work performance. However, the above psychological effects are caused by olfactory molecules, and may occur under unconscious or subconscious states of the brain, which are difficult to be accurately assessed by human subjective self-reports. Based on EEG signal analysis, this paper studies the olfactory effects on pleasure, wakefulness, and relaxation, and presents the computation method for taking both of the explicit and implicit parts of psychological effects into account comprehensively. Furthermore, the influences of rose and mint scents on working performance of human-machine collaboration are examined through MENSA IQ Test and Utrecht Work Engagement Scale. Research work of this paper provides an exploratory method for olfactory psychological computation, as well as the reference for human-machine collaborative environment construction.

Keywords: Human-machine collaboration · Olfactory effect · Psychological computation · EEG signal · Work performance

1 Introduction

In the work environment of human-machine collaboration, high stress or long-term working hours may cause physical fatigue and negative emotions of the human brain, and can severely affect the willingness to work, resulting in low efficiency and even operational errors. As one of the essential human senses, olfaction has significant impacts on human psychology and behaviors, which plays special roles in regulating human mental states [1, 2]. Therefore, an appropriate olfactory stimulation can be the effective way of improving work performance in man-machine collaborative environment construction.

However, the mechanism of human psychological effects caused by olfaction is different from that of hearing and vision. It is through the molecular movement of

Y. Sun et al. (Eds.): ChineseCSCW 2021, CCIS 1491, pp. 590–598, 2022.
https://doi.org/10.1007/978-981-19-4546-5_46

olfactory stimuli, and acts directly on human olfactory organ to produce physiology and psychological effects, which may occur under unconscious or subconscious states of the brain, and exists significant individual difference [3, 4]. This makes great difficulties in the description, evaluation, and computation of human olfactory psychological effects through the commonly-used methods which are mainly based on human subjective self-reports [5]. EEG (Electroencephalograph) signals can reflect the neural activities of human physiology and psychological changes even under the unconscious states of the brain, and provide great advantages on the study of olfactory effects [5, 6]. Based on EEG signal analysis, this paper studied the psychological effects evoked by different olfactory stimuli, explored the method for overcoming the existing computation difficulties, and conducted an empirical study to examine the influences of rose and mint scents on working performance, aiming to provide an effective method for olfactory psychological computation and the reference of olfactory environment construction for human-machine collaboration.

2 Olfactory Psychological Computation

2.1 Psychological Effects of Olfaction

Olfaction has significant regulating effects on human psychological and physiological states. For example, some scents favored by people such as those of fruits and flowers can induce positive emotions, and orange, mint, jasmine tea aroma, lavender, banana etc. can enhance pleasant experience, but butyric acid and acetic acid mainly produce negative emotions such as anger or disgust. In addition, olfactory stimuli can also affect physiological arousal. The relaxing scent of lavender can reduce heart rate and skin electricity, increase sleep duration, and peppermint can enhance alertness, as well as reduce daytime drowsiness.

The psychological effects evoked by olfaction are caused by the molecular motions acting directly on human sense organs. Especially, olfactory system is the only sensory channel that directly connects the higher cortex areas of human brain with the environment, bypassing the thalamus in the process of nerve signal transmission [1, 3]. Therefore, compared with other senses, the effect of olfactory regulation does not necessarily take place through the perception and processing at the level of consciousness. For example, smell can stimulate the contents and influence the mood in dreams, and olfactory cues can induce personal memories more effectively than visual and auditory cues [7]. The psychological effects of olfaction also vary from person to person, and display certain gender differences. Compared with male, female may demonstrate stronger positive emotions and weaker negative emotions to eugenol oil. In addition, the emotional experience of smell has much to do with the olfactory sensitivity and preferences of different persons.

In our previous study [5], we proposed an olfactory affective computation method based on EEG signal data, which showed better distinguishing performance and potential reliability than the self-reported scoring method in PAD (Pleasure-Arousal-Dominance) emotional space [8–10]. In that study, we adopted rose, wood, mint essential oils and 84 disinfectant (with the main chemical substance of NaClO) as olfactory stimuli, and obtained the EEG signal data from 23 qualified subjects with 10 males and 13 females, aged between 20 and 48, according to a specially designed experimental paradigm [5]. During the experiment, we also asked the subjects to make the assessments of olfactory effects on pleasure, wakefulness, and relaxation by the scores from −4 to + 4. The study of this paper will further explore the computation method of the above psychological effects based on the collected data. Table 1 shows the mean values and standard deviations of the subjects' assessment scores.

Table 1. Mean values and standard deviations of assessment scores.

Olfactory stimuli	Pleasure	Wakefulness	Relaxation
Rose	2.416 ± 1.084	2.022 ± 1.233	1.940 ± 1.112
Wood	2.382 ± 0.906	1.832 ± 1.321	2.267 ± 1.107
Mint	1.871 ± 1.224	2.348 ± 0.824	2.076 ± 1.378
Disinfectant	−1.962 ± 0.886	1.420 ± 1.153	−1.273 ± 1.081

From Table 1, we can see that the highest levels of pleasure (2.416), wakefulness (2.348), and relaxation (2.267) are evoked by rose essential oil, mint essential oil, and wood essential oil respectively. Therefore, those three scents can be used to improve the human-machine collaborative environment effectively. However, the assessment scores remain big standard deviations, which indicate that the olfactory psychological effects may exist great individual differences, and furthermore, the subjective assessment method can't acquire a precise result probably. This makes great difficulties in olfactory psychological computation.

2.2 Olfactory Computation Method

Due to the variety of molecules that may evoke different olfactory effects, and given the considerable differences and ambiguities of human experiences under the unconscious or subconscious states of the brain, commonly-used computation methods can hardly achieve the accurate results of olfactory psychological effects. The effective method seems to be explored based on the observation and analysis of neural activities evoked by olfactory stimulation.

EEG signals can be broken into wavelets and reconstructed as some typical waves with different frequency bands, such as δ (0.5–3 Hz), θ (4–7 Hz), α (8–13 Hz), β (14–30 Hz), and γ (>30 Hz). Among them, δ and θ waves are mostly related to the neural activities under unconscious and subconscious states of the brain; α wave reflects the conscious and quiet state, and β wave is closely related to tension, pressure, fatigue and the load of the brain; and γ wave is usually associated with the emotion states of anxiety and anger.

Our previous study showed that the feature parameters of PSD (Power Spectral Density) and ApEn (Approximate Entropy) of EEG signals can better reflect the affective effects of olfaction [5]. In order to get more accurate computation results, we extract those parameters from the following nine subdivided bands of EEG signals: B1-δ (0.5–3 Hz),

B2-θ (4–7 Hz), B3-low α (8–10 Hz), B4-high α (11–13 Hz), B5-low β (14–15 Hz), B6-midrange β (16–20 Hz), B7-high β (21–30 Hz), B8-low γ (31–40 Hz), and B9-midrange γ (41–50 Hz). Therefore, the computational problem of olfactory psychological effects can be described as follows:

$$P(i) = f_i(psd\,(j), ApEn(j)), i = 1, 2, 3; j = 1, 2, 3, ..., 9 \tag{1}$$

where, $P(i)$ stands for the psychological effects of pleasure, wakefulness, and relaxation ($i = 1, 2, 3$), and $psd\,(j)$, $ApEn(j)$ are the feature parameters of the nine subdivided waves from B1 to B9 ($j = 1, 2, 3, .., 9$).

However, the psychological effects that can be assessed by subjective scoring way are probably the only part under conscious states of the brain, so the whole psychological effects should be expressed as:

$$P(i) = P_e(i) + P_m(i), i = 1, 2, 3 \tag{2}$$

where, $P_e(i)$ stands for the explicit part of psychological effects that can be assessed under conscious states, while $P_m(i)$ represents the implicit part which is related to the unconscious and subconscious states.

Because the neural activities under conscious states of the brain are mainly reflected in α, β, and γ waves, so we use the feature parameter data extracted from B3 to B9 waves to estimate $P_e(i)$. Similarly, we apply the parameter data extracted from B1 and B2 to evaluate $P_m(i)$. Nevertheless, $P_m(i)$ can't be directly measured or subjectively assessed, and this leads to the difficulty in calibration and annotation, while using a machine learning method. In order to solve this problem, we introduce the following assumed prior knowledge:

$$P_m(i) = \frac{\mathrm{PSD}_m}{\mathrm{PSD}_e} P_e(i), i = 1, 2, 3 \tag{3}$$

where, PSD_m and PSD_e are the power spectral densities of B1–B2 (0.5–7 Hz) and B3–B9 (8–50 Hz) respectively for the same subject. PSD reflects the intensity of neural activities which are closely related to the strength of psychological effects, so Formula (3) is a reasonable assumption, because $P_m(i)$ and $P_e(i)$ are evoked through the same olfactory organs and nervous system for a certain individual subject.

Combining Formula (1), Formula (2), and Formula (3), we can further describe the computational problem as follows:

$$P_e(i) = \frac{1}{k+1} f_i(psd\,(j),\ ApEn(j)),\ i = 1,\ 2,\ 3;\ j = 3,\ 4,\ 5 ...,\ 9 \tag{4}$$

where, k represents $\frac{\mathrm{PSD}_m}{\mathrm{PSD}_e}$, which is depended on each different individual subjects. We first use the feature parameter data of $psd\,(j)$ and $ApEn(j)$ ($j = 3,\ 4,\ 5 ...,\ 9$) related to $P_e(i)$ for the computation. Finally, the whole psychological effects can be calculated as:

$$P(i) = (k + 1)P_e(i), i = 1, 2, 3 \tag{5}$$

Based on our previous experience [5, 11], we first use the LS-SVR (Least Squared Support Vector Regression) non-linear estimator [12] to realize the computation of Formula (4), and finally get the estimated whole psychological effects of $P(i)$ from Formula (5).

2.3 Computational Results and Analysis

In the computation process, different from a common way which usually takes one part of the data for training, and then uses the left data for test and accuracy evaluation, we first use all data for training, then estimate $P_e(i)$ for each subject with corresponding individual data by the trained LS-SVR estimator, and finally compute $P(i)$ according to Formula (5). In order to compare the estimated results of $P(i)$ with the subjective assessment scores, we show their mean values as in Fig. 1:

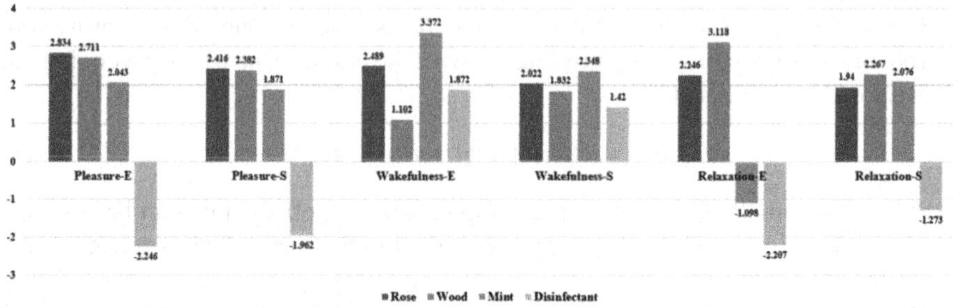

Fig. 1. Comparation of estimated results with subjective assessment scores in mean values.

In Fig. 1, Pleasure-E, Wakefulness-E, Relaxation-E are the mean values of estimated $P(i)$ for all subjects, and Pleasure-S, Wakefulness-S, Relaxation-S are the mean values of their subjective assessment scores as shown in Table 1. We can see that there are significant differences between them. For example, the subjective assessment of mint displays a high positive score of 2.076 on relaxation, but its estimated result based on EEG signal data indicates the negative effect of -1.098. Those differences can be explained as owing to the impacts of implicit psychological effects which can be hardly assessed by subjective self-reports.

Due to lack of an objective measurement and calibration way, the actual computation accuracy of $P(i)$ estimated by our proposed method is difficult to be precisely evaluated. However, we can analyze its resolving ability between different stimuli by comparing with the subjective assessment method. Because the four olfactory stimuli of rose, wood, mint, and disinfectant can evoke very different psychological effects obviously, so an effective computation method should be able to distinguish those effects of different stimuli. Table 2 shows the difference values of estimated results and subjective assessment scores respectively between each two different stimuli, for example, ΔP-E of Rose *vs.* Wood is calculated by subtracting the Pleasure-E value of rose from that of the wood: 2.834–2.711 = 0.123, and ΔP-S is obtained by subtracting the Pleasure-S value of rose from that of the wood: 2.416–2.382 = 0.034.

Table 2 reflects the resolving abilities of our proposed method and the subjective assessment method between different stimuli. All the absolute values of ΔP-E, ΔW-E, and ΔR-E are larger than the corresponding absolute values of ΔP-S, ΔW-S, and ΔR-S respectively, but except for the ΔR-E and ΔR-S of Mint *vs.* Disinfectant. Obviously, the average absolute values of the former are significantly greater than that of the later. It indicates that the computation method based on EEG feature parameters has higher

Table 2. Comparison of difference values between different stimuli.

Olfactory stimuli	ΔP-E	ΔP-S	ΔW-E	ΔW-S	ΔR-E	ΔR-S
Rose *vs.* Wood	0.123	0.034	1.387	0.190	−0.872	−0.327
Rose *vs.* Mint	0.791	0.545	−0.883	−0.326	3.344	−0.136
Rose *vs.* Disinfectant	5.080	4.378	0.617	0.602	4.453	3.213
Wood *vs.* Mint	0.668	0.511	−2.270	−0.516	4.216	0.191
Wood *vs.* Disinfectant	4.957	4.344	−0.770	0.412	5.325	3.540
Mint *vs.* Disinfectant	4.289	3.833	1.500	0.928	1.109	3.349
Average absolute value	2.651	2.274	1.238	0.4957	3.220	1.793

sensitivity and resolving ability than the subjective assessment way, because it can reflect the implicit part of psychological effects under unconscious and subconscious states of the brain. As for the exception of Mint *vs.* Disinfectant, our further analysis of EEG signals has verified that some subjects can't distinguish the wakefulness and relaxation effects evoked by mint clearly, which has actually the positive effects on wakefulness but the negative effects on relaxation, and the later negative effects were confounded as the former positive effects by those subjects in the experiment. This also shows that the computation method based on EEG signal data has more reliability than the subjective assessment way.

3 Olfactory Environment for Human-Machine Collaboration

Olfactory environment is very important for improving the working experience and efficiency of human-machine collaboration. In order to provide the reference for olfactory environment construction, we conducted an empirical study to examine olfactory influences on the working performance of human-machine collaboration. Table 1 shows that rose, mint, and wood essential oils have the highest positive effects on pleasure (2.416), wakefulness (2.348), and relaxation (2.267) respectively according to the subjective assessments, which has also been verified by the estimated results based on EEG signal data in Fig. 1. Nevertheless, Fig. 1 indicates that mint has a negative effect on relaxation (−1.098). This means that it can evoke the tension effect which is sometimes helpful in improving working performance. Therefore, we chose rose and mint scents for constructing the olfactory environment in our study.

The test was carried out in a computer laboratory by 41 university students with 17 males and 24 females, aged between 18 and 22, and each student had the better sense of smell. The laboratory environment was first made as unscented by an air purifier, then adjusted it with rose scent and mint scent respectively by an aroma distributing device, and between which the unscented environment was recovered in order to eliminate the residual scents. All students were asked to complete the 20 questions of MENSA IQ Test by computers under different olfactory environments. The above test results can reflect the working performance affected by the abilities of attention, observation, logical thinking, imagination, and memory comprehensively during the human-machine collaboration process. After MENSA IQ Test, the Chinese version of Utrecht Work Engagement Scale [13] was further used to investigate the engagement factors of work performance, which includes the questionnaires of three dimensions: work vigor, work dedication, and work absorption, with the scores from 0 to 7. Table 3 shows the mean values and standard deviations of the test results.

Table 3. Mean values and standard deviations of test results.

Olfactory environments	Work vigor	Work dedication	Work absorption	Working performance (IQ Scores)
Rose	4.041 ± 1.413	4.123 ± 1.251	4.013 ± 1.352	11.651 ± 1.227
Mint	3.932 ± 0.896	4.257 ± 0.786	4.425 ± 1.253	12.106 ± 1.327
Unscented	2.754 ± 1.026	3.483 ± 0.989	3.142 ± 1.019	9.032 ± 0.934

Table 3 shows that both of rose scent and mint scent can improve the working performance of human-machine collaboration and enhance the work engagement in all dimensions with minor standard deviations. We set the unscented environment as baseline, and take their incremental changes as the pure influences of rose and mint scents, as in Fig. 2:

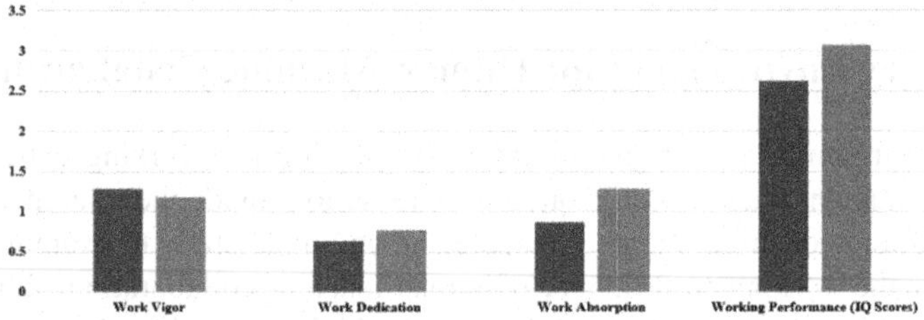

Fig. 2. Influences of rose scent and mint scent.

Figure 2 shows the higher influence of mint scent than rose scent on working performance, but the comparison results are not the same in different work engagement dimensions. The influence of rose scent is slightly higher than mint scent in the dimension of work vigor, but smaller and significantly less than mint scent in the dimensions of work dedication, and work absorption respectively. Therefore, the olfactory environment of human-machine collaboration needs to be adjusted from time to time by different scents, according to the situation of work engagement in different dimensions and the characteristics of different work tasks, so as to result in the highest working performance.

Actually, the three dimensions of work engagement have close correlations with the evoked psychological effects on pleasure, wakefulness, and relaxation. For example, work vigor is usually associated with work interest and physical fatigue, and a period of relaxation can help relieve the above fatigue. Work dedication and work absorption are related to responsibility, work willingness and work ability, etc., and the positive attitude of responsibility and work willingness can be reflected as pleasure, while the manifestation and effectiveness of work ability may be affected by wakefulness.

Therefore, in the construction of olfactory environment, we can use the proposed olfactory psychological computation method to analyze the specific effects of different olfactory stimuli, and design the optimal environmental adjustment scheme with comprehensive consideration of work task characteristics, working hours, human physiological rhythm, personality preferences, and work engagement feedback, etc. to achieve the best working performance.

4 Conclusion and Discussion

This paper studied the olfactory effects on pleasure, wakefulness, and relaxation evoked by rose, wood, mint essential oils and 84 disinfectant, and presented an olfactory psychological computation method based on feature parameters of EEG signals and LS-SVR estimator. Contrastive analysis indicates that the proposed method has higher sensitivity, resolving ability, and reliability than the subjective assessment way, perhaps because it can reflect the implicit part of psychological effects under unconscious and subconscious states of the brain.

Furthermore, an empirical study was conducted to examine the olfactory influences of rose and mint scents on working performance of human-machine collaboration. The result shows that both of those scents can improve working performance, and rose scent has a slightly higher influence on work vigor than mint scent, but smaller and significantly less influences on work dedication and work absorption respectively. In the construction of olfactory environment, we suggest to use the proposed computation method to analyze the specific effects of different olfactory stimuli, and design the optimal and dynamic environmental adjustment scheme with comprehensive consideration of all influence factories and feedbacks to achieve the best working performance.

This paper provides an exploratory method for olfactory psychological computation, and the reference for human-machine collaborative environment construction. Nevertheless, the following issues are worthy of further studies: the objective calibration method of olfactory psychological effects based on neural activity data analysis, the improvement of the proposed method with comparisons of some other machine learning approaches, and how to amend the subjective assessment results according to their possible relationships with the computation results so as to provide a convenient way for practical application.

Acknowledgements. This work was supported by National Natural Science Foundation of China (No. 71971066), Project of Ministry of Education of China (No.18YJA630019, No.19JZD010), and Undergraduate Program of Fudan University (No. 202007, No. 202008). Weihui Dai, Liu Liu, and Meilin Li are the joint first authors, and Weihui Dai and Lijuan Song are the joint corresponding authors of this paper. Many thanks to Ms Jingjie Hao and Professor Shuang Huang from Shanghai International Studies University for their help in language improvement.

References

1. Serby, M.J., Chobor, K.L.: Science of Olfaction. Springer-Verlag Inc., New York (1992). https://doi.org/10.1007/978-1-4612-2836-3
2. Zhuo, W., Feng, G.: Olfactory perception and its interplays with the emotional system. Adv. Psychol. Sci. **20**(1), 2–9 (2021)
3. Zheng, Q.Q., Shen, X.M., Wang, P., Ye, X.S.: Research progress of the olfactory neural system recognition model. J. Biomed. Eng. **25**(1), 200–203 (2008)
4. Liu, J., Wei, Y.X.: Analysis of factors related to individual difference of olfactory function. Chinese J. Otolaryngol. Head Neck Surg. **1**, 82–85 (2013)
5. Dai, W.H., et al.: Olfactory affective computation based on EEG signal data. In: Proceedings of 2021 IEEE International Conference on Progress in Informatics and Computing (PIC), pp. 432–436. IEEE (2021)
6. Yang, R.N.: Research on The Model of Olfactory System and The Extracting Method of Olfactory EEG. Nanjing University of Aeronautics and Astronautics, Nanjing (2007)
7. Herz, R.S.: Neuroimaging evidence for the emotional potency of odor-evoked memory. Neuropsychologia **42**(3), 371–378 (2004)
8. Mehrabian, A.: Pleasure-arousal-dominance: a general framework for describing and measuring individual differences in temperament. Current Psychol. Dev. Learn. Person. Soc. **14**(4), 261–292 (1996)
9. Liu, Y., Fu, X.L., Tao, L.M.: Emotion measurement based on PAD 3-d space. Commun. China Comput. Soc. **6**(5), 9–14 (2010)
10. Li, X.M., Fu, X.L., Deng, G.F.: Preliminary application of the abbreviated PAD emotion scale to Chinese undergraduates. Chin. Ment. Health J. **22**(5), 327–329 (2008)
11. Dai, W.H., Han, D.M., Dai, Y.H., Xu, D.R.: Emotion recognition and affective computing on vocal social media. Inf. Manag. **52**(7), 777–788 (2015)
12. Suykens, J.A.K., Vandewalle, J.: Least squares support vector machine classifiers. Neural Proc. Lett. **9**(3), 293–300 (1999)
13. Zhang, Y., Gan, Y.: The Chinese version of utrecht work engagement scale: an examination of reliability and validity. Chinese J. Clin. Psychol. **13**(3), 268–270, 281 (2005)

Merge Multiscale Attention Mechanism MSGAN-ACNN-BiLSTM Bearing Fault Diagnosis Model

Minglei Zheng[1], Qi Chang[1], Junfeng Man[1,2(✉)], Cheng Peng[1,2], Yi Liu[1,3], and Ke Xu[1]

[1] School of Computer, Hunan University of Technology, Zhuzhou 412007, China
mjfok@qq.com
[2] School of Computer, Central South University, Zhuzhou 412007, China
[3] National Advanced Rail Transit Equipment Innovation Center, Zhuzhou 412007, China

Abstract. To solve the problem that the sample of rolling bearing in actual working condition is seriously imbalanced, which leads to the poor performance on accuracy and generalization of fault diagnosis model. In this paper, A multi-scale bearing fault diagnosis model MSGAN-ACNN-BiLSTM with progressive generation and multi-scale attention mechanism is proposed for imbalanced data. Firstly, the original imbalanced fault samples are transformed into multi-scale frequency domain samples and input into the multi-scale generative adversarial network for training. After the network reaches Nash equilibrium, the progressive generated multi-scale fault samples are mixed into the original imbalanced samples, so as to solve the problem of serious imbalance data in actual conditions. Then, the re-balanced multi-scale datasets is input into the diagnostic model for training, which can extract multi-scale global and local feature information and improve the performance of the model, so as to realize the accurate classification of bearing fault diagnosis under imbalanced data. This experiment is based on the data set of UConn and CWRU. The experimental results show that the performance of the generated data quality and diagnosis accuracy of the model in each dataset is higher than other comparison methods, which proves the stability and effectiveness of the model.

Keywords: Fault diagnosis · Bearing · Imbalanced data · Multi-scale · GAN · Attention · Time series

1 Introduction

Rolling bearing is an important part in rotating machinery equipment [1], especially under high-speed and heavy-load operation for a long time, inner and outer rings and rolling body faults are easy to occur. Therefore, the research on fault diagnosis methods of rolling bearing has practical engineering significance and economic value, and is a hot spot in the field of mechanical fault diagnosis. According to incomplete statistics of relevant data, more than 30% of mechanical equipment fault on high-speed trains alone

Y. Sun et al. (Eds.): ChineseCSCW 2021, CCIS 1491, pp. 599–614, 2022.
https://doi.org/10.1007/978-981-19-4546-5_47

are caused by rolling bearings [2]. Therefore, the diagnosis method for rolling bearing fault can not only guarantee the operation quality of rotating machinery and equipment, but also avoid huge economic losses and casualties caused by disasters [3]. In recent years, the data-driven fault diagnosis method has gradually become a research hotspot and development trend in the field of rolling bearing and even mechanical fault diagnosis [4–6]. In actual working conditions, cracks in inner and outer rings of rolling bearing faults are the most common. According to statistics, inner and outer rings faults account for 90% of rolling bearing faults, and the rest of the parts account for only 10% [7]. Further, the number of fault signal samples that can be collected is generally far less than the normal status signal samples, which leads to serious imbalanced problem of the fault diagnosis dataset [8]. The model based on data-driven deep neural network will tend to improve the classification accuracy of more classes of samples in the continuous training process, and give up the classification performance on a small number of samples. This is a severe challenge in the field of fault diagnosis, because the negative samples in this field are in the absolute minority. At present, the over sampling method based on data generation technology is mostly used to deal with the problem of unbalanced data, and artificially generate new data to increase the amount of data to alleviate the problem of data imbalance. One of the traditional data generation methods is smote (synthetic minority oversampling Technology) and its improved method [9]. The other is the data generation method based on generative adversarial network [10].

In this paper, based on the ideas of GAN variants such as DCGAN [11], WGAN-GP [12], StackGAN [13], ProGAN [14] and the multi-scale mechanism, a bearing fault diagnosis method of multi-scale progressive generative adversarial network MSGAN combined with multi-scale attention fusion mechanism ACNN-BiLSTM is proposed. It is a well-structured and effective method with the advantages of high stability and rapid convergence. Local noise interpolation upsampling is proposed as an interpolation method with multi-scale progressive growth, and MMD-WGP is proposed as a loss function of MSGAN model. This method can stably generate high-quality multi-scale fault spectrum signal data from low-scale spectrum signal data by means of progressive growth. It can solve the problem of imbalanced data caused by the low proportion of fault samples, and improve the ability of fault diagnosis of rolling bearings under the condition of imbalanced data under actual working conditions.

2 Related Work

Since the GAN model was proposed, it has led the trend of data generation. Many scholars have proposed methods to solve the imbalanced data by using GAN model [15, 16] in different fields [17–19] such as image, audio, text, fault diagnosis, etc. Lee [20] studied and compared the GAN-based oversampling method and standard oversampling method on the data unbalance of the fault diagnosis of electric machines, and combined with the deep neural network model, proved that the GAN model generated data with higher classification accuracy. However, GAN still has many drawbacks, such as training instability, training failure, gradient disappearance, mode collapse. To solve these problems, researchers have proposed DCGAN based on convolution network structure, WGAN [21] using Wasserstein distance instead of Jensen-Shannon dispersion, and WGAN-GP with gradient penalty. These GAN methods improve the model from the network structure and loss function to make the network generate better data quality and the training process more stable. Shao et al. [22] used the improved framework of DCGAN to learn the original vibration data collected by the mechanical sensor, and generated one-dimensional signal data to alleviate data imbalance. Zhang et al. [23] proposed a method to generate a few categories of EEG samples based on conditional Wasserstein GAN, which enhanced the diversity of generated time series samples. Li et al. [24] presented a fault diagnosis method for rotating machinery based on auxiliary classifier and WGAN-GP, which improved the validity of generated samples and the accuracy of fault diagnosis.

In summary, the existing improved GAN generation methods have made breakthroughs in the design of GAN network structure and loss function, but training instability still exists in the experimental process of vibration signals based on time series. Therefore, in this paper, a stable multi-scale progressive generation GAN method is proposed to ensure the stability of training, speed up convergence, improve accuracy and robustness.

3 Description of the Algorithm

3.1 MSGAN: Multi-scale Generative Adversarial Network

Multi-scale Mechanism. Multi-scale mechanism can process time series signals at multiple scales to obtain time series signals with different scales. Different levels of features of time series signals can be observed at different scales. Therefore, multiscale mechanism has the ability to better characterize feature information and improve the performance of the network. In this paper, a multi-scale processing mechanism is designed to process the data in the frequency domain time series of fault vibration signals. The 1D maximum pool method is selected, and its step size is consistent with the core size. The maximum value in the sliding window can better preserve the instantaneous energy characteristics of the signal and filter out random noise and high frequency disturbance to a certain extent. This mechanism can obtain the original vibration signals of multiple time scales in time-frequency domain. It can extract more comprehensive information, take into account global and local features, and improve the performance of the model. In the training process, a set of vibration signals $\{x_1, \cdots, x_n, \cdots, x_N\}$, N is the length of the original input data, xn is the nth vibration value of the original input signal. The corresponding scale time series are obtained by one-dimensional maximum pooling with different steps, and the final data length is $\frac{N}{s}$. The multi-scale calculation process is expressed as,

$$\mathrm{M_{s,j}} = \max\{\, \mathrm{X_j'} \}, \; 1 \leq \mathrm{j} \leq \frac{\mathrm{N}}{\mathrm{S}} \tag{1}$$

where $M_{s,j}$ is an output signal obtained for multi-scale processing. M is the step size of one-dimensional max pooling, $X_j^{'}$ is the jth frequency domain signal sequence with scale S. Multi scale fault category frequency domain signals are divided into three scale types: 1 * 40, 1 * 100, 1 * 200.

Improved Gan Loss Function. WGAN proposes the measurement of Wasserstein distance to replace the JS divergence of the basic Gan model, keeps the loss function of the traditional Gan unchanged, removes the sigmoid layer of the discriminator D loss, and cancels the logarithmic process of generator G and discriminator D loss. In addition, because the Wasserstein distance has no upper and lower bounds, it may cause D to become larger and larger after multiple iterations and updates. However, the trick used in WGAN does not really make D satisfy that for any x, the magnitude of the gradient is less than or equal to 1, so as to meet the 1-Lipschitz condition. Therefore, problems such as training difficulties and slow convergence will still be encountered in practical. An improved method WGAN-GP was proposed. WGAN-GP really realizes the approximate 1-Lipschitz condition restriction on discriminator D by using gradient penalty instead of weight clipping method of directly clipping gradient value. It has achieved good performance in practice. The actual gradient penalty term of WGAN-GP is shown in formula (2). The original loss function of the discriminator is shown in formula (3), and the loss function of the discriminator of WGAN-GP is shown in formula (4).

$$GP = E_{x \sim P_{Penalty}}[(\|\nabla_x D(x)\|_2 - 1)^2] \tag{2}$$

$$L_{WGAN}(G, D) = E_{x \sim P_G}[D(x)] - E_{x \sim P_{data}}[D(x)] \tag{3}$$

$$L(D) = L_{WGAN} + GP \tag{4}$$

Although the loss function proposed by WGAN-GP has been successful in the field of GAN image generation, it still needs to be improved in the field of one-dimensional time series data failure sample generation. This paper presents MMD-WGP as a loss function of MSGAN model. On the basis of WGAN-GP, the maximum mean discrepancy (MMD) [25], which measures the similarity between source domain and target domain in migration learning domain is introduced to measure the similarity between generated samples and real failure samples. In the experiment, using WGAN-GP loss function in one-dimensional time series data generation task, the model converges too fast and the gradient disappears, which leads to inadequate training and the model is difficult to optimize. This method solves this problem by introducing MMD penalty of maximum mean difference, which makes the model training more stable and generates samples closer to the true fault signal. MMD is expressed as:

$$MMD[F, p, q] = \sup_{f \in F}(E_{x \sim p}[f(x)] - E_{x \sim q}[f(x)]) \tag{5}$$

where F denotes a given set of functions, p and q are two independent distributions, x and y obey p and q respectively, sup denotes an upper bound, and $f(\cdot)$ denotes a function mapping. MMD^2 needs to be used in the actual calculation to the generate sample set D_X and the real sample set D_Y in the actual calculation, which is shown in formula (6) is shown. The improved loss function MMD-WGP of the MSGAN model is shown in formula (7).

$$MMD^2[D_X, D_Y] = \|\frac{1}{x}\sum_{i=1}^{x} f(x_i) - \frac{1}{y}\sum_{j=1}^{y} f(y_i)\|^2 \tag{6}$$

$$L_{MSGAN}(G,D) = E_{x\sim P_G}[D(x)] - E_{x\sim P_{data}}[D(x)] + \lambda E_{x\sim P_{Penalty}}[(\|\nabla_x D(x)\|_2 - 1)^2] + \mu \| \frac{1}{x}\sum_{i=1}^{x} f(x_i) - \frac{1}{y}\sum_{j=1}^{y} f(y_i)) \|^2 \tag{7}$$

In Eq. (9), the first two are Wasserstein distance of WGAN-GP and gradient penalty. The last one is MMD penalty, which measures the distribution of generated failure samples and the distribution of real failure samples. Experiments show that compared with the original WGAN-GP loss function, the improved MMD-WGP loss for one-dimensional time series data can avoid premature convergence caused by the disappearance of MSGAN model gradient. It can Improve the stability of the model and the quality of the resulting failure samples.

Local Noise Interpolation Upsampling. In the training process of multi-scale generation adversarial network MSGAN, the progressive growth of generated samples requires the use of the up-sampling method, that is, the input of low-scale generated fault signal samples to higher-scale signal needs to be processed by upsampling. The main methods are nearest neighbor interpolation, bilinear interpolation, deconvolution, etc. These classical up-sampling methods are well applied in the GANs. In ProGAN [14], a progressively growing generation model, the conversion of pictures from lowdimensional pixels, 4 * 4, to higher-dimensional pixels, 8 * 8, is achieved through nearest neighbor interpolation. In its improved model StyleGAN [26], the core structure synthesis network uses deconvolution to convert the generated low-resolution pictures into higher-resolution pictures to double the resolution. In this paper, based on the features of one-dimensional spectral time series signals and MSGAN networks using input noise control to generate sample diversity, a local noise interpolation sampling method is proposed, that is, inserting adaptive Gaussian noise between two points of a low-dimensional time series signal. The mean σi and variance μi of noise are determined by the local values of the local window *i*. The distribution of adaptive Gaussian noise is expressed as

In this paper, based on the features of one-dimensional spectral time series signals and MSGAN networks using input noise control to generate sample diversity, a local noise interpolation sampling method is proposed, that is, inserting adaptive Gaussian noise between two points of a low-dimensional time series signal. The mean σ_i and variance μ_i of noise are determined by the local values of the local window i. The distribution of adaptive Gaussian noise is expressed as

$$p_G(x,a,b,i) = \frac{1}{b\sigma_i\sqrt{2\pi}} e^{-\frac{(x-a\mu_i)^2}{2(b\sigma_i)^2}} \tag{8}$$

where k value determines the local window size. Parameters a and b are coefficients of the mean and variance of the signals in the local window.

The Structure of MSGAN. The structure of MSGAN. The MSGAN presented in this paper is a stable and fast-convergent multiscale progressive generation GAN framework. The training generator G_1 achieves Nash equilibrium with discriminator D_1 by inputting low-scale normal-class frequency domain signal *XNormal* and low-scale true sample S_1^{real} with Gauss noise Z into generator G_1, and generates the same-scale fault spectrum signal sample S_1 for fault class. Then, the generated low-scale fault samples are sampled on the local noise interpolation to get the mesoscale fault sample $S_1^{'}$, and then the $S_1^{'}$ and the real sample S_1^{real} are input into the generator. After the Nash balance between the training generator G_2 and the discriminator D_2 is reached, a specified number of intermediate-scale fault frequency domain samples S_2 are generated. Use the same method to generate high-scale fault category spectrum signal S_3, or even higher-scale samples. Finally, multiscale fault frequency domain signal samples with different granularity (such as 40, 100, 200) can be generated stably. The structure of MSGAN is shown in Fig. 1. The MSGAN algorithm diagram is shown in Table 1.

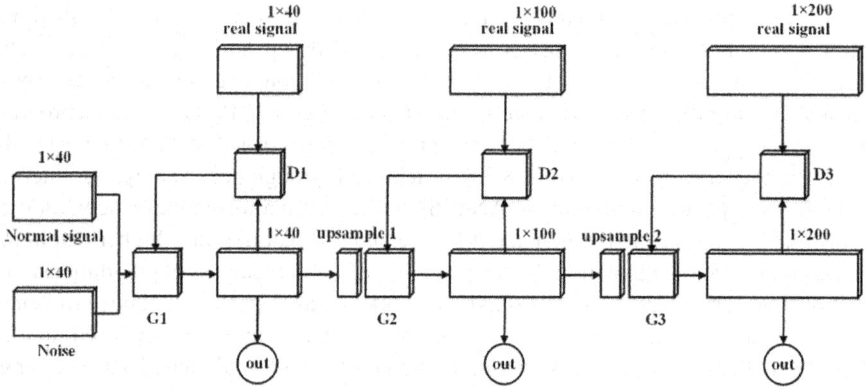

Fig. 1. The structure of MSGAN

3.2 MSGAN-ACNN-BiLSTM

In recent years, many experts and scholars have combined GAN or variants of GAN and CNN into a fault diagnosis model of deep convolution generation antagonistic network in the field of data imbalance. Hochreite et al. [27] proposed a long Short-Term Memory Network (LSTM), which has the ability to mine information from long-distance time series data, and is widely used in the field of fault prediction. The modified BiLSTM (bidirectional long short-term memory network) can learn the features from two-way directions of time series, so as to better extract the dependencies between sequences. The idea of combining CNN with BiLSTM is to extract high-dimensional features by using the abstraction ability of short sequence features of CNN and then make time

Table 1. The MSGAN algorithm

Algorithm 1 Multi-scale progressive generative algorithm

Input: $X_{Normal}, Z, S_1^{real}, S_2^{real}, S_3^{real}$

Output: S_1, S_2, S_3

function MSGAN($X_{Normal}, Z, S_1^{real}, S_2^{real}, S_3^{real}$):
  for i=1 to 3 do
    if k_i is 40:
      $G_1, D_1 \leftarrow X_{Normal}, Z, S_1^{real}$
      while G_1, D_1 Satisfy Nash equilibrium do
        $G_1, D_1 \leftarrow \min_D \max_G L_{MSGAN}(D_1, G_1)$
        $S_1 \leftarrow G_1(X_{Normal} + Z)$
    end if
    if k_i is 100 or 200:
      $S_{i-1}^{'} \leftarrow \text{upsampling}(S_{i-1})$
      $G_i, D_i \leftarrow S_{i-1}^{'}, S_i^{real},$
      while G_i, D_i Satisfy Nash equilibrium do
        $G_i, D_i \leftarrow \min_D \max_G L_{MSGAN}(D_i, G_i)$
        $S_i \leftarrow G_1(S_{i-1}^{'})$
    end if
  end for

series prediction by combining short sequence high-dimensional features of BiLSTM. But the importance of time series features in time dimension is not always the same. To solve this problem, Attention Mechanism (AM) Modeling the dependencies of data features on a global scale to obtain better expressive feature information can improve model performance.

At present, some studies have applied the attention mechanism to various fields, and the model performance has been effectively improved. Li Mei et al. [28] proposed an improved CNN-LSTM architecture by adding AM to process short sequence features ignored by the existing structure. However, this method lacks robustness, because it is easily disturbed by noise when using a single scale, which leads to unstable feature extraction. Therefore, this paper combines the multi-scale generation model MSGAN, puts forward the MSGAN-ACNN-BiLSTM model which combines the multi-scale attention mechanism to realize the fault diagnosis of rolling bearings under the imbalanced data in the practical application scenario. The network structure is shown in Fig. 2.

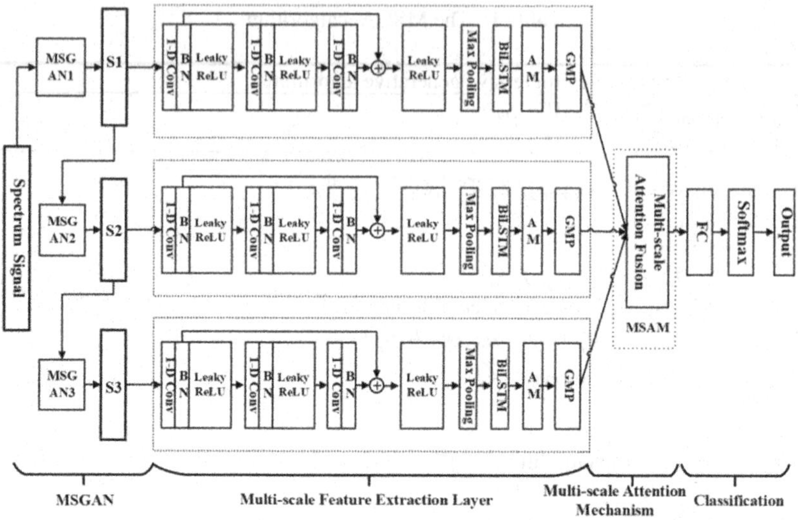

Fig. 2. The network structure of MSGAN-ACNN-BiLSTM.

4 Experiments

4.1 The Description of Datasets

In order to verify the validity and robustness of the proposed model in solving the problem of imbalanced sample of fault signals under actual itions, two different datasets are selected to validate the model.

Case1 UConn Dataset. The University of Connecticut (UConn) Gearbox Data Set is a gearbox vibration data set shared by Professor Tang Liang's team [29]. As shown in Fig. 3, the experimental equipment is a benchmark two-stage gearbox with replaceable gears. Nine different health states are introduced to the pinion on the input shaft, including healthy condition, missing tooth, root crack, spalling, and chipping tip with five different levels of severity.

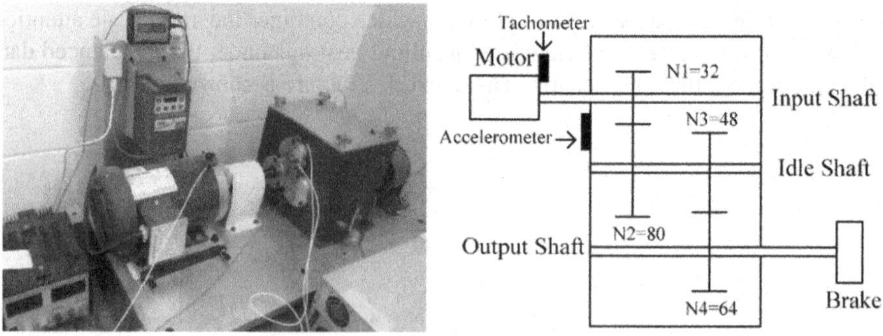

Fig. 3. The benchmark two-stage gearbox.

To verify the effectiveness and reliability of the methods proposed in this paper, three experimental datasets A, B, B' are designed from the vibration signal of UConn dataset, which have nine kinds of health states including health, mixing, crack, spalling and five degrees of gap fault states. On this basis, four experimental datasets C, D, C', D' are generated using the algorithm.

As shown in Table 2, dataset A is an imbalanced data, which is processed at an imbalanced rate of 0.1, including 312 normal samples and 32 fault samples in the other 9, totaling 586 samples. Dataset A as training data outputs multiscale generated balanced dataset C through MSGAN model. There are 312 samples in the normal category and 8 fault categories in C, including three different scales of data generated gradually by the model. Dataset C' contains only MSGAN-generated data from Balanced C, not the original data from F. It is the difference between C' and A. There are 280 generated samples for each of the 8fault categories. Dataset B and B' are test sets used to evaluate the training effect of the algorithm model. There are 104 samples in each class, 9 categories in H, 936 samples, 8 categories in H', 832 samples. These datasets are mainly used to verify the effectiveness and reliability of the multi-scale generation model proposed in this paper.

Table 2. The details of datasets from Case1

State	Location	A	B	C	D	B'	C'	D'	Length
0	Normal	312	104	312	312	–	–	–	200
1	Missing tooth	32	104	32 + 280	32 + 280	104	280	280	200
2	Root crack	32	104	32 + 280	32 + 280	104	280	280	200
3	Spalling	32	104	32 + 280	32 + 280	104	280	280	200
4	Chipping 5a	32	104	32 + 280	32 + 280	104	280	280	200
5	Chipping 4a	32	104	32 + 280	32 + 280	104	280	280	200
6	Chipping 3a	32	104	32 + 280	32 + 280	104	280	280	200
7	Chipping 2a	32	104	32 + 280	32 + 280	104	280	280	200
8	Chipping 1a	32	104	32 + 280	32 + 280	104	280	280	200

Case2 CWRU Dataset. In order to verify the overall performance of the proposed model, Case2 selects the authoritative data set in the field of bearing fault diagnosis: Case Western Reserve University (CWRU) bearing dataset. It is the standard bearing dataset published by the database of CWRU bearing center website. To simulate the imbalanced fault category data in real application scenarios and to validate the validity of the methods presented in this paper, ten different health states are selected for validation, and three datasets A, B and E are designed.

The dataset E is an imbalanced data set processed by an unbalanced ratio of 0.1. Its normal sample is 840, and the other 9 categories of faults are 84, total 1596 samples. The dataset F s an imbalanced data set processed by an unbalanced ratio of 0.0.5. Its normal sample is 840, and the other 9 categories of faults are 44, total 1236 samples. The generated balanced Datasets E', F' have 840 samples in each class. Dataset G is a test set with 360 samples in each class. The details of datasets is shown in Table 3.

Table 3. The details of datasets from Case2

State	Location	Degree	E	F	E'	F'	G	Length
0	Normal	0.000	840	840	840	840	360	200
1	Ball	0.007	84	44	84 + 756	44 + 796	360	200
2	Inner race	0.007	84	44	84 + 756	44 + 796	360	200
3	Outer race	0.007	84	44	84 + 756	44 + 796	360	200
4	Ball	0.014	84	44	84 + 756	44 + 796	360	200
5	Inner race	0.014	84	44	84 + 756	44 + 796	360	200
6	Outer race	0.014	84	44	84 + 756	44 + 796	360	200
7	Ball	0.021	84	44	84 + 756	44 + 796	360	200
8	Inner race	0.021	84	44	84 + 756	44 + 796	360	200
9	Outer race	0.021	84	44	84 + 756	44 + 796	360	200

Data Preprocessing. Compared with the original time domain signal, the frequency domain signal has a strong regularity and contains more useful information about the original signal, which can help to quantitatively analyze of the vibration signal [30]. However, traditional time-domain analysis and frequency-domain analysis are used to process vibration data which is less affected by noise or which has a simpler vibration signal. Under the actual working condition, the vibration signals of rolling bearings may have strong non-linearity and non-stationarity, so when the above two signal processing methods fail to meet the requirements, the time-frequency analysis method is needed. Therefore, considering the complex signal problems of practical engineering problems, the experiment uses Variational Mode Decomposition (VMD) in time-frequency analysis method to obtain frequency domain signals as data samples to train the model.

4.2 Experimental Results

Multiscale Sample Generation. To verify the feasibility of MSGAN-ACNN-BiLSTM to solve the imbalanced problem of vibration signal dataset of rotating machinery in application scenarios. The experimental samples are randomly cut from various original signals with a length of 400 time series segments, and the first half of symmetric frequency domain signals is taken after VMD processing, that is, frequency domain signals with a length of 200. In the experiment, dataset A, E and F are processed by multi-scale mechanism, and then multi-scale sample data with 1 * 40, 1 * 100 and 1 * 200 granularity are gradually generated by multi-scale MSGAN.

As shown in Fig. 4(a)-(b), The frequency domain signal map of the generated balanced dataset E' at 40, 100, and 200 scales. In the same way, imbalanced dataset A and F are used to obtain corresponding multi-scale balanced generated sample dataset C and F' respectively. Eventually, these multi-scale balanced data sets will realize fault diagnosis through ACNN-BiLSTM model of multi-scale attention mechanism.

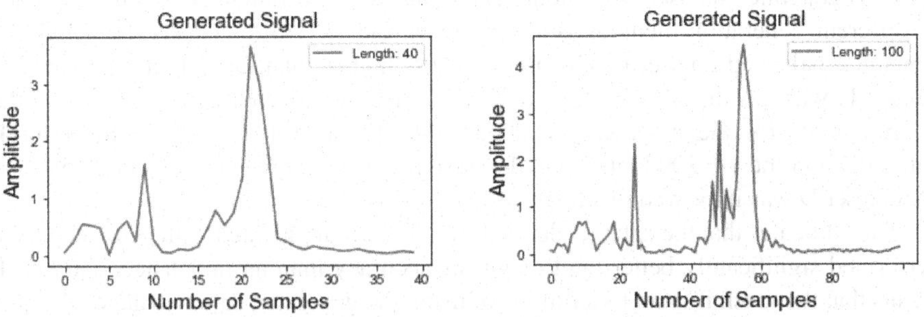

(a). low-scale Generated signal. **(b).** mesoscale Generated signal.

Fig. 4. The spectrum of multi-scale generated signal.

Figure 5(a)-(b) shows loss convergence without local noise interpolation for each fault class and loss convergence after using local noise interpolation during training process for generating dataset E', respectively. The experimental results show that loss convergence can be significantly improved by adding local noise interpolation during the progressive generation process of MSGAN.

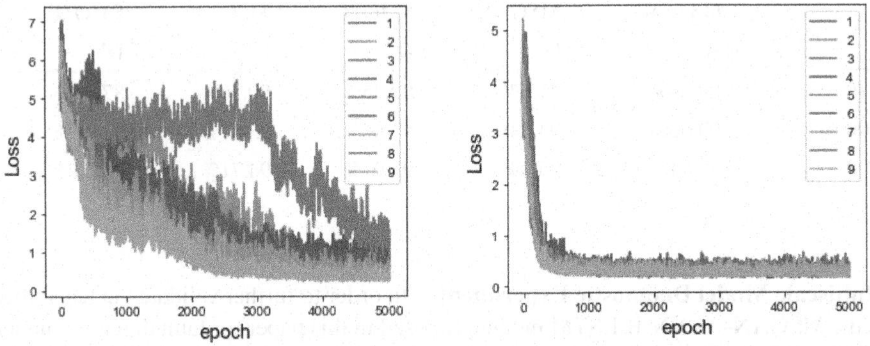

(a). not used the Local Noise Interpolation. **(b).** used the Local Noise Interpolation.

Fig. 5. Comparison of the local noise interpolation used in progressive generation.

As shown in Table 4, Case1 uses original imbalanced dataset A, multi-scale MSGAN-generated dataset C, C' and SMOTE-generated dataset D, D' as training data, respectively. The SVM algorithm, which has stable performance, is used as diagnostic model to evaluate the validity of generation model on test B and B'. Overall, the accuracy of the pure generated sample dataset C' from MSGAN is about 2.40% higher than that of the original imbalanced dataset A, 0.39% higher than that of the pure generated data D' from SMOTE, 3.07% higher than that of the imbalanced dataset A from MSGAN, and 1.11% higher than that of the original data. The balanced MSGAN-generated dataset C is about 3.07% higher than the unbalanced dataset A of the original data, and the balanced SMOTE-generated dataset D is about 1.11% higher. On different scales, the accuracy of different generation methods is different. On the 1 * 40 low-scale, the MSGAN-generated balanced dataset C was about 3.21% higher than the original imbalanced dataset F, whereas the SMOTE-generated dataset D was decreased by 1.32%. On the 1 * 100 mesoscale, the increases were about 3.74% for dataset C and 2.46% for SMOTE dataset D. On the 1 * 200 high-scale, the dataset C was improved by about 2.25% and the dataset D was improved by about 1.87%.

This indicates that the datasets derived from Case1, augmented with generated data, performed significantly better fault diagnosis accuracy than an imbalanced dataset. It means that the feasibility and usefulness of using the generated data to balance the data set. Secondly, on these datasets, the quality of MSGAN-generated samples is obviously better than that SMOTE-generated. In addition, the difference between different scales of the generated data indicates that the robustness of single scale is obviously lower than that of multi-scale model, which proves the necessity of fusing multi-scale data. The experimental results demonstrate the reliability and validity of the sample quality generated by multi-scale MSGAN proposed in this paper.

Table 4. Comparison of generated model.

Data scale	Imbalance	Generated balance		Pure generated	
	Original	MSGAN	SMOTE	MSGAN	SMOTE
	A	C	D	C'	D'
40	88.46%	91.67%	88.35%	90.50%	87.14%
100	90.60%	94.34%	93.06%	93.87%	92.31%
200	92.84%	95.09%	93.91%	94.71%	93.63%

Multiscale Model Diagnostic Experiments. In order to further validate the feasibility of the MSGAN-ACNN-BiLSTM model proposed in this paper for fault diagnosis under imbalanced data, several domains-recognized algorithms are selected for experimental comparison: VMD-SVM [31], DAE-DNN [32], 1D-CNN [33], BiLSTM [34], and ResNet [35]. VMD-SVM decomposes the original signal into several intrinsic mode functions IMFs by time-frequency analysis method VMD, filters the noise component by the steepness index, and finally inputs the filtered IMFs as fault features to SVM for fault diagnosis. SAE-DNN is an unsupervised pre-training of DNN by using stack auto-encoder with tie-weights, followed by fine-tuning of pre-training DNN using BP algorithm under supervised conditions. The pre-training process helps to mine fault features and fine-tuning process helps to obtain discriminant features for fault classification. 1D-CNN uses one-dimensional convolution neural network to extract local features of time series signals for fault diagnosis. BiLSTM makes use of the forward and reverse position sequences of known frequency domain signal data to perform bidirectional operations. BiLSTM can extract better sequence characteristics than unidirectional LSTM and obtain better effect in fault diagnosis. ResNet adds a short-circuit connection mechanism based on VGG-19 to implement the core residual unit, solves the degeneration problem of deep neural network, greatly improves the depth of neural network, and alleviases the problem of gradient disappearance, making ResNet a popular backbone of deep neural network. The 5 methods mentioned above and the method proposed in this paper were used for experimental comparison on the experimental datasets from Case1 and Case2. The experimental results are presented in Tables 5 and 6.

Table 5. Comparison of accuracy of various fault diagnosis models on Case1.

Data	Balance	Multi-scale	Method	VMD-SVM	SAE-DNN	1D-CNN	Bi-LSTM	Res-Net	Our
A	No	No	–	92.84%	93.38%	94.98%	89.21%	94.34%	–
D	Yes	Yes	SMOTE	93.91%	94.12%	91.25%	92.74%	94.97%	95.09%
C'	Yes	Yes	MSGAN	95.09%	93.483%	95.62%	91.88%	95.30%	96.26%

Table 6. Comparison of accuracy of various fault diagnosis models on Case2.

Data	Rate	Balance	Multi-scale	VMD-SVM	SAE-DNN	1D-CNN	Bi-LSTM	Res-Net	Our
E	0.1	No	No	95.50%	93.75%	95.47%	97.31%	96.97%	–
F	0.05	No	No	93.33%	92.61%	91.25%	96.14%	95.36%	–
E'	0.1	Yes	Yes	97.42%	97.43%	97.22%	97.53%	97.11%	98.47%
F'	0.05	Yes	Yes	96.33%	93.77%	95.28%	97.50%	95.84%	97.69%

The results of multi-scale data generation experiments and multi-scale model diagnostic experiments, it can be found that the classification performance of different algorithms on different dataset is significantly different. For example, on Case2, the average accuracy of 1D-CNN is 94.80, and that of BiLSTM is 97.12%. However, on Case1, the average accuracy of 1D-CNN was 95.62%, and that of BiLSTM was 90.54%. It show that the local and global time series feature of vibration dataset derived from different rotating machinery components are different and unstable in different scales. Such as the average accuracy of BiLSTM on Case2 is about 2.32% higher than that of 1D-CNN, but the average accuracy of 1D-CNN on Case1 is about 5% higher than that of BiLSTM. In contrast, the diagnostic accuracy of the three multi-scale balanced datasets C, E', F' is 96.26%, 98.47% and 97.69%, which are higher than that of other comparison models with the same imbalance rate. This proves that the multi-scale ACNN-BiLSTM fault diagnosis method used in this paper can combine the local feature extraction capability of CNN with the global timing feature extraction capability of BiLSTM. It has important application value for fault diagnosis because of its quite good performance on accuracy, robustness and generalization under different working conditions.

5 Conclusion

In order to deal with the serious imbalance of rolling bearing data in actual working conditions, this paper proposes a rolling bearing fault diagnosis model based on MSGAN-ACNN-BiLSTM. In this method, high-quality multi-scale fault sample data are gradually generated by the multi-scale generative adversarial network MSGAN, and then mixed with original imbalanced samples to obtain the balanced dataset. Then, the balanced dataset is input into the multi-scale ACNN-BiLSTM diagnostic model for training. Under the multi-scale mechanism, the diagnostic model obtains better representation ability of time series features from different scales of frequency domain signal samples, and further improves the performance of the model by fusing the multi-scale attention mechanism. Finally, it realizes the accurate diagnosis of the rolling bearing health state with imbalanced data under actual working conditions. In addition, the proposed model has better stability, diagnostic accuracy and generalization ability than other methods.

Acknowledgements. This work has been supported by the National Key R&D Program of the Ministry of Science and Technology, China (No. 2018YFB1003401), the National Natural Science Foundation, China (No. 61871432), the Natural Science Foundation of Hunan Province, China (No. 2019JJ60008, 2020JJ6086, 2020JJ4275, 2021JJ50049), Hunan Science and technology talent project - Young talents in Hunan (No. 2019RS2062).

References

1. Tang, H., Kang, H.-J.: A survey on deep learning based bearing fault diagnosis. Neurocomputing. **335**, 327–335 (2018)
2. Xing, L.: Study on state monitoring and fault diagnosis method of shock absorber of high-speed train. China Acad. Rail. Sci. (2018)
3. Xia, M., et al.: Fault diagnosis for rotating machinery using multiple sensors and convolutional neural networks. IEEE/ASME Trans. Mechatron. 23(1), 101–110 (2017)
4. Lei, Y., Feng, J.: Health monitoring method of mechanical equipment with big data based on deep learning theory. Chinese J. Mech. Eng. **51**(21), 49–56 (2015)
5. Zhou, Q., Shen, H.: Review and prospect of mechanical equipment health management based on deep learning. Mod. Mach. **2**(5), 19–27 (2018)
6. Islam, M.M.M., Kim, J.M.: Automated bearing fault diagnosis scheme using 21 representation of wavelet packet transform and deep convolutional neural network. Comput. Ind. **106**, 142–153 (2019)

7. Zhang, Y., Zhang, H., Sun, J.: Unbalanced data oversampling method based on Levy distribution. Comput. Eng. App. **55**(16) (2019)
8. Masoumeh, Z., Pourya, S., Yang, J.: Oversampling adversarial network for class-imbalanced fault diagnosis. Mech. Syst. Signal Process. **149**, 107175 (2021)
9. Shi, H., Chen, Y., Chen, X.: Summary of research on SMOTE oversampling and its improved algorithms. CAAI Trans. Intell. Syst. **14**(6), 1073–1083 (2019)
10. Goodfellow, J., et al.: Generative adversarial nets. In: Advances in Neural Information Processing Systems, pp. 2672–2680 (2014)
11. Radford, A.: Unsupervised Representation Learning with Deep Convolutional Generative Adversarial Networks. arXiv preprint arXiv:1511.06434v2 (2016)
12. Ishaan, G., et al.: Improved Training of Wasserstein GANs. arXiv preprint arXiv:1704.00028 (2017)
13. Han, Z.: StackGAN: Text to Photo-realistic Image Synthesis with Stacked Generative Adversarial Networks. ICCV (2017)
14. Tero, K.: Progressive Growing of GANS for Improved Quality, Stability, And Variation. ICLR (2018)
15. Hong, Y., Hwang, U.: How generative adversarial networks and their variants work. ACM Comput. Surv. (CSUR). **52**(1), 10 (2019)
16. Sun, J., Zhong, G.: Generative adversarial networks with mixture of t-distributions noise for diverse image generation. Neural Netw. **122**, 374–381 (2020)
17. Zheng, Y.J., et al.: Generative adversarial network based telecom fraud detection at the receiving bank. Neural Netw. **102**, 78–86 (2018)
18. Lu, Q., Tao, Q.: Sketch simplification based on conditional random field and least squares generative adversarial networks. Neurocomputing **16**, 178–189 (2018)
19. Gao, X., et al.: Data augmentation in fault diagnosis based on the Wasserstein generative adversarial network with gradient penalty. Neurocomputing **396**, 487–494 (2020)
20. Lee, Y.O., et al.: Application of deep neural network and generative adversarial network to industrial maintenance: a case study of induction motor fault detection. In: 2017 IEEE International Conference on Big Data (Big Data), pp. 3248–3253 (2018)
21. Martin, A., et al.: Wasserstein GAN. arXiv preprint arXiv:170107875 (2017)
22. Shao, S., et al.: Generative adversarial networks for data augmentation in machine fault diagnosis. Comput. Ind. **106**, 85–93 (2019)
23. Zhang, A., Su, L., Zhang, Y., Fu, Y., Wu, L., Liang, S.: EEG data augmentation for emotion recognition with a multiple generator conditional Wasserstein GAN. Complex Intell. Syst. **2021**, 1–13 (2021). https://doi.org/10.1007/s40747-021-00336-7
24. Zhenxiang, L., et al.: A novel method for imbalanced fault diagnosis of rotating machinery based on generative adversarial networks. IEEE Trans. Instrum. Meas. **70**, 1–17 (2021)
25. Gretton, A., et al.: A Kernel Method for the Two-Sample Problem. CoRR (2008)
26. Aliaksandr S.: Whitening and Coloring batch transform for GANs. arXiv preprint arXiv:1806.00420 (2019)
27. Hochreiter, S., Schmidhuber, J.: Long short-term memory. Neural Comput. **9**(8), 1735–1780 (1997)
28. Li, M., Ning, D., Guo, J.: CNN-LSTM model bas ed on attention Mechanism and its application. Comput. Eng. Appl. **55**(13), 20–27 (2019)
29. Cao, P., Zhang, S., Tang, J.: Preprocessing-free gear fault diagnosis using small datasets with deep convolutional neural network-based transfer learning. IEEE Access **6**, 26241–26253 (2018)
30. Zhang, Y., Chen, J., Wang, X.: Application of random forest to Rolling bearing fault diagnosis. Int. J. Comput. Sci. Technol. **2014**, 108–114 (2018)
31. Tang, X., Hu, B., Wen, H.: Fault diagnosis of hydraulic generator bearing by VMD-Based feature extraction and classification. Iranian J. Sci. Technol. Trans. Elect. Eng. **45**, 1–11 (2021)

32. Lei, Y.: Intelligent Fault Diagnosis and Remaining Useful Life Prediction of Rotating Machinery. 1st edn. Butterworth Heinemann Elsevier Ltd., Oxford (2016)
33. Eren, L., Ince, T., Kiranyaz, S.: A generic intelligent bearing fault diagnosis system using compact adaptive 1D CNN classifier. J. Signal Process. Syst. **91**(2), 179–189 (2018). https://doi.org/10.1007/s11265-018-1378-3
34. Rhanoui, M., et al.: A CNN-BiLSTM model for document-level sentiment analysis. Mach. Learn. Knowl. Extract. **1**(3), 832–847 (2019)
35. He, K., et al.: Deep residual learning for image recognition. In: Proceedings of IEEE Conference on Computer Vision and Pattern Recognition, 2016-DECEMBER, pp. 770–778 (2016)

A Semi-supervised Learning Based on Variational Autoencoder for Visual-Based Robot Localization

Kaiyun Liang, Fazhi He(✉), Yuanyuan Zhu, and Xiaoxin Gao

School of Computer Science and Technology, Wuhan University, Wuhan, Hubei, China
fzhe@whu.edu.cn

Abstract. Robot localization, the task of determining the current pose of a robot, is a crucial problem of mobile robotic. Visual-based robot localization, which using only cameras as exteroceptive sensors, has become extremely popular due to the relatively cheap cost of cameras. However, current approaches such as Bayes Filter based methods and Visual Odometry need knowledge of prior location and also rely on the feature points in images. This paper presents a novel semi-supervised learning method based on Variational Autoencoder (VAE) for visual-based robot localization, which does not rely on the prior location and feature points. Because our method does not need prior knowledge, it also can be used as a correction of dead reckoning. We adopt VAE as an unsupervised learning method to preprocess the environment images, followed by a supervised learning model to learn the mapping between the robot's location and processed images. Therefore, one merit of the proposed approach is that it can adopt any state-of-the-art supervised learning models. Furthermore, this semi-supervised learning scheme is also suitable for improving other supervised learning problems by adding extra unlabeled data to the training data set to solve the problem in a semi-supervised manner. We show that this semi-supervised learning scheme can get a high accuracy for pose prediction using a surprisingly small number of labeled images compared to other machine learning methods.

Keywords: Robot localization · Semi-supervised learning · Variational autoencoder · Neural network

1 Introduction

Self-localization is a crucial part of robots or self-driving cars' navigation systems. A robot must know its location when the robot needs to interact with the outer world.

The traditional ways for robot localization, such as Kalman filter and Monte Carlo Localization (MCL), use the historical sensor data and action commands

Y. Sun et al. (Eds.): ChineseCSCW 2021, CCIS 1491, pp. 615–627, 2022.
https://doi.org/10.1007/978-981-19-4546-5_48

to predict the current position then followed by a correct step that uses current sensor data. MCL is very useful when the robot moves continuously, but when a robot repeatedly senses the environment without moving or is kidnapped, this algorithm often fails [17, Chapter 8.3]. Although some variants of MCL can reduce the failure, they cannot completely tackle the problem.

Another approach, Visual Odometry (VO), by analyzing the associated camera frame to determines the motion of the mobile robots. The greatest advantage of VO is that it is applicable to all types of locomotion on any surface, unlike common wheel odometry. However, although the accuracy of VO is high, it can work effectively only when the environments have static scenes with enough texture [16].

Recently, using machine learning techniques in robot localization has become popular. One method [10] that uses machine learning techniques combining MCL gets a high accuracy but also cannot overcome the shortage of MCL.

Another method [5] that uses Convolutional Neural Network (CNN) to learn the mapping between images and positions but needs a large amount of labeled data, and this method also produces some bad predictions. This kind of deep learning approach guarantees a good prediction when a huge labeled training data set is provided. Nevertheless, in visual-based self-localization, labeled data is offten hard to get. Therefore, how to use unlabeled data, which is much easier to obtain, to improve the accuracy of prediction is a vitally important task.

Semi-supervised learning is a machine learning model between supervised and unsupervised learning, it uses both labeled and unlabeled data to train the model. Semi-supervised learning base on VAE has been successfully used in some tasks. A VAE followed by supervised learning model such as SVM and neural network, has successfully been used in image classifying and captioning [13].

In this paper, we present a novel scheme of semi-supervised learning for visual-based self-localization based on VAE, a generative model consists of an encoder and a decoder, and deep neural networks. A VAE trained in an unsupervised manner using only unlabeled data can learn to map an image to a lower dimension latent variable and map the latent variable back to an image. When the VAE has been trained, the encoder is used to preprocess the labeled images producing the latent variables of them, then a neural network trained in a supervised manner fed by these latent variables and corresponding locations is able to learn the mapping between latent variables and locations.

Major contributions of this work are as follows:

- A novel scheme of semi-supervised learning is developed for robot localization, which uses a small labeled data set and extra unlabeled data.
- A robot localization method that does not rely on prior knowledge of the location of the robot and the feature points in the images.
- A novel VAE setup implemented by a pair of symmetric CNNs, which use the same padding convolutional block to adjust the channels and use max-pooling and upsampling to decrease or increase the height and width of image data.

- This semi-supervised learning model is also suitable for improving other supervised learning problems by adding extra unlabeled data to the training data set to solve the problem in a semi-supervised manner.

We show that the proposed method can get a higher accuracy compared to other machine learning models.

2 Related Work

2.1 Robot Localization

Probabilistic localization is the classic algorithm in robot localization. This type of method is based on the Bayes Filter, which first predicts the probability distribution of the current location using historical sensor data and the previous location then corrects the location distribution by current sensor data. There are several variants of Bayes Filter based algorithm, such as Kalman Filter Localization, Extend Kalman Filter Localization. These two methods use a Gaussian probability distribution to approximate the real location distribution of the robot. Therefore when the real distribution is not a Gaussian, these methods tend to obtain a bad prediction of the current location. The most popular algorithm in Bayes Filter based methods is call Particle Filter, or Monte Carlo Localization (MCL) [19]. The Particle filter approximates the real location distribution by samples drawn from the real distribution. However, as the environment becomes complicated, the accuracy and the efficiency of MCL become unsatisfied to mobile robots. Although there are many disadvantages of MCL, it is indeed the most used mobile robot self-localization algorithm due to the simplicity of the implementation and the reasonable quality of the prediction.

Visual Odometry (VO) is a mature algorithm for robot localization, more often as a part of visual SLAM (Simultaneous Localization and Mapping). By analyzing consecutive frames captured by the camera, VO can estimate the motion of the camera (or robot). Oriented FAST and Rotated BRIEF (OBS) [15] is one of the most popular feature matching techniques, which builds on FAST keypoint detector and BRIEF descriptor, using in feature-based VO [12]. The effectiveness of keypoint detection and the efficiency of descriptor computing are crucial challenges for feature-based VO. Direct VO is more efficient than feature-based VO because it does not need to detect the keypoint and compute the descriptor. Although the direct method is not mature as the feature-based method, they have become more and more popular [2–4].

Recently deep learning visual-based localization method began to emerge. For example, poseNet [7] uses CNN and pre-trained networks in localization that works well both in indoor and outdoor environments. Another method [5] using CNN and CLSTM (Convolutional Long Short-term Memory) with images taken by a 360-degree camera to predict the pose of the agent in an indoor environment. These deep learning based methods usually can get a great result if we provide enough labeled data.

2.2 Variational Autoencoder

Autoencoder [9] or NLPCA (Nonlinear Principal Component Analysis) is the predecessor of VAE. It consists of an encoder and a decoder that try to learn an encoding (or latent variable z) for a set of data in an unsupervised manner. Although Autoencoder mainly uses for dimensional reduction (encoding), it is possible to use it as a generative model to synthesize data (decoding).

VAE [8] is a variant of Autoencoder that try to avoid overfitting in complex neural network and improve the ability of synthesis by encoding the data to a distribution of z instead of a single point encoding. It has been successfully used in image generation [6, 14] and text generation [21]. Recently, VAE is also used in a semi-supervised learning scheme to classify and caption images [13] (Fig. 1).

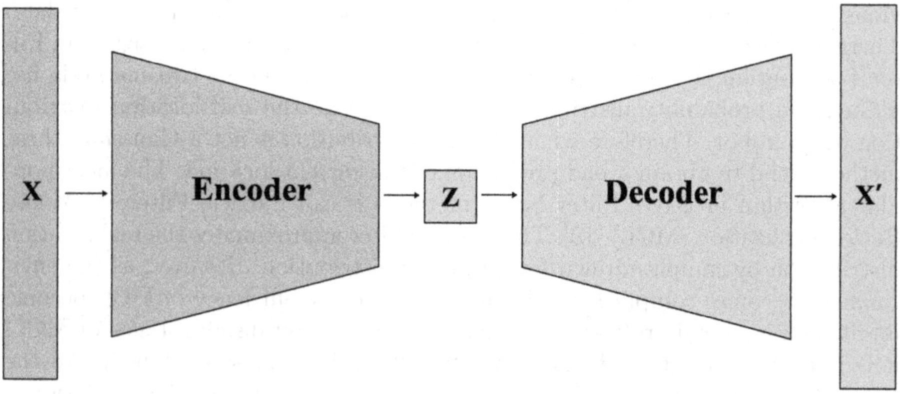

Fig. 1. Autoencoder. X is the original data, z is latent variable, X' is the reconstructed data decode from z. Basically an Autoencoder try to maximum the information z retained also minimize the error between X and X'.

3 Proposed Method

3.1 Overview

Let a mobile robot move in a 2-D environment, which is only equipped with cameras as exteroceptive sensors. Its location $\theta = (\theta_P, \theta_O) \in \mathbb{R}^3$ is a 3-dimensional vector that consists of its position $\theta_P \in \mathbb{R}^2$ and its orientation $\theta_O \in \mathbb{R}^1$. Let $\Theta \subset \mathbb{R}^3$, called Location Space (LS), denotes the set of all possible locations $\theta \in \Theta$ of the mobile robot.

An image $X \in \mathbb{R}^p$, which is made up of p pixels, captured in an arbitrary location θ_i is denoted by $X_i = \varphi(\theta_i)$, φ is called Image Modeling Function (IMF). $\mathcal{X} = X_i, i = 1, 2, ..., N$ is the set of all possible images (assume all images are distinct) X_i captured in LS Θ (Fig. 2):

$$\mathcal{X} = X_i = \varphi(\theta_i), i = 1, 2, ..., N, \theta \in \Theta \tag{1}$$

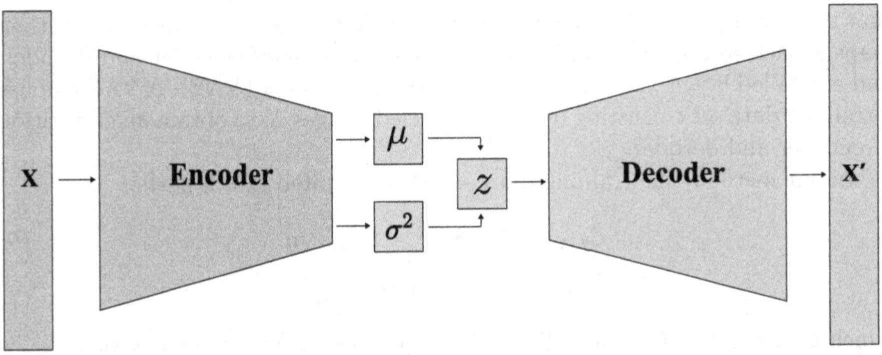

Fig. 2. VAE. Instead of encoding the data to a latent variable z, VAE encodes the data to a distribution (in this case, a Gaussian distribution represented by μ and σ^2) over latent space, then z is sampled from the distribution.

as a result, there must be a reverse function $\psi = \varphi^{-1}$:

$$\Theta = \theta_i = \psi(X_i), i = 1, 2, ..., N, X \in \mathcal{X} \tag{2}$$

called Image Localization Function (ILF).

If we have a training data set

$$\mathcal{S}_{\theta,X} = (X_i = \varphi(\theta_i), \theta_i), i = 1, 2, ..., N \tag{3}$$

consists of N labeled images, which are pairs of data included images and the corresponding location, a deep learning model can be used to learn ILF ψ, and the estimation of ILF ψ depends on the quality and quantity of training data set $\mathcal{S}_{\theta,X}$ and the complexity of the deep learning model. Consider another training data set

$$\mathcal{D}_{\theta,X} = (X_1, \theta_1), (X_2, \theta_2), ..., (X_n, \theta_n), X_{n+1}, ..., X_N \tag{4}$$

consists of n labeled images and $N - n$ unlabeled images, whose corresponding location is unknown, and $N = \alpha n, \alpha > 1$ is much larger than n, it means that in this data set, unlabeled images are much more than labeled images and can not use a straight forward deep learning model to get a good estimation of ILF ψ. In practice, a high quality and quantity data set like $\mathcal{S}_{\theta,X}$ is hard to get. More precisely, a large number of labeled images cannot be obtained easily. Even if labeled images are easy to get, there are unlabeled images can be utilized, which is very easy to collect. So, the problem is, when there is a data set like $\mathcal{D}_{\theta,X}$, how can we use the extra unlabeled images, which is extremely easy to obtain, to get a better estimation of ILF ψ than only using the labeled images, which is hard to obtained and sometimes impossible to obtained automatically and only can be obtained by hand.

Assuming that there is a pair of functions

$$X = g(z) = g(f(X)) \tag{5}$$

that maps image $X \in \mathbb{R}^p$ to a lower dimension vector $z \in \mathbb{R}^w$, which $w < p$, then maps z back to image X. This pair of functions is called encoder and decoder, and z is called latent variable in Variational Autoencoder (VAE). A VAE can use a training data set consisting of only unlabeled images X to obtain an estimation of encoder and decoder.

In our method, the training data set $\mathcal{D}_{\theta,X}$ is spited into 2 parts.

$$\mathcal{L}_{\theta,X} = (X_i, \theta_i), i = 1, 2, ..., n \tag{6}$$

$$\mathcal{I}_X = X_j, j = 1, 2, ..., m \tag{7}$$

which $\mathcal{L}_{\theta,X} \cup \mathcal{I}_X = \mathcal{D}_{\theta,X}$ and $\mathcal{L}_{\theta,X} \subset \mathcal{I}_x$. $\mathcal{I}_X$ contains all the images of $\mathcal{D}_{\theta,X}$, is called Image Set (IS), $\mathcal{L}_{\theta,X}$ contained all labeled images of $\mathcal{D}_{\theta,X}$, is called Label Image Set (LIS). In the first phase of our method, A VAE, implemented by a DCNN, uses IS $\mathcal{I}_X$ as training data set to obtain a pair of estimations, $\hat{g}$ and $\hat{f}$, of the encoder and the decoder is an unsupervised learning model, because all the images in IS $\mathcal{I}_X$ are unlabeled. The estimated encoder $\hat{f}$, utilizes the information of all images in the overall training data set $\mathcal{D}_{\theta,X}$, learns a mapping from very high dimension images, X to much lower dimension latent variables z

$$\hat{f} : \mathcal{X} \to Z = z_j = \hat{f}(X_j), j = 1, 2, ..., m \tag{8}$$

Let us reconsider ILF ψ, we can think that it is composed by 2 different functions

$$\theta = \psi(X) = \phi(f(X)) = \phi(z) \tag{9}$$

an encoder maps image X to latent variable z, and a Latent variable Localization Function (LLF) ϕ maps latent variable to location θ. The estimation of encoder f has already obtained from the former step. For obtaining an estimation for LLF ϕ from LIS $\mathcal{L}_{\theta,X}$, first the LIS $\mathcal{L}_{\theta,X}$ need to be preprocessed by encoder $\hat{f}$

$$\mathcal{L}'_{\theta,z} = (z_i = \hat{f}(X_i), \theta_i), i = 1, 2, ..., n \tag{10}$$

then the estimation of LLF ϕ can be obtained by solving a regression problem that given the sample labeled dataset $\mathcal{L}'_{\theta,z}$, recover the LLF ϕ. This can be done by neural network or other linear regression model.

3.2 Implementation Detail of VAE

The VAE is implemented by a pair of symmetric CNNs. After training, we can get an encoder and a decoder. The VAE is trained in an unsupervised manner. In our method, the encoder is implemented by CNN.

The original image is divided by 255 pixel-wise to scale to 0 to 1, then goes through several convolutional layers, pooling layers, finally gets two same dimension vectors, representing the mean and variance of the distribution of the latent variable. Finally, $z = \mu + \sigma\epsilon, \epsilon \sim \mathcal{N}(0, 1)$ is used to sample the latent variables with the mean and the standard deviation. As we can see, the same image will generate different latent variables because of the randomized sampling process (Fig. 3).

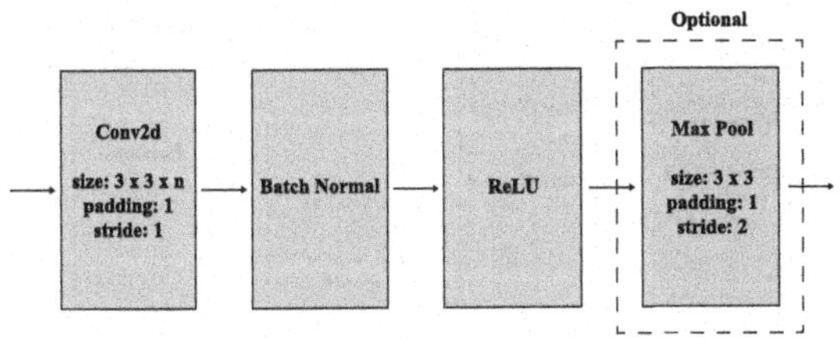

(a) Down Unit

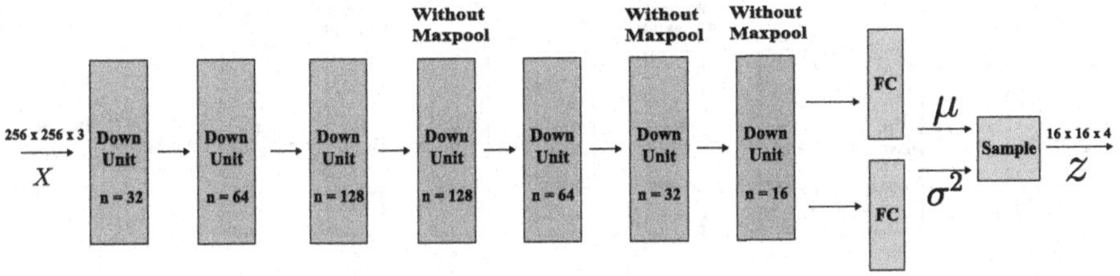

(b) Encoder

Fig. 3. Encoder of VAE.

In this model, every convolutional layer is same padding, i.e., the size of the output of the layer is identical to the size of the input. Reducing the size of input by a factor of 2 is done by several max-pooling layers, which reduce the coefficients of the neural network. Finally, we can get a much lower dimension of latent variables through those layers. The benefit of this structure is that a symmetric CNN can be used for image decoder. The batch-normal layers are used to regulate the CNN.

The image decoder is also implemented by a CNN, which takes the latent variables as input and outputs the reconstructed images.

After the FC layer, the latent variable vector is reshaped to a cubic in order to use convolutional layers and pooling layers to get an image back. Rest of the network is almost symmetric to the encoder except for the sigmoid layer, which forces every pixel in the decoded images to have a range from 0 to 1. All convolutional layers are same-padding to keep the output size unchanged. The upsampling layers increase the input size by a factor of 2 as a reverse of max-pooling layers. Also, we use batch-normal layers to regularize the neural network.

Since we use multivariate Gaussian distribution to represent the distribution of latent variables, and the output of the decoder is continuous, the loss function can be written as follow (Fig. 4):

$$L_{VAE} = \frac{1}{2}\sum_{j=1}^{J}(1 + \log(\sigma_j^2) - \mu_j^2 - \sigma_j^2) + C\|X - X'\|_2^2 \tag{11}$$

In our experiments, $J = 1024$ (dimension of latent variable) and $C = 1$ are used.

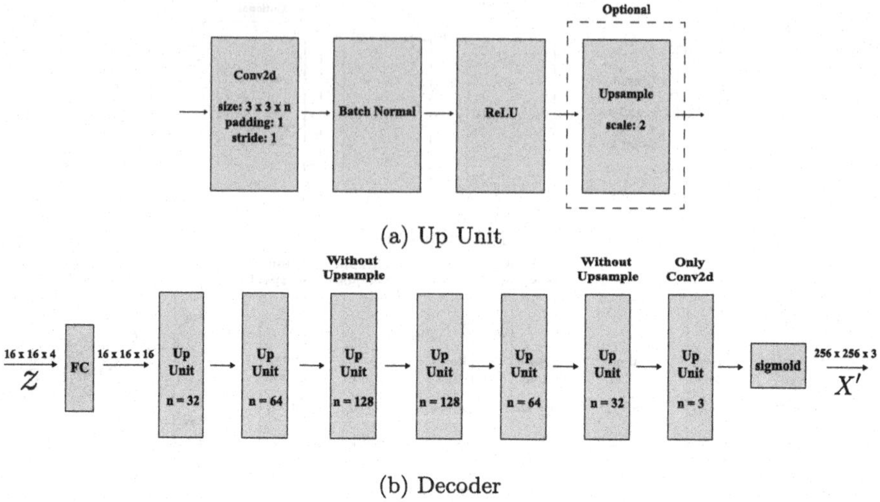

Fig. 4. Decoder of VAE.

3.3 Implementation Detail of Regression Model

After the unsupervised learning of VAE, we can get an image preprocessor, which can map the high dimension data, i.e., RGB images, to much lower dimension latent variables, i.e., 1-D vectors. In the preprocessing, all labeled images are fed to the encoder of VAE to get latent variables as their feature vectors. After the latent variables of labeled images are produced, a Fully Connected Neural Network (FCNN) is used to solve the regression model that learns the mapping between latent variables of images and corresponding locations of the images (Fig. 5).

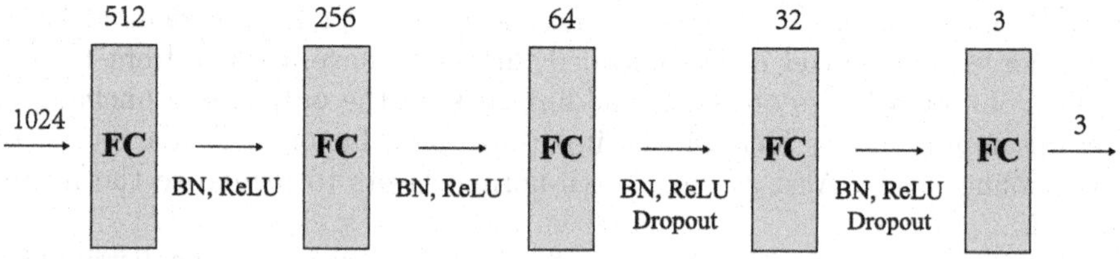

Fig. 5. FCNN model. Retaining rate of Dropout layer is 0.7, and mean square error (MSE) is used as loss function.

This model is simply a fully connected neural network combining several deep learning techniques to get a better regularization. Batch-normal (BN) layers and a technique called Dropout [18] are used for regularization. It has been shown that the Dropout technique does an excellent job of regularization.

4 Experimental Design

4.1 Dataset Description

"Multi-FoV" [20] synthetic dataset is used in our experiments. This dataset is generated using Blender, which simulates a vehicle moving in a city. When the vehicle is moving around, it captures images using different cameras and records the location in which the images are captured. The data set consists of 2500 images (480×640) and the corresponding pose (location and rotation). Figure 6 show the sample images provided in the dataset.

(a) Perspective (b) Fisheye (c) Catadioptric

Fig. 6. Images that captured by different visual system of vehicle from "Multi-FoV" dataset.

4.2 Experimental Setting

First, all images are randomly split into a 1750 images training set and a 750 images test set. Then we split the training data set into a labeled training set and an unlabeled training set. The labeled training set contains 30% (525) of the images of the training set. The unlabeled training set contains the rest of the images.

In the first step of our method, all 1750 images in the training set are used to train the VAE. After this unsupervised training, we get an encoder and a decoder. The encoder is used to preprocess the images.

Images in the labeled training set will be preprocessed by the encoder to latent variables. This process can be seen as feature extraction, which maps a higher dimensional data, i.e., image, to a low dimensional vector. Finally, because each image has a corresponding location in the labeled training set, we could use the features vector and locations to train a regression model.

The input of the regression model is the latent variables produced by the encoder, and the output is the corresponding locations. In the test part, the images in the test data set are preprocessed by the same encoder, then use the regression model to predict the locations of the images.

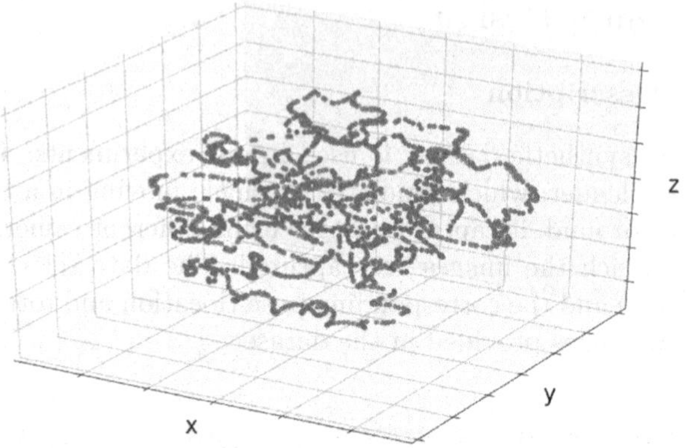

Fig. 7. Visualization of encoded data. First encode images to 1024 × 1 then use tSNE to reduce the dimension to 3.

4.3 Experimental Results

First, we want to show the latent variable z of images. Although the dimension of the encoded data (1024 × 1) is much lower than the original images, it is not enough to visualize in a plot. So we use t-SNE [11] to furthermore reduce the dimension to 2 and 3. As shown in Fig. 7, the blue dots (each dot represents an image) are connected to a string. Figure 8 shows an even clear pattern. Because the images are captured in a fixed time interval, if we plot the ground truth positions of images, they will form a string or, more precisely, a line. This pattern is what we expected. The position information of the images is maintained after encoding them to latent variables.

Figure 9 compares the input images to reconstructed images produced by VAE. We can see the reconstructed images are very close to the input images, although the compression rate of latent variables is extremely high, about 99.5% (1024 over 256 × 256 × 3). More interestingly, the reconstructed images keep the main structure and properties of the original images, such as building and sky, and parts unrelated to the main structure, such as street lamps and reflection in the mirrors, disappear.

Results of localization of our method compare to Grassmann & Stiefel Eigenmaps (GSE) [1] based localization method [10] and kernel nonparametric regression (KNR) based localization method [10] are presented in Table 1. GSE-based and KNR-based methods are trained using 1750 labeled images. The VAE is trained with 1000 epochs, and our regression model is trained with 1000 to 2000 epochs to get the most accurate rate. We can see that the results of fisheye images and catadioptric images outperform other methods but use much less labeled images. The relative poor accuracy of perspective images is due to the images' small field-of-view (FoV).

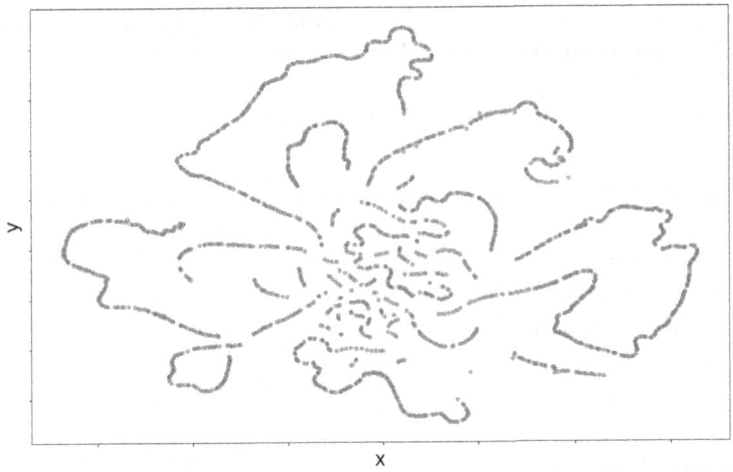

Fig. 8. Visualization of encoded data. First encode images to 1024 × 1 then use tSNE to reduce the dimension to 2.

Fig. 9. Comparision of input and reconstructed images. Upper part is the input images, and lower part is the reconstructed images.

Table 1. RRMSE for localization compare to GSE and KNR

Image types	Proposed (525 labeled)	GSE	KNR
Perspective (90° FoV)	0.076	0.045	0.063
Fisheye (180° FoV)	0.033	0.037	0.059
Catadioptric (360° FoV)	0.031	0.039	0.058

In order to furthermore show the advantage of our method, we compare it to a CNN-based localization method [5]. We use a different number of labeled images (525, 875) to train the CNN with 1000 epochs. As Table 2 shows, again, our method outperforms the CNN-based method.

Table 2. RRMSE for localization compare to CNN-based method

Image types	Proposed (525)	CNN (525)	CNN (875)
Perspective (90° FoV)	0.076	0.150	0.090
Fisheye (180° FoV)	0.033	0.095	0.037
Catadioptric (360° FoV)	0.031	0.073	0.037

5 Conclusions

This paper aimed to develop a method that is powered by the most advanced deep learning technique and does not rely on prior knowledge of the robot's location and feature points in the images for robot self-localization and dead reckon correction. As far as we know, this method is the first semi-supervised learning robot self-localization algorithm. Experiments showed that our method could get high accuracy of localization but use much less labeled data.

References

1. Bernstein, A.V., Kuleshov, A.P.: Manifold learning: generalization ability and tangent proximity. Int. J. Softw. Inform. **7**(3) (2013)
2. Engel, J., Koltun, V., Cremers, D.: Direct sparse odometry. IEEE Trans. Pattern Anal. Mach. Intell. **40**(3), 611–625 (2017)
3. Engel, J., Schöps, T., Cremers, D.: LSD-SLAM: large-scale direct monocular SLAM. In: Fleet, D., Pajdla, T., Schiele, B., Tuytelaars, T. (eds.) ECCV 2014. LNCS, vol. 8690, pp. 834–849. Springer, Cham (2014). https://doi.org/10.1007/978-3-319-10605-2_54
4. Forster, C., Pizzoli, M., Scaramuzza, D.: SVO: fast semi-direct monocular visual odometry. In: 2014 IEEE International Conference On Robotics and Automation (ICRA), pp. 15–22. IEEE (2014)
5. Hashimoto, S., Namihira, K.: Self-localization from a 360-o camera based on the deep neural network. In: Arai, K., Kapoor, S. (eds.) CVC 2019. AISC, vol. 943, pp. 145–158. Springer, Cham (2020). https://doi.org/10.1007/978-3-030-17795-9_11
6. Huang, H., Li, Z., He, R., Sun, Z., Tan, T.: Introvae: Introspective variational autoencoders for photographic image synthesis. arXiv preprint arXiv:1807.06358 (2018)
7. Kendall, A., Grimes, M., Cipolla, R.: PoseNet: a convolutional network for real-time 6-DOF camera relocalization. In: Proceedings of the IEEE International Conference on Computer Vision, pp. 2938–2946 (2015)
8. Kingma, D.P., Welling, M.: Auto-encoding variational Bayes. arXiv preprint arXiv:1312.6114 (2013)

9. Kramer, M.A.: Nonlinear principal component analysis using autoassociative neural networks. AIChE J. **37**(2), 233–243 (1991)
10. Kuleshov, A., Bernstein, A., Burnaev, E., Yanovich, Y.: Machine learning in appearance-based robot self-localization. In: 2017 16th IEEE International Conference on Machine Learning and Applications (ICMLA), pp. 106–112. IEEE (2017)
11. Van der Maaten, L., Hinton, G.: Visualizing data using t-SNE. J. Mach. Learn. Res. **9**(11), 1–27 (2008)
12. Mur-Artal, R., Montiel, J.M.M., Tardos, J.D.: Orb-slam: a versatile and accurate monocular slam system. IEEE Trans. Robot. **31**(5), 1147–1163 (2015)
13. Pu, Y., et al.: Variational autoencoder for deep learning of images, labels and captions. arXiv preprint arXiv:1609.08976 (2016)
14. Razavi, A., Oord, A., Vinyals, O.: Generating diverse high-fidelity images with VQ-VAE-2. arXiv preprint arXiv:1906.00446 (2019)
15. Rublee, E., Rabaud, V., Konolige, K., Bradski, G.: ORB: an efficient alternative to SIFT or SURF. In: 2011 International Conference on Computer Vision, pp. 2564–2571. IEEE (2011)
16. Scaramuzza, D., Fraundorfer, F.: Visual odometry [tutorial]. IEEE Robot. Autom. Mag. **18**(4), 80–92 (2011)
17. Thrun, S., Wolfram Burgard, D.F.: Probabilistic Robotics. The MIT Press, Cambridge (2005)
18. Srivastava, N., Hinton, G., Krizhevsky, A., Sutskever, I., Salakhutdinov, R.: Dropout: a simple way to prevent neural networks from overfitting. J. Mach. Learn. Res. **15**(1), 1929–1958 (2014)
19. Thrun, S., Fox, D., Burgard, W., Dellaert, F.: Robust monte Carlo localization for mobile robots. Artif. Intell. **128**(1–2), 99–141 (2001)
20. Zhang, Z., Rebecq, H., Forster, C., Scaramuzza, D.: Benefit of large field-of-view cameras for visual odometry. In: 2016 IEEE International Conference on Robotics and Automation (ICRA), pp. 801–808. IEEE (2016)
21. Zhao, T., Zhao, R., Eskenazi, M.: Learning discourse-level diversity for neural dialog models using conditional variational autoencoders. arXiv preprint arXiv:1703.10960 (2017)

Author Index

Printed in the United States
by Baker & Taylor Publisher Services